www.wadsworth.com

wadsworth.com is the World Wide Web site for Wadsworth and is your direct source to dozens of online resources.

At *wadsworth.com* you can find out about supplements, demonstration software, and student resources. You can also send email to many of our authors and preview new publications and exciting new technologies.

wadsworth.com
Changing the way the world learns®

GENDER BASICS

Feminist Perspectives on Women and Men

SECOND EDITION

Anne Minas
University of Waterloo

Wadsworth
Thomson Learning

Australia • Canada • Mexico • Singapore • Spain • United Kingdom • United States

Philosophy Editor: Peter Adams
Assistant Editor: Kerri Abdinoor
Editorial Assistants: Mindy Newfarmer/
    Mark Andrews
Marketing Manager: Dave Garrison
Project Editor: Matt Stevens
Print Buyer: April Reynolds

Permissions Editor: Joohee Lee
Production Service: Robin Gold/Forbes Mill Press
Copy Editor: Robin Gold
Cover Designer: Cuttriss and Hambleton
Compositor: Wolf Creek Press
Printer: Von Hoffmann Graphics

Printed in the United States of America
3 4 5 6 03 02

For more information, contact
Wadsworth/Thomson Learning
10 Davis Drive
Belmont, CA 94002-3098
USA
http://www.wadsworth.com

International Headquarters
Thomson Learning
International Division
290 Harbor Drive, 2nd Floor
Stamford, CT 06902-7477
USA

UK/Europe/Middle East/South Africa
Thomson Learning
Berkshire House
168-173 High Holborn
London WC1V 7AA
United Kingdom

Asia
Thomson Learning
60 Albert Street, #15-01
Albert Complex
Singapore 189969

Canada
Nelson Thomson Learning
1120 Birchmount Road
Toronto, Ontario M1K 5G4
Canada

Library of Congress
Cataloging-in-Publication Data

Gender basics : feminist perspectives on women and men / [edited by] Anne Minas.—
2nd ed.
    p. cm.
    Includes bibliographical references.
    ISBN 0-534-52839-2
    1. Sex role. 2. Feminist theory. I. Minas, Anne.

HQ1075.G462 2000
305.3—dc21   00-020517

 This book is printed on acid-free recycled paper.

Contents

Preface

Like its predecessor, the first edition of *Gender Basics,* this collection grew out of my course, that began its existence in 1976 as "Philosophy of Women." (The course title later became "Philosophy of Women and Men" and now is "Gender Issues.") The ideas that generated the course, and continue to fuel it in the form of multiple feminisms, were produced by the women's movement that began in the 1970s. However, student discussions and papers also were important in shaping the course. Classes insisted that men writers, especially those in touch with feminist ideas, ought to be incorporated in the course syllabus. Also, contemporary feminisms maintain that some attention should be paid to writers from racial and sexual minorities. Mainstream writers have no monopoly on good insights and argumentation. Finally, I found a course that addressed issues was more successful than one that incorporated a lot of theory. Most of my students seem to be interested in theory only insofar as it illuminates the issues they want to engage themselves in.

Because there is considerable lack of agreement in the area of gender issues, I have tried to include as many points of view as space allowed. The task of picking and choosing for this edition was even more difficult than for that of its predecessor because of the ever-increasing quantity of good solid readings in the arena. The increased lengths of the Further Readings for each part reflect some of this profusion. I also tried to pick readings that would be accessible to a first- or second-year student in her first women's studies course. Often I cut them to make them even more accessible. And, finally, although there is a strong theme of women's oppression running through the collection, I have tried to include writings that address other facets of gender issues. Thus, the collection should contain something to satisfy almost any mentality.

I compiled the first edition for my class that wanted a text like it to suit their needs. Now that gender issues are taking their rightful place in course curricula, there are texts like it which I often use myself, but I still want to update the first edition to take account of the new writings, yet still treat the same topics as the first edition.

I would like to thank the reviewers of this second edition:

Linda Damico, Kennesaw State College
Lori Gruen, Stanford University
Kate Mehuron, Eastern Michigan University
Anita Superson, University of Kentucky

I appreciate their valuable comments.

This second edition is again dedicated to my students, past, present, and future, and their counterparts everywhere. They embody our hopes for a future of both more thoughtful and better gender relations.

For the second edition, I thank Linda Daniel for her heroic typing and Robin Gold for shepherding the work through production. I also thank the writers for making available the writings I have incorporated in this volume.

Anne Minas
University of Waterloo

Introduction

WE LIVE OUR LIVES as gendered human beings. As children, we are either boys or girls. As adults, we are men or women. The fact that we are gendered means that we are called upon to think about certain issues and make decisions about them. Many of these issues are very important to us on a continuing basis.

A film is only a film. We see the film, it is over, we leave the theater and, if we read the reviews at all, we agree or disagree with them. The film may furnish material for interesting conversations with friends, but otherwise, once we have seen it, it is over for us.

Gender issues are not like films. As women and men, we confront choices such as whether we should pair up with a particular person, whether we should marry or remain single, whether we should have children, whether we should be productive members of the work force in a particular type of position, and whether we will be happy doing the kind of work the position requires. Despite the fact that we reach and implement decisions about such matters, the issues involved often continue to linger afterward. We married and had children, but was that really the best decision? We entered a certain line of work, but did we choose the one that was best for us? We decided to remain neutral about the issue of pornography, but should we have taken a position one way or another? Even irrevocable decisions have a tendency to come back and haunt us as issues, real or hypothetical dilemmas with no obvious solutions. Much as we are pleased with the three children we decided to have, they now seem to be at very difficult ages. This may lead us to wonder whether any two of them would have been more than enough.

Since such matters touch us directly, any reader must have already put thought into at least some of them. Thus, the subjects addressed by the writers in this collection should not be totally new to anyone. These writers have only, perhaps, put more thought into the topics than has the average person. In addition, many of the writers have interesting or unusual perspectives on their chosen subjects.

Many issues involving gender arise in what is sometimes called one's "personal life." This comprises the activities a person decides upon taking no one into account except herself plus those activities where she also considers other people to whom she is related by personal ties. One's relation to a doctor is not usually personal because interest in her is limited to the quality of medical care she offers. Any other doctor offering care of similar quality would do just as well. A spouse, child, or friend, by contrast, is not so interchangeable with someone else. For this reason, we think of our ties to them as personal. In personal relations, gender can make a difference. Our choice of spouse depends on gender and also on the qualities we think valuable (or productive of a valuable relationship with us), and we often see these qualities as gender related.

Gender issues are not, however, confined to private plots of life that can be cordoned off from the rest of human activity. We take our gender with us into the workplace and the rest of public life. Gender affects our perspectives on others and their perspectives on us, even when our relations with them cannot be classified as personal.

Very early in life we learn whether we are girls or boys and, accordingly, what we are expected to do or not do. Gender expectations for children (e.g., what types of clothing are appropriate for which gender) are relatively simple, however, compared with what is expected of adult women and men. Expectations for adults can be confining; also a particular sort of behavior can exact a much heavier price for one gender than for the other. For example, a certain posture that passes as "normal" for a man may precipitate unwelcome sexual attention if taken by a woman. Career paths in the work force are laid out according to gender; it is much easier for one gender than for the other to enter particular careers and to remain and progress in them. All told, it is difficult to find any segment of human life where gender fails to make a difference.

Accordingly, the topics selected for this collection are drawn from both private and public life. I tried to select subjects where gender clearly plays a major role and where the writers locate and explain this role for the reader.

Most of the writers acknowledge, in one way or another, an important problem in gendered life: the oppression of women. Even though some writers note it only in passing as they focus their discussion on other matters, it is the one problem that infuses the collection as a whole. Society is, in a word, sexist. It systematically favors men over women, and it engineers and maintains structures to ensure that men receive better treatment and have more options available to them. These structures are robust and effective in both private and public life. Feminism, the movement that has brought this matter to our attention, is discussed after a brief discussion of the two title words of the collection, "basics" and "gender."

Basics

What are "basics?" Insofar as a subject is based on experience, its basics are those elements that are as close to experience as the subject allows. Despite their proximity to experience, these elements are always beliefs, or experience that has been structured by thought. Because we are thinking beings, we bring thought to all experience; thought helps us make sense of the experience and incorporate it into the structure of beliefs we already have. Incorporation of a new experiential belief may strengthen this structure by giving us more confidence in the structure. Or the incorporation may require us to make changes in the existing structure because the new belief, which conflicts with some old ones in the structure, is more compelling.

As we know, people vary in important ways in what they believe. Since preexisting beliefs always structure experience, it is not surprising that people who bring different beliefs to the same situation receive different experiential messages. People may disagree, perhaps argumentatively, about what actually happened. They have developed an issue at the most basic (experiential) level, having arrived at points of view at this level that are initially incompatible.

Not everything that matters in life is intellectually important. Whether the flower garden would look better if it included petunias can turn into a very emotional matter, but the subject has little theoretical interest to recommend it. Philosophy focuses on more interesting issues—those that furnish material for thought—such as world hunger, punishment, and future generations. Moral philosophy focuses on what is right, wrong, allowable, mandatory, forbidden, and so on. When moral philosophy is directed to social issues, such as those just mentioned, it becomes social philosophy as well. Social philosophy works out moral positions on social institutions—those structures in which human beings live as members of society.

This volume deals with issues in social philosophy because the writings concern institutions that have been shaped by social forces. For example, both prostitution and marriage assume their present form because of their social histories and their places in a wider social context. Even though we may feel that our choice of whom and whether to marry is more under our control than, say, whether and how to end world hunger, the alternatives from which we choose in matters like marriage are socially formed entities. We may take steps to change these entities into something more suited and more valuable to us, but the socially formed structures we inherit are what we must begin with.

Gender issues are any controversies in which gender figures in a central way. Like other social and moral issues, gender issues can arise through conflict in our experiential beliefs about gendered human life. One perception of pornography is that it is simply one form of sexual material that can meet a particular sexual need or interest; it is relatively harmless unless it is misused, or contains depictions of persons being harmed as judged by standards external to sexuality. A quite different perception of pornography is that it portrays persons, women in particular, as sexual items that can be bought and sold. Thus, the same situation—marketing sexually explicit material—can generate different experiences because these experiences have been structured by different beliefs. The very contents of the experienced situation may thus become a matter of dispute.

The criterion for whether an issue is experientially basic is whether it can be described in terms that a lay thinker can comprehend. These terms would not be the property of any special theory that only particular groups of philosophers, sociologists, or scientists can understand. Instead the terms would belong to the large societywide vocabulary that we expect most educated persons to find intelligible. Persons acquainted with some subject matter, but lacking technical expertise in it, can then draw on this common vocabulary to think and converse with others about the subject. I have tried to select writings that can be understood without mastery of special theories. In these writings, thought, analysis, and argumentation are usually confined to concepts and terminology that do not rise above the level of conceptualization that any thoughtful person can understand. This is as close to experience as well-developed perspectives on gender issues can get.

Gender

"Gender" is one pervasive idea that structures experiential basics. Much of the world, the human world in particular, is perceived as male or female. Webster's[1] so defines "gender": "1 a. (archaic); kind, sort. b. sex 2. linguistics . . . any subclasses within a grammatical class . . . of a language that are partly arbitrary, but also partly based on distinguishable characteristics, such as . . . sex." The latter linguistic meaning of "gender" became familiar to most of us as we struggled to memorize the gender of nouns and pronouns in other languages. However, when we speak of human beings, we are not addressing linguistic items. What we need instead is something like the meaning of "gender" that Webster's equates with "sex." The ancestry of "gender" (kind) does not mandate that we restrict the word to the masculine/feminine dichotomy in linguistic items; we are quite correct in using it to mark the differences between male and female humans, apes, and parts of flowers. The current puzzle seems instead to be this: Why do we have two words, "sex" and "gender," each marking the dichotomy between men and women?

Meanings of words are always a bit messy. Perfectly formed language would perhaps contain no two words with identical meaning. However, our problems with "sex" and "gender" run deeper than simple synonymy. In addition, language is in a state of flux; words gradually make their way from one meaning to another. W. V. Quine's term for this is "language drift."[2] One cause of language drift is social change, which gives us new matters to discuss. However, only our old vocabulary is already in use in the linguistic community. People understand this vocabulary, at least well enough for it to be useful. So why mint new words that will be difficult for others to understand?

Sometimes a better strategy is to take vocabulary already entrenched and, by transporting it to a new context, give it the meaning needed for purposes at hand. If an old word is used with new meaning in a new context often enough, the new meaning may gradually become attached to the old word. According to Quine, this is just what happened with the word "sex."[3] Recently there have been an increased number of occasions for discussing human copulation. Street language furnishes us with ample terminology for such discussions, as do medicine and science. However, we do need a term for polite conversation. The word "sex" is the obvious choice, being neither too technical nor too crude for simple talk about these encounters. However, the frequency with which the word "sex" is used to describe copulation puts spin on its meaning in that direction, thus making "sex" less appropriate for speaking of male/female differences, especially those differences that are not biological.

We have become increasingly aware of the possibility that some of the differences between men and women have social causes. We need some way of saying so, especially if we want to discuss how social structures may function in creating particular differences. Perhaps if we can change the structures, we can change the differences they cause. (It hardly makes sense to direct social change at the genetic—the strictly biological—features.) Thus the word "sex" is coming to be restricted to biological, or genetic male/female differences, leaving its official synonym, "gender," free to drift toward meaning those differences that have social causes.

In fact, however, the matter is slightly more complicated; "gender" has drifted in two directions. Some use the word to talk about the differences between men and women (or boys and girls), that are caused by the social environment. [". . . at the risk of oversimplification, sex . . . is a biological given, gender is a social acquisition."[4]] Others, however, prefer to use the word "gender" in a way that leaves the matter open as to the cause of the differences. I support this latter use, and I think it is important that others try to use "gender" in this way for the following reasons.

Many differences between men and women have mixed origins, and many have origins that are not well understood. Male and female hormones are biologically caused, whereas dress codes for men and women are the work of society. But how do we categorize differences such as the relative volume of male/female voices? Girl and boy babies both seem quite capable of crying their lungs out with enormous volume relative to their size; later, girls may be encouraged to speak quietly, boys to yell. However, not every boy and girl receives this type of "encouragement," and some simply defy it. For example, a girl considered to be a tomboy may be quite vocal on the playing field. Toward adolescence, men's vocal chords undergo a change that gives them more depth and more volume capacity. Men also develop greater lung capacity than women. Women's voices can be trained, sometimes to the point of creating a Wagnerian soprano who is quite capable of being heard, over a large orchestra, in the back row of an opera house. But the singer may still be perceived as having a soft speaking voice because people pay less attention to the voices of women and don't listen to what they say as carefully as they would to the same thing said by a man.

Now where are we in the social/genetic distinction in differential male/female voice development? Because we are not in a position to make such distinctions, we should simply label this "gender difference," meaning that the difference could be biological, social, or some combination of the two. Or we could mean that the cause, although known, is difficult to categorize as either exclusively social or exclusively nonsocial. (What if our soprano's voice were reduced to a mere whisper because of industrial pollution in the area of the opera house? Is this industrial pollution social, physical, or both?)

It is worth mentioning, finally, that humans, other animals, and plants are not the only sorts of gendered beings imaginable. In fact, our imaginations seem generous in endowing their creations with gender. When inanimate natural objects come to life in our thinking, they almost always appear with gender. The sun, for example, is usually male when animated, whereas the moon is female. When extraterrestrials appear in films and on television screens, one of their most noticeable features is usually their gender. That even our most far-fetched imaginings include gender indicates the importance of this feature in human life.

Feminism

Feminism, as noted earlier, is the view that women have suffered oppression in virtually all areas of life. Christine Overall gives a fair definition of feminism.[5] The following is an amplification, with some modifications, of her definition.

Feminism is, first, a commitment to understanding women's own perceptions of their situations. These perceptions are what I have been calling gender basics, in this case the gender experiences from the perspective of women only. Feminists insist that because women as a group have been neglected in the past, we should make special efforts to pay attention to, understand, and respect women's reports of their experiences.

Because women have been oppressed, however, their experiences may have been altered by the instruments of oppression, and women may not possess the skills of communicating their experiences in ways that can be readily understood. Feminists, therefore, see part of their task as articulating women's reports or enabling women to articulate these reports themselves. Another task of the feminist is searching out and identifying the oppressive elements that have distorted women's experiences, including the experiences of feminists themselves.

These elements have threaded their way through all women's perceptions, so a feminist must do her best to search out the oppressive elements and analyze women's experiences without expecting perfect results. One feminist's ideas may conflict with those of other feminists, even though all are earnestly striving for the correct answer, or answers.

The situation is further complicated by the fact that women's experiences, including those involving oppression, are not uniform. Race and class, as well as sexual orientation (heterosexual or homosexual), lend genuine diversity to human experience. Some commonalities can be expected, but as a feminist learns to listen to her inner voice and respect what she believes, she must, at least initially, take the same attitude toward those whose differences seem to produce different messages.

Women who are feminists must have an awareness of women's oppression; this is Overall's second defining feature of feminism. Feminists maintain that oppression of women is codified in legal, educational, and religious systems and ingrained in our less formal relations to one another, as well as in our psychology and physiology. Women's oppression is also called "patriarchy" because feminists believe that this general organizational feature of society was initiated by men, continues to be maintained by men, and has men as its principal beneficiaries. A belief that patriarchy would be wrong *should* it happen to exist is insufficient for feminism. A feminist must believe in patriarchy's reality, beginning with her daily life as she experiences it.

Third, feminists are expected to have some explanation of patriarchy's origins and continuation. Male motivation to retain men's position as the advantaged gender is nearly always a large part of the explanation and may be the total one for many feminists. However, some feminists believe that other oppressive structures like capitalism or heterosexuality are essential buttresses of patriarchy. Some also maintain that the complicity of women is an important factor in explaining patriarchy's continuation.

Fourth, feminism is directed at social change. The objective is to end patriarchy either in particular areas or in its entirety. This is feminism's political aspect—political in that it is directed at influencing social policy. For many women, this is the most important part of feminism because they believe that the elimination of patriarchal structures is the ultimate reason for searching them out and developing theories about them.

This fourth aspect of feminism—translating thought into action—may be one cause of the unpopularity of feminism, even among women who might benefit from feminist action. No matter what line of action is taken, some separation from patriarchal structures is required. This can be a frightening experience to someone who has always accepted patriarchy and lived her life within its constraints. In addition, acting against the current social mores, especially against the entrenched powers of society, can be costly. One must usually pay, either immediately or in the long run, for such defiance. Anyone who openly takes a stand as a feminist must be prepared for negative responses from others. Antifeminism is subtle and pervasive. Many women internalize their antifeminism and are conflicted about whether to take openly feminist action even when they believe in a cause clearly aligned with feminist belief. For example, a woman may support rape prevention but deny she is a feminist in doing so.

The principal theory in opposition to feminism is biological determinism. This view recognizes social differences between women and men, and it may even acknowledge the oppression of women; but it asserts that biology causes all gender differences which, in turn, totally explain women's relative social position. One popular view of biological determinism is that a woman's biology justifies her destiny as a wife in a heterosexual marriage, which is the role of bearing children and nurturing all family members, including her husband.

Writings that express this type of opposition to feminism are not included in this collection because of their speculative nature, even though biological determinism has a long history and has been associated with prominent thinkers, including philosophers from Aristotle to Hegel. A commitment to approaching gender issues through experience rules out any views based on speculation.

For a strikingly similar reason, no writings are included that address Overall's final feature of feminism: "a feminist perspective is characterized by the deliberate and self-conscious (in a positive sense) nature of its world view."[6] Feminists are developing theories of knowledge, ontologies, ethical systems, and theories of art, film, and even logic. However, these endeavors do leave the field of experiential basics and attempt to build theoretical structures. Such structures are quite often successful in illuminating women's experience or, more generally, the experience of both women and men as seen from the perspective of their respective genders. Since the more experiential writings use only the language, concepts, and theory of everyman/everywoman, as explained earlier, they furnish a more suitable place to begin any study of gender, including studies from a feminist perspective.

We Are Demiurges

Philosophers may have first heard of the demiurge as the lesser god of Plato's *Timeaus,* who fashioned (as best he could) the world as we know it. However, in its first origins (in Homer, for example) a *demiourgos* was simply a workman or craftsman. *Demi* has its Greek root in *demos* (man, person) and *ourgos* (worker). In Plato's philosophy, *demiourgos* acquired connotations of creative, spiritual power as well. The word retains this meaning today; "demiurgic" is: "pertaining to a demiurge or creative power."[7]

Feminists could well perceive themselves as demiurges. We have less power than the forces of patriarchy (as the demiurge of Plato was a lesser god). Nonetheless, we must coordinate our thoughts and powers to create a better world, as we try to rid institutions such as education, law, art, as well as our own bodies and spirits, of elements of patriarchal oppression.

However, we have at present two serious problems: factionalism and hubris. (Hubris is unjustified pride and overconfidence in oneself and one's own point of view.) In a fairly obvious way, hubris generates factionalism. If I get overconfident about my perspective and you develop a similar attitude about yours, we will have a difficult time listening to each other and identifying our commonalities and differences. We will also have a difficult time joining forces to do new things in feminism on the basis of both these commonalities and differences. For example, if I am indigenous and you are an immigrant, I may want to talk about *our* national experience as women as if only experiences of my kind are worth talking about and yours can be ignored. I could do the same with my race, ethnicity, sexual orientation, or class. In short, I could adopt the mentality of patriarchy toward you because you are different from me. I thus miss the point that we have a common cause in oppression as women and that, if we want to join forces, we must find some way of coming to terms with our differences. Ideally, these differences among us should function as a source of strength, furnishing us a variety of sources of thought and energy about how to approach our problems.

My own view, not shared by all feminists, is that we need to develop new relations with men as well, now that the patriarchal structures that kept us in separate spheres are showing the first signs of decay. We should be prepared to address differences of gender in much the same spirit as race or class difference. As long as different gender perspectives exist, neither gender has a monopoly on insight into gender issues, including the all-important matter of women's oppression, just as this is not the prerogative of any one race or class. Our best hope at present, then, is to pool perspectives from different races, classes, sexual orientations, and genders. Surely we can expect the results to be better than if we had limited our field of vision by eliminating one or more of these perspectives.

I compiled this collection of writings with as much variety as I could as a hopeful step in the direction of better understanding of gender matters and the more effective resolution of problems related to gender, especially the problem of women's oppression.

NOTES

1. *Webster's Third New International Dictionary of the English Language* (Unabridged).

2. W. V. Quine. *Quiddities: An Intermittently Philosophical Dictionary* (Cambridge, MA: Belknap Press of Harvard University Press, 1987), pp. 111–114.

3. *Ibid.,* pp.78–82.

4. Casey Miller and Kate Swift. *Words and Women* (New York: Anchor, 1976), p. 47.

5. Christine Overall. *Ethics and Human Reproduction: A Feminist Analysis* (Winchester, MA: Allen and Unwin, 1987), pp. 2–4.

6. *Ibid.,* p. 3f.

7. *Webster's New 20th Century Dictionary,* Unabridged, Second Edition.

Part I

Oppression

Introduction

THE CENTRAL THEME of this collection is that patriarchy—male control—is a serious form of oppression that affects the lives of women (and men along with them, to some extent) in detrimental ways. Other forms of oppression compound patriarchal oppression. This section contains descriptions and explanations of oppressive structures. Frye, de Beauvoir, and Kaufman focus on the oppression of women by men; McIntosh, Lorde, Daseler, and the U.S. Commission on Human Rights speak to oppression that results from racism and social stratification; McIntosh also discusses the oppression of homosexuals by systems favoring heterosexuals; Wendell describes the oppression of the disabled.

I.1   Oppression

MARILYN FRYE

Marilyn Frye compares the oppression of women to the situation of a bird in a cage. A woman can become caught in a bind where, no matter what she chooses to think, say, or do, a bar puts difficulties in her path. These barriers are often difficult to recognize, because it is not easy to perceive them as parts of a configuration and because of the attempts made to hide their more pernicious aspects. This configuration of bars restricts men, as well. But the system, as a whole, benefits men.

Frye teaches philosophy and feminist theory at Michigan State University. Her writings are based directly on her life as a woman and lesbian. (Selections by Marilyn Frye are also included in Parts IV and VI.)

Reading Questions

1. What is the difference between being miserable and being oppressed?
2. What is the difference between having limits set for you, having barriers put in your way, and being oppressed?
3. What is the difference between frustration and oppression?

IT IS A FUNDAMENTAL CLAIM of feminism that women are oppressed. The word "oppression" is a strong word. It repels and attracts. It is dangerous and dangerously fashionable and endangered. It is much misused, and sometimes not innocently.

The statement that women are oppressed is frequently met with the claim that men are oppressed too. We hear that oppressing is oppressive to those who oppress as well as to those they oppress. Some men cite as evidence of their oppression their much-advertised inability to cry. It is tough, we are told, to be masculine. When the stresses and frustrations of being a man are cited as evidence that oppressors are oppressed by their oppressing, the word "oppression" is being stretched to meaninglessness; it is treated as though its scope includes any and all human experience of limitation or suffering, no matter the cause, degree, or consequence. Once such usage has been put over on us, then if ever we deny that any person or group is oppressed, we seem to imply that we think they never suffer and have no feelings. We are accused of insensitivity; even of bigotry. For women, such accusation is particularly intimidating, since sensitivity is one of the few virtues that has been assigned to us. If we are found insensitive, we may fear we have no redeeming traits at all and perhaps are not real women. Thus are we silenced before we begin: the name of our situation drained of meaning and our guilt mechanisms tripped.

But this is nonsense. Human beings can be miserable without being oppressed, and it is perfectly consistent to deny that a person or

Abridged from "Oppression" in The Politics of Reality: Essays in Feminist Theory *(Trumansburg, NY: The Crossing Press, 1983) pp. 1–16.*

group is oppressed without denying that they have feelings or that they suffer.

We need to think clearly about oppression, and there is much that mitigates against this. I do not want to undertake to prove that women are oppressed (or that men are not), but I want to make clear what is being said when we say it. We need this word, this concept, and we need it to be sharp and sure.

I

The root of the word "oppression" is the element "press." *The press of the crowd; pressed into military service; to press a pair of pants; printing press; press the button.* Presses are used to mold things or flatten them or reduce them in bulk, sometimes to reduce them by squeezing out the gasses or liquids in them. Something pressed is something caught between or among forces and barriers which are so related to each other that jointly they restrain, restrict, or prevent the thing's motion or mobility. Mold. Immobilize. Reduce.

The mundane experience of the oppressed provides another clue. One of the most characteristic and ubiquitous features of the world as experienced by oppressed people is the double bind—situations in which options are reduced to a very few, and all of them expose one to penalty, censure, or deprivation. For example, it is often a requirement upon oppressed people that we smile and be cheerful. If we comply, we signal our docility and our acquiescence in our situation. We need not, then, be taken note of. We acquiesce in being made invisible, in our occupying no space. We participate in our own erasure. On the other hand, anything but the sunniest countenance exposes us to being perceived as mean, bitter, angry, or dangerous. This means, at the least, that we may be found "difficult" or unpleasant to work with, which is enough to cost one one's livelihood; at worst, being seen as mean, bitter, angry or dangerous has been known to result in rape, arrest, beat-

ing, and murder. One can only choose to risk one's preferred form and rate of annihilation.

Another example: It is common in the United States that women, especially younger women, are in a bind where neither sexual activity nor sexual inactivity is all right. If she is heterosexually active, a woman is open to censure and punishment for being loose, unprincipled, or a whore. The "punishment" comes in the form of criticism, snide and embarrassing remarks, being treated as an easy lay by men, scorn from her more restrained female friends. She may have to lie and hide her behavior from her parents. She must juggle the risks of unwanted pregnancy and dangerous contraceptives. On the other hand, if she refrains from heterosexual activity, she is fairly constantly harassed by men who try to persuade her into it and pressure her to "relax" and "let her hair down"; she is threatened with labels like "frigid," "uptight," "man-hater," "bitch," and "cocktease." The same parents who would be disapproving of her sexual activity may be worried by her inactivity because it suggests she is not or will not be popular, or is not sexually normal. She may be charged with lesbianism. If a woman is raped, then if she has been heterosexually active she is subject to the presumption that she liked it (since her activity is presumed to show that she likes sex), and if she has not been heterosexually active, she is subject to the presumption that she liked it (since she is supposedly "repressed and frustrated"). Both heterosexual activity and heterosexual nonactivity are likely to be taken as proof that you wanted to be raped, and hence, of course, weren't *really* raped at all. You can't win. You are caught in a bind, caught between systematically related pressures.

Women are caught like this, too, by networks of forces and barriers that expose one to penalty, loss, or contempt whether one works outside the home or not, is on welfare or not, bears children or not, raises children or not, marries or not, stays married or not, is heterosexual, lesbian, both, or neither. Economic necessity; confinement to racial and/or sexual job ghettos; sexual harassment; sex discrimination; pressures of competing expectations and judgments about *women, wives,* and *mothers* (in the society at large, in racial and ethnic subcultures and in one's own mind); dependence (full or partial) on husbands, parents, or the state; commitment to political ideas; loyalties to racial or ethnic or other "minority" groups; the demands of self-respect and responsibilities to others. Each of these factors exists in complex tension with every other, penalizing or prohibiting all of the apparently available options. And nipping at one's heels, always, is the endless pack of little things. If one dresses one way, one is subject to the assumption that one is advertising one's sexual availability; if one dresses another way, one appears to "not care about oneself" or to be "unfeminine." If one uses "strong language," one invites categorization as a whore or slut; if one does not, one invites categorization as a "lady"—one too delicately constituted to cope with robust speech or the realities to which it presumably refers.

The experience of oppressed people is that the living of one's life is confined and shaped by forces and barriers which are not accidental or occasional and hence avoidable, but are systematically related to each other in such a way as to catch one between and among them and restrict or penalize motion in any direction. It is the experience of being caged in: All avenues, in every direction, are blocked or booby trapped.

Cages. Consider a birdcage. If you look very closely at just one wire in the cage, you cannot see the other wires. If your conception of what is before you is determined by this myopic focus, you could look at that one wire, up and down the length of it, and be unable to see why a bird would not just fly around the wire any time it wanted to go somewhere. Furthermore, even if, one day at a time, you myopically inspected each wire, you still could not see why a bird would have trouble going past the wires to get anywhere. There is no physical property of any one wire, *nothing* that the closest scrutiny could discover, that will reveal how a bird could be inhibited or harmed by it except in the most accidental way. It is only when you step back, stop looking at the wires one by one, microscopically, and take a macroscopic view of the whole cage, that you can see why the bird does not go anywhere; and then you will see it in a moment. It will require no great subtlety of mental powers. It is perfectly *obvious* that the bird is surrounded by a network of systematically related barriers, no one of which would be the least hindrance to its flight, but which, by their relations to each other, are as confining as the solid walls of a dungeon.

It is now possible to grasp one of the reasons why oppression can be hard to see and recognize: one can study the elements of an oppressive structure with great care and some good will without seeing the structure as a whole, and hence without seeing or being able to understand that one is looking at a cage and that there are people there who are caged, whose motion and mobility are restricted, whose lives are shaped and reduced.

The arresting of vision at a microscopic level yields such common confusion as that about the male door-opening ritual. This ritual, which is remarkably widespread across classes and races, puzzles many people, some of whom do and some of whom do not find it offensive. Look at the scene of the two people approaching a door. The male steps slightly ahead and opens the door. The male holds the door open while the female glides through. Then the male goes through. The door closes after them. "Now how," one innocently asks, "can those crazy women'slibbers say that is oppressive? The guy *removed* a barrier to the lady's smooth and unruffled progress." But each repetition of this ritual has a place in a pattern, in fact in several patterns. One has to shift the level of one's perception in order to see the whole picture.

The door-opening pretends to be a helpful service, but the helpfulness is false. This can be seen by noting that it will be done whether or not it makes any practical sense. Infirm men and men burdened with packages will open doors for able-bodied women who are free of physical burdens. Men will impose themselves awkwardly and jostle everyone in order to get to the door first. The act is not determined by convenience or grace.

Furthermore, these very numerous acts of un-needed or even noisome "help" occur in counter-point to a pattern of men not being helpful in many practical ways in which women might wel-come help. What *women* experience is a world in which gallant princes charming commonly make a fuss about being helpful and providing small services when help and services are of little or no use, but in which there are rarely ingenious and adroit princes at hand when substantial assistance is really wanted either in mundane affairs or in sit-uations of threat, assault, or terror. There is no help with the (his) laundry; no help typing a re-port at 4:00 A.M.; no help in mediating disputes among relatives or children. There is nothing but advice that women should stay indoors after dark, be chaperoned by a man, or when it comes down to it, "lie back and enjoy it."

The gallant gestures have no practical mean-ing. Their meaning is symbolic. The door-opening and similar services provided are services which really are needed by people who are for one reason or another incapacitated—unwell, burdened with parcels, etc. So the message is that women are incapable. The detachment of the acts from the concrete realities of what women need and do not need is a vehicle for the message that women's actual needs and interests are unimportant or irrelevant. Finally, these gestures imitate the behavior of servants toward masters and thus mock women, who are in most respects the servants and caretakers of men. The message of the false helpfulness of male gallantry is female dependence, the invisibility or insignificance of women, and contempt for women.

One cannot see the meanings of these rituals if one's focus is riveted upon the individual event in all its particularity, including the particularity of the individual man's present conscious inten-tions and motives and the individual woman's conscious perception of the event in the mo-ment. It seems sometimes that people take a de-liberately myopic view and fill their eyes with things seen microscopically in order not to see macroscopically. At any rate, whether it is delib-erate or not, people can and do fail to see the oppression of women because they fail to see

macroscopically and hence fail to see the various elements of the situation as systematically related in larger schemes.

As the cageness of the bird cage is a macro-scopic phenomenon, the oppressiveness of the situations in which women live our various and different lives is a macroscopic phenomenon. Neither can be *seen* from a microscopic perspec-tive. But when you look macroscopically you can see it—a network of forces and barriers which are systematically related and which con-spire to the immobilization, reduction, and molding of women and the lives we live . . .

III

It seems to be the human condition that in one degree or another we all suffer frustration and limitation, all encounter unwelcome barriers, and all are damaged and hurt in various ways. Since we are a social species, almost all of our be-havior and activities are structured by more than individual inclination and the conditions of the planet and its atmosphere. No human is free of social structures, nor (perhaps) would happiness consist in such freedom. Structure consists of boundaries, limits, and barriers; in a structured whole, some motions and changes are possible, and others are not. If one is looking for an ex-cuse to dilute the word "oppression," one can use the fact of social structure as an excuse and say that everyone is oppressed. But if one would rather get clear about what oppression is and is not, one needs to sort out the sufferings, harms, and limitations and figure out which are ele-ments of oppression and which are not.

From what I have already said here, it is clear that if one wants to determine whether a particu-lar suffering, harm, or limitation is part of some-one's being oppressed, one has to look at it *in context* in order to tell whether it is an element in an oppressive structure: one has to see if it is part of an enclosing structure of forces and barriers which tends to the immobilization and reduction of a group or category of people. One has to look at how the barrier or force fits with others and to whose benefit or detriment it works. As soon as one looks at examples, it becomes obvious that not everything which frustrates or limits a person is oppressive, and not every harm or damage is due to or contributes to oppression.

If a rich white playboy who lives off income from his investments in South African diamond mines should break a leg in a skiing accident at Aspen and wait in pain in a blizzard for hours before he is rescued, we may assume that in that period he suffers. But the suffering comes to an end; his leg is repaired by the best surgeon money can buy and he is soon recuperating in a lavish suite, sipping Chivas Regal. Nothing in this picture suggests a structure of barriers and forces. He is a member of several oppressor groups and does not suddenly become oppressed because he is injured and in pain. Even if the accident was caused by someone's malicious negligence, and hence someone can be blamed for it and morally faulted, that person still has not been an agent of oppression.

Consider also the restriction of having to drive one's vehicle on a certain side of the road. There is no doubt that this restriction is almost unbearably frustrating at times, when one's lane is not moving and the other lane is clear. There are surely times, even, when abiding by this regulation would have harmful consequences. But the restriction is obviously wholesome for most of us most of the time. The restraint is imposed for our benefit, and does benefit us; its operation tends to encourage our *continued* motion, not to immobilize us. The limits imposed by traffic regulations are limits most of us would cheerfully impose on ourselves given that we knew others would follow them too. They are part of a structure which shapes our behavior, not to our reduction and immobilization, but rather to the protection of our continued ability to move and act as we will.

Another example: The boundaries of a racial ghetto in an American city serve to some extent to keep white people from going in, as well as to keep ghetto dwellers from going out. A particular white citizen may be frustrated or feel deprived because s/he cannot stroll around there

and enjoy the "exotic" aura of a "foreign" culture, or shop for bargains in the ghetto swap shops. In fact, the existence of the ghetto, of racial segregation, does deprive the white person of knowledge and harm her/his character by nurturing unwarranted feelings of superiority. But this does not make the white person in this situation a member of an oppressed race or a person oppressed because of her/his race. One must look at the barrier. It limits the activities and the access of those on both sides of it (though to different degrees). But it is a product of the intention, planning, and action of whites for the benefit of whites, to secure and maintain privileges that are available to whites generally, as members of the dominant and privileged group. Though the existence of the barrier has some bad consequences for whites, the barrier does not exist in systematic relationship with other barriers and forces forming a structure oppressive to whites; quite the contrary. It is part of a structure which oppresses the ghetto dwellers and thereby (and by white intention) protects and furthers white interests as dominant white culture understands them. This barrier is not oppressive to whites, even though it is a barrier to whites.

Barriers have different meanings to those on opposite sides of them, even though they are barriers to both. The physical walls of a prison no more dissolve to let an outsider in than to let an insider out, but for the insider they are confining and limiting while to the outsider they may mean protection from what s/he takes to be threats posed by insiders—freedom from harm or anxiety. A set of social and economic barriers and forces separating two groups may be felt, even painfully, by members of both groups and yet may mean confinement to one and liberty and enlargement of opportunity to the other.

The service sector of the wives/mommas/assistants/girls is almost exclusively a woman-only sector; its boundaries not only enclose women but to a very great extent keep men out. Some men sometimes encounter this barrier and experience it as a restriction on their movements, their activities, their control or their choices of "life-style."

Thinking they might like the simple nurturant life (which they may imagine to be quite free of stress, alienation, and hard work), and feeling deprived since it seems closed to them, they thereupon announce the discovery that they are oppressed, too, by "sex roles." But that barrier is erected and maintained by men, for the benefit of men. It consists of cultural and economic forces and pressures in a culture and economy controlled by men in which, at every economic level and in all racial and ethnic subcultures, economy, tradition—and even ideologies of liberation—work to keep at least local culture and economy in male control.*

The boundary that sets apart women's sphere is maintained and promoted by men generally for the benefit of men generally, and men generally do benefit from this existence, even the man who bumps into it and complains of the inconvenience. That barrier is protecting his classification and status as a male, as superior, as having a right to sexual access to a female or females. It protects a kind of citizenship which is superior to that of females of his class and race, his access to a wider range of better paying and higher status work, and his right to prefer unemployment to the degradation of doing lower status or "women's" work.

If a person's life or activity is affected by some force or barrier that person encounters, one may not conclude that the person is oppressed simply because the person encounters that barrier or force; nor simply because the encounter is unpleasant, frustrating, or painful to that person at that time; nor simply because the existence of the barrier or force, or the processes which maintain or apply it, serve to deprive that person of something of value. One must look at the barrier or force and answer certain questions about it. Who constructs and maintains it? Whose interests are served by its existence? Is it part of a structure which tends to confine, reduce, and immobilize

some group? Is the individual a member of the confined group? Various forces, barriers, and limitations a person may encounter or live with may be part of an oppressive structure or not, and if they are, that person may be on either the oppressed or the oppressor side of it. One cannot tell which by how loudly or how little the person complains.

IV

Many of the restrictions and limitations we live with are more or less internalized and self-monitored and are part of our adaptations to the requirements and expectations imposed by the needs and tastes and tyrannies of others. I have in mind such things as women's cramped postures and attenuated strides and men's restraint of emotional self-expression (except for anger). Who gets what out of the practice of those disciplines, and who imposes what penalties for improper relaxations of them? What are the rewards of this self-discipline?

Can men cry? Yes, in the company of women. If a man cannot cry, it is in the company of men that he cannot cry. It is men, not women, who require this restraint and men not only require it, they reward it. The man who maintains a steely or tough or laid-back demeanor (all are forms which suggest invulnerability) marks himself as a member of the male community and is esteemed by other men. Consequently, the maintenance of that demeanor contributes to the man's self-esteem. It is felt as good, and he can feel good about himself. The way this restriction fits into the structures of men's lives is as one of the socially required behaviors which, if carried off, contribute to their acceptance and respect by significant others and to their own self-esteem. It is to their benefit to practice this discipline.

Consider, by comparison, the discipline of women's cramped physical postures and attenuated stride. This discipline can be relaxed in the company of women; it generally is at its most

---

* Of course this is complicated by race and class. Machismo and "Black manhood" politics seem to help keep Latin or Black men in control of more cash than Latin or Black women control; but these politics seem to me also to ultimately help keep the larger economy in *white* male control.

strenuous in the company of men.* Like men's emotional restraint, women's physical restraint is required by men. But unlike the case of men's emotional restraint, women's physical restraint is not rewarded. What do we get for it? Respect and esteem and acceptance? No. They mock us and parody our mincing steps. We look silly, incompetent, weak, and generally contemptible. Our exercise of this discipline tends to low esteem and low self-esteem. It does not benefit us. It fits in a network of behaviors through which we constantly announce to others our membership in a lower caste and our unwillingness and/or inability to defend our bodily or moral integrity. It is degrading and part of a pattern of degradation.

Acceptable behavior for both groups, men and women, involves a required restraint that seems in itself silly and perhaps damaging. But the social effect is drastically different. The woman's restraint is part of a structure oppressive to women; the man's restraint is part of a structure oppressive to women.

V

One is marked for application of oppressive pressures by one's membership in some group or category. Much of one's suffering and frustration befalls one partly or largely because one is a member or that category. In the case at hand, it is the category, *woman*. Being a woman is a major factor in my not having a better job than I do; being a woman selects me as a likely victim of sexual assault or harassment; it is my being a woman that reduces the power of my anger to a proof of my insanity. If a woman has little or no economic or political power, or achieves little of what she wants to achieve, a major causal factor in this is that she is a woman. For any woman of any race or economic class, being a woman is significantly attached to whatever disadvantages and deprivations she suffers, be they great or small.

None of this is the case with respect to a person's being a man. Simply being a man is not what stands between him and a better job; whatever assaults and harassments he is subject to, being male is not what selects him for victimization; being male is not a factor which would make his anger impotent—quite the opposite. If a man has little or no material or political power, or achieves little of what he wants to achieve, his being male is no part of the explanation. Being male is something he has going *for* him, even if race or class or age or disability is going against him.

Women are oppressed, *as women*. Members of certain racial and/or economic groups and classes, both the males and the females, are oppressed *as* members of those races and/or classes. But men are not oppressed *as men*.

. . . and isn't it strange that any of us should have been confused and mystified about such a simple thing?

---

*Cf. *Let's Take Back Our Space: "Female" and "Male" Body Language as a Result of Patriarchal Structures,* by Marianne Wex (Frauenliteratureverlag Hermine Fees, West Germany, 1979), especially p. 173. This remarkable book presents literally thousands of candid photographs of women and men, in public, seated, standing, and lying down. It vividly demonstrates the very systematic differences in women's and men's postures and gestures.

Further Questions

1. Think of a situation that is an example of being caught in the type of birdcage Frye describes. Can a person's confinement in such a birdcage be seen only by viewing the larger situation, as Frye claims?

2. Frye says that the action of a man opening a door for a woman is part of an oppressive structure. Do you agree?

3. Frye believes that men's inability to cry is not a form of oppression. Does she make too little of this constraint on men's behavior?

Woman Is Not Our Brother   I.2

SIMONE DE BEAUVOIR

Referring to Laforgue, Simone de Beauvoir claims that "woman is not our brother." Men and women are always in a state of tension with respect to each other. These conflicts are due to their roles of oppressor and oppressed; each blames the other for their respective situations. De Beauvoir hopes for a future where social and economic equality of men and women will bring about a flourishing of new and better forms of relations among them.

Simone de Beauvoir (1908–1986) was one of the leaders of the existentialism movement and wrote many essays and books developing themes of existentialism. She is perhaps best remembered, however, for her two-volume study of women, *The Second Sex,* which became a new watershed for feminist thinking all over the world. (Selections from this work are also included in Parts IV, V, and XII)

Reading Questions

1. Are many women intent on "trapping a man"? If so, what might be the cause of this motivation?
2. Do many men try to spare women burdens of responsibility and decision making? Is this helping women?
3. If a person finds herself in an underprivileged position with no evident means of escape, is cruelty to her oppressor an option that would naturally occur to her?

"NO, WOMAN IS NOT OUR BROTHER; through indolence and depravity we have made of her a being apart, unknown, having no weapon other than her sex, which not only means constant strife but is moreover an unfair weapon of the eternal little slave's mistrust—adoring or hating, but never our frank companion, a being set apart as if in *esprit de corps* and freemasonry."

Many men would still subscribe to these words of Laforgue; many think that there will always be "strife and dispute," as Montaigne put it, and that fraternity will never be possible. The fact is that today neither men nor women are satisfied with each other. But the question is to know whether there is an original curse that condemns them to rend each other or whether the conflicts in which they are opposed merely mark a transitional moment in human history. . . .

. . . Society, being codified by man, decrees that woman is inferior: she can do away with this inferiority only by destroying the male's superiority. She sets about mutilating, dominating man, she contradicts him, she denies his truth and his values. But in doing this she is only defending herself; it was neither a changeless essence nor a mistaken choice that doomed her

. . . to inferiority. They were imposed upon her. All oppression creates a state of war. And this is no exception. . . .

. . . The "feminine" woman in making herself prey tries to reduce man, also, to her carnal passivity; she occupies herself in catching him in her trap, in enchaining him by mens of the desire she arouses in him in submissively making herself a thing. The emancipated woman, on the contrary, wants to be active, a taker, and refuses the passivity man means to impose on her. . . . But the "modern" woman accepts masculine values: she prides herself on thinking, taking action, working, creating, on the same terms as men; instead of seeking to disparage them, she declares herself their equal.

In so far as she expresses herself in definite action, this claim is legitimate, and male insolence must then bear the blame. But in men's defense it must be said that women are wont to confuse the issue. A Mabel Dodge Luhan intended to subjugate D. H. Lawrence by her feminine charms so as to dominate him spiritually thereafter; many women, in order to show by their successes their equivalence to men, try to secure male support by sexual means; they play on both sides, demanding old-fashioned respect and modern esteem, banking on their old magic and their new rights. It is understandable that a man becomes irritated and puts himself on the defensive; but he is also double-dealing when he requires woman to play the game fairly while he denies them the indispensable trump cards through distrust and hostility. Indeed, the struggle cannot be clearly drawn between them. . . . When she makes weapons at once of her weakness and of her strength, it is not a matter of designing calculation: She seeks salvation spontaneously in the way that has been imposed on her, that of passivity, at the same time when she is actively demanding her sovereignty; and no doubt this procedure is unfair tactics, but it is dictated to her by the ambiguous situation assigned her. Man, however, becomes indignant when he treats her as a free and independent being and then realizes that

she is still a trap for him; if he gratifies and satisfies her in her posture as prey, he finds her claims to autonomy irritating; whatever he does, he feels tricked and she feels wronged. . . .

. . . It is vain to apportion praise and blame. The truth is that if the vicious circle is so hard to break, it is because the two sexes are each the victim at once of the other and of itself. Between two adversaries confronting each other in their pure liberty, an agreement could be easily reached: the more so as the war profits neither. But the complexity of the whole affair derives from the fact that each camp is giving aid and comfort to the enemy; woman is pursuing a dream of submission, man a dream of identification. . . . Man is concerned with the effort to appear male, important, superior; he pretends so as to get pretense in return; he, too, is aggressive, uneasy; he feels hostility for women because he is afraid of them, he is afraid of them because he is afraid of the personage, the image, with which he identifies himself. What time and strength he squanders in liquidating, sublimating, transferring complexes, in talking about women, in seducing them, in fearing them! He would be liberated himself in their liberation. But this is precisely what he dreads. And so he obstinately persists in the mystifications intended to keep woman in her chains. . . .

That she is being tricked, many men have realized. "What a misfortune to be a woman? And yet the misfortune, when one is a woman, is at bottom not to comprehend that it is one," says Kierkegaard. For a long time there have been efforts to disguise this misfortune. . . . To forbid her working, to keep her at home, is to defend her against herself and to assure her happiness. We have seen what poetic veils are thrown over her monotonous burdens of housekeeping and maternity: in exchange for her liberty she has received the false treasures of her "femininity." Balzac illustrates this maneuver very well in counseling man to treat her as a slave while persuading her that she is a queen. Less cynical, many men try to convince themselves that she is really privileged. There are American sociologists who seriously teach today the theory of "low-class gain." In France, also, it has often been proclaimed—although in a less scientific manner—that the workers are very fortunate in not being obliged to "keep up appearances" and still more so the bums who can dress in rags and sleep on the sidewalks, pleasures forbidden to the Count de Beaumont and the Wendels. Like the carefree wretches gaily scratching at their vermin, like the merry Negroes laughing under the lash and those joyous Tunisian Arabs burying their starved children with a smile, woman enjoys that incomparable privilege: irresponsibility. Free from troublesome burdens and cares, she obviously has "the better part." But it is disturbing that with an obstinate perversity—connected no doubt with original sin—down through the centuries and in all countries, the people who have the better part are always crying to their benefactors: "It is too much! I will be satisfied with yours!" But the munificent capitalists, the generous colonists, the superb males, stick to their guns: "Keep the better part, hold on to it!"

It must be admitted that the males find in woman more complicity than the oppressor usually finds in the oppressed. And in bad faith they take authorization from this to declare that she has *desired* the destiny they have imposed on her. . . . If a child is taught idleness by being amused all day long and never being led to study, or shown its usefulness, it will hardly be said, when he grows up, that he chose to be incapable and ignorant; yet this is how woman is brought up, without ever being impressed with the necessity of taking charge of her own existence. So she readily lets herself come to count on the protection, love, assistance, and supervision of others, she lets herself be fascinated with the hope of self-realization without *doing* anything. She does wrong in yielding to the temptation; but man is in no position to blame her, since he has led her into the temptation. When conflict arises between them, each will hold the other responsible for the situation; she will reproach him with having made her what she is:

"No one taught me to reason or to earn my own living"; he will reproach her with having accepted the consequences: "You don't know anything, you are an incompetent," and so on. Each sex thinks it can justify itself by taking the offensive; but the wrongs done by one do not make the other innocent.

The innumerable conflicts that set men and women against one another come from the fact that neither is prepared to assume all the consequences of this situation which the one has offered and the other accepted. The doubtful concept of "equality in inequality," which the one uses to mask his despotism and the other to mask her cowardice, does not stand the test of experience: in their exchanges, woman appeals to the theoretical equality she has been guaranteed, and man the concrete inequality that exists. The result is that in every association an endless debate goes on concerning the ambiguous meaning of the words *give* and *take:* she complaints of giving her all, he protests that she takes his all. Woman has to learn that exchanges—it is a fundamental law of political economy—are based on the value the merchandise offered has for the buyer, and not for the seller: she has been deceived in being persuaded that her worth is priceless. The truth is that for man she is an amusement, a pleasure, company, an inessential boon; he is for her the meaning, the justification of her existence. The exchange, therefore, is not of two items of equal value.

This inequality will be especially brought out in the fact that the time they spend together—which fallaciously seems to be the same time—does not have the same value for both partners. During the evening the lover spends with his mistress he could be doing something of advantage to his career, seeing friends, cultivating business relationships, seeking recreation; for a man normally integrated in society, time is a positive value: money, reputation, pleasure. For the idle, bored woman, on the contrary, it is a burden she wishes to get rid of; when she succeeds in killing time, it is a benefit to her: the man's presence is pure profit. In a liaison what most clearly interests the man, in many cases, is the sexual benefit he gets from it: If need be, he can be content to spend no more time with his mistress than is required for the sexual act; but—with exceptions—what she, on her part, wants is to kill all the excess time she has on her hands; and—like the storekeeper who will not sell potatoes unless the customer will take turnips also—she will not yield her body unless her lover will take hours of conversation and "going out" into the bargain. A balance is reached if, on the whole, the cost does not seem too high to the man, and this depends, of course, on the strength of his desire and the importance he gives to what is to be sacrificed. But if the woman demands—offers—too much time, she becomes wholly intrusive, like the river overflowing its banks, and the man will prefer to have nothing rather than too much. Then she reduces her demands; but very often the balance is reached at the cost of a double tension: she feels that the man has "had" her at a bargain, and he thinks her price is too high. This analysis, of course, is put in somewhat humorous terms: but—except for those affairs of jealous and exclusive passion in which the man wants total possession of the woman—this conflict constantly appears in cases of affection, desire, and even love. He always has "other things to do" with his time; whereas she has time to burn; and he considers much of the time she gives him not as a gift but as a burden.

As a rule he consents to assume the burden because he knows very well that he is on the privileged side, he has a bad conscience; and if he is of reasonable good will he tries to compensate for the inequality by being generous. He prides himself on his compassion, however, and at the first clash he treats the woman as ungrateful and thinks, with some irritation: "I'm too good to her." She feels she is behaving like a beggar when she is convinced of the high value of her gifts, and that humiliates her.

Here we find the explanation of the cruelty that woman often shows she is capable of practicing; she has a good conscience because she is on the unprivileged side; she feels she is under no obligation to deal gently with the favored caste, and her only thought is to defend herself. She will even be very happy if she has occasion to show her resentment to a lover who has not been able to satisfy all her demands: since he does not give her enough, she takes savage delight in taking back everything from him. At this point the wounded lover suddenly discovers the value *in toto* of a liaison each moment of which he held more or less in contempt: he is ready to promise her everything, even though he will feel exploited again when he has to make good. He accuses his mistress of blackmailing him: she calls him stingy; both feel wronged.

Once again it is useless to apportion blame and excuses: Justice can never be done in the midst of injustice. A colonial administrator has no possibility of acting rightly toward the natives, nor a general toward his soldiers; the only solution is to be neither colonist nor military chief; but a man could not prevent himself from being a man. So there he is, culpable in spite of himself and laboring under the effects of a fault he did not himself commit; and here she is, victim and shrew in spite of herself. Sometimes he rebels and becomes cruel, but then he makes himself an accomplice of the injustice, and the fault becomes really his. Sometimes he lets himself be annihilated, devoured, by his demanding victim; but in that case he feels duped. Often he stops at a compromise that at once belittles him and leaves him ill at ease. A well-disposed man will be more tortured by the situation than the woman herself: In a sense it is always better to be on the side of the vanquished; but if she is well-disposed also, incapable of self-sufficiency, reluctant to crush the man with the weight of her destiny, she struggles in hopeless confusion.

In daily life we meet with an abundance of these cases which are incapable of satisfactory solution because they are determined by unsatisfactory conditions. A man who is compelled to go on materially and morally supporting a woman whom he no longer loves feels he is victimized; but if he abandons without resources the woman who has pledged her whole life to him, she will be quite as unjustly victimized. The evil originates not in the perversity of individuals—and bad faith first appears when each blames the other—it originates rather in a situation against which all individual action is powerless. Women are "clinging," they are a dead weight, and they suffer for it; the point is that their situation is like that of a parasite sucking out the living strength of another organism. Let them be provided with living strength of their own, let them have the means to attack the world and wrest from it their own subsistence, and their dependence will be abolished—that of man also. There is no doubt that both men and women will profit greatly from the new situation. . . .

But is it enough to change laws, institutions. customs, public opinion, and the whole social context, for men and women to become truly equal? "Women will always be women," say the skeptics. Other seers prophesy that in casting off their femininity they will not succeed in changing themselves into men and they will become monsters. This would be to admit that the woman of today is a creation of nature; it must be repeated once more that in human society nothing is natural and that woman, like much else, is a product elaborated by civilization. The intervention of others in her destiny is fundamental: if this action took a different direction, it would produce a quite different result. Woman is determined not by her hormones or by mysterious instincts, but by the manner in which her body and her relation to the world are modified through the action of others than herself. . . . It is not a question of abolishing in woman the contingencies and miseries of the human condition, but of giving her the means for transcending them.

Woman is the victim of no mysterious fatality; the peculiarities that identify her as specifically a woman get their importance from the significance placed upon them. They can be surmounted, in the future, when they are regarded in new perspectives. . . .

I shall be told that all this is utopian fancy, because woman cannot be "made over" unless so-

ciety has first made her really the equal of man. Conservatives have never failed in such circumstances to refer to that vicious circle; history, however, does not revolve. If a caste is kept in a state of inferiority, no doubt it remains inferior; but liberty can break the circle. Let the Negroes vote and they become worthy of having the vote; let woman be given responsibilities and she is able to assume them. The fact is that oppressors cannot be expected to make a move of gratuitous generosity; but at one time the revolt of the oppressed, at another time even the very evolution of the privilege caste itself, creates new situations; thus men have been led, in their own interest, to give partial emancipation to women: it remains only for women to continue their ascent, and the successes they are obtaining are an encouragement for them to do so. It seems almost certain that sooner or later they will arrive at complete economic and social equality, which will bring about an inner metamorphosis. . . .

Let us not forget that our lack of imagination always depopulates the future; for us it is only an abstraction; each one of us secretly deplores the absence there of the one who was himself. But the humanity of tomorrow will be living in its flesh and in its conscious liberty; that time will be its present and it will in turn prefer it. New relations of flesh and sentiment of which we have no conception will arise between the sexes; already, indeed, there have appeared between men and women friendships, rivalries, complicities, comradeships—chaste or sensual—which past centuries could not have conceived. To mention one point, nothing could seem to me more debatable than the opinion that dooms the new world to uniformity and hence to boredom. I fail to see that this present world is free from boredom or that liberty ever creates uniformity.

To begin with, there will always be certain differences between man and woman; her eroticism, and therefore her sexual world, have a special form of their own and therefore cannot fail to engender a sensuality, a sensitivity, of a special nature. This means that her relations to her own body, to that of the male, to the child, will never be identical with those the male bears to his own body, to that of the female, and to the child; those who make much of "equality in difference" could not with good grace refuse to grant me the possible existence of differences in equality. Then again, it is institutions that create uniformity. Young and pretty, the slaves of the harem are always the same in the sultan's embrace; Christianity gave eroticism its savor of sin and legend when it endowed the human female with a soul; if society restores her sovereign individuality to woman, it will not thereby destroy the power of love's embrace to move the heart.

It is nonsense to assert that revelry, vice, ecstasy, passion, would become impossible if man and woman were equal in concrete matters; the contradictions that put the flesh in opposition to the spirit, the instant to time, the swoon of immanence to the challenge of transcendence, the absolute of pleasure to the nothingness of forgetting, will never be resolved; in sexuality will always be materialized the tension, the anguish, the joy, the frustration, and the triumph of existence. To emancipate woman is to refuse to confine her to the relations she bears to man, not to deny them to her; let her have her independent existence and she will continue none the less to exist for him *also:* mutually recognizing each other as subject, each will yet remain for the other an *other.* The reciprocity of their relations will not do away with the miracles—

desire, possession, love, dream, adventure—worked by the division of human beings into two separate categories; and the words that move us—giving, conquering, uniting—will not lose their meaning. On the contrary, when we abolish the slavery of half of humanity, together with the whole system of hypocrisy that it implies, then the "division" of humanity will reveal its genuine significance and the human couple will find its true form. "The direct, natural, necessary relation of human creatures is the *relation of man to woman*," Marx has said.[1] "The nature of this relation determines to what point man himself is to be considered as a *generic being*, as mankind; the relation of man to woman is the most natural relation of human being to human being. By it is shown, therefore, to what point the *natural* behavior of man has become *human* or to what point the *human* being has become his *natural* being, to what point his *human nature* has become his *nature.*"

The case could not be better stated. It is for man to establish the reign of liberty in the midst of the world of the given. To gain the supreme victory, it is necessary, for one thing, that by and through their natural differentiation men and women unequivocally affirm their brotherhood.

NOTE

1. *Philosophical Works,* Vol. VI (Marx's italics).

Further Questions

1. Do you believe that relations between men and women would acquire a more creative dimension under conditions of greater equality?

2. In particular, is companionship of equals an important goal in relations between women and men?

3. If a man and a woman spend time together, is the time taken out of the rest of his life more important to him than her time is to her? If so, what are possible solutions to this problem?

Men, Feminism, and Men's Contradictory Experiences of Power

I.3

MICHAEL KAUFMAN

Michael Kaufman maintains that the power men have in a system of patriarchy is combined in a "contradictory" way with pain. Men learn to suppress emotions that then come to keep men in their grip. Ignorance of these emotions becomes alienation and isolation. The feminist movement has increased men's pain relative to men's power but promises to diminish men's pain along with diminution of their power.

Kaufman taught from 1979 to 1992 at York University, Toronto, and now works full time writing and doing educational and training work on gender issues.

Reading Questions

1. What forms of control are likely to be found in a society where there is male domination? How does power as control differ from power to develop one's human capacities?
2. What kinds of emotions and needs do men learn to suppress because these needs and emotions might restrict men's ability to control themselves, or those around them?
3. How do suppressed emotions return to have a strange sort of hold on the man whose emotions they are?

IN A WORLD dominated by men, the world of men is, by definition, a world of power. That power is a structured part of the economies and systems of political and social organization; it forms part of the core of religion, family, forms of play, and intellectual life. On an individual level, much of what we associate with masculinity hinges on a man's capacity to exercise power and control.

But men's lives speak of a different reality. Though men hold power and reap the privileges that come with our sex, that power is tainted.[1]

There is, in the lives of men, a strange combination of power and powerlessness, privilege and pain. Men enjoy social power and many forms of privilege by virtue of being male. But the way we have set up that world of power causes immense pain, isolation, and alienation not only for women but also for men. This is not to equate men's pain with the systemic and systematic forms of women's oppression. Rather, it is to say that men's worldly power—as we sit in our homes or walk the street, apply ourselves at work or march through history—comes with a price for us. This combination of power and pain is the hidden story in the lives of men. This is men's contradictory experience of power.

The idea of men's contradictory experiences of power suggests not simply that there is both

Abridged from "Men, Feminism, and Men's Contradictory Experiences of Power" in Theorizing Masculinities. *Harry Brod and Michael Kaufman, eds. (Thousand Oaks, CA: Sage Publications, 1994, pp. 142–163). Reprinted by permission of the publisher.*

power and pain in men's lives. Such a statement would obscure the centrality of men's power and the roots of pain within that power. The key, indeed, is the relationship between the two. As we know, men's social power is the source of individual power and privilege, but as we shall see, it is also the source of the individual experience of pain and alienation. That pain can become an impetus for the individual reproduction—the acceptance, affirmation, celebration, and propagation—of men's individual and collective power. Alternatively, it can be an impetus for change.[2]

The existence of men's pain cannot be an excuse for acts of violence or oppression at the hands of men. After all, the overarching framework for this analysis is the basic point of feminism—and here I state the obvious—that almost all humans currently live in systems of patriarchal power that privilege men and stigmatize, penalize, and oppress women.[3] Rather, knowledge of this pain is a means to better understand men and the complex character of the dominant forms of masculinity.

The realization of men's contradictory experiences of power allows us to better understand the interactions of class, race, sexual orientation, ethnicity, age, and other factors in the lives of men—which is why I speak of contradictory experiences of power in the plural. It allows us to better understand the process of gender acquisition for men. It allows us to better grasp what we might think of as the *gender work* of a society.

An understanding of men's contradictory experiences of power enables us, when possible, to reach out to men with compassion, even as we are highly critical of particular actions and beliefs and challenge the dominant forms of masculinity. It can be one vehicle to understand how good human beings can do horrible things and how some beautiful baby boys can turn into horrible adults. It can help us understand how the majority of men can be reached with a message of change. It is, in a nutshell, the basis for men's embrace of feminism. . . .

MEN'S CONTRADICTORY EXPERIENCES OF POWER

Power and Masculinity

Power, indeed, is the key term when referring to hegemonic masculinities. As I argue at greater length elsewhere,[8] the common feature of the dominant forms of contemporary masculinity is that manhood is equated with having some sort of power.

There are, of course, different ways to conceptualize and describe power. Political philosopher C. B. Macpherson points to the liberal and radical traditions of the last two centuries and tells us that one way we have come to think of human power is as the potential for using and developing our human capacities. Such a view is based on the idea that we are doers and creators able to use rational understanding, moral judgment, creativity, and emotional connection.[9] We possess the power to meet our needs, the power to fight injustice and oppression, the power of muscles and brain, and the power of love. All men, to a greater or lesser extent, experience these meanings of power.

Power, obviously, also has a more negative manifestation. Men have come to see power as a capacity to impose control on others and on our own unruly emotions. It means controlling material resources around us. This understanding of power meshes with the one described by Macpherson because, in societies based on hierarchy and inequality, it appears that all people cannot use and develop their capacities to an equal extent. You have power if you can take advantage of differences between people. I feel I can have power only if I have access to more resources than you do. Power is seen as power over something or someone else.

Although we all experience power in diverse ways, some that celebrate life and diversity and others that hinge on control and domination, the two types of experiences are not equal in the eyes of men, for the latter is the dominant conception of power in our world. The equation of power with domination and control is a definition that has emerged over time in societies in which various divisions are central to the way we have organized our lives: One class has control over economic resources and politics, adults have control over children, humans try to control nature, men dominate women, and, in many countries, one ethnic, racial, or religious group, or group based on sexual orientation, has control over others. There is, though, a common factor to all these societies; all are societies of male domination. The equation of masculinity with power is one that developed over centuries. It conformed to, and in turn justified, the real-life domination of men over women and the valuation of males over females.

Individual men internalize all this into their developing personalities because, born into such a life, we learn to experience our power as a capacity to exercise control. Men learn to accept and exercise power this way because it gives us privileges and advantages that women or children do not usually enjoy. The source of this power is in the society around us, but we learn to exercise it as our own. This is a discourse of social power, but the collective power of men rests not simply on transgenerational and abstract institutions and structures of power but on the ways we internalize, individualize, and come to embody and reproduce these institutions, structures, and conceptualizations of men's power. . . .

The Price

In more concrete terms the acquisition of hegemonic (and most subordinate) masculinities is a process through which men come to suppress a range of emotions, needs, and possibilities, such as nurturing, receptivity, empathy, and compassion, which are experienced as inconsistent with the power of manhood. These emotions and needs do not disappear; they are simply held in check or not allowed to play as full a role in our lives as would be healthy for ourselves and those around us. We dampen these emotions because they might restrict our ability and desire to control ourselves or dominate the human beings around us on whom we depend for love and

friendship. We suppress them because they come to be associated with the femininity we have rejected as part of our quest for masculinity.

These are many things men do to have the type of power we associate with masculinity: We've got to perform and stay in control. We've got to conquer, be on top of things, and call the shots. We've got to tough it out, provide, and achieve. Meanwhile we learn to beat back our feelings, hide our emotions, and suppress our needs.

Whatever power might be associated with dominant masculinities, they also can be the source of enormous pain. Because the images are, ultimately, childhood pictures of omnipotence, they are impossible to obtain. Surface appearances aside, no man is completely able to live up to these ideals and images. For one thing we all continue to experience a range of needs and feelings that are deemed inconsistent with manhood. Such experiences become the source of enormous fear. In our society, this fear is experienced as homophobia or, to express it differently, homophobia is the vehicle that simultaneously transmits and quells the fear.

Such fear and pain have visceral, emotional, intellectual dimensions—although none of these dimensions is necessarily conscious—and the more we are the prisoners of the fear, the more we need to exercise the power we grant ourselves as men. In other words, men exercise patriarchal power not only because we reap tangible benefits from it. The assertion of power is also a response to fear and to the wounds we have experienced in the quest for power. Paradoxically, men are wounded by the very way we have learned to embody and exercise our power.

A man's pain may be deeply buried, barely a whisper in his heart, or it may flood from every pore. The pain might be the lasting trace of things that happened or attitudes and needs acquired 20, 30, or 60 years earlier. Whatever it is, the pain inspires fear for it means not being a man, which means, in a society that confuses gender and sex, not being a male. This means losing power and ungluing basic building blocks of our personalities. This fear must be suppressed for it itself is inconsistent with dominant masculinities.

As every woman who knows men can tell us, the strange thing about men's trying to suppress emotions is that it leads not to less but to more emotional dependency. By losing track of a wide range of our human needs and capacities and by blocking our need for care and nurturance, men lose our emotional common sense and our ability to look after ourselves. Unmet, unknown, and unexpected emotions and needs do not disappear but rather spill into our lives at work, on the road, in a bar, or at home. The very emotions and feelings we have tried to suppress gain a strange hold over us. No matter how cool and in control, these emotions dominate us. I think of the man who feels powerlessness who beats his wife in uncontrolled rage. I walk into a bar and see two men hugging each other in a drunken embrace, the two of them able to express their affection for each other only when plastered. I read about the teenage boys who go out gay-bashing and the men who turn their sense of impotence into a rage against blacks, Jews, or any who are convenient scapegoats.

Alternatively, men might direct buried pain against themselves in the form of self-hate, self-deprecation, physical illness, insecurity, or addictions. Sometimes this is connected with the first. Interviews with rapists and batterers often show not only contempt for women but also an even deeper hatred and contempt for oneself. It is as if, not able to stand themselves, they lash out at others, possibly to inflict similar feelings on another who has been defined as a socially acceptable target, possibly to experience a momentary sense of power and control.[14] We can think of men's pain as having a dynamic aspect. We might displace it or make it invisible, but in doing so we give it even more urgency. This blanking out of a sense of pain is another way of saying that men learn to wear a suit of armor, that is, to maintain an emotional barrier from those around us in order to keep fighting and winning. The impermeable ego barriers discussed in feminist psychoanalysis simultaneously protects men and keeps us locked in a prison of our own creation.

Power, Alienation, and Oppression

Men's pain and the way we exercise power are not just symptoms of our current gender order. Together they shape our sense of manhood, for masculinity has become a form of alienation. Men's alienation is our ignorance of our own emotions, feelings, needs, and potential for human connection and nurturance. Our alienation also results from our distance from women and our distance and isolation from other men. In his book *The Gender of Oppression,* Jeff Hearn suggests that what we think of as masculinity is the result of the way our power and our alienation combine. Our alienation increases the lonely pursuit of power and emphasizes our belief that power requires an ability to be detached and distant.[15]

Men's alienation and distance from women and other men takes on strange and rather conflicting forms. Robert Bly and those in the mythopoetic men's movement have made a lot out of the loss of the father and the distance of many men, in dominant North American cultures anyway, from their own fathers. Part of their point is accurate and simply reaffirms important work done over the past couple of decades on issues around fathers and fathering.[16] Their discussion of these points, however, lacks the richness and depth of feminist psychoanalysis that holds, as a central issue, that the absence of men from most parenting and nurturing tasks means that the masculinity internalized by little boys is based on distance, separation, and a fantasy image of what constitutes manhood, rather than on the type of oneness and inseparability that typifies early mother-child relationships.

The distance from other men is accentuated, in many contemporary heterosexual men's cultures at least, by the emotional distance from other males that begins to develop in adolescence. Men might have buddies, pals, workmates, and friends, but they seldom have the level of complete trust and intimacy enjoyed by many women. Our experience of friendship is limited by the reduced empathy that becomes the masculine norm.[17] As a result we have the paradox that most heterosexual men (and even many gay men) in the dominant North American culture are extremely isolated from other men. In fact, as I have argued elsewhere, many of the institutions of male bonding—the clubs, sporting events, card games, locker rooms, workplaces, professional and religious hierarchies—are a means to provide safety for isolated men who need to find ways to affirm themselves, find common ground with other men, and collectively exercise their power.[18] Such isolation means that each man can remain blind to his dialogue of self-doubt about making the masculine grade—the self-doubts that are consciously experienced by virtually all adolescent males and then consciously or unconsciously by them as adults. In a strange sense, this isolation is key in preserving patriarchy: To a greater or lesser extent it increases the possibility that all men end up colluding with patriarchy—in all its diverse myths and realities—because their own doubts and sense of confusion remain buried.

It is not only other men from whom most men, and certainly most straight men, remain distant. It is also from women. Here another important insight of feminist psychoanalysis is key: Boys' separation from their mother or mother figure means the erection of more or less impermeable ego barriers and an affirmation of distinction, difference, and opposition to those things identified with women and femininity. Boys repress characteristics and possibilities associated with mother/women/the feminine, unconsciously and consciously. Thus Bly and the mythopoetic theorists have it all wrong when they suggest that the central problem with contemporary men (and by this they seem to mean North American middle-class, young to middle-aged, white, straight urban men) is that they have become feminized. The problem as suggested above is the wholesale repression and

suppression of those traits and possibilities associated with women.[19]

These factors suggest the complexity of gender identity, gender formation, and gender relations. It appears that we need forms of analysis that allow for contradictory relationships between individuals and the power structures from which they benefit. It is a strange situation when men's very real power and privilege in the world hinges not only on that power but also on an experience of alienation and powerlessness—rooted in childhood experiences but reinforced in different ways as adolescents and then adults. These experiences, in turn, become the spur at the individual level (in addition to the obvious and tangible benefits) to recreate and celebrate the forms and structures through which men exercise power.

But as we have seen, there is no single masculinity or one experience of being a man. The experience of different men, their actual power and privilege in the world, is based on a range of social positions and relations. The social power of a poor white man is different from a rich one, a working-class black man from a working-class white man, a gay man from a bisexual man from a straight man, a Jewish man in Ethiopia from a Jewish man in Israel, a teenage boy from an adult. Within each group, men usually have privileges and power relative to the women in that group, but in society as a whole, things are not always so straightforward. . . .

MEN AND FEMINISM

An analysis of men's contradictory experiences of power gives us useful insights into the potential relation of men to feminism. The power side of the equation is not anything new and, indeed, men's power and privileges form a very good reason for men to individually and collectively oppose feminism.

But we do know that an increasing number of men have become sympathetic to feminism (in content if not always in name) and have embraced feminist theory and action (although, again, more often in theory than in action). There are different reasons for a man's acceptance of feminism. It might be outrage at inequality; it might result from the influence of a partner, family member, or friend; it might be his own sense of injustice at the hands of other men; it might be a sense of shared oppression, say because of his sexual orientation; it might be his own guilt about the privileges he enjoys as a man; it might be horror at men's violence; it might be sheer decency.

Although the majority of men in North America would still not label themselves profeminist, a strong majority of men in Canada and a reasonable percentage of men in the United States would sympathize with many of the issues as presented by feminists. As we know, this sympathy does not always translate into changes of behavior, but, increasingly ideas are changing and in some cases, behavior is starting to catch up.

How do we explain the growing number of men who are supportive of feminism and women's liberation (to use that term that was too hastily abandoned by the end of the 1970s)? Except for the rare outcast or iconoclast, there are few examples from history where significant numbers of a ruling group supported the liberation or those over whom they ruled and from whose subordination they benefited.

One answer is that the current feminist wave—whatever its weaknesses and whatever backlash might exist against it—has had a massive impact during the past two and a half decades. Large numbers of men, along with many women who had supported the status quo, now realize that the tide has turned and, like it or not, the world is changing. Women's rebellion against patriarchy holds the promise of bringing patriarchy to an end. Although patriarchy in its many different social and economic forms still has considerable staying power, an increasing number of its social, political, economic, and emotional structures are proving unworkable. Some men react with rearguard actions while others step tentatively or strongly in the direction of change.

This explanation of men's support for change catches only part of the picture. The existence of contradictory experiences of power suggests there is a basis for men's embrace of feminism that goes beyond swimming with a change in the tide.

The rise of feminism has shifted the balance between men's power and men's pain. In societies and eras in which men's social power went largely unchallenged, men's power so outweighed men's pain that the existence of this pain could remain buried, even nonexistent. When you rule the roost, call the shots, and are closer to God, there is not a lot of room left for pain, at least for pain that appears to be linked to the practices of masculinity. But with the rise of modern feminism, the fulcrum between men's power and men's pain has been undergoing a rapid shift. This is particularly true in cultures where the definition of men's power had already moved away from tight control over the home and tight monopolies in the real world of work.[20]

As men's power is challenged, those things that came as a compensation, a reward, or a lifelong distraction from any potential pain are progressively reduced or, at least, called into question. As women's oppression becomes problematized, many forms of this oppression become problems for men. Individual gender-related experiences of pain and disquietude among men have become increasingly manifest and have started to gain a social hearing and social expression in widely diverse forms, including different branches of the men's movement—from reactionary antifeminists, to the Bly-type mythopoetic movement, to pro-feminist men's organizing.

In other words, if gender is about power, then as actual relations of power between men and women and between different groups of men (such as straight and gay men) start to shift, then our experiences of gender and our gender definitions must also begin to change. The process of gender work is ongoing and includes this process of reformulation and upheaval. . . .

RISING SUPPORT AND LEARNING PITFALLS

On the psychodynamic level—the realm in which we can witness the interplay between social movements and the individual psyche—the challenge of feminism to men is one of dislodging the hegemonic masculine psyche. This is not a psychological interpretation of change because it is the social challenge to men's power and the actual reduction of mens' social power that is the source of change. What was once a secure relationship between power over others, control over oneself, and the suppression of a range of needs and emotions is under attack. What had felt stable, natural, and right is being revealed as both a source of oppression for others and the prime source of pain, anguish, and disquietude for men themselves.

The implication of all this is that the feminists challenge to men's power has the potential of liberating men and helping more men discover new masculinities that will be part of demolishing gender altogether. Whatever privileges and forms of power we will certainly lose will be increasingly compensated by the end of the pain, fear, dysfunctional forms of behavior, violence experienced at the hands of other men, violence we inflict on ourselves, endless pressure to perform and succeed, and the sheer impossibility of living up to our masculine ideals.

Our awareness of men's contradictory experiences of power give us the tools to simultaneously challenge men's power and speak to men's pain. It is the basis for a politics of compassion and for enlisting men's support for a revolution that is challenging the most basic and long-lasting structures of human civilization.

NOTES

1. Although it may be somewhat awkward for women readers, I often refer to men in the first person plural—we, us, our—to acknowledge my position within the object of my analysis.

2. My thanks to Harry Brod who several years ago cautioned me against talking about men's power and men's pain as two sides of the same coin, a comment that led me to focus on the relationship between the two. Thanks also to Harry and to Bob Connell for their comments on a draft of this article. I'd particularly like to express my appreciation to Michael Kimmel both for his comments on the draft and for our ongoing intellectual partnership and friendship.

3. Although there has been controversy over the applicability of the term *patriarchy*—see for example, Michel Barrett and Mary MacIntosh's reservations in *The Anti-Social Family* (London: Verso, 1982)—I follow others who use it as a broad descriptive term for male-dominated social systems.

8. *Cracking the Armour: Power, Pain, and the Lives of Men* (Toronto: Viking Canada, 1993).

9. C. B. Macpherson, *Democratic Theory* (London: Oxford University Press, 1973).

14. See, for example, the accounts in Sylvia Levine and Joseph Koenig, eds., *Why Men Rape* (Toronto: Macmillan of Canada, 1980) and Timothy Beneke, *Men on Rape* (New York: St. Martin's, 1982).

15. Jeff Hern, *The Gender of Oppression* (Brighton, UK: Wheatsheaf, 1987).

16. For numerous sources on fatherhood, see Michael E. Lamb, ed., *The Role of the Father in Child Development* (New York: John Wiley, 1981); Stanley H. Cath, Alan R. Gurwitt, and John Munder Ross, *Father and Child* (Boston: Little, Brown, 1982). Also see Michael W. Yogman, James Cooley, & Daniel Kindlon, "Fathers, Infants, Toddlers: Developing Relationship" and others in Phyllis Bronstein and Carolyn Pape Cowan, *Fatherhood Today* (New York: John Wiley, 1988); and Kyle D. Pruett, "Infants of Primary Nurturing Fathers," in *The Psychoanalytic Study of the Child,* vol. 38, 1983; and for a different approach, see Samuel Osherson, *Finding our Fathers* (New York: Free Press, 1986).

17. Lillian Rubin, *Intimate Strangers* (New York: Harper Colophon, 1984). See also Peter M. Nardi, ed., *Mens' Friendships* (Newbury Park, CA: Sage, 1992).

18. Kaufman, *Cracking the Armour,* op. cit.

19. The mythopoetic framework is discussed at length by Michael Kimmel and Michael Kaufman in chapter 14 of this volume.

20. One fascinating account of total patriarchal control of the home is Naguib Mahfouz's 1956 book *Palace Walk* (New York: Anchor Books, 1990).

Further Questions

1. What role does fear play in the experiences of power, needs, and feelings?
2. How do isolation and alienation function to preserve patriarchal power?
3. How has feminism diminished men's power and brought their pain to the surface?
How might feminism liberate men by helping end the pain of fear of patriarchy?

White Privilege and Male Privilege:
A Personal Account of Coming to See Correspondences
I.4 # Through Work in Women's Studies*

PEGGY McINTOSH

Peggy McIntosh compares privileges of being white with male privilege. Both are protected by being denied. Those possessing such privileges, in particular, are taught not to recognize them as such. She lists 46 types of circumstances in which white skin is an unearned advantage. She also lists 8 areas in which being heterosexual is an (unearned) social asset, like white skin in being taken for granted by persons so advantaged.

McIntosh is Associate Director of the Center for Research on Women at Wellesley College, Wellesley, MA.

Reading Questions

1. Think of some everyday situations where you are advantaged/disadvantaged by race or class. Then compare your list with McIntosh's. What were the highlights of this comparison?
2. Think of some everyday situations in which you are advantaged/disadvantaged by sexual orientation (homosexual or heterosexual). How do your experiences in this area compare with those mentioned by McIntosh?

* I have appreciated commentary on this paper from the Working Papers Committee of the Wellesley College Center for Research on Women, from members of the Dodge seminar, and from many individuals, including Margaret Andersen, Sorel Berman, Joanne Braxton, Johnella Butler, Sandra Dickerson, Marnie Evans, Beverly Guy-Sheftall, Sandra Harding, Eleanor Hinton Hoytt, Pauline Houston, Paul Lauter, Joyce Miller, Mary Norris, Gloria Oden, Beverly Smith, and John Walter.

THROUGH WORK to bring materials and perspectives from Women's Studies into the rest of the curriculum, I have often noticed men's unwillingness to grant that they are overprivileged in the curriculum, even though they may grant that women are disadvantaged. Denials that amount to taboos surround the subject of advantages that men gain from women's disadvantages. These denials protect male privilege from being fully recognized, acknowledged, lessened, or ended.

Thinking through unacknowledged male privilege as a phenomenon with a life of its own, I realized that since hierarchies in our society are interlocking, there was most likely a phenomenon of white privilege that was similarly denied and protected, but alive and real in its effects. As a white person, I realized I had been taught about racism as something that puts others at a disadvantage, but had been taught not to see one of its corollary aspects, white privilege, which puts me at an advantage.

I think whites are carefully taught not to recognize white privilege, as males are taught not to recognize male privilege. So I have begun in an untutored way to ask what it is like to have white privilege. This paper is a partial record of my personal observations and not a scholarly analysis. It is based on my daily experiences within my particular circumstances.

I have come to see white privilege as an invisible package of unearned assets that I can count on cashing in each day, but about which I was "meant" to remain oblivious. White privilege is like an invisible weightless knapsack of special provisions, assurances, tools, maps, guides, codebooks, passports, visas, clothes, compass, emergency gear, and blank checks.

Since I have had trouble facing white privilege, and describing its results in my life, I saw parallels here with men's reluctance to acknowledge male privilege. Only rarely will a man go beyond acknowledging that women are disadvantaged to acknowledging that men have unearned advantage, or that unearned privilege has not been good for men's development as human beings, or for society's development, or that privilege systems might ever be challenged and *changed*.

I will review here several types or layers of denial that I see at work protecting, and preventing awareness about, entrenched male privilege. Then I will draw parallels, from my own experience, with the denials that veil the facts of white privilege. Finally, I will list forty-six ordinary and daily ways in which I experience having white privilege, by contrast with my African American colleagues in the same building. This list is not intended to be generalizable. Others can make their own lists from within their own life circumstances.

Writing this paper has been difficult, despite warm receptions for the talks on which it is based.[1] For describing white privilege makes one newly accountable. As we in Women's Studies work reveal male privilege and ask men to give up some of their power, so one who writes about having white privilege must ask, "Having described it, what will I do to lessen or end it?"

The denial of men's overprivileged state takes many forms in discussions of curriculum change work. Some claim that men must be central in the curriculum because they have done most of what is important or distinctive in life or in civilization. Some recognize sexism in the curriculum but deny that it makes male students seem unduly important in life. Others agree that certain *individual* thinkers are male oriented but deny that there is any *systemic* tendency in disciplinary frameworks or epistemology to overempower men as a group. Those men who do grant that male privilege takes institutionalized and embedded forms are still likely to deny that male hegemony has opened doors for them personally. Virtually all men deny that male overreward alone can explain men's centrality in all the inner sanctums of our most powerful institutions. Moreover, those few who will acknowledge that male privilege systems have overempowered them usually end up doubting that we could dismantle these privilege systems. They may say they will work to improve women's status, in the society or in the university, but they can't or won't support the idea of lessening men's. In curricular terms, this is the point at which they say that they regret they cannot use any of the interesting new scholarship on women because the syllabus is full. When the talk turns to giving men less cultural room, even the most thoughtful and fair-minded of the men I know will tend to reflect, or fall back on, conservative assumptions about the inevitability of present gender relations and distributions of power, calling on precedent or sociobiology and psychobiology to demonstrate that male domination is natural and follows inevitably from evolutionary pressures. Others resort to arguments from "experience" or religion or social responsibility or wishing and dreaming.

After I realized, through faculty development work in Women's Studies, the extent to which men work from a base of unacknowledged privilege, I understood that much of their oppressiveness was unconscious. Then I remembered the frequent charges from women of color that white women whom they encounter are oppressive. I began to understand why we are justly seen as oppressive, even when we don't see ourselves that way. At the very least, obliviousness of one's privileged state can make a person or group irritating to be with. I began to count the ways in which I enjoy unearned skin privilege and have been conditioned into oblivion about its existence, unable to see that it put me "ahead" in any way, or put my people ahead, overrewarding us and yet also paradoxically damaging us, or that it could or should be changed.

My schooling gave me no training in seeing myself as an oppressor, as an unfairly advantaged person, or as a participant in a damaged culture. I was taught to see myself as an individual whose moral state depended on her individual moral will. At school, we are not taught about slavery in any depth; we are not taught to see slaveholders as damaged people. Slaves were seen as the only group at risk of being dehumanized. My schooling followed the pattern which Elizabeth

Minnich has pointed out: whites are taught to think of their lives as morally neutral, normative, and average, and also ideal, so that when we work to benefit others, this is seen as work that will allow "them" to be more like "us." I think many of us know how obnoxious this attitude can be in men.

After frustration with men who would not recognize male privilege, I decided to try to work on myself at least by identifying some of the daily effects of white privilege in my life. It is crude work, at this stage, but I will give here a list of special circumstances and conditions I experience that I did not earn but that I have been made to feel are mine by birth, by citizenship, and by virtue of being a conscientious law-abiding "normal" person of goodwill. I have chosen those conditions that I think in my case *attach somewhat more to skin-color privilege* than to class, religion, ethnic status, or geographical location, though these other privileging factors are intricately intertwined. As far as I can see, my Afro-American co-workers, friends, and acquaintances with whom I come into daily or frequent contact in this particular time, place, and line of work cannot count on most of these conditions.

1. I can, if I wish, arrange to be in the company of people of my race most of the time.

2. I can avoid spending time with people whom I was trained to mistrust and who have learned to mistrust my kind or me.

3. If I should need to move, I can be pretty sure of renting or purchasing housing in an area which I can afford and in which I would want to live.

4. I can be reasonably sure that my neighbors in such a location will be neutral or pleasant to me.

5. I can go shopping alone most of the time, fairly well assured that I will not be followed or harassed by store detectives.

6. I can turn on the television or open to the front page of the paper and see people of my race widely and positively represented.

7. When I am told about our national heritage or about "civilization," I am shown that people of my color made it what it is.

8. I can be sure that my children will be given curricular materials that testify to the existence of their race.

9. If I want to, I can be pretty sure of finding a publisher for this piece on white privilege.

10. I can be fairly sure of having my voice heard in a group in which I am the only member of my race.

11. I can be casual about whether or not to listen to another woman's voice in a group in which she is the only member of her race.

12. I can go into a book shop and count on finding the writing of my race represented, into a supermarket and find the staple foods that fit with my cultural traditions, into a hairdresser's shop and find someone who can deal with my hair.

13. Whether I use checks, credit cards, or cash, I can count on my skin color not to work against the appearance that I am financially reliable.

14. I could arrange to protect our young children most of the time from people who might not like them.

15. I did not have to educate our children to be aware of systemic racism for their own daily physical protection.

16. I can be pretty sure that my children's teachers and employers will tolerate them if they fit school and workplace norms; my chief worries about them do not concern others' attitudes toward their race.

17. I can talk with my mouth full and not have people put this down to my color.

18. I can swear, or dress in secondhand clothes, or not answer letters, without having people attribute these choices to the bad morals, the poverty, or the illiteracy of my race.

19. I can speak in public to a powerful male group without putting my race on trial.

20. I can do well in a challenging situation without being called a credit to my race.

21. I am never asked to speak for all the people of my racial group.

22. I can remain oblivious to the language and customs of persons of color who constitute the world's majority without feeling in my culture any penalty for such oblivion.

23. I can criticize our government and talk about how much I fear its policies and behavior without being seen as a cultural outsider.

24. I can be reasonably sure that if I ask to talk to "the person in charge," I will be facing a person of my race.

25. If a traffic cop pulls me over or if the IRS audits my tax return, I can be sure I haven't been singled out because of my race.

26. I can easily buy posters, postcards, picture books, greeting cards, dolls, toys, and children's magazines featuring people of my race.

27. I can go home from most meetings of organizations I belong to feeling somewhat tied in, rather than isolated, out of place, outnumbered, unheard, held at a distance, or feared.

28. I can be pretty sure that an argument with a colleague of another race is more likely to jeopardize her chances for advancement than to jeopardize mine.

29. I can be fairly sure that if I argue for the promotion of a person of another race, or a program centering on race, this is not likely to cost me heavily within my present setting, even if my colleagues disagree with me.

30. If I declare there is a racial issue at hand, or there isn't a racial issue at hand, my race will lend me more credibility for either position than a person of color will have.

31. I can choose to ignore developments in minority writing and minority activist programs, or disparage them, or learn from them, but in any case, I can find ways to be more or less protected from negative consequences of any of these choices.

32. My culture gives me little fear about ignoring the perspectives and powers of people of other races.

33. I am not made acutely aware that my shape, bearing, or body odor will be taken as a reflection on my race.

34. I can worry about racism without being seen as self-interested or self-seeking.

35. I can take a job with an affirmative action employer without having my co-workers on the job suspect that I got it because of my race.

36. If my day, week, or year is going badly, I need not ask of each negative episode or situation whether it has racial overtones.

37. I can be pretty sure of finding people who would be willing to talk with me and advise me about my next steps, professionally.

38. I can think over many options, social, political, imaginative, or professional, without asking whether a person of my race would be accepted or allowed to do what I want to do.

39. I can be late to a meeting without having the lateness reflect on my race.

40. I can choose public accommodation without fearing that people of my race cannot get in or will be mistreated in the places I have chosen.

41. I can be sure that if I need legal or medical help, my race will not work against me.

42. I can arrange my activities so that I will never have to experience feelings of rejection owing to my race.

43. If I have low credibility as a leader, I can be sure that my race is not the problem.

44. I can easily find academic courses and institutions that give attention only to people of my race.

45. I can expect figurative language and imagery in all of the arts to testify to experiences of my race.

46. I can choose blemish cover or bandages in "flesh" color and have them more or less match my skin.

I repeatedly forgot each of the realizations on this list until I wrote it down. For me, white privilege has turned out to be an elusive and fugitive subject. The pressure to avoid it is great, for in facing it I must give up the myth of meritocracy. If these things are true, this is not such a free country; one's life is not what one makes it; many doors open for certain people through no virtues of their own. These perceptions mean also that my moral condition is not what I had been led to believe. The appearance of being a good citizen rather than a troublemaker comes in large part from having all sorts of doors open automatically because of my color.

A further paralysis of nerve comes from literary silence protecting privilege. My clearest memories of finding such analysis are in Lillian Smith's unparalleled *Killers of the Dream* and Margaret Andersen's review of Karen and Mamie Field's *Lemon Swamp*. Smith, for example, wrote about walking toward black children on the street and knowing they would step into the gutter; Andersen contrasted the pleasure that she, as a white child, took on summer driving trips to the south with Karen Fields' memories of driving in a closed car stocked with all necessities lest, in stopping, her black family should suffer "insult, or worse." Adrienne Rich also recognizes and writes about daily experiences of privilege, but in my observation, white women's writing in this area is far more often on systemic racism than on our daily lives as light-skinned women.[2]

In unpacking this invisible knapsack of white privilege, I have listed conditions of daily experience that I once took for granted, as neutral, normal, and universally available to everybody, just as I once thought of a male-focused curriculum as the neutral or accurate account that can speak for all. Nor did I think of any of these perquisites as bad for the holder. I now think that we need a more finely differentiated taxonomy of privilege, for some of these varieties are only what one would want for everyone in a just society, and others give license to be ignorant, oblivious, arrogant, and destructive. Before proposing some more finely tuned categorization, I will make some observations about the general effects of these conditions on my life and expectations.

In this potpourri of examples, some privileges make me feel at home in the world. Others allow me to escape penalties or dangers that others suffer. Through some, I escape fear, anxiety, insult, injury, or a sense of not being welcome, not being real. Some keep me from having to hide, to be in disguise, to feel sick or crazy, to negotiate each transaction from the position of being an outsider or, within my group, a person who is suspected of having too close links with a dominant culture. Most keep me from having to be angry.

I see a pattern running through the matrix of white privilege, a pattern of assumptions that were passed on to me as a white person. There was one main piece of cultural turf; it was my own turf, and I was among those who could control the turf. I could measure up to the cultural standards and take advantage of the many options I saw around me to make what the culture would call a success of my life. *My skin color was an asset for any move I was educated to want to make.* I could think of myself as "belonging" in major ways and of making social systems work for me. I could freely disparage, fear, neglect, or be oblivious to anything outside of the dominant cultural forms. Being of the main culture, I could also criticize it fairly freely. My life was reflected back to me frequently enough so that I felt, with regard to my race, if not to my sex, like one of the real people.

Whether through the curriculum or in the newspaper, the television, the economic system, or the general look of people in the streets, I received daily signals and indications that my people counted and that others *either didn't exist or must be trying, not very successfully, to be like people of my race.* I was given cultural permission not to hear voices of people of other races or a tepid cultural tolerance for hearing or acting on such voices. I was also raised not to suffer seriously from anything that darker-skinned people might say about my group, "protected," though perhaps I should more accurately say *prohibited,* through the habits of my economic class and social group, from living in racially mixed groups or being reflective about interactions between people or differing races.

In proportion as my racial group was being made confident, comfortable, and oblivious, other groups were likely being made unconfident, uncomfortable, and alienated. Whiteness protected me from many kinds of hostility, distress, and violence, which I was being subtly trained to visit in turn upon people of color.

For this reason, the word "privilege" now seems to me misleading. Its connotations are too positive to fit the conditions and behaviors which "privilege systems" produce. We usually think of privilege as being a favored state, whether earned, or conferred by birth or luck. School graduates are reminded they are privileged and urged to use their (enviable) assets well. The word "privilege" carries the connotation of being something everyone must want. Yet some of the conditions I have described here work to systematically overempower certain groups. Such privilege simply *confers dominance,* gives permission to control, because of one's race or sex. The kind of privilege that gives license to some people to be, at best, thoughtless and, at worst, murderous should not continue to be referred to as a desirable attribute. Such "privilege" may be widely desired without being in any way beneficial to the whole society.

Moreover, though "privilege" may confer power, it does not confer moral strength. Those who do not depend on conferred dominance have traits and qualities that may never develop in those who do. Just as Women's Studies courses indicate that women survive their political circumstances to lead lives that hold the human race together, so "underprivileged" people of color who are the world's majority have survived their oppression and lived survivors' lives from which the white global minority can and must learn. In some groups, those dominated have actually become strong through *not* having all of these unearned advantages, and this gives them a great deal to teach the others. Members of so-called privileged groups can seem foolish, ridiculous, infantile, or dangerous by contrast.

I want, then, to distinguish between earned strength and unearned power conferred systemically. Power from unearned privilege can look like strength when it is, in fact, permission to escape or to dominate. But not all of the privileges on my list are inevitably damaging. Some, like the expectation that neighbors will be decent to you, or that your race will not count against you in court, should be the norm in a just society and should be considered as the entitlement of everyone. Others, like the privilege not to listen to less powerful people, distort the humanity of the holders as well as the ignored groups. Still others, like finding one's staple foods everywhere, may be a function of being a member of a numerical majority in the population. Others have to do with not having to labor under pervasive negative stereotyping and mythology.

We might at least start by distinguishing between positive advantages that we can work to spread, to the point where they are not advantages at all but simply part of the normal civic and social fabric, and negative types of advantage that unless rejected will always reinforce our present hierarchies. For example, the positive "privilege" of belonging, the feeling that one belongs within the human circle, as Native Americans say, fosters development and should not be seen as privilege for a few. It is, let us say, an entitlement that none of us should have to

earn; ideally it is an *unearned entitlement*. At present, since only a few have it, it is an *unearned advantage* for them. The negative "privilege" that gave me cultural permission not to take darker-skinned Others seriously can be seen as arbitrarily conferred dominance and should not be desirable for anyone. This paper results from a process of coming to see that some of the power that I originally saw as attendant on being a human being in the United States consisted in *unearned advantage* and *conferred dominance,* as well as other kinds of special circumstance not universally taken for granted.

In writing this paper I have also realized that white identity and status (as well as class identity and status) give me considerable power to choose whether to broach this subject and its trouble. I can pretty well decide whether to disappear and avoid and not listen and escape the dislike I may engender in other people through this essay, or interrupt, answer, interpret, preach, correct, criticize, and control to some extent what goes on in reaction to it. Being white, I am given considerable power to escape many kinds of danger or penalty as well as to choose which risks I want to take.

There is an analogy here, once again with Women's Studies. Our male colleagues do not have a great deal to lose in supporting Women's Studies, but they do not have a great deal to lose if they oppose it either. They simply have the power to decide whether to commit themselves to more equitable distributions of power. They will probably feel few penalties whatever choice they make; they do not seem, in any obvious short-term sense, the ones at risk, though they are, we are all at risk because of the behaviors that have been rewarded in them.

Through Women's Studies work I have met very few men who are truly distressed about systemic, unearned male advantage and conferred dominance. And so one question for me and others like me is whether we will be like them, or whether we will get truly distressed, even outraged, about unearned race advantage and conferred dominance and if so, what we will do to lessen them. In any case, we need to do more work in identifying how they actually affect our daily lives. We need more down-to-earth writing by people about these taboo subjects. We need more understanding of the ways in which white "privilege" damages white people, for these are not the same ways in which it damages the victimized. Skewed white psyches are an inseparable part of the picture, though I do not want to confuse the kinds of damage done to the holders of special assets and to those who suffer the deficits. Many, perhaps most, of our white students in the United States think that racism doesn't affect them because they are not people of color; they do not see "whiteness" as a racial identity. Many men likewise think that Women's Studies does not bear on their own existences because they are not female; they do not see themselves as having gendered identities. Insisting on the universal "effects" of "privilege" systems, then, becomes one of our chief tasks, and being more explicit about the *particular* effects in particular contexts is another. Men need to join us in this work.

In addition, since race and sex are not the only advantaging systems at work, we need to similarly examine the daily experience of having age advantage, or ethnic advantage, or physical ability, or advantage related to nationality, religion, or sexual orientation. Professor Marnie Evans suggested to me that in many ways the list I made also applies directly to heterosexual privilege. This is a still more taboo subject than race privilege: the daily ways in which heterosexual privilege makes some persons comfortable or powerful, providing supports, assets, approvals, and rewards to those who live or expect to live in heterosexual pairs. Unpacking that content is still more difficult, owing to the deeper imbeddedness of heterosexual advantage and dominance and stricter taboos surrounding these.

But to start such an analysis I would put this observation from my own experience: The fact that I live under the same roof with a man triggers all kinds of societal assumptions about my worth, politics, life, and value and triggers a host of unearned advantages and powers. After

recasting many elements from the original list I would add further observations like these:

1. My children do not have to answer questions about why I live with my partner (my husband).

2. I have no difficulty finding neighborhoods where people approve of our household.

3. Our children are given texts and classes that implicitly support our kind of family unit and do not turn them against my choice of domestic partnership.

4. I can travel alone or with my husband without expecting embarrassment or hostility in those who deal with us.

5. Most people I meet will see my marital arrangements as an asset to my life or as a favorable comment on my likability, my competence, or my mental health.

6. I can talk about the social events of a weekend without fearing most listeners' reactions.

7. I will feel welcomed and "normal" in the usual walks of public life, institutional and social.

8. In many contexts, I am seen as "all right" in daily work on women because I do not live chiefly with women.

Difficulties and dangers surrounding the tasks of finding parallels are many. Since racism, sexism, and heterosexism are not the same, the advantages associated with them should not be seen as the same. In addition, it is hard to isolate aspects of unearned advantage that derive chiefly from social class, economic class, race, religion, region, sex, or ethnic identity. The oppressions are both distinct and interlocking, as the Combahee River Collective statement of 1977 continues to remind us eloquently.[3]

One factor seems clear about all of the interlocking oppressions. They take both active forms that we can see and embedded forms that members of the dominant group are taught not to see. In my class and place, I did not see myself as racist because I was taught to recognize racism only in individual acts of meanness by members of my group, never in invisible systems conferring racial dominance on my group from birth. Likewise, we are taught to think that sexism or heterosexism is carried on only through intentional, individual acts of discrimination, meanness, or cruelty, rather than in invisible systems conferring unsought dominance on certain groups. Disapproving of the systems won't be enough to change them. I was taught to think that racism could end if white individuals changed their attitudes; many men think sexism can be ended by individual changes in daily behavior toward women. But a man's sex provides advantage for him whether or not he approves of the way in which dominance has been conferred on his group. A "white" skin in the United States opens many doors for whites whether or not we approve of the way dominance has been conferred on us. Individual acts can palliate, but cannot end, these problems. To redesign social systems, we need first to acknowledge their colossal unseen dimensions. The silences and denials surrounding privilege are the key political tool here. They keep the thinking about equality or equity incomplete, protecting unearned advantage and conferred dominance by making these taboo subjects. Most talk by whites about equal opportunity seems to me now to be about equal opportunity to try to get into a position of dominance while denying that *systems* of dominance exist.

Obliviousness about white advantage, like obliviousness about male advantage, is kept strongly inculturated in the United States so as to maintain the myth of meritocracy, the myth that democratic choice is equally available to all. Keeping most people unaware that freedom of confident action is there for just a small number of people props up those in power and serves to keep power in the hands of the same groups that have most of it already. Though systemic change takes many decades, there are pressing questions for me and I imagine for some others like me if we raise our daily consciousness on the perquisites of being light-skinned. What will we do with such knowledge? As we know from watching men, it is an open question whether we will choose to use unearned advantage to weaken invisible privilege systems and whether we will use any of our arbitrarily awarded power to try to reconstruct power systems on a broader base.

Notes

1. This paper was presented at the Virginia Women's Studies Association conference in Richmond in April, 1986, and the American Educational Research Association conference in Boston in October, 1986, and discussed with two groups of participants in the Dodge seminars for Secondary School Teachers in New York and Boston in the spring of 1987.

2. Andersen, Margaret, "Race and the Social Science Curriculum: A Teaching and Learning Discussion." *Radical Teacher,* November, 1984, pp. 17–20. Smith, Lillian, *Killers of the Dream,* New York: W. W. Norton, 1949.

3. "A Black Feminist Statement," The Combahee River Collective, pp. 13–22 in G. Hull, P. Scott, B. Smith, Eds., *All the Women Are White, All the Blacks Are Men, But Some of Us Are Brave: Black Women's Studies,* Old Westbury, NY: The Feminist Press, 1982.

Further Questions

1. If you are of the advantaged race or sexual orientation, do you easily forget the unearned advantages that come your way because of this?

2. Do you agree that unearned privileges confer only power and dominance and do not necessarily make advantaged groups morally correct or morally strong?

3. How does recognition of white and heterosexual privileges enlighten you about the system of male privilege?

The Uses of Anger: Women Responding to Racism[*] I.5

AUDRE LORDE

Audre Lorde discusses anger as a response to racism; her comments, however, apply to oppression of any sort. She is angry that white women believe in the inevitability of systems that put whites at the center, women of color somewhere on the fringe. She sees no reason to refrain from expressing this anger out of fear of provoking guilt feelings either in herself or in the white women at which it is directed. Anger can be a positive force in bringing differences to the surface and making productive use of them.

Lorde taught English at Hunter College in New York City. Many of her poems, essays, fiction, and speeches are articulate statements of her experience as a black lesbian feminist. (Another writing by Audre Lorde appears in Part XII.)

Reading Questions

1. What is your idea of racism, and what is your response to it? Would your response be different if you were of a different race?
2. Is responding to racism among women too much of a distraction from the more important tasks of destroying patriarchy?
3. What productive response can you make to someone who is angry about your solidarity with a group that is oppressing her group?

RACISM. THE BELIEF in the inherent superiority of one race over all others and thereby the right to dominance, manifest and implied.

Women respond to racism. My response to racism is anger. I have lived with that anger, ignoring it, feeding upon it, learning to use it before it laid my visions to waste, for most of my life. Once I did it in silence, afraid of the weight. My fear of anger taught me nothing. Your fear of that anger will teach you nothing, also.

Women responding to racism means women responding to anger; the anger of exclusion, of unquestioned privilege, of racial distortions, of silence, ill-use, stereotyping, defensiveness, misnaming, betrayal, and co-optation.

My anger is a response to racist attitudes and to the actions and presumptions that arise out of those attitudes. If your dealings with other women reflect those attitudes, then my anger and your attendant fears are spotlights that can be used for growth in the same way I have used learning to express anger for my growth. But for corrective surgery, not guilt. Guilt and defensiveness are bricks in a wall against which we all flounder; they serve none of our futures.

[*]*Keynote presentation at the National Women's Studies Association Conference, Storrs, Connecticut, June 1981.*

"The Uses of Anger" in Sister Outsider *by Audre Lorde (Freedom, CA: The Crossing Press, 1984). Reprinted by permission of the publisher and author.*

Because I do not want this to become a theoretical discussion, I am going to give a few examples of interchanges between women that illustrate these points. In the interest of time, I am going to cut them short. I want you to know there were many more.

For example:

- I speak out of direct and particular anger at an academic conference, and a white woman says, "Tell me how you feel but don't say it too harshly or I cannot hear you." But is it my manner that keeps her from hearing, or the threat of a message that her life may change?

- The Women's Studies Program of a southern university invites a Black woman to read following a week-long forum on Black and white women. "What has this week given to you?" I ask. The most vocal white woman says, "I think I've gotten a lot. I feel Black women really understand me a lot better now; they have a better idea of where I'm coming from." As if understanding her lay at the core of the racist problem.

- After fifteen years of a women's movement which professes to address the life concerns and possible futures of all women, I still hear, on campus after campus, "How can we address the issues of racism? No women of Color attended." Or, the other side of that statement, "We have no one in our department equipped to teach their work." In other words, racism is a Black women's problem, a problem of women of Color, and only we can discuss it.

- After I read from my work entitled "Poems for Women in Rage,"* a white woman asks me: "Are you going to do anything with how we can deal directly with *our* anger? I feel it's so important."

I ask "How do you use *your* rage?" And then I have to turn away from the blank look in her eyes, before she can invite me to participate in her own annihilation. I do not exist to feel her anger for her.

- White women are beginning to examine their relationships to Black women, yet often I hear them wanting only to deal with little colored children across the roads of childhood, the beloved nursemaid, the occasional second-grade classmate—those tender memories of what was once mysterious and intriguing or neutral. You avoid the childhood assumptions formed by the raucous laughter at Rastus and Alfalfa, the acute message of your mommy's handkerchief spread upon the park bench because I had just been sitting there, the indelible and dehumanizing portraits of Amos 'n Andy and your daddy's humorous bedtime stories.

- I wheel my two-year-old daughter in a shopping cart through a supermarket in Eastchester in 1967, and a little white girl riding past in her mother's cart calls out excitedly, "Oh look, Mommy, a baby maid!" And your mother shushes you, but she does not correct you. And so fifteen years later, at a conference on racism, you can still find that story humorous. But I hear your laughter is full of terror and dis-ease.

- A white academic welcomes the appearance of a collection by non-Black women of Color.† "It allows me to deal with racism without dealing with the harshness of Black women," she says to me.

- At an international cultural gathering of women, a well-known white american woman poet interrupts the reading of the

---

*One poem from this series is included in *Chosen Poems: Old and New* (W. W. Norton and Company, New York, 1978), pp. 105–108.

† *This Bridge Called My Back: Writings by Radical Women of Color* edited by Cherríe Moraga and Gloria Anzaldua (Kitchen Table: Women of Color Press, New York, 1984), first published in 1981.

work of women of Color to read her own poem, and then dashes off to an "important panel."

If women in the academy truly want a dialogue about racism, it will require recognizing the needs and the living contexts of other women. When an academic woman says, "I can't afford it," she may mean she is making a choice about how to spend her available money. But when a woman on welfare says, "I can't afford it," she means that she is surviving on an amount of money that was barely subsistence in 1972, and she often does not have enough to eat. Yet the National Women's Studies Association here in 1981 holds a conference in which it commits itself to responding to racism, yet refuses to waive the registration fee for poor women and women of Color who wished to present and conduct workshops. This has made it impossible for many women of Color—for instance, Wilmette Brown, of Black Women for Wages for Housework—to participate in this conference. Is this to be merely another case of the academy discussing life within the closed circuits of the academy?

To the white women present who recognize these attitudes as familiar, but most of all, to all my sisters of Color who live and survive thousands of such encounters—to my sisters of Color who like me still tremble their rage under harness, or who sometimes question the expression of our rage as useless and disruptive (the two most popular accusations)—I want to speak about anger, my anger, and what I have learned from my travels through its dominions.

Everything can be used / except what is wasteful / (you will need / to remember this when you are accused of destruction.)*

Every woman has a well-stocked arsenal of anger potentially useful against those oppressions, personal and institutional, which brought

that anger into being. Focused with precision it can become a powerful source of energy serving progress and change. And when I speak of change, I do not mean a simple switch of positions or a temporary lessening of tensions, nor the ability to smile or feel good. I am speaking of a basic and radical alteration in those assumptions underlying our lives.

I have seen situations where white women hear a racist remark, resent what has been said, become filled with fury, and remain silent because they are afraid. That unexpressed anger lies within them like an undetonated device, usually to be hurled at the first woman of Color who talks about racism.

But anger expressed and translated into action in the service of our vision and our future is a liberating and strengthening act of clarification, for it is in the painful process of this translation that we identify who are our allies with whom we have grave differences, and who are our genuine enemies.

Anger is loaded with information and energy. When I speak of women of Color, I do not only mean Black women. The woman of Color who is not black and who charges me with rendering her invisible by assuming that her struggles with racism are identical with my own has something to tell me that I had better learn from, lest we both waste ourselves fighting the truths between us. If I participate, knowingly or otherwise, in my sister's oppression and she calls me on it, to answer her anger with my own only blankets the substance of our exchange with reaction. It wastes energy. And yes, it is very difficult to stand still and to listen to another woman's voice delineate an agony I do not share, or one to which I myself have contributed.

In this place we speak removed from the more blatant reminders of our embattlement as women. This need not blind us to the size and complexities of the forces mounting against us and all that is most human within our environment. We are not here as women examining racism in a political and social vacuum. We operate in the teeth of a system for which racism

---

* From "For Each of You," first published in *From a Land Where Other People Live* (Broadside Press, Detroit, 1973), and collected in *Chosen Poems: Old and New* (W. W. Norton and Company, New York, 1982), p. 42.

and sexism are primary, established, and necessary props of profit. Women responding to racism is a topic so dangerous that when the local media attempt to discredit this conference they choose to focus upon the provision of lesbian housing as a diversionary device—as if the Hartford *Courant* dare not mention the topic chosen for discussion here, racism, lest it become apparent that women are in fact attempting to examine and to alter all the repressive conditions of our lives.

Mainstream communication does not want women, particularly white women, responding to racism. It wants racism to be accepted as an immutable given in the fabric of your existence, like eveningtime or the common cold.

So we are working in a context of opposition and threat, the cause of which is certainly not the angers which lie between us, but rather that virulent hatred leveled against all women, people of Color, lesbians and gay men, poor people—against all of us who are seeking to examine the particulars of our lives as we resist our oppressions, moving toward coalition and effective action.

Any discussion among women about racism must include the recognition and the use of anger. This discussion must be direct and creative because it is crucial. We cannot allow our fear of anger to deflect us nor seduce us into settling for anything less than the hard work of excavating honesty; we must be quite serious about the choice of this topic and the angers entwined within it because, rest assured, our opponents are quite serious about their hatred of us and of what we are trying to do here.

And while we scrutinize the often painful face of each other's anger, please remember that it is not our anger which makes me caution you to lock your doors at night and not to wander the streets of Hartford alone. It is the hatred which lurks in those streets, that urge to destroy us all if we truly work for change rather than merely indulge in academic rhetoric.

This hatred and our anger are very different. Hatred is the fury of those who do not share

our goals, and its object is death and destruction. Anger is a grief of distortions between peers, and its object is change. But our time is getting shorter. We have been raised to view any difference other than sex as a reason for destruction, and for Black women and white women to face each other's angers without denial or immobility or silence or guilt is in itself a heretical and generative idea. It implies peers meeting upon a common basis to examine difference, and to alter those distortions which history has created around our difference. For it is those distortions which separate us. And we must ask ourselves: who profits from all this?

Women of Color in america have grown up within a symphony of anger, at being silenced, at being unchosen, at knowing that when we survive, it is in spite of a world that takes for granted our lack of humanness, and which hates our very existence outside of this service. And I say *symphony* rather than *cacophony* because we have had to learn to orchestrate those furies so that they do not tear us apart. We have had to learn to move through them and use them for strength and force and insight within our daily lives. Those of us who did not learn this difficult lesson did not survive. And part of my anger is always libation for my fallen sisters.

Anger is an appropriate reaction to racist attitudes, as is fury when the actions arising from those attitudes do not change. To those women here who fear the anger of women of Color more than their own unscrutinized racist attitudes, I ask: Is the anger of women of Color more threatening than the women-hatred that tinges all aspects of our lives?

It is not the anger of other women that will destroy us but our refusals to stand still, to listen to its rhythms, to learn within it, to move beyond the manner of presentation to the substance, to tap that anger as an important source of empowerment.

I cannot hide my anger to spare you guilt, nor hurt feelings, nor answering anger; for to do so insults and trivializes all our efforts. Guilt is not a response to anger; it is a response to one's own actions or lack of action. If it leads to change then it can be useful, since it is then no longer guilt but the beginning of knowledge. Yet all too often, guilt is just another name for impotence, for defensiveness destructive of communication; it becomes a device to protect ignorance and the continuation of things the way they are, the ultimate protection for changelessness.

Most women have not developed tools for facing anger constructively. CR groups in the past, largely white, dealt with how to express anger, usually at the world of men. And these groups were made up of white women who shared the terms of their oppressions. There was usually little attempt to articulate the genuine differences between women, such as those of race, color, age, class, and sexual identity. There was no apparent need at that time to examine the contradictions of self, woman as oppressor. There was work on expressing anger, but very little on anger directed against each other. No tools were developed to deal with other women's anger except to avoid it, deflect it, or flee from it under a blanket of guilt.

I have no creative use for guilt, yours or my own. Guilt is only another way of avoiding informed action, of buying time out of the pressing need to make clear choices, out of the approaching storm that can feed the earth as well as bend the trees. If I speak to you in anger, at least I have spoken to you: I have not put a gun to your head and shot you down in the street; I have not looked at your bleeding sister's body and asked, "What did she do to deserve it?" This was the reaction of two white women to Mary Church Terrell's telling of the lynching of a pregnant Black woman whose baby was then torn from her body. That was in 1921, and Alice Paul had just refused to publicly endorse the enforcement of the Nineteenth Amendment for all women—by refusing to endorse the inclusion of women of Color, although we had worked to help bring about that amendment.

The angers between women will not kill us if we can articulate them with precision, if we listen to the content of what is said with at least as much intensity as we defend ourselves against the manner of saying. When we turn from anger we turn from insight, saying we will accept only the designs already known, deadly and safely familiar. I have tried to learn my anger's usefulness to me, as well as its limitations.

For women raised to fear, too often anger threatens annihilation. In the male construct of brute force, we were taught that our lives depended upon the good will of patriarchal power. The anger of others was to be avoided at all costs because there was nothing to be learned from it but pain, a judgment that we had been bad girls, come up lacking, not done what we were supposed to do. And if we accept our powerlessness, then of course any anger can destroy us.

But the strength of women lies in recognizing differences between us as creative, and in standing to those distortions which we inherited without blame, but which are now ours to alter. The angers of women can transform difference through insight into power. For anger between peers births change, not destruction, and the discomfort and sense of loss it often causes is not fatal, but a sign of growth.

My response to racism is anger. That anger has eaten clefts into my living only when it remained unspoken, useless to anyone. It has also served me in classrooms without light or learning, where the work and history of Black women was less than a vapor. It has served me as fire in the ice zone of uncomprehending eyes of white women who see in my experience and the experience of my people only new reasons for fear or guilt. And my anger is no excuse for not dealing with your blindness, no reason to withdraw from the results of your own actions.

When women of Color speak out of the anger that laces so many of our contacts with white women, we are often told that we are "creating a mood of hopelessness," "preventing white women from getting past guilt," or "standing in the way of trusting communication and action." All these quotes come directly from letters to me from members of this organization within the last two years. One woman wrote, "Because you are Black and Lesbian, you seem to speak with the moral authority of suffering." Yes, I am Black and Lesbian, and what you hear in my voice is fury, not suffering. Anger, not moral authority. There is a difference.

To turn aside from the anger of Black women with excuses or the pretexts of intimidation is to award no one power—it is merely another way of preserving racial blindness, the power of unaddressed privilege, unbreached, intact. Guilt is only another form of objectification. Oppressed peoples are always being asked to stretch a little more, to bridge the gap between blindness and humanity. Black women are expected to use our anger only in the service of other people's salvation or learning. But that time is over. My anger has meant pain to me but it has also meant survival, and before I give it up I'm going to be sure that there is something at least as powerful to replace it on the road to clarity.

What woman here is so enamoured of her own oppression that she cannot see her heel print upon another woman's face? What woman's terms of oppression have become precious and necessary to her as a ticket into the fold of the righteous, away from the cold winds of self-scrutiny?

I am a lesbian woman of Color whose children eat regularly because I work in a university. If their full bellies make me fail to recognize my commonality with a woman of Color whose children do not eat because she cannot find work, or who has no children because her insides are rotted from home abortions and sterilization; if I fail to recognize the lesbian who chooses not to have children, the woman who remains closeted because her homophobic community is her only life support, the woman who chooses silence instead of another death, the woman who is terrified lest my anger trigger the explosion of hers; if I fail to recognize them as other faces of myself, then I am contributing not only to each of their oppressions but also to my own, and the anger which stands between us then must be used for clarity and mutual empowerment, not for evasion by guilt or for further separation. I am not

free while any woman is unfree, even when her shackles are very different from my own. And I am not free as long as one person of Color remains chained. Nor is any one of you.

I speak here as a woman of Color who is not bent upon destruction, but upon survival. No woman is responsible for altering the psyche of her oppressor, even when that psyche is embodied in another woman. I have suckled the wolf's lip of anger and I have used it for illumination, laughter, protection, fire in places where there was no light, no food, no sisters, no quarter. We are not goddesses or matriarchs or edifices of divine forgiveness; we are not fiery fingers of judgment or instruments of flagellation; we are women forced back always upon our woman's power. We have learned to use anger as we have learned to use the dead flesh of animals, and bruised, battered, and changing, we have survived and grown and, in Angela Wilson's words, we *are* moving on. With or without uncolored women. We use whatever strengths we have fought for, including anger, to help define and fashion a world where all our sisters can grow, where our children can love, and where the power of touching and meeting another woman's difference and wonder will eventually transcend the need for destruction.

For it is not the anger of Black women which is dripping down over this globe like a diseased liquid. It is not my anger that launches rockets, spends over sixty thousand dollars a second on missiles and other agents of war and death, slaughters children in cities, stockpiles nerve gas and chemical bombs, sodomizes our daughters and our earth. It is not the anger of Black women which corrodes into blind, dehumanizing power, bent upon the annihilation of us all unless we meet it with what we have, our power to examine and to redefine the terms upon which we will live and work; our power to envision and to reconstruct, anger by painful anger, stone upon heavy stone, a future of pollinating difference and the earth to support our choices.

We welcome all women who can meet us, face to face, beyond objectification and beyond guilt.

Further Questions

1. Should you refrain from becoming angry about oppression because you might create a situation where you or someone else feels guilty?

2. Is someone's guilt reaction to anger at bottom a response to her own attitudes and actions?

3. Can anger be a useful force in breaking down ignorance and developing alternatives to continuation of an undesirable status quo?

Asian Americans Battle "Model Minority" Stereotype   I.6

ROBERT DASELER

Robert Daseler gives some views of the "Model Minority" stereotype of Asian Americans held by Asian Americans themselves. The stereotype imposes expectations from without, often ignoring the real need of Asian Americans, and biases their relations with other minorities. Despite the fact that Asian Americans can as easily be impoverished and disadvantaged as they can be economically successful, mainstream culture could use the successful stereotype to deny that racial prejudice was a factor in unfavourable conditions among other minorities.

Reading Questions

1. The cultural determinism in the model minority myth can be harmful for Asian Americans who are not superstars. Discuss this contention in relation to some examples.
2. Daseler maintains that Asian American students are expected to do well in technical and scientific fields and "do not have the freedom to be mediocre"; nor are they encouraged to enter the humanities. Discuss, with reference to some examples.
3. Does holding up one minority as "model" help foster suspicion and factionalism among minorities? Discuss with some examples.

FOR DECADES, ASIAN AMERICANS have borne the peculiar burden of being the "model minority." Their signal success, especially in technical and scientific fields, has resulted in their being viewed more favorably than other American minorities, who supposedly lack their initiative.

The idea that Asians can serve as a model for other minorities seems to have originated in the 1960s, during the heyday of the civil rights movement. In a 1966 *New York Times Magazine* article, Berkeley sociologist William Petersen wrote: "By any criterion of good citizenship that we choose, the Japanese Americans are better

From Pomona College Today, *Summer 1994. Reprinted by permission of the editor.*

than any other group in our society, including native-born whites. They have established this remarkable record, moreover, by their own almost totally unaided effort."

Later in the article, Petersen, having further elaborated the accomplishments of Japanese Americans, made the invidious comparison to other minorities: "This is not true (or, at best, less true) of such 'non-whites' as Negroes, Indians, Mexicans, Chinese, and Filipinos."

Despite the fact that Petersen included Chinese and Filipinos on his list of less successful minorities, the idea spread that Asians generally work hard, send their children to college, rise rapidly in American society, and are "by any criterion of good citizenship that we choose" better than, for example, African Americans, Latinos, and Native Americans.

Although Petersen did not explicitly state that other minorities ought to emulate Japanese Americans or other Asian Americans, the notion of Asians as a model minority acquired a certain popular acceptance in the 1970s and 1980s.

According to . . . Ruth Gim, a Pomona College psychologist whose family emigrated to this country from Korea in 1970, the "model minority" tag stereotypes Asians, denying their many social, psychological, and financial difficulties and falsifying the actual record of their assimilation into American culture.

In Gim's view, the model minority image is dangerous to Asian Americans because it results in the denial of their actual needs, it imposes a set of expectations for Asian Americans that they do not create for themselves ("Someone else is prescribing to us what we should be"), and it biases their relations with other minorities.

Gim also believes that there was an implicit message behind the development of the myth of the model minority: "It was sending a message to the other minorities, saying, 'Why can't you be like them?' It was trying to use one minority group to send a message to another minority group." Many Asian Americans came quite naturally to resent the dubious distinction of being hailed as models for other minorities.

A study, released by UCLA in May, pointed out that Asian Americans are just as likely to be impoverished and disadvantaged as they are to be economically successful. According to Paul Ong, editor of the report, "It's been an uphill battle to get decision-makers and the population overall to realize that the Asian Pacific American population is a diverse one." The UCLA study paints a picture of a rapidly growing population (the 1990 Census said the nation's Asian and Pacific Islander population totaled 7,273,662, more than double the 1980 total whose veneer of success camouflages some disturbing struggles.

At a series of luncheons sponsored by Pomona's Asian American Resource Center during the spring semester, Gim, who directs the center, and other speakers examined the myth, trying to understand its origins, the reasons for its wide-spread acceptance (even among many Asian Americans), and its dangers.

PROMOTING SUPER-ACHIEVERS

Gim, who teaches courses in Asian American studies and psychology at Pomona, was the lead-off speaker in the series. Promoting Asians as super-achievers was, in effect, a tactic that conservatives could use to undercut criticism of mainstream culture by dissidents within the minority communities, Gim said.

In fact, Petersen, in his 1966 piece, emphasized the point that discrimination against Japanese Americans had been, if anything, more virulent than discrimination against other minorities. The implication of the Petersen article was clear: if both minorities did not prosper, it was because they are not as industrious or as determined as the Japanese.

By holding up Asian Americans as a model for other minorities, mainstream culture could, in effect, deny that racial prejudice was to blame for unemployment and poverty among African Americans, Latinos, and others. Drawing attention to the success of thousands of

Asian Americans was, in other words, an indirect way of placing the blame for racial inequality upon the minorities themselves, rather than the dominant culture.

Gim believes that embedded in the model minority myth was an assumption of cultural determinism: that Asian cultures are superior to other cultures, and for that reason, Asians tend to rise to the top of whatever culture they enter. She asserts that this presumption of Asian superiority is actually harmful for Asian Americans, especially those who are not academic superstars.

Gim also notes, ironically, that the model minority portrayal of Asian Americans is in stark contrast to the "Yellow Peril" image of them promulgated earlier in the century.

In the years prior to World War II, the prevailing view of Asians was represented by the figure of Charlie Chan, the movie detective who outwitted (usually Irish) policeman to solve crimes. Chan was an icon of the "inscrutable" Oriental: astute, mysterious, and ultimately risible. (Although he possessed a good vocabulary, his grammar was defective.)

Gim points out that many Asian Americans have internalized the "model minority" image, resulting in a narrowing of their social horizons. They know they are expected to enter technical and scientific fields—mathematics, engineering, medicine, economics—but not the humanities. Asian American students who do *not* do well in math or technical subjects often feel that they have not lived up to the expectations they have inherited. Asian American students do not have the freedom to be mediocre.

Furthermore, those who want to study history, sociology, or art often feel they are stepping over an invisible line between what is and is not an appropriate career path.

Contrary to the myth of invulnerability, Asian American students have a significantly higher rate of major depression and diagnosed schizophrenia than European Americans. "The superficial view seems to support the model minority image," Gim says, "but when you dig deeper, you find that cultural factors influence the underutilization of psychological services by Asian American students."

Moreover, the severity of psychiatric problems reported by Asian American students belies the image of them as programmed automatons.

The pressure on these students is coming not only from the culture, of course, but primarily from their families, who often steer the students into traditional and lucrative professions.

The concluding speaker in the series, Linus Yamane, as assistant professor of economics at Pitzer College, further debunked the myth by noting that, while the average family income of Asian Americans, $42,250, is higher than that for European Americans, $36,920, the proportion of Asian Americans living below the poverty line is much higher than for European Americans.

Yamane also pointed out that Asian American families tend to be larger than families of European Americans, somewhat vitiating their higher average income.

Yamane drew a complex picture of Asians in the United States, saying that poverty rates for Chinese, Japanese, and Korean families are lower than for European Americans, while poverty rates for Filipino and Native American families are higher.

Yamane also argued that discrimination against Asians in the work force varies with their ethnic background. Japanese and Korean males are found to do as well as European American males with comparable education, but Chinese and Filipino males do less well, and Native American men earn about 30 percent less, on the average, than European American males with comparable education.

MANAGEMENT GLASS CEILING

Yamane believes that there is a "glass ceiling" for Asian Americans in management. Studies appear to show that, while Asian Americans rise rapidly in the lower ranks of organizations, they are excluded from higher managerial positions.

Between Gim and Yamane came three other speakers. One of these was David Yoo, a historian at Claremont McKenna College, whose specialty is ethnicity, immigration, and race. Yoo characterized the model minority view of Asian Americans as just the latest wrinkle in the evolution of the stereotype of Asians in America.

Proclaiming Asian Americans to be a model minority "works against the true notion of a multicultural America," Yoo says. "It reinforces a racial hierarchy, which is kept intact if you can pit one minority against another."

Yoo believes that embracing Asians as exemplary gives people an excuse not to ask more fundamental questions about race and inequality.

While debunking the model-minority image as a myth, Gim, Yamane, and Yoo agree that there is some truth to the characterization of Asian Americans as high achievers. The proportion of Asian American students at highly selective colleges and universities is itself an indicator that at least a few ethnic groups within the Asian American community place high status on education, discipline, and intellectual distinction.

In March, homosexuality in the Asian Pacific Islander communities was discussed by Eric Reyes, a member of the Asian Pacific AIDS Intervention Team in Los Angeles, and Alice Y. Hom, a doctoral candidate in history at The Claremont Graduate School; and Jack Ling, a psychologist and environmental consultant, spoke on the subject of Asian American gangs. Reyes, Hom, and Ling highlighted aspects of the Asian American experience that conflict with the model-minority stereotype.

The number of Asian American students at The Claremont Colleges and in the University of California system does not signify that the story of Asian Americans is one of unalloyed success and social advance. Stereotyping, a pervasive sense of being suspended between two strong cultures, high stress levels, and a concern about loss of identity also are elements in the story.

Asian American students tend, for the most part, to associate with one another, and sometimes this leads to resentment by European American students, who view the Asians as cliquish and unfriendly.

A Pomona sophomore, who asked that his name not be mentioned, is a good example of the Asian American student who has taken the traditional path toward a career. With a double major in chemistry and Chinese, he is conforming, at least for the moment, to his father's expectation that he should become a doctor.

"He has one thing in mind," this young man says of his father, who was raised in Taiwan. "He thinks medicine is the best way to go."

A graduate of a prep school at which there was "a substantial" number of Asian students, the young man associated primarily with other Asian students in high school. At Pomona College, too, he associates with other Asians more than with Caucasian students. "Just for some reason, a lot of the people I knew happen to be Asian," he says. He thinks that Koreans tend to be more cliquish than other Asians, though.

This sophomore learned about the model minority myth when he took Ruth Gim's "Asian American Perspectives" class as a freshman.

"You can apply it to some people," he says, "but I don't think you can apply it to Asians as a whole. Asians do work hard and try to do well in school. I think the model-minority myth could be applied to a lot of my friends, but a lot of my Caucasian friends would fit the myth, too, if they were Asians."

A recent graduate, who also asked for anonymity, chose a nontraditional major for a student whose parents are born, as the sophomore's were, in Taiwan. She majored in sociology and Women's Studies, and in her senior thesis, she compared the cultural sensitivity of two centers for battered women: one mainstream, the other for Pacific Islanders and Asians.

Except for her social sciences major, she believes that "I do fall into what people would call a model-minority category." That is, she works hard, attends a prestigious college, and will pursue graduate studies. She also acknowledges the generational linguistic and class privileges that have allowed her to achieve these goals.

She is troubled by the stereotype, however, "I think it's very dangerous," she says. "It creates suspicion between groups, and it prevents us from forming coalitions in our similar struggle."

She says that majoring in sociology and Women's Studies wasn't something she planned. "I could barely do the natural sciences," she admits. So she switched into a field in which she had an interest . . . and could excel.

She graduated from a high school in Cerritos, California, in which the Asian Pacific Islander enrollment was 75 percent.

"It was the most comfortable social environment I was ever in or that I expect I ever will be in," she says. "It was difficult adjusting to Pomona, where suddenly I was the minority. I was not a part of the dominant culture."

Although being in the majority was pleasant, she now believes that "she would have benefitted more from high school if there had been a greater diversity of students, particularly more African American and Latino students."

She took a course from Gim, who helped her put the Asian American experience in perspective. "It really allowed me to see the Asian American contributions to American history," she says.

Growing up in Riverside and Orange counties, Gim found that there were two ways for her to compensate for being a minority: "I made sure I did better academically [than other students]. I don't think I really was smarter than other kids, but I made sure I worked harder. The other defense mechanism was that I dressed well."

Gim hopes that the increasing number of Asian American courses will help Asian American students find their own identity in a dominantly European American culture, without having to rely upon stereotypes imposed either by that culture or by their own minority culture.

"I am more American than most Americans walking around," Gim asserts. "I really believe that. I don't think most people realize what it is to be an American. I believe I have a better understanding and appreciation of what it means to be an American because of my bicultural background."

Further Questions

1. If your culture, and your parents especially, wanted you to excel in technical subjects and become a doctor or an engineer, how easy would you find it to enter a field like history or sociology? Would you feel that too much pressure was being applied to you in your decisions about what to study?

2. Should minorities have one of their number held up to them as a "model minority"? Is the intention or effect to deny that racial discrimination exists with respect to any of the minorities? Does this weaken the ability of the minorities to act together to combat racial discrimination?

3. Does stereotyping a group as "model" lead to overlooking problems that individuals in the group might be encountering? Does it mean that these individuals can expect less help with their problems? Give some examples.

I.7   Indian Tribes: A Continuing Quest for Survival

U.S. COMMISSION ON HUMAN RIGHTS

The U.S. Commission on Human Rights briefly describes how Indian rights have fared compared with the system of legal rights taken for granted in the United States. Racism has been prominent in the treatment of Indians, which has ranged from deprivation of land and religion to genocide.

Reading Questions

1. Ought Indians to be assimilated into the dominant society? Are good reasons for the proposal that Indians should be deprived of self-determination to be found in the belief that they have an inferior life style?
2. What is the fair way to allocate land to the Indians? Can non-Indians carry out this allocation without consulting the Indians on the ground that Indians have an inferior right to own property?
3. Should the dominant society be able to determine what is best for Indians through educating Indian children in the skills that are most useful in a white society.

TRADITIONAL CIVIL RIGHTS, as the phrase is used here, include those rights that are secured to individuals and are basic to the United States system of government. They include the right to vote and the right to equal treatment without discrimination on the basis of race, religion, or national origin, among others, in such areas as education, housing, employment, pubic accommodations, and the administration of justice.

In order to understand where American Indians stand today with respect to these rights, it is important to look at historical developments of the concept of Indian rights along with the civil rights movement in this country. The consideration given to these factors here will not be exhaustive but, rather, a brief look at some of the events that are most necessary to a background understanding of this area.

A basic and essential factor concerning American Indians is that the development of civil rights issues for them is in reverse order from other minorities in this country. Politically, other minorities started with nothing and attempted to obtain a voice in the existing economic and political structure. Indians started with everything and have gradually lost much of what they had to an advancing alien civilization. Other minorities have had no separate governmental institutions. Their goal primarily has been and continues to be to make the existing system involve them and work for them. Indian tribes have always been separate political entities interested in maintaining their own institutions and beliefs. Their goal has been to prevent the dismantling of their own systems. So while other minorities have sought integration into the larger society, much of Indian society is motivated to retain its political and cultural separateness.

Although at the beginning of the colonization process Indian nations were more numerous and better adapted to survival on this continent than the European settlers, these advantages were quickly lost. The colonization period saw the rapid expansion of non-Indian communities in numbers and territory covered and a shift in the balance of strength from Indian to non-Indian communities and governments. The extent to which Indians intermingled with non-Indian society varied by time period, geographical location, and the ability of natives and newcomers to get along with one another. As a general matter, however, Indians were viewed and treated as members of political entities that were not part of the United States. The Constitution acknowledges this by its separate provision regarding trade with the Indian tribes.[1] Indian tribes today that have not been forcibly assimilated, extinguished, or legally terminated still consider themselves to be and are viewed in American law, as separate political units.

THE RACIAL FACTOR

An important element in the development of civil rights for American Indians today goes beyond their legal and political status to include the way they have been viewed racially. Since colonial times Indians have been viewed as an "inferior race"; sometimes this view is condescendingly positive—the romanticized noble savage—at other times this view is hostile—the vicious savage—at all times the view is racist. All things Indian are viewed as inherently inferior to their counterparts in the white European tradition. Strong racist statements have appeared in congressional debates, presidential policy announcements, court decisions, and other authoritative public utterances. This racism has served to justify a view now repudiated, but which still lingers in the public mind, that Indians are not entitled to the same legal rights as others in this country. In some cases, racism has been coupled with apparently benevolent motives, to "civilize" the "savages," to teach them Christian principles. In other cases, the racism has been coupled with greed; Indians were "removed" to distant locations to prevent them from standing in the way of the development of the new Western civilization. At one extreme

the concept of inferior status of Indians was used to justify genocide; at the other, apparently benevolent side, the attempt was to assimilate them into the dominant society. Whatever the rationale or motive, whether rooted in voluntary efforts or coercion, the common denominator has been the belief that Indian society is an inferior lifestyle.

> It sprang from a conviction that native people were a lower grade of humanity for whom the accepted cannons [sic] of respect need not apply; one did not debase oneself by ruining a native person. At times, this conviction was stated explicitly by men in public office, but whether expressed or not, it generated decision and action.[2]

Early assimilationists like Thomas Jefferson proceeded from this assumption with benevolent designs.

> Thus, even as they acknowledged a degree of political autonomy in the tribes, their conviction of the natives' cultural inferiority led them to interfere in their social, religious, and economic practices. Federal agents to the tribes not only negotiated treaties and tendered payments; they pressured husbands to take up the plow and wives to learn to spin. The more conscientious agents offered gratuitous lectures on the virtues of monogamy, industry, and temperance.

The same underlying assumption provided the basis for Andrew Jackson's attitude. "I have long viewed treaties with the Indians an absurdity not to be reconciled to the principles of our government," he said. As President he refused to enforce the decisions of the U.S. Supreme Court upholding Cherokee tribal autonomy, and he had a prominent role in the forced removal of the Cherokees from Georgia and the appropriation of their land by white settlers. Other eastern tribes met a similar fate under the Indian Removal Act of 1830.[3]

Another Federal Indian land policy, enacted at the end of the 19th century and followed until 1934, that shows the virulent effect of racist assumptions was the allotment of land parcels to individual Indians as a replacement for tribal ownership. Many proponents of the policy were considered "friends of the Indians," and they argued that the attributes of individual land ownership would have a great civilizing and assimilating effect on American Indians. This action, undertaken for the benefit of the Indians, was accomplished without consulting them. Had Congress heeded the views of the purported beneficiaries of this policy, allotment might not have been adopted. Representatives of 19 tribes met in Oklahoma and unanimously opposed the legislation, recognizing the destructive effect it would have upon Indian culture and the land base itself, which was reduced by 90 million acres in 45 years.

An important principle established by the allotment policy was that the Indian form of land ownership was not "civilized," and so it was the right of the Government to invalidate that form. It is curious that the principle of the right to own property in conglomerate form for the benefit of those with a shareholder's undivided interest in the whole was a basis of the American corporate system, then developing in strength. Yet a similar form of ownership when practiced by Indians was viewed as a hallmark of savagery. Whatever the explanation for this double standard, the allotment policy reinforced the notion that Indians are somehow inferior, that non-Indians in power knew what was best for them, and that these suppositions justified the assertion that non-Indians had the power and authority to interfere with the basic right to own property.

Religion is another area in which non-Indians have felt justified in interfering with Indian beliefs. The intent to civilize the natives of this continent included a determined effort to Christianize them. Despite the constitutional prohibition, Congress, beginning in 1819, regularly appropriated funds for Christian missionary efforts. Christian goals were visibly aligned with Federal Indian policy in 1869 when a Board of Indian Commissioners was established by Congress under President Grant's administration. Representative of the spectrum of Christian denominations, the independently wealthy members

of the Board were charged by the Commissioner of Indian Affairs to work for the "humanization, civilization, and Christianization of the Indians." Officials of the Federal Indian Service were supposed to cooperate with this Board.

The benevolent support of Christian missionary efforts stood in stark contrast to the Federal policy of suppressing tribal religions. Indian ceremonial behavior was misunderstood and suppressed by Indian agents. In 1892 the Commissioner of Indian Affairs established a regulation making it a criminal offense to engage in such ceremonies as the sun dance. The spread of the Ghost Dance religion, which promised salvation from the white man, was so frightening to the Federal Government that troops were called in to prevent it, even though the practice posed no threat to white settlers.

The judiciary of the United States, though it has in many instances forthrightly interpreted the law to support Indian legal claims in the face of strong, sometimes violent opposition, has also lent support to the myth of Indian inferiority. For example, the United States Supreme Court in 1883, in recognizing the right of tribes to govern themselves, held that they had the exclusive authority to try Indians for criminal offenses committed against Indians. In describing its reasons for refusing to find jurisdiction in a non-Indian court in such cases, the Supreme Court said:

> It [the non-Indian court] tries them, not by their peers, nor by the customs of their people, nor the law of their land, but by *superiors* of a different race, according to the law of a social state of which they have an imperfect conception, and which is opposed to the traditions of their history, to the habits of their lives, to the strongest prejudices of their *savage nature;* one which measures the red man's revenge by the maxims of the white man's morality.[4] (emphasis added)

In recognizing the power of the United States Government to determine the right of Indians to occupy their lands, the Supreme Court expressed the good faith of the country in such matters with these words: "the United States will be governed by such considerations of justice as will control a Christian people in their treatment of an ignorant and dependent race."[5]

Another example of racist stereotyping to be found in the courts is this example from the Supreme Court of Washington State:

> The Indian was a child, and a dangerous child, of nature, to be both protected and restrained. . . . True, arrangements took the form of treaty and of terms like "cede," "relinquish," "reserve." But never were these agreements between equals . . . [but rather] that "between a superior and an inferior."[6]

This reasoning, based on racism, has supported the view that Indians are wards of the Government who need the protection and assistance of Federal agencies and it is the Government's obligation to recreate their governments, conforming them to a non-Indian model, to establish their priorities, and to make or approve their decisions for them.

Indian education policies have often been examples of the Federal Government having determined what is "best" for Indians. Having judged that assimilation could be promoted through the indoctrination process of white schools, the Federal Government began investing in Indian education. Following the model established by army officer Richard Pratt in 1879, boarding schools were established where Indian children are separated from the influences of tribal and home life. The boarding schools tried to teach Indians skills and trades that would be useful in white society, utilizing stern disciplinary measures to force assimilation. The tactics used are within memory of today's generation of tribal leaders who recall the policy of deterring communication in native languages. "I remember being punished many times for . . . singing one Navajo song, or a Navajo word slipping out of my tongue just in an unplanned way, but I was punished for it."

Federal education was made compulsory, and the policy was applied to tribes that had sophisticated school systems of their own as well as to tribes that really needed assistance to establish educational systems. The ability of the tribal school to educate was not relevant, given

that the overriding goal was assimilation rather than education.

Racism in Indian affairs has not been sanctioned recently by political or religious leaders or other leaders in American society. In fact, public pronouncements over the last several decades have lamented past evils and poor treatment of Indians.[7] The virulent public expressions of other eras characterizing Indians as "children" or "savages" are not now acceptable modes of public expression. Public policy today is a commitment to Indian self-determination. Numerous actions of Congress and the executive branch give evidence of a more positive era for Indian policy.[8] Beneath the surface, however, the effects of centuries of racism still persist. The attitudes of the public, of State and local officials, and of Federal policymakers do not always live up to the positive pronouncements of official policy. Some decisions today are perceived as being made on the basis of precedents mired in the racism and greed of another era. Perhaps more important, the legacy of racism permeates behavior and that behavior creates classic civil rights violations. . . .

NOTES

1. U.S. Const. Art. 1, §8.
2. D'Arcy McNickel, *Native American Tribalism* (New York: Oxford University Press, 1973). p. 56.
3. Act of May 28, 1830, ch. 148, 4 Stat. 411.
4. *Ex Parte Crow Dog*, 109 U.S. 556, 571 (1883).
5. *Missouri, Kansas, and Texas Railway Co. v. Roberts*, 152 U.S. 114, 117 (1894).
6. *State v. Towessnute*, 154 P. 805, 807 (Wash. Sup. Ct. 1916), quoting *Choctaw Nation v. United States*, 119 U.S. 1, 27 (1886).
7. See, e.g., President Nixon's July 8, 1970, Message to the Congress, Recommendations for Indian Policy, H. Doc. No. 91-363, 91st Cong., 2d sess. (hereafter cited as *Recommendations for Indian Policy*).
8. Ibid; Indian Self-Determination and Education Assistance Act, Pub. L. No. 93-638, 88 Stat. 2203 (1975); Indian Child Welfare Act of 1978, Pub. L. No. 95-608, 92 Stat. 3096; U.S. Department of the Interior, *Report on the Implementation of the Helsinki Final Act* (1979).

Further Questions

1. If Indian society wishes to retain its own political and cultural systems, separate from those of the dominant society, to what extent should this wish be respected?

2. What role is there, if any, for Christian missionary efforts in the religious life of Indians? Explain.

3. Should Indians be permitted to have their own judicial system? Why or why not? What judicial system should be in charge of offenses of Indians against non-Indians or non-Indians against Indians?

I.8   The Flight from the Rejected Body

SUSAN WENDELL

Susan Wendell mentions some attitudes of rejection of bodies and their experiences when these bodies and experiences fail to measure up to the ideas of normality set by our demanding culture. One prominent social attitude is the myth that illnesses and other weaknesses can be controlled, which leads doctors to postulate the patient's psychological interference when her condition does not yield to diagnosis or treatment. Another version of the myth is that people are themselves to blame when bad things happen to them.

Wendell is Associate Professor of Women's Studies at Simon Fraser University, British Columbia.

Reading Questions

1. Give some examples of standards of bodily normality that can cause harmful attitudes toward those people who fall short of these ideals. How are such ideals harmful to the disabled in particular?

2. Are expectations of doctors' control over the ailing body too high? Why do doctors often hypothesize psychiatric conditions when they fail to find the answers they are looking for?

3. Why is it difficult to believe that bad things happen to people for reasons beyond their control?

IN THE COMMERCIAL-MEDIA-SOAKED societies of North America,[1] the body is idealized and objectified to a high degree; these cultural practices foster demand to control our bodies and to attempt to perfect them, which in turn create rejection, shame, and fear in relation to both failures to control the body and deviations from body ideals. Implied in any idealization of the body is the rejection of some kinds of bodies or some aspects of bodily life. I use the terms "rejected body" and "negative body" to refer to those aspects of bodily life (such as illness, disability, weakness, and dying), bodily appearance (usually deviations from the cultural ideals of the body), and bodily experience (including most forms of bodily suffering) that are feared, ignored, despised, and/or rejected in a society and its culture. In this chapter I discuss some forms of idealization and objectification of the body, how they affect people with and without disabilities, and how they contribute to cultural demands that we control our bodies. I then describe and criticize some influential contemporary versions of the myth that the body can be controlled.

Our real human bodies are exceedingly diverse—in size, shape, colour, texture, structure, function, range and habits of movement, and development—and they are constantly changing. Yet many cultures, especially modern commercial cultures, do not seem to absorb or reflect these simple facts. Instead, they idealize the human body; the ideals change from time to time, but there always seem to be ideals. Body ideals include not only ideals of appearance, which are particularly influential for women (Bartky, 1990), but also ideals of strength, energy, movement, function, and proper control; the latter are unnoticed assumptions for most people who can meet them, but they leap to the foreground for those who are sick or disabled. In Canada and the United States, we are bombarded everywhere with images of these ideals, demands for them, and offers of products and services to help us achieve them.

Clearly, idealization of the body is related in complex ways to the economic processes of a consumer society. Idealization now generates tremendous profits, and the quest for profit demands that people be reminded constantly of existing body ideals and presented regularly with new ideals. Moreover, never before in history have images of real people who meet the latest cultural ideals of beauty, health, and physical performance been so often presented to so many people. Now it is possible for the images of a few people to drive out the reality of most people we actually encounter. (For example, I find that few people realize that the average North American woman is much fatter than the average woman we see on television.) This tends to conflate body ideals with our concept of what is physically "normal," increasing the number of people whose bodies are regarded by themselves and others as abnormal and socially unacceptable.

Idealization also contributes to objectification of the body, along with other factors, such as the cultural splitting of mind from body and derogation of the body, strong cultural emphasis on physical appearance, medical ways of seeing and treating the body, sexual exploitation, pressures to perform, and some forms of competition. To objectify another person's body is to ignore (at least temporarily) the consciousness that is embodied there and to fail to concern oneself with her/his subjective bodily experience. Objectifying one's own body is more complex; one must, in a sense, split one's consciousness from it and ignore one's inner subjective experience of it in order to regard or treat it as another person might. Widely accepted current forms of objectifying one's own body include treating it primarily as an instrument for accomplishing one's goals, regarding it as a physical object to be viewed, used, and manipulated, and treating it as a material possession to be maintained, exploited, and traded (Sheets-Johnstone, 1992b). They all assume and require considerable control of the body in order to maintain its suitability as an object of that type. Observing and participating in constant cultural objectification of other people's bodies encourages us to objectify our own. Some objectification of one's own body is probably inevitable, and not always harmful, but if it becomes the primary mode of experiencing one's body, it is a source of profound alienation from feeling, from nature, from the unconscious, from every aspect of oneself and others that resists control.

THE DISCIPLINES OF NORMALITY

The disciplines of normality are preconditions of participation in every aspect of social life, yet they are unnoticed by most adults who can conform to them without conscious effort. Children are very aware of the requirements of normality; among children, conformity to standards of normality in body size, carriage, movement, gesture, speech, emotional expression, appearance, scent, ways of eating, and especially control of bodily functions such as salivation, passing gas, urination, and defecation, are enforced by teasing, taunting, and the threat of social ostracism, beginning at an early age. (When I was a child in New York City public schools, peeing in your pants in school or on the playground was one of the most shameful things that could happen to you; nothing you might do deliberately, no matter how morally rotten, could compare in shamefulness.) Those of us who can learn to be or seem "normal" do so, and those of us who cannot meet the standards of normality usually achieve the closest approximation we can manage.

The disciplines of normality, like those of femininity, are not only enforced by others but internalized. For many of us, our proximity to the standards of normality is an important aspect of our identity and our sense of social acceptability, an aspect of our self-respect. We are unlikely to notice this until our ability to meet the standards is threatened in some way. An injury or a prolonged illness often draws the attention of non-disabled people to this previously unnoticed facet of their self-images. For people who already have disabilities, the prospect of more disability can have the same effect. Shame and self-hatred when we cannot measure up to the standards of normality are indications that they are enforced by a powerful internalized disciplinarian.

People who do not appear to act physically "normal" draw attention to the disciplines of normality, just as women who do not practice the disciplines of femininity make them more

apparent. In both cases, there are rules at work, but most of us are trying to ignore the existence of the rules, trying to pretend that things are "naturally" and effortlessly the way they seem, not socially enforced. (Consider how rarely anyone admits in public that s/he is depressed, having intestinal cramps, or even just desperate for a toilet, compared to how often you feel that way. Stating such a thing would be at least as embarrassing as a woman's remarking in public that she did not have time to shave her legs.) Moreover, since almost everyone tries to appear as "normal" as possible, those who appear clearly "abnormal" according to their society's standards are constant reminders to those who are currently measuring up that they might slip outside the standards. In this aspect, people with disabilities arouse fear. But they are also reassuring, in that encountering them can make "normals" feel more "normal" by comparison (which in turn may arouse guilt).[2] These reactions are completely understandable, given the disciplines of normality, and they all contribute to the "Otherness" of people with disabilities.

It is not easy to distinguish standards of physical normality from *ideals* of health, appearance, and performance, just as it is not easy to distinguish between feminine body ideals and minimal standards of femininity. One would expect the range of social normality (not medical "normality," which is different) to be considerably broader than the physical ideals of a culture, because otherwise very few people would be considered normal. Nevertheless, in practice, the two are linked. When the ideals of physical health, appearance, and performance become more difficult to meet, the social standards of normality follow suit, threatening more of us with the possibility of falling below the minimum required for self-esteem and social acceptability. Moreover, for many people, falling within the "normal" range is not enough, especially when they are constantly pressured and encouraged to try to meet the ideal. By pursuing the cultural ideal, people can raise the standards of normality.

Kathryn Pauly Morgan discusses this phenomenon in relation to plastic surgery for women:

> In the technical and popular literature on cosmetic surgery, what have previously been described as *normal* variations of female body shapes or described in the relatively innocuous language of "problem areas," are increasingly described as "deformities," "ugly protrusions," "inadequate breasts," and "unsightly concentrations of fat cells"—a litany of descriptions designed to intensify feelings of disgust, shame, and relief at the possibility of recourse for these "deformities." Cosmetic surgery promises virtually all women the creation of beautiful, youthful-appearing bodies. As a consequence, more and more women will be labelled "ugly" and "old" in relation to this more select population of surgically created beautiful faces and bodies. ... I suspect that the naturally "given," so to speak, will increasingly come to be seen as the technologically "primitive"; the "ordinary" will come to be perceived and evaluated as the "ugly." (Morgan 1991, 41)[3]

Other ideals can sneak up on us, becoming standards of normality because they enter into a society's competitive structure. For example, when the pace of life increases, stamina becomes more important to participation in every aspect of society, and what was once regarded as an ideal level of energy gradually comes to be regarded as normal. Everyone who cannot keep up is urged to take steps (or medications) to increase their energy, and bodies that were once considered normal are pathologized. In my society, I have noticed that it has become increasingly unacceptable to "slow down" as one ages, when not long ago it was expected.

Some people can have the temporary self-acceptance that comes from believing that their bodies are "close enough" to current body ideals, but this gives them an investment in the ideals and draws them into the endless task of reconciling reality with them. Most people learn to identify with their own strengths (by cultural standards) and to hate, fear, and neglect their own weaknesses. Everyone is subjected to cultural pressure to deny bodily weaknesses, to dread old age, to feel ashamed of and responsible for their distance from the ideals, and to objectify their own bodies at the expense of subjective bodily awareness. These pressures foster a desire to gain/maintain control of our bodies; conversely, the myth that we can control our bodies encourages us to strive to meet body ideals.

Most people with disabilities cannot even attempt to make their bodies fit the physical ideals of their culture. They may wish for bodies they cannot have, with frustration, shame, and sometimes self-hatred; they may reject the physical ideals as narrow, unimaginative, and/or oppressive; or, like myself, they may fluctuate irrationally between the points of view. In any case, they must struggle harder than non-disabled people for a self-image that is both realistic and positive, and this is made more difficult by other people's reactions to them.[4] In a society that idealizes the body, people who cannot come close enough to the ideals, and those whose bodies are out of control, become devalued people because of their devalued bodies (Hannaford, 1985). Moreover, they are constant reminders to the temporarily "normal" of the rejected body—of what the "normal" are trying to avoid, forget, and ignore (Lessing, 1981).

Of course, it is not just from fear of being or becoming abnormal that the rejected body is shunned. It is also shunned from fear of pain, illness, limitation, suffering, and dying. Yet the cultural banishment of the rejected body contributes to fear of those experiences by fostering ignorance of them. Even though everyone has or will have experiences of the negative body, if the cultural concept of the "normal" body is a young, healthy, energetic, pain-free body with all parts present and a maximum range of graceful movement, then experiences of the negative body need not be confronted and understood. They belong to those with disabilities and illnesses, who are marginalized, not "ordinary" people, not "us."

People with disabilities and illnesses learn that most people do not want to know about the suffering they experience because of their bodies. Curiosity about medical diagnoses, physical appearance, and the sexual and other intimate aspects of disability is common; interest in the subjective experience is rare (Matthews, 1983). This is also understandable. If we tell people about our pain, for example, we remind them of the existence of pain, the imperfection and fragility of the body, the possibility of their own pain, the *inevitability* of it. The less willing they are to accept all these, the less they will want to know. If they cannot avoid confronting pain in our presence, they can avoid us. They may even blame us for being in pain. They may tell themselves that we could have avoided it, in order to believe that they can avoid it. They may want to believe they are not like us, not vulnerable to this; if so, they will cling to our differences, and we will become "the Others." Our shared culture offers this solution and makes the distance between our experiences difficult to bridge. It is not surprising that many people who can, hide their disabilities from everyone but their closest friends.

THE MYTH OF CONTROL

A major obstacle to coming to terms with the full reality of bodily life is the widespread myth that the body can be controlled. Conversely, people embrace the myth of control in part because it promises escape from the rejected body. The essence of the myth of control is the belief that it is possible, by means of human actions, to have the bodies we want and to prevent illness, disability, and death. Like many myths, the myth of control contains a significant element of truth; we do have some control over the conditions of our bodies, for example through the physical risks we take or avoid and our care for our health. What makes it a myth is that people continue to cling to it even where there is overwhelming evidence against it, and that most

versions of it are formulated in such a way that they are invulnerable to evidence against them.

When people are blamed or made to feel responsible for having nonideal bodies despite their reasonable care, when unprovable theories are generated to explain how someone could have avoided becoming ill, when people with disabilities are seen as having their psychological, moral, or spiritual failures written upon their bodies, and when every death is regarded as a defeat of human efforts, the myth of control is at work. This myth is shared by scientific, nonscientific, and antiscientific worldviews. It persists in many forms, but I will focus my discussion on those forms that most affect people with disabilities and illnesses in my society.

SCIENTIFIC WESTERN MEDICINE AND THE MYTH OF CONTROL

The myth that the body can be controlled is part of the general assumption of the modern Western scientific project that nature can be controlled. Neither the larger assumption about nature nor the more specific myth about the body is seriously questioned in the light of failures; they are heuristics, guiding long-term goals and scientific projects not propositions meant to be tested by experience. Yet there is a strong tendency in scientific medicine to pretend that the myth of control is the truth. Collectively, doctors and medical researchers exhibit very little modesty about their knowledge, rarely admitting to patients or the public the vast remaining gaps in scientific medicine's understanding of the human body or their inability to repair or heal most physical conditions that cause suffering, limitation, and death. Scientific medicine participates in and fosters the myth of control by focusing overwhelmingly on cures and lifesaving medical interventions, and by tending to neglect chronic illnesses, rehabilitation, pain management, and the quality of patients' experiences, including their experiences of dying. Research, funding, medical care, and the numbers and status of various types of medical professionals all reflect this emphasis.

Sherwin Nuland (1993, 71), points out that there are only 4,084 geriatricians (they specialize in total care of elderly patients), but 17,000 heart specialists in the United States. Those specializations that involve surgery and saving lives carry by far the most prestige; they also bolster the illusion of control much better than does the long, patient process of rehabilitation or the management of long-term illness. These latter, less visible functions of medicine tend to be performed by nurses, physiotherapists, and other low-prestige members of the profession, and by some primary-care physicians, whose prestige and income are much lower than those of physicians who specialize in cures.

All doctors in the Western scientific tradition are trained to do something to control the body, to "make it better" (Kleinman, 1988). Moreover, people who crave control may be attracted to medicine. Nuland, a surgeon of many years and a teacher of surgery and the history of medicine, says that he has observed in many doctors "a need to control that exceeds in magnitude what most people would find reasonable" (Nuland, 1993, 258); he believes this need often leads them to deal badly with loss of control over a patient's condition.

> There is a specific form of abandonment that is particularly common among patients near death from cancer, and it requires comment. I refer here to abandonment by doctors. Doctors rarely *want* to give up. As long as there is any possibility of solving The Riddle, they will keep at it, and sometimes it takes the intervention of a family or the patient himself to put an end to medical exercises in futility. When it becomes obvious, though, that there is no longer a Riddle on which to focus, many doctors lose the drive that sustained their enthusiasm. As the long siege drags on and one after another treatment has begun to fail, those enthusiasms tend to fall by the wayside. Emotionally, doctors then tend to disappear; physically, too, they sometimes all but disappear. (Nuland, 1993, 257–258)

It would be too easy to blame this and other manifestations of medicine's participation in the myth of control on the personalities and socialized attitudes of doctors. Doctors seek heroic control in part because they are cast as the heroes of medicine. They may enjoy being in the role of hero, but the rest of us also like them in that role and try to keep them there, because *we* want to believe that someone can always "make it better." We (nondoctors) are allowed to maintain this illusion partly because the most obvious loss of control over the body, death, has been medicalized, hidden from us and "managed" by medical institutions. Eighty percent of Americans now die in hospitals, compared to 50 percent in 1949 (Nuland 1993, 255).[9] Nuland has this to say about the neglect of dying in a society that does not want to know about death:

> We live today in the era not of the art of dying, but of the art of saving life, and the dilemmas of that art are multitudinous. As recently as half a century ago, that other great art, the part of medicine, still prided itself on its ability to manage the process of death, making it as tranquil as professional kindness could. Except in the too-few programs such as hospice, that part of the art is now mostly lost, replaced by the brilliance of rescue and, unfortunately, the all-to-common abandonment when rescue proves impossible. (Nuland 1993, 265).

MIND OVER BODY AND THE MYTH OF CONTROL

The influence of psychoanalysis on both the medicine and popular culture has contributed the concepts of psychosomatic illness and imagined illness to the myth of control, and it has strengthened the older and vaguer notion that the mind can control the body. Although there may be genuine psychosomatic conditions and forms of mental illness in which people imagine physical symptoms, both these explanations are employed too readily by medical practitioners and lay people when they can find no other explanation for a patient's complaints or when a patient does not benefit from medical treatment.

In 1972, Irving Zola warned of the re-introduction, through psychosomatic diagnoses, of the idea that individuals are responsible for their illnesses:

> It is not clear that the issues of morality and individual responsibility have been fully banished from the etiological scene itself. At the same time as the label "illness" is being used to attribute "diminished responsibility" to a whole host of phenomena, the issue of "personal responsibility" seems to be re-emerging within medicine itself. Regardless of the truth and insights of the concepts of stress and the perspective of psychosomatics, whatever else they do, they bring man, *not* bacteria to the center of the stage and lead thereby to a re-examination of the individual's role in his own demise, disability and even recovery. (Zola, 1972, 491)[12]

The literature describing experiences of disabilities and chronic illnesses abounds with accounts of early diagnoses of "psychosomatic illness," even when the patients had diseases and conditions well known to medical science. For example, in a study of 21 women and 14 men with multiple sclerosis in Canada, Susan Russell found that 7 of the women and 1 of the men (note the gender difference), that is 22.8 percent of the 35 patients, had been told by physicians that their symptoms were psychological in origin (Russell, 1985, 56).[13] No doubt the physicians would reply in their own defense that MS is notoriously difficult to diagnose, presenting as it often does at first with fatigue, dizziness, or brief episodes of numbness. But if they know that MS (and certainly this is true of many other physical ailments as well) is difficult to diagnose, why are they telling their patients that their symptoms have psychological causes, instead of telling them that they do not yet know what is wrong and they must wait and see?

If patients with well known physical diseases and conditions are likely to receive diagnoses of psychosomatic illness, patients with little-known or unknown physical problems are in great danger of being told that their symptoms are psychological in origin. Toni Jeffreys, who was so ill with ME in the late 1970s (before ME was more widely recognized) that she could not walk, was repeatedly told that her illness was psychosomatic. When she was completely bedridden, her partner Jim, who had made an emergency call to a specialist they had consulted because he was frightened by the severity of Toni's symptoms, was advised by the doctor to abandon her: "He said you'd soon pull yourself together" (Jeffreys, 1982, 85). Since I am a somewhat public person with ME, I have been contacted by dozens of people with ME who have discussed their experiences with me. If they became ill before about 1988 (when ME, or chronic fatigue immune dysfunction syndrome, began to be recognized as a "legitimate" physical illness in medical circles, most notably at the Centers for Disease Control), they were usually sent to psychiatrists. If they became ill after 1988, they were not. The difference was not in the symptoms, but in their doctors' recognition of physical disease. Psychosomatic illness was not being diagnosed on the basis of positive evidence of psychological problems; it was a *default* diagnosis for physical symptoms.[14] Why do physicians burden their patients with self-doubt, not to mention expensive and unnecessary psychological treatment, when they could admit that they do not know what is wrong?

MORE VERSIONS OF THE MYTH

There are other popular versions of the myth of control. One is the belief that if you take proper care of your body, you will stay well and fit until you die (presumably death will be both instantaneous and inexplicable). This has the ugly implication that if you are ill or disabled, you must have failed to take care of yourself. Another is that people "make themselves" ill or disabled by mismanaging their lives, their psyches, or their spirits in some way.

I spent a lot of the time I was confined to bed probing the question of whether I fell ill because I had mismanaged my life in some way. I find this is the most common hypothesis among women who, like myself, were struck down suddenly by ME in the midst of busy lives. This may be due partly to the popular media characterization of ME as a disease of "overachievers." It may also reflect feelings of guilt or uncertainty about having worked toward goals which were widely considered "inappropriate" for us. It may be part of a rationalizing rejection of one's former, healthy self, in order to adjust to a new body and a new way of life. I discarded the mismanagement hypothesis eventually, partly on the reasoned basis that I know dozens of healthy people who have always taken far worse care of themselves than I ever did, and partly on the emotional basis that I liked (and still do like) the woman I used to be, even though I have become a different woman. If I mismanaged my life, it was not in any way I could have known at the time nor in any way I can see now.

When people remake their lives in order to live with an illness or disability, and especially when they come to like their new lives better or find them more fulfilling than their previous lives, they and others often infer that they became ill or disabled *in order* to change their lives or because their lives needed changing. And, as I have mentioned, when people make their illnesses or disabilities meaningful in their lives, the meanings they give them are often interpreted as the *reasons* for their having become ill or disabled. Both these responses strike me as manifestations of the myth of control, as well as attempts to believe that nothing really devastating happens without a good purpose.

The mismanagement hypothesis is not the only one of the control hypotheses I explored personally. Several friends suggested that conflicts we were having at the time might have been responsible for my falling ill. Some suggested that unconscious hostility toward me, which they had since become aware of, might have hurt me physically. These attempts to take

responsibility were both touching and rather frightening. They made me think about possible forms of vulnerability I had not seriously considered. I did not and do not dismiss them, because I do not imagine that my own worldview is complete or even very accurate, and because I know that wise and compassionate people believe that such things happen and live according to those beliefs.[20] But because neither the friend who suggested them nor I come from cultures in which these hypotheses are supported, their suggestions, and my reactions, made me realize how hard we were all trying to believe that we had some control over my being ill.

BAD THINGS HAPPEN

Feminist theorists have probed the causes of European patriarchal cultures' demands for control of the body, postulating fear of death, fear of the strong impulses and feelings the body gives us, fear of nature, and fear and resentment of the mother's power over the infant (Beauvoir, 1952; Dinnerstein, 19756; Griffin, 1981). I will not rehearse these theories here, since they are widely available in better form than I could give them. I think the evidence is strong that all four factors, in addition to the idealizations and objectifications of the body by a culture, contribute to the demand for control of the body. But I think there is another, more general contributor.

Most people are deeply reluctant to believe that bad things happen to people who do not deserve them, or seek them, or risk them, or fail to take care of themselves. To believe this as a general proposition is to acknowledge the fragility of one's own life; to realize it in relation to someone one knows is to become acutely aware of one's own vulnerability.

The philosopher Susan Brison, who survived rape and attempted murder by a stranger, eloquently describes the reluctance to believe in unavoidable disaster that she encountered:

My sense of unreality was fed by the massive denial of those around me—a reaction I learned is an almost universal response to rape. Where the facts would appear to be incontrovertible, denial takes the form of attempts to explain the assault in ways that leave the observer's world view unscathed. Even those who are able to acknowledge the existence of violence try to protect themselves from the realization that the world in which it occurs is their world and so they find it hard to identify with the victim. They cannot allow themselves to imagine the victim's shattered life, or else their illusions about their own safety and control over their lives might begin to crumble. The most well-meaning individuals, caught up in the myth of their own immunity, can inadvertently add to the victim's suffering by suggesting that the attack was avoidable or somehow her fault. One victim's assistance coordinator, whom I had phoned for legal advice, stressed that she herself had never been a victim and said that I would benefit from the experience by learning not to be so trusting of people and to take basic safety precautions like not going out late at night. She didn't pause long enough during her lecture for me to point out that I was attacked suddenly, from behind, in broad daylight. (Brison, 1993, 11)

Reactions to illness or accident are often similar to the reactions Brison describes. Most people cannot resist suggesting ways in which it was avoidable, or at least seeking causal factors over which a person might exert control to avoid it. The ill and injured themselves, like the victims of any personal disaster, usually prefer blaming themselves to believing that they could not have prevented it. Brison says: "I felt angry, scared and helpless, and I wished I could blame myself for what had happened so that I would feel less vulnerable, more in control of my life" (Brison, 1993, 13).

Of the vulnerability that people with disabilities both symbolize for others and feel themselves, Mary Jane Owen says:

Those of us with disabilities are precisely the people who prove to society how frail and vulnerable the human creature is. We prove in every way that "it" can happen to anyone, anywhere, anytime. That reality often frightens non-disabled people into avoiding us.

It also frightens many of us. We know, from the gut out, what it feels like to have some system of the body fall apart. The sword has fallen and broken our thin thread of potential perfection. We are already flawed. *And if it happened once, it can happen again and again.*

Maybe we have learned to compensate at our present level of functioning. But what about the next assault? How much can we be expected to overcome? We are vulnerable, in the worst way, to the future. (Owen, 1994, 8)

Affirming that bad things happen to people who do not deserve them, or seek them, or risk them, or fail to take care of themselves not only frightens most of us, it also raises challenging religious or spiritual issues for people who believe that God is omnipotent, omniscient, and benevolent, for those who believe that one or more powerful transcendent beings are caring for them, and for those who believe (or just feel) that the universe itself is, if not benevolent, at least benign. On rereading *Job,* I was amused to discover that Job's friends and colleagues offered (unsolicited) many theories of how he had brought an unremitting plague of misfortunes upon himself by his own actions and omissions. Reactions to other people's disasters do not seem to have changed much. The book also portrays Job's own agonized attempts to understand why God is punishing him so harshly. In fact, as the reader knows, God is not punishing him but allowing Satan to test Job's faith. That God would allow God's faithful servant to be tortured for so long to prove a point to a fallen angel does not offer an attractive or comforting picture of God. *Job* is a vivid story of terrible things happening to someone who did not deserve them, seek them, risk them, or fail to take care of himself, with which the writer forces the reader to think beyond a religious faith based on the fantasy of the perfect parent. *Job* presents the spiritual challenge: Can you love and seek to know God even if God might be like this? Or, put more generally (in Platonic terms): Can you love and seek to know Reality even if Reality might be like this? Desire to avoid such spiritual challenges is liable to lead religious people to attribute too much responsibility to victims of disaster and to look for moral and spiritual flaws in those whose lives have been devastated by violence, accident, or disease.

NOTES

1. I refer to the "commercial-media-soaked societies of North America" to distinguish them from social groups who inhabit the North American continent while maintaining (or struggling to maintain) their own cultures and social forms. Prominent among the latter are native societies in Canada and the United States that, although they are inevitably influenced by the cultures imported and developed here by invading Europeans, have values and practices which are radically different from them and based in independent traditions. It is not accurate to refer to a single "European-based culture, " because groups such as the Hasidic Jews and the Amish also came from Europe and yet maintain a way of life as separate from the commercial cultures created by Europeans as that of many native people. Nor is there only one, homogeneous commercial-media-soaked society in North America; there are sufficient differences in values and practice between Canada and the United States to make them different societies (as well as different nation states), and there are equally significant differences among regions within Canada and the United States. In this discussion, I try to stick to cultural trends and influences that I observe in media which reach all regions of the United States and Canada and that are discussed by observers of both Canadian and American societies.

2. For a discussion of some psychological aspects of the reactions of "normals" to "abnormality," see Fiedler, 1984.

3. Ironically, Kathy Davis defends the reasonableness of choosing cosmetic surgery on the basis that there is no clear distinction (even within the standards of a particular society) between the normal and the abnormal: "Where is the line between the 'normal' deficiency, to be dealt with within the usual routines of body maintenance and improvement, and the abnormally ugly, that which can no longer be endured?" (Davis, 1991, 37).

4. Disabled women suffer more than disabled men from the demand that people have ideal, or at least "normal," bodies, because in most male-dominated cultures women are judged more by their bodies than are men (Campling, 1981; Matthews, 1983; Hannaford, 1985; Fine and Asch, 1988; Driedger and Gray, 1992).

8. Thanks to Joyce Frazee for pointing this out to me years ago.

9. Fear of losing control of the body has, I believe, contributed to the medicalization of both death and birth. I will say more about the medicalization of birth in chapter 5.

12. Zola also pointed out that this medical re-introduction of individual moral responsibility for illness fit well with "the beliefs of the man in the street" (Zola, 1972, 491).

13. There is more evidence along the same lines. Jeffreys (1982, 177–78) reports: "A recent study showed that of twenty-six patients with proven myasthenia gravis, a disease causing seriously impaired muscle functioning, nine had been given initial diagnoses of hypochondriasis, depression, or hysteria (T. Sneddon, 'Myasthenia Gravis—the Difficult Diagnosis,' *British Journal of Psychiatry*, 136:92–93, 1980.)"

14. In an in-depth interview study of 8 women who had eventually been diagnosed with ME, Ingrid Deringer found that they had previously received a total of eight psychological diagnoses (some had received none, some more than one), including depression, stress, anorexia, psychosomatic disorder, and dementia (Deringer, 1992, 56–59).

20. For example, my rather sketchy understanding of what some aboriginal people in Canada call "bad medicine" is that it involves psychological action at a distance that can make a person sick.

REFERENCES

Bartky, Sandra Lee. 1990. *Femininity and Domination: Studies in the Phenomenology of Oppression.* New York: Routledge.

Beauvoir, Simone de. 1952. *The Second Sex.* New York: Alfred A. Knopf.

Brison, Susan J. 1993. "Surviving Sexual Violence: A Philosophical Perspective." *Journal of Social Philosophy* 24 (1): 5–22.

Campling, Jo, ed. 1981. *Images of Ourselves— Women with Disabilities Talking.* London: Routledge and Kegan Paul.

Davis, Kathy. 1991. "Remaking the She-Devil: A Critical Look at Feminist Approaches to Beauty." *Hypatia: A Journal of Feminist Philosophy* 6 (2): 21–43.

Deringer, Ingrid C. 1992. "Women's Experiences of Myalgic Encephalomyelitis/Chronic Fatigue Syndrome." Unpublished MA Thesis in the Department of Women's Studies, Simon Fraser University.

Dinnerstein, Dorothy. 1976. *The Mermaid and the Minotaur: Sexual Arrangements and Human Malaise*. New York: Harper.

Driedger, Diane, and Susan Gray, eds. 1992. *Imprinting Our Image: An International Anthology by Women with Disabilities*. Canada: Gynergy Books.

Fiedler, Leslie A. 1984. "The Tyranny of the Normal." *The Hastings Center Report* April: 40–42.

Fine, Michelle, and Adrienne Asch, eds. 1988. *Women with Disabilities: Essays in Psychology, Culture and Politics*. Philadelphia: Temple University Press.

Griffin, Susan. 1981. *Pornography and Silence: Culture's Revenge Against Nature*. New York: Harper.

Hannaford, Susan. 1985. *Living Outside Inside. A Disabled Woman's Experience. Towards A Social and Political Perspective*. Berkeley: Canterbury Press.

Jeffreys, Toni. 1982. *The Mile-High Staircase*. Sydney: Hodder and Stoughton.

Kleinman, Arthur, MD. 1988. *The Illness Narratives: Suffering, Healing, and the Human Condition*. New York: Basic Books.

Lessing, Jill. 1981. "Denial and Disability." *Off Our Backs* 11 (5): 21.

Matthews, Gwyneth Ferguson. 1983. *Voices from the Shadows: Women with Disabilities Speak Out*. Toronto: The Women's Press.

Morgan, Kathryn. 1991. "Women and the Knife. Cosmetic Surgery and the Colonization of Women's Bodies." *Hypatia: A Journal of Feminist Philosophy* 6 (3): 25–53.

Nuland, Sherwin B. 1992. *How We Die: Reflections on Life's Final Chapter*. New York: Vintage Books.

Owen, Mary Jane. 1994. "Like Squabbling Cubs." In *The Ragged Edge: The Disability Experience from the Pages of The First Fifteen Years of The Disability Rag,* ed. Barrett Shaw, 7–10. Louisville, KY: Advocado Press.

Russell, Susan. 1985. "Social Dimensions of Disability: Women and M.S." In *Women and Disability. Resources for Feminist Research* 14 (1): 56–58.

Sheets-Johnstone, Maxine, ed. 1992b. *Giving the Body Its Due*. Albany: State University of New York Press.

Wade, Cheryl Marie. 1994a. "It Ain't Exactly Sexy." In *The Ragged Edge: The Disability Experience from the Pages of The First Fifteen Years of The Disability Rag,* ed. Barrett Shaw, 88–90. Louisville, KY: Advocado Press. (Article originally published in 1991.)

Zola, Irving Kenneth. 1972. "Medicine as an Institution of Social Control." *Sociological Review* 20: 487–504.

Further Questions

1. What is "objectification" of the body, according to Wendell? Why is it a source of alienation and from what does it alienate us?

2. Suppose you had a disability that could be at least partly concealed. Which people would you like to know about it and from which people would you try to conceal it?

3. In the *Book of Job,* Job's advisors search for something Job has done that explains his misfortunes. Is the true explanation more unsettling than the possibility that Job has directly brought his misfortunes upon himself?

Further Readings for Part 1: Oppression

We live in a hierarchical society that contains many possibilities for oppression. Good, accessible works on the subject are too numerous to mention. What follows is only a small, selected sample. Many cover a wide variety of topics within the general category of oppression and outside of it as well.

I. RACIAL OPPRESSION

Jean Adleman and Gloria Enguìdanos, eds. *Racism in the Lives of Women: Testimony, Theory and Guides to Antiracist Practice* (Binghamton, NY: Harrington Park, 1995).

K. Anthony Appiah and Amy Gutmann. *Color Conscious: The Political Morality of Race* (Princeton, NJ: Princeton University Press, 1996).

Gloria Anzaldúa, ed. *Making Face, Making Soul: Haciendo Caras; Creative and Critical Perspectives by Feminist of Color* (San Francisco: Aunt Lute Books, 1990).

Asian Women United of California, eds. *Making Waves: An Anthology of Writings by and about Asian American Women* (Boston: Beacon, 1989).

Maxine Baca Zinn and Bonnie Thornton Dill, eds. *Women of Color in U.S. Society* (Philadelphia: Temple University Press, 1994).

Bernard R. Boxill. *Blacks and Social Justice, Revised Edition* (Lanham, MD: Rowman & Littlefield, 1992).

Carol Camper, ed. *Miscegenation Blues: Voices of Mixed Race Women* (Toronto, ON: Sister Vision, 1994).

Esther Ngan-Ling Chow, Doris Wilkinson, Maxine Baca Zinn, eds. *Race, Class and Gender: Common Bonds, Different Voices* (Thousand Oaks, CA: Sage, 1996).

Patricia Hill Collins. *Black Feminist Thought: Knowledge, Consciousness and the Politics of Empowerment* (New York: Routledge, 1991).

Lillian Comas-Díaz and Beverly Greene, eds. *Women of Color: Integrating Ethnic and Gender Identities in Psychotherapy* (New York: Guilford, 1994).

J. David, ed. *The American Indian: The First Victim* (New York: Morrow, 1972).

Angela Y. Davis. *Women, Culture, Politics* (New York: Vintage, 1990).

Richard Delgado, ed. *Critical Race Theory: The Cutting Edge* (Philadelphia: Temple University Press, 1995).

Diana L. Fowlkes. *White Political Women: Paths from Privilege to Empowerment* (Knoxville: University of Tennessee Press, 1992).

Ruth Frankenberg. *White Women, Race Matters: The Social Construction of Whiteness* (Minneapolis: University of Minnesota Press, 1993).

Alma M. García, ed. *Chicana Feminist Thought. The Basic Historical Writings* (New York: Routledge, 1997).

Beverly Guy-Sheftall, ed. *Words of Fire: An Anthology of African-American Feminist Thought* (New York: New Press, 1995).

bell hooks. *Talking Back: Thinking Feminist, Thinking Black* (Boston: South End, 1989).

———. *Yearning: Race, Gender and Cultural Politics* (Boston: South End, 1990).

———. *Killing Rage: Ending Racism* (New York: Holt, 1995).

Elaine H. Kim, Lilia V. Villanueva and Asian Women United of California, eds. *Making More Waves; New Writing by Asian American Women* (Boston: Beacon, 1997).

Audre Lorde. *Sister Outsider: Essays and Speeches* (Freedom, CA: Crossing, 1984).

Mari J. Matsuda. *Where Is Your Body and Other Essays on Race, Gender, and the Law* (Boston: Beacon, 1996).

Charles W. Mills. *Blackness Visible: Essays on Philosophy and Race* (Ithaca, NY: Cornell University Press, 1998).

Joan Moore and Harry Pachon. *Hispanics in the U.S.* (Englewood Cliffs, NJ: Prentice Hall, 1985).

Michael Omi and Harold Winnat. *Racial Formations in the United States* (New York: Routledge and Kegan Paul, 1986).

Lucus T. Outlaw (Jr.). *On Race and Philosophy* (New York: Routledge, 1996).

Paula S. Rothenberg, ed. *Race, Class, and Gender in the United States* (New York: St. Martin's, 4th Edition, 1998).

Elizabeth V. Spelman. *Inessential Woman: Problems of Exclusion in Feminist Thought* (Boston: Beacon, 1988).

Robert Staples. *Black Masculinity: The Black Male's Role in American Society* (San Francisco: Black Scholar, 1982).

———. *The Black Woman in America: Sex, Marriage and the Family* (Chicago: Nelson-Hall, 1973).

John Stone, ed. *Race, Ethnicity and Social Change* (Belmont, CA: Wadsworth, 1997).

Cornel West. *Race Matters* (Boston: Beacon, 1993).

Winged Words; American Indian Writers Speak (Lincoln: University of Nebraska Press, 1990).

Patricia J. Williams. *The Alchemy of Race and Rights: Diary of a Law Professor* (Cambridge, MA: Harvard University Press, 1991).

Naomi Zack, ed. *Race/Sex: Their Sameness, Difference, and Interplay* (New York: Routledge, 1997).

2. CLASS OPPRESSION

Paul Blumberg. *Inequality in an Age of Decline* (New York: Oxford University Press, 1980).

Katie de Koster and Bruno Leone, eds. *Poverty: Opposing Viewpoints* (San Diego: Greenhaven, 1994).

Elliot Liebow. *Tell Them Who I Am: The Lives of Homeless Women* (New York: Penguin, 1993).

Daniel Moynihan, ed. *On Understanding Poverty* (New York: Basic, 1969).

Kevin Phillips. *The Politics of the Rich and the Poor* (New York: Random House, 1990).

Lillian B. Rubin. *Worlds of Pain: Life in the Working Class Family* (New York: Basic, 1976).

Tamara L. Roleff. *The Homeless: Opposing Viewpoints* (San Diego: Greenhaven, 1996).

Richard Sennet and Jonathan Cobb. *The Hidden Injuries of Class* (New York: Vintage, 1973).

William J. Wilson. *The Truly Disadvantaged: The Inner City, The Underclass and Public Policy* (Chicago: University of Chicago Press, 1987).

3. OPPRESSION OF THE DISABLED

Esther Boylan, ed. *Women and Disability* (Atlantic Highlands, NJ: Zed, 1990).

Jo Campling, ed. *Images of Ourselves—Women with Disabilities Talking* (London: Routledge and Kegan Paul, 1981).

Michelle Fine and Adrienne Asch, eds. *Women with Disabilities: Essays in Psychology, Culture and Politics* (Philadelphia: Temple University Press, 1988).

Susan Hannaford. *Living Outside Inside. A Disabled Woman's Experience: Towards a Social and Political Perspective* (Berkeley, CA: Canterbury, 1985).

Benedict Instad and Susan Reynolds White, eds. *Disability and Culture* (Berkeley: University of California Press, 1995).

Gwyneth Ferguson Matthews. *Voices from the Shadows: Women with Disabilities Speak Out* (Toronto: Women's Educational, 1983).

Karen Thompson and Julie Andrzejewski. *Why Can't Sharon Kowalski Come Home?* (San Francisco: Spinsters, Aunt Lute, 1988).

Mary Willmuth and Lillian Holcombe, eds. *Women With Disabilities: Found Voices* (Binghamton, NY: Harrington Park, 1993).

4. GENDER OPPRESSION

(a) Classics on women's oppression from the beginning of the Women's Liberation Movement, around 1970.

Simone de Beauvoir. *The Second Sex* (New York: Knopf, 1953).
Shulamith Firestone. *The Dialectic of Sex: The Case for Feminist Revolution* (New York: Morrow, 1970).
Vivian Gornick and Barbara K. Moran, eds. *Women in Sexist Society* (New York: Signet, 1972).
Kate Millett. *Sexual Politics* (New York: Ballantine, 1969).
Juliet Mitchell. *Women's Estate* (New York: Pantheon, 1971).
Robin Morgan, ed. *Sisterhood is Powerful: An Anthology of Writings from the Women's Liberation Movement* (New York: Vintage, 1970).

(b) Early responses by men to women's oppression.

Marc Feigen Fasteau. *Male Machine* (New York: Dell, 1975).
Michael Korda. *Male Chauvinism! How It Works* (New York: Ballantine, 1973).
John Stuart Mill. "The Subjection of Women" in *Essays on Sex Equality* by John Stuart Mill and Harriet Taylor Mill, Alice S. Rossi, ed. (Chicago: University of Chicago Press, 1970).

5. FURTHER READINGS FOR HETEROSEXIST OPPRESSION (OPPRESSION OF GAYS AND LESBIANS)

These can be found in Further Readings for Part VI: "Sex and Sexuality."

Suggested Moral of Part 1

While we are surveying the world with a feminist eye, trying to discern control of women by men, we should not overlook other forms of oppression. Writers in this section have shown the pervasiveness of oppression of homosexuals, non-whites, and the disabled. The expected result of the presence of these other oppressive structures is a certain amount of diversity in patriarchal oppression. Feminism must be prepared to confront this diversity with a pluralistic approach. It should not expect problems of, or solutions to, male control to be the same for all races, classes, sexual orientations, or levels of ability or disability.

Part II

Messages on the Surface: Looks and Language

Introduction

LOOKS (PERSONAL APPEARANCE) AND LANGUAGE have two important functions in patriarchy and other oppressive structures. First, they convey messages about which segments of society are in control. And second, they maintain that control. Looks and language are phenomena on the surface (easy to see or hear), even though their messages are often not easy to decipher.

Adams and Ware discuss some of the sexist messages of the English language; hooks claims that "talking back" can contest forms of control; Pronger writes of being gay but passing as straight on the basis of appearance; Wolf explains how pressures to be thin can generate eating disorders in women; Dull and West maintain that cosmetic surgery answers to pressures to perfect one's appearance that fall disproportionately upon women.

II.1   Sexism and the English Language: The Linguistic Implications of Being a Woman

KAREN L. ADAMS AND NORMA C. WARE

Karen L. Adams and Norma C. Ware note that language is a kind of "social mirror" and that, in particular, much can be learned about the social status of women by looking at words referring to women. Such words can sexualize women, trivialize them, or refer to them as dependent on or secondary to men. There is also the distinct possibility that language shapes and reinforces social attitudes about women.

Karen L. Adams is Associate Professor of English at Arizona State University. Norma C. Ware is a research fellow in the program in medical anthropology at Harvard Medical School.

Reading Questions

1. Give some examples of sexual terminology referring to women. Does its presence in language mean that sexuality is considered a woman's most important feature, even when the sexual terms are pejorative?
2. Give some examples of terms that trivialize women. Is the use of "lady" or "girl" a trivializing device?
3. Give some examples of terms referring to women that are derivatives of more basic male forms. Does such terminology mean that women are described from a male point of view as secondary beings?

TO ANALYZE SEXISM IN the English language—what it looks like, and how it affects the way women think, feel, and act in our society[1]—we must look at two aspects of the relationship of language to society: references and usage. First, how are female human beings referred to in English, what are the cultural attitudes these kinds of references suggest, and what are their implications for the ways women see themselves and their role in society? Second, what are characteristic speech habits of both women and men, and how do these speech habits affect the

way women lead their lives? Then we can take up the question of change: What is being done to combat linguistic sexism, and what more could be done?

REFERRING TO WOMEN

One of the most intriguing characteristics of language is that it acts as a kind of social mirror, reflecting the organization and dynamics of the society of which it is a part. Because of this, we

From Women: A Feminist Perspective. *Fifth Edition. Jo Freeman, editor. Copyright © 1995 by Mayfield Publishing Company. Reprinted by permission of the publisher. As in the third and fourth editions of this book, "Sexism and the English Language," originally coauthored, appears here with additions and revisions by Karen L. Adams.*

can learn a great deal about our society by looking at some of the words used in English to refer to women.

The Sexualization of Women

English words used to refer to women are often "sexually weighted." This is evident in some sex-specific pairs of nouns that are similar in meaning but in which the female form has taken on sexual overtones. A prime example is the set of terms *master* and *mistress*. Both of these words refer to someone who possesses or has power over someone or something else, as in "He is the master of his fate," or "She is the mistress of a great fortune." However, as Lakoff has pointed out, the word *mistress* has acquired a sexual connotation that its masculine counterpart has not.[2] Thus, we can use a sentence like "Jane is Tom's mistress" to report the fact that Jane and Tom are sleeping together and be understood perfectly, while to attempt to describe the same situation with the expression "Tom is Jane's master" is to invite communicational disaster. The latter sentence fails to express its intended meaning because the word *master* is devoid of sexual connotations.

This kind of asymmetrical relationship between what are ostensibly male-female equivalents is not restricted to a single example. In the pair *sir* and *madam,* the latter refers to the proprietor of a brothel as well as serving as a term of address. Even the words *man* and *woman* may be seen to conform to this pattern. The sexual overtones inherent in the word *woman* show through clearly in a sentence such as: "After six months at sea, the first thing Bill wanted to do on leave was to find a woman." Then there is the case of the male academician who objected to the title of a new course because it was "too suggestive"—the title was "Women in the Social Order."[3]

Another indication of the sexualization of women in English is that the language seems to have so many more ways of describing women in terms of their sexuality than it has for men. Schulz reports the findings of two investigators who, as part of a larger study of slang, managed to collect

over five hundred synonyms for *prostitute,* but only sixty-five for the masculine sexual term *whoremonger,* and she herself "located roughly a thousand words and phrases describing women in sexually derogatory ways. There is nothing approaching this multitude for describing men."[4] A 1989 dictionary of college slang shows the same pattern persisting since Schulz's article appeared over fifteen years ago. The dictionary contains over five times as many terms (fifteen versus five) for sexually active women as for men and twice as many terms (six versus three) with sexual overtones for unpleasant women.[5]

Many once quite neutral terms relating to women have degenerated into terms that have sexual or negative connotations or both. Schulz explains how the word *hussy,* for example, is derived from the Old English *huswif* (house wife), whose meaning was simply "female head of the household." A *spinster* was originally someone who operated a spinning wheel. A *broad* was simply a young woman, and *tart* and *biddy* were terms of endearment![6]

Linguists generally agree that an elaborate vocabulary on a given topic in a language mean that this topic is of particular concern or importance to a particular group or to the society as a whole. What, then, can we conclude from the fact that English has so many terms describing women in specifically sexual ways, including its slang terminology, which is largely considered a male creation?[7] Is it that a woman's sexuality is considered the most salient aspect of her being, rivaling or even outweighing her humanity in importance? Furthermore, why are so many of these terms pejorative? Is it due to the well-known "sex is dirty" attitude that is characteristic of our culture? If this is true, it leaves women in the position of having the essence of their existence defined in terms of something that is considered unclean and distasteful. The implications of this are sobering at best.

The Trivialization of Women

A look at the kinds of people and things with which women tend to be grouped in the English language can also tell us a great deal about how our culture regards the female sex. Consider, for example, stock phrases such as *women and children first,* or *wine, women, and song.* Less proverbial but no less significant classifications have been offered by various prominent individuals. For instance, during the Vietnam War former Harvard President Nathan Pusey is reputed to have lamented the draining effect of the draft on male brainpower at the university with the words, "We shall be left with *the blind, the lame, and the women.*"[8]

Examples like these are not difficult to find. The question is, what do these groupings imply about the kind of people women are considered to be? For us, at least, the implication is that women are immature (like children), frivolous (to be indulged in for entertainment purposes, like wine and song), and handicapped (like the blind and the lame). Singly or in combination, these presumed female attributes provide a convenient excuse for not taking women seriously; they serve to trivialize the female sex.

This trivialization effect appears elsewhere in the language as well. The college dictionary of slang mentioned above has ten times as many words for stupid and/or superficial women, e.g., *dimbo* and *fifi,* than for men. More formal, non-slang situations also provide examples of trivialization. Lakoff has pointed out, for example, "that if, in a particular sentence, both *woman* and lady might be used, the use of the latter tends to trivialize the subject matter under discussion, often subtly ridiculing the woman involved." The expressions *lady atheist* (which appeared in the *San Francisco Chronicle,* January 31, 1972) and *lady sculptor,* with their connotation of eccentricity and frivolousness, are cited as cases in point.[9]

Similar in effect to the substitution of *lady* for *woman* is the common practice of referring to adult females as *girls.* Although the suggestion of youth may be a desirable one in our youth-oriented culture, it is also true that the association carries certain decidedly negative connotations—irresponsibility, immaturity, "smallness" of body or mind, etc. What is associated with youth tends

to lack stature, and therefore importance, almost by definition.

The parallel terms for men, *gentlemen* and *boys,* can have the same sort of trivializing effect, as in *gentleman scholar,* for example. However, the issue here is one of frequency. Males are referred to as *boys* or *gentlemen* much less often than females are called *girls* or *ladies.*[10]

Woman in Terms of Man

The English language also has a tendency to define women as a sort of male appendage. A woman's linguistic existence is in many cases expressed in essentially male terms, from a male point of view, or with male interests in mind. One example of this tendency is the fact that many of the nouns that refer to women performing various activities or roles are linguistically marked as derivatives of the basic (male) form. Thus, we have poet*ess* and actr*ess,* songstr*ess,* steward*ess,* usher*ette,* major*ette,* and stud*ette* (slang), not to mention proper names such as *Jeannette.* Only in matters of marriage and the few female-dominated professions is the female form the primary one. Thus, we have widow*er,* *male* nurse, and *male* prostitute.

Another way in which English tends to classify women in essentially male terms is in social titles that make the declaration of a woman's marital status—i.e., her relationship to a man—obligatory. Until very recently, women had no choice but to reveal whether they were single or (ever) married every time they wanted to refer to themselves in the conventional title-plus-last-name manner. A woman was either *Miss* Somebody-or-other, or *Mrs.* Somebody-or-other.[11] Now, of course, one can be *Ms.* Somebody-or-other and supposedly avoid the whole issue. However, the use of *Ms.* is on occasion interpreted to mean "unmarried, and slightly ashamed of the fact." As one writer reports, "After four attempts to convince a travel agent that I was not 'Miss' or 'Mrs.' but 'Ms.,' she finally responded with 'Oh, I'm not married either, but it doesn't bother me.'"[12]

One of the more subtle ways in which the English language represents the female as a derivative, or subset, of the male is by means of the linguistic convention known as "generic man." In English, the same word that is used to refer to male human beings is also used in the generic sense to refer to all human beings: that word is, of course, *man*. English grammar books assure us that persons of both sexes are meant to be included in expressions such as *man the hunter, the man in the street, goodwill to men,* and *all men are created equal.* But is this really the case? If *man* is really generic, why is there something decidedly funny about the sentence, "My brother married a spaceman who works for NASA"?[13]

That generic man is not always quite what he appears to be is particularly well illustrated by the following incident: At the end of one of the hour-long segments of Jacob Bronowski's highly acclaimed series "The Ascent of Man," "the host of the series chatted for a few minutes with a guest anthropologist about what women were doing during this early period in the ascent of man."[14]

The same generic principle that makes *man* both male and female is supposed to apply to pronouns as well. We have all been taught that the third person singular pronoun *he* is both masculine and sex-indefinite. But again, if this is true, shouldn't the following statement sound perfectly natural: "No person may require another person to perform, participate in, or undergo an abortion against his will"?[15]

Research provides experimental evidence of the male bias in generic *man*. Two sociologists at Drake University asked college students to submit appropriate photographs for the various chapters of an introductory sociology textbook. One group of students was given a list of chapter titles, in which the generic term was not used (e.g., "Culture," "Family," "Urban Life," "Political Life," "Social Life"). Another group was given a list in which some of the titles had been changed to read "Urban Man," "Political Man," "Social Man," etc. Sixty-four percent of the students given the *man* titles submitted male-only pictures, whereas only 50 percent of the students given neutral labels submitted male-only pictures.[16]

Studies on generic *he* also offer clear evidence that, despite what the grammar books tell us, in actual use this generic term does not apply equally to men and women. Khosroshahi compared the images drawn by female and male students after they read paragraphs with sex unspecified for the person involved. The paragraphs were composed using generic *he, he or she,* or *they.* The students had been divided according to use in their own compositions of generic *he* and sex-inclusive pronouns such as *he or she.* According to the study generic "*He* was found to be least likely to evoke female referents, *he or she* most likely, and *they* in between." Only the women who used sex-inclusive pronouns in their own writing drew more images of women than men.[17] As reported twenty years ago by Bem and Bem, the use of generic *he* and the masculine images it evokes can have practical consequences. High school women in their study responded to job advertisements with generic *he* less often than to those with *she* even though they were qualified for jobs in both types of advertisements.[18]

All this is not to say, however, that generic terms are never interpreted generically. Grammar-book definitions and years of English composition classes have presumably had some impact, and sentences such as the following may well be taken as referring to both sexes:

1. Man the life boats!
2. Each student should pick up his paper upon entering the room.

But the impact appears to be minor. In Khosroshahi's study, the interpretation of *he* as generic accounted for less than an eighth of the images drawn by the students.[19]

The continued use of the so-called generic sense exacerbates, rather than solves, the problem. Because *man* and *he* are both generic and nongeneric, women find themselves caught in a linguistic contradiction of rather formidable proportions: they discover that they are being defined as both *man* and *not man* at the same time.[20] The generic *man* convention sets up a linguistic structure whereby women can be portrayed in English *either* as women *or* as people, but not both.

Finally, we note that other words can be used in such a way as to exclude females from human groups. A television commentator was heard to say: "People won't give up power. They'll give up anything else first—money, home, wife, children—but not power."[21]

Implications and Consequences
(Or, So What?)

How does all this affect the way women live in the world? There are two views of the relationship of language to society and its effect on society. Some people maintain that the relationship between language and society is one of representation only, whereby language serves as a social mirror, reflecting the implicit values, attitudes, and prejudices of the society in which it is embedded but having no power to influence the perceptions or interactions of the people in that society. From this argument it follows that, while the picture the English language paints of women may be distasteful to us, that picture has no real effect on the way women think, the way they feel about themselves, or the way they lead their lives.

A considerable number of people disagree with this position, however. These people maintain that language not only reflects social values, attitudes, etc., but also reinforces them. In any language, it is easier to talk about some things than about others. Since many of the words that English offers for referring to women also have sexual connotations, it is easy to talk about women in a sexual way.

With the habit of talking about things in certain ways comes the habit of thinking about them in those ways. Thus, the language-based predisposition to talk about women in sexual terms makes it more likely that a speaker will think about them in those terms. It is in this sense, then, that language may be said to reinforce, as well as to reflect, prevailing social opinion.

One implication of this argument is that the ability of language to reinforce the status quo helps to perpetuate sexist attitudes and practices and to inhibit social change. Another implication is that, according to this theory, women are likely to come to "see themselves as the language sees them"—in the case of English, as sex objects, as trivial, as ambivalent about their status as complete human beings, etc.

Consider again the use of generic *he*. In Khosroshahi's study all men and the women who did not normally use sex-neutral pronouns drew more male than female images in all contexts. They drew the most with generic *he* and the fewest with *he or she*. The results fit studies on memory that show that the presentation of a word brings to mind all its associated meanings; thus, generic *he* will bring to mind the non-generic sex-specific interpretation; *he or she* will introduce female-specific images. The women who used sex-neutral pronouns in their own writing and drew more female than male images in all cases show that a speaker can consciously override an image in a controlled context. The use of generic male terminology is so ubiquitous that this override process requires vigilance.[22]

The consequences of this relationship of language to society can be even more serious for minority women. Not only are sexist attitudes perpetuated through language, but so also are racist attitudes. Moreover, in bilingual communities, women may have to deal with additional stereotyping in another language. The result of this ability of language to reinforce negative attitudes and practices can be overwhelming in such cases.[23] . . .

CONCLUSION

A few years ago, the principal question being asked by those who recognized and objected to sexism in the English language was can sexist language be changed? Is it in fact possible to legislate the changes necessary to wipe out language's sexist bias? The question is now well on its way to being answered affirmatively. In an attempt to eliminate sexist references to women, people have proposed many changes, and many of these are in use. Best known among them are the title *Ms.* to replace *Miss* and *Mrs.;* sex-indefinite substitutes such as sales*person,* mail *carrier,* spokes*person,* and *human*kind for the ambiguous generic *man* constructions; and substitutes for generic *he,* such as extension of the use of *they* to the singular, the alternation of *she* or *he* with *he* or *she,* and the newly coined *s/he.*

Some of these proposed changes have become institutionalized. For example, the U.S. Department of Labor's *Dictionary of Occupational Titles* has set the standard for nonsexist job designations. Since the publication of the *American Heritage School Dictionary* in 1972 (the first of its kind to employ definitions and sample sentences premeditatedly nonsexist in nature), efforts to eliminate sexism for the country's reading matter have also grown steadily. The *Random House Webster's College Dictionary* released in 1991 created some stir by including words like *herstory, waitron,* and *wimmin,* but its guidelines for avoiding sexist language did not. Newspaper policies developed in the mid to late 1970s for the most part have resulted in a uniform style of referring to women and men by name and title. Other major textbook publishers and professional organizations have also distributed guidelines for nonsexist writing to authors and editors. *Language, Gender, and Professional Writing,* published by the Modern Language Association, is a fine example of this. Library catalogers have worked to eradicate sexism in card catalogues, and various religious organizations have reworded hymns and other materials used in their services.[52]

Along with these institutional efforts, the ongoing, day-to-day struggle of individual women to combat sexist language must be recognized. For example, more and more women are refusing to be called, or to call themselves, *girls* or to be referred to as *lady golfer* or addressed as *chairman.* Many professional women have also insisted upon the title *Ms.* A midwestern recruiting firm found that a majority of female executives

under forty years of age preferred the title *Ms.,* and a recent study found that women using *Ms.* as a title as opposed to *Mrs.* or *Miss* are more likely to be perceived by other people as having the qualities of a manager.[53] These efforts have been all the more praiseworthy because they have often been undertaken knowing that one result may be ridicule by others.

The fact that many such changes are under way, however, only gives rise to another, equally important question: will the eradication of sexism in the English language help to eliminate this bias from other parts of society? The answer is yes. Language does, indeed, have the power to influence other parts of society; it can reinforce the status quo, or it can work to facilitate change. An awareness of sexist language is essential if we are to understand the traditional rules of interaction between women and men. Once we know these rules, we can work to modify them, to defy them, and to use them to our own advantage. Men and women can only benefit from the eradication of sexism in the English language.

NOTES

1. This article does not include information on the relationships between women and language in other societies, and what is true of English may not necessarily be true of other languages. Also, most of the data on usage that we describe are for white middle-class speakers, although when possible we have added data for women of color. Unfortunately, such research has often been neglected. A discussion of this neglect for Hispanic women can be found in D. Letticia Galindo, "Dispelling the Male-Only Myth: Chicanas and Caló," *The Bilingual Review/La Revista Bilingue* 17 (Jan.–April 1992), 3–35.

2. Robin Lakoff, *Language and Woman's Place* (New York: Harper and Row, 1975), 29. The extent to which the original meaning of *mistress* is still in use is open to question. Lakoff argues that it is "practically restricted to its sexual sense." However, one of us maintains that she quite comfortably refers to herself as mistress of her pet dog and cat. Also Betty Lou Dubois and Isabel Crouch, in "The Question of Tag Questions

in Women's Speech: They Don't Really Use More of Them, Do They?" *Language in Society* 4 (1975), 289–94, criticize Lakoff and include the following quotes in which the word is used in a nonsexual sense: "It was not that she would make any demonstration; she just did not want to be looked at when she was not quite *mistress* of herself." (Italics added.) Oliver La-Farge, *Laughing Boy* (Boston: Houghton Mifflin, 1927, p. 26; reprinted 1957). "The walls are full of pictures of famous people, from President Nixon to President Sadat of Egypt, all of them autographed to the *mistress* of the house—former movie star Shirley Temple Black." (Italics added.) P. J. Oppenheimer, "Shirley Temple Black Talks about Her Times of Tears, Her Times of Triumph," *Family Weekly,* Nov. 1974, pp. 9–11.

3. Laurel Richardson Walum, *The Dynamics of Sex and Gender: A Sociological Perspective* (Chicago: Rand McNally College Publishing Co., 1977), 18. Walum also notes that the same word can have both sexual and nonsexual meanings, depending on whether it is used to refer to a male or to a female. She points out that "a male *tramp* is simply a hobo but a female *tramp* is a slut." Ibid.

4. Muriel R. Schulz, "The Semantic Derogation of Women," in Barrie Thorne and Nancy Henley, eds., *Language and Sex: Difference and Dominance* (Rowley, Mass.: Newbury House Publishers, 1975), 72. The original study cited in Schulz, p. 75, is J. S. Farmer and W. E. Henley, *Slang and Its Analogues* (New York: Kraus Reprint Corporation, 1965 [reprint of seven volumes published 1890–1904]).

5. The dictionary in question, Pamela Munro et al., *Slang U* (New York: Harmony Books, 1989), contains words collected by and from UCLA students. Karen L. Adams, "Still a Dimbo After All These Years" (manuscript, Arizona State University, 1992), compared all nouns in the dictionary that referred specifically to either women or men and found that in addition to the sexually explicit vocabulary, words describing women as unattractive, e.g., *broomhilda* or *heifer,* were three times more common than words for unattractive men. Words for attractive men, e.g., *adonis* and *beauhunk,* were slightly more common than words for attractive women. The small numbers in this study in comparison to the one by Farmer and Henley mentioned above reflect the limited scope and specialized topic of the dictionary itself. A study of slang among Australian adolescents, Vivian de Klerk, "Slang: A Male Domain?" *Sex Roles* 22:9/10 (1990), 589–605, which

also found an abundance of terms for girls rather than boys, supports the argument that the patterns of unevenness continue in contemporary society.

6. Schulz, "The Semantic Derogation of Women," 66–68.

7. De Klerk, "Slang: A Male Domain?" 592–93.

8. This example appears in Mary Ritchie Key, *Male/Female Language* (Metuchen, N.J.: Scarecrow Press, 1975), 82.

9. Lakoff, *Language and Woman's Place,* 23.

10. What is more likely to happen, we think, is that men will be referred to as *guys* rather than *boys*—a term that seems distinctly less trivializing somehow. This could be one reason why young women seem so often to refer to one another as *guys* as well.

11. Even more striking in this regard is the fact that a woman was and still is in many cases expected to take her husband's name upon marriage, so that she becomes not only *Mrs.* Somebody-or-other, but even *Mrs. John* Somebody-or-other. For example, Hillary Clinton initially kept her own name but was forced to assume her husband's when he ran for governor of Arkansas and her independence became a political liability. Related also is the familiar practice of referring to a married couple as "man and wife," now rapidly becoming obsolete.

12. Walum, *The Dynamics of Sex and Gender,* 19, note 2.

13. This example originally appears in A. P. Nilsen, "Grammatical Gender and Its Relationship to the Equal Treatment of Males and Females in Children's Books" (Ph.D. dissertation, College of Education in the Graduate College, University of Iowa, Iowa City, 1973), 86–87. We discovered it in Casey Miller and Kate Swift, *Words and Women* (Garden City, N.Y.: Anchor Press/Doubleday, 1976), 29.

14. Miller and Swift, *Words and Women,* 20.

15. This example appears in Key, *Male/Female Language,* 89. It is interesting to note that *he* has not always been considered the correct third-person pronoun for referring to a single human being of indeterminate sex. Until about the eighteenth century, the correct choice of a pronoun for such a purpose was *they* or *he or she.* It was only when certain eighteenth-century grammarians decided that there was something inherently plural about *they,* and so prescribed a substitute for use in the singular, that our present generic *he* was born. Ann Bodine, "Androcentrism in Prescriptive Grammar: Singular 'They,' Sex-Indefinite 'He,' and 'He or She,'" *Language in Society* 4 (Aug. 1975), 129–46.

16. Joseph W. Schneider and Sally W. Hacker, "Sex Role Imagery and Use of Generic 'Man' in Introductory Texts: A Case in the Sociology of Sociology," *American Sociology* 8 (Feb. 1973), 12–18.

17. Fatemeh Khosroshahi, "Penguins Don't Care, but Women Do: A Social Identity Analysis of a Whorfian Problem," *Language in Society* 18 (Dec. 1989), 505. Khosroshahi's study is only one of many demonstrating the nongeneric interpretation of generic *he*. Donald G. MacKay, "Prescriptive Grammar and the Pronoun Problem," in Barrie Thorne, Cheris Kramarae, and Nancy Henley, eds., *Language, Gender and Society* (Rowley, Mass.: Newbury House Publishers, Inc., 1982), 38–53, is another such study, which also systematically addresses and counters linguistic arguments put forward as to why generic *he* should not or even cannot be changed. Mykol C. Hamilton, "Using Masculine Generics: Does Generic *He* Increase Male Bias in the User's Imagery," *Sex Roles* 19:11/12 (1988), 785–99, demonstrates that the bias in interpreting generic *he* as male occurs not only when students are presented with sentences written by the experimenter but also, even more importantly, when students write their own generic *he* versus sex-inclusive sentences.

18. S. L. Bem and D. J. Bem, "Does Sex-Biased Job Advertising 'Aid and Abet' Sex Discrimination?" *Journal of Applied Social Psychology* 3 (1973), 6–18.

19. Khosroshahi, "Penguins Don't Care, But Women Do," 515.

20. Note that this same contradictory quality could also conceivably serve as a convenient way of covering up the exclusion of women. One can always claim to be using *man* in the generic sense, whether one actually is or not. Thus, the ambiguity inherent in the meaning and the usage of the word *man* effectively turns the term into yet another weapon in the arsenal of those who have an interest, for whatever reason, in keeping women in the social backwaters and out of the mainstream.

21. The late Frank McGee on *Today Show*, NBC-TV, June 19, 1972, quoted in Miller and Swift, *Words and Women*, 37.

22. Does the fact that the male students who used sex-neutral pronouns in their own writing but still drew consistently male images argue against the influence of language and thought? According to Khosroshahi, no. The relationship between change in action and change in thought is a complex one. Their use of sex-neutral pronouns is probably in response to external pressures that have not yet affected more unconscious processes. However, social theory accepts the notion that change in action can trigger change in ways of thinking (Khosroshahi, "Penguins Don't Care, But Women Do," 516–22).

23. For examples, see Patricia Bell Scott, "The English Language and Black Womanhood: A Low Blow at Self-Esteem," *Journal of Afro-American Issues* 2 (1974), 218–24.

52. Miller and Swift, *Words and Women*, 145–47, discuss some of the earlier efforts. Discussion of newspaper policies can be found in Ralph Fasold, Haru Yamada, David Robinson, and Steven Barish, "The Language Planning Effect on Newspaper Editorial Policy: Gender Differences in *The Washington Post*," *Language in Society* 19 (1990), 521–39. Some variation in naming practice still occurs in nonnews type stories. See Lisa Mamula, "An Examination of Media Coverage of Gender-Related Differences Using Five 1990 Gubernatorial Races (undergraduate honors thesis, Arizona State University, 1990). However, Fasold et al., Mamula, and Michael Geis (*The Language of Politics* [New York: Springer-Verlag, 1987]) are among several studies demonstrating many other important differences in the description and amount of coverage given women and men in news stories. The full reference for the specific nonsexist guidelines mentioned here is Francine Wattman Frank and Paula A. Treichler, *Language, Gender, and Professional Writing: Theoretical Approaches and Guidelines for Nonsexist Usage* (New York: The Modern Language Association of America, 1989).

53. "Call Me Madam? No, Sir, Call me Ms. and Smile When You Say It" *Canadian Business* 60:7 (1987), 12; and Kenneth L. Dion and Regina A. Schuller, "Ms. and the Manager: A Tale of Two Stereotypes," *Sex Roles* 22:9/10 (1990), 569–77. Karen L. Adams and Alleen P. Nilsen, "Multifaceted Self-Images: Terms of Address for Faculty in Academia" (manuscript, Arizona State University, 1992), found a similar pattern. Several women with Ph.D. degrees also preferred to use *Dr.* rather than *Ms.* or *Mrs.* to show their status and to avoid any controversy about marital status or political views. Other aspects of naming are related to these changes in title. Most women in Adams and Nilsen considered the use of *Mrs. John Smith* archaic and in a professional context maintained their own birthname or former last name upon marriage or remarriage.

Further Questions

1. Can the title "Ms." be used in a way that totally bypasses a woman's marital status? Is "Ms." always preferable to the use of "Miss" or "Mrs."?

2. Is there such a thing as a generic use of "man" with no connotations of maleness? If so, how would one distinguish between generically human and specifically male uses of the word?

3. Can the pronoun "he" be used in a generic way to mean "he or she"? If so, how do you explain studies where "he" is much less likely to call female referents to mind than is "he or she"?

4. Do you believe that sexist attitudes are perpetrated through language? If so, suggest some changes in language that would make for less sexist attitudes.

II.2   Talking Back

BELL HOOKS

bell hooks talks of her experiences of breaking through the surface of male-dominated language by "talking back." This means disagreeing, as an equal, with an authority figure, being seen as well as heard. Her craving to be heard was awakened, as a child, by talk among the black women in her home. She found her own empowerment to talk back through adopting an ancestor, bell hooks, as a mentor and as her own identity as a writer.

hooks is Distinguished Professor of English at City College of New York and has written widely from the perspective of a black feminist. Another selection by hooks appears in Part IV.

Reading Questions

1. If you were silenced as a child, how did this make you feel? What effect did this have on your later life?
2. In your experience, can the voices of men usually drown out the voices of women?
3. Have you found it easier, on occasion, to express disagreement with a more powerful person if you think of yourself as being someone else?

IN THE WORLD of the southern black community I grew up in, "back talk" and "talking back" meant speaking as an equal to an authority figure. It meant daring to disagree and sometimes it just meant having an opinion. In the "old school," children were meant to be seen and not heard. My great-grandparents, grandparents, and parents were all from the old

Abridged from "Talking Back" in Talking Back: Thinking Feminist, Thinking Black *(Boston: South End Press, 116 Saint Botolph St., 1989), pp. 5–9. Reprinted by permission of the publisher.*

school. To make yourself heard if you were a child was to invite punishment, the back-hand lick, the slap across the face that would catch you unaware, or the feel of switches stinging your arms and legs.

To speak then when one was not spoken to was a courageous act—an act of risk and daring. And yet it was hard not to speak in warm rooms where heated discussions began at the crack of dawn, women's voices filling the air, giving orders, making threats, fussing. Black men may have excelled in the art of poetic preaching in the male-dominated church, but in the church of the home, where the everyday rules of how to live and how to act were established, it was black women who preached. There, black women spoke in a language so rich, so poetic, that it felt to me like being shut off from life, smothered to death if one were not allowed to participate.

It was in that world of woman talk (the men were often silent, often absent) that was born in me the craving to speak, to have a voice, and not just any voice but one that could be identified as belonging to me. To make my voice, I had to speak, to hear myself talk—and talk I did—darting in and out of grown folks' conversations and dialogues, answering questions that were not directed at me, endlessly asking questions, making speeches. Needless to say, the punishments for these acts of speech seemed endless. They were intended to silence me—the child—and more particularly the girl child. Had I been a boy, they might have encouraged me to speak believing that I might someday be called to preach. There was no "calling" for talking girls, no legitimized rewarded speech. The punishments I received for "talking back" were intended to suppress all possibility that I would create my own speech. That speech was to be suppressed so that the "right speech of womanhood" would emerge.

Within feminist circles, silence is often seen as the sexist "right speech of womanhood"— the sign of woman's submission to patriarchal authority. This emphasis on woman's silence may be an accurate remembering of what has taken place in the households of women from WASP backgrounds in the United States, but in black communities (and diverse ethnic communities), women have not been silent. Their voices can be heard. Certainly for black women, our struggle has not been to emerge from silence into speech but to change the nature and direction of our speech, to make a speech that compels listeners, one that is heard.

Our speech, "the right speech of womanhood," was often the soliloquy, the talking into thin air, the talking to ears that do not hear you—the talk that is simply not listened to. Unlike the black male preacher whose speech was to be heard, who was to be listened to, whose words were to be remembered, the voices of black women—giving orders, making threats, fussing—could be tuned out, could become a kind of background music, audible but not acknowledged as significant speech. Dialogue— the sharing of speech and recognition—took place not between mother and child or mother and male authority figure but among black women. I can remember watching fascinated as our mother talked with her mother, sisters, and women friends. The intimacy and intensity of their speech—the satisfaction they received from talking to one another, the pleasure, the joy. It was in this world of woman speech, loud talk, angry words, women with tongues quick and sharp, tender sweet tongues, touching our world with their words, that I made speech my birthright—and the right to voice, to authorship, a privilege I would not be denied. It was in that world and because of it that I came to dream of writing, to write.

Writing was a way to capture speech, to hold onto it, keep it close. And so I wrote down bits and pieces of conversations, confessing in cheap diaries that soon fell apart from too much handling, expressing the intensity of my sorrow, the anguish of speech—for I was always saying the wrong thing, asking the wrong questions. I could not confine my speech to the necessary corners and concerns of life. I hid these writings under my bed, in pillow stuffings, among faded underwear. When my sisters found and read them, they ridiculed and mocked me—poking fun. I felt violated, ashamed, as if the secret parts of my self had been exposed, brought into the open, and hung like newly clean laundry, out in the air for everyone to see. The fear of exposure, the fear that one's deepest emotions and inner-most thoughts will be dismissed as mere non-sense, felt by so many young girls keeping diaries, holding and hiding speech, seems to me now one of the barriers that women have always needed and still need to destroy so that we are no longer pushed into secrecy or silence.

Despite my feelings of violation, of exposure, I continued to speak and write, choosing my hiding places well, learning to destroy work when no safe place could be found. I was never taught absolute silence, I was taught that it was important to speak but to talk a talk that was in itself a silence. Taught to speak and yet beware of the betrayal of too much heard speech, I experienced intense confu-sion and deep anxiety in my efforts to speak and write. Reciting poems at Sunday afternoon church service might be rewarded. Writing a poem (when one's time could be "better" spent sweeping, ironing, learning to cook) was luxurious activity, indulged in at the expense of others. Questioning authority, raising issues that were not deemed ap-propriate subjects brought pain, punishments—like telling mama I wanted to die before her because I could not live without her—that was crazy talk, crazy speech, the kind that would lead you to end up in a mental institution. "Little girl," I would be told, "if you don't stop all this crazy talk and crazy acting you are going to end up right out there at Western State."

Madness, not just physical abuse, was the punishment for too much talk if you were fe-male. Yet even as this fear of madness haunted me, hanging over my writing like a monstrous shadow, I could not stop the words, making thought, writing speech. For this terrible mad-ness which I feared, which I was sure was the destiny of daring women born to intense speech (after all, the authorities emphasized this point daily), was not as threatening as imposed si-lence, as suppressed speech.

Safety and sanity were to be sacrificed if I was to experience defiant speech. Though I risked them both, deep-seated fears and anxieties char-acterized my childhood days. I would speak but I would not ride a bike, play hardball, or hold the gray kitten. Writing about the ways we are traumatized in our growing up years, psychoan-alyst Alice Miller makes the point in *For Your Own Good* that it is not clear why childhood wounds become for some folk an opportunity to grow, to move forward rather than backward in the process of self-realization. Certainly, when I reflect on the trials of my growing-up years, the many punishments, I can see now that in resistance I learned to be vigilant in the nour-ishment of my spirit, to be tough, to coura-geously protect that spirit from forces that would break it.

While punishing me, my parents often spoke about the necessity of breaking my spirit. Now when I ponder the silences, the voices that are not heard, the voices of those wounded and/or oppressed individuals who do not speak or write, I contemplate the acts of persecution, torture—the terrorism that breaks spirits, that makes creativity impossible. I write these words to bear witness to the primacy of resistance struggle in any situation of domination (even within family life); to the strength and power that emerges from sustained resistance and the profound conviction that these forces can be healing, can protect us from dehumanization and despair. . . .

. . . For us, true speaking is not solely an ex-pression of creative power; it is an act of resis-tance, a political gesture that challenges politics of domination that would render us nameless and voiceless. As such, it is a courageous act—as such, it represents a threat. To those who wield oppressive power, that which is threatening must necessarily be wiped out, annihilated, silenced.

Recently, efforts by black women writers to call attention to our work serve to highlight both our presence and absence. Whenever I pe-ruse women's bookstores, I am struck not by the rapidly growing body of feminist writing by black women, but by the paucity of available published material. Those of us who write and are published remain few in number. The context of silence is varied and multi-dimensional. Most obvious are the ways racism, sexism, and class exploitation act to suppress and silence. Less obvious are the inner struggles, the efforts made to gain the necessary confidence to write, to rewrite, to fully develop craft and skill—and the extent to which such efforts fail.

Although I have wanted writing to be my life-work since childhood, it has been difficult for me to claim "writer" as part of that which identifies and shapes my everyday reality. Even after publishing books, I would often speak of wanting to be a writer as though these works did not exist. And though I would be told, "you are a writer," I was not yet ready to fully affirm this truth. Part of myself was still held captive by domineering forces of history, of familial life that had charted a map of silence, of right speech. I had not completely let go of the fear of saying the wrong thing, of being punished. Somewhere in the deep recesses of my mind, I believed I could avoid both responsibility and punishment if I did not declare myself a writer.

One of the many reasons I chose to write using the pseudonym bell hooks, a family name (mother to Sarah Oldham, grandmother to Rosa Bell Oldham, great-grandmother to me), was to construct a writer-identity that would challenge and subdue all impulses leading me away from speech into silence. I was a young girl buying bubble gum at the corner store when I first really heard the full name bell hooks. I had just "talked back" to a grown person. Even now I can recall the surprised look, the mocking tones that informed me I must be kin to bell hooks—a sharp-tongued woman, a woman who spoke her mind, a woman who was not afraid to talk back. I claimed this legacy of defiance, of will, of courage, affirming my link to female ancestors who were bold and daring in their speech. Unlike my bold and daring mother and grandmother, who were not supportive of talking back, even though they were assertive and powerful in their speech, bell hooks as I discovered, claimed, and invented her was my ally, my support.

That initial act of talking back outside the home was empowering. It was the first of many acts of defiant speech that would make it possible for me to emerge as an independent thinker and writer. In retrospect, "talking back" became for me a rite of initiation, testing my courage, strengthening my commitment, preparing me for the days ahead—the days when writing, rejection notices, periods of silence, publication, ongoing development seem impossible but necessary.

Moving from silence into speech is for the oppressed, the colonized, the exploited, and those who stand and struggle side by side a gesture of defiance that heals, that makes new life and new growth possible. It is that act of speech, of "talking back," that is no mere gesture of empty words, that is the expression of our movement from object to subject—the liberated voice.

Further Questions

1. What was your most successful effort at challenging authority by "talking back"?

2. What was the most successful effort made against you, as an authority, by someone "talking back" to you?

3. Is abandoning silence and expressing disagreement important for ending oppressive structures like racism and patriarchy? Think of a good example where spoken or written disagreement (or defiance) has caused a major change in an oppressive structure.

II.3   Gay Irony

BRIAN PRONGER

Brian Pronger speaks of how gay men can pass as straight in a society that takes heterosexuality as the norm and presumes that everyone fits in. Sexual orientation can be placed beneath the surface of appearance, allowing gays to assume the status of an invisible minority on occasions in which they wish to pass. Pronger calls this dissimulation "gay irony" and writes that it is highlighted by "radical drag": a man with a masculine, muscled body dressed as a slinky, sensuous woman.

Pronger is an associate researcher at the School of Physical and Health Education, University of Toronto (Toronto, Ontario).

Reading Questions

1. You go into a (same sex) locker room. What, if anything, do you assume about the sexual orientation of the people using it?
2. Imagine yourself homosexual but not visible as such. Do you sometimes feel a tension between the way you appear and the way you are?
3. Are there occasions when you dress in a way clearly appropriate to your gender because this will make life easier for you, even though this results in a discrepancy between the way you look and the way you feel?

THE FLUIDITY OF BEING GAY AND PASSING AS STRAIGHT

GAY MEN PASS IN AND OUT of gay contexts, moment to moment, day to day, and through different periods of their lives. Gay contexts are created not only by the presence of gay men but also by their decisions to interpret a situation as gay. Consequently, it is possible for a gay man to go to a gymnasium, be completely involved in the athleticism of his workout, and experience that time as being simply athletic, devoid of any gay significance as far as he is concerned. Another day, he may go to the same gymnasium and find the same men there doing much the same exercises as they were previously; this time, however, he sees the experience as a gay experience. That is, he may find the situation sexy; he may find it ironic (as I will explain shortly); he may decide that he is with only other gay men and experience a sense of gay fraternity. The gay context depends on the man's interpretation. Self-concept also depends upon personal interpretation. A man who is a runner may enter the Boston marathon, an event that he considers to be very important to himself athletically. His concerns are whether he will finish, what his time might be, or how painful the experience will be. Here, his concept of himself is overwhelmingly that of a runner. The same man could enter the same marathon another year, and having decided to wear a singlet with a large pink triangle emblazoned with the word *gay*, he sees himself as a gay runner and his participation in this race as an expression of his pride in being gay.

The fluidity of homosexuality is enhanced by the fact that gay men can and often do pass as straight men. In a society that assumes that everyone is heterosexual, it is relatively easy for homosexual men to "pass." This ability is a distinguishing feature of the homosexual minority; people of colour cannot easily pass as white, and women have a difficult time passing as men. Passing is particularly important in mainstream athletic culture where heterosexuality is expected (Kidd, 1987; Kopay & Young, 1977). Certainly, it is usually necessary for gay men to pass as straight in the potentially sexual situations of men's locker rooms and showers.

Afraid of losing their positions on teams, as a result of the compulsory heterosexuality of sport, many gay athletes find it necessary to hide their homosexuality by passing as straight. I interviewed an international competitive rower who said it was essential to seem to be heterosexual:

> You did everything you could to hang on to your seat, to make the crew, that you would never jeopardize—you wouldn't even tell the coach you had a cold. You could be *crippled* and you'd hide it from the coach, because if there's any perceived weakness, they'll put somebody else in the boat. So to hint that I was gay was to kiss rowing goodbye.

THE IRONIC GAY SENSIBILITY

. . . Gay irony is a unique way of knowing that has its origins in the social construction of heterosexist society. The ways that gay men think are very much the results of having to deal with homophobia. To avoid suffering in potentially homophobic settings like athletic teams and locker rooms, gay men learn to pass as straight. Passing predisposes gay men to a sense of irony.

From an early age, gay men are aware of this important irony—they seem to be heterosexual when in fact they are not. Most social relations are organized around heterosexuality. For boys, the social side of sports is heterosexual. One's team-mates form a "boys-wanting-girls club." When a young male athlete socializes with his teammates, inside or outside the locker room, talk is often about sex with girls and the problems of dating. Bars, clubs, or athletic dances held to mark the end of a sporting season or a school victory are always heterosexual functions. In their early years, most young gay people follow this social pattern.

A gay man may follow these patterns, but because he is not really part of the heterosexual action, the budding gay man is aware of himself as an outsider, an observer. The position of the observer is an ironic stance (Muecke, 1982). A young homosexual person can be aware of himself as an outsider without having understood himself as homosexual. In fact, this sense of being an outsider may lead to one's self-identification as homosexual. During this time the foundation for a young gay person's sense of irony develops. In his position as an observer, the young gay man, probably unconsciously, masters some of the basic skills of the ironist. As he grows older he becomes increasingly aware of himself as the observer who seems to be part of the action. Although he may never define his world as ironic, the gay man may, nevertheless, employ irony unwittingly. (One need not analyze and define the formal structure of a way of thinking or being in order to use that structure in day-to-day-life.) Growing up in a world in which heterosexuality is taken for granted, then, gay people may be introduced to the rudiments of irony. By developing this sense and seeing his world as ironic, the gay man can manipulate the socially constructed incompatibility of the appearance and the reality of his sexuality.

Wayne Booth (1974) says that fundamental to irony is its invitation to reconstruct something deeper than what is apparent on the surface. While inviting one to see deeper than the superficial appearance and thereby understand what is actually meant, irony preserves the appearance. The total truth includes both appearance and reality. This technique for understanding reality while maintaining a cosmetic appearance is very useful to gay men while passing as straight. It is a technique that many of us learn to use at very young ages simply in order to survive. Because gay men feel at home with irony, even when "the closet" is not an issue, they continue to interpret their worlds ironically. Because irony brings with it a sense of superiority, a sense of looking at the world from a higher place (Muecke, 1982), each gay ironic experience is a sublime reaffirmation of a gay worldview.

Gay irony is a way of thinking, communicating, and being that emerges out of the experience of being gay in a society in which people tend to believe that everyone is straight. It is a sensibility that is essentially fluid both through the lives of individuals and throughout society. The phenomenon of being gay is a matter of context; so too is the invocation of gay irony. Not all homosexual people see themselves as "gay," and not all gay people use irony. Being gay and the use of irony are conceptual dispositions and techniques that people use to think about themselves and interpret their worlds. Irony is a form of interpretation, a way of understanding that develops out of the experience of individuals' interactions with sexual and gender categories. Gay irony, therefore, is best understood as a tendency to interpret experience ironically rather than a consistent standpoint shared by all gay men. . . .

Anagnorisis

Gay men subtly communicate their shared worldview by using irony. This subtlety has important implications for gay men; it allows them to remain undiscovered by the uninitiated, thereby affording them some protection from the expressions of homophobia that frequently accompany detection. Especially important in gay irony is *anagnorisis,* which is the observer's recognition of the ironist as an ironist with a deeper intent than that which is immediately apparent on the surface. Anagnorisis occurs when the interpreter of the irony realizes the irony in the situation. In anagnorisis, the gay ironist not only reveals meanings that have been concealed by appearances, he also reveals himself. Eye contact is the way gay men usually recognize each other in non-gay settings. One manifestation of this eye contact can be a subtle, knowing look, which can be the clue for mutual anagnorisis. One

man told me about being in a university weight room and watching an athlete to whom he was attracted lifting a weight. To most observers, the scenario would appear to be quite straight. A man whom he didn't know was standing nearby and watching the same athlete. Moving from the athlete to each other, their admiring eyes met, and with no more obvious gesture than a slight pause in their gazes, they became aware of their secret fraternity. In their sententious exchange of glances, having, as novelist John Fowles said, "the undeclared knowledge of a shared imagination," their worlds touched. They uttered not a word.

Acting versus Being

As a result of coming out in some contexts, gay men become more consciously aware of passing in others; gay men can start to see others' uses of masculinity as a technique for passing. This insight can bring them to a heightened awareness of their uses of masculinity as an ironic form. Rather than thinking of themselves as being masculine, gay men can come to think of themselves as acting masculine. In the 1970s, the disco group "The Village People" epitomized this masculine (and I think intensely ironic) act. Their outfits were ironic caricatures of masculinity: construction worker, policeman, Indian, and a hyper masculine-looking man with a mustache (a style known as the "clone"). One of their hit songs had the lyrics, "Macho, macho, man; I wanna be a macho man." The clue to their irony lies in the fact that they don't say they are macho men; rather, they "wanna be" macho men. That is, they look like macho men when in fact they are not. The macho look, especially that of the clone, became very popular in gay ghettos across North America and parts of Europe. The deep and sometimes subliminal irony of the gay masculine clone style[1] may best be appreciated in the light of Wallace Stevens (1977): "The final belief is to believe in a fiction, which you know to be a fiction, there being nothing else. The exquisite truth is to know that it is a fiction and that you believe in it willingly" (p. 163). . . .

This gay ironic play with masculinity is highlighted in radical drag. A man with bulging biceps and thunderous thighs wearing a slinky dress and a tiara is, through the juxtaposition of a masculine body and feminine clothes, expressing the overt irony of seeming to be "masculine" when he is also "feminine". . . .

NOTE

1. The fluidity of being gay should be kept in mind here; that is, there are men who may practice homosexuality who see their masculine behaviours not in this gay context but in a traditional patriarchal one. Moreover, they may switch from a traditional context to a gay one from time to time, depending on the situation.

BIBLIOGRAPHY

Booth, W. (1974). *A rhetoric of irony.* Chicago: University of Chicago Press.
Kidd, B. (1987). Sports and masculinity. In M. Kaufman (Ed.), *Beyond patriarchy: Essays by men on pleasure, power, and change* (pp. 250–265). Toronto: Oxford University Press.
Kopay, D., & Young, P. (1977). *The David Kopay story: An extraordinary self revelation.* New York: Arbor House.
Muecke, D. (1982). *Irony and the ironic.* London: Methuen.
Stevens, W. (1977). *Opus posthumous.* New York: Knopf.

Further Questions

1. Do you ever wear clothing, cosmetics, hairstyles, and so forth that are usually worn only by the other gender? If so, why do you do this?
2. Do you find a man in obviously feminine clothing upsetting? If so, why? Is a woman in masculine clothing equally upsetting?
3. Do you have days when you think most of what you do in the sight of others is pure "fiction," not an expression of what you are really thinking or feeling?

Hunger   II.4

NAOMI WOLF

Naomi Wolf deplores the new culture of food deprivation that has afflicted women, creating anorexics, bulimics, and other women who feel they must go hungry to fit into a predetermined body mold that Wolf calls The Iron Maiden. Her contention is that the psychological effects of hunger in women are sought to cancel out the dangerous effects of the new liberation brought by the women's movement.

Reading Questions

1. Wolf claims that the eating disorders that afflict young women would not be tolerated in a population of young men. Is she right?
2. Wolf maintains "whom a society values it feeds well" and, conversely, those with less social value are fed less well. Is this borne out in your experience? Give some examples or counter-examples.
3. Are hunger and dieting institutions in place to control the new liberties, self-esteem, and power women recently have come to acquire, as Wolf claims? What sort of evidence would support or fail to support this claim?

I saw the best minds of my generation destroyed by madness, starving. . . .

—Allen Ginsberg, "Howl"

THERE IS A DISEASE spreading. It taps on the shoulder America's firstborn sons, its best and brightest. At its touch, they turn away from food. Their bones swell out from receding flesh. Shadows invade their faces. They walk slowly, with the effort of old men. A white spittle forms on their lips. They can swallow only pellets of bread, and a little thin milk. First tens, then hundreds, then thousands, until, among the most affluent families, one young son in five is stricken. Many are hospitalized, many die.

The boys of the ghetto die young, and America has lived with that. But these boys are the golden ones to whom the reins of the world are to be lightly tossed: the captain of the Princeton football team, the head of the Berkeley debating club, the editor of the *Harvard Crimson*. Then a quarter of the Dartmouth rugby team falls ill; then a third of the initiates of Yale's secret societies. The heirs, the cream, the fresh delegates to the nation's forum selectively waste away.

The American disease spreads eastward. It strikes young men at the Sorbonne, in London's Inns of Court, in the administration of The Hague, in the Bourse, in the offices of *Die Zeit,* in the universities of Edinburgh and Tübingen and Salamanca. They grow thin and still more thin. They can hardly speak aloud. They lose their libido, and can no longer make the effort to joke or argue. When they run or swim, they look appalling: buttocks collapsed, tailbones protruding, knees knocked together, ribs splayed in a shelf that stretches their papery skin. There is no medical reason.

The disease mutates again. Across America, it becomes apparent that for every well-born living skeleton there are at least three other young men, also bright lights, who do something just as strange. Once they have swallowed their steaks and Rhine wine, they hide away, to thrust their fingers down their throats and spew out all the nourishment in them. They wander back into Maury's or "21,"shaking and pale. Eventually they arrange their lives so they can spend hours each day hunched over like that, their highly trained minds telescoped around two shameful holes: mouth, toilet; toilet, mouth.

Meanwhile, people are waiting for them to take up their places: assistantships at *The New York Times,* seats on the stock exchange, clerkships with federal judges. Speeches need to be written and briefs researched among the clangor of gavels and the whir of fax machines. What is happening to the fine young men, in their brush cuts and khaki trousers? It hurts to look at them. At the expense-account lunches, they hide their medallions of veal under lettuce leaves. Secretly they purge. They vomit after matriculation banquets and after tailgate parties at the Game. The men's room in the Oyster Bar reeks with it. One in five, on the campuses that speak their own names proudest.

How would America react to the mass self-immolation by hunger of its favorite sons? How would Western Europe absorb the export of such a disease? One would expect an emergency response: crisis task forces convened in congressional hearing rooms, unscheduled alumni meetings, the best experts money can hire, cover stories in newsmagazines, a flurry of editorials, blame and counterblame, bulletins, warnings, symptoms, updates; an epidemic blazoned in boldface red. The sons of privilege *are* the future; the future is committing suicide.

Of course, this is actually happening right now, only with a gender difference. The institutions that shelter and promote these diseases are hibernating. The public conscience is fast asleep. Young women are dying from institutional catatonia: four hundred dollars a term from the college endowment for the women's

---

center to teach "self-help"; fifty to buy a noon-time talk from a visiting clinician. The world is not coming to an end because the cherished child in five who "chooses" to die slowly is a girl. And she is merely doing too well what she is expected to do very well in the best of times.

Up to one tenth of all young American women, up to one fifth of women students in the United States, are locked into one-woman hunger camps. When they fall, there are no memorial services, no intervention through awareness programs, no formal message from their schools and colleges that the society prefers its young women to eat and thrive rather than sicken and die. Flags are not lowered in recognition of the fact that in every black-robed ceremonial marches a fifth column of death's-heads.

The weight-loss cult recruits women from an early age, and eating diseases are the cult's bequest. Anorexia and bulimia are female maladies: From 90 to 95 percent of anorexics and bulimics are women. America, which has the greatest number of women who have made it into the male sphere, also leads the world with female anorexia. Women's magazines report that there are up to a million American anorexics, but the American Anorexia and Bulimia Association states that anorexia and bulimia strike a million American women *every year;* 30,000, it reports, also become emetic abusers.

Each year, according to the association, 150,000 American women die of anorexia. If so, every twelve months there are 17,024 more deaths in the United States alone than the total number of deaths from AIDS tabulated by the World Health Organization in 177 countries and territories from the beginning of the epidemic until the end of 1988; if so, more die of anorexia in the United States each year than died in ten years of civil wars in Beirut. Beirut has long been front-page news. As criminally neglectful as media coverage of the AIDS epidemic has been, it still dwarfs that of anorexia; so it appears that the bedrock question—why must Western women go hungry—is one too dangerous to ask even in the face of a death toll such as this.

Joan Jacobs Brumberg in *Fasting Girls: The Emergence of Anorexia Nervosa as a Modern Disease* puts the number of anorexics at 5 to 10 percent of all American girls and women. On some college campuses, she believes, one woman student in five is anorexic. The number of women with the disease has increased dramatically throughout the Western world starting twenty years ago. Dr. Charles A. Murkovsky of Gracie Square Hospital in New York City, an eating diseases specialist, says that 20 percent of American college women binge and purge on a regular basis. Kim Chernin in *The Hungry Self* suggests that at least half the women on campuses in the United States suffer at some time from bulimia or anorexia. Roberta Pollack Seid in *Never Too Thin* agrees with the 5- to 10-percent figure for anorexia among young American women, adding that up to six times that figure on campuses are bulimic. If we take the high end of the figures, it means that of ten young American women in college, two will be anorexic and six will be bulimic; only two will be well. The norm, then, for young, middle-class American women, is to be a sufferer from some form of the eating disease.

The disease is a deadly one. Brumberg reports that 5 to 15 percent of hospitalized anorexics die in treatment, giving the disease one of the highest fatality rates for a mental illness. *The New York Times* cites the same fatality rate. Researcher L.K.G. Hsu gives a death rate of up to 19 percent. Forty to 50 percent of anorexics never recover completely, a worse rate of recovery from starvation than the 66 percent recovery rate for famine victims hospitalized in the war-torn Netherlands in 1944–45.

The medical effects of anorexia include hypothermia, edema, hypotension, bradycardia (impaired heartbeat), lanugo (growth of body hair), infertility, and death. The medical effects of bulimia include dehydration, electrolyte imbalance, epileptic seizure, abnormal heart rhythm, and death. When the two are combined, they can result in tooth erosion, hiatal hernia, abraded esophagus, kidney failure, osteoporosis and death. Medical literature is starting to report that babies and children underfed by weight-conscious mothers are suffering from stunted growth, delayed puberty, and failure to thrive.

. . . In fact, "there is very little evidence to support the claim that fatness causes poor health among women. . . . The results of recent studies have suggested that women may in fact live longer and be generally healthier if they weigh ten to fifteen percent *above* the life-insurance figures *and* they refrain from dieting," asserts *Radiance;* when poor health is correlated to fatness in women, it is due to chronic dieting and the emotional stress of self-hatred. The National Institutes of Health studies that linked obesity to heart disease and stroke were based on male subjects; when a study of females was finally published in 1990, it showed that weight made only a fraction of the difference for women that it made for men. The film *The Famine Within* cites a sixteen-country study that fails to correlate fatness to ill health. Female fat is not in itself unhealthy.

But female fat is the subject of public passion, and women feel guilty about female fat, because we implicitly recognize that under the myth, women's bodies are not our own but society's, and that thinness is not a private aesthetic, but hunger a social concession expected by the community. A cultural fixation on female thinness is not an obsession about female beauty but an obsession about female obedience. Women's dieting has become what Yale psychologist Judith Rodin calls a "normative obsession," a never-ending passion play given international coverage out of all proportion to the health risks associated with obesity, and using emotive language that does not figure even in discussions of alcohol or tobacco abuse. The nations seize with compulsive attention on this melodrama because women and men understand that it is not about cholesterol or heart rate or the disruption of a line of tailoring, but about how much social freedom women are going to get away with or concede. The media's convulsive analysis of the endless saga of female fat and the battle to vanquish it are actually bulletins of the sex war: what women are gaining or losing in it, and how fast.

The great weight shift must be understood as one of the major historical developments of the century, a direct solution to the dangers posed by the women's movement and economic and reproductive freedom. Dieting is the most potent political sedative in women's history; a quietly mad population is a tractable one. Researchers S. C. Wooley and O. W. Wooley confirmed what most women know too well—that concern with weight leads to "a virtual collapse of self-esteem and sense of effectiveness." Researchers J. Polivy and C. P. Herman found that "prolonged and periodic caloric restriction" resulted in a distinctive personality whose traits are "passivity, anxiety, and emotionality."

It is those traits, and not thinness for its own sake, that the dominant culture wants to create in the private sense of self of recently liberated women in order to cancel out the dangers of their liberation.

Women's advances had begun to give them the opposite traits—high self-esteem, a sense of effectiveness, activity, courage, and clarity of mind. "Prolonged and periodic caloric restriction" is a means to take the teeth out of this revolution. The great weight shift and its One Stone Solution followed the rebirth of feminism so that women just reaching for power would become weak, preoccupied, and, as it evolved, mentally ill in useful ways and in astonishing proportions. To understand how the gaunt toughness of the Iron Maiden has managed spectacularly to roll back women's advances toward equality, we have to see that what is really at stake is not fashion or beauty or sex, but a struggle over political hegemony that has become—for women, who are often unaware of the real issues behind our predicament—one of life and death.

We need to reexamine all the terms again, then, in the light of a public agenda. What, first, is food? Certainly, within the context of the intimate family, food is love, and memory, and language. But in the public realm, food is status and honor.

Food is the primal symbol of social worth. Whom a society values, it feeds well. The piled plate, the choicest cut, say: We think you're worth this much of the tribe's resources. Samoan women, who are held in high esteem, exaggerate how much they eat on feast days. Publicly apportioning food is about determining power relations, and sharing it is about cementing social equality: When men break bread together, or toast the queen, or slaughter for one another the fatted calf, they've become equals and then allies. The word *companion* comes from the Latin for "with" and "bread"— those who break bread together.

But under the beauty myth, now that all women's eating is a public issue, our portions testify to and reinforce our sense of social inferiority. If women cannot eat the same food as men, we cannot experience equal status in the community. As long as women are asked to bring a self-denying mentality to the communal table, it will never be round, men and women seated together; but the same tradition hierarchical dais, with a folding table for women at the foot.

In the current epidemic of rich Western women who cannot "choose" to eat, we see the continuation of an older, poorer tradition of women's relation to food. Modern Western female dieting descends from a long history. Women have always had to eat differently from men: less and worse. In Hellenistic Rome, reports classicist Sarah B. Pomeroy, boys were rationed sixteen measures of meal to twelve measures allotted to girls. In medieval France, according to historian John Boswell, women received two thirds of the grain allocated to men. Throughout history, when there is only so much to eat, women get little, or none: A common explanation among anthropologists for female infanticide is that food shortage provokes it. According to UN publications, where hunger goes, women meet it first: In Bangladesh and Botswana, female infants die more frequently than male, and girls are more often malnourished, because they are given smaller portions.

In Turkey, India, Pakistan, North Africa, and the Middle East, men get the lion's share of what food there is, regardless of women's caloric needs. "It is not the caloric value of work which is represented in the patterns of food consumption" of men in relation to women in North Africa, "nor is it a question of physiological needs. . . . Rather these patterns tend to guarantee priority rights to the 'important' members of society, that is, adult men." . . .

The affluent West is merely carrying on this traditional apportioning. Researchers found that parents in the United States urged boys to eat, regardless of their weight, while they did so with daughters only if they were relatively thin. In a sample of babies of both sexes, 99 percent of the boys were breast-fed, but only 66 percent of the girls, who were given 50 percent less time to feed. "Thus," writes Susie Orbach, "daughters are often fed less well, less attentively, and less sensitively than they need." Women do not feel entitled to enough food because they have been taught to go with less than they need since birth, in a tradition passed down through an endless line of mothers; the public role of "honored guest" is new to us, and the culture is telling us through the ideology of caloric restriction that we are not welcome finally to occupy it.

What, then, is fat? Fat is portrayed in the literature of the myth as expendable female filth; virtually cancerous matter, an inert or treacherous infiltration into the body of nauseating bulk waste. The demonic characterizations of a simple body substance do not arise from its physical properties but from old-fashioned misogyny, for above all fat is female; it is the medium and regulator of female sexual characteristics.

Fat is sexual in women; Victorians called it affectionately their "silken layer." The leanness of the Iron Maiden impairs female sexuality. One fifth of women who exercise to shape their bodies have menstrual irregularities and diminished fertility. The body of the model, remember, is 22 to 23 percent leaner than that of the average woman; the average woman wants to be as lean as the model; infertility and hormone imbalance are common among women whose fat-to-lean ratio falls below 22 percent. Hormonal imbalances promote ovarian and endometrial cancer and osteoporosis. Fat tissues store sex hormones, so low fat reserves are linked with weak estrogens and low levels of all the other important sex hormones, as well as with inactive ovaries. Rose E. Frisch in *Scientific American* refers to the fatness of Stone Age fertility figures, saying that "this historical linking of fatness and fertility actually makes biological sense" since fat regulates reproduction. Underweight women double their risk of low-birth-weight babies.

What, finally, is dieting? "Dieting," and, in Great Britain, "slimming," are trivializing words for what is in fact self-inflicted semistarvation. In India, one of the poorest countries in the world, the very poorest women eat 1,400 calories a day, or 600 more than a Western woman on the Hilton Head Diet. "Quite simply," writes Seid, dieters "are reacting the way victims of semi-starvation react . . . semi-starvation, even if caused by self-imposed diets, produces startlingly similar effects on all human beings."

The range of repulsive and pathetic behaviors exhibited by women touched by food diseases is portrayed as quintessentially feminine, proof positive of women's irrationality (replacing the conviction of menstrual irrationality that had to be abandoned when women were needed for the full-time work force). In a classic study done at the University of Minnesota, thirty-six volunteers were placed on an extended low-calorie diet and "the psychological, behavioral, and physical effects were carefully documented." The subjects were young and healthy, showing "high levels of ego strength, emotional stability, and good intellectual ability." They "began a six-month period . . . in which their food intake was reduced by half—a typical weight reduction technique for women.

"After losing approximately 25% of their original body weight, pervasive effects of semi-starvation were seen." The subjects "became increasingly preoccupied with food and eating, to the extent that they ruminated obsessively about meals and food, collected recipes and cookbooks, and showed abnormal food rituals, such as excessively slow eating and hoarding of food related objects." Then, the majority "suffered some form of emotional disturbance as a result of semistarvation, including depression, hypochondriasis, hysteria, angry outbursts, and, in some cases, psychotic levels of disorganization." Then, they "lost their ability to function in work and social contexts, due to apathy, reduced energy and alertness, social isolation, and decreased sexual interest." Finally, "within weeks of reducing their food intake," they "reported relentless hunger, as well as powerful urges to break dietary rules. Some succumbed to eating binges, followed by vomiting and feelings of self-reproach. Ravenous hunger persisted, even following large meals during refeeding." Some of the subjects "found themselves eating continuously, while others engaged in uncontrollable cycles of gorging and vomiting." The volunteers "became terrified of going outside the experiment environment where they would be tempted by the foods they had agreed not to eat . . . when they did succumb, they made hysterical, half-crazed confessions." They became irritable, tense, fatigued, and full of vague complaints. "Like fugitives, [they] could not shed the feeling they were being shadowed by a sinister force." For some, doctors eventually had to prescribe tranquilizers.

The subjects were a group of completely normal healthy college men.

During the great famine that began in May 1940 during the German occupation of the Netherlands, the Dutch authorities maintained rations at between 600 and 1,600 calories a day, or what they characterized as the level of semistarvation. The worst sufferers were defined as starving when they had lost 25 percent of their body weight, and were given precious supplements. Photos taken of clothed starving Dutch women are striking for how preternaturally modern they look.

At 600–1,600 calories daily, the Dutch suffered semistarvation; the Diet Centers' diet is fixed at 1,600 calories. When they had lost 25 percent of their body weight, the Dutch were given crisis food supplementation. The average healthy woman has to lose almost exactly as much to fit the Iron Maiden. In the Lodz Ghetto in 1941, besieged Jews were allotted starvation rations of 500–1200 calories a day. At Treblinka, 900 calories was scientifically determined to be the minimum necessary to sustain human functioning. At "the nation's top weight-loss clinics," where "patients" are treated for up to a year, the rations are the same.

The psychological effects of self-inflicted semistarvation are identical to those of involuntary semistarvation. By 1980 more and more researchers were acknowledging the considerable emotional and physical consequences of chronic dieting, including "symptoms such as irritability, poor concentration, anxiety, depression, apathy, lability of mood, fatigue, and social isolation." Magnus Pyke, describing the Dutch famine, writes that "starvation is known to affect people's minds and these people in Holland became mentally listless, apathetic, and constantly obsessed with thoughts of food." Bruch notes that with involuntary progressive semistarvation, "there is a coarsening of emotions, sensitivity, and other human traits." Robert Jay Lifton found that World War II victims of starvation "experienced feelings of guilt over having done something bad for which they are now being punished, and dreams and fantasies of food of every kind in limitless amounts." Starving destroys individuality; "anorexic patients," like others who starve, asserts Hilde Bruch, "exhibited remarkably uniform behavior and emotional patterns until they gained some weight." "Food deprivation," Roberta Pollack Seid sums it up, "triggers food obsessions for both physical and psychological reasons. . . . undernourishment produces lassitude, depression, and irritability. Body metabolism slows down. . . . And hunger drives the hungry person to obsess about food." The psychological terror of hunger is cross-cultural: Orphans adopted from poor countries cannot control their compulsion to smuggle and hide food, sometimes even after living for years in a secure environment.

Authoritative evidence is mounting that eating diseases are caused mainly by dieting. Ilana Attie and J. Brooks-Gunn quote investigators who found "chronic, restrained eating" to "constitute a cumulative stress of such magnitude that dieting itself may be 'a sufficient condition for the development of anorexia nervosa or bulimia.'" Roberta Pollack Seid reaches the same conclusion. "Ironically, dieting . . . itself may provoke obsessive behaviour and binge-eating. It may indeed *cause* both eating disorders and obesity itself." Sustained caloric deprivation appears to be a severe shock to the body that it remembers with destructive consequences. Seid writes that "women's problems with food seem to stem . . . from their effort to get an ultra-lean body. . . . The only way 95 percent can get it is by putting themselves on deprivatory diets." Attie and Brooks-Gunn concur: "Much of the behavior thought to cause anorexia nervosa and bulimia may actually be a consequence of starvation. . . . The normal weight dieter who diets to look and feel thin also is vulnerable to disturbed emotional, cognitive, and behavioral patterns by virtue of the constant stress of trying to stay below the body's 'natural' or biologically regulated weight." Dieting and fashionable thinness make women seriously unwell.

Now, if female fat is sexuality and reproductive power; if food is honor; if dieting is semistarvation; if women have to lose 23 percent of their body weight to fit the Iron Maiden and chronic psychological disruption sets in at a body weight loss of 25 percent; if semistarvation is physically and psychologically debilitating, and female strength, sexuality, and self-respect pose the threats explored earlier against the vested interests of society; if women's journalism is sponsored by a $33-billion industry whose capital is made out of the political fear of women; then we can understand why the Iron Maiden is so thin. The thin "ideal" is not beautiful aesthetically; she is beautiful as a political solution.

The compulsion to imitate her is not something trivial that women choose freely to do to ourselves. It is something serious being done to us to safeguard political power. Seen in this light, it is inconceivable that women would not have to be compelled to grow thin at this point in our history.

The ideology of semistarvation undoes feminism; what happens to women's bodies happen to our minds. If women's bodies are and have always been wrong whereas men's are right, then women are wrong and men are right. Where feminism taught women to put a higher value on ourselves, hunger teaches us how to erode our self-esteem. If a woman can be made to say, "I hate my fat thighs," it is a way she has been made to hate femaleness. The more financially independent, in control of events, educated and sexually autonomous women become in the world, the more impoverished, out of control, foolish, and sexually insecure we are asked to feel in our bodies.

Further Questions

1. If you are a woman, do you sometimes envy men for not having to maintain your level of concern with your weight? If you are a man, are you pleased to be free of worrying about your weight in the way women do? Is there something unfair in this gender situation?

2. What should be done about the fact that there are so many anorexics and bulimics? How difficult will it be to change this situation?

3. Should a woman want to be as thin as a model even if loss of that much weight can cause unwanted psychological changes that will make her dysfunctional? Would educational programs about the effects of starvation and semi-starvation be helpful here?

Accounting for Cosmetic Surgery: The Accomplishment of Gender

II.5

DIANA DULL AND CANDACE WEST

Diana Dull and Candace West suggest that women see cosmetic surgery as "normal" and "natural" whereas men do not because women have been taught they must look good and be as pretty as possible. More so than men, women wish to change their racial and ethnically determined features such as noses. Because our culture contains a double standard of aging, whereby women but not men with wrinkled skin look old, women also have the majority of face lifts and eyelid reconstructions.

At the time this article was written, Dull was a graduate student at the University of California, Santa Cruz. West is a Professor of Sociology at the University of California, Santa Cruz.

© 1991 by the Society for the Study of Social Problems. Reprinted from Social Problems, Vol. 38, No. 1 (February 1991), p. 54–70 by permission.

Reading Questions

1. What is cosmetic surgery? Is undergoing such a procedure to improve one's looks as normal as applying make-up or getting one's hair done?
2. Is cosmetic surgery a natural response to the wrinkled skin of aging? Should the answer to this question be different for men and women?
3. Can it improve one's appearance to have one's racially typical nose or other features changed through cosmetic surgery? How important is it to have such features made to conform to those of white Anglo-Saxon Protestants?

WITHIN THE UNITED STATES, physicians claim a professional mandate to define the nature and treatment of disease (Hughes, 1958, 78; Thorne, 1973, 36–37). For most surgeons, this mandate includes the right to evaluate patients' complaints, to determine what should be done about them, and to assess post-operative results.[1] For plastic surgeons, however, the mandate is not so clear. The field of plastic surgery encompasses two categories of operations: (1) reconstructive procedures, which restore or improve physical function and minimize disfigurement from accidents, diseases, or birth defects, and (2) cosmetic procedures, which offer elective aesthetic improvement through surgical alterations of facial and bodily features (American Society of Plastic and Reconstructive Surgeons, 1988). In the case of reconstructive surgery, the professional mandate rests on the surgeon's ability to improve physical function and minimize disfigurement. But in the case of cosmetic surgery, the evaluation of patients' complaints, the determination of what should be done about them, and the assessment of post-operative results must be negotiated in relation to *what* "aesthetic improvement" might consist of, and to *whom*. This, then, is the central dilemma of cosmetic surgery.

The disproportionate number of women who undergo cosmetic operations suggests the importance of gender to understanding how this dilemma is resolved. For example, in 1988 more than half a million people in the United States had cosmetic surgery, with the available evidence indicating that the vast majority were women.[2] Although official statistics do not distinguish between cosmetic and reconstructive operations, they do indicate a decided bias. In 1985, 61 percent of all rhinoplasty (nose surgery), 86 percent of all eyelid reconstruction, and 91 percent of all facelifts were performed on women (U.S. National Center for Health Statistics, 1987). The American Society of Plastic and Reconstructive Surgeons estimates that 90,000 men opted for cosmetic surgery in 1988, but that number represents only 16 percent of the total cosmetic operations identified.

METHODS

Our primary data consists of interviews with surgeons who perform cosmetic surgery and with individuals who have undergone such operations. By law, any licenced medical doctor may perform cosmetic surgery, but we limited our study to surgeons certified to do so through boards recognized by the American Board of Medical Specialties. Eight of the ten surgeons in this sample are certified by the American Board of Plastic Surgery and two, by the American Board of Otolaryngology. We obtained these interviews through a snowball sample, yielding one woman and nine men surgeons, all white. With the exception of one surgeon outside California (whom we interviewed by phone), we conducted all our physician interviews in person at surgeons' offices. Each interview was recorded on audiotape and lasted approximately one hour.

Given the sensitive nature of the topic, we gave people who had undergone cosmetic surgery two interview options. The first option, chosen by 7 of the total 23, was to be interviewed on audiotape face to face. The second option, chosen by 16 of the 23, was to complete an open-ended questionnaire with a follow-up discussion over the phone if clarification was needed. In the analysis that follows we found no differences among people's perspectives on cosmetic surgery according to which of the options they selected. These interviews were also obtained through a snowball sample.

Nineteen of the 23 persons interviewed were women whose surgical experiences included face lifting, upper and lower eyelid reduction, rhinoplasty, chin implantation, breast augmentation, breast reduction, and liposuction of the hips, thighs, and knees. Two of the interviews were with men who had undergone eyelid reduction or face lifting. Our secondary data consist of two further interviews with men who ultimately decided against cosmetic surgery. Given that both had seriously contemplated aesthetic rhinoplasty and were among only four men we were able to locate who had ever consulted plastic surgeons, we decided to include their views with those of our other interviewees—setting them off in our analysis as anomalous cases.[3] Four of the women and one of the men had undergone more than one surgery, and in at least two cases later operations were performed in order to correct the results of an earlier procedure.

THE ACCOMPLISHMENT OF GENDER

Elsewhere, we advance an ethnomethodological view of gender as an *accomplishment,* that is, an achieved property of situated social action (Fenstermaker, West, & Zimmerman, 1990; West & Fenstermaker, forthcoming; West & Zimmerman, 1987). From this perspective, gender is not simply something one is; rather, it is something one does in ongoing interaction with others. Following Heritage (1984, 179), we argue that to

the extent that members of society know their actions are accountable, they will design their actions with an eye to how others might see and characterize them. Moreover, insofar as sex categories (e.g., "girl" or "boy," "woman" or "man") are omnirelevant to social life (Garfinkel, 1967, 111; Goffman, 1977, 324), they provide an ever-ready resource for characterizing social action (e.g., as consistent with women's or men's "essential nature"). Accordingly, "people involved in virtually *any* activity may hold themselves accountable and be held accountable for their performance of that activity as *women* or as *men*" (West and Fenstermaker, forthcoming, 7).

In the data presented in this paper, we find that accounts of cosmetic surgery rest ultimately on the accomplishment of gender. For example, throughout our interviews with surgeons and former patients, we found implicit claims that what was "normal" and "natural" for a woman was *not* normal or natural for a man. Surgeons were united in the view that women's concerns for their appearance are *essential* to their nature as women. They observed that women are, after all, taught to look good and disguise their real or imagined "defects." Hence, they said, it is taken for granted that a woman "wants to primp and look pretty as she can." Her desire may not be biologically ordained—as they noted, she is a product of our society and how she was brought up. But, they pointed out, by the time a woman has been "brought up," her consciousness of her appearance as a matter of self image is "intrinsic" to her nature as a *woman* (cf. Cahill, 1982, 1986a, 1986b).

By contrast, surgeons characterized men's concerns for their appearance as extrinsic to their nature as men. They observed that men are taught "to deal with little defects here and there," and that therefore, "they don't have the psychological investment in it that women do." They further observed that men must rely on their wives to buy their clothes or tell them what looks good, and that men only attend to their appearance in instrumental fashion, for example, to attain a more prestigious job.

Women are more concerned about their appearance than men are as a basic rule. Now that is not something you can apply to every person. Obviously you'll see that the success level is related to their appearance level. People who don't take some care in how they appear don't seem to be in supervisory or professional positions. And I guess people, as they're educated, I guess, as they attempt to reach some goal in life, find that their appearance relates to achieving those goals. Women, conversely, are intrinsically . . . concerned about their appearance, not just in a goal-oriented fashion, but as a matter of self image.

Here, a surgeon notes that educated "people" (meaning men) may discover that their appearance has an impact on their "attempt to reach some goal in life," but he does not attribute that discovery to any natural order of things. In fact, a concern for appearance is so unnatural for men that, as another surgeon notes, some men may deliberately misrepresent it in surgeons' offices, for example complaining that they "can't breathe" to cover up their wishes for "a better-looking nose."

Our interviews with former patients also suggested that what was "normal" and "natural" for a woman was not normal or natural for a man. As noted above, women referred to cosmetic surgery as what "anyone" would do, extolled its benefits for "everyone," and compared it to "wearing makeup" or "having your hair done." By contrast, the only grounds on which men characterized the pursuit of cosmetic surgery as "normal" were job-related concerns. One man, a cosmetologist who underwent upper eyelid reduction, felt his upper lids were a distraction in his work. Another, who had undergone a facelift, explained that as a dentist, he felt patients liked "younger persons working on them." Still another man we spoke with who underwent reconstructive rhinoplasty for a deviated septum—but decided against cosmetic alteration—stated that he would only consider cosmetic surgery if he "were disfigured or something." And a man who consulted a surgeon about cosmetic rhinoplasty—but then decided against it—told us,

> I like my nose. It's a little on the large side, and I was teased about it when I was younger, but it's the nose I grew up with. . . . Besides, would I lie to the kids I have some day? They're going to grow up with these noses and say, "Where did this come from?" My philosophy is that you work with what you've got.

Of course, the men in the last two excerpts were accounting for something they did not do, while those in the first two excerpts were accounting for something they did. We can, therefore, understand why the last two excerpts would emphasize good reasons for not having surgery, and the first two, good reasons for having it. But what is noteworthy in all four descriptions is the assumption that a desire for aesthetic improvement must be *justified* (either on the basis of job-related concerns or in the case of "disfigurement"). Clearly, it was not seen as "natural."

Our interviewees further distinguished women from men in their descriptions of "objective" indicators for surgery. Many surgeons acknowledged that our culture and its double standard of aging are responsible for women's and men's differential experiences as they get older. Thus, they explained the fact that a man with wrinkles looks "acceptable" while a woman with wrinkles does not on the basis of cultural conceptions, rather than any objective standard. Surgeons, however, relied *on those same cultural conceptions* to select candidates for surgery:

> Our society has got a very strange double standard and it can be summarized that when a man gets old, he gets sophisticated, debonair [and] wise; but when a woman gets old, she gets old. A man with a wrinkly face doesn't necessarily look bad in our society. A woman with a wrinkly face looks old. So when a man comes in and he wants a facelift, I have to be able to get considerably more skin than I would on a woman. . . . And usually there is something else going on. . . . Usually, they're getting rid of their wife.

In requiring "considerably more [excess] skin" for men than women, the surgeon constructs an "objective indicator" for doing surgery—as well as "objective differences" between women and men.

Another surgeon contended that there *are* objective differences that make women more likely to "need" surgery:

> Men don't seem to have the lipodystrophy [i.e., deposition of fat in tissue] that women do. They don't have subcutaneous fat layers and uh ... I guess I've only done one man with love handles. ... I think it is more of a gender-related difference than uh, psychological. ... men dermabrade their face with a razor every morning. You have thick hair follicles that support the skin so that it doesn't get wrinkled ... like your upper lip, for instance. Men hardly ever have any problem with that and women, sometimes by age 50, need their lip peeled or something.

Our concern here is *not* the physiological differences this surgeon attests to (although we note that he ignores potbellies in this description). Rather, we are interested in how these differences are invoked to legitimize one course of activity and discredit another. If women's bodies are seen as *essentially* "in need of repair," then surgery on women can be seen as a moral imperative instead of an aesthetic option. But if men "hardly ever have any problem with that," then surgery on men will require elaborate justification.

Such justification was apparent in our interviews with men who had undergone cosmetic surgery. For example, in contrast to the woman patient who said that "when your eyelids start to come down" and "you start to get that 'crepeyness' in your neck" it is simply "time to do it," one man said that *his wife's appearance* motivated him to have a facelift, as he did not want his wife "to look much younger." Here, he eschewed a description of "objective" signs of aging for an explanation of how he might appear in relation to his spouse. Another man stated that following his upper eyelid reduction, he "once again looked like [his] old self." As a

result, he indicated he "felt better" and did not "get as tired," attributing the difference to psychological effect.

The notion of gender as an interactional accomplishment also advances our analysis of how race and ethnicity were constituted as "objective" grounds for surgery. References to Michael Jackson notwithstanding, the descriptions of most surgeons focused on what *women* in various racial and ethnic groups "have" and "need," not on men. Even while former patients relied on white, Anglo Saxon, Protestant features as the unmarked case, they described their post-operative benefits not only as looking "less exotic," but also, "prettier," and "more attractive to men."

In short, we contend that our interviewees' accounts would not have been possible without the accomplishment of gender. This is the mechanism that allows them to see the pursuit of elective aesthetic improvement as "normal" and "natural" for a woman, but not for a man. The accountability of persons to particular sex categories provides for their seeing women as "objectively" needing repair and men as "hardly ever" requiring it. The fact that gender is an *interactional* accomplishment explains why surgeons prefer patients who are "doing it for themselves" but actively participate in the construction of patients' preferences.

The evidence indicates that the selection of "good candidates" for cosmetic surgery relies not merely on the creation of patients with "appropriate" levels of concern and the reduction of patients' faces and bodies to a series of component parts. It also relies on the simultaneous accomplishment of gender. Following Berk (1985), we contend that there are actually two processes here: (1) the selection of "good candidates" for surgery, and (2) the accomplishment of gender. The "normal," "natural" character of each process is made sensible in relation to the other, and since they operate simultaneously, the relationship between the two processes and their outcomes "is virtually impossible to question" (West and Fenstermaker, forthcoming, 14). Thus, the assessment of "appropriate levels of concern" ensures patients who will agree with a surgeon's perceptions of their problems, and at the same time, it furnishes the opportunity to affirm the pursuit of cosmetic surgery as an essentially "gendered" activity:

> A lot of guys come in and the classic one is that they want their nose fixed. And you look at the guy and he's got this big, God-awful nose. So does Anthony Quinn! Uh, a man can get away with that kind of nose. So what is normal for a man would not be . . . well, let's say what is *acceptable* for a man would not necessarily be acceptable for a woman.

The point, then, is not merely that pursuing cosmetic surgery is seen as something women do, but that for a woman to seek it while a man does not displays the "essential" nature of each.

NOTES

1. The surgeon's mandate to assess post-operative results works in at least two way. First, it affords surgeons the authority to appraise likely outcomes of operations in advance of their occurrence (and thereby, to determine whether operations should be performed). Second, it affords surgeons the authority to judge results of particular procedures after the fact (and thus, to pronounce procedures as "successful"). The later mandate is especially important in cases of malpractice suits, where the expert testimony of other surgeons weighs heavily in litigation.

2. This figure should be treated as a conservative estimate, insofar is it only includes operations performed by the 2,550 active physician members of the American Society of Plastic and Reconstructive Surgeons. However, statistics on the actual incidence of cosmetic surgery are virtually impossible to maintain. For example, the U.S. National Center for Health Statistics reports figures independently of physicians' and surgeons' Board affiliations and society memberships, but it does not include operations performed outside hospitals. Since 95 percent of cosmetic procedures are said to be performed in private offices or clinics (American Society of Plastic and Reconstructive Surgeons, 1988), the National Center for Health Statistics offers an even less reliable estimate of their actual incidence.

3. Ideally, we also would have obtained interviews with women who consulted plastic surgeons, but decided against cosmetic surgery. We were unable to locate such women through our snowball sample. However, insofar as the accomplishment of gender involves the *accountability* of persons to particular sex categories (not deviance or conformity per se), this "gap" in our data does not constitute a problem for our analysis.

REFERENCES

American Society of Plastic and Reconstructive Surgeons. 1988. Press Release: "Estimated number of cosmetic procedures performed by ASPRS members." Department of Communications, Arlington Heights, Ill.

Berk, Sarah F. 1985. *The Gender Factory: The Apportionment of Work in American Households.* New York: Plenum.

Berscheid, Ellen and Steve Gangestad. 1982. "The social psychological implications of facial physical attractiveness." *Clinics in Plastic Surgery* 9:289–296.

Berscheid, Ellen and Elaine H. Walster. 1969. *Interpersonal Attraction.* Reading, Mass.: Addison-Wesley.

Cahill, Spencer E. 1982. "Becoming boys and girls." Ph.D. dissertation, Department of Sociology, University of California, Santa Barbara.

Cahill, Spencer E. 1986a. "Childhood socialization as recruitment process: Some lessons from the study of gender development." In *Sociological Studies of Child Development,* ed. Patricia and Peter Adler, 163–186. Greenwich, Conn.: JAI Press.

Cahill, Spencer E. 1986b. "Language practices and self-definition: The case of gender identity acquisition." *The Sociological Quarterly* 27: 295–311.

Fenstermaker, Sarah, Candace West, and Don H. Zimmerman. 1990. "Gender inequality: New conceptual terrain." In *Gender, Family and Economy: The Triple Overlap,* ed. Rae Lesser Blumberg, 289–307. Beverly Hills: Sage.

Garfinkel, Harold. 1967. *Studies in Ethnomethodology.* Englewood Cliffs, N.J.: Prentice Hall.

Goffman, Erving. 1977. "The arrangement between the sexes." *Theory and Society* 4: 301–331.

Heritage, John. 1984. *Garfinkel and Ethnomethodology.* Cambridge, England; Polity Press.

Hughes, Everett C. 1958. *Men and Their Work.* Glencoe, Ill.: The Free Press.

Thorne, Barrie. 1973. "Professional education in medicine." In *Education for the Professions of Medicine, Law, Theology and Social Welfare* (a report for the Carnegie Commission on Higher Education), by Everett C. Hughes, Barrie Thorne, Agostino M. DeBaggis, Arnold Gurin and David Williams, 17–99. New York: McGraw Hill.

U.S. National Center for Health Statistics. 1987. *Detailed Diagnoses and Surgical Procedures.* Washington, D.C.: U.S. Government Printing Office.

West, Candace and Sarah Fenstermaker. Forthcoming. "Power, inequality and the accomplishment of gender: An ethnomethodological view." In *Theory on Gender/Feminism on Theory,* ed. Paula England. New York: Aldine.

West, Candace and Don H. Zimmerman. 1987. "Doing gender." *Gender & Society 1*: 125–151.

Further Questions

1. Would you ever consider undergoing cosmetic surgery? Would it make a difference to your answer if you were of the other gender or in a different line of work?

2. Does the popularity of liposuction testify to the fact that cultural standards of obesity are too stringent, especially for women? Should breast augmentation and breast reduction be as popular as they are at present?

3. What can be said about a society where most of the cosmetic surgery is performed on women? If the situation is to be rectified, should more men or fewer women elect to have cosmetic surgery?

II.6   A Hair Piece: Perspectives on the Intersection of Race and Gender

PAULETTE M. CALDWELL

Paulette M. Caldwell speaks to the issue of an employer's forbidding an employee to wear a braided hairstyle in the workplace. She begins by citing *Rogers v. American Airlines,* where the right of the employer to prohibit the braided hairstyle was upheld, and takes the reader through a journey of her own experiences with braided and unbraided hair. She argues that the issue of braids falls on the "intersection" of race and gender because it is an issue for black women, not for all women, and not for all blacks; hence it is illustrative of the interdependence of racism and sexism.

Caldwell is Professor of Law at New York University Law School.

Reading Questions

1. What message does *Rogers v. American Airlines* convey about the rights of an employer over his employees and his black women employees in particular? What does it have to say, in turn, about the status of these black women employees?

2. Does the fact that braids are an artifice of culture, rather than a natural hairstyle like an Afro, strengthen an employer's case against braids?

3. All over the world black women braid their hair and have done so for four centuries. Therefore, does it bolster an employer's case against braids that braids were made more generally popular by Bo Derek in *10*? What does the reference to Bo Derek imply about blacks' contribution to culture?

THE CASE OF *ROGERS V. AMERICAN AIRLINES*[1] upheld the right of employers to prohibit the wearing of braided hairstyles in the workplace. The plaintiff, a black woman, argued that American Airlines' policy discriminated against her specifically as a black woman. In effect, she based her claim on the interactive effects of racial and gender discrimination. The court chose, however, to base its decision principally on distinctions between biological and cultural conceptions of race. More importantly, it treated the plaintiff's claims of race and gender discrimination in the alternative and independent of each other, thus denying any interactive relationship between the two.

Although *Rogers* is the only reported decision that upholds that categorical exclusion of braided hairstyles,[2] the prohibition of such styles in the workforce is both widespread and longstanding. Protests surrounding recent cases in Washington, D.C., sparked national media attention. Nearly fifty women picketed a Hyatt hotel, and black political leaders threatened to boycott hotels that prohibit black women from wearing braids. Several employees initiated legal action by filing complaints with federal or local fair employment practices agencies; most cases were settled shortly thereafter. No court has yet issued an opinion that controverts *Rogers*.

I discovered *Rogers* while reading a newspaper article describing the actual or threatened firing of several black women in metropolitan Washington, D.C., solely for wearing braided hairstyles. The article referred to *Rogers* but actually focused on the case of Cheryl Tatum, who was fired from her job as a restaurant cashier in a Hyatt hotel under a company policy that prohibited "extreme and unusual hairstyles."

The newspaper description of the Hyatt's grooming policy conjured up an image of a ludicrous and outlandishly coiffed Cheryl Tatum, one clearly bent on exceeding the bounds of workplace taste and discipline. But the picture that accompanied the article revealed a young, attractive black woman whose hair fell neatly to her shoulder in an all-American, common, everyday pageboy style, distinguished only by the presence of tiny braids in lieu of single strands of hair.

Whether motivated by politics, ethnic pride, health, or vanity, I was outraged by the idea that an employer could regulate or force me to explain something as personal and private as the way that I groom my hair. I resented the implication that I could not be trusted to choose standards appropriate for the workplace and that my right to work could be conditioned on my disassociation with my race, gender, and culture. Mostly, I marveled with sadness that something as simple as a black woman's hair continues to threaten the social, political, and economic fabric of American life.

Why Would Anyone Want to Wear Their Hair That Way

Should I be put to the task of choosing a logical, credible, "legitimate," legally sympathetic justification out of the many reasons that may have motivated me and other black women to braid our own hair? Perhaps we do so out of concern for the health of our hair, which many of us risk losing permanently after years of chemical straighteners; or perhaps because we fear that the entry of chemical toxins into our bloodstreams through our scalps will damage our unborn or breast-feeding children. Some of us choose the positive expression of ethnic pride not only for ourselves but also for our children, many of whom learn, despite all of our teachings to the contrary, to reject association with black people and black culture in search of a keener nose or bluer eye. Many of us wear braids in the exercise of private, personal prerogatives taken for granted by women who are not black.

TO CHOOSE MYSELF: INTERLOCKING FIGURATIONS IN THE CONSTRUCTION OF RACE AND GENDER

SUNDAY. School is out, my exams are graded, and I have unbraided my hair a few days before my appointment at the beauty parlor to have it braided again. After a year in braids, my hair is healthy again; long and thick and cottony soft. I decide not to french roll it or twist it or pull it into a ponytail or bun or cover it with a scarf. Instead, I comb it out and leave it natural, in a full and big "Angela Davis" afro style. I feel full and big and regal. I walk the three blocks from my apartment to the subway. I see a white male colleague walking in the opposite direction and I wave to him from across the street. He stops, squints his eyes against the glare of the sun, and stares, trying to figure out who has greeted him. He recognizes me and starts to cross over to my side of the street. I keep walking, fearing the possibility of his curiosity and needing to be relieved of the strain of explanation.

MONDAY. My hair is still unbraided, but I blow it out with a hair dryer and pull it back into a ponytail tied at the nape of my neck before I go to the law school. I enter the building and run into four white female colleagues on their way out to a white female lunch. Before I can say hello, one of them blurts out, "It IS weird!" Another drowns out the first: "You look so young, like a teenager!" The third invites me to join them for lunch while the fourth stands silently, observing my hair. I mumble some excuse about lunch and interject, almost apologetically, that I plan to get my hair braided again the next day. When I arrive at my office suite and run into the white male I had greeted on Sunday, I realize immediately that he has told the bunch on the way to lunch about our encounter the day before. He mutters something about how different I look today, then asks me whether the day before I had been on my way to a ceremony. He and the others are generally nice colleagues, so I half-smile, but say nothing in response. I feel a lot less full and big and regal.

TUESDAY. I walk to the garage under my apartment building, again wearing a big, full "Angela Davis" afro. Another white male colleague passes me by, not recognizing me. I greet him and he smiles broadly, saying that he has never seen me look more beautiful. I smile back, continue the chit chat for a moment more, and try not to think about whether he is being disingenuous. I slowly get into my car, buckle up, relax, and turn on the radio. It will take me about forty-five minutes to drive up-town to the beauty parlor, park my car, and get something to eat before beginning the long hours of sitting and braiding. I feel good, knowing that the braider will be ecstatic when she sees the results of her healing handiwork. I keep my movements small, easy, and slow, relishing in a rare, short morning of being free.

My initial outrage notwithstanding, *Rogers* is an unremarkable decision. Courts generally protect employer-mandated hair and dress codes, often according the greatest deference to ones that classify individuals on the basis of socially conditioned rather than biological differences. All in all, such cases are generally considered only marginally significant in the battle to secure equal employment rights.

But *Rogers* is regrettably unremarkable in an important respect. It rests on suppositions that are deeply imbedded in American culture—assumptions so entrenched and so necessary to the maintenance of interlocking, interdependent structures of domination that their mythological bases and political functions have become invisible, especially to those to whom their existence is most detrimental. *Rogers* proceeds from the premise that, although racism and sexism share much in common, they are nonetheless fundamentally unrelated phenomena—a proposition proved false by history and contemporary reality. Racism and sexism are interlocking, mutually reinforcing components of a system of dominance rooted in patriarchy. No significant and lasting progress in combating either can be made until this interdependence is acknowledged, and until the perspectives gained from considering their interaction are reflected in legal theory and public policy.

Cases arising under employment discrimination statutes illustrate both the operation in law and the effect on the development of legal theory of the assumptions of race-sex correspondence and difference. These cases also demonstrate the absence of any consideration of either race-sex interaction or the stereotyping of black womanhood. Focusing on cases that involve black female plaintiffs, at least three categories emerge.

In one category, courts have considered whether black women may represent themselves or other race or gender discriminatees. Some cases deny black women the right to claim discrimination as a subgroup distinct from black men and white women.[6] Others deny black women the right to represent a class that includes white women in a suit based on sex discrimination, on the ground that race distinguishes them.[7] Still other cases prohibit black women from representing a class in a race discrimination suit that includes black men, on the ground of gender differences.[8] These cases demonstrate the failure of courts to account for race-sex intersection and are premised on the assumptions that discrimination is based on either race or gender, but never both.

A second category of case concerns the interaction of race and gender in determining the limits of an employer's ability to condition work on reproductive and marital choices associated with black women.[9] Several courts have upheld the firing of black women for becoming pregnant while unmarried if their work involves association with children—especially black teenage girls. These decisions rest on entrenched fears of and distorted images about black female sexuality, stigmatize single black mothers (and by extension their children), and reinforce "culture of poverty" notions that blame poverty on poor people themselves. They also reinforce the notion that the problems of black families are attributable to the deviant and dominant roles of black women and the idea that racial progress depends on black female subordination.

A third category concerns black women's physical images. These cases involve a variety of mechanisms to exclude black women from jobs that involve contact with the public—a tendency particularly evident in traditionally female jobs in which employers place a premium on female attractiveness—including a subtle, and often not so subtle, emphasis on female sexuality. The latter two categories sometimes involve in addition to the intersection of race and gender, questions that concern the interaction of race, gender, and culture.

The failure to consider the implications of race-sex interaction is only partially explained, if at all, by the historical or contemporary development of separate political movements against racism and sexism. Rather, this failure arises from the inability of political activists, policymakers, and legal theorists to grapple with the existence and political functions of the complex of myths, negative images, and stereotypes regarding black womanhood. These stereotypes, and the culture of prejudice that sustains them, exist to define the social position of black women as subordinate on the basis of gender to all men, regardless of color, and on the basis of race to all other women. These negative images also are indispensable to the maintenance of an interlocking system of oppression based on race and gender that operates to the detriment of all women and all blacks. Stereotypical notions about white women and black men are not only developed by comparing them to white men but also by setting them apart from black women.

The Rogers *Opinion*

The *Rogers* decision is a classic example of a case concerning the physical image of black women. Renee Rogers, whose work for American Airlines involved extensive passenger contact, charged that American's prohibition of braided hairstyles in certain job classifications discriminated against her as a woman in general, and as a black woman in particular.[10] The court did not attempt to limit the plaintiff's case by forcing her to proceed on either race or gender grounds, nor did it create a false hierarchy between the two bases by treating one as grounded in statutory law and the other as a "plus" factor that would explain the application of law to a subgroup not technically recognized as a protected group by law. The court also appeared to recognize that the plaintiff's claim was not based on the cumulative effects of race and gender.

However, the court treated the race and sex claims in the alternative only. This approach reflects the assumption that racism and sexism always operate independently even when the claimant is a member of both a subordinated race and a subordinated gender group. The court refused to acknowledge that American's policy need not affect all women or all blacks in order to affect black women discriminatorily. By treating race and sex as alternative bases on which a claim might rest, the court concluded that the plaintiff failed to state a claim of discrimination on either ground. The court's treatment of the issues made this result inevitable—as did its exclusive reliance on the factors that it insisted were dispositive of cases involving employee grooming or other image preferences.

The distinct history of black women dictates that the analysis of discrimination be appropriately tailored in interactive claims to provide black women with the same protection available to other individuals and groups protected by antidiscrimination law. The *Rogers* court's approach permitted it to avoid the essence of overlapping discrimination against black women and kept it from applying the basic elements of an-

tidiscrimination analysis: a focus on group history; identification of recurring patterns of oppression that serve over time to define the social and economic position of the group; analysis of the current position of the group in relation to other groups in society; and analysis of the employment practice in question to determine whether, and if so how, it perpetuates individual and group subordination.

The court gave three principal reasons for dismissing the plaintiff's claim. First, in considering the sex discrimination aspects of the claim, the court disagreed with the plaintiff's argument that, in effect, the application of the company's grooming policy to exclude the category of braided hairstyles from the workplace reached only women. Rather, the court stressed that American's policy was even-handed and applied to men and women alike.[11] Second, the court emphasized that American's grooming policy did not regulate or classify employees on the basis of an immutable gender characteristic.[12] Finally, American's policy did not bear on the exercise of a fundamental right.[13] The plaintiff's racial discrimination claim was analyzed separately but dismissed on the same grounds; neutral application of American's anti-braid policy to all races and absence of any impact of the policy on an immutable racial characteristic or of any effect on the exercise of a fundamental right.

The court's treatment of culture and cultural associations in the racial context bears close examination. It carefully distinguished between the phenotypic and cultural aspects of race. First, it rejected the plaintiff's analogy between all-braided and Afro, or "natural," hairstyles. Stopping short of concluding that Afro hairstyles might be protected under all circumstances, the court held that "an all-braided hairstyle is a different matter. It is not the product of natural hair growth but of artifice."[14] Second, in response to the plaintiff's argument that, like Afro hairstyles, the wearing of braids reflected her choice for ethnic and cultural identification, the court again distinguished between the immutable aspects of race and characteristics that are "socioculturally associated with a particular race or nationality"[15] However, given the variability of so-called immutable racial characteristics such as skin color and hair texture, it is difficult to understand racism as other than a complex of historical, sociocultural associations with race.

The court conceived of race and the legal protection against racism almost exclusively in biological terms. Natural hairstyles—or at least some of them, such as Afros—are permitted because hair texture is immutable, a matter over which individuals have no choice. Braids, however, are the products of artifice—a cultural practice—and are therefore mutable, i.e., the result of choice. Because the plaintiff could have altered the all-braided hairstyle in the exercise of her own volition, American was legally authorized to force that choice upon her.

In support of this view that the plaintiff had failed to establish a factual basis for her claim that American's policy had a disparate impact on black women, thus destroying any basis for the purported neutral application of the policy, the court pointed to American's assertion that the plaintiff had adopted the prohibited hairstyle only shortly after it had been "popularized" by Bo Derek, a white actress, in the film *10*.[16] Notwithstanding the factual inaccuracy of American's claim, and notwithstanding the implication that there is no relationship between braided hair and the culture of black women, the court assumed that black and white women are equally motivated (i.e., by the movies) to adopt braided hairstyles.

Wherever they exist in the world, black women braid their hair. They have done so in the United States for more than four centuries. African in origin, the practice of braiding is as American—black American—as sweet potato pie. A braided hairstyle was first worn in a nationally televised media event in the United States—and in that sense "popularized"—by a black actress, Cicely Tyson, nearly a decade before the movie *10*.[17] More importantly, Cicely Tyson's choice to popularize (i.e., to "go public" with) braids, like her choice of acting roles, was a political act made on her own behalf and on behalf of all black women.[18]

The very use of the term "popularized" to describe Bo Derek's wearing of braids—in the sense of rendering suitable to the majority—specifically subordinates and makes invisible all of the black women who for centuries have worn braids in places where they and their hair were not overt threats to the American aesthetic. The great majority of such women worked exclusively in jobs where their racial subordination was clear. They were never permitted in any affirmative sense of the word any choice so closely related to personal dignity as the choice—or a range of choices—regarding the grooming of their hair. By virtue of their subordination—their clearly defined place in the society—their choices were simply ignored.

The court's reference to Bo Derek presents us with two conflicting images, both of which subordinate black women and black culture. On the one hand, braids are separated from black culture and, by implication, are said to arise from whites. Not only do blacks contribute nothing to the nation's or the world's culture, they copy the fads of whites. On the other hand, whites make fads of black culture, which, by virtue of their popularization, become—like all "pop"—disposable, vulgar, and without lasting value. Braided hairstyles are thus trivialized and protests over them made ludicrous.

To narrow the concept of race further—and, therefore racism and the scope of legal protection against it—the *Rogers* court likened the plaintiff's claim to ethnic identity in the wearing of braids to identity claims based on the use of languages other than English. The court sought refuge in *Garcia v. Gloor*, a decision that upheld the general right of employers to prohibit the speaking of any language other than English in the workplace without requiring employers to articulate a business justification for the prohibition.[19] By excising the cultural component of racial or ethnic identity, the court reinforces the view of a homogeneous, unicultural society, and pits blacks and other groups against each other in a battle over minimal deviations from cultural norms. Black women cannot wear their hair in braids because Hispanics cannot speak Spanish at work. The court cedes to private employers the power of family patriarchs to enforce a numbing sameness, based exclusively on the employers' whim, without the obligation to provide a connection to work performance or business need, and thus deprives employees of the right to be judged on ability rather than on image or sound.

HEALING THE SHAME

Eliminating the behavioral consequences of certain stereotypes is a core function of antidiscrimination law. This function can never be adequately performed as long as courts and legal theorists create narrow, inflexible definitions of harm and categories of protection that fail to reflect the actual experience of discrimination. Considering the interactive relationship between racism and sexism from the experiential standpoint and knowledge base of black women can lead to the development of legal theories grounded in reality, and to the consideration by all women of the extent to which racism limits their choices as women and by black and other men of color of the extent to which sexism defines their experiences as men of subordinated races.

Creating a society that can be judged favorably by the way it treats the women of its darkest race need not be the work of black women alone, nor will black women be the exclusive or primary beneficiaries of such a society. Such work can be engaged in by all who are willing to take seriously the everyday acts engaged in by black women and others to resist racism and sexism and to use these acts as the basis to develop legal theories designed to end race and gender subordination.

Resistance can take the form of momentous acts of organized, planned, and disciplined protests, or it may consist of small, everyday actions of seeming insignificance that can nevertheless validate the actor's sense of dignity and worth—such as refusing on the basis of inferiority to give up a seat on a bus or covering one's self in shame it can arise out of the smallest conviction, such as knowing that an old woman can transmit an entire culture simply by touching a child. Sometimes it can come from nothing more than a refusal to leave a grandmother behind.

NOTES

1. 527 F. Suppl. 229 (S.D.N.Y. 1981).

2. *Rogers* relied on *Carswell v. Peachford Hosp.*, 27 Fair Empl. Prac. Cas. (BNA) 698 (N.D. Ga. 1981) (1981 WL 224). In *Carswell,* the employer discharged the plaintiff for wearing beads woven into a braided hairstyle. The prohibition applied to jewelry and other items and was justified by safety precautions for employees working in a hospital for psychiatric and substance-abusing patients. Significantly, the court noted that the hospital did not categorically prohibit the wearing of either braided or Afro hairstyles.

6. See, e.g., *DeGraffenreid v. General Motors Assembly Div.,* 413 F. Suppl. 142, 145 (E.D. Mo. 1976) (Title VII did not create a new sub-category of "black women" with standing independent of black males).

7. See, e.g., *Moore v. Hughes Helicopter, Inc.,* 708 F.2d 475, 480 (9th Cir. 1983) (certified class includes only black females, as plaintiff black female inadequately represents white females' interests).

8. See, e.g., *Payne v. Travenol.* 673 F.2d 798, 810–12 (5th Cir. 1982) (interests of black female plaintiffs substantially conflict with interests of black males, since females sought to prove that males were promoted at females' expense notwithstanding the court's finding of extensive racial discrimination).

9. See *Chambers v. Girls Club of Omaha,* 834 F.2d 697 (8th Circ. 1987).

10. *Rogers v. American Airlines, Inc.,* 527 F. Supp. 229, 231 (S.D.N.Y. 1981). Rogers sued under the thirteenth amendment, 42 U.S.C. § 1981 (1988), and Title VII of the Civil Rights Act of 1964, 42 U.S.C. § 2000e (1988). The court disposed of the thirteenth amendment claim on the ground that the amendment prohibits practices that constitute badges and incidents of slavery. Unless the plaintiff could show that she did not have the option to leave her job, her claim could not be maintained. *Rogers,* 527

F. Supp. at 231. The court also noted that the Title VII and section 1981 claims were indistinguishable in the circumstances of the case and were, therefore, treated together. Id.

11. Id. at 231.
12. Id.
13. Id.
14. Id. at 232.
15. Id.
16. Id. at 232.

17. Tyson is most noted for her roles in the film *Sounder* (20th Century Fox 1972) and in the television special *The Autobiography of Miss Jane Pitman* (CBS Televison Broadcast, Jan. 1974).

18. Her work is political in the sense that she selects roles that celebrate the strength and dignity of black women and avoids roles that do not.

19. *Garcia v. Gloor,* 618 F.2d 264, 267–69 (5th Cir. 1980); cf. *Gutierrez v. Municipal Court,* 838 F.2d 1031, 1040–41 (9th Cir.), vacated, 409 U.S. 1016 (1988).

Further Questions

1. Might the choice of braids for black women be an intelligent one when braids are compared with chemical straighteners that are quite possibly dangerous? Are black women acting legitimately when they wear braids as a source of ethnic pride?

2. Should black women have the right to claim discrimination as a group distinct from black men and white women? Should black women also be able to claim discrimination jointly with white women and with black men? What are examples other than braids where black women ought to be able to claim discrimination as a group?

3. Ought an employer have rights to prohibit anything he doesn't like in his workplace without relating it to work performance or business need? If so, explain the impact on his employees. If not, what sort of lines should be drawn that he has no right to step over?

Further Readings for Part II:
Messages on the Surface: Looks and Language

1. LOOKS

Diane Bartnel. *Putting on Appearances: Gender and Advertising* (Philadelphia: Temple University Press, 1988). Women are persuaded by advertising to accept their low self image and the advertisers' solutions.

Susan Bordo. *Unbearable Weight: Feminism, Western Culture, and the Body* (Berkeley: University of California Press, 1993). Cultural meanings of the female body with emphasis on the cult of slenderness.

Susan Brownmiller. *Femininity* (New York: Ballantine, 1984). Detailed analysis of oppressive elements in feminine appearances and life-styles.

Vern L. Bullough and Bonnie Bullough. *Cross Dressing, Sex, and Gender* (Philadelphia: University of Pennsylvania Press, 1993). Historical and contemporary overview of cross dressing.

Kathy Davis. *Reshaping the Female Body: The Dilemma of Cosmetic Surgery* (New York: Routledge, 1995).

Shulamith Firestone. *The Dialectic of Sex: A Case for Feminist Revolution* (New York: Morrow, 1970), Chapter 7. Brief, pointed account of women's confusing their appearance with their individuality.

Barry Glassner. *Bodies. Why We Look the Way We Do* (New York: Putnam, 1988). Contains an especially interesting account of the importance of muscle to male appearance.

Germaine Greer. *The Female Eunuch* (New York: McGraw Hill, 1971), especially Part I, "Body." Depiction of women as tailored to male specifications, *inter alia,* in appearance.

Sara Halprin. *"Looking at My Ugly Face": Myths and Musings on Beauty and other Perilous Obsessions with Women's Appearance* (New York: Penguin, 1995). Myth-strewn discussions of beauty and gender.

Elizabeth Haiken. *Venus Envy: A History of Cosmetic Surgery* (Baltimore, MD: Johns Hopkins University Press, 1997).

Lina A. Jackson. *Physical Appearance and Gender: Sociological and Sociocultural Perspectives* (Albany: State University of New York Press, 1992). How gender similarities and differences affect the impact our physical appearance has on other people.

Duncan Kennedy. *Sexy Dressing, Etc.: Essays on the Power and Politics of Cultural Identity* (Cambridge, MA: Harvard University Press, 1993). Argues that women's sexy dressing may mean an invitation to abuse but may also mean the eroticization of female autonomy.

Richard Majors and Janet Mancino Billson. *Cool Pose: Dilemmas of Black Manhood in America* (New York: Touchstone, 1992). Appearance, image, and style of cool as a coping strategy for problems of black men.

Susan Orbach. *Fat is a Feminist Issue* (New York: Berkeley, 1978). Develops the thesis that fat is a response to social pressures; to lose weight, you must understand these pressures and learn to like yourself.

Roberta Pollack Seid. *Never Too Thin: Why Women Are at War with Their Bodies* (New York: Prentice Hall, 1989). Thorough discussion of myth that thinner is healthier, sexier, happier, and more beautiful.

Matra Robertson. *Starving in the Silences: An Exploration of Anorexia Nervosa* (New York: New York University Press, 1992). The meaning of anorexia in feminism and medicine and the issues it raises.

Becky W. Thompson. *A Hunger So Wide and So Deep: A Multiracial View of Women's Eating Problems* (Minneapolis: University of Minnesota Press, 1996). An argument that eating problems are ways of coping with stresses of classism, racism, sexism, homophobia, and emotional, physical, and sexual abuse.

Andrew Wernick. "From Voyeur to Narcissist: Imaging Men in Contemporary Advertising" in *Beyond Patriarchy, Essays by Men on Pleasure, Power and Change,* Michael Kaufmann, ed. (New York: Oxford University Press, 1987). Argument that men as well as women have their appearances shaped by advertising.

Naomi Wolf. *The Beauty Myth* (New York: Vintage, Random House, 1991). Women are straitjacketed by beauty requirements. Germaine Greer says it's "The most important feminist publication since [Greer's own] *The Female Eunuch.*"

LANGUAGE*

Maryann Neely Ayim, *The Moral Parameters of Good Talk: A Feminist Analysis* (Waterloo, ON: Wilfrid Laurier University Press, 1997). How racist and sexist speech fails the moral test of freedom of expression for all.

Dennis Baron. *Grammar and Gender* (New Haven, CT: Yale University Press, 1986). Comprehensive but rewarding book. Chapter on pronouns is especially interesting.

Francis J. Beckwith and Michael E. Bauman, eds. *Are You Politically Correct? Debating America's Cultural Standards* (Buffalo, NY: Prometheus, 1993). Lively discussion of a timely topic.

Deborah Cameron, ed. *The Feminist Critique of Language* (New York: Routledge, 1990). Anthology of feminist writings on language, Virginia Woolf to the present.

Thanks to Maryann Ayim and Diane Goossens for suggestions for these readings.

Louise Gouëffic. *Breaking the Patriarchal Code: The Linguistic Basis of Sexual Bias* (Manchester, CT: Knowledge, Ideas, and Trends, 1996). Elaborate examination of forms of gender biased language together with suggestions for change.

Christina Hendricks and Kelly Oliver, eds. *Language and Liberation: Feminism, Philosophy, and Language* (Albany: State University of New York Press, 1999). Feminist interventions into the use of language.

Charles R. Lawrence, Mari J. Matsuda, Richard Delgado, and Kimberlè Williams Crenshaw. *Words That Wound: Critical Race Theory Assaultive Speech and the First Amendment* (Boulder, CO: Westview, 1993). Four thoughtful authors address important racial issues in language.

Julia Penelope. *Speaking Freely. Unlearning the Lies of the Fathers' Tongues* (New York: Pergamon, 1990). Lively challenges to patriarchal forms of speech.

Stephen Richer and Lorna Weir, eds. *Beyond Political Correctness: Toward the Inclusive University* (Toronto, ON: University of Toronto Press, 1995). The debate concerning political correctness and university ideals.

Philip M. Smith. *Language, the Sexes and Society* (New York: Basil Blackwell, 1985). Discussion of language as used to subordinate or devalue women.

Mary M. Talbot. *Language and Gender: An Introduction* (Malden, MA: Blackwell, 1998). Nice, well-written accessible book in the area of language and gender.

Dale Spender. *Man Made Language* (London: Routledge & Kegan Paul, 1980). Radical and angry statement of how language, and research on language, oppresses women.

Mary Vetterling-Braggin, ed. *Sexist Language: A Modern Philosophical Analysis.* (Littlefield, Adams, 1981). Philosophers address themselves to sexist problems in language.

Everyone should have a guide for using language in a non-sexist manner. Two recommendations are:

Rosalie Maggio. *The Non-Sexist Word Finder: A Dictionary of Gender-Free Usage* (Boston: Beacon, 1988).

Casey Miller and Kate Swift. *The Handbook of Non-Sexist Writing* (New York: Harper & Row, 1980).

Suggested Moral of Part II

We respond to the surface aspects of social life because this is what we first catch a glimpse of: what people look like and what they say. We can expect power structures to be in evidence in some way on the surface, even though we may need thought and some ideas of what is going on beneath the surface to decide the messages. Patriarchy evidences itself in words that demean or neglect women. Also, the rules about appearance are much more stringent for women than for men because it is men, past and present, who make and maintain the rules for both genders.

Part III

The Workplace

Introduction

THE GENDER STRUCTURE of the workplace deserves close examination because, in today's industrialized world, opportunities for meaningful activity are increasingly becoming organized around job positions in the workplace. In addition, a person's place in the work force is often a major source of his worth, as measured by the income, prestige, and power he gains through his job performance.

Lips discusses the social handicaps from which women often suffer in the workplace; Sokoloff explains how women and blacks gain or fail to gain certain positions in the workforce; Minas argues for target hiring as a device for overcoming discrimination; Comas-Díaz and Green explain tokenism and stereotyping; Paul contests the idea of pay equity; Gray describes his experiences of men learning to share the shop floor with women. Williams discusses the glass escalator men often occupy in predominantly female professions; Chang deplores the plight of illegal immigrant women who must work as nannies or other household help under a private arrangement with their employer.

III.1   Women and Power in the Workplace

HILARY M. LIPS

Hilary M. Lips maintains that women's personal features and circumstances have been overplayed in explaining the continuation of male dominance in the workplace. The reality is that men use a variety of techniques, including considerable mythology about male and female psychology, to maintain their relative position.

Lips has taught psychology of sex and gender at the University of Winnipeg (Winnipeg, Manitoba) and has contributed numerous chapters, articles, and books in her field.

Reading Questions

1. As a woman, do you think that the likeliest way to be successful in your chosen career is to follow the model of the successful man?
2. Do you think the world is a reasonably fair and just place and that there are explanations adequate to justify why people hold the positions they do in the work force?
3. Are women in a double bind in trying to exercise power, because power is held to be unfeminine?

DURING MOST OF OUR RECENT HISTORY, the major thrust of women's struggle for power has been toward increased access to the major institutions in society. The struggle simply not to be excluded—from voting rights, jobs, organisations, full legal status as persons—has taken up much of women's collective energy for decades. A strong emphasis in the struggle has been on access to and equality in the world of paid employment, for women have intuited rightly that the income, status, knowledge, and social networks that come with employment are crucial resources on which power, both individual and collective, can be based.

Power, it should be noted at the outset, is the capacity to have an impact on one's environ-ment, to be able to make a difference through one's actions. It is the opposite of helplessness. There is no use in debating whether or not women should really want power, or whether it is appropriately feminist to strive for power. Such debates are based on a long outdated, narrow notion of power as a static quality possessed only by tyrants. In talking about women increasing their power, I am referring to an increase in effectiveness of influence, in strength.

More power for women means two things: increasing women's access to resources and to the positions from which these resources are controlled; and increasing women's impact on the formation of policy about how our institutions function. Because women have a long history of

Abridged from "Women and Power in the Workplace" in Women and Men: Interdisciplinary Readings in Gender. Greta Hoffman Neminoff, Ed. (Richmond Hill, Ontario: Fitzhenry and Whiteside Ltd., 1987) pp. 403–415. Reprinted by permission of the author and publisher.

exclusion, the initial focus in the struggle to increase women's power has been to gain access for women to a variety of institutions.

The universities are a good case in point. For years, women were excluded from higher education on the grounds that we were unsuited for it and might even be damaged by it. Some "experts" even went so far as to argue that too much use of a woman's brain would damage her reproductive organs and thus endanger her vital childbearing function (see Shields, 1975). Universities in many countries accept female students as a matter of course now. In Canada, we have come a long way from the time when the principal of a Laval University-affiliated college for women had to placate critics of her institution by interspersing piano recitals and afternoon teas with normal academic pursuits. Such activities were supposedly necessary to keep her delicate female students from breaking under the strain of uninterrupted intellectual work (Danylewycz, 1981). However, arguments about damaging the reproductive system are still being used in some quarters to exclude women from various arenas of professional and amateur sports. . . .

. . . [T]he sense of power that comes with women's perception of an increased range of career choices may be short-lived. Statistics on women's employment indicate that they may often get in the door, but no further. Females in almost every professional field, for example, are underemployed and underpaid relative to their male counterparts (Abella, 1984) and women in trade occupations still have a great deal of difficulty finding employment (Braid, 1982). Moreover, the research bleakly suggests that, as women grow more numerous in a particular profession or occupation, its status declines (Touhey, 1974).

Thus, although women's problems with access to the workplace are far from over, there is an increasing recognition that simply being allowed in—to a profession, a business organisation, a trade union—is only half the battle. How can women avoid being marginal members of the workplace community—tokens whose presence supposedly illustrates that "women can make it," but who are not at the centre of decision making and who are powerless to rise to the top of, or change the shape of, the institutions in which they work?

Much advice has been aimed at women in an effort to answer this question. Most of it boils down to a prescription that women carefully observe and follow the models provided by successful men. Successful businesswomen profiled in the media are (like their male counterparts) often heard to comment that, in the service of success, they have given up their social life, hobbies, and recreation, and find it difficult to make time for family and friendship.

Such an ideal, based on the model of a small number of high-achieving, powerful, visible men in high-status jobs, creates discomfort among many women. For some, the discomfort may stem from a fear of being labelled tough, competitive or ambitious—qualities that are incongruent with our culture's definition of femininity. For others, the idea of subordinating all other priorities to one's paid work seems unrealistic and unpleasant. The first objection is easily dealt with, at least in theory. The attention paid to the concept of androgyny in recent years has, if nothing else, shown that the qualities associated with strength are not necessarily antithetical to the traditional "feminine" virtues of nurturence, sensitivity, and care for others (Colwill and Lips, 1978). It is possible to be tough without losing sight of what is fair, to be ambitious without trampling on everyone else on one's way to the top—and if women are going to make an impact in the workplace or anywhere else they are simply going to have to figure out how to blend these qualities.

The second objection, however, is one to be taken more seriously. How realistic, how desirable is it for women to adopt wholesale the myth that gaining success and power requires the subordination of all other activities, values, and interests to one's career? This model, which is held out to men as an ideal, is unworkable and destructive even for most of *them,* even though they have been socialized toward it and are provided by society with many more supports for this life style than are women (Harrison, 1978).

In order to devote all of her energy to a career, a woman needs someone taking care of the other aspects of her life: feeding her, cleaning up after her, making sure she has clean clothes, making dental appointments for her, keeping her social life organised, looking after her children, and so on. She needs, in essence, a wife. Employed women do not have wives, and it is simply impractical to try to follow the male model for career success without one. Now that fewer career men have wives who fill the traditional role, perhaps the male career model itself will begin to change. At any rate, business and professional women will have to develop their own model for career success.

The male model, presented in such glowing terms, is largely a myth. It is an ideal that is used to keep men in line, and there is no reason why women should fall in line behind them. While popular writers are exhorting women to map out career strategy years in advance the way men supposedly do, research suggests that, despite the ideal, most men do not plan their careers any more carefully than women do (Harlan and Weiss, 1980). While the advice-mongers are saying knowingly that women have not got what it takes to wheel and deal in the business world because they have never learned not to take conflict personally, many business and professional women have found to their chagrin that their male counterparts grow silent, withdraw, or become bitter and vindictive in their relationships to colleagues after being opposed on some policy or economic issue. While popular writers are fond of saying that women lack the training necessary to be good "team players" because they never passed through the proving ground of football, basketball, and hockey, many a male ex-athlete will admit that his main legacy from high school football was a recurring knee injury and a sense of failure.

The writers who say these things have taken our society's definition of the male role and life pattern and elevated it unquestioningly to an ideal. If the shoe were on the other foot, if women were in the majority in business and the professions, these same writers would be telling aspiring career men that they were at a disadvantage in knowing how to be part of a co-operative business partnership because they had never gone through the "proving ground" of rearing children. Instead of advising women to bone up on football and hockey so that they would not feel left out of casual conversations with the men in the office, the experts (presuming traditional gender roles in this mythical situation) would be advising men to read romance novels, keep up with the latest recipes, talk about their children, and follow the careers of the great women runners and tennis players. Since men hold the majority of powerful business and professional positions, it is assumed that there must be something right about men's upbringing and life style—something that leads them into powerful positions—and if women would only emulate that pattern they too could make it to "the top" in large numbers. Not only does this analysis overlook the fact that our society is arranged in a way that makes it horribly impractical for the majority of women to follow the male model (i.e., not only do most women *not* have partners who fulfill the role of the traditional wife, but also they *do* have children for whom they usually have primary responsibility), but also the whole approach is rooted in our all-too-human need to rationalise the status quo.

Psychologists have been finding for years that people in general like to believe that the world is a reasonably fair and just place, that there is an order to things, and that people basically get what they deserve (e.g., Lerner, 1974). Thus, people are very good at thinking up reasons why things are the way they are—at justifying and rationalising our social arrangements rather than questioning them. It is easier, for example, to think of women as "unassertive" or poorly trained for leadership in order to explain how few women reach visible leadership positions than to think that there may be something askew with a system or an organization in which this is the case. Since men are on top and women are on the bottom, such thinking goes, what women are doing must be wrong . . . and men are the ones doing it right. Teach the women how to act like men, and their problems will be solved.

Perhaps the clearest way to see how this type of rationalisation works is to imagine the changes in explanation for the status quo that would be required if the positions of the two groups were reversed. Gloria Steinem provides an amusing example of this process in her article. "If Men Could Menstruate" (Steinem, 1983). She fantasises that if men and not women had menstrual cycles, menstruation would be regarded as a sign of superiority. The fact that men were "in tune" with nature and the cycles of the moon would be thought to give them an advantage in making important decisions, and women's non-cyclic nature would be used as a reason for excluding them from high positions. In fact, women's menstrual cycle has been cited repeatedly (on very flimsy evidence) as a handicap that makes them unfit for certain possible positions. Here too, though, the only logic in the argument is that relating it to the status quo. Nowhere is it argued that, since women supposedly become so unreliable and irrational at certain times of the month, they should be relieved of the delicate job of caring for small, helpless children during such times. Similar logic asserts that women's allegedly superior manual dexterity makes them uniquely fit to be typists, while ignoring the possibility that it might make them uniquely fit to be surgeons or television repairpersons.

It is reasonable to be suspicious of any approach that purports to explain women's failure to advance, or their lack of impact, solely on the basis of flaws in their own behaviour. Of course there are things most women can learn to make themselves more effective, but that is also true for most men. What *may* be more true for women than for men in many organisations, however, is that support and security from the organisation is lacking. Women, while inside an organisation, often find that they are still outsiders. As Rosa-beth Kanter's (1977) work shows, the issue is not whether or not women know how to play on teams, but whether a token woman can play on a team that does not want her on it.

It is becoming clear, then, that having broken down many initial access barriers, women taking up their newly-won positions in mainstream organizations often find that they are still far from the centre of power. Having dealt with many of the formal barriers to career participation, they find themselves blocked by less tangible but equally frustrating obstacles. They feel invisible. They feel (and they are often right) that no one takes them seriously. Such feelings are not limited to women in business, engineering, or other male-dominated professions, or to women in "white-collar" jobs. Women in teaching, nursing, secretarial work, carpentry and other trades, and factory work all report similar frustrations in their struggles to make an impact in their work environment. Understanding of the dilemmas faced by women trying to be effective in the workplace can be enhanced by examining their problems within the framework provided by psychological research on power.

Psychologists argue that power—the ability to make an impact or to get others to do what one wants them to do—is based on a person's access to certain resources that can be used to "back up" her influence attempts (French and Raven, 1959). In other words, in order for a person (or a group) to exert power, there have to be reasons—fear, respect, admiration, greed, loyalty—for others in the environment to co-operate or comply. The resources that provide the reasons for compliance include control over rewards (for example, the capacity to reward a person who complies with one's wishes by promoting her, giving her a raise, giving her the day off, giving her a gift) and control over punishments (such as the capacity to discipline someone, fire her, take something away from her). The resources on which power is based also include legitimacy, expertise, personal attractiveness or likableness, and the sheer amount of knowledge or information one can muster to support one's arguments. The amount of power or influence a person can wield depends at least partly on how much access she has, and is seen to have, to these kinds of resources.

A person's ability to influence others depends not only on her actual access to resources, but also on the amount of control over these resources that others see her as having. If a woman is an expert in a given field, for instance, that expertise will not provide her with a source of power with respect to others who do not recognise her as an expert. While women are often blocked from control over certain kinds of resources in their work settings, it is just as often true that the resources they do have go unrecognised. In the case of expertise, the stereotype of feminine incompetence often works against the perception of women as experts, particularly in traditionally male fields. In the case of legitimacy, not only do women rarely find themselves in positions of authority, but, even when they do, their automatic low status as women acts to contradict and undermine their authority in the eyes of others.

A consequence of these difficulties is that women sometimes find themselves relying more than they should or would like to on the resources of personal attractiveness or likableness to exert influence in the workplace. They smile a lot, try to win the friendship and good will of the people they must influence, and may sometimes use their sexuality in overt or covert ways as a basis of power. This is a strategy that often does work, but it tends to be a trap if relied on exclusively. A person using it does not enhance anyone's view of her competence and must be rather too careful about staying on everyone's good side. . . .

Not the least of the problems a person can face in trying to wield power is a negative bias in her own view of the resources she controls. If a person who is an expert lacks confidence in her own expertise, she will have difficulty exerting influence based on that expertise. Since women are continually being given the message that they are not expected to be experts, that people are pleasantly surprised when they know anything about important issues, lack of confidence is a dangerously seductive trap for them. Men too feel inadequate when they compare themselves to their colleagues. Our culture's specialised, competitive workplaces tend to foster this feeling. Men, however, have developed more strategies than women have for hiding this feeling of inadequacy. What must be kept in mind is that the exercise of power depends not only on what kinds of resources one controls, but also on the way one thinks one's own resources compare to everyone else's. In other words, how powerful a person or group feels can make a difference in how powerful they are.

A person's exercise of power is also affected by what she and others see as appropriate behaviour. Since "feminine" behaviour is, almost by definition, powerless behaviour, the woman trying to act in a powerful way is placed in a double bind. There may be times when she has the resources and knows she has the resources to wield power, but holds back out of a fear of being labelled pushy, aggressive, tough, or just plain not nice.

The three factors just described (what resources a person controls, how powerful she feels, and what she and others see as appropriate behaviour) affect not only the amount of impact she can have in a particular situation, but also the style or strategy of influence she employs. Her style of influence may be more or less direct, for example (Johnson, 1976). Someone who uses a direct style of influence asks for or demands openly what she wants, making it clear that she is the one who wants it. Someone using a very indirect style of influence, on the other hand, tries to get what she wants to happen without acknowledging that she is the source of the influence. A common example of the latter is the strategy of talking to someone behind the scenes rather than personally bringing up an issue at a meeting.

Both styles carry some risks, especially at the extremes. The person using the direct approach to influence may be viewed as abrasive, may be disliked, and may often find herself involved in conflict. The payoff is that, when she gets something positive to happen, she gets credit for it—credit that adds to her competence and expertise in the eyes of others and thus adds to the store of resources she can draw on in future situations.

The person using the indirect approach to influence, on the other hand, avoids the risk of being openly associated with an idea that turns out to be unpopular or unworkable, while keeping the opportunity for private satisfaction when she is the source of an initiative that works. However, sometimes this satisfaction can be a little too private. No matter how many good ideas she generates, a person can never build up her credibility if she is never seen as the originator of these ideas, if her influence is always indirect.

Clearly, to increase one's competence in the eyes of others, it is necessary to use influence directly and openly, at least some of the time. However, this is not to say that women should always avoid using indirect strategies. There are times when it is simply more important to get something done than to make an issue of it or get credit for it. In some organisations, for instance, people have managed to advance the cause of women considerably without ever being so obvious about it that they generated a fight.

Since it seems to be important to use influence directly and openly at least some of the time, it would seem to be a simple matter for women to get the message and start using more direct power styles in order to enhance their personal effectiveness and increase their acceptance within institutions. This, in essence, is what assertiveness training is supposed to be about: teaching people, especially women, to exert influence directly. Men rarely sign up for assertiveness training. Does this mean men have no trouble exerting influence openly? Perhaps, but it could also mean that men are more reluctant than women to accept for themselves the label of "unassertive." Also, many of the programmes are geared to women, on the unproven assumption that women need the training more. In fact, some Canadian research suggests that women are actually more appropriately assertive than men in many situations (Wine, Smye, and Moses, 1980).

But while basic skills in assertiveness can only be helpful, they provide no magic cure for the power problems that women face in their working lives. How direct a woman is able to be in her attempts to exert influence depends only in a limited way on these skills. More importantly, it depends on the degree of actual control over resources that she brings to an interaction, how powerful she feels, and what kinds of behaviour she and those around her see as appropriate.

Women are often accused of relying on indirect or hidden power styles— manipulative and sneaky rather than open when trying to exert influence. In cases where this accusation is true, there are probably a number of factors operating that favour an indirect strategy. For example, the more resources one can command to back up one's requests or demands, the easier it is to be direct. This is particularly true of such resources as legitimacy, status, and support. The more authority a person has in her position, the higher her status, and the more backing she feels from her co-workers, the easier it is for her to make strong, clear demands on people. For this reason, a teacher may have no hesitation about making certain clear demands on her students, but may be wary about adopting the same strong, direct style with school administrators. When dealing with students, she is operating from a position of recognised authority and of higher status within the institution. Moreover, she usually knows she is working within guidelines that are accepted by and will be supported by her colleagues. If she had no recognised authority over the people she was trying to influence, if she were operating from a position of lower status, if she felt isolated from her colleagues on a particular issue (all of which are more likely to be the case when she is trying to exert influence over an administrator instead of a student), it would be more difficult for her to be direct and assertive.

For women (or men, for that matter) who find themselves at the bottom of the ladder in a workplace that operates on a very hierarchical basis, it is unrealistic to expect a lot of direct, open use of power. This is doubly true if a woman has no network of support among her co-workers—a problem that plagues women who are breaking ground in a traditionally male job. Finally, it must be noted that women tend to start with a strike against them when it comes to status. The status ascribed to females in many jobs is automatically lower than that ascribed to men in the same job. Simply trying to teach or convince women to be more assertive and direct under these conditions is not the answer. Most women know how to be assertive under the right circumstances, but they avoid behaviour that is going to get them into more trouble than they want to handle.

Intervention to increase women's capacity to exert power in a direct way should not focus mainly on the behaviour of individual women. Rather, a more useful focus is on finding ways to increase women's access to resources, and to change the culture's image of femininity so that it is no longer synonymous with weakness or incompetence.

How can such changes be accomplished? They have already begun to happen. A crucial aspect of increasing women's access to resources in the workplace is the formation of support groups. Such groups not only provide much needed support (a resource in itself) for women who are isolated or ignored in male-dominated workplaces, they also enable women to share information and expertise—thus potentially increasing the competence (another resource) of all members. In some situations, these groups can also provide the political clout to help attain certain kinds of change beneficial to women (yet another resource). Also, the existence of network groups may provide a significant source of encouragement for more women to enter certain fields, an eventuality that will make it less common for women to find themselves isolated as tokens in their jobs.

It does not take a psychologist to tell most women that another extremely important aspect of increasing women's access to the resources on which power is based involves eliminating wom-

en's "double shift." Time and energy are themselves precious resources on which all attempts to have influence or make an impact on the world are based. For years, women's time and energy have been stolen from them by economic and cultural systems that have allocated to women virtually all of the responsibility for child care and the daily maintenance functions of cooking, cleaning, shopping, and errand-running. Even in countries where serious attempts have been made to "socialise" child care functions, women are the ones faced with the housework when they return from work each day. And in Sweden, where new fathers and mothers are equally entitled to parental leave at 90 per cent of salary, few fathers avail themselves of the opportunity to stay home with their infants. No modern economic system has yet solved this problem of women's double day.

On an individual level, a woman is seriously handicapped in her attempts to have an impact outside of her own family by its double burden of labour. On a group level, the double shift weakens and dilutes women's impact on the values that shape the political process, the educational process, the arts, our own culture, and the future of the world. In the power terms discussed in this chapter, the cultural requirement that women perform a disproportionately large share of home-related work interferes with their access to almost every type of resource on which power can be based. Household responsibilities may make a woman less available for the extra meetings or social events where information is exchanged and contacts that lead to promotions and better jobs are made. They slow down her education, keeping her at a lower level in the job market. Thus, her access to information and expertise is curtailed, as is her access to the reward and punishment power that accompanies control over economic resources, and to the legitimacy that comes with holding a position of recognised authority. The only power base that is not guaranteed to be adversely affected by this situation is that of personal attractiveness or likability—and there is many a bleary-eyed, irritable woman with no time for exercise or sleep who will say that even that traditional source of female power is compromised by the double shift. Clearly, for women as individuals or for women as a group to have a greater impact on our cultural institutions, the relegation to women of most child care and household responsibilities would have to be changed.

The "powerless/incompetent" impact of femininity would also have to be changed. While that change is beginning to happen as strong, competent women become more visible, efforts in some specific areas are called for. Ripe for revision, for instance, is the notion that women are incompetent to handle all things mathematical and technical. The pernicious stereotype of women as beings who cannot deal with numbers and who are too muddleheaded to balance a chequebook is not only wrong, it is dangerous in an age that is increasingly dominated by the computer. It will be helpful to remember that when the typewriter was first invented, it was thought to be too complicated a machine for women to handle!

It would also be useful to work against the idea that women must be physically weak. Not only is this view of women an obstacle to their employment in a variety of jobs requiring strength and stamina, but it may also be related to the general perception of women's effectiveness and their sense of power. Being weak fosters a need for protection from men—and this generates an attitude of protectiveness on men's part that generalises far beyond the physical realm into other aspects of women's lives.

A third aspect of the femininity stereotype that would-be powerful women need to challenge is that women are quiet, soft-spoken, and polite. A growing body of research in psychology shows that, in the first place, people who talk more in groups tend to be accorded more status in those groups; and, in the second place, men tend to discourage women from speaking up in group situations by interrupting them and by ignoring their input. These tactics used by men tend to subdue women's efforts at participation in the discussion, allowing the men conversational control. Then, in a vicious circle, women are discounted more and more as they become increasingly silent, and they try less and less often to enter the conversation as they feel increasingly ignored. One approach to this problem is for women to try to train their male colleagues to stop interrupting them, but such training may not come easily. It is a rare and lucky woman who, after bringing the problem to the attention of the men she works with, finds she is never interrupted again! More probably, she will have to work actively to invalidate the feminine stereotype of politeness by refusing to defer to male speakers who try to interrupt her and by protesting such interruptions again and again. Since old habits die hard, and since change is more in women's interest than men's, it is unrealistic to rely too heavily on men to relinquish their conversational control tactics without continuous pressure from women.

As women gain more access to the resources on which power is based, they will find it easier to challenge the "powerless" image of femininity. And, concurrently, as the powerless image fades, women will find it easier to be recognised as strong, as competent, as experts. Thus, in a reversal of a "vicious circle," the two processes will feed into each other, ultimately making it easier for women to use such resources as expertise, information, and legitimacy. These resources become springboards for acquiring access to other resources—tangible ones such as money and control over decision making—and for opening the doors to these resources to other women. This is an optimistic perspective to be sure, but one that is consistent with the way many advances for women have been achieved over the years. For women, as for any relatively powerless group, the key to starting the "nonvicious circle" rolling is to use their most available resource: their numbers, their collectivity, pooled energy, and shared support. The payoff may well be not only more access to and impact in the workplace for women, but a more humane workplace for everyone.

REFERENCES

Abella, R. S. *Equality in Employment: A Royal Commission Report.* Ottawa: Canadian Government Publishing Centre, 1984.

Astin, A. W., King., M. R., and Richardson, G. T. *The American Freshman: National Norms for Fall 1975.* Los Angeles: University of California Laboratory for Research in Higher Education, 1975.

Braid, K. "Women in Trades in British Columbia." In M. Fitzgerald, C. Guberman, and M. Wolfe (eds.), *Still Ain't Satisfied! Canadian Feminism Today.* Toronto: Woman's Press, 1982.

Colwill, N. L., and Lips, H. M. "Masculinity, Femininity, and Androgyny: What Have You Done for Us Lately?" Chapter in H. M. Lips and N. L. Colwill, *The Psychology of Sex Differences.* Englewood Cliffs, N.J.: Prentice-Hall, 1978.

Danylewycz, M. "Changing Relationships: Nuns and Feminists in Montréal, 1890–1925." *Histoire Sociale—Social History,* 14:28 (1981), 413–434.

French, J. P. R., and Raven, B. "The Bases of Social Power." In D. Cartwright (ed.), *Studies in Social Power.* Ann Arbor: Institute for Social Research, University of Michigan, 1959.

Harlan, A., and Weiss, C. L. "Moving Up: Women in Managerial Careers." Third progress report. Wellesley, Mass.: Wellesley College Center for Research on Women, 1980.

Harrison, J. "Warning: The Male Sex Role May Be Dangerous to Your Health." *Journal of Social Issues,* 34:1 (1978), 65–86.

Johnson, P. "Women and Power: Toward a Theory of Effectiveness." *Journal of Social Issues,* 32:3 (1976), 99–110.

Kanter, R. M. *Men and Women of the Corporation.* New York: Basic Books, 1977.

Lerner, M. J. "Social Psychology of Justice and Interpersonal Attraction." In T. L. Huston (ed.), *Foundations of Interpersonal Attraction.* New York: Academic Press, 1974.

Shields, S. A. "Functionalism, Darwinism, and the Psychology of Women: A Study in Social Myth." *American Psychologist,* 30:7 (1975), 739–754.

Steinem, G. *Outrageous Acts and Everyday Rebellions.* New York: Holt, Rinehart, and Winston, 1983.

Touhey, J. C. "Effects of Additional Women Professionals on Rating of Occupational Prestige and Desirability." *Journal of Personality and Social Psychology* 29: (1974), 86–89.

Wine, J. D., Smye, M. D., and Moses, B. "Assertiveness: Sex Differences in Relationships between Self-report and Behavioural Measures." In C. Stark-Adamec (ed.), *Sex Roles: Origins, Influences, and Implications for Women.* Montreal: Eden Press, 1980.

Further Questions

1. Is it desirable for a person to put his or her career first, subordinating everything else to this one part of life?

2. Is there something valuable about the way in which men have been brought up and about the arrangement of their lifestyles (and conversely, perhaps, something lacking in these areas for women) that explains why men get ahead of women in the workplace?

3. Does a woman's ability to be direct in particular circumstances partly depend on the character of the circumstances? If so, how?

The Half-Empty Glass: Can It Ever Be Filled?   III.2

NATALIE J. SOKOLOFF

Natalie J. Sokoloff contends that there is still job segregation by race and gender, with white men at the top and black women at the bottom of the hierarchy. Movement of disadvantaged groups into jobs once held by white men means only that these jobs have declined in attractiveness or more of them have opened up and that white men have gone on to jobs that are better paying and have more autonomy, better career prospects, more prestige, and other desirable features. In like manner, black men and white women have abandoned less desirable jobs which are then filled with black women.

Reading Questions

1. Explain the ideas of a labor queue and a job queue and illustrate them with some examples from the text.
2. Why is it misleading to cite numbers of entries from disadvantaged groups into previously white male dominated professions as evidence that race and gender hierarchies are disappearing? Discuss with reference to some examples from the text.
3. Should the entry of black women into jobs previously held by white women be regarded as racial progress? Use some examples from the text in your discussion.

TWENTY YEARS OF CHANGE: A SUMMARY OF WHAT HAPPENED IN THE PROFESSIONS 1960–1980

Introduction

The period between 1960 and 1980 was a time of remarkable change in the United States. The political and economic expansion of the post-World War II era was manifested, among other things, in a general increase in the sixties and seventies in what are considered to be the "good jobs"—particularly professional occupations. Not only were more of the prized jobs available, but the civil-rights and women's movements catalyzed legislation mandating that these jobs be open to everyone. My purpose in this book has been to investigate the degree to which black women and white women, in rela-

tion to black men and white men, were able to participate in these increasing opportunities in the occupational arena. To this end, I have explored the changes experienced by these men and women in the wide array of jobs available in the professional/technical labor force in the United States between 1960 and 1980.

What we have seen is that from one perspective, the glass was half-full by 1980; from another, it was half-empty. Although virtually all major groups in the society benefited from the economic expansion, there were other equally important but not so positive developments. These included the deterioration in job security, autonomy, promotion prospects and real earnings for many jobs in the economy, including many of the professions. If we look at these changes in work processes and in professional/

From Black Women and White Women in the Professions *by Natalie Sokoloff. Routledge, Inc. 1992. Reprinted by permission from the publisher.*

technical job rewards, questions are raised about the character of what first appeared to be increased opportunities for women and black men. For just one example, it is true that the disadvantaged groups of white women, black women, and black men all gained substantial access to what had been the white male-dominated professions of accounting, design, and nonspecific college teaching. But something else was happening to these professions. Even as they were opening to groups that had been excluded, these professions were in the process of losing their autonomy, relatively high status, and high-level job rewards. As their conditions of work deteriorated, white men moved on to other, more privileged occupations, leaving these deteriorating professions to groups that had heretofore been excluded from them.

In short, disadvantaged groups continued to have *less than equal opportunities;* and when they were offered better jobs, it was more than likely that these jobs were undergoing substantial changes, leading to their decline in attractiveness to the more privileged groups holding them. Although there was a new, much larger glass, many of the jobs contained within it in 1980 had deteriorated from what they had been in the smaller glass of 1960. Because the contents had changed over those 20 years, it becomes no simple matter to say whether by 1980 the glass was half-full or half-empty.

Occupations Providing the Greatest Access to Disadvantaged Groups

The period between 1960 and 1980 was one of rapid changes in the professions, not the least of which were changes in who occupied them. As the media consistently reported, women and minority men made definite progress in the professions, to some extent even in those customarily associated with white men. However, the media did not often report that white men participated in those gains as well, particularly in the most desirable male-dominated professions. While it is true that, over these 20 years of major social change, *disadvantaged groups* gained greater access to professional/technical

occupations considered as a whole, when we look at these fields individually, we find that only *certain occupations* opened up significantly to women and minority men. And considering these occupations as a whole, race/gender hierarchies continued unchanged or reconstituted themselves with white men at the top of the professional/technical occupational ladder and black women at the bottom.

On the whole, white men retained dominance in the most desired professions as doctors, lawyers, engineers, and the like. A few male-dominated professions lower down the socioeconomic ladder created new opportunities primarily for white women, and secondarily for black men and black women; these included accounting, design, and nonspecific college teaching. Blacks, both men and women, did best in relation to white men *outside* male-dominated professions in such gender-neutral professions as personnel and labor relations, and vocational and educational counseling. Finally, the female-dominated professions/technical areas, typically the domain of white women, provided the greatest openings to black women, especially social work, prekindergarten and kindergarten teaching, elementary education, and clinical-laboratory work.

Increased Segregation and Increased Access

For all four groups of men and women, changes were channeled in several different directions throughout the professions simultaneously. Thus, while some occupations became integrated (i.e., each race gender group became represented according to its percents in the labor force as a whole), most did not. Rather, they were primarily either preserved for white men or reserved for disadvantaged groups. In both cases, the occupations changed enough to provide openings to other groups, while remaining substantially segregated. Finally, another group of occupations appeared to have really opened up to disadvantaged groups, only to close again, trapping them in jobs that restrict disadvantaged incumbents to them—a form of group resegregation within occupations.[1]

As we have seen, out of the 30 large professions and technical areas[2] studied (which include about four-fifths of all professionals and technicians), very few occupations became *genuinely integrated*. This appears to have been the case for only three male professions: accounting, design, and nonspecific college teaching. (Even here white women moved the closest toward parity with white men; black men and black women were less able to close the gap.) All three of these occupations, even at the beginning of the period, were at the lowest end of the status and income range for male professions, and by the end of the period they had experienced serious deterioration in occupational advantage. Only one gender-neutral profession, personnel and labor relations, which had been a predominantly white occupation in 1960, became perfectly integrated over time for all race/gender groups. In short, most of the desired white male professions remained substantially segregated, with only very modest gains for disadvantaged race/gender groups.

In contrast to the overall increased access, some occupations remained or became increasingly dominated by white men. As we have seen, this is often obscured because an occupation can be preserved for the more advantaged group of white men and still allow women and minority men greater opportunities to enter it in those sectors white men deem as less desirable. This appears to have been the case throughout the elite and most of the nonelite male professions and male technical fields. In such a scenario, women and minority men in no way reach parity of representation with white men in the most desired of professional jobs, white men continue to have access to the "best" jobs, and white men do not "lose" such jobs to disadvantaged groups.

For example, as physicians, clergy, and engineers of many kinds, white men *increased* their overrepresentation in these professions in comparison to their representation in the labor force as a whole. Not only did these professions expand greatly during the period under study, but they also were able to include their traditional population of white men while allowing somewhat greater access to previously excluded groups. In

short, as the glass expanded, so did the area allotted to disadvantaged groups. Yet the area reserved for white men grew even more! White men were able to retain or enter higher-tier, more autonomous sectors of these male-dominated professions, while black women, white women, and black men were able to gain access primarily to expanding numbers of routinized and more poorly paid jobs within the very same profession or technical field (see, e.g., Carter and Carter, 1981; Luxemberg, 1985; Robinson and McIlwee, 1989; Roach, 1990).

A major theoretical explanation for this set of circumstances was developed by Barbara F. Reskin and Patricia A. Roos in *Job Queues, Gender Queues* (1990). According to Reskin and Roos, job assignment is part of a "queuing" (i.e., ranking) system. Employers' preferences for workers and workers' preferences for jobs are both queued: "*labor queues* order groups of workers in terms of their attractiveness to employers, and *job queues* rank jobs in terms of their attractiveness to workers" (p. 29). This system determines who is hired in which positions: "employers hire workers from as high in the labor queue as possible, and workers accept the best jobs available to them. As a result the best jobs go to the most preferred workers, and less attractive jobs go to workers lower in the labor queue; bottom-ranked workers may go jobless, and the worst jobs may be left unfilled" (p. 30. Interestingly, this idea was first developed on the basis of race, not gender, by Thurow, 1972).

Reskin and Roos apply these general principles to women and men in male-dominated jobs throughout the U.S. labor force during the approximate period of my study. Women are hired at the bottom of a given occupation and cannot move up until men abandon the positions at the top. During the 1970s, this movement accelerated due to a number of factors, including deskilling of jobs (making them less desirable to men), changes in technology and work settings, declining wages and other rewards (autonomy, career prospects, etc.), the weakening of male labor unions, changing demand for worker, and affirmative-action policies. The result was an influx of women into jobs that men no longer wanted. Certain male occupations had undergone, in Reskin and Roos's phrase, "occupational feminization."

Let us extend their analysis beyond the two gender groups to the four race/gender groups that I studied. As we have seen, white men in the professions either held on to their superior rewards or moved on to something better. Only when white men moved on from the top jobs (which had deteriorated in some way) could the three disadvantaged race/gender groups move up from the bottom. Likewise, although white women were clearly disadvantaged in relation to white men, they were more advantaged in relation to black women (and in some ways in relation to black men, although the picture is mixed).

In the higher-status professions, black men did not significantly improve their position relative to white men but they were able to gain greater access relative to white women. This was true for most engineering specialties, chemistry, and medicine. Thus black men and white women became concentrated in *different* male professions, depending on the degree to which they were able to gain access. And as white women moved out of lower-status female professions and into higher-level gender-neutral and male professions, black women gained access to places from which they had previously been excluded by preferences for and by white women. Thus black women were last in line to be able to pursue their goals. It was only in those occupations or sectors of occupations that other groups deem less desirable that black women were able to gain access. And once in them, they tended to be trapped there, nominally professionals but unable to move out into other, more prestigious professions.

It is important to understand that even though other groups may filter into a given occupation, that occupation may remain heavily segregated (i.e., largely filled by a given race/gender group). This is true not only for the more prestigious occupations, but of the less prestigious as well. Thus, while all of the large

female-dominated professions/technical fields showed significant declines in white women's overrepresentation in comparison to men, white women remained heavily overrepresented.

Although occupational gender segregation has persisted in the female fields, racial factors have also remained significant. Although the much larger numbers of white women ensured that they remained the numerical majority in these occupations, as certain of these fields declined in power, autonomy, and rewards, those white women that were able moved out and into the lower rungs of the male and gender-neutral professions. Black women thus moved into (i.e., became better represented in) social work, nursing, preschool and elementary education, and librarianship as these jobs became increasingly routinized, deskilled, and under male supervision and control (e.g., see Dressel, 1987). At the same time, once in them, black women tended to be restricted to these—and a very few other—professions. Because of their small numbers, however, black women (and black men) could simultaneously be channeled into a few fields and yet have no chance of ever becoming the numerical majority in them.

In sum, both gender and race/gender segregation operated in 1980 as well as in 1960, although the nature of the jobs as well as the exact race/gender composition changed. What did *not* change is that the most privileged occupations remained by and large reserved for white men, and the less privileged remained the province of black women, white women, and—to some extent—black men.

The Greatest Increases in Occupational Segregation, 1960–1980. Outside the already highly segregated male occupations, increased segregation occurred chiefly on the basis of race, although gender itself and race/gender were also important. For example, both black men and black women became overrepresented (in proportion to their share of the overall labor force) or increased their overrepresentation in comparison to white men as counselors, social workers, and clinical-laboratory technicians. However, these were also some of the very occupations in which black women were more heavily overrepresented than black men, when these two groups are compared. In addition, black women were also more likely to be overrepresented than white men as secondary-school teachers and teachers/nec. In short, while segregation was on the rise for black men and black women in certain gender-neutral and female professions/technical areas, it was more severe for black women than for black men.

Increasing segregation occurred also on the basis of gender; for example, in the profession of painting/sculpting. However, two other gender-neutral professions were already disproportionately occupied by white women in 1960: counseling and editing/reporting. Twenty years later, segregation in these occupations had intensified. Again, it is crucial to realize that some jobs became not just feminized, but "race/genderized." When black women and white women are compared, the following occupations moved from being overrepresented by white women to being overrepresented by black women between 1960 and 1980: vocational and educational counseling, social work, and prekindergarten and kindergarten teaching. Given the trend toward increased racial segregation among women, it is quite possible that those occupations in which black women finally reached parity with white women by 1980 will become increasingly occupied by black women. These occupations include a not insignificant number of middle- and lower-level large professions/technical areas: personnel and labor relations, elementary education, clinical-laboratory technology, and electrical-engineering technology.

As Reskin and Roos made clear in their analysis of gender, and as my study points out for race/gender as well, occupational segregation has continued to benefit primarily white men. However, we must also be careful to recognize the advances that individual members of disadvantaged race/gender groups have made. Opening up of professional and technical jobs

has meant that some women and minority men have been able to get an education and use their skills to an extent that 20 years earlier would have been impossible. The irony, of course, is that most of these opportunities have come in the less prestigious occupations, and that many of the benefits of professionalism obtained 20 years previously have been seriously eroded. Thus the social and political conditions of professionalism have changed drastically—and often not for the better—in conjunction with the entrance of the previously excluded.

Access to the Elite Professions, 1960–1980. On the one hand, some members of the disadvantaged race/gender groups have indeed been able to enter the domain of white men. On the other hand, these fortunate individuals are just that—individuals—and their success, no matter how hard won and how well deserved, does not signify an advance for their group overall. For example, in the elite male profession of medicine, *black women* might have shown a threefold increase; but because their numbers were so small in comparison to white men, the fortunes *of the group* of black women hardly changed at all. Over the 20 years, black women physicians increased from 0.02 percent to 0.06 percent of all employed black women. Likewise, *black men* not only experienced enormous rates of growth in engineering specialties, but also increased their representation *in relation to white women* (thereby belying the claim that white women take important male-dominated jobs away from black men). Yet black men still represented only 2 percent of all engineers by 1980, far less than their 5.8 percent representation in the overall labor force. In short, despite the many changes in access to an occupation, that change may not be consequential in terms of the group's fortunes.

As we have seen, no matter what changes occurred in a profession, white men did not lose out. Instead, they maintained or increased their overrepresentation over time throughout most of the elite and nonelite male professions and male technical fields. So long as the occupation continued to expand, white men were able to take the best positions for themselves. Either women and minorities entered the lower-tier jobs in elite male professions, as other researchers have shown, or they gained access to occupations that themselves were the lower levels of the nonelite male professions, as my research has shown. In both cases, disadvantaged groups were faced with occupations that were deteriorating in quality and increasing in numbers while white men kept control of the best positions.[3]

A Structural Analysis of Increased Access to the Professions

As we have seen throughout this book, increased opportunities for women and minority men in the 1960–1980 period took place in professions that were undergoing substantial structural change. There are three major structural factors common to occupations that provided greater access: (1) increasing size, (2) decreasing status and/or deteriorating conditions of work, and (3) political pressure on behalf of disadvantaged groups.

Increased Size. One structural factor that correlates positively with increased job opportunities for disadvantaged groups is an increasing number of jobs in a given field. Women and black men were able to gain greater access, both inside and outside the male-dominated professions, to those occupations that expanded greatly in size. In some occupations, such as the nonelite male profession of accounting, expansion was so rapid that there were not enough white men to fill the new positions; thus all three disadvantaged race/gender groups were able to enter this field in large numbers. Other professions/technical areas where women and black men gained greater representation did not increase as much as accounting. Nevertheless, all increased the number of new jobs at a rate much faster than the average growth of most occupations.[4] Thus there were enough jobs so that white men (or white women in the female-dominated professions) could simultaneously increase their numbers and allow other groups in.

Low Status and Job Deterioration. Another important structural feature concerns the changing nature and conditions of work in those occupations that disadvantaged groups have been able to enter. As Reskin and Roos (1990: 317) concluded in their study, "the structural change in queues that contributed most to women's inroads in the case study occupations . . . [was] men's reordering of the job queue. By downranking jobs in customarily male occupations, men abandoned them to women. It is this source of occupational feminization that seems most likely to contribute to *nominal* desegregation in the future." In my study, great integration, as well as increased segregation, occurred in those professions in which working conditions and/or occupational rewards had been deteriorating over time. Most important, in the male professions, greater access for disadvantaged groups occurred mostly in the least desirable professions, if occupational status and level of income are used as criteria. For example, using the Nam-Powers (1983) occupational-status scores (described in Chapter 1), accounting, design, and nonspecific college teaching had the lowest ratings and the lowest average incomes of all but one of the large male professions, the ministry.[5]

However, not only were these occupations less desirable to white men to begin with, but they became increasingly so over time. For example, design and nonspecific college teaching experienced some of the largest drops in income for women compared to men between 1960 and 1980.[6] In addition, both historical and case-study analyses of accounting and college teaching have described the relationship between the deterioration of these professions in autonomy, control, skill requirements, working conditions, and income (in short, their proletarianization) and their increasing feminization.

A similar argument can be made about some of the occupations (especially in the gender-neutral and some of the female professions) that became increasingly segregated by race and gender. As was suggested earlier, the increase of blacks and white women in vocational and educational counseling may well have been related to the enormous expansion of two-year and community colleges in the 1960s. Many black, third-world, and poorer students of all racial/ethnic backgrounds were the first in their families to be able to go to college. The vast number of students requiring vocational and educational counseling mushroomed. Counselors' caseloads expanded greatly, while the job itself became more narrowly focused and with fewer rewards than those traditionally associate with counseling well-to-do students attending elite colleges and universities. The situation was similar for book editors: the decline in autonomy, creativity, job security, and income paved the way for increasing feminization of that occupation.

Social work, a classic female profession, likewise became increasingly transformed after the mid-1960s as certain aspects of social-welfare work were automated, intake procedures were separated from casework, income-maintenance activities were separated from the provision of social services, and jobs were reclassified, allowing larger jobs to be broken into smaller tasks and female workers to become increasingly less likely to control their own work process under the direction of male supervisors (Dressel, 1987). The de-skilling of social work has led not only to further subordination of women in the social welfare labor process, as Dressel argues; according to my data, it has also led to the access of black women to professional jobs previously held by white women.

In short, it appears that increased access to the professions for disadvantaged groups was largely related to the growth of a large number of jobs newly created in the professions that were deteriorating in power, prestige, income, and authority. This was true whether they were male professions (e.g., accounting, design, and college teaching) that became less desirable to white men; gender-neutral professions (e.g.,

editing/reporting and counseling) that were again, less desirable particularly to white men; or female professions (e.g., social work, and prekindergarten and kindergarten teaching) that were less desirable to white women, given other options available higher up the professional hierarchy. In each case, race/gender groups lower down the occupational hierarchy gained access to professions/technical arenas that favored groups deemed as less desirable.

Political Pressures. A structural analysis also requires us to look at the ways in which race, gender, and class underlie the organization of basic social relations. How these social relations became transformed through political pressure from oppressed groups is part of the dynamics of change that led to the emergence of more women and the new black middle class in particular professions. So, for example, the growth of blacks in counseling, personnel and labor relations, and social work was not only part of the process of occupational proletarianization; it was also directly linked to the changes that emerged in the 1960s as government employed educated blacks in public-service occupations that served poor and black populations. At that time, poor and minority people were demanding more rights, services, and participation in the society. Also at that time, there were widespread riots and disturbances in deteriorating inner cities that were increasingly becoming ghettos for the black and third-world underclasses.

As earlier in U.S. history when racial segregation was legal, black professionals were able to provide services where whites would not go. This time, however, the new black middle class was more integrated occupationally into white society. Moreover, many blacks were hired by government or private corporations as affirmative-action officers in the 1960s and 1970s, only to be let go in the 1980s once the political and economic climate became less hospitable to blacks. These phenomena help explain the increasing segregation (or incredible overconcentration) of black men and women in such gender-neutral and female-dominated professions as counseling, social work, school teaching at all levels, and personnel and labor relations. That black women were overrepresented in these professions when compared to black men makes it clear that the forces of race and gender are intimately intertwined.

In short, political pressures clearly resulted in the growth of many of these jobs. This helps us to understand why these professions grew, why they grew using the labor of blacks and women, and why this growth did not represent a growth in power, earnings, or prestige to the extent that one would have expected.

In conclusion, certainly there was some integration of professions between 1960 and 1980, but it came about largely because of the growth and substantial change in character of the jobs themselves. Finally, many of these changes occurred because politically less powerful groups pushed for changes in the kinds of jobs and services they needed.

RACIAL AND GENDER SEGREGATION, 1980 TO THE PRESENT

The changes within professions have been so great that, in a sense, it no longer is adequate to talk about doctors or lawyers, engineers or pharmacists. The difference between a lawyer "working" the district court in a city like New York and the corporate counsel of a Wall Street firm, the difference between the pharmacist working for a multimillion-dollar research-based firm and one filling prescriptions in the local drugstore are so great that there well may be more that distinguishes the various positions *within* the professions than there are similarities. Increasingly the major aspect of the profession that they seem to share is the name. Likewise, a lawyer in a large, prestigious corporation and a vocational counselor in a public high school often share little more than the fact that they are both designated as "professionals."

While the degree of segregation seems high, even when we examine the detailed occupational data used in this research, it is clearly an underestimation of both gender and race segregation and stratification *within* an occupation. Several examples are pertinent here. Bielby and Baron (1986) studied gender segregation in occupations using firm-specific job titles. They found that even when men and women worked in the very same occupation, they were given different job titles, and were employed in different firms and geographic locations with different occupational opportunities and rewards. This held true for both professional and nonprofessional jobs. Despite women's increasing access to male-dominated jobs, the researchers concluded that gender segregation was continually being reestablished.

Likewise, Higginbotham (1987) argued that although more blacks may have found their way into professions traditionally associated with whites, they have been slotted into racially segregated positions. Thus during the 1970s, although more black men and black women were working as doctors and nurses, they were employed in public hospitals and municipal clinics as salaried workers servicing poor and minority populations. Such workers are "colonized" professionals. Higginbotham concluded in her study comparing black and white women in the professions that

> The patterns of employment for professional Black women must be discussed. Otherwise as we pass through the 1980s and into the 1990s, we will continue to find Black women teaching in public schools, nursing in public hospitals, and coping with heavy caseloads as social workers for the department of welfare. They will still be colonized professionals, caught in either public sector jobs or the few occupational opportunities in the private sector of the Black community. Maybe then researchers will cease to sing the praises of the tiny minority of Black women in formerly traditional male professions who are able to secure employment in the private sector. (1987: 90)

Moreover,

> the minority of Black women who enter tradi-
> tionally male professions also tend to be ghet-
> toized in the public defender's office, city-run
> hospitals, dental clinics, and minority relations
> for corporate firms. These patterns illustrate the
> persistence of racial stratification, even in the de-
> velopment of a Black middle class (1987: 75).

Within the black community the degree of
gender segregation and stratification is likewise
evident. For example, in the traditionally male
clergy, women numbered as many as one-third
of all ministers in some of the historically black
denominations in 1989 (Goldman, 1990). Yet
black female clergy report they are unable to
achieve pulpits of their own, which more recently has led them to open new churches on
their own. While white female pastors said they
have some similar problems in achieving major
pulpits, black women clergy argued "that their
plight was intensified by the fact that the church
has traditionally been the primary vehicle of
black men to exercise both religious and political power" (Goldman, 1990: 28).

In science and engineering, another remarkable gender difference has emerged. In the mid-
1980s, a landmark was reached when black
women received, for the first time, more than
half of all doctorates, including science and engineering, awarded to all black American citizens. However, only 6 percent of all science
degrees awarded to black women were in the
higher-paying and more prestigious areas of engineering, mathematics, and physical science.
Black men predominated here. Black women's
majority was in the less powerful and less lucrative life and social/behavioral sciences (Malcolm, 1989).

Ghettoization and Resegregation

Much of the literature on gender and race that
emerged in the late 1980s and early 1990s
began to discuss ghettoization of women into
female enclaves and into lower-status, lower-
paying segments of male professions. It also
began to document the stratification of black
women in relation to white women at all levels
of the professional (and managerial) hierarchy in
both female- and male-dominated professions.

Looking at gender segregation, Reskin and
Roos (1990) and their colleagues reported on an
important set of case studies on the feminization
of male occupations. As we saw earlier in this
chapter, they argued that the numerical increase
of women in male occupations during the 1970s
reflected both women's *ghettoization* in certain
jobs within some of these male occupations (i.e.,
women held a restricted number of lower-level
jobs) and the *resegregation* of others (i.e., men
moved out and women became the majority).
Genuine gender integration, they concluded,
was indeed rare in the 1970s. The professions
that experienced, first, ghettoization of women,
then resegregation (i.e., became feminized) during this time included systems analysis, pharmacy, book editing, public relations, accounting
and auditing, and reporting. Note that none of
these are among the elite male professions. Thus,
for example, among public-relations specialists,
men were more likely to be promoted into public-relations management, while women ended
up overrepresented as lower-level "communications technicians." Among pharmacists, men
were more likely to be found in management positions in retail pharmacy and in research, while
women were located in salaried hospital settings.
Not only did women become ghettoized in public relations, the occupation also became resegregated. Retail pharmacy followed suit in the
1980s: women replaced men as the statistical majority in the occupation. Gender resegregation
likewise occurred among book editors in the
1970s. Their analysis, they concluded, "does not
offer a very rosy prognosis for desegregation,
much less for genuine integration, during the
1990s" (p. 381).

Other research indicates that these trends
continued beyond 1980. Blau (1989) found
that by 1987, personnel, training, and labor relations; educational and vocational counseling;
and public relations were among the male or

gender-mixed professions that had become predominantly female. It appears that as male occupations change to permit women to participate, they often reach some kind of "tipping point" and become resegregated, only this time with women instead of men.

Lest one think that the elite male professions are exempt from these processes, it is important to recognize the continued ghettoization of women in newly expanding as well as older areas in law, medicine, engineering, and the like. This is in large part related to the increasing proletarianization of labor even in elite male professions. Thus even doctors, lawyers, and college professors are becoming more bureaucratized, with more outside interference in their monopoly over the profession. As Carter and Carter (1981) have argued, many of the tasks have become deskilled in such a way that a split in the profession emerged between prestigious jobs with good pay, autonomy, and opportunity for growth and development, and a new class of more routinized, poorly paid jobs with little autonomy. This latter segment is unconnected by promotion ladders to prestigious jobs in the profession. And although this de-skilling process affects both men and women, Carter and Carter have predicted that "it is precisely in the newer, more routinized sector of professional employment that women's employment will be overwhelmingly concentrated" (p.478). Thus the smaller upper tier of semiautonomous, highly paid jobs will continue to exist, will continue to be male dominated, and will maintain institutional barriers that make access from the newly created routinized jobs difficult to achieve.

Recent examples in law, medicine, and engineering are becoming plentiful. In-house corporate legal counsel is the fastest-expanding segment of the legal profession. Women lawyers are more likely to be recruited as in-house legal counseling financial services (which is lower salaried, with more women employed in nonlegal jobs as well) than into more profitable manufacturing corporations (Roach, 1990). In medicine, increasing bureaucratization combined with de-

clining profitability, entrepreneurial potential, and social status to weaken men's involvement in medicine and open up certain sectors to women (Luxenberg, 1985; Nesbitt, 1986; Leslie, 1987). Likewise, one study concludes that in engineering, even when women and men are virtually identical in educational qualifications and time on the job, and have similar occupational attitudes, women are less likely than men to hold high-status jobs in design or management:

> The men outrank women in structural arenas where the profession of engineering itself flourishes—where authority relations are least bureaucratic, growth and technical innovation are greatest, and engineers have the most status and power (i.e., in electrical engineering and high tech firms). Women achieve equality with men where there are resources specifically designed for them (affirmative action), where the work of engineers is most routine, the power of engineers is relatively low, and the work place is most bureaucratic in structure (i.e., in mechanical engineering and aerospace). That is, opportunities for women appear greatest where the power of engineers is offset by other forces. (Robinson and McIlwee, 1989: 462–463)

At the highest levels of the professional and corporate world, we have only recently recognized that despite all the changes women have made, only a minuscule number are able to reach the top, even with the passage of time (Schafran, 1987). Thus *Fortune* asked, "Why Women Still Don't Hit the Top" (Fierman, 1990) in a survey of 4,012 people listed as the highest-paid officers and directors of the 1,000 largest U.S. industrial and service companies. Only 19 women—less than 1 percent—were identified among the more than 4,000 executives. Structural barriers, as well as stereotyping and discrimination, are among the impediments cited to advancement. In the legal profession, although women increased from 2.8 percent of all partners in the 250 largest firms at the beginning of the 1980s, by 1989 they were less than 1 in 10 (9.2 percent) of the partners in these top firms (Jensen, 1990; see also Stille, 1985; Weisenhaus, 1988). Even when women lawyers are not limited to the "mommy track" (Kingson, 1988), they "... Aren't Yet Equal Partners" either (Goldstein, 1988; Menkel-Meadow, 1987–88). And women may well be better able to become partners—even in top law firms—precisely when these partnerships become less desirable (Cowan, 1992). Even in more typically female professions such as education, school superintendents have usually been men. Today that still continues to be the case. For example, in 1988 only 3.8 percent of all superintendents of independent school districts and 6.2 percent of dependent school districts in New York State were women (Rush, 1989).

The continued domination of white men in top positions where professionally trained people are likely to be employed throughout the economy is repeated today in almost every study cited: the centers of power surrounding the president in the White House and the Cabinet (Dowd, 1991); the Federal Reserve, the government's most influential economic policy-making institution (Crustinger, 1990); top executives in the defense industry (Hyde, 1989); managers and professionals at the upper reaches of the corporate world (Silver, 1990; Skrzycki, 1990); deans and heads of departments in medical schools (Altman, 1988) as well as chief executives of national medical organizations (Hilts, 1991); scientists elevated to the rolls of the National Academy of Sciences (Angier, 1991); partners in prestigious law firms (Weisenhaus, 1988; Brenner, 1990; Jensen, 1990). The list goes on. Not only do white women fail to reach top positions throughout executive and professional domains—the proverbial "glass ceiling" is reached—but, as much of this same research shows, this situation is much worse for minorities—both men and women.

Segregation and Stratification: Black Women in the Professions

Recent research has likewise suggested that segregation and stratification within professions for black women have continued to rise, and have had a distinctive impact on this race/gender group. Specifically, there are two somewhat contradictory aspects of increasing opportunity for black women. The first is the degree to which opportunity has changed from one generation to another. The second is the degree to which, in any one generation, people can make choices among the full range of jobs available in the economy. In the first case, there certainly have been changes for black women: It makes a tremendous difference that one can now become a social worker or an accountant rather than a secretary or a cleaning woman. In the second case, there is virtually no difference: Black women are no more free to choose among the wide array of different sorts of work now than they were a generation ago. If they were, black women would not be concentrated in the lowest levels of the professional/technical labor force, nor would they have to wait for better jobs until white women are able to find better opportunities themselves outside the traditional female professions.

Studies have consistently shown that black women are concentrated in different jobs than white women throughout the labor force, including the professions (Almquist, 1979; Wallace, 1980; Malveaux, 1981, 1985, 1990; Westcott, 1982; Dill, Cannon, and Vanneman, 1987; Amott and Matthaei, 1991). Black women are primarily overrepresented in occupations outside the professions—more so than white women. And within the professions, black women are concentrated in far fewer jobs than white women.

For example, in 1980, among the top 40 occupations in which black women were overconcentrated, the only professional/technical jobs were social worker, prekindergarten and kindergarten teacher, dietician, and licensed practical nurse. In contrast, white women, although overrepresented in these occupations, were also heavily concentrated as librarians, health professors, home-economics professors, registered nurses, dental hygienists, occupational therapists, speech therapists, and health-record technicians (Dill, Cannon, and Vanneman, 1987).[7]

The fact that black women have become more highly concentrated in a few female professions/technical areas while white women have found employment in a wider variety is important for at least two reasons: first, for the greater limitations placed on black women; second, because the occupations in which black women are concentrated tend to pay so much less than those in which white women are concentrated (Dill, Cannon, and Vanneman, 1987).

Although there are very few detailed occupational studies that have compared black and white women in the professions, there have been a larger number of popular and scholarly articles on blacks in management, some of which have focused on black women. The degree of racial segregation and stratification is apparent throughout this literature. For example, Malveaux (1981) pointed out that black women are more likely to be management trainees at McDonald's franchises than at more financially and socially well-off corporations. Further, Malveaux reports on a survey of several elite universities and their M.B.A. programs between 1975 and 1980, which found that no black women were on "fast tracks" and no black women were hired at management jobs paying more than $40,000. This was in sharp contrast to white men, black men, and white women, who were able to find first jobs in these categories. Almost a decade later, in 1988, black women constituted only 2 percent of all managers in companies with at least 100 employees.[8] Moreover, once in the door, the few black women managers suffered from isolation, lack of mentors, and stereotyping. They reported they were usually the only black women in management, were bypassed for promotions, and were relegated to staff positions that were not on the fast track and thus were vulnerable to corporate streamlining (Alexander, 1990). The continuing level of discrimination against black women once they have gained access to managerial and professional jobs persists. This is also documented in other recent studies that include black women managers (Fulbright,

1985–86; Nkomo, 1986; Alston, 1987; DiTomaso and Thompson, 1988; and S. Collins, 1989). Recently opportunities for black women to gain entry to the upper echelons of corporate America also have been recognized. So, too, have the very significant barriers (King, 1988; Silver, 1990).

NOTES

1. Because the numbers of black men and black women in the professions are so small, it is impossible for a profession/technical field to become a "black" occupation—that is, over 50 percent black. However, black men or black women may be concentrated in a particular occupation, making it likely that, as a group, they will become locked into certain positions in the professions/technical areas. This is a form of segregation. For example, in New York City in 1990, the Human Resources Administration has become predominantly black in its managerial staff (Human Resources Administration Report, 1991). This leads many whites to argue that this is proof of blacks getting all the advantages. I would argue, instead, that this is part of the process whereby blacks are resegregated into certain occupations and sectors of an organization (here a city bureaucracy), with the higher-level, still highly valued positions or sectors remaining predominantly white and male.

2. Professions and technical fields as a group, as well as the 30 large ones, expand at a much faster rate than other jobs in the economy as a whole. Some of the smaller professions and technical fields (with less than 100,000 occupants in 1970) may operate differently.

3. A young white man, sitting in the audience at a professional sociology meeting where I presented some of my findings, offered the following relevant observation: On the one hand, my findings suggest it is inappropriate to talk about the "displacement" of white men by women and minorities in the more advantaged professions; white men clearly are still in control. On the other hand, he continued, it may well be the case that the increasing number of white women, black women, and black men challenges white male "hegemony" in certain professions, creating a new sense of unease for this traditionally privileged group of white men.

4. The fastest *growth rates* occurred in nonspecific college teaching, engineering (nec), counseling,

personnel and labor relations, computer programming, social work, and clinical laboratory technology. In addition, growth rates were above average for all professions and technical fields in law, accounting, research work, library work, elementary education, electronic technology and engineering and science technology/nec.

5. Despite the fact that the ministry traditionally has been an important occupation for black men, my data show that not only were white men severely overrepresented, but they became *more so* between 1960 and 1980.

6. These were also occupations where men's incomes declined, but less than women's.

7. The authors defined black women as overconcentrated in a profession if they were at least twice as likely to be represented in that profession as in the labor force as a whole.

8. Here black men made up 3 percent, white women 23 percent, and white men 67 percent of managers.

REFERENCES

Alexander, Keith. 1990. "Minority Women Feel Racism, Sexism Are Blocking the Path to Management." *Wall Street Journal,* July 25:B1.

Almquist, Elizabeth McTaggart. 1989. *Minorities, Gender and Work.* Lexington, Mass.: D. C. Heath.

Alston, Denise A. 1987. "Black Women in Management: Solving Problems; Asserting Authority." Paper presented at Fourth Annual Women and Work Conference, University of Texas at Arlington.

Altman, Lawrence K. 1988. "Few Women Attain Top Positions on Faculty." *New York Times,* December 15:B23.

Angier, Natalie. 1991. "Women Swell Ranks of Science, but Remain Invisible at the Top." *New York Times,* May 21:C1,C12.

Bielby, William T., and James N. Baron. 1986. "Men and Women at Work: Sex Segregation and Statistical Discrimination." *American Journal of Sociology* 91 (January): 759–799.

Blau, Francine. 1989. "Occupational Segregation by Gender: A Look at the 1980s." Revised paper presented at the 1988 American Economics Association meetings, New York.

Brenner, Joel Glenn. 1990. "Minority Lawyers Missed Out on Hiring Boom." *Washington Post,* February 13: A8.

Carter, Michael, and Susan Boslego Carter. 1981. "Women's Recent Progress in the Professions; or, Women Get a Ticket to Ride after the Gravy Train Has Left the Station." *Feminist Studies* 7 (Fall): 477–504.

Collins, Sharon M. 1989. "The Marginalization of Black Executives." *Social Problems* 36 (October): 317–331.

Cowan, Alison Leigh. 1992. "The New Letdown: Making Partner." *New York Times,* April 1: D1, D8.

Crustinger, Martin. 1990. "Study: Men in Most Top Jobs at Fed." *Washington Post,* September 4:B8.

Dill, Bonnie Thornton, Lynn Weber Cannon, and Reeve Vanneman. 1987. "Race and Gender in Occupational Segregation." In *Pay Equity: An Issue of Race, Ethnicity and Sex,* 10–69. Washington, D.C.: National Committee on Pay Equity.

DiTomaso, Nancy, and Donna E. Thompson. 1988. "Minority Success in Corporate Management." In Donna E. Thompson and Nancy Di Tomaso (eds.), *Ensuring Minority Success in Corporate Management,* 3–24. New York: Plenum.

Dowd, Maureen. 1991. "Bush Appoints More Women, but It's All-Male Club at Top." *New York Times,* May 20:A1,B6.

Dressel, Paula. 1987. "Patriarchy and Social Welfare Work." *Social Problems* 34 (June):294–309.

Fierman, Jaclyn. 1990. "Why Women Still Don't Hit the Top." *Fortune* 122 (July 30):40–42, 46, 50, 62.

Fulbright, Karen. 1985–86. "The Myth of the Double-Advantage: Black Female Managers." *Review of Black Political Economy* 14 (Fall–Winter): 33–45.

Goldman, Ari L. 1990. "Black Women's Bumpy Path to Church Leadership." *New York Times,* July 29:1,28.

Goldstein, Tom. 1988. "Women in the Law Aren't Yet Equal Partners." *New York Times,* February 12:B7.

Higginbotham, Elizabeth. 1987. "Employment for Professional Black Women in the Twentieth Century." In Christine Bose and Glenna Spitze (eds.). *Ingredients for Women's Employment Policy,* 73–91. Albany: SUNY Press.

Hilts, Philip J. 1991. "Women Still Behind in Medicine." *New York Times,* September 10:C7.

Human Resources Administration. 1991. *EEO Quarterly Statistical Summary Report.* New York City. October–December.

Hyde, James C. 1989. "Defense Industry's Top Ranks Hold Few Women Execs." *Armed Forces Journal International* 127:55–57.

Jensen, Rita Henley. 1990. "Minorities Didn't Share in Firm Growth." *National Law Journal,* Volume 12, 4, February 19:1, 28, 29, 31, 35, 36.

King, Sharon R. 1988. "Special Report: Black Women in Corporate America: At the Crossroads." *Black Enterprise* (August):45–61.

Leslie, Connie. 1987. "Making Doctors Human." *Newsweek on Campus* (September):39–40.

Luxenberg, Stan. 1985. *Roadside Empires.* New York: Viking.

Malcolm, Shirley. 1989. "Increasing the Participation of Black Women in Science and Technology." *Sage: A Scholarly Journal on Black Women* 6 (Fall):15–17.

Malveaux, Julianne. 1981. "Shifts in the Occupational and Employment Status of Black Women: Current Trends and Future Implications." In *Black Working Women. Proceedings of a Conference on Black Working Women in the U.S.,* 133–168. Berkeley: University of California.

———. 1985. "The Economic Interests of Black and White Women: Are They Similar?" *Review of Black Political Economy* 14 (Summer): 5–27.

———. 1990. "Gender Difference and Beyond: An Economic Perspective on Diversity and Commonality among Women." In Deborah L. Rhode (ed.), *Theoretical Perspectives on Sexual Difference,* 226–238. New Haven and London: Yale University Press.

Menkel-Meadow, Carrie J. 1987–88. "The Comparative Sociology of Women Lawyers: The 'Feminization' of the Legal Profession." Institute for Social Science Research Working Papers in the Social Sciences, vol. 3, no. 4, University of California, Los Angeles.

Nam, Charles B., and Mary G. Power. 1983. *The Socioeconomic Approach to Status Measurement.* Houston: Cap and Gown.

Nesbitt, Paula D. 1986. "Implications of Gender Mobility on Organization Communication: An Occupational Analysis." Unpublished manuscript, Harvard University.

Nkomo, Stella. 1986. "Race and Sex: The Forgotten Case of the Black Female Manager." Paper presented at Sixth Annual International Conference on Women in Organizations. N.P.

Reskin, Barbara F., and Patricia A. Roos. 1990. *Job Queues, Gender Queues: Explaining Women's Inroads into Male Occupations.* Philadelphia: Temple University Press.

Roach, Sharon L. 1990. "Men and Women Lawyers in In-House Legal Departments: Recruitment and Career Patterns." *Gender & Society* 4 (June):207–219.

Robinson, J. Gregg, and Judith S. McIlwee. 1989. "Women in Engineering: A Promise Unfulfilled?" *Social Problems* 36 (December):455–472.

Rush, Marjorie E. 1989. "Women in School Administration: Two Views." *Women in Government* 12 (Fall):4. SUNY, Albany: Center for Women in Government.

Schafran, Lynn Hecht. 1987. "Practicing Law in a Sexist Society." In Laura L. Crites and Winifred L. Hepperle (eds.), *Women, The Courts, and Equality,* 191–207. Newbury Park, Calif.: Sage.

Silver, Lori. 1990. "Few Women, Minorities at the Top." *Washington Post,* August 14:A1.

Skrzycki, Cindy. 1990. "Efforts Fail to Advance Women's Jobs: 'Glass Ceiling' Intact Despite New Benefits." *Washington Post,* February 20:A1.

Stille, Alexander. 1985. "Outlook Better for Women, Asians: Little Room at the Top for Blacks, Hispanics." *National Law Journal,* December 23:1,6–10.

Thurow, Lester. 1972. "Education and Economic Equality." *Public Interest* 28 (Summer):66–81.

Wallace, Phyllis. 1980. *Black Women in the Labor Force.* Cambridge, Mass.: MIT Press.

Weisenhaus, Doreen. 1988. "Still a Long Way to Go for Women, Minorities. " *National Law Journal,* February 8:1, 48, 50, 53,

Westcott, Diane Nilsen. 1982. "Blacks in the 1970s: Did They Scale the Job Ladder?" *Monthly Labor Review* 105 (June):29–38.

Further Questions

　　1. Did anything in the reading suggest to you that white men are losing ground in the job market to other racial or gender groups?

　　2. Can political movement help open job opportunities for disadvantaged groups? Should white men see it as a threat to their favored positions in the work force?

　　3. What are ghettoization and resegregation, and how do these function in the job market?

　　4. Did anything in the reading suggest that particular gender and racial groups occupy the lower rungs of the job hierarchy because that is their preference?

Target Hiring　　　　　　　　　　　　　　　　　　III.3

ANNE MINAS

This writing supports gender targets—setting in place goals of hiring certain percentages of women over a specified time, with the aim of increasing the numbers of women in certain positions. It is argued that this gives both genders fair opportunities for these positions and, at universities, is indispensable to fulfilling the proper function of these institutions.

Reading Questions

1. If gender is a factor in a decision to hire a certain candidate, does this mean that this candidate is less qualified than is someone else who was considered for the position but not hired?
2. If a person has spent considerable time qualifying himself for a position with the belief that his gender would be favored in hiring decisions, is it fair to him to put in place targets that make it more likely that members of the other gender will be hired?
3. Do colleges and universities have an obligation to society at large to provide thoughtful ideas about gender relations?

I

AN UNFORTUNATE LEGACY OF PATRIARCHY is the inflated perception of male qualification—the belief that being male adds to a persons qualifications. Gender targets in hiring are devices to remedy that misperception. When an employer has a target (sometimes called a "soft quota") to hire a certain proportion of women, he is forced to recruit women and to look closely at their credentials. If women and men in the same candidate pool appear equally qualified or have credentials that seem commensurate with each other, the employer must give women benefit of doubt; he must hire women in such situations until he has met his gender target. A gender target forces an employer to examine his thinking to make sure he is not favoring males.

These targets usually mandate that a certain proportion of women be hired or that explanations be given—in terms of recruitment efforts, credentials of candidates, and procedures for judging these credentials—as to why that proportion of qualified women could not be found. There is, then, no real conflict between target hiring and hiring according to qualification; in both, qualification is given its maximum weight in hiring decisions. Targets merely specify procedures that must be used in recruiting and judging candidates to ensure that these processes are not interfered with by external forces like patriarchy.

We assume all institutions have an interest in turning out a high quality product. The institution may be in a situation in which its product must be marketed in competition with like products of other institutions. Alternatively, an institution might have a particular clientele to whom it owes quality production, as universities owe high quality teaching and research to their communities, benefactors, students, and governments. In either case, unless interfered with by other forces, institutions will gravitate toward hiring personnel who are competent to turn out such products.

Far from interfering with such gravitation toward competence, targets give institutions additional incentive to exercise care in hiring those who are best qualified. Suppose a gender target provides pressure to hire a woman. Those who have doubts about the competence of women for the position will react by carefully scrutinizing the credentials of the women candidates. Such persons are also likely to try to find a qualified man and to prove that he has better credentials than any of the female candidates. We can anticipate that such a situation will result in a detailed, careful investigation and recording of the recruitment procedures and the judgments about the credentials of the leading candidates of both genders. The fact that a gender target is in place virtually precludes hasty judgments in which gender is a major factor.[1]

II

Gender targets thus help eliminate patriarchal bias in hiring practices and ensure that women will have better opportunities to attain positions. The expectation is that this will encourage more interested women to qualify themselves and apply. The only way to discover the level of interest that women have, for example, in philosophy, is to open the doors and see how many women walk in and apply for such positions. An institution that makes known its gender targets is taking active steps to recruit qualified women. It can be even more forceful in these recruitment efforts if it goes out and tries to find such women instead of simply waiting for the women to find it.

An institution may or may not have obligations to hire the best qualified candidates. However, as we have just seen, gender targets do give maximum weight to qualifications as a consideration in hiring. Their force is to ensure that the gender that was previously neglected in hiring practices receives adequate consideration of its credentials. The idea is that the only effective way to ensure this is to opt for the woman when there is no perceived difference between her qualifications and those of the man being considered. Men as a gender already have adequate attention drawn to their credentials (even though factors like color and class still make a difference within both genders between those whose credentials are adequately considered and those whose credentials are relatively neglected.) Men will continue to receive attention as long as targets require hiring specific numbers from each gender. Targets that mandate taking the woman in case she has perceived qualifications equal in weight to those of the man (until the gender target is met) serve only to offset the inflated perception of males' qualifications as mentioned earlier.

III

However, there is more at stake in gender target hiring than simply fairness to applicants of both genders. Studies of Jewish populations have shown that Jews, as individuals, can be assimilated into a society until their percentage of the population in that society reaches about 10 percent. In numbers above that percentage, Jews become visible enough to become subject to persecution. However, when their numbers reach 30 percent to 40 percent, Jews become strong enough to forestall or resist persecution efforts, provided the Jews have enough internal cohesiveness.[2]

The report to the Canadian Philosophical Association from the Committee to Study Hiring Policies Affecting Women, May 1991,[3] states, strikingly, that 13 percent of tenured and tenure-track positions in Canadian philosophy departments are held by women. The report recommends that the percentage of women in permanent faculty positions should be raised to 27 percent by the year 2000 and to 40 percent by the year 2010. These numbers would presumably make women strong enough so that they would not be vulnerable to victimization by male coalitions. The report also recommends that gender targets should exceed the current proportion of women in the candidate pool of new PhD recipients, which presently stands at about 28 percent. The message of the report is fairly clear. It encourages women to pursue careers in philosophy by attaining doctorates and applying for positions, so that philosophy departments and universities can meet their teaching and research responsibilities.

Our heritage has committed us to a tradition of democracy, which usually means rule by the majority. Sometimes, however, a majority becomes a coalition, acting in unison in pursuit of its interest at the expense of some group. This is often called "oligarchy." Patriarchy is a form of self-interested oligarchy, rule by men to benefit men at the expense of women. When men acquire and retain most of the positions connected with prestige, opportunities, and power—especially the power to determine who is hired, retained, or promoted—men can exclude women and, at the extreme, treat them ruth-

lessly. As long as the number of women hired is kept small, men can hold on to this power. According to the study of Jewish populations cited earlier, such patriarchal activity can function well in an environment in which 13 percent of the positions are held by women.

In addition, academic freedom gives all faculty a right to express themselves and behave toward each other as they see fit, within certain obvious limits. This can subject minority groups, including women, to what has become known as "a ton of feathers." Continual bombardment by patriarchally minded individuals speaking and acting individually can make women feel that there is something not quite right about them and that they lack full legitimacy as faculty members. A multitude of actions (e.g., general or quite specific questions about women's competence, exclusion from discussions where decision-making takes place, failure to consider women for positions of power, continually interrupting women, subjecting women to higher standards than male counterparts in everything from personal appearance and personal life to quality of teaching and research) can, in their totality, be quite devastating. The energy of women faculty is often dissipated on these brush fires, and their teaching and research may suffer. Yet even in such an environment, women are deemed inadequate if they fall short in their responsibilities as faculty members. Paradoxically, we women are often required to perform extraordinary feats of *machismo,* as when Peter O'Toole, as Lawrence of Arabia, leaves his hand in the candle flame saying, "The trick, you see, is not to *care* that it hurts." For example, a woman is not supposed to care if her chairman (as mine did) cuts her pay increase to, as he put it, "teach you a lesson."

The original intention of democracy and academic freedom in universities was to ensure a favorable climate for scholarship and teaching. But like many institutions that can be used to promote good, these can be used to promote just the opposite. Academic freedom leaves people free to say and do quite harmful things to one another. Democracy allows a majority to oppress a minority. In particular, men can use these two institutions to keep women in a subordinate position according to the principle of "might makes right."

Universities also see the odd phenomenon of the converse of this principle—right also makes might: ". . . because one knows what is morally right, it is morally appropriate . . . to dominate others. One understands one's agency as that of the judge, teacher/preacher, director, administrator."[4] Too many men still think themselves possessed of a moral vision that is superior to that of women, which allows them to exercise their patriarchal power to full capacity. This includes structuring hiring practices for new positions. For example, when my philosophy department set its gender hiring quotas in the fall of 1990, none of our three women faculty were consulted. The decision was made by a small coalition of "right-thinking" men, apparently so sure of their vision that they simply announced it to the department as a whole as a *fait accompli*. (The coalition left out some of the men in the department as well. However, because the decision was about the relative gender composition of the department in the future, it was a real anomaly that representatives of only one gender were consulted.) Thus patriarchy perpetuates itself by shutting out voices of women as long as it has power to do so.

A university does not properly serve its students or its community by promulgating a single way of thinking, that of the white, able-bodied, ethnically correct, financially secure, heterosexual male. Graduates should not leave a university with the idea that philosophy, leadership, moral correctness, or anything else is the prerogative of just one kind of person. Universities should be about diversity as well as about whatever content of the disciplines remains constant through diversity. In particular, universities should not teach students that patriarchy is a form of justice, or that there are no alternative way of organizing society.

Many women who presently hold faculty positions have lived though quite brutal encounters with patriarchy. Many of us hope our experiences were not in vain—that somehow things will be better for our younger counterparts. Gender target hiring until we become strong enough in numbers to resist patriarchy by democratic procedures may not be the only solution, but it is one solution.

NOTES

1. This is something like Mary Ann Warren's argument regarding quota hiring. Each occasion on which an employer favored gender A over qualification would have to be compensated on a later occasion by his favoring gender B over qualification to make his quotas come out properly. (Mary Ann Warren, "Secondary Sexism and Quota Hiring," reprinted in *Philosophy and Women,* Sharon Bishop and Marjorie Weinzweig, eds., (Belmont, CA: Wadsworth, 1979), 243. Warren's argument should assuage anyone's worries about targets hardening into quotas in cases where targets specify the same gender proportions as those in the candidate pool. The employer would have no incentive to favor gender over qualifications.

2. Stanislav Andreski, "An Economic Interpretation of Antisemitism" in *Race, Ethnicity and Social Change,* John Stone, ed. (Belmont, CA: Wadsworth, 1977), 126–127.

3. Report to the Canadian Philosophical Association from the Committee to Study Hiring Policies Affecting Women, May 1991, Brenda Baker, Josiane Boulad Ayoub, Lorraine Code, Michael McDonald, Kathleen Okruhlik, Susan Sherwin, Wayne Summer (unpublished; copies circulated to all members of the Canadian Philosophical Association).

4. Marilyn Frye, "A Response to *Lesbian Ethics*" in *Feminist Ethics,* Claudia Card, ed. (Lawrence, KS: University Press of Kansas, 1991), 54.

Further Questions

1. In a situation of target hiring, should a candidate's credentials be made light of, or scrutinized with extra care?

2. Do men possess better leadership qualities than women, so that they should take charge of all matters in the workplace, including hiring decisions?

3. If middle-aged men have been the beneficiaries of gender discrimination in past hiring decisions, ought they be forced to step down from their positions so that gender targets will not lower the chances of younger men's being hired?

Tokenism and Stereotyping: Objectification   III.4

LILLIAN COMAS-DÍAZ AND BEVERLY GREENE

Lillian Comas-Díaz and Beverly Greene discuss the matters of tokenism and stereotyping for women of color in the professions. Being hired, or being believed to be hired, as a token implies a belief that the woman is not qualified for her position. Women can also be degraded in the workplace by being stereotyped as mothers, sisters, daughters, wives, mistresses, prostitutes, or care-givers.

Comas-Díaz is Executive Director of the Transcultural Mental Health Institute and a clinical psychologist in private practice in Washington, DC. Greene is Associate Professor of Psychology at St. John's University and a clinical psychologist in private practice in New York City.

Reading Questions

1. If you saw very few women of color in a work place, would you assume that they had been hired as tokens? Would you think that they had been hired as a result of a policy of affirmative action? Would you assume they were unqualified?

2. If you were assumed to be a token, would you expect have to work doubly hard to get your achievements noticed? Would you mind the heightened visibility for you that came with being seen as a token?

3. If you, as a token, were taken to be representative of all women of color, or of all women of your ethnic group, would you feel that you had shouldered a heavy burden? Do you think it would interfere with your own tasks and goals at work?

Excerpts from Women of Color: Integrating Ethnic and Gender Identities in Psychotherapy *(New York: The Guilford Press, 1994). Reprinted by permission.*

TOKENISM

In an era of declining support for affirmative action policies revealed by such things as reverse discrimination lawsuits and financial constraints (cited as the reason for not meeting minority quotas), why and how women and people of color have been professionally advanced has become an issue of public discussion (Romero & Garza, 1986). According to Greider (1991), whenever people are losing their jobs and socioeconomic decline is visible, it is often easier to blame the troubles on racial minorities—especially those who have made some advancement—than it is to confront the political leaders who are responsible. Women of color may be particularly targeted by such scapegoating, because of their dual "categories," gender and race, and long-standing negative stereotypes about women and people of color. This double discrimination in the professional domain takes its form in claims of tokenism.

Being the only woman of color (or one of the very few) in a professional setting means becoming a token, a symbol of how women of color do, a role model for all women of color. Often, a token position is designed to give affirmative action credibility to an institution. As a double minority, a woman of color can be perceived as a double token—filling two affirmative action categories (female and race/ethnicity) in a single person (Wyche & Graves, 1992). Although many of the professional women of color may not experience direct blatant discrimination on the job, there is a tendency to question their qualifications by presuming that their gender and race and not their merit got them the position or gave them an advantage.

In a poignant discussion of tokenism among women in the corporate world, Kanter (1977) observes that it is the proportionally small numbers of women, rather than femaleness per se, that breeds the dynamics of tokenism. She states that the charge of tokenism, like powerlessness, sets in motion self-perpetuating cycles that reinforce the low numbers of women in professional settings and maintains the perception of them as tokens.

Being hired as a token, or being perceived that way by coworkers is a form of racism because it implies that the woman of color with professional status is not qualified for her position. Although women of color get attention and heightened visibility by being tokens, and thus the token does not have to work hard to be noticed, paradoxically, the woman of color has to work extraordinarily hard to have her achievements noticed. According to Kanter (1977), the presence of a token causes members of the dominant group to become more aware of their commonality, and to preserve their commonality they try to keep the token slightly outside. This has detrimental consequences for the token, such as loneliness and alienation. Indeed, many of the women that Kanter studied had higher turnover and failure rates than their male counterparts.

Being a token means encountering special pressures. As an illustration, women of color may alternate between being showcased (being highly visible) and being invisible. They may be showcased by their employers as documentation of conforming to affirmative action policies, but also as proving that by hiring a woman of color they have progressive attitudes and are above prejudice. In other words, showcasing a professional woman of color may be an example of being politically correct. However, being showcased can affect negatively the performance of the professional woman, as we see in the following vignette.

> Maria, an American Indian woman, was repeatedly asked to represent her department during interagency meetings. The majority of these meetings had nothing to do with Maria's actual position in the agency. When she complains about the inordinate time spent attending these meetings, her supervisors replied that her department needed minority representation and that she was the only person of color. After 6 months, Maria was formally counseled by her immediate supervisor because of a decrease in her work productivity. Consequently, Maria felt that by being showcased at the expense of her work, she was indirectly penalized for being a woman of color in a professional setting.

The converse dynamic of a token's visibility is invisibility. The heightened awareness of hiring women of color who are professionals can paradoxically result in making them invisible. Castro (1990) investigated the tokens' invisibility in a study on the multicultural labor force in the United States conducted by Rutgers University. The study found that white women and women of color suffer from an invisibility syndrome, in which white male managers commonly tend to ignore them in meetings and thus overlook their contributions.

Tokens tend to perform their jobs under public and symbolic conditions different from those of the members of the majority group. The token visibility phenomenon makes women of color public figures, at times causing them to lose their individuality and privacy. Because their lives are put in the limelight, their work and behavior are more closely scrutinized than that of other employees. Their mistakes and intimate relationships also become public knowledge (Kanter, 1977). Women of color may feel that their freedom of action is restricted and that they have less independence than members of the dominant group.

Being a symbol or a representative of all women of color, of all persons of color, of all African Americans (Latinos, Asian Americans, American Indians, etc.) can be potentially draining (Wiltz, 1991). For example, in discussing the dilemmas faced by African American women in leadership positions, Dumas (1980) states that these women are torn between their symbolic image to others in the organization and their own professional tasks and goals. Regardless of their professional expertise, women of color may be asked to provide an ethnic minority perspective, or a woman's perspective, or both. The extended symbolic consequences of their behavior are powerful for many of these women, who have real reasons to feel that their performance could affect the prospects of other women and men of color in the professional setting. Indeed, the existence of successful ethnic minority role models can help to counteract racist opinions that people of color cannot succeed (Williams, 1990). Although some women of color may embrace this symbolism and decide to represent some or all people of color, they may do so at the expense of their own individual needs. They may also make themselves easy scapegoats in this regard. For example, women of color may be punished if what they say makes those in power uncomfortable or contradicts their view of themselves as liberal minded.

Tokenism can also involve not being taken seriously at work, resulting in being assigned tasks below one's capacity, bearing minimal responsibilities, or being placed in a dead-end job. For example, Jenkins (1985) argues that for African American women, significant barriers in the labor market often relegate these women to marginal positions within the workplace, threatening their well-being.

Tokenism may afford an initial access to professional positions for women of color. However, being perceived as a token also entails a denial of the woman's capabilities. For instance, many majority group members often attribute people of color's successes to luck or other situational factors, while attributing failures to laziness, stupidity, or other internal factors (Weitz & Gordon, 1993). Likewise, professional women of color carry the burden of needing to prove that their achievement is more than the result of affirmative action policies. As Carter (1991) asserts, some individuals suspect that all people of color with professional status achieved their status because of affirmative action policies, and not because of their merit. He terms this suspicion the "qualification question."

Paradoxically, if women of color become too successful, they run the risk of being penalized. This penalization is translated into retaliation by the members of the dominant group. Kanter (1977) argues that when a token does well enough to out-perform members of the dominant group, it cannot be kept a secret, since the token's behavior is public and therefore it is more difficult to avoid being publicly humiliated by a colleague from the dominant group. On the other hand, the woman's success may be kept conspicuously secret or minimized. It may be hard for some women of color to maintain the fine balancing act between doing well and doing too well, thus generating peer resentment.

The culture within professional settings appears to have institutionalized a practice to impede women of color from becoming too successful (i.e., more successful than members of the dominant group). The glass ceiling phenomenon is an illustration of such a practice. Women and ethnic minorities encounter an invisible barrier that limits their advancement toward upper management in organizations in the United States. The phrase "glass ceiling" refers to a barrier so subtle that it is transparent, yet so strong that it prevents women and people of color from moving up in the management hierarchy (Morrison & Von Glinow, 1990; Wiltz, 1991).

STEREOTYPING: OBJECTIFICATION BASED ON GENDER AND RACE

Ingrained cultural conditioning socializes men to think of women in terms of stereotypes. As Lott (1991) argues, expectations of status and power are embedded in gender. These stereotyped attributions are carried into the workplace. For example, Harragan (1977) argues that many men have had no prior experience in dealing with women as autonomous individuals, instead, in the workplace they assign them the stereotyped role of mother, sister, daughter, wife, mistress, prostitute, or nurturer of some kind (nurse, teacher, etc.). Empirical research seems to corroborate some of these notions. As an illustration, McKenzie-Mohr and Zanna (1990) found that men previously identified as strongly gender schematic were found more often than other men to have sexual feelings about a woman in a professional situation after being exposed to nonviolent pornography.

Most women of color have been socially and legally perceived as paradigmatic sex objects in the United States. As an illustration, hooks (1991) argues that African American women have been the recipients of white male misog-

yny, and white women defended against it by the denying and/or justifying African American women's scapegoating. Additionally, African American women have been portrayed in the literature and media as being mammies or matriarchs, or as sexually promiscuous, castrating, or masculinized females (Carey, 1990; Gilkes, 1982; Greene, 1990, 1994; McGoldrick et al., 1989). This type of stereotyping has serious implications for African American women who are assertive and/or are in authority positions.

Latinas may tend to be stereotyped into the Madonna/whore or Virgin Mary/Eve complex (Almquist, 1989; Comas-Díaz, 1989; Espín, 1986). On the one hand they are perceived as being overly sexual, promiscuous, sexually available (whore), and self-serving temptresses (Eve), while on the other, they are perceived to be virginal, chaste, sexually repressed, altruistic, martyred, and madonna-like woman (Virgin Mary) (Almquist, 1989; Espín, 1986). This type of objectification, reinforced in the popular media, makes it difficult for some males to take Latinas who have professional status seriously.

Asian American women are stereotyped as being submissive, shy, quiet, gentle, unassertive (Chow, 1989; McGoldrick et al., 1982), but also sexually attractive and available (Chan, 1987). There are also the more specific stereotypes of them as sexually exotic and eager to please (geisha) (Chan, 1987), as monstrously threatening (dragon lady) if they are too strong and assertive, or as gender neutral (i.e. as a sexless worker bee) (Loo, 1988; True, 1990). Furthermore, True (1990) states that due to the persistence of stereotyping Asian American women as hardworking and uncomplaining handmaidens, they are often exploited in their work. The sexual and racial stereotypes often affect the peer relationships of professional women of color, for example, a Chinese American woman developed a confrontational interpersonal style with her colleagues because she was tired of being perceived as a China doll.

American Indian women are the most invisible women of color (Almquist, 1989). They represent perhaps the least researched group of people in the United States (Snipp, 1990). According to Allen (1986), self-image constitutes the central issue with which American Indian women must come to terms. She argues that negative images of American Indians in the media and educational materials profoundly affect American Indian women's sense of self, how they behave, and how they relate to others. Nonetheless, some American Indian women in professional settings may attempt to embody exotic and mythical images for the benefit of coworkers. Although there is wide diversity among American Indian women, members of mainstream society often stereotype them as the American Indian princess or Pocahontas figure (Green, 1976). Seeing an American Indian woman as a Pocahontas involves attributing to her courage, resourcefulness, and a devotion to whites that historical accounts ascribe to this historical figure (Stevens, 1950). Conversely, a different stereotype involves assuming that American Indian professional women are too culturally committed, making their priorities the family and the cultural group as opposed to the job (Teresa LaFromboise, personal communication, 1992). This stereotype implies that American Indian women may not be properly committed to their professional work, and thus, should not be taken seriously. There are of course other stereotypes of American Indian women with professional status resulting from an objectification based on race and gender.

REFERENCES

Allen, P. G. (1986). *The sacred hoop: Recovering the feminism in American Indian traditions.* Boston: Beacon.

Almquist, E. (1989). The experience of minority women in the United States. In J. Freeman (Ed.), *Women: A feminist perspective* (4th ed., pp. 414–445). Mountain View, CA: Mayfield.

Carey, P. M. (1990). Beyond superwoman: On being a successful black administrator. *Journal of National Association for Women Deans, Administrators, and Counselors, 53,* 15–19.

Carter, S. T. (1991). *Reflections of an affirmative action baby.* New York: Basic Books.

Castro, J. (1990, Fall). Get set: Here they come! *Time* [Special Issue, *Women: The road ahead*], *136,* 50–52.

Chan, C. S. (1987). Asian American women: Psychological responses to sexual exploitation and cultural stereotypes. *Women and Therapy, 6,* 33–38.

Chow, E. N. (1989). The feminist movement: Where are all the Asian American women? In Asian Women United of California (Ed.), *Making waves: An anthology of writings by and about Asian American women.* Boston: Beacon.

Comas-Díaz, L. (1989). Culturally relevant issues and treatment implications for Hispanics. In D. R. Koslow & E. Salett (Eds.), *Crossing cultures in mental health* (pp. 31–48). Washington, DC: Society for International Education Training and Research (SIETAR).

Dumas, R. (1980). Dilemmas of black females in leadership. In L. Rodgers-Rose (Ed.), *The black woman* (pp. 201–215). Newbury Park, CA: Sage.

Espín, O. M. (1986). Cultural and historical influences on sexuality in Hispanic/Latin women. In J. Cole (Ed.), *All American women* (pp. 272–284). New York: Free Press.

Gilkes, C. T. (1982). Successful rebellious professionals: The Black woman's professional identity and community commitment. *Psychology of Women Quarterly,*

Green, R. (1976). The Pocahontas perplex: The image of Indian women in American culture. *Massachusetts Review, 14,* 698–714.

Greene, B. (1990). Sturdy bridges: The role of African American mothers in the socialization of African American children. *Women and Therapy, 10,* 205–225.

Greene, B. (1994). Diversity and difference: The issue of race in feminist therapy. In M. P. Mirkin (Ed.), *Women in context: Toward a feminist reconstruction of psychotherapy* (pp. 333–351). New York: Guilford.

Greider, W. (1991, September 5). The politics of diversion: Blame it on the Blacks. *Rolling Stone,* pp. 32–33, 96.

Harragan, B. L. (1977). *Games mother never taught you: Corporate gamemanship for women.* New York: Warner.

hooks, b. (1981). *Black Women and Feminism.* Boston, MA. South End Press.

Jenkins, I. M. (1985). The integration of psycho-therapy-vocational interventions: Relevance for Black women. *Psychotherapy, 22,* 394–397.

Kanter, E. R. (1977). *Men and women of the corporation.* New York: Basic Books.

Lott, B. (1991). Social psychology: Humanistic roots and feminist future. *Psychology of Women Quarterly, 15,* 505–519.

Loo, C. (1988, August). *Socio-cultural barriers to the achievement of Asian American women.* Paper presented at the 96th annual convention of the American Psychological Association, Atlanta, GA.

McGoldrick, M., Pearce, J. K., & Giordano, J. (Eds.). (1982). *Ethnicity and family therapy.* New York: Guilford.

McKenzie-Mohr, D., & Zanna, M. P. (1990). Treating women as sexual objects: Look to the (gender schematic) male who has viewed pornography. *Personality and Social Psychology Bulletin, 16,* 296–308.

Morrison, A. M., & Von Glinow, M. A. (1990). Women and minorities in management. *American Psychologist, 45,* 200–208.

Romero, G. J., & Garza, R. T. (1986). Attributions for the occupational success/failure of ethnic minority and nonminority women. *Sex Roles, 14,* 445–452.

Snipp, C. M. (1990). A portrait of American Indian women and their labor force experiences. In S. E. Rix (Ed.), *The American woman, 1990–91: A status report* (pp. 265–272). New York: Norton.

Stevens, W. (1950). *Famous women of America.* New York: Dodd, Meade.

True, R. H. (1990). Psychotherapeutic issues with Asian American women. *Sex Roles, 22,* 477–486.

Weitz, R., & Gordon, L. (1993). Images of Black women among Anglo college students, *Sex Roles, 28,* 19–34.

Williams, L. E. (1990). The challenges before Black women in higher education. *Journal of the National Association for Women Deans, Administrators, and Counselors, 53,* 1–2.

Wiltz, T. (1991, May). Glass-ceiling survival. *Essence, 35,* 37.

Wyche, K. F., & Graves, S. B. (1992). Minority women in Academia: Access and barriers to professional participation. *Psychology of Women Quarterly, 16,* 429–437.

Further Questions

1. As a token, would you have the potential problem of outperforming members of the dominant group and being penalized for it? At the same time, would you need to prove that you achieved your status through merit and that your successes were not due to sheer luck?

2. Name some problems that a woman in the work place might have if she is perceived chiefly through one or more stereotypes.

3. What kinds of problems does a woman of color have if she is stereotyped as an African American, a Latina, an Asian American, or an American Indian woman?

The Comparable Worth Debate   III.5

ELLEN FRANKEL PAUL

Ellen Frankel Paul discusses the concept of comparable worth, comparing two types of occupations to determine whether they are different or equal in value. Advocates of making such comparisons argue that women are often clustered in occupations equal in value to those in which men predominate, and therefore deserve to be paid the same as men in these comparable positions. Paul disagrees with these advocates.

Paul is research director and professor of political science at the Social Philosophy and Policy Center at Bowling Green State University. She is author of numerous articles and books in political, economic, and moral theory.

Reading Questions

1. Do different types of work have objective qualities that can be used to set the value of the work of each type?
2. Is one line of work better in all respects than a second line of work if it is paid a better wage?
3. Is an unregulated market a "democratic" way of setting prices and wages, since we all participate in the market by buying and selling goods and services?

COMPARABLE WORTH, or pay equity in its newer guise, is an attractive concept: if only employers could be required to pay female employees in traditionally female occupations the same salaries as males in male-dominated jobs of comparable value to their employers, then the wage gap would largely disappear. Advocates for women's equality have become increasingly enthusiastic about this strategy for achieving their goals, as they have seen other legal remedies—the Equal Pay Act, Title VII of the Civil Rights Act—fail to secure to women this elusive equality.

Comparable worth in the 1980s has achieved remarkable strides, virtually sweeping the country. Despite comparable worth's seeming novelty—it is a concept that has caught fire only recently—the idea has been around for quite a while. In fact, the notion of "comparable work"

was employed by the National War Labor Board during World War II. The board required equal pay for comparable work and made job evaluations within plants between dissimilar jobs to determine whether any pay inequities existed. Every Congress since 1945 has entertained a comparable work bill of various types.[1]

"Equal pay for equal work" is not the objective of the comparable worth advocates, for that standard has been the law of the land since 1963, when the Equal Pay Act was approved by Congress as an amendment to the Fair Labor Standards Act. Since then, it has been illegal to pay women less than men doing "substantially equal" work.[2] For many advocates of women's equality, however, this standard does not go nearly far enough. It leaves important gaps in the protection afforded to women workers; for example,

Abridged from "Introduction" and "Some Philosophical Considerations" in Equity and Gender: The Comparable Worth Debate *(New Brunswick, NJ: Transaction Publishers, 1989), pp. 1–7, 109–130. Reprinted by permission of the publisher and author.*

women who labor in jobs with no equivalent male jobs available for purposes of comparison are left unprotected as are women whose work is comparable to men's but not equal by the "substantially equal" standard. If over half the women in the United States work in jobs that are 75 percent dominated by women, then more must be done to alleviate their lot than simply securing them equal pay for equal work.[3]

However, comparable worth's advocates are not merely pointing to a lacunae in the law. They seek sweeping reforms that would question the very foundation of our market-based economic system. What they doubt is not the efficiency of the market but its justice. Why, they ask, should a female registered nurse whose skills require years of training and whose responsibility for the preservation of human life is so great be paid less than a garbage man? Why should a social worker, another female-dominated job classification, receive less pay than a truck driver, when the social worker requires years of schooling and must exercise considerable judgment in guiding the lives of others? Why do women working full-time earn a mere 64 cents to men's one dollar? Something must be radically amiss in a market system that produces such patent inequities, the advocates conclude. . . .

Despite Marx's abhorrence of this fact, labor power is as much a commodity as anything else. The price of any particular kind of labor is set by the same criteria as any other good. The market price equates supply and demand; each laborer is paid the equivalent of his marginal productivity, his contribution to the enterprise. Marginal utility theory, thus, overcame another problem inherent in a labor theory of value: that every factor of production—labor, land, entrepreneurship—required a different theory to explain how its price was set.

Now, what bearing does all of this have on comparable worth? Comparable worth shares with the labor theory of value a desire to discover some objective characteristics of worth or value apart from the valuations in the marketplace derived from the choices of actual buyers. For comparable worth, the hours of labor embodied in a

thing no longer set its value, but rather, the value of labor itself can be determined by assessing its components: knowledge, skills, mental demands, accountability, working conditions.

What comparable worth's proponents are searching for is some identifiable, objective qualities that are transferable from job to job and that everyone could, at least theoretically, agree upon. But are they not searching in vain? The perpetual squabbles among evaluators performing studies in the states, the instructions of consultants to the evaluation committees that they should go with their gut instincts in assessing points, and the reevaluations that go on once the scores have been assembled are empirical evidence of a problem that really lies on the theoretical level.

If there is no intrinsic value to a job, then it cannot be measured. Let us look at the wage-setting process as it unfolds in the market to see what the price of labor means, if it does not mean a measurement of intrinsic value.

A job has value to someone who creates it and is willing to pay someone to do it. The price of that job is set in the labor market, which is nothing more than an arena for satisfying the demands for labor of various sorts by numerous employers. What an employer is willing to pay for the type of labor he needs depends on his assessment of what that labor can contribute to the ultimate product and what price he thinks those products will command in the market. The labor market is an impersonal process. In most cases, employers and potential employees do not know each other before the process is begun. It is impersonal in another way, also. No individual employer can exercise much influence over the price of labor of the kind he needs. Only in the rarest of cases, where no alternative employers are available to willing workers, will any one employer have much of an impact on the overall job market. Such influence characterizes centrally planned, government-owned economies much more than it does market economies. To the extent that markets are distorted by government-imposed monopolies or cartels, the actual market departs from the theoretical one.

The supporters of comparable worth consider this view of the market naive. Rather, they say, markets are dominated by monopolies that dictate wages to workers who by-and-large have no other options. The problem with this argument is that it is simply not true that the labor market in the United States is largely dominated by monopolies. What has characterized capitalist economies since the Industrial Revolution is precisely the options that workers have, the fluidity of labor markets, and the ever-changing possibilities the market creates. Unlike the Middle Ages, where workers' options were essentially limited to following the paternal occupation and where class status was very nearly immutable, capitalism presents workers with a plethora of options.

Another problem with this quest for objective value or worth is that it confuses oral language with economic language. Surely, economists talk about value: They mean by the value of a commodity what it will trade for at any particular time in the marketplace. There is nothing mysterious, no essence that lies buried beneath this market value (at least since the labor theory of value was abandoned).

What the comparable worth people mean by value is something essential to any particular type of labor. They are looking for some higher order moral principle that, irrespective of the market, can compare the work of the plumber to the tree-trimmer to the grocer to the secretary to the nurse. Within our society, there is no agreement about higher order moral principles: about what contributes to the good life; what activities are worthy of pursuit in their own right; what kinds of behavior contribute to the welfare of society. How can we expect individuals in society to agree about how particular jobs contribute to ends, when those ends themselves are in dispute?

Wouldn't it be an unpleasant world if people did agree about values, if those values could be objectively measured as they were exemplified in different jobs, and if they were paid accordingly? Then, if Michael Jackson earned a million dollars for each performance while an emergency room nurse received $20 for her work during the same two hours, we would know that he was really worth 50,000 times as much as she; that is, that society valued her contribution so very much less. We would know, simply by the salary paid to each person in such a society, exactly what his social contribution and, presumably, his social status was. But on a market we cannot even infer that a plumber making $10 an hour is worth more or less to his employer than a teacher who earns the same wage is worth to hers. Such comparisons are vacuous. One's worth, in the moral sense, is not measured in the marketplace by one's wage. Price and salary are economic terms, and they depend upon the available supply and the demand for particular kinds of labor. Value and worth are moral terms, as comparable worth's supporters intend them, and they do not equate well at all with price in the marketplace. Thus, even the market cannot equate the worth (in the moral sense) of one job with another; all it shows is that at any particular time secretaries are paid more or less than zoo keepers.

Any attempt to employ "objective" job assessment criteria must be inherently discretionary. That blanket statement stands unrefuted by the comparable worth camp. I believe it is logically impossible for them to surmount this difficulty: for they cannot find objectivity by appealing to the views of experts who, as human beings, bring their prejudices to any assessment; nor can they find it by abandoning the market and embracing central planning, which is nothing more than personal whims enshrined in decrees. Either way, the judgments of bureaucrats or judges would be forcibly substituted for the assessments of those who are the actual purchasers of labor services. This is unavoidable, since there is no intrinsic value to any job. The impersonal forces of the market would have to be replaced by subjective judgments, by the opinions of "experts." Even if these "experts" were bereft of all tastes—which is, of course, inconceivable—they could not implement a system of objective measurement. Where is the metric? None is to be found. While each person can order his own preferences, these separate preference orders cannot be equated. Similarly, different jobs cannot be equated on any objective scale, at least not until everyone is in agreement about ultimate moral values. Even then, their particular application would be open to differences of opinion.

The comparable worth critics are correct: there is no intrinsic value to any job, and, hence, they can neither be measured or compared. . . .

. . . if an employer, through discriminatory motivation or any other reason, wishes to pay less than the prevailing wage for a certain kind of labor, one of three things will normally happen. He will get no takers. He will get fewer takers than he needs. Or the quality of the applicant pool will be lower than the job requires. Conversely, if he wishes to pay more, he will get many applicants and some of them will be of higher quality than normal in that job classification.

In the former case, the employer jeopardizes his business by presumably making his products less marketable and his operation less efficient; in the latter case, the employer may benefit his business if his more skilled employees produce more products or a better product that the consumers are willing to pay a higher price to acquire. The consumer, however, may not be willing, and then the business would be jeopardized.

Thus, employers are, in the normal case, pretty much tied to paying prevailing market wages. Those employers who discriminate for irrelevant reasons—like race, sex, religion—put themselves at a competitive disadvantage by restricting the pool of labor from which they can select workers. If discrimination against blacks or women, for example, were prevalent in the society, the price of such labor would be lower than for comparable labor provided by members of other groups. Those employers willing to hire the despised will benefit from lower prices for their labor and will enjoy a competitive edge. In the absence of laws enshrined by governments to perpetuate discrimination, the market should correct for it over time by penalizing discriminatory employers and rewarding the others. Eventually, the wages of the discriminated will rise.

If jobs have no intrinsic worth, then the comparable worth position has been severely wounded, for it bases its case on precisely such an assumption. What I have argued is that jobs have no intrinsic value within the context of a market economy. Now, that is an important caveat. A competing system, one that sets the prices for all goods, services, and labor by a central planning agency could provide an alternative framework to the market. But would the price of various types of labor be objectively set in such a system? All we could say is that the planners would tell everyone else what each job was worth. Via job evaluations, direct flashes of insight, or whatever methodology they chose, the wages of labor would be set and everyone would abide by those directives. One might call such a system objective in the sense that departures from the assigned wages might be punishable, but using the term in the way we normally do, it seems like rampant subjectivism. As John Stuart Mill wrote a century ago:

A fixed rule, like that of equality, might be acquiesced in, and so might chance, or an external necessity; but that a handful of human beings should weight everybody in the balance, and give more to one and less to another at their *sole* pleasure and judgment, would not be borne unless from persons believed to be more than men, and backed by supernatural terrors . . .[4]

. . . there is something else fundamentally flawed about the proponents' line of argument. Comparable worth cannot eliminate discrimination from the labor market, and neither can any other scheme, including the market. The purpose of any hiring process is precisely to discriminate. A personnel director does not only look for skills in hiring an applicant. Such intangibles as personality, looks, motivation, and so forth play a factor. Just as any employer discriminates in hiring, so the consulting firms or wage boards would impose their tastes and value judgments.

One kind of discrimination that is particularly invidious is government-imposed discrimination. Apartheid is one example; the policies toward Hungarians in Rumania and Turks in Bulgaria, are others. What makes this kind of discrimination so odious is that it is government-imposed, and hence nearly inescapable. Discrimination in the market is haphazard and usually escapable: one employer may not like women, another doesn't like blacks but doesn't mind women, while most look for the best person to do the job. If you don't like the wages or the conditions in one firm, you can join another or start your own. The comparable worth consulting firms, and what I see as the inevitable wage boards, court-appointed masters, or judicial "wage boards," denote more the apartheid and less the market kind of discrimination. The standards would be government mandated and inescapable, except by leaving the country. . . .

If discrimination—meaning tastes—is irremediable, why should we prefer comparable worth and the discrimination of "experts" to the market and the discrimination generated by the free choices of all of us? . . .

MARKETS EXPRESS CONSUMER SOVEREIGNTY

Employers are consumers of labor, but they are also intermediaries between the ultimate consumers of their products and their laborers. Employers produce goods by combining various factors of production, and they hope these goods will mesh with what consumers want. They do so as efficiently as their competitors, or else they are soon out of business. Thus, comparable worth is not simply an attempt to replace the decisions of employers with the decisions of "experts," bureaucrats, and judges: Comparable worth seeks ultimately to replace the decisions of consumers themselves about how they wish to spend their money.

To most comparable worth advocates, those who embrace comparable worth because they see it as a means for bettering women's earnings, the tendency of comparable worth to undermine consumer sovereignty ought to be disturbing. Women are consumers, and they ought to value the liberty that has created the abundance we all enjoy. The more radical supporters of comparable worth, however, understand that the concept

is a wedge they can use to undermine our free market economy, and I expect that they are not at all disconcerted by the tendency of comparable worth to replace the choice of consumers with the opinions of "experts." These radicals constitute, however, only a small proportion of those who support comparable worth.

MARKETS ARE IMPERSONAL

If secretaries and nurses on average receive lower salaries than accountants and auto mechanics, it is not because any one group of "experts" has determined that the latter are more worthy than the former. It is simply a function of supply and demand. While individual employers may operate their businesses as idiosyncratically as they like (within, of course, the current labor and civil rights laws of the United States), they follow discriminatory wage policies at their peril. If fewer women choose to become nurses and secretaries, these occupations will receive higher remuneration in the future.

To condemn the marketplace because some employers discriminate, as comparable worth does, and to expect that a system that eliminates discrimination can be devised, is to search for the Holy Grail. Such utopian quests typically end in disaster, in inflicting on human beings infinitely worse suffering than they endured before the revolutionaries tried to remake mankind. Our collective experience as a species with attempts to better society by placing decisions in the hands of enlightened experts, those who know the truth, have all been colossal failures. The record of revolutionary societies in our century in the treatment of minorities is much worse than the record of free market societies, South Africa included. If one doubts this, examine the lot of the Chinese in Vietnam, the Crimean Tatars, Jews, Germans, and other non-Russian peoples in the Soviet Union, the Turks in Bulgaria, the Hungarians in Rumania, the Eritreans in Ethiopia . . .

My purpose in adverting to this list of human atrocities is not to equate support for comparable worth with support for the gulags. Rather, I would caution the supporters of comparable worth that the attempt to make society dramatically better by perfecting the results of the free choices of real people is more often than not—dare I say, always—calamitous. Those we place in power to perfect us are human, too, and whatever failings they have tend to be magnified by the possession of power over other people's lives. To the extent that comparable worth replaces impersonal market forces with the opinions of "experts," it flirts with the potential of doing great harm.

MARKETS ARE EFFICIENT

In contrast to centrally planned economies, which have proven notoriously inefficient, market systems produce bounties undreamt of in past centuries. Comparable worth seems to require courts or wage boards to intervene continuously in the operations of all firms. With all the disruptions and inefficiencies such intervention would cause, a movement to explicit central planning of the economy would be the logical next step. Something would have to provide a "cure" for the dislocations caused by perpetual comparable worth evaluations, and since the market is out, central planning would be the only logical alternative. . . .

MARKETS ALLOW FREEDOM OF EXIT AND ENTRY

If a woman does not like the terms of employment offered to her, if she thinks the proffered wage is too low, she is perfectly free to seek another employer or strike out on her own. No one is perpetually tied to a job, as has been the practice off and on in some centrally planned economies. If one feels that as a secretary one is being discriminated against in relation to an office manager, one can acquire new skills and become an office manager or go into an entirely different line of work.

Comparable worth's advocates deride such a fluid vision of women's choices: "Aren't women stuck in the low-paying jobs they've trained for? Millions of women have invested their time in becoming nurses, secretaries, teachers, and social workers. Let's make sure they are paid more; let's not demand that they change their occupations."

Where this line of argument misfires is in assuming that millions of women would have to change jobs to increase their wages. This simply is not true. If enough women (at the margin, to use the economist's term) moved out of these jobs, or more realistically, if younger women did not replace their departing older sisters in sufficient numbers, the wages for those remaining would rise—without comparable worth and just as a result of natural market forces.

Women should not expect to eat their cake and have it too. If they want to flock to these traditionally female occupations—for some perfectly good reasons relating to family responsibilities—they should understand that one of the drawbacks to making the same choice as millions of others is that one contributes to the oversupply of labor in one's chosen field. Men know this. If there are too many middle managers and the economy takes a nose dive, then middle managers will be pounding the pavement. If there are too many lawyers, their salaries will decline.

As free individuals, women have choices. Older women, if they are dissatisfied with their salaries as teachers or nurses, can retrain for other more lucrative jobs or can start businesses of their own, as indeed, many of them have done. Younger women can train for traditionally male occupations, as indeed, millions of them have. To insist, as comparable worth activists do, that women are entitled to remain secretaries and nurses, but that their pay should be jury-rigged upward, is to appear childish, dependent and unknowledgeable about how the world of work functions. . . .

Comparable worth is a detour—not to say, a dead end—that will not aid women in the long run, will not encourage them to pursue new paths, to explore new possibilities. Rather than condemning the market system, feminists ought to be glorying in it, for it has proved remarkably adaptable to women's evolving desire to work full-time, to work throughout their lives, and to work in new and challenging jobs. Why do comparable worth supporters view women as requiring special dispensations from government to advance in the marketplace, precisely at the time when women have made such great advances in the professions, in business, and in nontraditional vocations? Why emphasize women's disadvantages—their alleged victimization, their helplessness—when feminism rightly understood should glory in women's remarkable advances?

Indeed, it is the opponents of comparable worth, rather than its advocates, who have a positive attitude toward women's abilities, who see women as capable of determining what is in their own best interests and of competing and working for these goals in the marketplace alongside men, without any special privileges.

NOTES

1. *County of Washington v. Gunther,* 452 U.S. 161 (1981), Rehnquist dissent at 185 n. 1.

2. The Equal Pay Act is Section 6 of the Fair Labor Standards Act of 1938. The "substantially equal" definition of equal work is judicially defined language. See: *Shultz v. Wheaton Glass Co.,* 421 F. 2d 259, *cert. denied,* 398 U.S. 905 (1970); *Brennan v. Prince William Hospital Corp.,* 503 F. 2d 282, *cert. denied,* 420 U.S. 972 (1975).

3. *Who's Working for Working Women,* National Committee on Pay Equity and the National Women's Political Caucus, 1984.

4. John Stuart Mill, *Principles of Political Economy,* Book I, chap. ii, par. 4; as quoted in F. A. Hayek, *The Road to Serfdom* (Chicago: University of Chicago Press, 1944), p. 112.

Further Questions

1. If we are not in agreement about what constitutes the good life, how can we assess the value of an occupation according to the contribution it makes to human life?

2. If a job, like nursing, fails to attract qualified applicants because of its low wages, can we expect that the resulting shortage of nurses will make wages rise, that qualified applicants will then apply, and that the shortage will vanish?

3. When women are making too little money because of the occupation they are in, is it a viable solution for them to move to another occupation that pays more? That is, are women always in a position where they can make such a move?

Sharing the Shop Floor   III.6

STAN GRAY

Stan Gray writes about his experience as shop steward in admitting women into an all-male factory floor. It was not an easy task, because the sexist attitudes of the men would not allow women to work alongside them.

Gray is now an independent advocate for workers and unions, focusing on representing workers in the areas of workers compensation, health and safety, and human rights.

Abridged from "Sharing the Shop Floor" by Stan Gray from Canadian Dimension 18, *June 1984. Reprinted by permission of the author and publisher.*

Reading Questions

1. Can the ways men talk and act in a factory environment be so rough that women should not be allowed to work in such an environment?
2. Are factory workers and other blue-collar workers used as objects, dehumanized, and treated as faceless bodies in much the same way feminists claim that women are?
3. Is a woman who works normally robbing a male breadwinner of adequate income for his family?

MY EDUCATION BEGINS

... MY EDUCATION IN THE PROBLEMS of the Westinghouse women began in November 1978, when I was recalled to work following a bitter and unsuccessful five-month strike. The union represented eighteen hundred workers in three plants that produced turbines, motors, transformers, and switchgear equipment. When I was recalled to work it wasn't to my old Beach Road plant—where I had been a union steward and safety rep—but to an all-female department in the Switchgear plant and to a drastic drop in my labor grade. The plant was mostly segregated; in other words, jobs (and many departments) were either male or female. There were separate seniority lists and job descriptions. The dual-wage, dual-seniority system was enshrined in the collective agreement signed and enforced by both company and union.

At Switchgear I heard the complaints of the women, who worked the worst jobs in terms of monotony, speed, and work discipline but received lower pay, were denied chances for promotion, and were frequently laid off. They complained too of the union, accusing the male leadership of sanctioning and policing their inferior treatment. In cahoots with management, it swept the women's complaints under the carpet. From the first day it was obvious to me that the company enforced harsher standards for the women. They worked harder and faster, got less break time, and were allowed less leeway than the men. When I was later transferred to the all-male machine shop, the change was from night to day.

Meanwhile the men's club that ran the union made its views known to me early and clearly. The staff rep told me that he himself would never work with women. He boasted that he and his friends in the leadership drank in the one remaining all-male bar in the city. The local president was upset when he heard that I was seriously listening to the complaints of the women workers. He told me that he always just listened to their unfounded bitching, said "yes, yes, yes," and then completely ignored what he had been told. I ought to do the same, was his advice. Although I had just been elected to the executive in a rank-and-file rebellion against the old guard, he assumed that a common male bond would override our differences. When I persisted in taking the women's complaints seriously, the leadership started to ridicule me, calling me "the Ambassador" and saying they were now happy that I was saving them the distasteful task of listening to the women's bitching.

Then in 1979 the boom fell at Switchgear: the company announced it would close the plant. For the women, this was a serious threat. In the new contract the seniority and wage lists had been integrated, thanks to a new Ontario Human Rights Code. But would the women be able to exercise their seniority and bump or transfer to jobs in the other Hamilton plants, or would they find themselves out in the street after years at Switchgear?

DIVIDE AND CONQUER

By this time I had been recalled to my old department at the Beach Road plant, thanks to shop-floor pressure by the guys. There was a lot of worry in the plants about the prospect of large-scale transfers of women from Switchgear. A few women who had already been transferred had met with harassment and open hostility from the men. Some of us tried to raise the matter in the stewards' council, but the leadership was in no mood to discuss and confront sexism openly. The union bully boys went after us, threatening, shouting, breast beating, and blaming the women for the problems.

Since the union structures weren't going to touch the problem, we were left to our own resources in the shop. I worked in the Transformer Division, which the management was determined to keep all male. As a steward I insisted that the Switchgear women had every right to jobs in our department, at least to training and a trial period as stipulated by seniority. Since this was a legal and contractual right, management developed a strategy of Divide and Rule: present the women as a threat to men's jobs; create splits and get the hourly men to do the bosses' dirty work for them. Management had a secondary objective here, which was to break our shop-floor union organization. Since the trauma of the strike and post-strike repression, a number of stewards and safety reps had patiently rebuilt the union in the plant, block by block—fighting every grievance, hazard, and injustice with a variety of tactics and constructing some shop-floor unity. We did so in the teeth of opposition from both company and union, whose officials were overly anxious to get along peacefully with each other. A war of the sexes would be a weapon in management's counteroffensive against us.

For months before the anticipated transfers, foremen and their assorted rumor mongers stirred up the pot with the specter of the Invasion of the Women. Two hundred Switchgear women would come and throw all Beach Road breadwinners out in the street; no one's job would be safe. Day after day, week after week, we were fed the tales: for example, that fourteen women with thirty years' seniority were coming to the department in eight days and no male would be protected. Better start thinking now about unemployment insurance. . . .

For weeks before their arrival, the department was hyper-alive, everyone keyed to the Invasion of the Women. I was approached by one of the guys, who said that a number of them had discussed the problem and wanted me, as their steward, to tell management the men didn't want the women in here and would fight to keep them out.

The moment was a personal watershed for me. As I listened to him, I knew that half measures would no longer do. I would now have to take the bull by the horns. . . .

I told this guy, "No. These women from Switchgear are our sisters, and we have fought for them to come into our department. They are our fellow workers with seniority rights, and we want them to work here rather than get laid off. If we deny them their seniority rights, it hurts us, for once that goes down the drain, none of us has any protection. It is our enemies, the bosses, who are trying to do them out of jobs here. There's enough work for everyone; even if there weren't, seniority has to rule. For us as well as for them. The guys should train the women when they come and make them feel welcome." . . .

It was easy to tease guys with the contradictions that male double standards led them to. Although they were afraid the women would overproduce, at the same time they insisted that women wouldn't be physically strong enough to do our "man's work." Either they could or they couldn't was the answer to that one, and if they could, they deserved the jobs. It would be up to us to initiate them into the department norms. Many of the guys said that the women would never be able to do certain of the heavy and rotten jobs. As steward and safety rep I always jumped on that one: We shouldn't do those jobs either. Hadn't we been fighting to make them safer and easier for ourselves? Well, they answered, the women would still not be able to do all the jobs. Right, I would say, but how many guys here have we protected from doing certain jobs because of back or heart problems, or age, or simply personal distaste? If the women can't do certain jobs, we treat them the same way as men who can't. We don't victimize people who can't do everything the company wants them to. We protect them: as our brothers, and as our sisters.

By pointing out the irrationalities of the sexist double standards, we were pushing the guys to apply their class principles—universal standards of equal treatment. Treat the women just as we treat men regarding work tasks, seniority, illness, and so on.

COUNTERING SEXISM

Male sexist culture strives to degrade women to nothing but pieces of flesh, physical bodies, mindless animals . . . something less than fully human, which the men can then be superior to. Name-calling becomes a means of putting women in a different category from *us*, to justify different and inferior treatment.

Part of the fight to identify the women as coworkers was therefore the battle against calling them "cunts" or "bitches." It was important to set the public standard whereby the women were labeled as part of us, not *them*. I wouldn't be silent with anyone using these sexist labels and pushed the point very aggressively. Eventually everyone referred to "the women."

After a while most of the men in the department came to agree that having the women in and giving them a chance was the right thing to do by any standard of fairness, unionism, or solidarity, and was required by the basic human decency that separates *us* from *them*. But then the focus shifted to other areas. Many men came back with traditional arguments against women in the work force. They belong at home with the kids, they're robbing male breadwinners of family income and so forth. But others disagreed: Most of the guys' wives worked outside the home or had done so in the past; after all a family needed at least two wages these days. Some men answered that in bad times a family should have only one breadwinner so all would have an income. Fine, we told them, let's be really fair and square: you go home and clean the house and leave your wife at work. Alright, they countered, they could tolerate women working who supported a family, but not single women. And

so I picked out four single men in our department and proposed they be immediately sacked.

Fairness and equality seemed to triumph here too. The guys understood that everyone who had a job at Westinghouse deserved equal protection. But then, some men found another objection. As one, Peter, put it, "I have no respect for any women who could come into work here in these rotten conditions." The comeback was sharp: "What the hell are *you* putting up with this shit for? Why didn't you refuse to do that dirty job last month? Don't *you* deserve to be treated with respect?"[1]

As the Invasion Date approached I got worried. Reason and appeals to class solidarity had had a certain impact. Most of the guys were agreeing, grudgingly, to give the women a chance. But the campaign had been too short; fear and hostility were surfacing more and more. I was worried that there would be some ugly incident the first day or two that would set a pattern.

Much of the male hostility had been kept in check because I, as the union steward, had fought so aggressively on the issue. I decided to take this one step further and use some intimidation to enforce the basics of public behavior. In a tactic I later realized was a double-edged sword, I puffed myself up, assumed a cocky posture, and went for the jugular. I loudly challenged the masculinity of any worker who was opposed to the women. What kind of man is afraid of women? I asked. Only sissies and wimps are threatened by equality. *A real man* has nothing to be afraid of; he wants strong women. Any man worth his salt doesn't need the crutch of superiority over his sisters; he fears no female. A real man lives like an equal, doesn't step on women, doesn't degrade his sisters, doesn't have to rule the roost at home in order to affirm his manhood. Real men fight the boss, stand up with self-respect and dignity, rather than scapegoat our sisters.

I was sarcastic and cutting with my buddies: "This anti-woman crap of yours is a symbol of weakness. Stand up like a real man and behave and work as equals. The liberation of the women is the best thing that ever came along. . . . It's in *our* interests." To someone who boasted of how he made his wife cook his meals and clean his floors, I'd ask if she wiped his ass too? To the porno addicts I'd say, "You like that pervert shit? What's wrong with the real thing? Can you only get it up with those fantasies and cartoon women? Afraid of a real woman?" I'd outdo some of the worst guys in verbal intimidation and physical feats. Then I'd lecture them on women's equality and on welcoming our sisters the next week. I zeroed in on one or two of the sick types and physically threatened them if they pulled off anything with the women.

All of this worked, as I had hoped. It established an atmosphere of intimidation; no one was going to get smart with the women. Everyone would stand back for a while, some would cooperate, some would be neutral, and those I saw as "psycho-sexists" would keep out.

The tactic was effective because it spoke directly to a basic issue. But it was also effective because it took a leaf from the book of the psycho-sexists themselves.

At Westinghouse as elsewhere, some of the men were less chauvinistic and more sensible than others, but they often kept quiet in a group. They allowed the group pattern to be set by the most sexist bullies, whose style of woman baiting everyone at least gave in to. The psycho-sexists achieved this result because they challenged, directly or by implication, the masculinity of any male who didn't act the same way. All the men, whatever their real inclinations, are intimidated into acting or talking in a manner degrading to women. I had done the same thing, but in reverse. I had challenged the masculinity of any worker who would oppose the women. I had scared them off.

THE DAY THE WOMEN ARRIVED

The department crackled with tension the morning The Women arrived. There were only two of them to start with. The company was ev-

idently scared by the volatile situation it had worked so hard to create. They backed off a direct confrontation by assigning my helper George and me to work with the women.

The two women were on their guard: Betty and Laura, in their late thirties, were expecting trouble. They were pleasantly shocked when I said matter-of-factly that we would train them on the job. They were overjoyed when I explained that the men had wanted them in our department and had fought the bosses to bring them here.

It was an unforgettable day. Men from all corners of the plant crept near the iron-stacking area to spy on us. I explained the work and we set about our tasks. We outproduced the standard rate by just a hair so that the company couldn't say the women weren't able to meet the normal requirements of the job.

My strategy was to get over the hump of the first few days. I knew that once the guys got used to the women being there, they'd begin to treat them as people, not as "women" and their hysteria would go away. It was essential to avoid incidents. Thus I forced the guys to interact with them. Calling over one of the male opponents, I introduced him as Bruce the Slinger who knew all the jobs and was an expert in lifts and would be happy to help them if asked and could always be called on to give a hand. This put him on the spot. Finally he flashed a big smile, and said, "Sure, just ask and I'd be pleased to show you anything, and to begin with, here's what to watch out for. . . ."

The morning went by. There were no incidents. From then on it was easy. More guys began to talk to the two women. They started to see them as Betty with four kids who lived on the mountain and knew wiring and was always cheerful; or Laura, who was a friend of John's uncle and was cranky early in the morning, who could easily operate the crane but had trouble with the impact gun, and who liked to heat up meat pies for lunch. After all, these men lived and worked with women all of their lives outside the plant—mothers, sisters, wives, in-laws, friends, daughters, and girlfriends. Having women at work was no big deal once they got over the trauma of the invasion of this male preserve. Just like helping your sister-in-law hang some wallpaper.

As the news spread, more and more women applied to transfer to our department. They were integrated with minimum fuss. The same thing happened in several adjoining departments. Quickly, men and women began to see each other as people and co-workers, not as enemies. Rather than man vs. woman it was John, Mary, Sue, Peter, Alice, George, and Laura. That Christmas we had a big party at someone's home—men and women of the department, drinking and dancing. The photos and various raucous tales of that night provided the basis for department storytelling for the next three months.

Was this, then, peace between the sexes? The integration of men and women as co-workers in the plant? Class solidarity triumphing over sex antagonism? Not quite. Although they were now together, it was not peace. The result was more complicated, for now the war between the sexes was being extended from the community into the workplace.

WORKPLACE CULTURE

As our struggle showed, sexism coexists and often is at war with class consciousness and with the trade union solidarity that develops among factory men. Our campaign was successful to the extent that it was able to sharply polarize and push the contradictions between these two tendencies in each individual. With most of the men, their sense of class solidarity triumphed over male chauvinism.

Many of the men had resisted the female invasion of the workplace because for them it was the last sanctum of male culture. It was somewhere they could get away from the world of women, away from responsibility and children and the civilized society's cultural restraints. In the plant they could revel in the rough and

tumble of a masculine world of physical harshness, of constant swearing and rough behavior, of half-serious fighting and competition with each other and more serious fighting with the boss. It was eight hours full of filth and dirt and grease and grime and sweat—manual labor and a manly atmosphere. They could be vulgar and obscene, talk about football and car repairs, and let their hair down. Boys could be boys.

The male workplace culture functions as a form of rebellion against the discipline of their society. Outside the workplace, women are the guardians of the community. They raise the kids and enforce some degree of family and collective responsibility. They frequently have to force this upon men, who would rather go drinking or play baseball while the women mind the kids, wash the family's clothes, attend to problems with the neighbors and in-laws, and so on. Like rebellious teenage sons escaping mother's control, male wage earners enter the factory gates, where in their male culture they feel free of the restraints of these repressive standards.

Even if all factory men don't share these attitudes, a large proportion do, to a greater or lesser degree.

The manly factory culture becomes an outlet for accumulated anger and frustration. But this is a vicious circle because the tedious work and the subordination to the bosses is in large part the very cause of the male worker's dissatisfaction. He is bitter against a world that has kept him down, exploited his labor power, bent him to meet the needs of production and profit, cheated him of a better life, and made the daily grind so harsh. Working men are treated like dirt everywhere: At work they are at the bottom of the heap and under the thumb of the boss; outside they are scorned by polite society. But, the men can say, we are better than them all in certain ways; we're doing men's work; it's physically tough; women can't do it; neither can the bankers and politicians. Tough work gives a sense of masculine superiority that compensates for being stepped on and ridiculed. All that was threatened by the Women's Invasion.

However, this male workplace culture is not one-sided, for it contains a fundamentally positive sense of class value. The workingmen contrast themselves to other classes and take pride in having a concrete grasp of the physical world around them. The big shots can talk fancy and manipulate words, flout their elegance and manners. But we control the nuts and bolts of production, have our hands on the machines and gears and valves, the wires and lathes and pumps, the furnaces and spindles and batteries. We're the masters of the real and the concrete; we manipulate the steel and the lead, the wood, oil, and aluminum. What we know is genuine, the real and specific world of daily life. Workers are the wheels that make a society go round, the creators of social value and wealth. There would be no fancy society, no civilized conditions if it were not for our labor.

The male workers are contemptuous of the mild-mannered parasites and soft-spoken vultures who live off our daily sweat: the managers and directors, the judges and entertainers, the lawyers, the coupon clippers, the administrators, the insurance brokers, the legislators . . . all those who profit from the shop floor, who build careers for themselves with the wealth we create. All that social overhead depends upon our mechanical skills, our concrete knowledge, our calloused hands, our technical ingenuity, our strained muscles and backs.

The Dignity of Labor, but society treats us like a pack of dumb animals, mere bodies with no minds or culture. We're physical labor power; the intelligence belongs to the management class. Workers are sneeringly regarded as society's bodies, the middle class as society's mind. One is inferior; the other is superior and fully human. The workers are less than human, close to animals, society's beasts of burden.

The male workplace culture tends to worship this self-identity of vulgar physicalness. It is as if the men enjoy wallowing in a masculine filth. They brag of being the wild men of the factory. Say it loud: I'm a brute and I'm proud.

Sexism thus undermines and subverts the proud tradition of the dignity of labor. It turns a class consciousness upside down by accepting and then glorifying the middle-class view of manual labor and physical activity as inferior, animalistic, and crude. When workers identify with the savages that the bosses see them as, they develop contempt for themselves. It is self-contempt to accept the scornful labels, the negative definitions, the insulting dehumanized treatment, the cartoon stereotypes of class chauvinism the super masculine menials, the industrial sweathogs.

Remember Peter, who couldn't respect a woman who would come to work in this hellhole. It was obviously a place where he felt he had lost his own self-respect. My reply to him was that he shouldn't put up with that rotten treatment, *that the men also deserved better*. We should be treated with dignity. Respect yourself—fight back like a man, not a macho fool who glorifies that which degrades him.

Everything gets turned inside out. It is seen as manly to be treated as less than a man, as just a physical, instinctual creature. But this is precisely how sexist society treats women: as mindless bodies, pieces of flesh . . . "biology is destiny." You would think that male factory workers and the women's movement would be natural allies, that they'd speak the same language. They share a common experience of being used as objects, dehumanized by those on top. Men in the factory are treated not as persons, but as bodies, replaceable numbers, commodities, faceless factors of production. The struggles of workingmen and of women revolve around similar things. The right to choice on abortion, for example, revolves around the right for women to control their own bodies. Is this not what the fight for health and safety on the shop floor is all about? To have some control over our bodies, not to let the bastards do what they want with our lives and limbs, to wreck us in their search for higher profits.

But male chauvinism turns many workingmen away from their natural allies, away from a rational and collective solution to their problems, diverting them from class unity with their sisters into oppressors and degraders of their sisters. Robbed of their real manhood—their humanity as men—they get a false sense of manhood by lording over women.

PLAYING THE FOREMAN AT HOME

Many men compensate for their wage-labor status in the workplace by becoming the boss at home. Treated terribly in the factory, he plays foreman after work and rules with authority over his wife and kids. He thus gains at home that independence he loses on the shop floor. He becomes a part-time boss himself with women as his servants. This becomes key to his identity and sense of self-esteem. Working-class patriarchs, rulers of the roost.

This sense of authority has an economic underpinning. The male worker's role as primary breadwinner gives him power over the family and status in society. It also makes him the beneficiary of the woman's unpaid labor in the household.

A wage laborer not only lacks independence, he also lacks property, having nothing but his labor power to sell. Sexism gives him the sense of property, as owner of the family. His wife or girlfriend is his sexual property. As Elvis sang, "You are my only possession, you are my everything." This domination and ownership of a woman are basic to how he sees himself.

These things are powerful pressures toward individualism, a trait of the business class: foreman of the family, man of property, possessiveness. They elevate the wage earner above the category of the downtrodden common laborer, and in doing so divert him from the collective struggle with his brothers and sisters to change their conditions. Capitalism is based on competitiveness and encourages everyone to be better than the next guy, to rise up on the backs of your neighbors. Similarly the male chauvinist seeks superiority over others, of both sexes. Men tend to be competitive, always putting one another down, constantly playing one-upmanship. Men even express appreciation and affection for each other through good-natured mutual insults.

Sexist culture thus undermines the working-class traditions of equality and solidarity and provides a recruiting ground for labor's adversaries. Over the years at Westinghouse I had noticed that a high proportion of workers who became foremen were extreme chauvinists—sexual braggarts, degraders of women, aggressive, individualistic, ambitious, ever willing to push other workers around. Male competition is counterproductive in the shop or union, where we ought to cooperate as equals and seek common solutions. The masculine ego makes for bad comradeship, bad brotherhood. It also makes it difficult for chauvinistic men to look at and deal objectively with many situations because their fragile egos are always on the line. They have to keep up a facade of superiority and are unable to handle criticism, no matter how constructive. Their chauvinistic crutches make them subjective, irrational, unreliable, and often self-destructive, as with men who want to work or drive dangerously.

Workingmen pay a high price for the limited material benefits they get from sexist structures. It is the bosses who make the big bucks and enjoy the real power from the inferior treatment of women. . . .

. . . the fight against sexism is also a fight for men. Sexism is destructive of the labor movement and the workingman's struggle. It has led men to confuse our class interests, to side with the boss time after time, to seek false and illusory solutions to our situation as exploited wage earners, and to escape the injustices of class by lording it over the women.

Sexism instills the ideas and values of the enemy class in our ranks. It ingrains false ideas of manhood and strength. It cultivates individualistic attitudes and competitive behavior when what we need is collective struggle. It deludes men and pushes them into irrational actions. It channels men's anger and rebellion along destructive paths—destructive to themselves as well as to our sisters. This sexist madness is part of how capitalism keeps male workers in line. It's anti-labor and anti-working class. We should so label it and treat it. In doing so we are fighting for our own liberation, as well as that of our sisters. . . .

Authoritarianism, intimidation, aggression—these are a basic part of sexism. You can't separate aggression from sexism. Aggressive ways of relating to people are part of what sexism is. To be a male chauvinist is to establish a competitive power relationship to your own people, to seek to dominate your brothers and sisters, to treat *us* as *them*.

You can't combat sexism by reinforcing the fear of authority or by intimidating the men, by becoming the loudest shouter at the male lunch table. The peaceful women's table was stronger because it was collective and noncompetitive. During some of the campaigns at the plant, I saw that management was a lot more frightened of the quiet women than they were of the mouthy men. Force and authority can outlaw discriminatory practices and structures, but sexist attitudes cannot be fought with the weapons of authority. Authoritarianism itself must be undermined.

Labor has to go beyond paper resolutions and do more than place women in top positions. We have to deepen the struggle against sexism where it really counts—on the shop floor and within the locals.

Militant men in the labor movement have to organize themselves and speak out publicly. We need to express an anti-sexist position that reflects men's experiences, speaks in a masculine voice, and develops a language of our own. Such a position would label sexism as antilabor and show how it is harmful to women *and* to

male wage earners. This rank-and-file male voice would be distinct from the women's voice but allied to it in a common fight.

Men need to speak to men about sexism. Men need to learn from the women who have been playing a dynamic part in the labor movement, and we must confront on our own the issues the women's movement has raised: equal treatment, union democracy, non-competitive structures, a humanization of the use of power, the relation between community and workplace problems, the family, sexuality, repression, authoritarianism. Men need to debate these issues in our own way, developing our own non-sexist answers.

The experience of women is enriching and strengthening the world of labor in many ways. Men have to recognize and appreciate these contributions. This means recasting our conception of work and labor as something uniquely masculine and accepting and learning from the distinct methods, rhythms, and styles of women assemblers, machinists, miners.

Workingmen share basic common interests with our sisters. When more of us recognize this, define and speak about these interests in our own way, and act in common with women, then we will be able to start moving the mountains that stand in our way.

NOTE

1. The names of the plant workers in this article are not their real ones.

Further Questions

1. Is it in the best interest of a community for the women to stay at home to guard the community's standards, while the men go to the workplace where they are allowed to break these standards?

2. If a job is too dirty and nasty for a woman, isn't it too dirty and nasty for a man as well?

3. Do men get a false sense of manhood by maintaining themselves in positions where they can control or exclude women?

The Glass Escalator: Hidden Advantages for Men in the "Female" Professions

III.7

CHRISTINE L. WILLIAMS

Christine L. Williams describes her study on men's underrepresentation in four predominantly female occupations: nursing, librarianship, elementary school teaching, and social work. Many people interviewed said that there is a preference for hiring men in these four occupations. Moreover, once hired, men can be put on a "glass escalator": they are tracked into the better paying and more prestigious areas of the occupation, administration in particular.

Williams is Associate Professor of Sociology at the University of Texas at Austin.

Reading Questions

1. Is it wrong to favor the underrepresented gender in hiring decisions in an occupation? Is there something to be said in favor of such hiring bias?
2. Is it wrong to put men on a "glass escalator" so that they more easily advance to positions with better pay and more prestige? What is the effect on a profession when such a "glass escalator" for men is in operation?
3. One effect of the "glass escalator" for men is that men are more likely to be supervised by a member of their own gender. Does this put women workers at a disadvantage? Explain, using examples.

THE SEX SEGREGATION of the U.S. labor force is one of the most perplexing and tenacious problems in our society. Even though the proportion of men and women in the labor force is approaching parity (particularly for younger cohorts of workers) (U.S. Department of Labor, 1991: 18), men and women are still generally confined to predominantly single-sex occupations. Forty percent of men or women would have to change major occupational categories to achieve equal representation of men and women in all jobs (Reskin and Roos, 1990: 6), but even this figure underestimates the true degree of sex segregation. It is extremely rare to

find specific jobs where equal numbers of men and women are engaged in the same activities in the same industries (Bielby and Baron, 1984).

Most studies of sex segregation in the work force have focused on women's experiences in male-dominated occupations. Both researchers and advocates for social change have focused on the barriers faced by women who try to integrate predominantly male fields. Few have looked at the "flip-side" of occupational sex segregation: the exclusion of men from predominantly female occupations (exceptions include Shreiber 1979; Williams, 1989; Zimmer, 1988). But the fact is that men are less likely to enter

This research was funded in part by a faculty grant from the University of Texas at Austin. I also acknowledge the support of the sociology departments of the University of California, Berkeley; Harvard University; and Arizona State University. I would like to thank Judy Auerbach, Martin Button, Robert Nye, Teresa Sullivan, Debra Umberson, Mary Waters, and the reviewers at Social Problems for their comments on earlier versions of this paper. © 1992 by The Society for the Study of Social Problems. Reprinted from Social Problems, Vol. 39, No. 3 (August 1992) p. 253–267, by permission.

female sex-typed occupations than women are to enter male-dominated jobs (Jacobs, 1989). Reskin and Roos, for example, were able to identify 33 occupations in which female representation increased by more than nine percentage points between 1970 and 1980, but only three occupations in which the proportion of men increased as radically (1990: 20–21).

In this paper, I examine men's underrepresentation in four predominantly female occupations—nursing, librarianship, elementary school teaching, and social work. Throughout the twentieth century, these occupations have been identified with "women's work"—even though prior to the Civil War, men were more likely to be employed in these areas. These four occupations, often called the female "semi-professions" (Hodson and Sullivan, 1990), today range from 5.5 percent male (in nursing) to 32 percent male (in social work). (See Table 25.1.) These percentages have not changed substantially in decades. In fact, as Table 25.1 indicates, two of these professions—librarianship and social work—have experienced declines in the proportions of men since 1975. Nursing is the only one of the four experiencing noticeable changes in sex composition, with the proportion of men increasing 80 percent between 1975 and 1990. Even so, men continue to be a tiny minority of all nurses.

METHODS

I conducted in-depth interviews with 76 men and 23 women in four occupations from 1985–1991, Interviews were conducted in four metropolitan areas: San Francisco/Oakland, California; Austin, Texas; Boston, Massachusetts; and Phoenix, Arizona. These four areas were selected because they show considerable variation in the proportions of men in the four professions. For example, Austin has one of the highest percentages of men in nursing (7.7 percent), whereas Phoenix's percentage is one of the lowest (2.7 percent) (U.S. Bureau of the Census, 1980). The sample was generated using

Table 25.1 Percent male in selected occupations, selected years

Profession	1990	1980	1975
Nurses	5.5	3.5	3.0
Elementary teachers	14.8	16.3	14.6
Librarians	16.7	14.8	18.9
Social workers	31.8	35.0	39.2

SOURCE: U.S. Department of Labor. Bureau of Labor Statistics. *Employment and Earnings* 38:1 (January 1991), Table 22 (Employed civilians by detailed occupation), 185; 28:1 (January 1981), Table 23 (Employed persons by detailed occupation), 180; 22:7 (January 1976), Table 2 (Employed persons by detailed occupation), 11.

"snowballing" techniques. Women were included in the sample to gauge their feelings and responses to men who enter "their" professions.

Like the people employed in these professions generally, those in my sample were predominantly white (90 percent).[1] Their ages ranged from 20 to 66 and the average age was 38. The interview questionnaire consisted of several open-ended questions on four broad topics: motivation to enter the profession; experiences in training; career progression; and general views about men's status and prospects within these occupations. I conducted all the interviews, which generally lasted between one and two hours. Interviews took place in restaurants, my home or office, or the respondent's home or office. Interviews were tape-recorded and transcribed for the analysis.

In this paper, I review individuals' responses to questions about discrimination in hiring practices, on-the-job rapport with supervisors and co-workers, and prejudice from clients and others outside their profession.

DISCRIMINATION IN HIRING

Contrary to the experiences of many women in the male-dominated professions, many of the men and women I spoke to indicated that there is a *preference* for hiring men in these four occupations. A Texas librarian at a junior high school said that his school district "would hire a male over a female."

I: Why do you think that is?
R: Because there are so few, and the . . . ones that they do have, the library directors seem to really . . . think they're doing great jobs. I don't know, maybe they just feel they're being progressive or something, [but] I have had a real sense that they really appreciate having a male, particularly at the junior high. . . . As I said, when seven of us lost our jobs from the high schools and were redistributed, there were only four positions at junior high, and I got one of them. Three of the librarians, some who had been here longer than I had with the school district, were put down in elementary school as librarians. And I definitely think that being male made a difference in my being moved to the junior high rather than an elementary school.

Many of the men perceived their token status as males in predominantly female occupations as an *advantage* in hiring and promotions. I asked an Arizona teacher whether his specialty (elementary special education) was an unusual area for men compared to other areas within education. He said,

Much more so. I am extremely marketable in special education. That's not why I got into the field. But I am extremely marketable because I am a man.

In several cases, the more female-dominated the specialty, the greater the apparent preference for men. For example, when asked if he encountered any problem getting a job in pediatrics, a Massachusetts nurse said,

No, no, none. . . . I've heard this from managers and supervisory-type people with men in pediatrics: "It's nice to have a man because it's such a female-dominated profession."

However, there were some exceptions to this preference for men in the most female-dominated specialties. In some cases, formal policies actually barred men from certain jobs. This was the case in some rural Texas school districts, which refused to hire men in the youngest grades (K–3). Some nurses also reported being excluded from positions in obstetrics and gynecology wards, a policy encountered more frequently in private Catholic hospitals.

But often the pressures keeping men out of certain specialties were more subtle than this. Some men described being "tracked" into practice areas within their professions which were considered more legitimate for men. For example, one Texas man described how he was pushed into administration and planning in social work, even though "I'm not interested in writing policy; I'm much more interested in research and clinical stuff." A nurse who is interested in pursuing graduate study in family and child health in Boston said he was dissuaded from entering the program specialty in favor of a concentration in "adult nursing." A kindergarten teacher described the difficulty of finding a job in his specialty after graduation: "I was recruited immediately to start getting into a track to become an administrator. And it was men who recruited me. It was men that ran the system at that time, especially in Los Angeles."

This tracking may bar men from the most female-identified specialties within these professions. But men are effectively being "kicked upstairs" in the process. Those specialties considered more legitimate practice areas for men also tend to be the most prestigious, better paying ones. A distinguished kindergarten teacher, who had been voted city-wide "Teacher of the Year," told me that even though people were pleased to see him in the classroom, "there's been some encouragement to think about administration, and there's been some encouragement to think about teaching at the university level or something like that, or supervisory-type position." That is, despite his aptitude and interest in staying in the classroom, he felt pushed in the direction of administration.

The effect of this "tracking" is the opposite of that experienced by women in male-dominated occupations. Researchers have reported that many women encounter a "glass ceiling" in their efforts to scale organizational and professional hierarchies. That is, they are constrained by invisible barriers to promotion in their careers, caused mainly by sexist attitudes of men in the highest positions (Freeman, 1990).[2] In contrast to the "glass ceiling," many of the men I interviewed seem to encounter a "glass escalator." Often, despite their intentions, they face invisible pressures to move up in their professions. As if on a moving escalator, they must work to stay in place.

A public librarian specializing in children's collections (a heavily female-dominated concentration) described an encounter with this "escalator" in his very first job out of library school. In his first six-months' evaluation, his supervisors commended him for his good work in storytelling and related activities, but they criticized him for "not shooting high enough."

> Seriously. That's literally what they were telling me. They assumed that because I was a male— and they told me this—and that I was being hired right out of graduate school, that somehow I wasn't doing the kind of management-oriented work that they thought I should be doing. And as a result, really they had a lot of bad marks, as it were, against me on my evaluation. And I said I couldn't believe this!

Throughout his ten-year career, he has had to struggle to remain in children's collections.

The glass escalator does not operate at all levels. In particular, men in academia reported some gender-based discrimination in the highest positions due to their universities' commitment to affirmative action. Two nursing professors reported that they felt their own chances of promotion to deanships were nil because their universities viewed the position of nursing dean as a guaranteed female appointment in an otherwise heavily male-dominated administration. One California social work professor reported his university canceled its search for a dean because no minority male or female candidates had been placed on their short list. It was rumored that other schools on campus were permitted to go forward with their searches—even though they also failed to put forward names of minority

candidates—because the higher administration perceived it to be "easier" to fulfill affirmative action goals in the social work school. The interviews provide greater evidence of the "glass escalator" at work in the lower levels of these professions.

Of course, men's motivations also play a role in their advancement to higher professional positions. I do not mean to suggest that the men I talked to all resented the informal tracking they experienced. For many men, leaving the most female-identified areas of their professions helped them resolve internal conflicts involving their masculinity. One man left his job as a school social worker to work in a methadone drug treatment program not because he was encouraged to leave by his colleagues, but because "I think there was some macho shit there, to tell you the truth, because I remember feeling a little uncomfortable there . . .; it didn't feel right to me." Another social worker, employed in the mental health services department of a large urban area in California, reflected on his move into administration:

> The more I think about it, through our discussion, I'm sure that's a large part of why I wound up in administration. It's okay for a man to do the administration. In fact, I don't know if I fully answered a question that you asked a little while ago about how did being male contribute to my advancing in the field. I was saying it wasn't because I got any special favoritism as a man, but . . . I think . . . because I'm a man, I felt a need to get into this kind of position. I may have worked harder toward it, may have competed harder for it, than most women would do, even women who think about doing administrative work.

Elsewhere I have speculated on the origins of men's tendency to define masculinity through single-sex work environments (Williams, 1989). Clearly, personal ambition does play a role in accounting for men's movement into more "male-defined" arenas within these professions. But these occupations also structure opportunities for males independent of their individual desires or motives.

The interviews suggest that men's under-representation in these professions cannot be attributed to discrimination in hiring or promotions. Many of the men indicated that they received preferential treatment because they were men. Although men mentioned gender discrimination in the hiring process, for the most part they were channeled into the more "masculine" specialties within these professions, which ironically meant being "tracked" into better paying and more prestigious specialties.

SUPERVISORS AND COLLEAGUES: THE WORKING ENVIRONMENT

Researchers claim that subtle forms of work place discrimination push women out of male-dominated occupations (Jacobs, 1989; Reskin and Hartmann, 1986). In particular, women report feeling excluded from informal leadership and decision-making networks, and they sense hostility from their male co-workers, which makes them feel uncomfortable and unwanted (Carothers and Crull, 1984). Respondents in this study were asked about their relationships with supervisors and female colleagues to ascertain whether men also experienced "poisoned" work environments when entering gender atypical occupations.

A major difference in the experience of men and women in nontraditional occupations is that men in these situations are far more likely to be supervised by a member of their own sex. In each of the four professions I studied, men are overrepresented in administrative and managerial capacities, or, as in the case of nursing, their positions in the organizational hierarchy are governed by men (Grimm and Sterm, 1974; Phenix, 1987; Schmuck, 1987; Williams, 1989; York, Henley, & Gamble, 1987). Thus, unlike women who enter "male fields," the men in these professions often work under the direct supervision of other men.

Many of the men interviewed reported that they had good rapport with their male supervi-

sors. Even in professional school, some men reported extremely close relationships with their male professors. For example, a Texas librarian described an unusually intimate association with two male professors in graduate school:

> I can remember a lot of times in the classroom there would be discussions about a particular topic or issue, and the conversation would spill over into their office hours, after the class was over. And even though there were . . . a couple of the other women that had been in on the discussion, they weren't there. And I don't know if that was preferential or not . . . it certainly carried over into personal life as well. Not just at the school and that sort of thing. I mean, we would get together for dinner . . .

These professors explicitly encouraged him because he was male:

> **I:** Did they ever offer you explicit words of encouragement about being in the profession by virtue of the fact that you were male? . . .
> **R:** Definitely. On several occasions. Yeah. Both of these guys, for sure, including the Dean who was male also. And it's an interesting point that you bring up because it was, oftentimes, kind of in a sign, you know. It wasn't in the classroom, and it wasn't in front of the group, or if we were in the student lounge or something like that. It was . . . if it was just myself or maybe another one of the guys, you know, and just talking in the office. It's like . . . you know, kind of an opening-up and saying, "you know, you're really lucky that you're in the profession because you'll really go to the top real quick, and you'll be able to make real definite improvements and changes. And you'll have a real influence," and all this sort of thing. I mean, really, I can remember several times.

Although I did not interview many supervisors, I did include 23 women in my sample to ascertain their perspectives about the presence of men in their professions. All of the women I interviewed claimed to be supportive of their male colleagues, but some conveyed ambivalence. For example, a social work professor said she would like to see more men enter the social work profession, particularly in the clinical specialty (where they are underrepresented). Indeed, she favored affirmative action hiring guidelines for men in the profession. Yet, she resented the fact that her department hired "another white male" during a recent search. I questioned her about this ambivalence:

> I: I find it very interesting that, on the one hand, you sort of perceive this preference and perhaps even sexism with regard to how men are evaluated and how they achieve higher positions within the profession, yet on the other hand, you would be encouraging of more men to enter the field. Is that contradictory to you, or . . .?
>
> R: Yeah, it's contradictory.

It appears that women are generally eager to see men enter "their" occupations. Indeed, several men noted that their female colleagues had facilitated their careers in various ways (including mentorship in college). However, at the same time, women often resent the apparent ease with which men advance within these professions, sensing that men at the higher levels receive preferential treatment which closes off advancement opportunities for women.

Even outside work, most of the men interviewed said they felt fully accepted by their female colleagues. They were usually included in informal socializing occasions with the women—even though this frequently meant attending baby showers or Tupperware parties. Many said that they declined offers to attend these events because they were not interested in "women's things," although several others claimed to attend everything: The minority men I interviewed seemed to feel the least comfortable in these informal contexts. One social worker in Arizona was asked about socializing with his female colleagues:

> I: So in general, for example, if all the employees were going to get together to have a party, or celebrate a bridal shower or whatever, would you be invited along with the rest of the group?
>
> R: They would invite me, I would say, somewhat reluctantly. Being a black male, working

with all white females, it did cause some outside problems. So I didn't go to a lot of functions with them . . .

> I: You felt that there was some tension there on the level of your acceptance . . .?
>
> R: Yeah. It was OK working, but on the outside, personally, there was some tension there. It never came out, that they said, "Because of who you are we can't invite you" (laughs), and I wouldn't have done anything anyway. I would have probably respected them more for saying what was on their minds. But I never felt completely in with the group.

DISCRIMINATION FROM "OUTSIDERS"

The most compelling evidence of discrimination against men in these professions is related to their dealings with the public. Men often encounter negative stereotypes when they come into contact with clients or "outsiders"—people they meet outside of work. For instance, it is popularly assumed that male nurses are gay. Librarians encounter images of themselves as "wimpy" and asexual. Male social workers describe being typecast as "feminine" and "passive." Elementary school teachers are often confronted by suspicions that they are pedophiles. One kindergarten teacher described an experience that occurred early in his career which was related to him years afterwards by his principal:

> He indicated to me that parents had come to him and indicated to him that they had a problem with the fact that I was a male. . . . I recall almost exactly what he said. There were three specific concerns that the parents had: One parent said, "How can he love my child; he's a man." The second thing that I recall, he said the parent said, "He has a beard." And the third thing was, "Aren't you concerned about homosexuality?"

Such suspicions often cause men in all four professions to alter their work behavior to guard against sexual abuse charges, particularly in those specialties requiring intimate contact with women and children.

Men are very distressed by these negative stereotypes, which tend to undermine their self-esteem and to cause them to second-guess their motivations for entering these fields. A California teacher said,

> If I tell men that I don't know, that I'm meeting for the first time, that that's what I do, . . . sometimes there's a look on their faces that, you know, "Oh, couldn't get a real job?"

When asked if his wife, who is also an elementary school teacher, encounters the same kind of prejudice, he said,

> No, it's accepted because she's a woman. . . . I think people would see that as a . . . step up, you know. "Oh, you're not a housewife, you've got a career. That's great . . . that you're out there working. And you have a daughter, but you're still out there working. You decided not to stay home, and you went out there and got a job." Whereas for me, it's more like I'm supposed to be out working anyway, even though I'd rather be home with [my daughter].

Unlike women who enter traditionally male professions, men's movement into these jobs is perceived by the "outside world" as a step down in status. This particular form of discrimination may be most significant in explaining why men are underrepresented in these professions. Men who otherwise might show interest in and aptitudes for such careers are probably discouraged from pursuing them because of the negative popular stereotypes associated with the men who work in them. This is a crucial difference from the experience of women in nontraditional professions: "My daughter, the physician," resonates far more favorably in most people's ears than "My son, the nurse."

Of course, there are additional factors besides societal prejudice contributing to men's underrepresentation in female-dominated professions. Most notably, those men I interviewed mentioned as a deterrent the fact that these professions are all underpaid relative to comparable

"male" occupations, and several suggested that instituting a "comparable worth" policy might attract more men. However, I am not convinced that improved salaries will substantially alter the sex composition of these professions unless the cultural stigma faced by men in these occupations diminishes. Occupational sex segregation is remarkably resilient, even in the face of devastating economic hardship. During the Great Depression of the 1930s, for example, "women's jobs" failed to attract sizable numbers of men (Blum, 1991: 154). In her study of American Telephone and Telegraph (AT&T) workers, Epstein (1989) found that some men would rather suffer unemployment than accept relatively high paying "women's jobs" because of the damage to their identities this would cause. She quotes one unemployed man who refused to apply for a female-identified telephone operator job:

> I think if they offered me $1000 a week tax free, I wouldn't take that job. When I . . . see those guys sitting in there [in the telephone operating room], I wonder what's wrong with them. Are they pansies or what? (Epstein, 1989: 577)

This is not to say that raising salaries would not affect the sex composition of these jobs. Rather, I am suggesting that wages are not the only—or perhaps even the major—impediment to men's entry into these jobs. Further research is needed to explore the ideological significance of the "woman's wage" for maintaining occupational stratification.[3]

NOTES

1. According to the U.S. Census, black men and women constitute 7 percent of all nurses and librarians, 11 percent of all elementary school teachers, and 19 percent of all social workers (calculated from U.S. Census 1980: Table 278, 1–197). The proportion of blacks in social work may be exaggerated by these statistics. The occupational definition of "social worker" used by the Census Bureau includes welfare workers

and pardon and parole officers, who are not considered "professional" social workers by the National Association of Social Workers. A study of degreed professionals found that 89 percent of practitioners were white (Hardcastle, 1987).

2. In April 1991, the Labor Department created a "Glass Ceiling Commission" to "conduct a thorough study of the underrepresentation of women and minorities in executive, management, and senior decision-making positions in business" (U.S. House of Representatives, 1991: 20).

3. Alice Kessler-Harris argues that the lower pay of traditionally female occupations is symbolic of a patriarchal order that assumes female dependence on a male breadwinner. She writes that pay equity is fundamentally threatening to the "male worker's sense of self, pride, and masculinity" because it upsets his individual standing in the hierarchical ordering of the sexes (1990: 125). Thus, men's reluctance to enter these occupations may have less to do with the actual dollar amount recorded in their paychecks, and more to do with the damage that earning "a woman's wage" would wreak on their self-esteem in a society that privileges men. This conclusion is supported by the interview data.

REFERENCES

Bielby, William T., and James N. Baron. 1984. "A woman's place is with other women: Sex segregation within organizations." In *Sex Segmentation in the Workplace: Trends, Explanations, Remedies,* ed. Barbara Reskin, 27–55. Washington, D.C.: National Academy Press.

Blum, Linda M. 1991. *Between Feminism and Labor: The Significance of the Comparable Worth Movement.* Berkeley and Los Angeles: University of California Press.

Carothers, Suzanne C., and Peggy Crull. 1984. "Contrasting sexual harassment in female-dominated and male-dominated occupations." In *My Troubles Are Going to Have Trouble with Me: Everyday Trials and Triumphs of Women Workers,* ed. Karen B. Sacks and Dorothy Remy, 220–227. New Brunswick, N.J.: Rutgers University Press.

Epstein, Cynthia Fuchs. 1989. "Workplace boundaries: Conceptions and creations." *Social Research* 46: 571–590.

Freeman, Sue J. M. 1990. *Managing Lives: Corporate Women and Social Change.* Amherst, Mass.: University of Massachusetts Press.

Grimm, James W., and Robert N. Stern. 1974. "Sex roles and internal labor market structures: The female semi-professions." *Social Problems* 21: 690–705.

Hardcastle, D. A. 1987. "The social work labor force." Austin, Tex.: School of Social Work, University of Texas.

Hodson, Randy, and Teresa Sullivan. 1990. *The Social Organization of Work.* Belmont, Calif. Wadsworth Publishing Co.

Jacobs, Jerry. 1989. *Revolving Doors: Sex Segregation and Women's Careers.* Stanford, Calif.: Stanford University Press.

Kessler-Harris, Alice. 1990. *A Woman's Wage: Historical Meanings and Social Consequences.* Lexington: Kentucky University Press.

Phenix, Katharine. 1987. "The status of women librarians." *Frontiers* 9: 36–40.

Reskin, Barbara, and Heidi Hartmann. 1986. *Women's Work, Men's Work: Sex Segregation on the Job.* Washington, D.C.: National Academy Press.

Reskin, Barbara, and Patricia Roos. 1990. *Job Queues, Gender Queues: Explaining Women's Inroads into Male Occupations.* Philadelphia: Temple University Press.

Schmuck, Patricia A. 1987. "Women school employees in the United States." In *Women Educators: Employees of Schools in Western Countries,* ed. Patricia A. Schmuck, 75–97. Albany: State University of New York Press.

Schreiber, Carol. 1979. *Men and Women in Transitional Occupations.* Cambridge, Mass.: MIT Press.

U.S. Bureau of the Census. 1980. *Detailed Population Characteristics,* Vol. 1, Ch. D. Washington, D.C.: Government Printing Office.

U.S. Congress. House. 1991. *Civil Rights and Women's Equity in Employment Act of 1991.* Report. (Report 102-40, Part I.) Washington, D.C.: Government Printing Office.

U.S. Department of Labor. Bureau of Labor Statistics. 1991. *Employment and Earnings.* January. Washington, D.C.: Government Printing Office.

Williams, Christine L. 1989. *Gender Differences at Work: Women and Men in Nontraditional Occupations.* Berkeley: University of California Press.

York, Reginald O., H. Carl Henley, and Dorothy N. Gamble. 1987. "Sexual discrimination in social work: Is it salary or advancement?" *Social Work* 32: 336–340.

Zimmer, Lynn. 1988. "Tokenism and women in the workplace." *Social Problems* 35: 64–77.

Further Questions

   1. If there are few members of one gender in an occupation, social occasions might be awkward for them. What is a good way to resolve this potential problem?

   2. Describe some of the negative stereotypes associated with men in nontraditional fields. Is there any way to dismantle such stereotypes? Is there a way to solve the problem that entering a predominantly female area can be perceived as a step-down in status for men?

   3. If you were in charge of hiring in a traditionally female occupation, what attitude would you take toward favoring men applicants? If you were in charge of promotions, would you favor men candidates?

Undocumented Latinas:
III.8 The New "Employable Mothers"

GRACE CHANG

Grace Chang describes some of the hardships endured by undocumented immigrant women who are employed for child care and domestic work by the more privileged class. In some cases their condition is almost slavery or indentured servitude. They cannot escape these hardships because they lack the documentation to get themselves better positions.

   When she wrote this article, Chang was completing her Ph.D. in ethnic studies at the University of California at Berkeley.

Reading Questions

1. Should someone receive the minimum wage for child-care even though the employer can get away with paying less? Can an employer force her nanny employee to work 16 hour days with no time off?
2. What should be done about the fact that an immigrant nanny must often leave her own children in the care of others while she cares for her employer's children?
3. Should regulations be changed so that household employers may hire "illegal" immigrants or should household workers be given special visas? What problems would such changes solve? What problems would such changes create?

THE NOMINATION OF ZOE BAIRD for U.S. Attorney General in 1993 forced a confession that provoked a public uproar. Baird admitted to employing two undocumented Peruvian immigrants, as a baby-sitter and a driver, in clear violation of current immigration law prohibiting the hiring of "illegal" aliens. Responses to Baird's disclosure indicate her "crime" is a pervasive phenomenon.[1] Deborah Sontag reported in the *New York Times* that two-career, middle-class families employing so-called illegal immigrants to do child care and domestic work is so common that employment agencies routinely recommend undocumented immigrants to their clients. As the director of one Manhattan nanny agency said, "It's just a reality of life that without the illegal girls, there wouldn't be any nannies, and the mommies would have to stay home and mind their own kids."[2] Another agency's director said bluntly, "It all comes down to money . . . the reason that people hire immigrants without papers is that they're looking to save. If they want legal, they can get it, but it costs."[3] According to a survey of eighteen New York agencies, "illegal" workers earned as little as 175 dollars a week and "legal" workers as much as six hundred dollars.[4]

Thus the uproar surrounding Zoe Baird was not so much a response to the discovery that some people flouted the law by employing undocumented workers. This was hardly news. Rather, the public outcry was a reflection of resentment that this practice was so easily accessible to the more privileged classes while others, that is, working-class, "working" mothers, struggled to find any child care. As one critic of Baird commented, "I don't think it's fair. I raised my kids while I was working. I worked days. My husband worked nights at the post office. Our in-laws filled in when they had to."[5] Another woman pointed out "Average working mothers don't make nearly what she makes, and yet we are obligated to follow the law."[6]

What was conspicuously absent from most of the commentary on the Baird controversy was concern for the plight of the undocumented workers themselves. Ironically, two other news stories involving immigrant women working in private households appeared in a California newspaper at the same time Zoe Baird's situation was making headlines across the nation; yet these stories did not receive comparable attention. The first of these involved Claudia Garate, who immigrated from Chile at the age of nineteen in order to take a job as an au pair for a professional couple. Ms. Garate testified before the state Labor Commissioner in Sonoma County that she slept on the floor and worked on call twenty-four hours a day, seven days a week as a maid, baby-sitter, cook and gardener for fifty dollars a month. Garate's employers held on to her visa and passport, and withheld her pay for thirteen months, claiming they would deposit it in a bank account for her. The second case involved Maria de Jesus Ramos Hernandez, who left her three children in Mexico to work as a housekeeper in California. Once here, her employer repeatedly raped her, telling her that he had paid her way here and would have her jailed if she did not submit to him.[7]

Evidence indicates that while Garate's and Hernandez's cases may have been extreme, abuses of undocumented women working in private households were not uncommon. Lina Avidan, program director for the San Francisco-based Coalition for Immigrant and Refugee Rights and Services (CIRRS), said "I have clients who work . . . seven days a week, doing child care from 6 A.M. to 10 P.M. [for] $200 a month. Clearly, they are working in the homes of the wealthy and they're not even getting minimum wage."[8] Spokeswomen for Mujeres Unidas y Activas, a San Francisco-based advocacy group for Latina immigrants, said they had heard countless reports from Latinas working as domestics who endure conditions approaching slavery or indentured servitude.[9] These statements were echoed by undocumented household workers in New York. For example, Dorothea Grant, a Jamaican woman who received a green card after working as a nanny for seven years, explained why American-born workers rarely apply for nanny jobs: "These days, most Americans see it as some kind of slavery."[10] Others reported that because their employers agreed to sponsor them for legal residency they felt like indentured servants in the interim, sometimes waiting up to ten years. One woman from Guyana who had applied for residency six years before was working on call round the clock as a housekeeper for her sponsoring family.[11]

Taken together, these accounts indicate that middle-class households often make exploitative use of immigrant women to do child care and domestic work. They also suggest that the advances of many middle-class, white women in the work force have been largely predicated on the exploitation of poor, immigrant women. While middle- and upper-class women entrust their children and homes to undocumented immigrant women, the immigrant women often must leave their own children in order to work. Some leave their children with family in their home countries, hoping to earn enough to return or send money back to them. Thus, middle- and upper-class women are readily able to find "affordable" care for their children at the expense of poor immigrant women and their children. The employment of undocumented women in dead-end, low-wage, temporary service jobs—often under exploitative conditions—makes it possible for middle- and upper-class women to pursue salaried jobs, and not have to contend with the "second shift" when they come home.

A predictable outgrowth of the Baird controversy has been the proposal that the existing law, the Immigration Reform and Control Act (IRCA) of 1986, be changed so that household employers are exempted from the prohibition against hiring "illegal" immigrants, or that household workers are given special visas. If the law were changed to meet this "popular demand," it would only serve to perpetuate—and authorize by law—the exploitation of thousands of undocumented immigrants. Certainly there is much historical precedent for government-sanc-

tioned exploitation of immigrants as cheap laborers in the U.S. For example in response to the wartime demands of Southwestern agricultural employers for laborers, the Bracero Program was instituted in 1942, allowing for the importation of millions of Mexicans as temporary workers. These workers were bound to fixed low wages, and obliged to stay on certain farms until they were to be returned to Mexico at the end of their contractual periods. Following this model, agribusiness lobbyists succeeded in getting provisions for agricultural "guest workers" written into IRCA, enabling growers to continue to draw on immigrants as a superexploitable labor pool. The current proposals raise the specter of a counterpart to these agricultural "guest workers" in private household work: "disposable nannies" who may be dumped once babies become older or newer immigrants can be found who are willing to work for even lower wages. . . .

THE IMMIGRATION REFORM AND CONTROL ACT OF 1986: A COMPROMISE

The IRCA emerged in 1986 after nearly a decade of debate in Congress and in the public domain about what impact immigration, particularly "illegal" immigration, had on the U.S. economy. The Act had two main objectives that were possibly contradictory: to stem the tide of illegal immigration, and to provide rights and the chance to legalize their status to those undocumented immigrants who had already lived and/or worked in the country. Unable to reconcile these conflicting impulses, Congress incorporated a number of provisions into the law as concessions to various interest groups. First, to discourage illegal immigration, the law established employer sanctions against those who knowingly employed "illegal" immigrants. Second, to provide rights and protections to undocumented persons. The amnesty program offered those who could prove they had lived in the country "illegally" since at least 1982 the chance to apply for temporary resident status. Finally, in response to the concerns of growers about how the law might affect the availability of agricultural labor, Congress created three special classes of those who could enter the country or gain residency as agricultural workers.

Some of the most heated debate surrounding IRCA centered around the issue of whether immigrants contribute to or deplete the public coffers. This debate led lawmakers to include in IRCA two provisions, the public charge exclusion and the five-year bar, governing whether those perceived as potentially welfare-dependent should be able to gain residency, and what entitlements "legalized persons" should be allowed to receive. Before examining these provisions more closely, it will be useful to look at some of the dimensions of this debate, in order to understand the political context in which these provisions were formulated and implemented. In the past, most public views and scholarly discussions on the "costs and benefits" of immigrants have emphasized the charge that male migrant laborers steal jobs from "native" workers. In the last decade, however, this concern has been drowned out by cries that immigrants impose a heavy welfare burden on "natives." A 1986 CBS/*New York Times* poll found that forty-seven percent of Americans believed that "most immigrants wind up on welfare."[12] In a review of studies on the economic impacts of immigration to the U.S., Annie Nakao reported for the *San Francisco Examiner,* "What is generally accepted is that immigrants do not take jobs from natives. . . ."[13] The abundance of studies examining how immigrants affect the U.S. economy disagree on many points, but most recent works seem to agree that Americans should be more worried about protecting public revenues than their jobs.

Thus, a new twist in anti-immigrant rhetoric has emerged, with a focus on immigrants as economic welfare burdens. For example, Governor Pete Wilson deployed this rhetoric in marketing his proposals for slashing social service funds in California's 1992 budget. In his administration's report "The Growing Taxpayer Squeeze,"

Wilson called immigrants "tax receivers" and identified the "rising foreign immigrant population" as a major cause of growing tax expenditures for welfare, Medi-Cal, and public schools.[14] The new emphasis on the alleged depletion of public revenues by immigrants signals an implicit shift in the main target of anti-immigrant attacks. Men as job stealers are no longer seen as the "immigrant problem." Instead, immigrant women as idle, welfare-dependent mothers and inordinate breeders of dependents are seen as the great menace. Thus, a legislative analyst on Governor Wilson's staff reported that Latinas have an AFDC dependency rate twenty-three percent higher than the rate for all other women.[15] Such "findings" are almost always coupled with statements about higher birth rates among immigrant women and the threat they pose to controlling population growth.

Perhaps this new strategy, identifying immigrant women (and particularly Latinas) as the major threat to American public resources, reflects a growing awareness of changes that have occurred in the composition and nature of Mexican migration to the U.S. in the last two decades. Wayne Cornelius, of the Center for U.S.-Mexican Studies, reports that, beginning in the 1970s and through the 1980s, there was a shift in Mexican migration from that dominated by "lone male" (single or unaccompanied by dependents), seasonally employed, and highly mobile, migrant laborers to a "de facto" permanent Mexican immigrant population including more women, children, and entire families.[16] The change consists of more migration by whole families, more family reunification, and more migration by single women. Cornelius explains that Mexico's crisis has driven more women to migrate to the United States, where there is "an abundance of new employment opportunities for which women are the preferred labor source," including child care, cleaning, and laundry work.

Cornelius's analysis of U.S. Census Bureau (1988) data suggests that, as a result of this expanded female migration, females may now represent the majority of "settled" undocumented

Mexican immigrants. In her study of undocumented Mexican immigrant communities, Pierette Hondagneu reports that it is the women who advocate and mobilize families toward permanent settlement in the U.S. Thus, she theorizes, U.S. xenophobia has come to focus on women because they are perceived as the leaders of this threatening demographic shift.[17]

Heightened awareness of these new demographics contributed to hysteria about protecting public revenues and guarding against the growth of a population of welfare dependents. These concerns undoubtedly influenced the inclusion of two provisions of IRCA, the public charge exclusion and the five-year bar, to restrict aliens' access to social services and public benefits. Clearly, these restrictions were formulated with the goal of limiting welfare expenditures. In executing IRCA, the INS went even further, utilizing an interpretation of the law that effectively denied amnesty to those seen as potential welfare abusers, that is, undocumented women with children. . . .

CONCLUSION

Some feminists have proposed that subsidies to women with children should be expanded in the recognition that full-time mothering is work and should be properly rewarded. Wendy Sarvasy, for example, has called for us to recapture some of the original principles behind the Mothers' Pension program: that mothers be seen as civil servants and provided with pensions as compensation for their services in nurturing future citizens.[18] Such proposals repeat the original flaw of the Mothers' Pension program: limiting support to an elite group of women by defining "deserving" mothers as full-time mothers, while few women actually find full-time mothering viable. Under the current racial division of reproductive labor, some women cannot stay at home with their own children while they mother other people's children and keep other people's homes. Ironically, the assumption of these reproductive functions by

women of color and immigrant women of white middle-class or professional women allows the latter group *not* to choose full-time mothering, opting for careers and other pursuits which may be more rewarding economically or personally. Thus, proposals to reward full-time mothering offer nothing to most women of color, for whom this occupation is rarely an option.

Furthermore, women of color may not view full-time mothering as the ideal. Historically, women of color have had to work, even while raising small children, either to supplement inadequate wages garnered by their men, or to provide for families in the absence of male providers. In response, communities of color have often constructed alternatives to dominant society's model of the family in which men are providers and women primarily dependents and consumers. For example, Carol Stack and Linda Burton report that male, female, old, and young members of low-income African-American families negotiated shared caretaking responsibilities, enabling women to earn wages during early childbearing years.[19] Similarly, the Mexican mothers in Denise Segura's study viewed employment as compatible with mothering, as it enabled them to contribute toward the collective good of the family.[20]

Thus, proposals to reform the welfare system through revaluing the work of full-time mothering fail to address the needs of women of color and further marginalize them in their struggles to provide for their families. A more radical proposition—and one which might begin to address the plight of women of color who are poor working mothers—would be to recognize and reward women for the services they provide through both their productive and reproductive labors. . . . This would necessitate a demystification of these women as welfare-dependents, and a recognition that they are working mothers, often heads of household or at least significant providers for their families. More importantly, such a demystification might compel the states to recognize the many ways in which these women benefit American capital and society at large—through paid (but grossly undercompensated) productive labor, through reproductive labor for others, and through the reproductive functions they perform within their own families. The fact that they too, in raising their own children, provide a service in nurturing future adult citizens should not be obscured by public ignorance casting their children as somehow less worthy.

In return for all of these contributions, these women should at least be afforded access to citizenship. This would mean that they would not jeopardize their chances to gain legal status in seeking public assistance, including AFDC, for their children, many of whom are American citizens by birth and therefore fully entitled to these benefits. The professed goal of AFDC is to give temporary support to poor mothers so that ultimately they may be able to provide for their families through wage earning. If this is indeed the objective of AFDC, then denying amnesty to undocumented women who have received aid for their children contradicts this purpose by undermining these women's abilities to increase their employment options and earning powers. As we have seen, government policies have been utilized to handicap rather than support undocumented mothers. These practices facilitate U.S. employers' ability to extract cheap labor from these women and at the same time allow the state to evade responsibility for the welfare of citizen children. Undocumented women have been forced to choose between aid for their children or the possibility to gain legal status. Those who "choose" aid for their children condemn themselves to remain in an underclass, unrecognized as "productive citizens," yet functioning as perhaps the ultimate servants of our society.

NOTES

1. The *San Francisco Chronicle* reported that, although no precise figures exist, "experts believe a large percentage of the estimated 3 million undocumented workers now residing in the United States are employed in child-care and domestic work." "Hiring of

Aliens Is a Widespread Practice," "San Francisco Chronicle" (January 15, 1993), p. A6.

2. Deborah Sontag, "Increasingly, Two-Career Family Means Illegal Immigrant Help," *New York Times* (January 24, 1993), p. A-1.

3. Ibid., p. A-13.

4. Ibid.

5. Felicity Barringer, "What Many Say About Baird: What She Did Wasn't Right," *New York Times* (January 22, 1993), p. A1.

6. Ibid., p. A10.

7. Carla Marinucci, "Immigrant Abuse: 'Slavery—Pure and Simple,'" *San Francisco Examiner* (January 10, 1993), pp. A-1, A-8.

8. Carla Marinucci, pp. A1, A8.

9. Carla Marinucci, "Silence Shields Abuse of Immigrant Women," *San Francisco Examiner* (January 11, 1993), pp. A-1, A-10.

10. Sontag, p. A13.

11. Ibid.

12. CBS/*New York Times* poll, July 14, 1986, cited in Julian Simon, *The Economic Consequences of Immigration* (Cambridge: Basil Blackwell, Inc., 1989), p. 105.

13. Annie Nakao, "Assessing the Cost of Immigration," *San Francisco Examiner* (December 1, 1991), pp. B-1, B-3.

14. Terri Lobdell and Lewis Butler, "Tending Our Future Together," *California Perspectives* (November, 1991), pp. 31–41; and California Department of Finance, "California's Growing Taxpayer Squeeze," *California Perspectives* (November, 1991), p. 4.

15. Nakao, p. B-3.

16. Wayne Cornelius, "From Sojourners to Settlers: The Changing Profile of Mexican Migration to the U.S." (San Diego: Center for U.S.-Mexican Studies, University of California, San Diego, August 15, 1990), p.17; published in Jorge Bustamante, Raul Hinojosa, and Clark Reynolds, eds., *U.S.-Mexico Relations: Labor Market Interdependence* (Stanford, CA: Stanford University Press, 1991).

17. Pierrette M. Hondagneu, "Gender and the Politics of Mexican Undocumented Immigrant Settlement," Ph.D. Dissertation, University of California (1990), p. 249.

18. Wendy Sarvasy, "Reagan and Low-Income Mothers: A Feminist Recasting of the Debate," in M. K. Brown, ed., *Remaking the Welfare State: Retrenchment and Social Policy in America and Europe* (Philadelphia: Temple University Press, 1988), pp. 253–276.

19. Carol Stack and Linda Burton, "Kinscripts: Reflections on Family, Generation, and Culture," in E. Nakano Glenn, G. Chang, and L. Rennie Forcey, eds., *Mothering: Ideology, Experience, and Agency* (New York: Routledge, 1993).

20. Denise Segura, "Working at Motherhood: Chicana and Mexican Immigrant Mothers and Employment," in E. Nakano Glenn, G. Chang, and L. Rennie Forcey, eds., *Mothering: Ideology, Experience, and Agency* (New York: Routledge, 1993).

Further Questions

1. Is the new Latina migration by more women, children, and families in response to the new opportunities for women in domestic service likely to pose a threat to the American public resource system?

2. Should full-time mothering work be rewarded by the public resource system? How would this affect mothers of color who must work outside the home?

3. Would you ever consider an undocumented Latina as a nanny for your children? Would you prefer it if she were documented but had a poor array of other job options? If you hire her, how much would you pay her and what kind of hours would you expect her to work?

Further Readings for Part III: The Workplace

Lisa Adkins. *Gendered Work: Sexuality, Family and the Labour Market* (Bristol, PA: Open University Press, 1995). Gendered nature of the labour market in Britain.

Pat Armstrong and Hugh Armstrong. *The Double Ghetto: Canadian Women and Their Segregated Work* (Toronto, ON: McClelland and Stewart, Revised Edition, 1989). Argument that gender segregation in the labor force mirrors and is influenced by the division of domestic work by gender.

Barbara R. Bergman. *The Economic Emergence of Women* (New York, NY: Basic Books, 1986). Knowledgeable tracing of the exodus of women from home into the workforce, only to be occupationally segregated and become major victims of discrimination. Multifaceted agenda for change.

Jessie Bernard. *Academic Women* (New York, NY: Meridian, 1964). Discussion of the forces in academic life which hold women back by affecting their motivation, creativity, and productivity.

Martha Blaxall and Barbara Regan, eds. *Women and the Workplace: The Implications for Occupational Segregation* (Chicago, IL: The University of Chicago Press, 1976). Workplace gender segregation, its roots and consequences and some strategies for combatting it.

Eileen Boris and Elisabeth Prügl. *Homeworkers in Global Perspective: Invisible No More* (New York, NY: Routledge, 1996). The conduct of home-based labor by women in the U.S. and in an international context.

Steven M. Cahn, ed. *The Affirmative Action Debate* (New York, NY: Routledge, 1995). Classics in the field, mainly by philosophers.

Nicholas Capaldi. *Out of Order: Affirmative Action and the Crisis of Doctrinaire Liberalism* (Buffalo, NY: Prometheus Books, 1985). Thoroughgoing critique of affirmative action.

David L. Collinson. "Engineering Humor: Masculinity and Conflict in Shop Floor Relations," in *Organizational Studies*, 1988 9/2, pp. 181–199. Reprinted in Michael S. Kimmel and Michael A. Messner, eds. *Men's Lives* (New York, NY: Macmillan, 2nd Edition, 1992) pp. 232–246. The role of joking among men on the shop floor.

D. S. David and R. Brannon, eds. *The Forty-nine Percent Majority: The Male Sex Role* (Reading, MA: Addison-Wesley, 1976). Some good discussions of the workplace functioning as a primary component of masculinity.

Ann Duffy and Norene Pupo. *Part-time Paradox: Connecting Gender, Work and Family* (Toronto, ON: McClelland and Stewart Inc. 1992). Part-time work is ghettoized and poorly paid. Almost three-quarters of Canada's part-time workers are women.

Gertrude Ezorsky. *Racism and Justice: The Case for Affirmative Action* (Ithaca, NY: Cornell University Press, 1991). Good, thoughtful arguments for affirmative action in a racist society. Some are applicable to a sexist society as well.

Judy Fudge and Patricia McDermott, eds. *Just Wages: A Feminist Assessment of Pay Equity* (Toronto, ON: University of Toronto Press, 1991). Impact of pay equity legislation upon public service, the public sector and the private sector.

Robert K. Fullenwider. *The Reverse Discrimination Controversy. A Moral and Legal Analysis* (Totowa, NJ: Rowan and Littlefield, 1981). Well organized discussion of aspects of affirmative action.

Charlene Gannage. *Double Day, Double Bind: Women Garment Workers* (Toronto: The Women's Press, 1986). Bad situations experienced by women garment workers, especially immigrant workers.

Winona Giles and Sedet Arat-Koç, eds. *Maid in the Market: Women's Paid Domestic Labour* (Halifax, NS: Fernwood Publishing, 1994). Discussion of how domestic work is subordinated and devalued when done for a wage.

Alan H. Goldman. *Justice and Reverse Discrimination* (Princeton, NJ: Princeton University Press, 1979). Affirmative action again. Drier discussion than Ezorsky and Fullenwider.

Mona Harrington. *Women Lawyers: Rewriting the Rules* (New York, NY: Penguin Books, 1993). What happens to women lawyers in the male-dominated legal profession.

Pat Heim with Susan K. Golant. *Hardball for Women: Winning at the Game of Business* (New York, NY: Penguin Books, 1993). How to be a woman who succeeds in the man's world of business.

Kevin D. Henson. *Just a Temp* (Philadelphia, PA: Temple University Press, 1996). Issues in temporary work.

Rosanna Hertz. *More Equal Than Others: Women and Men in Dual-Career Marriages* (Berkeley, CA: University of California Press, 1986). Both husband and wife suffer in a dual-career situation (especially if there are children) if the marriage retains its traditional structure.

Martin P. Levine. "The Status of Gay Men in the Workplace" in Michael S. Kimmel and Michael A. Messner, eds. *Men's Lives* (New York, NY: Macmillan, 2nd Edition, 1992) pp. 251–266.

Martin P. Levine and Robert Leonard. "Discrimination Against Lesbians in the Workforce," in *Signs* 9 (4) pp. 700–710.

Richard R. Peterson. *Women, Work and Divorce* (Albany, NY: State University of New York Press, 1989). Divorce is an economic hardship on women, but it generally improves the position of women in the workplace. Work now appears to be better than marriage for a woman's economic security.

J. H. Pleck and J. Sawyer, eds. *Men and Masculinity* (Englewood Cliffs, NJ: Prentice Hall, 1974). More on breadwinner problems in the male role. The collection features Robert E. Gould's "Measuring Masculinity by the Size of a Paycheck."

Judith Posner. *The Feminine Mistake: Women, Work and Identity* (New York, NY: Warner Books, 1992). The mistake is believing that as a woman you can have it all—work in the fast track, and also be a supermom and a perfect wife. Slow down and find your own solution.

Rosemary Pringle. *Secretaries Talk: Sexuality, Power, and Work* (New York, NY: Verso, 1988). Interviews with almost 500 secretaries from a wide range of workplaces.

Maeve Quaid. *Job Evaluation: The Myth of Equitable Assessment* (Toronto, ON: University of Toronto Press, 1993). Careful demonstration that jobs cannot be compared for purposes of establishing pay equity.

Barbara Reskin and Irene Pactavíc. *Women and Men at Work* (Thousand Oaks, CA: Pine Forge Press, 1994). The gendered nature of paid and unpaid work.

Barbara F. Reskin and Patricia A. Roos. *Job Queues, Gender Queues: Explaining Women's Inroads into Male Occupations* (Philadelphia, PA: Temple University Press, 1990).

Mary Romero. *Maid in U.S.A.* (New York, NY: Routledge, Chapman and Hall, Inc., 1992). How domestic work creates hierarchies of gender, race, and class.

Ellen Israel Rosen. *Bitter Choices: Blue Collar Women In and Out of Work* (Chicago, IL: The University of Chicago Press, 1987). Includes the impact of class and gender on blue collar work.

Anne Statham, Eleanor M. Miller, Haus O. Mauksch, eds. *The Worth of Women's Work* (Albany, NY: State University of New York Press, 1988). Women's work experiences in thirteen professions, from domestic service to policewoman.

Judith Hicks Stiehm. *Arms and the Enlisted Woman* (Philadelphia, PA: Temple University Press, 1989). Issues affecting the enlisted woman in the armed services.

Judith Hicks Stiehm, ed. *It's Our Military, Too: Women and the U.S. Military* (Philadelphia, PA: Temple University Press, 1996). Women write of women's experiences in the U.S. military.

Deborah J. Swiss and Judith P. Walker. *Women and the Work/Family Dilemma: How Today's Professional Women are Confronting the Maternal Wall* (New York, NY: John Wiley and Sons, Inc., 1993). Women speak of their conflicts between their careers and their children, focusing on the maternal wall which prevents mothers from following certain career choices.

Christine Williams. *Gender Differences at Work: Women and Men in Non-Traditional Occupations* (Berkeley, CA: University of California Press, 1991). Lively descriptions of experiences of men working in traditionally women's fields and vice-versa and the impact of such work on gender identity.

S. J. Wilson. *Women, the Family and the Economy* (New York, NY: McGraw-Hill Ryerson, 1982). Clear, lively discussion of the gender division of labor in the family and workplace.

Mary Wollstonecraft. *A Vindication of the Rights of Women*, C. H. Poston, ed. (New York: Norton, 1975; original work published in 1792). Early insight into women's needs for intellectual and physical exercise.

Virginia Woolf. *A Room of One's Own* (Harmondsworth, England: Penguin Books, Ltd., 1945). "A woman must have money and a room of her own if she is to write fiction." Woolf's thesis is that women's creativity can flourish only if women are allowed the requisite privacy and free time.

Suggested Moral of Part III

Opportunities for women in the workplace are not yet equal to those for men. Because workplace positions are becoming, increasingly, the locus of opportunity to do anything worthwhile, the lives of women are, accordingly, impoverished. In addition, gender discrepancies in power, prestige, and money that originate in the workplace find their way into relations between men and women in other parts of their lives in a society that is still organized by gender.

Part IV

Love and Relationships

Introduction

LOVE IS A TOPIC OF CONTINUING CURIOSITY because it has such an important place in human life. Romantic relationships and friendships seem to receive as much attention as work in questions concerning what human existence is all about. Romantic love is an area where we recognize the importance of gendered life because gender is an essential element of the beloved and because romantic love makes us feel our own gender so keenly.

Nozick explores romantic love; Strikwerda and May discuss intimacy in male friendship; de Beauvoir critiques the situation of the woman in love; Frye distinguishes arrogance from love; Ewing, hooks, and Richie and Kanuha speak to the problem of violence in personal relationships.

IV.1   Love's Bond

ROBERT NOZICK

Robert Nozick claims that infatuation becomes love when one develops the desire to form a "we" with the other person. He has some interesting ideas on why the "we" aspect of love precludes ideas of "trading up" to a better embodiment of the qualities appreciated in the beloved.

Nozick is Arthur Kingsley Porter Professor of Philosophy at Harvard University and author of *Anarchy, State and Utopia, Philosophical Explanations,* and *The Nature of Rationality.* "Love's Bond," from *The Examined Life,* contains some of Nozick's thoughts about life and living. Another selection from *The Examined Life* appears in Part VI.

Reading Questions

1. How would you be able to tell whether a feeling was the real thing (love) this time, rather than a simple infatuation?
2. We think of romantic love as having a unique object. Only this particular person will do as the beloved; someone with identical qualities, or better versions of them, will not do. Why is this?
3. When you are contemplating beginning a romantic relationship with someone, is it appropriate to ask, as Nozick suggests, "Will it be fun?"

THE GENERAL PHENOMENON of love encompasses romantic love, the love of a parent for a child, love of one's country, and more. What is common to all love is this: Your own well-being is tied up with that of someone (or something) you love. When a bad thing happens to a friend, it happens to her and you feel sad for her; when something good happens, you feel happy for her. When something bad happens to one you love, though, something bad also happens *to you.* . . .

This extension of your own well-being (or ill-being) is what marks all the different kinds of love: the love of children, the love of parents, the love of one's people, of one's country. Love is not necessarily a matter of caring equally or more about someone else than about yourself. These loves are large, but love in some amount is present when your well-being is affected to whatever extent (but in the same direction) by another's. As the other fares, so (to some extent) do you. The people you love are included inside your boundaries, their well-being is your own.

Being "in love," infatuation, is an intense state that displays familiar features: almost always thinking of the person; wanting constantly to touch and to be together; excitement in the other's presence; losing sleep; expressing one's feelings through poetry, gifts, or still other ways to delight the beloved; gazing deeply into each other's eyes; candlelit dinners; feeling that short separations are long; smiling foolishly when remembering actions and remarks of the other; feeling that the other's minor foibles are delightful; experiencing joy at having found the other and at being found by the other; and (as Tolstoy depicts Levin in *Anna Karenina* as he learns Kitty loves him) finding *everyone* charming and nice, and thinking they all must sense one's happiness. Other concerns and responsibilities become minor background details in the story of the romance, which become the predominant foreground event of life. (When major public responsibilities such as commanding Rome's armies or being king of England are put aside, the tales engross.) The vividness of the relationship can carry artistic or mythic proportions—lying together like figures in a painting, jointly living a new tale from Ovid. Familiar, too, is what happens when the love is not equally reciprocated: melancholy, obsessive rumination on what went wrong, fantasies about its being set right, lingering in places to catch a glimpse of the person, making telephone calls to hear the other's voice, finding that all other activities seem flat, occasionally having suicidal thoughts.

However and whenever infatuation begins, if given the opportunity it transforms itself into continuing romantic love or else it disappears. With this continuing romantic love, it feels to the two people that they are united to form and constitute a new entity in the world, what might be called a "we."* You can be in romantic love with someone, however, without actually forming a *we* with her or him—that other person might not be in love with you. Love, romantic love, is *wanting* to form a *we* with that particular person, feeling, or perhaps wanting, that particular person to be the right one for you to form a *we* with, and also wanting the other to feel the same way about you. (It would be kinder if the realization that the other person is not the right one with whom to form a *we* al-

*For a discussion of love as the formation of a *we*, see Robert Solomon, *Love* (Garden City, N.Y.: Anchor Books, 1981).

ways and immediately terminated the desire to form it.) The desire to form a *we* with that other person is not simply something that goes along with romantic love, something that contingently happens when love does. That desire is intrinsic to the nature of love, I think; it is an important part of what love intends.

In a *we*, the two people are not bound physically like Siamese twins; they can be in distant places, feel differently about things, carry on different occupations. In what sense, then, do these people together constitute a new entity, a *we*? That new entity is created by a new web of relationships between them which makes them no longer so separate. Let me describe some features of this web: I will begin with two that have a somewhat cold and political-science sound.

First, the defining feature we mentioned which applies to love in general: Your own well-being is tied up with that of someone you love romantically. Love, then, among other things, can place you at risk. Bad things that happen to your loved one happen to you. But so too do good things; moreover, someone who loves you helps you with care and comfort to meet vicissitudes—not out of selfishness although her doing so does, in part, help maintain her own well-being too. Thus, love places a floor under your well-being; it provides insurance in the face of fate's blows. . . .

People who form a *we* pool not only their well-being but also their autonomy. They limit or curtail their own decision-making power and rights; some decisions can no longer be made alone. Which decisions these are will be parceled differently by different couples: where to live, how to live, who friends are and how to see them, whether to have children and how many, where to travel, whether to go to the movies that night and what to see. Each transfers some previous rights to make certain decisions unilaterally into a joint pool; somehow, decisions will be made together about how to be together. If your well-being so closely affects and is affected by another's, it is not surprising that decisions that importantly affect well-being, even in the first instance primarily your own, will no longer be made alone.*

The term *couple* used in reference to people who have formed a *we* is not accidental. The two people also view themselves as a new and continuing unit, and they present that face to the world. They want to be perceived publicly as a couple, to express and assert their identity as a couple in public. Hence those homosexual couples unable to do this face a serious impediment.

To be part of a *we* involves having a new identity, an additional one. This does *not* mean that you no longer have any individual identity or that your sole identity is as part of the *we*. However, the individual identity you did have will become altered. To have this new identity is to enter a certain psychological stance; and each party in the *we* has this stance toward the other. Each becomes psychologically part of the other's identity. How can we say more exactly what this means? To say that something is part of your identity when, if that thing changes or is lost, you feel like a different person, seems only to reintroduce the very notion of identity that needs to be explained. Here is something more helpful: To love someone might be, in part, to devote alertness to their well-being and to your connection with them. (More generally, shall we say that something is part of your identity when you continually make it one of your few areas of special alertness?) There are empirical tests of alertness in the case of your own separate identity—for example, how you hear your name mentioned through the noise of a conversation

you were not consciously attending to; how a word that resembles your name "jumps out" from the page. We might find similar tests to check for that alertness involved in loving someone. For example, a person in a *we* often is considerably more worried about the dangers of traveling—air crashes or whatever—when the other is traveling alone than when both travel together or when he himself or she herself is traveling alone; it seems plausible that a person in a *we* is alert, in general, to dangers to the other that would necessitate having to go back to a single individual identity, while these are made especially salient by a significant physical separation. Other criteria for the formation of a joint identity also might be suggested, such as a certain kind of division of labor. A person in a *we* might find himself coming across something interesting to read yet leaving it for the other person, not because he himself would not be interested in it but because the other would be more interested, and one of them reading it is sufficient for it to be registered by the wider identity now shared, the *we*. If the couple breaks up, they then might notice themselves reading all those things directly; the other person no longer can do it for *them*. (The list of criteria for the *we* might continue on to include something we discuss later, not seeking to "trade up" to another partner.) Sometimes the existence of the *we* can be very palpable. Just as a reflective person can walk along the street in friendly internal dialogue with himself, keeping himself company, so can one be with a loved person who is not physically present, thinking what she would say, conversing with her, noticing things as she would, for her, because she is not there to notice, saying things to others that she would say, in her tone of voice, carrying the full *we* along.

If we picture the individual self as a closed figure whose boundaries are continuous and solid, dividing what is inside from what is outside, then we might diagram the *we* as two figures with the boundary line between them erased where they come together. (Is that the traditional heart shape?) The unitive aspects of sexual experience,

---

* This curtailment of unilateral decision-making rights extends even to a decision to end the romantic love relationship. This decision, if any, you would think you could make by yourself. And so you can, but only in certain ways at a certain pace. Another kind of relation might be ended because you feel like it or because you find it no longer satisfactory, but in a love relationship the other party "has a vote." This does not mean a permanent veto; but the other party has a right to have his or her say, to try to repair, to be convinced. After some time, to be sure, one party may insist on ending the relationship even without the other's consent, but what they each have forgone, in love, is the right to act unilaterally and swiftly.

two persons flowing together and intensely merging, mirror and aid the formation of the *we.* Meaningful work, creative activity, and development can change the shape of the self. Intimate bonds change the boundaries of the self and alter its *topology*—romantic love in one way and friendship (as we shall see) in another.

The individual self can be related to the *we* it identifies with in two different ways. It can see the *we* as a very important *aspect* of itself, or it can see itself as part of the *we,* as contained within it. It may be that men more often take the former view, women the latter. Although both see the *we* as extremely important for the self, most men might draw the circle of themselves containing the circle of the *we* as an aspect *within* it, while most women might draw the circle of themselves within the circle of the *we.* In either case, the *we* need not consume an individual self or leave it without any autonomy. . . .

The heart of the love relationship is how the lovers view it from the inside, how they feel about their partner and about themselves within it, and the particular ways in which they are good *to* each other. Each person in love delights in the other, and also in giving delight; this often expresses itself in being playful together. In receiving adult love, we are held worthy of being the primary object of the most intense love, something we were not given in the childhood oedipal triangle. Seeing the other happy with us and made happy through our love, we become happier with ourselves.

To be englowed by someone's love, it must be we ourselves who are loved, not a whitewashed version of ourselves, not just a portion. In the complete intimacy of love, a partner knows us as we are, fully. It is no reassurance to be loved by someone ignorant of those traits and features we feel might make us unlovable. Sometimes these are character traits or areas of incompetence, clumsiness, or ignorance; sometimes these are personal bodily features. Complex are the ways parents make children uncomfortable about sites of pleasure or elimination, and these feelings can be soothed or transformed in the closest attentive and loving sexual intimacy. In the full intimacy of love, the full person is known and cleansed and accepted. And healed.

To be made happy with yourself by being loved, it must be you who is loved, not some feature such as your money. People want, as they say, to be loved "for themselves." You are loved for something else when what you are loved for is a peripheral part of your own self-image or identity. However, someone for whom money, or the ability to make it, was central to his identity, or for whom good looks or great kindness or intelligence was, might not be averse to love's being prompted by these characteristics. You can fall in love with someone because of certain characteristics and you can continue to delight in these; but eventually you must love the person himself, and not *for* the characteristics, not, at any rate, for any delimited list of them. But what does this mean, exactly?

We love the person when being together with that person is a salient part of our identity as we think of it: "being with Eve," "being with Adam," rather than "being with someone who is (or has) such-and-such. . . ." How does this come about? Characteristics must have played some important role, for otherwise why was not a different person loved just as well? Yet if we continue to be loved "for" the characteristics, then the love seems conditional, something that might change or disappear if the characteristics do. Perhaps we should think of love as like imprinting in ducks, where a duckling will attach itself to the first sizable moving object it sees in a certain time period and follow that as its mother. With people, perhaps characteristics set off the imprint of love, but then the person is loved in a way that is no longer based upon retaining those characteristics. This will be helped if the love is based at first upon a wide range of characteristics; it begins as conditional, contingent upon the loved person's having these desirable characteristics, yet given their range and tenacity, it is not insecure.

However, love between people, unlike imprinting with ducks, is not unalterable. Though no longer dependent upon the particular characteristics that set it off, it *can* be overcome over time by new and sufficiently negative other characteristics. Or perhaps by a new imprinting onto another person. Yet this alteration will not be sought by someone with a *we*. If someone were loved "for" certain desirable or valuable characteristics, on the other hand, then if someone else came along who had those characteristics to a greater extent, or other even more valuable characteristics, it seems you should love this new person more. And in that case, why merely wait for a "better" person to turn up; why not actively seek to "trade up" to someone with a "higher score" along valuable dimensions? (Plato's theory is especially vulnerable to these questions, for there it is the Form of Beauty that is the ultimate and appropriate object of love; any particular person serves merely as a bearer of characteristics that awaken in the lover a love of the Form, and hence any such person should be replaceable by a better awakener.*)

A readiness to trade up, looking for someone with "better" characteristics, does not fit with an attitude of love. An illuminating view should explain why not, yet why, nevertheless, the attitude of love is not irrational. One possible and boring explanation is economic in form. Once you have come to know a person well, it would take a large investment of time and energy to reach the comparable point with another person, so there is a barrier to switching. (But couldn't the other person promise a greater return, even taking into account the new costs of investment?) There is uncertainty about a new person; only after long time and experience together, through arguments and crises, can one come to know a person's trustworthiness, reliability, resiliency, and compassion in hardships. Investigating another candidate for coupledom, even an apparently promising one, is likely eventually to reach a neg-

ative conclusion and it probably will necessitate curtailing or ending one's current coupled state. So it is unwise to seek to trade up from a reasonably satisfactory situation; the energy you'd expend in search might better be invested in improving your current *we*.

These counsels of economic prudence are not silly—far from it—but they are external. According to them, nothing about the nature of love itself focuses upon the particular individual loved or involves an unwillingness to substitute another; rather, the likelihood of losses from the substitution is what militates against it. We can see why, if the economic analysis were so, we would welcome someone's directing an attitude of love toward us that includes commitment to a particular person, and we can see why we might have to trade the offering or semblance of such an attitude in order to receive it. But why would we want actually to give such a commitment to a particular person, shunning all other partners? What special value is reached through such a love relationship committed to particularism but in no other way? To add that we care about our partners and so do not want to cause them hurt by replacing them is true, yet does not answer the question fully.

Economic analysis might even provide somewhat more understanding.† Repeated trading with a fixed partner with special resources might make it rational to develop in yourself specialized assets for trading with that partner (and similarly on the partner's part toward you); and this specialization gives some assurance that you will continue to trade *with that party* (since the invested resources would be worth much less in exchanges with any third party). Moreover, to shape yourself and specialize so as to better fit and trade with that partner, and therefore to do so less well with others, you will want some commitment and guarantee that the party will continue to trade with you, a guarantee that

---

* See Gregory Vlastos, "The Individual as an Object of Love in Plato," in his *Platonic Studies* (Princeton: Princeton University Press, 1973), pp. 3–34.

† This paragraph was suggested by the mode of economic analysis found in Oliver Williamson, *The Economic Institutions of Capitalism* (New York: The Free Press, 1986).

goes beyond the party's own specialization to fit you. Under some conditions it will be economically advantageous for two such trading firms to combine into *one* firm, with all allocations now becoming internal. Here at last we come to something like the notion of a joint identity.

The intention in love is to form a *we* and to identify with it as an extended self, to identify one's fortunes in large part with its fortunes. A willingness to trade up, to destroy the very *we* you largely identify with, would then be a willingness to destroy your self in the form of your own extended self. One could not, therefore, intend to link into another *we* unless one had ceased to identify with a current one—unless, that is, one had already ceased to love. Even in that case, the intention to form the new *we* would be an intention to *then* no longer be open to trading up. It is intrinsic to the notion of love, and to the *we* formed by it, that there is not that willingness to trade up. One is no more willing to find another partner, even one with a "higher score," than to destroy the personal self one identifies with in order to allow another, possibly better, but discontinuous self to replace it. (This is not to say one is unwilling to improve or transform oneself.) Perhaps here lies one function of infatuation, to pave and smooth the way to uniting in a *we;* it provides enthusiasm to take one over the hurdles of concern for one's own autonomy, and it provides an initiation into *we* thinking too, by constantly occupying the mind with thoughts of the other and of the two of you together. A more cynical view than mine might see infatuation as the temporary glue that manages to hold people together until they are stuck.

Part of the process by which people soften their boundaries and move into a *we* involves repeated expression of the desire to do so, repeatedly telling each other that they love each other. Their statement often will be tentative, subject to withdrawal if the other does not respond with similar avowals. Holding hands, they walk into the water together, step by step. Their caution may become as great as when two suspicious groups or nations—Israel and the Palestinians

might be an example—need to recognize the legitimacy of one another. Neither wants to recognize if the other does not, and it also will not suffice for each to announce that it will recognize if the other one does also. For each then will have announced a conditional recognition, contingent upon the other's unconditional recognition. Since neither one has offered this last, they haven't yet gotten started. Neither will it help if each says it will recognize conditional upon the other's conditional recognition: "I'll recognize you if you'll recognize me if I'll recognize you." For here each has given the other a three-part conditional announcement, one which is contingent upon, and goes into operation only when there exists, a two-part conditional announcement for the other party; so neither one has given the other exactly what will trigger that other's recognition, namely a two-part announcement. So long as they both symmetrically announce conditionals of the same length and complexity, they will not be able to get started. Some asymmetry is needed, then, but it need not be that either one begins by offering unconditional recognition. It would be enough for the first to offer the three-part recognition (which is contingent upon the other's simple two-part conditional recognition), and for the second to offer the two-part conditional recognition. The latter triggers the first to recognize outright and this, in turn, triggers the second to do the same. Between lovers, it never becomes this complicated explicitly. Neither makes the nested announcement "I will love you if you will love me if I will love you," and if either one did, this would not (to put it mildly) facilitate the formation of a *we*. Yet the frequency of their saying to each other, "I love you," and their attention to the other's response, may indicate a nesting that is implicit and very deep, as deep as the repeated triggering necessary to overcome caution and produce the actual and unconditional formation of the *we*. . . .

The desire to have love in one's life, to be part of a *we* someday, is not the same as loving a particular person, wanting to form a *we* with that person in particular. In the choice of a particular partner, reasons can play a significant role, I think. Yet in addition to the merits of the other person and her or his qualities, there also is the question of whether the thought of forming a *we* with that person brings excitement and delight. Does that identity seem a wonderful one for you to have? Will it be *fun*? Here the answer is as complicated and mysterious as your relation to your own separate identity. Neither case is completely governed by reasons, but still we might hope that our choices do meet what reasoned standards there are. (The desire to continue to feel that the other is the right partner in your *we* also helps one surmount the inevitable moments in life together when that feeling itself becomes bruised.) The feeling that there is just "one right person" in the world for you, implausible beforehand—what lucky accident made that one unique person inhabit your century?—becomes true after the *we* is formed. Now your identity is wrapped up in that particular *we* with that particular person, so for the particular *you* you now are, there *is* just one other person who is right.

In the view of a person who loves someone romantically, there couldn't be anyone else who was better as a partner. He might think that person he is in love with could be better somehow—stop leaving toothpaste in the sink or whatever—but any description he could offer of a better mate would be a description of his mate changed, not one of somebody *else*. No one else would do, no matter what her qualities. Perhaps this is due to the particularity of the qualities you come to love, not just a sense of humor but that particular one, not just some way of looking mock-stern but that one. Plato got the matter reversed, then; as love grows you love not general aspects of traits but more and more particular ones, not intelligence in general but that particular mind, not kindness in general but those particular ways of being kind. In trying to imagine a "better" mate, a person in romantic love will require her or him to have a very particular constellation of very particular traits and—

leaving aside various "science fiction" possibilities—no other person *could* have precisely those traits; therefore, any imagined person will be the same mate (perhaps) somewhat changed, not somebody else. (If that same mate actually alters, though, the romantic partner may well come to love and require that new constellation of particulars.) Hence, a person in romantic love *could not* seek to "trade up"—he would have to seek out the very same person. A person not in love might seek someone with certain traits, yet after finding someone, even (remarkably) a person who has the traits sought, if he loves that person she will show those traits in a particularity he did not initially seek but now has come to love—her particular versions of these traits. Since a romantic mate eventually comes to be loved, not for any general dimensions or "score" on such dimensions—that, if anything, gets taken for granted—but for his or her own particular and nonduplicable way of embodying such general traits, a person in love could not make any coherent sense of his "trading up" to *another*. . . .

This does not yet show that a person could not have many such different focused desires, just as she might desire to read this particular book and also that one. I believe that the romantic desire is to form a *we* with that particular person *and* with no other. In the strong sense of the notion of identity involved here, one can no more be part of many *wes* which constitute one's identity than one can simultaneously have many individual identities. (What persons with multiple personality have is not many identities but not quite one.) In a *we*, the people *share* an identity and do not simply each have identities that are enlarged. The desire to share not only our life but our very identity with another marks our fullest openness. What more central and intimate thing could we share? . . .

It is instructive here to consider friendship, which too alters and recontours an individual's boundaries, providing a distinct shape and character to the self. The salient feature of friendship is *sharing*. In sharing things—food, happy occasions, football games, a concern with problems, events to celebrate—friends especially want these to be had together; while it might constitute something good when each person has the thing separately, friends want that it be had or done by both (or all) of them *together.* To be sure, a good thing does get magnified for you when it is shared with others, and some things can be more fun when done together—indeed, fun, in part, is just the sharing and taking of delight in something together. Yet in friendship the sharing is not desired simply to enlarge our individual benefits.

A friendship does not exist *solely* for further purposes, whether a political movement's larger goals, an occupational endeavor, or simply the participant's separate and individual benefits. Of course, there can be many further benefits that flow within friendship and from it, benefits so familiar as not to need listing. Aristotle held one of these to be most central; a friend, he said, is a "second self" who is a means to your own self-awareness. (In his listing of the virtuous characteristics one should seek in a friend, Aristotle takes your parents' view of who your friends should be.) Nevertheless, a relationship is a friendship to the extent that it shares activities for no further purpose than the sharing of them.

People seek to engage in sharing beyond the domain of personal friendship also. One important reason we read newspapers, I think, is not the importance or intrinsic interest of the news; we rarely take action whose direction depends upon what we read there, and if somehow we were shipwrecked for ten years on an isolated is-land, when we returned we would want a summary of what had happened meanwhile, but we certainly would not choose to peruse the back newspapers of the previous ten years. Rather, we read newspapers because we want to *share* information with our fellows, we want to have a range of information in common with them, a common stock of mental contents. We already share with them a geography and a language, and also a common fate in the face of large-scale events. That we also desire to share the daily flow of information shows how very intense our desire to share is.

Nonromantic friends do not, in general, share an *identity.* In part, this may be because of the crisscrossing web of friendships. The friend of your friend may be your acquaintance, but he or she is not necessarily someone you are close to or would meet with separately. As in the case of multiple bilateral defense treaties among nations, conflicts of action and attachment can occur that make it difficult to delineate any larger entity to which one safely can cede powers and make the bearer of a larger identity. Such considerations also help explain why it is not feasible for a person simultaneously to be part of multiple romantic couples (or of a trio), even were the person to desire this. Friends want to share the things they do *as* a sharing, and they think, correctly, that friendship is valuable partly *because* of its sharing—perhaps specially valuable because, unlike the case of romantic love, this valued sharing occurs *without* any sharing of identity. . . .

Further Questions

1. Would you think of your beloved as being part of yourself (or vice versa)? What exactly does this mean to you?

2. Do you find that a love relationship changes you in some ways? If you are positive about this, what explanation can you give for your attitude?

3. Why is it important that the person you love, love you as well?

4. Why can one have many friends, although, normally, only one person with whom one is in love?

IV.2   Male Friendship and Intimacy

ROBERT A. STRIKWERDA AND LARRY MAY

Robert A. Strikwerda and Larry May discuss some of the difficulties men have in forming male friendships. Intimacy requires a reciprocal relationship, mutual knowledge and understanding, and mutual trust built on shared experience. But to engage in self-disclosure people must be aware of the feelings they wish to disclose. Men, however, have been taught to ignore their feelings; feelings also are suppressed by homophobia, competitiveness, and callousness.

Strikwerda teaches philosophy at Indiana University, Kokomo. May teaches philosophy at Washington University in St. Louis.

Reading Questions

1. What are the differences between friendship based on intimacy and caring and the comradeship typified in combat situations? What are the differences between friendships and the companionship generated by "parallel play"?
2. Why is the loyalty of comradeship more fragile than more intimate forms of bonding? What sort of understanding is involved in intimate bonding? Why is it important that this knowledge and understanding be mutual? Why is mutual trust important?
3. What is callousness, and why does it pose an obstacle to male friendship?

Life is so very different when you have a good friend. I've seen people without special friends, close friends. Other men, especially. For some reason men don't often make and keep friends. This is a real tragedy, I think, because in a way, without a tight male friend, you never really are able to see yourself. That is because part of shaping ourselves is done by others; and a lot of our shaping comes from that one close friend who is something like us.

—Mr. Hal[1]

The "tradition" in the West has made comradeship between men the paradigm of friendship. Friendships in their purest form have been thought to exist more often among men than among women. Vera Brittain summarizes:

From the days of Homer the friendships of men have enjoyed glory and acclamation, but the friendships of women, despite Ruth and Naomi, have usually been not merely unsung, but mocked, belittled. . . .[2]

For the most part the characteristics of loyalty, fellow feeling, and concern for the other's interests have been stressed much more heavily than intimacy in male friendships. Moreover, the presence of these characteristics has been thought to make male friendship superior to female friendship.

In contrast, recent studies of Americans indicate that men tend not to have same-sex friendships that are as satisfying to them as same-sex friendships are to women.[3] And men are begin-

Abridged from Rethinking Masculinity: Philosophical Explorations Light of Feminism (Lanham, MD: Rowman and Littlefield, 1992) p. 95–110. Reprinted by permission.

ning to wonder why this is so. Daniel Levinson writes that in "our interviews, friendship was largely noticeable by its absence. As a tentative generalization, we would say that close friendship with a man or a woman is rarely experienced by American men."[4] In 1985, after a ten-year study of 5,000 American men and women, Michael McGill stated:

> To say that men have no intimate friends seems on the surface too harsh. . . . But the data indicate that it is not far from the truth. . . . Their relationships with other men are superficial, even shallow.[5]

I. COMRADESHIP AND MALE BONDING

Male friendships often resemble the relationships between very young children who engage in "parallel play." These children want to be close to each other in the sandbox, for example, but they just move the sand around without sharing or helping and *usually* without hurting each other. They don't really interact *with* each other; they merely play side-by-side—hence the term parallel play.

Here is a rather common adult example of parallel play. Two men sit in a bar, each sipping his third beer. Every few minutes one speaks, more by way of a speech (about last night's baseball game or the new beer on tap); the other nods in agreement but waits a while before speaking himself, and then often on a different topic altogether. The men are not concerned by the lack of conversation; indeed, they might tell you that they know each other so well that they don't need to have lengthy conversations, adding that it is the peace and quiet of one another's company that they each prize most highly. When they depart for home, they clasp hands or perhaps merely salute one another.[8]

Such companionship is enjoyable; at least, we have enjoyed it. Our point is not to criticize such relationships. Not every friendship needs to be intimate. However, it seems to us that if *all* of one's friendships display such a lack of intimacy, then one's life will be impoverished and unsatisfying. Such friendships are not in themselves impoverished, but a steady diet of them may lead one either to nutritional deficiency or to hunger for something more. Similarly, if men are open to intimacy only with female friends or partners, they cut themselves off from deeply rewarding relationships with other men, as well as help perpetuate a debilitating gender pattern in which women do the emotional work for men.

Some traditional male experiences have led to a form of friendship that may pass for intimacy—what we call comradeship. The sharing of certain kinds of experiences—such as those of teenage boys in a summer resort community, of soldiers in the trenches, or of sailors on long sea voyages—provides the occasion for mutual self-disclosure among males. In these situations, one is in a period of some stress, whether puberty or physical danger, with plenty of time and not enough activity to fill it. In war, men are forced to be with one another, and they report that in this situation they often reflect on aspects of their lives they normally would block. Soldiers not only fight shoulder to shoulder, but they sit for long hours in cramped quarters wondering if their lives will end in the next barrage of gunfire. Such occasions can bring men to talk about deeply personal matters in their lives and hence to form bonds with one another that may last long after the common experiences have ended.[9]

Loyalty clearly plays a significant role in comradeship. In *The Warriors,* J. Glenn Gray provides a phenomenological account of the experiences of comradeship that develop in combat settings.

> Near the front it was impossible to ignore, consciously or unconsciously, the stark fact that out there were men who would gladly kill you, if and when they got the chance. As a consequence, an individual was dependent on others . . . [and] in turn he was of interest only as a center of force, a wielder of weapons, a means

of security and survival. This confraternity of danger and exposure is unequaled in forging links among people of unlike desire and temperament. . . .[10]

In combat situations, some men recognize that they are exposed and vulnerable in ways men normally do not acknowledge. From the position of mutual vulnerability, they come to seek out others on whom they can depend, rather than withdraw into their own self-contained egos.

Interestingly, in wartime situations comrades come to see each other in abstract rather than highly personal terms. As Gray points out, "comrades are loyal to each other spontaneously, and without any need for reasons."[11] But, as Gray also notes, this loyalty is fragile since it is not necessarily connected to "spontaneous liking and the feeling of belonging."[12] Indeed, the bonding that epitomizes comradeship is strictly non-particularistic. "Men are true comrades only when each is ready to give up his life for the other, without reflection and without thought of personal loss."[13]

Comrades are not necessarily intimate friends, for they are often bound to one another as generalized others, not in terms of who each one is as a unique member of the human race. Somewhat paradoxically, comrades are loyal to each other not out of concern for the particularity of the individual other, but out of an almost impartial respect for people of a certain type or in a certain situation: fellow soldiers, compatriots, coworkers, etc. Thus there can be a wide diversity of background and personality types among comrades in combat, without the reciprocal willingness to sacrifice one's life for the other varying as a result. Comradeship is a deontological regard for a generalized other and, in this sense, is quite different from intimate friendships, which are based on a regard for a particularized other and where consequences and contexts matter quite a bit.

In intimate friendship, the psychic boundary that normally encloses the male self, allowing for the characteristically self-confident, competent, single-minded pursuit of one's public roles, is temporarily opened to allow a new focus to develop, one that includes the man and another person. It is not the formation of a new boundary as typical in comradeship, but an expansion of one's concentration of attention from self to include the other. This new concentration may look similar to our stereotyped notion of male bonding. What often passes for intimate male bonding is really the deep loyalty of comradeship, which is based on so little information about the person to whom one is loyal that it is quite fragile and likely to change as new people come to instantiate the type to whom the comrade is loyal. In contrast, because intimate bonding is based on particular characteristics of the other, it will not generally break apart unless the people themselves change significantly.

Perhaps the following analogy is apropos. Just as some anthropologists describe the typical American marriage pattern as "serial monogamy" (just one spouse at a time), so for many men having friends is "serial best-friendship." As Stanley Bing puts it, a bit facetiously, "I don't miss my formerly essential friends, because I have been able to re-create over and over again the same satisfying infantile relationship with any number of adult males within lunching distance. Every one of these guys is precious, and every one can be replaced."[16] Similarly, we have friends who are "workfriends" or "next-door friends" or "racketball partners," involving more or less constricted friendships, limited in time, place, or social situation. Thus these friendships are likely to change when the situation does. As in marriages, "divorces" and "remarriages" occur in friendships, but perhaps it is time to reconsider what intimacy in a relationship is when one is marrying for the fifth time or, as Bing would put it, "re-creating one's fifth set of essential friends."

II. THE NATURE AND VALUE OF INTIMACY

Intimacy paradigmatically occurs in a reciprocal relationship between two or more people.

Knowing oneself intimately seems to us a derivative notion, though we will suggest self-knowledge does have an essential role to play in enabling reciprocal intimacy. Although there is a substantial knowledge element involved in intimacy, there is also a degree of what one might call understanding. It is not simply knowledge of facts about the person, or an ability to predict behavior, but also an understanding of why something is the way it is, of priorities and relations. As one might expect from its etymological roots (as the superlative form of *interior*—"innermost"), intimacy typically involves a sense of a deep or profound relationship. Finally, intimacy includes an element of warmth in two dimensions, that of caring receptivity and that of being comfortable, as in "an intimate club."

Intimacy in a friendship involves a mutual relation; one cannot really be an intimate friend without a reciprocity of intimacy from another. Indeed, the reciprocal enrichment and enjoyment that typically flow from intimate relationships may constitute the chief value of such relationships. Consider the friendships that might start with one coworker asking another, "Wanna get some lunch?" Having once learned something about the other person and liking him, one typically acts to further the relationship, not just with a directly work-related suggestion, but with something that is optional. If one finds another person interesting but that person is not willing to make time for lunch or a beer, the relationship is unlikely to get off the ground. He has not given a sign of the mutuality of interest and respect that grounds intimate friendship. Nor is there a place for the simple enjoyment of each other's company or conversation.

Genuine intimacy involves a deep or intense mutual knowledge that allows the participants to grow in both self-understanding and understanding of others. That knowledge includes understanding the defining personal characteristics of an individual, conjoined with enjoyment of and loyalty to that person. Whereas one can speak of certain kinds of friends—for example sports buddies—that one doesn't know very

well, one wouldn't say this about an intimate friend. One might say, after some unexpected event, "I guess I didn't know my friend very well, but he's still my friend," but it would be quite odd to say, "I don't know him very well, but we're still intimate friends."

Even if mutual knowledge is linked to strongly positive emotional feelings for one another, these are not enough to constitute intimate friendship. It is possible for two people to know a great deal about each other and feel positively toward each other without that counting as intimate friendship. The relationship of counselor and counselee, especially when they both like each other, may involve knowledge and positive feelings without being an intimate friendship. The constrained nature and the distinctly different roles of the two people make it something other than an intimate friendship, at least until some other dimensions are added to their relationship.

Perhaps the most significant step in friendship is the achievement of a mutual trust based on some form of shared experience. To attain this trust, people usually need time in each other's company. Over time, that common experience leads to self-disclosure as a sign of trust. This trust engenders a corresponding loyalty and a further relaxation to heighten each other's enjoyment of shared activities.

As we saw in the examination of comradeship, to be intimate with another person one cannot be loyal to that person as a mere abstract other. Intimacy is not mere "fellow feeling" or mutual respect, although intimacy shares much in common with each of these concepts. Intimacy involves the kind of self-revelatory disclosures that go beyond what is necessary to generate sympathy or respect. Indeed, self-disclosure by itself often makes sympathy and respect more difficult. That is why one wants a sign of trustworthiness before one becomes intimate friends with another. When these elements of knowledge, positive feelings, trust, and reciprocity coalesce, then self-disclosure is a form of mutual enclosure in which two selves create a new, inclusive focus of attention, what Aristotle terms a complete friendship.

III. OBSTACLES TO INTIMACY IN MALE FRIENDSHIPS

As we have noted, many male friendships lack the dimension of mutual self-disclosure. The women we know report forming friendships through self-revealing discussion, whereas the men we know report that they typically form friendships based on common activities, such as work or participation in some sport, with self-revelation being at best tangential to the activity. On one level, it is certainly easier to engage in self-disclosure through discussion than by other, less-straightforward means, since one is able to disclose one's feelings with the least ambiguity by simply saying how one feels. But that presupposes capacities that many men currently lack. It is not a logical necessity that self-disclosure occur by means of discussion. Insofar as what we are is created by what we do as much as the reverse, action can be as vital a form of disclosure as speech.[17]

However, if one cannot accompany another person in the various aspects of the other's life, full disclosure through action is virtually impossible, and thus disclosure via speech becomes a practical necessity. Actions cannot easily disclose the past or project into the future without words to set the context. When one shares a past with another and shares a variety of activities—working at the same place, shopping at the same stores, attending the same church or synagogue—one can expect to disclose oneself gradually through action. The increasing diversity and mobility of North American life means that the route to intimacy through a shared past linked with shared present activities is not open to many of us. Thus, self-disclosure through speech is the only realistic possibility we have found.

The difficulties are not simply social or logistical. In order to be able to engage in self-disclosure, persons must be able to gain access to the feelings they are trying to disclose to their friends. And in order to gain this access, they must in some sense be aware of having certain feelings and be able to conceptualize them. Yet males in contemporary Western culture are encouraged not to show their feelings; indeed, from the dispassionate reasoner model of the philosopher to the Clint Eastwood image of manhood, males are encouraged not to let their feelings interfere at all with the conduct of their lives.[18] The culturally ingrained habit of hiding, rejecting, and denying legitimacy to one's feelings makes it much harder for these males, for us, to gain access to feelings and impedes the disclosure of these feelings to intimate friends.[19] We need others to help understand ourselves, as G. H. Mead has stressed, yet without some degree of self-awareness or self-intimacy we can only with great difficulty communicate what is most important about ourselves.

Larry had a revealing experience several years ago. Right before setting out for his grandfather's funeral, several friends remarked that he was keeping remarkably cool in the face of what must have been very emotionally difficult times. In reflecting on this on the way to the funeral, he discovered, much to his own amazement, that he simply had no feelings about the death of his grandfather. It was not that he and his grandfather had been distant or enemies; indeed, they had once been fairly close. But over the years, he had let the thought of his grandfather become less and less important until there simply were no positive or negative feelings attached to him. While there were no feelings here, except indifference, to disclose to his friends, the very lack of emotions could have been, but was not at that time, a basis for self-disclosure and self-realization.

It is our experience that most males we know have fewer and/or less complex emotional responses to situations than do most females. It is also true that men have been socialized to display callousness in those situations where their feelings might otherwise manifest themselves. Callousness is a lack of emotional response, or a diminished emotional responsiveness, to certain stimuli. Culturally ingrained callousness may lead to a lack of feeling, just as the metaphor suggests: The finger that has a callous will not feel as much pain as the finger without one. Callousness in men is produced by, among other ways, habitual association of a negative emotional response with images of people who are not considered (good or real) men. Negative psychological association stifles emotional feeling, just as the encrusting of nerve endings deadens sensory feeling. Over time, callousness may lead to the elimination of a certain kind of emotional response.[20] In our culture, men may disclose fewer feelings than do women simply because they have been socialized to be less aware of the few feelings they do have. They may thus be content with comradeship as we have described it as their paradigm of friendship. This socialization helps many men avoid dealing with the emotional consequences for others of their acts, at least for the short term.

At the very least, many men, ourselves included, report that they have been bewildered by the task of understanding their own feelings. For men, feelings simply seem inchoate in ways that generally do not seem to be true for women. A number of years ago Bob was almost entirely stymied when he tried to role-play the part of a woman friend in a variation of a common male-female interaction. He could recall how she had acted in the past but could not place himself in her position. He tried and failed, whereas she could play the male much better. He could not imaginatively experience how she might have felt and acted. This seems to be a much more typically male incapacity.[21] And this limits reciprocity and may also help explain why males report fewer intimate relationships than women do.

In order to have strongly positive emotional feelings for another person, as well as sustained mutual self-disclosure, it is important to be able both to have such feelings and to express them. To express such feelings, one must be able to trust another person. Yet sociological studies indicate that the dominant model is one of competition rather than trust between men.[22]

Competition creates bonds between teammates but it also makes men reluctant to reveal things about themselves that would make them vulnerable, and hence cause them to risk being taken advantage of. Completing this paper took longer than anticipated because Bob's inability to admit that he simply works more slowly than Larry made it difficult to maintain their work schedule. Instead of working cooperatively, albeit differently, Bob slipped into seeing Larry more as a competitor and less as a partner. And this took some time to acknowledge. To have the openness to allow the mutual expressions of positive feelings toward one another, the people involved cannot be worrying about becoming more vulnerable than the other.

Men in American culture are clearly stymied in pursuing intimacy with other males because of fears involving their sexuality, especially culturally inbred homophobia. As teenagers, we learned not to display feelings toward other boys on pain of being ridiculed as "queers"; Bob and his brother were called "homos" for putting their arms around each other. The taboo against males touching, except in the firm public handshake, continues these teenage prohibitions. Such restrictions and taboos dampen the expression of deep feelings among males in much of American culture. And yet, in sports contexts for instance, there are clearly accepted exceptions to these taboos, such as the pat on the backside of a teammate. Perhaps here manliness is somehow assured. Homophobia is not an insurmountable obstacle to male intimacy, but it certainly does contribute to the difficulties that men have in expressing their deeply held feelings.

We see a complex of interacting factors—including homophobia, competitiveness, callousness, taboos against the expression of feelings, and social and cultural patterns—that culminate in many men in our society not being as well suited for intimacy as women are. The lack of socialization either to seek out the personal, defining characteristics of another person or to seek this information about oneself is significant. We don't ask! Rather, males best relate with one another on the basis of shared experiences, such as sports or work, rather than shared details of one another's personal life.

V. RESOURCES FOR GREATER MALE INTIMACY

The fact that some men have developed intimacy in relationships that began as comradeships lends hope. Only if men were somehow blocked from realizing the value of intimacy would there be cause for despair. There are emotional resources that males have available to them that could, but normally do not, lead them to form intimate friendships. Among these are the ability to find common ground with those one meets for the first time, the ability to be constructively critical without adversely affecting the future of a relationship, and the ability to form long-lasting bonds of loyalty with other males. Indeed, there are several types of feeling that men are generally socialized to express more readily than do women. Just as men already feel entitled to express anger, rage, and hostility, there is no reason to think that other feelings will be permanently blocked. Surely, though, what is most in need of change here is the current lack of attention on the part of most males in Western culture toward an understanding of their own feelings.

How can men learn to become intimate with each other? Not quickly, but most likely through a process of learning while doing things together and talking about themselves. Indeed, achieving intimacy is a process, as opposed to an event to make happen or a goal to be achieved. The situation seems similar to the hedonistic paradox that those who directly seek happiness are often least likely to achieve that goal, since happiness often comes in the seeking of other things. Recently, Bob drew back from a new friend because that friend's personal disclosures made Bob quite uncomfortable; fortunately, because they continued to work together a greater *mutual* openness developed. We have not participated in the workshops or "gatherings" of the so-called Men's Movement, and so we hesitate to comment on it. If these do allow many men moments of intimacy with selves and others, they are still very different from the building of an intimate friendship.

In our own interactions, it seems that we have gotten to know each other best—achieved greater intimacy—in those conversations where we relaxed our boundaries and simply talked. We felt the tug of hesitations, inhibitions each of us has to confront one by one. Should I mention this, should I criticize or let it pass, should I ask about that, can I admit to this? Opportunities are lost, disclosure prevented. And men—we—need to develop a greater ability and inclination to reflect, both as individuals and as friends. This requires us to approach our relationships as more than "undigested interactions,"[32] as things upon which we are already reflecting, and make that more explicit. Instead of just swapping stories about our childhoods, we grew by asking ourselves questions such as, "Why did Bob react to his father in one way when disciplined and Larry to his father in a different fashion?" and, "Why did we not mention our mothers in this respect?" Here the beginnings of intimacy can enable more intimacy.

This process will not teach us to become caring, but how to develop and express our caring. We do not want to be interpreted as claiming that many men do not care about one another. Men do care, often very deeply, but at the same time in a stunted and inchoate fashion. The narrowness of our relations hinders the realization and expression of care. A friend's brother dies unexpectedly and we realize that we have little idea of what sort of relationship the two had. We don't know what to say. Perhaps they were intense rivals, drifting apart as one gained more success than the other. Perhaps not. We don't know.

Men can, however, come to know each other. We can learn to form together the intimate friendships that many women have. And just like women's friendships, eventually intimate male friendships can benefit us all.[33]

NOTES

1. Alice Walker, *The Temple of My Familiar* (New York: Harcourt, Brace, Jovanovich, 1989), p. 114.

2. Vera Brittain, *Testament of Friendship: The Story of Winifred Holtby* (London: Macmillan, 1947). This passage is quoted by Blanche Cook in "Female Support Networks and Political Activism: Lillian Wald, Crystal Eastman, and Emma Goldman," *Chrysalis,* vol. 3 (1977), p. 44, who also perceptively discusses the scholarly disregard of female friendships.

3. See the summary of this research in Chapter 13 of Letty Cottin Pogrebin's *Among Friends* (New York: McGraw-Hill, 1987). See also Drury Sherrod, "The Influence of Gender on Same-Sex Friendships," in *Close Relationships,* edited by Clyde Hendrick (Newbury Park, CA: Sage Publishing Co., 1989); and Barry McCarthy, "Adult Friendships," in *Person to Person,* edited by George Graham and Hugh LaFollette (Philadelphia: Temple University Press, 1989).

4. Cited in Pogrebin, ibid., p. 253.

5. Ibid.

8. Gerry Philipsen, in "Speaking 'like a man' in Teamsterville: Cultural Patterns of Role Enactment in an Urban Neighborhood," *Quarterly Journal of Speech,* vol. 61 (1975), pp. 13–22, insightfully examines how situational expectations govern male speech in one American community.

9. For a cautionary note on the durability of these relationships, see Roger Little, "Friendships in the Military Community," in *Friendship,* volume 2 of *Research in the Interweave of Social Roles,* edited by Helena Znaniecka Lopata and David Maines (Greenwich, CT: JAI Press, 1981).

10. J. Glenn Gray, *The Warriors* (New York: Harper Torchbooks, 1959), pp. 26–27 (p. 24 of this volume).

11. Ibid., p. 40 (p. 30 of this volume).

12. Ibid. (p. 30 of this volume).

13. Ibid., p. 46 (p. 33 of this volume).

16. Stanley Bing, "No Man is an Isthmus," *Esquire,* August 1989, p. 53.

17. See Sherrod, op. cit., for a discussion of this question.

18. Judith Mayne explores some of the often overlooked complexities of Clint Eastwood movies in her essay "Walking the Tightrope of Feminism and Male Desire," in *Men and Feminism,* edited by Alice Jardine and Paul Smith (New York: Methuen, 1987).

19. See Susan Pollack and Carol Gilligan, "Images of Violence in Thematic Apperception Test Stories," *Journal of Personality and Social Psychology,* vol. 42 (1982), pp. 159–67.

20. See Larry May's essay "Insensitivity and Moral Responsibility," *Journal of Value Inquiry,* vol. 26 (1992), pp. 7–22.

21. Lillian B. Rubin, *Intimate Strangers: Men and Women Together* (New York: Harper and Row, 1983), pp. 69–70.

22. See, for example, *Beyond Patriarchy,* edited by Michael Kaufman (Toronto: Oxford University Press, 1987).

32. This phrase was borrowed from Steve Duck and Kris Pond, "Friends, Romans, Countrymen: Rhetoric and Reality in Personal Relationships," in *Close Relationships,* op. cit.

33. We have benefited from the comments of Marilyn Friedman, Penny Weiss, Clark Rountree, and those who attended our presentation of an earlier version of this paper in the Purdue University Women's Studies Program Spring 1990 "Brown Bag Lecture Series." We also thank the referees and editor at *Hypatia* for valuable comments on the penultimate version of this paper.

Further Questions

1. Why does competition pose obstacles to male friendship? How do homophobia and taboos on expressing feelings create such obstacles?

2. What are some of the resources men have available for forming male friendships? Why is speech important in this enterprise?

3. If you wanted to convert a comradeship into a relationship with the intimacy of a friendship, how do you think you would go about it?

IV.3   The Woman in Love

SIMONE DE BEAUVOIR

Simone de Beauvoir maintains that there are significant gender differences, in heterosexual romantic relationships, caused by differences in social situations. Love plays a bigger part in the life of women because men have more other important things they must do. We have already seen how men are advantaged in the workplace. Accordingly, success for men depends to a large extent on workplace achievement. Women's best course to success in life, on the other hand, is often through romantic attachments. As might be expected, this disparity skews romantic relationships in undesirable ways.

Other selections by de Beauvoir appear in Parts I, V, and XII.

Reading Questions

1. Should a woman expect to abandon her own personality, likes, dislikes, habits, and activities when she enters a romantic relationship and replace them with those of her beloved? Should a man expect to abandon these things to the same extent?
2. Is serving the other person an appropriate approach to a romantic relationship?
3. Can the fact that you have an ongoing relationship justify your existence?

THE WORD *LOVE* has by no means the same sense for both sexes, and this is one cause of the serious misunderstandings that divide them. Byron well said: "Man's love is of man's life a thing apart; 'Tis woman's whole existence." Nietzsche expresses the same idea in *The Gay Science:*

> The single word love in fact signifies two different things for man and woman. What woman understands by love is clear enough: it is not only devotion, it is a total gift of body and soul, without reservation, without regard for anything whatever. This unconditional nature of her love is what makes it a *faith*,[1] the only one she has. As for man, if he loves a woman, what he *wants* is that love from her, he is in consequence far from postulating the same sentiment for himself as for woman; if there should be men who also felt that desire

for complete abandonment, upon my word, they would not be men.

Men have found it possible to be passionate lovers at certain times in their lives, but there is not one of them who could be called "a great lover"[2]; in their most violent transports, they never abdicate completely; even on their knees before a mistress, what they still want is to take possession of her; at the very heart of their lives they remain sovereign subjects; the beloved woman is only one value among others; they wish to integrate her into their existence and not to squander it entirely on her. For woman, on the contrary, to love is to relinquish everything for the benefit of a master. As Cécile Sauvage puts it: "Woman must forget her own personality when she is in love. It is a law of nature. A woman is nonexistent without a master. Without a master, she is a scattered bouquet."

The fact is that we have nothing to do here with laws of nature. It is the difference in their situations that is reflected in the difference men and women show in their conceptions of love. The individual who is a subject, who is himself, if he has the courageous inclination toward transcendence, endeavors to extend his grasp on the world: he is ambitious, he acts. But an inessential creature is incapable of sensing the absolute at the heart of her subjectivity; a being doomed to immanence cannot find self-realization in acts. Shut up in the sphere of the relative, destined to the male from childhood, habituated to seeing in him a superb being whom she cannot possibly equal, the woman who has not repressed her claim to humanity will dream of transcending her being toward one of these superior beings, of amalgamating herself with the sovereign subject. There is no other way out for her than to lose herself, body and soul, in him who is represented to her as the absolute, as the essential. Since she is anyway doomed to dependence, she will prefer to serve a god rather than obey tyrants—parents, husband, or protector. She chooses to desire her enslavement so ardently that it will seem to her the expression of her liberty; she will try to rise above her situation as inessential object by fully accepting it; through her flesh, her feelings, her behavior, she will enthrone him as supreme value and reality: she will humble herself to nothingness before him. Love becomes for her a religion. . . .

. . . [W]hat woman wants in the first place is to serve; for in responding to her lover's demands, a woman will feel that she is necessary; she will be integrated with his existence, she will share his worth, she will be justified. Even mystics like to believe, according to Angelus Silesius, that God needs man; otherwise they would be giving themselves in vain. The more demands the man makes, the more gratified the woman feels. Although the seclusion imposed by Victor Hugo on Juliette Drouet weighed heavily on the young woman, one feels that she

is happy in obeying him: to stay by the fireside is to do something for the master's pleasure. She tries also to be useful to him in a positive way. She cooks choice dishes for him and arranges a little nest where he can be at home; she looks after his clothes. "I want you to tear your clothes as much as possible," she writes to him, "and I want to mend and clean them all myself." She reads the papers, clips out articles, classifies letters and notes, copies manuscripts, for him. She is grieved when the poet entrusts a part of the work to his daughter Léopoldine.

Such traits are found in every woman in love. If need be, she herself tyrannizes over herself in her lover's name; all she is, all she has, every moment of her life, must be devoted to him and thus gain their *raison d'être;* she wishes to possess nothing save in him; what makes her unhappy is for him to require nothing of her, so much so that a sensitive love will invent demands. She at first sought in love a confirmation of what she was, of her past, of her personality; but she also involves her future in it, and to justify her future she puts it in the hands of one who possesses all values. . . .

The woman who finds pleasure in submitting to male caprices also admires the evident action of a sovereign-free being in the tyranny practiced on her. It must be noted that if for some reason the lover's prestige is destroyed, his blows and demands become odious; they are precious only if they manifest the divinity of the loved one. But if they do, it is intoxicating joy to feel herself the prey of another's free action. An existent finds it a most amazing adventure to be justified through the varying and imperious will of another; one wearies of living always in the same skin, and blind obedience is the only chance for radical transformation known to a human being. Woman is thus slave, queen, flower, hind, stained-glass window, wanton, servant, courtesan, muse, companion, mother, sister, child, according to the fugitive dreams, the imperious commands, of her lover. She lends herself to these metamorphoses with ravishment as long as she does not realize that all the time her lips have retained the unvarying savor of submission. On the level of love, as on that of eroticism, it seems evident that masochism is one of the bypaths taken by the unsatisfied woman, disappointed in both the other and herself; but it is not the natural tendency of a happy resignation. Masochism perpetuates the presence of the ego in a bruised and degraded condition; love brings forgetfulness of self in favor of the essential subject.

The supreme goal of human love, as of mystical love, is identification with the loved one.[3] The measure of values, the truth of the world, are in his consciousness; hence it is not enough to serve him. The woman in love tries to see with his eyes; she reads the books he reads, prefers the pictures and the music he prefers; she is interested only in the landscapes she sees with him, in the ideas that come from him; she adopts his friendships, his enmities, his opinions; when she questions herself, it is his reply she tries to hear; she wants to have in her lungs the air he has already breathed; the fruits and flowers that do not come from his hands have no taste and no fragrance. Her idea of location in space, even, is upset: the center of the world is no longer the place where she is, but that occupied by her lover; all roads lead to his home, and from it. She uses his words, mimics his gestures, acquires his eccentricities and his tics. "I am Heathcliffe," says Catherine in *Wuthering Heights;* that is the cry of every woman in love; she is another incarnation of her loved one, his refection, his double: she is *he.* She lets her own world collapse in contingence, for she really lives in his.

The supreme happiness of the woman in love is to be recognized by the loved man as a part of himself; when he says "we," she is associated and identified with him, she shares his prestige and reigns with him over the rest of the world; she never tires of repeating—even to excess—this delectable "we." As one necessary to a being who is absolute necessity, who stands forth in the world seeking necessary goals and who gives her back the world in necessary form the woman in love acquires in her submission that magnifi-

cent possession, the absolute. It is this certitude that gives her lofty joys; she feels exalted to a place at the right hand of God. Small matter to her to have only second place if she has *her* place, forever, in a most wonderfully ordered world. So long as she is in love and is loved by and necessary to her loved one, she feels herself wholly justified: she knows peace and happiness. . . .

But this glorious felicity rarely lasts. No man really is God. The relations sustained by the mystic with the divine Absence depend on her fervor alone; but the deified man, who is not God, is present. And from this fact are to come the torments of the woman in love. . . . [W]oman, in assuming her role as the inessential, accepting a total dependence, creates a hell for herself. Every woman in love recognizes herself in Hans Andersen's little mermaid who exchanged her fishtail for feminine legs through love and then found herself walking on needles and live coals. It is not true that the loved man is absolutely necessary, above chance and circumstance, and the woman is not necessary to him; he is not really in a position to justify the feminine being who is consecrated to his worship, and he does not permit himself to be possessed by her.

An authentic love should assume the contingence of the other; that is to say, his lacks, his limitations, and his basic gratuitousness. It would not pretend to be a mode of salvation, but a human inter-relation. Idolatrous love attributes an absolute value to the loved one, a first falsity that is brilliantly apparent to all outsiders. "*He* isn't worth all that love," is whispered around the woman in love, and posterity wears a pitying smile at the thought of certain pallid heroes, like Count Guibert. It is a searing disappointment to the woman to discover the faults, the mediocrity of her idol. Novelists, like Colette, have often depicted this bitter anguish. The disillusion is still more cruel than that of the child who sees the father's prestige crumble, because the woman has herself selected the one to whom she has given over her entire being.

Even if the chosen one is worthy of the profoundest affection, his truth is of the earth, earthy, and it is no longer this mere man whom the woman loves as she kneels before a supreme being; she is duped by that spirit of seriousness which declines to take values as incidental—that is to say, declines to recognize that they have their source in human existence. . . . She offers him incense, she bows down, but she is not a friend to him since she does not realize that he is in danger in the world, that his projects and his aims are as fragile as he is; regarding him as the Faith, the Truth, she misunderstands his freedom—his hesitancy and anguish of spirit. This refusal to apply a human measuring scale to the lover explains many feminine paradoxes. The woman asks a favor from her lover. Is it granted? Then he is generous, rich, magnificent; he is kingly, he is divine. Is it refused? Then he is avaricious, mean, cruel; he is a devilish or a bestial creature. One might be tempted to object: If a "yes" is such an astounding and superb extravagance, should one be surprised at a "no"? If the "no" discloses such abject selfishness, why wonder so much at the "yes"? Between the superhuman and the inhuman is there no place for the human?

A fallen god is not a man: he is a fraud; the lover has no other alternative than to prove that he really is this king accepting adulation—or to confess himself a usurper. If he is no longer adored, he must be trampled on. In virtue of that glory with which she has haloed the brow of her beloved, the woman in love forbids him any weakness; she is disappointed and vexed if he does not live up to the image she has put in his place. If he gets tired or careless, if he gets hungry or thirsty at the wrong time, if he makes a mistake or contradicts himself, she asserts that he is "not himself" and she makes a grievance of it. In this indirect way she will go so far as to take him to task for any of his ventures that she disapproves; she judges her judge, and she denies him his liberty so that he may deserve to remain her master. . . .

It is one of the curses afflicting the passionate woman that her generosity is soon converted into exigence. Having become identified with another, she wants to make up for her loss; she must take possession of that other person who has captured her. She gives herself to him entirely; but he must be completely available to receive this gift. She dedicates every moment to him, but he must be present at all times; she wants to live only in him—but she wants to live, and he must therefore devote himself to making her live. . . .

And yet she is not willing for him to be nothing but her prisoner. This is one of the painful paradoxes of love: a captive, the god is shorn of his divinity. Woman preserves her transcendence by transferring it to him; but he must bring it to bear upon the whole world. If two lovers sink together in the absolute of passion, all their liberty is degraded into immanence; death is then the only solution. That is one of the meanings of the *Tristan and Isolde* myth. Two lovers destined solely for each other are already dead: they die of ennui, of the slow agony of a love that feeds on itself.

Woman is aware of this danger. Save in crises of jealous frenzy, she herself demands that man be all project, all action, for he is no more a hero if he engages in no exploits. The knight departing for new adventures offends his lady, yet she has nothing but contempt for him if he remains at her feet. This is the torture of the impossible love; the woman wants to possess the man wholly, but she demands that he transcend any gift that could possibly be possessed: a free being cannot be *had*. . . .

Even in mutual love there is fundamental difference in the feelings of the lovers, which the woman tries to hide. The man must certainly be capable of justifying himself without her, since she hopes to be justified through him. If he is necessary to her, it means that she is evading her liberty; but if he accepts his liberty, without which he would be neither a hero nor even a man, no person or thing can be necessary to him. The dependence accepted by woman comes from her weakness; how, therefore, could she find a reciprocal dependence in the man she loves in his strength?

A passionately demanding soul cannot find repose in love, because the end she has in view is inherently contradictory. Torn and tortured, she risks becoming a burden to the man instead of his slave, as she had dreamed; unable to feel indispensable, she becomes importunate, a nuisance. This is, indeed, a common tragedy. If she is wiser and less intransigent, the woman in love becomes resigned. She is not all, she is not necessary: it is enough to be useful; another might easily fill her place: she is content to be the one who is there. She accepts her servitude without demanding the same in return. Thus she can enjoy a modest happiness; but even within these limits it will not be unclouded. . . .

Genuine love ought to be founded on the mutual recognition of two liberties; the lovers would then experience themselves both as self and as other: neither would give up transcendence, neither would be mutilated; together they would manifest values and aims in the world. For the one and the other, love would be revelation of self by the gift of self and enrichment of the world. . . .

Men have vied with one another in proclaiming that love is woman's supreme accomplishment. "A woman who loves as a woman becomes only the more feminine," says Nietzsche; and Balzac: "Among the first-rate, man's life is fame, woman's life is love. Woman is man's equal only when she makes her life a perpetual offering, as that of man is perpetual action." But therein, again, is a cruel deception, since what she offers, men are in no wise anxious to accept. Man has no need of the unconditional devotion he claims, nor of the idolatrous love that flatters his vanity; he accepts them only on condition that he need not satisfy the reciprocal demands these attitudes imply. He preaches to woman that she should give—and her gifts bore him to distraction; she is left in embarrassment with her useless offerings, her empty love. On the day when it will be possible for woman to love not in her weakness but in her strength, not to escape herself but to find herself, not to abase herself but to assert herself—on that day love will become for her, as for man, a source of life and not of mortal danger. In the meantime, love represents in its most touching form the curse that lies heavily upon woman confined in the feminine universe, woman mutilated, insufficient unto herself. The innumerable martyrs to love bear witness against the injustice of a fate that offers a sterile hell as ultimate salvation. . . .

NOTES

1. Nietzsche's italics.
2. In the sense that a woman may sometimes be called "*une grande amoureuse.*"—TR.
3. See T. Reik's *Psychology of Sex Relations* (Farrar, Straus & Co., 1945).—TR.

Further Questions

1. Is love one good way of escaping "living always in the same skin"?
2. Can someone who puts herself in your hands in the name of love eventually turn out to be more of a burden than a benefit?
3. Are we ready for a time in heterosexual romance when two people meet each other halfway, each allowing the other the same amount of liberty of thought, choice, and action as he takes for himself?

The Arrogant Eye, the Loving Eye, and the Beloved   IV.4

MARILYN FRYE

Marilyn Frye distinguishes between the arrogant eye, whose aim is to appropriate for itself, and the loving eye, which recognizes the independence of the other. Her hope is that women who love women will be a positive force in helping women to free themselves from the arrogant eye of men and to realize and appreciate the independence of women.

Other selections by Marilyn Frye appear in Parts I and VI.

Reading Questions

1. Can you think of a situation in which a person consistently behaved in a certain way largely because this was expected of her and in which these expectations were organized largely around someone else's interests?
2. Should we unconditionally praise those who serve others, or should we look into the circumstances and assess the service accordingly?
3. Can a person love someone, but still recognize where her own interests leave off and the other person's interests begin?

THE ARROGANT EYE

. . . THE IDEA OF THERE BEING more than one body's worth of substance, will, and wit lined up behind one's projects has its appeal. As one woman said, after going through the reasons, "My God, who *wouldn't* want a wife?"[1] Ti-Grace Atkinson pointed out in her analysis of the roots of oppression that there is an enormous gap between what one can do and what one can imagine doing. Humans have what she referred to as a "constructive imagination" which, though obviously a blessing in some ways, also is a source of great frustration. For it provides a constant tease of imagined accomplishments and imagined threats—to neither of which are we physically equal.[2] The majority of people do not deal with this problem and temptation by enslaving others overtly and by force

. . . But many, many people, most of them male, are in a cultural and material position to accomplish, to a great degree, the same end by other means and under other descriptions, means and descriptions which obscure to them and to their victims the fact that their end is the same. The end: acquisition of the service of others. The means: variations on the theme of enslavement—dis-integrating an integrated human organism and grafting its substance to oneself. . . .

The Bible says that all of nature (including woman) exists for man. Man is invited to subdue the earth and have dominion over every living thing on it, all of which is said to exist "to you" "for meat."[3] Woman is created to be man's helper. This captures in myth Western Civilization's primary answer to the philosophical question of man's place in nature: everything that is is resource for man's exploitation. With this

Abridged from "In and Out of Harm's Way: Arrogance and Love," in The Politics of Reality: Essays in Feminist Theory *(Trumansburg, NY: The Crossing Press, 1983), pp. 52–83.*

world view, men see with arrogant eyes which organize everything seen with reference to themselves and their own interests. The arrogating perceiver is a teleologist, a believer that everything exists and happens for some purpose, and he tends to animate things, imagining attitudes toward himself as the animating motives. Everything is either "for me" or "against me." This is the kind of vision that interprets the rock one trips on as hostile, the bolt one cannot loosen as stubborn, the woman who made meatloaf when he wanted spaghetti as "bad" (though he didn't say what he wanted). The arrogant perceiver does not countenance the possibility that the Other is independent, indifferent. The feminist separatist can only be a man-hater; Nature is called "Mother."

The arrogant perceiver falsifies—the Nature who makes both green beans and *Bacillus botulinus* doesn't give a passing damn whether humans live or die[4]—but he also coerces the objects of his perception into satisfying the conditions his perception imposes. He tries to accomplish in a glance what the slave master and batterers accomplish by extended use of physical force, and to a great extent he succeeds. He manipulates the environment, perception, and judgment of her whom he perceives so that her recognized options are limited, and the course she chooses will be such as coheres with his purposes. The seer himself is an element of her environment. The structures of his perception are as solid a fact in her situation as are the structures of a chair which seats her too low or of gestures which threaten.

How one sees another and how one expects the other to behave are in tight interdependence, and how one expects another to behave is a large factor in determining how the other does behave. Naomi Weisstein, in "Psychology Constructs the Female," reviewed experiments which show dramatically that this is true.

For instance, in one experiment subjects were to assign numbers to pictures of men's faces, with high numbers representing the subject's judgment that the man in the picture was a successful person, and low numbers representing the subject's judgment that the man in the pic-

ture was an unsuccessful person. One group of experimenters was told that the subjects tended to rate the faces high; another group of experimenters was told that the subjects tended to rate the faces low. Each group of experimenters was instructed to follow precisely the same procedure: they were required to read to subjects a set of instructions and to *say nothing else*. For the 375 subjects run, the results show clearly that those subjects who performed the task with experimenters who expected high ratings gave high ratings, and those subjects who performed the task with experimenters who expected low ratings gave low ratings.[5]

When experimenters think the rats they are working with were bred for high intelligence, the rats they are working with learn faster; when the experimenters think their rats were bred for low intelligence, the rats learn less well. And children believed by their teachers to have high IQs show dramatic increases in their IQs. Weisstein concludes: "The concreteness of the changed conditions produced by expectations is a fact, a reality. . . . In some extremely important ways, people are what you expect them to be, or at least they behave as you expect them to behave."[6]

The experiments only boldly outline something we all know from experience. Women experience the coerciveness of this kind of "influence" when men perversely impose sexual meanings on our every movement. We know the palpable pressure of a man's reduction of our objection to an occasion for our instruction. Women do not so often experience ourselves imposing expectations on situations and making them stick, but some of the most awesome stories of women's successful resistance to male violence involve a woman's expecting the male assailant into the position of a little boy in the power of his mother.* The power of expectations is enormous; it should be engaged and responded to attentively and with care. The

* I refer here to some experience of my own, and to such stories as the Success Stories included in "Do It Yourself Self-Defense," by Pat James, in *Fight Back: Feminist Resistance to Male Violence,* edited by Frederique Delacoste & Felice Newman (Cleis Press, 1981), p. 205.

arrogant perceiver engages it with the same unconsciousness with which he engages his muscles when he writes his name.

The arrogant perceiver's expectation creates in the space about him a sort of vacuum mold into which the other is sucked and held. But the other is not sucked into his structure always, nor always without resistance. In the absence of his manipulation, the other *is* not organized primarily with reference to his interests. To the extent that she is not shaped to his will, does not fit the conformation he imposes, there is friction, anomaly, or incoherence in his world. To the extent that he notices this incongruity, he can experience it in no other way than as something wrong with her. His perception is arrogating; his senses tell him that the world and everything in it (with the occasional exception of other men) is in the nature of things there *for* him, that she is by her constitution and *telos* his servant. He believes his senses. If woman does not serve man, it can only be because he is not a sufficiently skilled master or because there is something wrong with the woman. He may try to manage things better, but when that fails he can only conclude that she is defective: unnatural, flawed, broken, abnormal, damaged, sick. His norms of virtue and health are set according to the degree of congruence of the object of perception with the seer's interests. This is exactly wrong.

Though anyone might wish, for any of many reasons, to contribute to another's pursuit of her or his interests, the health and integrity of an organism is a matter of its being organized largely toward its own interests and welfare. The arrogant perceiver knows this in his own case, but he *arrogates* everything to himself and thus perceives as healthy or "right" everything that relates to him as his own substance does when he is healthy. But what's sauce for the gander is sauce for the goose. *She* is healthy and "working right" when *her* substance is organized primarily on principles which align it to *her* interests and welfare. Cooperation is essential, of course, but it will not do that I arrange everything so that you get enough exercise: for me to be healthy, *I* must get enough exercise.

My being adequately exercised is logically independent of your being so. . . .

The procurer-enslaver, working with overt force, constructs a situation in which the victim's pursuit of her own survival or health and her attempt to be good always require, as a matter of practical fact in that situation, actions which serve him. In the world constructed by the arrogant eye, this same connection is established not by terror but by definition.*

The official story about men who batter women is that they do so in large part because they suffer "low self-esteem." What this suggests to me is that they suffer a lack of arrogance and cannot fully believe in themselves as centers about which all else (but some other men) revolves and to which all else refers. Because of this they cannot effectively exercise the power of that expectation. But as men they "know" they are supposed to be centers of universes, so they are reduced to trying to create by force what more successful men, men who can carry off masculinity better, create by arrogant perception. This is, perhaps, one reason why some of the men who do not batter have contempt for men who do.

THE LOVING EYE

The attachment of the well-broken slave to the master has been confused with love. Under the

---

* Neither the arrogant perceiver nor the procurer works in a vacuum, of course. They are supported by a culture which in many ways "softens up" their victims for them, an economy which systematically places women in positions of economic dependence on men, and a community of men which threatens women with rape at every turn. Also, the existence of the procurers support the arrogant perceiver by making him seem benign by comparison. The arrogant perceiver, in addition, has the support of a community of arrogant perceivers, among whom are all or most of the most powerful members of the community at large. I do want to claim that the power of perception, even exercised without "community support," is great; but as we normally experience it, it is augmented enormously by its being an instance of the "normal" perceiving among those who control the material media of culture and most other economic resources.

name of Love, a willing and unconditional servitude has been promoted as something ecstatic, noble, fulfilling, and even redemptive. All praise is sung for the devoted wife who loves the husband and children she is willing to live for, and of the brave man who loves the god he is willing to kill for, the country he is willing to die for.

We can be taken in by this equation of servitude with love because we make two mistakes at once: We think, of both servitude and love, that they are selfless or unselfish. We tend to think of them as attachments in which the person is not engaged because of self-interest and does not pursue self-interest. The wife who married for money did not marry for love, we think; the mercenary soldier is despised by the loyal patriot. And the slave, we think, is selfless because she *can* do nothing but serve the interests of another. But this is wrong. Neither is the slave selfless, nor is the lover.

It is one mark of a voluntary association that the one person can survive displeasing the other, defying the other, dissociating from the other. The slave, the battered wife, the not-so-battered wife, is constantly in jeopardy. She is in a situation where she cannot, or reasonably believes she cannot, survive without the other's provision and protection, and where experience has made it credible to her that the other may kill her or abandon her if and when she displeases him. . . .

One who loves is not selfless either. If the loving eye is in any sense disinterested, it is not that the seer has lost herself, has no interests, or ignores or denies her interests. Any of these would seriously incapacitate her as a perceiver. What *is* the case, surely, is that unlike the slave or the master, the loving perceiver can see without the presupposition that the other poses a constant threat or that the other exists for the seer's service; nor does she see with the other's eye instead of her own. Her interest does not blend the seer and the seen, either empirically by terror or *a priori* by conceptual links forged by the arrogant eye. One who sees with a loving eye is separate from the other whom she sees. There are boundaries between them; she and

the other are two; their interests are not identical; they are not blended in vital parasitic or symbiotic relations, nor does she believe they are or try to pretend they are.

The loving eye is a contrary of the arrogant eye.

The loving eye knows the independence of the other. It is the eye of a seer who knows that nature is indifferent. It is the eye of one who knows that to know the seen, one must consult something other than one's own will and interests and fears and imagination. One must look at the thing. One must look and listen and check and question.

The loving eye is one that pays a certain sort of attention. This attention can require a discipline but *not* a self-denial. The discipline is one of self-knowledge, knowledge of the scope and boundary of the self. What is required is that one know what are one's interests, desires and loathings, one's projects, hungers, fears and wishes, and that one know what is and what is not determined by these. In particular, it is a matter of being able to tell one's own interests from those of others and of knowing where one's self leaves off and another begins. Perhaps in another world this would be easy and not a matter of discipline, but here we are brought up among metaphysical cannibals and their robots. Some of us are taught we can have everything, some are taught we can have nothing. Either way we will acquire a great wanting. The wanting doesn't care about truth: It simplifies, where the truth is complex; it invents, when it should be investigating; it expects, when it should be waiting to find out; it would turn everything to its satisfaction; and what it finally thinks it cannot thus maneuver it hates. But the necessary discipline is not a denial of the wanting. On the contrary, it is a discipline of knowing and owning the wanting: identifying it, claiming it, knowing its scope, and through all this, knowing its distance from the truth.

The loving eye does not make the object of perception into something edible, does not try to assimilate it, does not reduce it to the size of the seer's desire, fear, and imagination, and hence does not have to simplify. It knows the complexity of the other as something which will forever present new things to be known. The science of the loving eye would favor The Complexity Theory of Truth and presuppose The Endless Interestingness of the Universe.

The loving eye seems generous to its object, though it means neither to give nor to take, for not-being-invaded, not-being-coerced, not-being-annexed must be felt in a world such as ours as a great gift.

THE BELOVED

We who would love women, and well, who would change ourselves and change the world so that it is possible to love women well, we need to imagine the possibilities for what women might be if we lived lives free of the material and perceptual forces which subordinate women to men. The point is not to imagine a female human animal unaffected by the other humans around it, uninfluenced by its woman and others' perceptions of others' interests, unaffected by culture. The point is only to imagine women not enslaved, to imagine these intelligent, willful, and female bodies not subordinated in service to males, individually or via institutions (or to anybody, in any way); not pressed into a shape that suits an arrogant eye.

The forces which we want to imagine ourselves free of are a guide to what we might be when free of them. They mark the shape they mold us to, but they also suggest by implication the shapes we might have been without that molding. One can guess something of the magnitude and direction of the tendencies the thing would exhibit when free by attending to the magnitudes and directions of the forces required to confine and shape it. For instance, much pressure is applied at the point of our verbal behavior, enforcing silence or limiting our speech.[7] One can reason that without that force we might show ourselves to be loquacious and

perhaps prone to oratory, not to mention prone to saying things unpleasant to male ears. The threat of rape is a force of great magnitude which is, among other things, applied against our movement about the cities, towns, and countryside. The implication is that without it a great many women might prove to be very prone to nomadic lives of exploration and adventure—why else should so much force be required to keep us at home?

But to speak most generally: The forces of men's materials and perceptual violence mold Woman to dependence upon Man, in every meaning of "dependence": contingent upon; conditional upon; necessitated by; defined in terms of; incomplete or unreal without; requiring the support or assistance of; being a subordinate part of; being an appurtenance to.

Dependence is forced upon us. It is not rash to speculate that without this force, much, most, or all of what most or all of us are and do would not be contingent upon, conditional upon, necessitated by, or subordinate to any man or what belongs to or pertains to a man, men, or masculinity. What we are and how we are, or what we would be and how we would be if not molded by the arrogating eye, is: *not molded to man, not dependent.*

I do not speak here of a specious absolute independence that would mean never responding to another's need and never needing another's response. I conceive here simply of a being whose needs and responses are not *bound* by concepts or by terror in a dependence upon those of another. The loving eye makes the correct assumption: The object of the seeing is *another* being whose existence and character are logically independent of the seer and who may be practically or empirically independent in any particular respect at any particular time.

. . . [T]here is in the fabric of our lives, not always visible but always affecting its texture and strength, a mortal dread of being outside the field of vision of the arrogant eye. That eye gives all things meaning by connecting all things to each other by way of their references to one point—Man. We fear that if we are not in that web of meaning there will be no meaning: our work will be meaningless, our lives of no value, our accomplishments empty, our identities illusory. The reason for this dread, I suggest, is that for most of us, including the exceptional, a woman existing outside the field of vision of man's arrogant eye is really inconceivable.

This is a terrible disability. If we have no intuition of ourselves as independent, unmediated beings in the world, then we cannot conceive ourselves surviving our liberation; for what our liberation will do is dissolve the structures and dismantle the mechanisms by which Woman is mediated by Man. If we cannot imagine ourselves surviving this, we certainly will not make it happen.

There probably is really no distinction, in the end, between imagination and courage. We can't imagine what we can't face, and we can't face what we can't imagine. To break out of the structures of the arrogant eye we have to dare to rely on ourselves to make meaning and we have to imagine ourselves beings capable of that: capable of weaving the web of meaning which will hold us in some kind of intelligibility. We do manage this, to some extent; but we also wobble and threaten to fall, like a beginner on a bicycle who does not get up enough momentum, partly for lack of nerve. . . .

We need to know women as independent: subjectively in our own beings, and in our appreciations of others. If we are to know it in ourselves, I think we may have to be under the gaze of a loving eye, the eye which presupposes our independence. The loving eye does not prohibit a woman's experiencing the world directly, does not force her to experience it by way of the interested interpretations of the seer in whose visual field she moves. In this situation, she *can* experience directly in her bones the contingent character of her relations to all others and to Nature. If we are to know women's independence in the being of others, I think we may have to cast a loving eye toward them . . . and wait, and see.

NOTES

1. "Why I Want A Wife," by Judy Syfers, *Radical Feminism,* edited by Anne Koedt, Ellen Levine, and Anita Rapone (Quadrangle, New York, 1973), pp. 60–62.

2. *Amazon Odyssey,* by Ti-Grace Atkinson (Links Books, New York, 1974), "Metaphysical Cannibalism."

3. Genesis 1:29.

4. Due to Catherine Madsen, from her review of *Wanderground,* by Sally Gearhart (Persephone Press, Watertown, Massachusetts, 1979), in *Conditions No. 7,* p. 138.

5. "Psychology Constructs the Female," by Naomi Weisstein, in *Woman in Sexist Society,* edited by Vivian Gornick and Barbara K. Moran (Basic Books, Inc., New York, 1971), pp. 138–139.

6. Ibid.

7. Cf., *Man-Made Language,* by Dale Spender (Routledge & Kegan Paul, London, 1980), pp. 43–50.

Further Questions

1. Is someone who fails to be of service when this is expected of her flawed, abnormal, or sick for that reason alone?

2. Is it too much to ask someone to devote herself entirely to the service of another?

3. Do women have reason to fear relinquishing men's mediation between the world and themselves? Do they have reason to overcome such a fear?

The Civic Advocacy of Violence   IV.5

WAYNE EWING

Wayne Ewing recommends that "the abusive male is every man" and recounts the items in the cycle of male batterers. He argues that society not only tolerates male abusiveness but actually encourages it.

Reading Questions

1. Do you think that some deficiency in the childhood or background of a batterer excuses his violence and abusiveness?
2. Do you think that more attention has been paid to victims of battering than to their batterers because victims tend to bring battering upon themselves?
3. Batterers are often contrite and remorseful afterwards about their battering. Why is this?

THE RULING PARADIGM for male supremacy remains, to this hour physical violence. This paradigm remains unchecked and untouched by change. Critically, the permissive environment of male violence against women is supported by a civic advocacy of violence as socially acceptable, appropriate, and necessary. Physically abusive men, particularly men who batter their spouses, continue for the most part to be a protected population. And the sources which provide us with what we know of the batterer—largely clinical and treatment models—have themselves remained too isolated from sexual politics and from a social analysis of male cultures. Until the code of male violence is read, translated, and undone, male batterers will not be largely affected by what we are coming to know about them.

PROFILING THE MALE BATTERER

I sometimes think that none of the literature will ever move our knowledge dramatically further than Erin Pizzey's observation that all batterers are either alcoholics or psychotics or psychopaths or just plain bullies. That is good common sense applied to the all too ordinary affair of men beating up women. I also think that the following observation, more often than not made rhetorically and politically, has a measure of significance that we can draw on. When the question is raised, "Who is the male batterer?," the answer is sometimes given, "Every man!" Without pushing too quickly let me simply point out here that this observation is accurate. It is not simply an attention-getter. Attempts to profile the male batterer always wind up with a significant body of information which points to . . . every man.

I believe the most striking example of this is found in those studies which support the—in my estimation, accurate—view of male violence as a learned behavior. Depending on the study, 81 to 63 percent of the population of batterers researched have either experienced abuse as victims in the home of their childhood or have witnessed their fathers beat their mothers. While that is significant enough to support our forming knowledge that socialization into violence in the home perpetuates violence, and that individual men can be conditioned to domestic violence as normal, I do not believe we have spent enough time looking at the chilling fact that remains: from 19 to 37 percent of these populations have literally invented violence in an intimate relationship. It is clear that the experience as victim or observer of physical violence is not necessary to "produce" a violent, abusive man.

And so it is with any of the many categories of inquiry applied to populations of male batterers. I will tick some of these off here, and in each case refer to the batterers with whom I work in Denver. *Ethnic backgrounds,* for example, will closely parallel the ethnic makeup of the community in which the study is made. In intake interviews of men either volunteering or ordered by the Courts into the men's groups of our project in Denver, the statistics generated on ethnicity are the statistics available about our community in general. *Age* is not a major factor. While most physically abusive men are in their 20s or early 30s, batterers are also under 20 and over 50. The fact that slightly more than half the men we deal with in Denver are in their 20s is attributable to so many other possibilities, that the fact itself recedes insignificance. *Education* is not a major determinant. While a majority of batterers may have a high school education, the ones we know are equally balanced on either side by men with undergraduate, graduate, and professional degrees and men with less than a high school education. *Income* studies do not support the popular idea that battering men are low income earners. Over a third of the men studied in Denver have incomes of $15,000 and above; and regular employment is as much a feature of the batterer as is infrequent employment. The *onset and frequency of violence* within a relationship are not consistent indicators of the behavior profile of the male batterer. The only conclusion safely drawn from these inquiries is that the probability of maiming and permanently crippling injury for the victim rises with the increase of frequency, and that the period of contrition on the part of the batterer becomes briefer between episodes as frequency increases. *Substance abuse* may as easily accompany battering episodes as not. In Denver, it is involved in a little over a third, while in other populations studies, substance abuse may figure in as much as 80 percent of battering episodes. And of course the self-reported "causes" of violence from both victims and abusers runs from sex to in-laws to money to housework to children to employment and around and around and around. There is no real clue to the profile of the abusive male in these reported occasions for battering episodes. With respect to the *psychological makeup* of the abusive male, there is considerable consensus that these men evidence low self-esteem, dependency needs, unfamiliarity with their emotions, fear of intimacy, poor communication skills, and performance orientation. But what is intriguing about these observations is that they span all of these other indicators.

And so I end this brief review where I started. The abusive male—that is, the violent man of low self-esteem, high dependency need, slow on affect, fearful of intimacy, poor in communicating emotions, and oriented to performance—the abusive male is every man.

THE CYCLE OF VIOLENCE

How is it we know so little, then, about the male batterer? In part this is due to the fact that the movement begun by the female victims of male violence has not spawned a fervent desire to look at the abuser. The simple fact is that as massive as male domestic violence is, we know more about the victims than we do about the abusers. There are some very obvious realities at work here. If we are to serve, counsel, protect, renurture, and heal victims, we must come to know them, to understand the cycle of violence in which they are terrorized and victimized. We need to elicit from them the motivation to break the cycle of violence. But if we are to intervene in the cycle of violence in society at large—which is after all, the sustainer of violence from men toward women—the batterer must be known as well. For every female victim who is freed from the cycle of violence without intervening in the actual behavior of the male abuser, we still have a battering male-at-large.

We do know that a particular characteristic of the cycle of male violence—the period of contrition—is critical to how the cycle repeats itself in relationships: the building up of tension and conflict; the episode of battering; the time of remorse; the idyllic time of reconciliation. And then the cycle begins again. What is going on in the time of remorse? How is it that this apparent recognition of violent behavior is insufficient to provoke change and to begin a cycle of nonviolent behaviors? It seems to me that remorse is a time-honored device, within male-dominant, sexist cultures, for "making things right" again. I refer of course to the Judeo-Christian model of "making things right"—as it was always stated until very recently in the texts of theology and of devotion—between "God and man." This whole pattern of remorse, guilt, repentance, newly invigorated belief, and forgiveness has had one of the most profound symbolic impacts on Western male consciousness.

When a man physically abuses a woman, it is a matter of course for him to fall back on this model. Things can be "made right," not by actual change, but by feeling awful, by confessing it, and by *believing* that the renewal of the relationship is then effected. That this is more hocus-pocus than authentically religious hardly matters. A crippling consequence of this major model of renewal and change—remorse followed by forgiveness-taken-for-granted—is an almost guaranteed start up of the previous behavior once again. The *non* resolution which we violent men rehearse by remorse and "resolve" is vacuous. It is the exercise of a mere accompaniment to violence. And particularly where our dependency on the female victim of our abuse is so strong, the simple telling of the "resolve" not to be violent again is seen as establishing how good we are in fact.

Actually, the interweaving of the violence and the remorse is so tight that the expression of remorse to the victim establishes how good we have been, and how good we are. The remorse is not even a future-oriented "resolve"; it is more an internalized benediction we give to the immedi-

ately preceding episode of battery. Thee is no shock of recognition here in the cycle of violence. It is not a matter of "Oh my god, did I do that?" It is a matter of *stating* "Oh my god, I couldn't have done that," implying that *I in fact did not do it.* The confession of remorse then only reinforces the self-perception that I did not do it. Remorse, in this model of "making things right" again, literally wipes the slate clean. Over and over again we violent men are puzzled as to how it is our victims come to a place where they will not tolerate our violence and so report us or walk out on us. Can't they see that the violence no longer counts as real, because I said I was sorry?

Whatever clinical research reveals to us about the population of batterers, the fact of denial built into the cycle of violence itself veils from both us and the batterer the reality of the violence. Over and over again, abusive men will ask what the fuss is all about. They hold as a right and privilege the behavior of assault and battery against "their" women. Our groups in Denver are filled with men from all walks and circumstances of life to whom it has never occurred that battering is wrong. In other words, one reason we know so little about male batterers is that they only reluctantly come to *speak* of battering at all.

Another factor further veils this population from us. Male batterers continue to be deliberately protected in the careful construction of familial silence; in the denial of neighbors, friends, clergy, teachers, and the like that battering can be "true" for John and Mary; in the failure of law enforcement to "preserve and protect" the victims of domestic violence; in the unwillingness of local and state governments to provide shelter for victims; or in the editorializing of the Eagle Forum that the safe house movement is an anti-male, lesbian conspiracy. Male violence has become the ordinary, the expected, the usual.

THE CIVIC ADVOCACY OF VIOLENCE

What remains is for us to deal with what very few of us want to confront: American life remains sexist and male supremacist in spite of the strides of the second wave of American Feminism. Whether it be snide—"You've come a long way, baby"—or whether it be sophisticated—George Gidler's *Sexual Suicide*—the put down of women's quest for equality, dignity, and freedom from male oppression is damn near total in the America of the 1980s. I contend that the ultimate put down is the continuing advocacy of violence against women, and that until we confront that advocacy with integrity and resolve, the revolution in men's consciousness and behavior cannot get underway.

I used to think that we simply tolerated and permitted male abusiveness in our society. I have now come to understand rather, that we *advocate* physical violence. Violence is presented as effective. Violence is taught as the normal, appropriate, and necessary behavior of power and control.

We apparently have no meaningful response to violence. I am convinced that until the voices that say "No!" to male violence are more numerous than those that say "Yes!," we will not see change. Nor will we men who want to change our violent behaviors find the support necessary to change. And silence in the face of violence is heard as "Yes!"

Under the governing paradigm of violence as effective and normal, every man can find a place. The individual male who has not beaten a woman is still surrounded by a civic environment which claims that it *would* and *could* be appropriate for him to beat a woman. He is immersed in a civic advocacy of violence which therefore contends that should he have committed battery, it is normal; and should he have not committed battery, it is only that he has not *yet* committed battery, given the ordinary course of affairs. In sexual political terms, we men can simply be divided into pre-battery and post-battery phases of life.

The teaching of violence is so pervasive, so totally a part of male experience, that I think it best to acknowledge this teaching as a *civic*, rather than as a cultural or as a social phenomenon. Certainly there are social institutions which form pieces of the total advocacy of violence:

marriage and family; ecclesiastical institutions; schools; economic and corporate institutions; government and political institutions. And there are cultural and sub-cultural variations on the theme and reality of violence, of course. I believe, however, that if we are to crack the code of violent male behavior, we must begin where the environment of advocacy is total. Total civic advocacy is the setting of all the varieties of cultural adaptations from which violent men come.

For this total, pervasive advocacy of violence, I can find no better word that *civic*. The word has a noble ring to it, and calls up the manner in which the people of a nation, a society, a culture are schooled in basic citizenship. That's precisely what I want to call up. Civic responsibilities and civil affairs are what we come to expect as normal, proper, and necessary. Violence, in male experience, *is* just such an expectation. Violence is *learned* within the environment of civic advocacy.

Demonstrating this is perhaps belaboring the obvious. But when we fail to belabor the obvious, the obvious continues to escape us and becomes even in its pervasiveness, part of an apparently innocent environment or backdrop. "Oh, say can you see. . . ." Our National Anthem can perhaps be thought of as simply romanticizing war, mayhem, bloodshed, and violence. But more than that, reflection on the content of the song shows that we pride ourselves, civically, on the fortress mentality of siege, endurance, and battle. The headier virtues of civic responsibility—freedom and justice—are come to only in the context of violence. "The rockets' red glare, the bombs bursting in air," are as ordinary to us as the school event, the sporting event, the civic sanction in which we conjure up hailing America "o'er the ramparts."

"I pledge allegiance. . . ." The flag of violence becomes the object of fidelity and devotion for American children even before they know the meaning of "allegiance." Yet feudal-like obeisance—the hand over the heart and devotional hush to the recitation—to the liege lords of violence is sanctioned as appropriate behavior quite calmly with this ritual.

We might assume of course that because this is ritual no one takes it seriously. That's precisely my point. We don't take it seriously at all. We just take it, live it, breathe it, feel awkward when we don't participate in the ritual, feel condemnatory when others around us don't participate in the ritual, and so on. The environment of civic advocacy of violence *is* ordinary, and not extraordinary.

THE EVERYDAY LANGUAGE OF VIOLENCE

Language is not innocent of meaning, intent and passion. Otherwise, there would be no communication between us at all. Yet words fall from our mouths—even in the civil illustrations above—as if there were no meaning, intent, and passion involved. What I make of this is that the advocacy of violence is so pervasive that the human spirit somehow, someway, mercifully inures itself to the environment. We are numbed and paralyzed by violence, and so continue to speak the language of violence as automatons.

I am not referring to the overt, up front renditions of violence we men use in describing battery and battering. "Giving it to the old woman" and "kicking the shit out of her" however, are phenomenologically on the same level of meaning, intention, and passion as assaulting a problem; conquering fear, nature, a woman; shooting down opinions; striking out at injustices; beating you to the punch; beating an idea to death; striking a blow for free enterprise, democracy; whomping up a meal; pounding home an idea; being under the gun to perform; "It strikes me that. . . ." You can make your own list of violent language. Listen to yourself. Listen to those around you. The meaning, intent, and passion of violence are everywhere to be found in the ordinary language of ordinary experience.

Analyses which interweave the advocacy of male violence with "Super Bowl Culture" have never been refuted. It is too obvious. Civic expectations—translated into professionalism, financial commitments, city planning for recreational space, the raising of male children of competitive sport, the corporate ethics of business ownership of athletic teams, profiteering on entertainment—all result in the monument of the National Football League, symbol and reality at once of the advocacy of violence. How piously the network televison cameras turn away from out-and-out riots on the fields and in the stands. But how expertly the technologies of the television medium replay, stop action, and replay and replay and replay "a clean hit." Like the feelies of George Orwell's *1984,* giant screens in bars and homes can go over and over the bone-crunching tackle, the quarterback sack, the mid-air hit—compared in slow motion to dance and ballet, sophisticating violence in aesthetic terms. We love it. We want it. We pay for it. And I don't mean the black market price of a Bronco season ticket or the inflated price of the beer, automobile accessories and tires, as having equipment and the like which put the violence on the screen. I mean the human toll, the broken women and children of our land, and we frightened men who beat them. And even if I were to claim that neither you nor I is affected by the civic advocacy of violence in commercialism and free enterprise, we would still have to note that the powers and scions of industry *believe*—to the tune of billions of dollars a year—that we are so affected.

Pornography is no more a needed release for prurient sexual energies than would be the continuation of temple prostitutes. But it is sanctioned, and the civic advocacy of violence through pornography is real. It is not on the decrease. Soft porn is no longer *Charlie's Angels* or the double entendres of a Johnny Carson-starlet interview; that's simply a matter of course. Soft porn is now *Playboy, Penthouse,* and *Oui,* where every month, right next to the chewing gum and razor blades at the corner grocery, air-sprayed photographs play into male masturbatory fantasies. Hard porn itself is becoming more "ordinary" every day; child porn and snuff films lead the race in capturing the male market for sex and violence. We love it. We want it. And we pay for it. Violence works.

Insofar as violence works, the male batterer is finally, and somewhat definitively, hidden from us. I would not denigrate or halt for a moment our struggle to know the male batterer through clinical research models. But I would call all who are interested in knowing him and in intervening in and ending the cycle of the violence of men against women, to the larger context of the civic advocacy of violence. There, I believe, is the complement of the analysis generated by profiling the male batterer.

Until the code of male violence is undone, male dominance and sexism will prevail. Until the commerce in violence against women ceases, and we finally create an environment in which violence is no longer acceptable or conceivable, male supremacy will remain a fact of life for all of us.

Further Questions

1. Can someone have a right or privilege of abusing or assaulting another human being?
2. Is it in any way normal and only to be expected that someone batters someone else?
3. Is it true that men batter, in part, because they see all around them the fact that violence works? *Should* violence work?

IV.6   Violence in Intimate Relationships: A Feminist Perspective

BELL HOOKS

How much violence is tolerable in an intimate relationship? bell hooks claims that no violence is tolerable in this context. Such violence strips the victim of her dignity and signals lack of integrity in the relationship.

Another selection by hooks appears in Part II.

Reading Questions

1. Is "battered woman" a stigmatizing term, inhibiting women from breaking the silence about problems of family violence? What would be a better word to use?
2. Does even occasional hitting occasion a breach of trust? Explain.
3. Can sharing intimate details of our lives (for example, how we were abused as children) open up areas of vulnerability that partners can then exploit by creating similar scenarios?

Abridged from "Violence in Intimate Relationships: A Feminist Perspective" in Talking Back: Thinking Feminist. Thinking Black by bell hooks (Boston: South End Press, 1989), pp.84–91. Reprinted by permission of the publisher and the author.

RECENTLY, I BEGAN a conversation with a group of black adults about hitting children. They all agreed that hitting was sometimes necessary. A professional black male in a southern family setting with two children commented on the way he punished his daughters. Sitting them down, he would first interrogate them about the situation or circumstance for which they were being punished. He said with great pride, "I want them to be able to understand fully why they are being punished." I responded by saying that "they will likely become women whom a lover will attack using the same procedure you who he loved them so well used and they will not know how to respond." He resisted the idea that his behavior would have any impact on their responses to violence as adult women. I pointed to case after case of women in intimate relationships with men (and sometimes women) who are subjected to the same form of interrogation and punishment they experienced as children, who accept their lover assuming an abusive, authoritarian role. Children who are the victims of physical abuse—whether one beating or repeated beatings, one violent push or several—whose wounds are inflicted by a loved one, experience an extreme sense of dislocation. The world one has most intimately known, in which one felt relatively safe and secure, has collapsed. Another world has come into being, one filled with terrors, where it is difficult to distinguish between a safe situation and a dangerous one. A gesture of love and a violent, uncaring gesture. There is a feeling of vulnerability, exposure, that never goes away, that lurks beneath the surface. I know. I was one of those children. Adults hit by loved ones usually experience similar sensations of dislocation, of loss, of new found terrors.

Many children who are hit have never known what it feels like to be cared for, loved without physical aggression or abusive pain. Hitting is such a widespread practice that any of us are lucky if we can go through life without having this experience. One undiscussed aspect of the reality of children who are hit finding themselves as adults in similar circumstances is that we often share with friends and lovers the framework of our childhood pains, and this may determine how they respond to us in difficult situations. We share the ways we are wounded and expose vulnerable areas. Often, these revelations provide a detailed model for anyone who wishes to wound or hurt us. While the literature about physical abuse often points to the fact that children who are abused are likely to become abusers or be abused, there is no attention given to sharing woundedness in such a way that we let intimate others know exactly what can be done to hurt us, to make us feel as though we are caught in the destructive patterns we have struggled to break. When partners create scenarios of abuse similar, if not exactly the same, to those we have experienced in childhood, the wounded person is hurt not only by the physical pain but by the feeling of calculated betrayal. Betrayal. When we are physically hurt by loved ones, we feel betrayed. We can no longer trust that care can be sustained. We are wounded, damaged—hurt to our hearts.

Feminist work calling attention to male violence against women has helped create a climate where the issues of physical abuse by loved ones can be freely addressed, especially sexual abuse within families. Exploration of male violence against women by feminists and non-feminists shows a connection between childhood experience of being hit by loved ones and the later occurrence of violence in adult relationships. While there is much material available discussing physical abuse of women by men, usually extreme physical abuse, there is not much discussion of the impact that one incident of hitting may have on a person in an intimate relationship, or how the person who is hit recovers from that experience. Increasingly, in discussions with women about physical abuse in relationships, irrespective of sexual preference, I find that most of us have had the experience of being violently hit at least once. There is little discussion of how we are damaged by such experiences (especially if we have been hit as children), of the ways we cope and recover from this wounding. This is an important area for feminist research precisely because many cases of extreme physical abuse begin with an isolated incident of hitting. Attention must be given to understanding and stopping these isolated incidents if we are to eliminate the possibility that women will be at risk in intimate relationships.

Critically thinking about issues of physical abuse has led me to question the way our culture, the way we as feminist advocates focus on the issue of violence and physical abuse by loved ones. The focus has been on male violence against women and, in particular, male sexual abuse of children. Given the nature of patriarchy, it has been necessary for feminists to focus on extreme cases to make people confront the issue, and acknowledge it to be serious and relevant. Unfortunately, an exclusive focus on extreme cases can and does lead us to ignore the more frequent, more common, yet less extreme case of occasional hitting. Women are also less likely to acknowledge occasional hitting for fear that they will then be seen as someone who is in a bad relationship or someone whose life is out of control. Currently, the literature about male violence against women identifies the physically abused woman as a "battered woman." While it has been important to have an accessible terminology to draw attention to the issue of male violence against women, the terms used reflect biases because they call attention to only one type of violence in intimate relationships. The term "battered woman" is problematical. It is not a term that emerged from feminist work on male violence against women; it was already used by psychologists and sociologists in the literature on domestic violence. This label "battered woman" places primary emphasis on physical assaults that are continuous, repeated, and unrelenting. The focus is on extreme violence, with little effort to link these cases with the everyday acceptance within intimate relationships of physical abuse that is not extreme, that may not be repeated. Yet these lesser forms of physical abuse damage individuals psychologically and, if not properly addressed and recovered from, can set the stage for more extreme incidents.

Most importantly, the term "battered woman" is used as though it constitutes a separate and unique category of womanness, as though it is an identity, a mark that sets one apart rather than being simply a descriptive term. It is as though the experience of being repeatedly violently hit is the sole defining characteristic of a woman's identity and all other aspects of who she is and what her experience has been are submerged. When I was hit, I too used the popular phrases "batterer," "battered woman," "battering" even though I did not feel that these words adequately described being hit once. However, these were the terms that people would listen to, would see as important, significant (as if it is not really significant for an individual, and more importantly for a woman, to be hit once). My partner was angry to be labelled a batterer by me. He was reluctant to talk about the experience of hitting me precisely because he did not want to be labelled a batterer. I had hit him once (not as badly as he had hit me) and I did not think of myself as a batterer. For both of us, these terms were inadequate. Rather than enabling us to cope effectively and positively with a negative situation, they were part of all the mechanisms of denial; they made us want to avoid confronting what had happened. This is the case for many people who are hit and those who hit.

Women who are hit once by men in their lives, and women who are hit repeatedly do not want to be placed in the category of "battered woman" because it is a label that appears to strip us of dignity, to deny that there has been any integrity in the relationships we are in. A person physically assaulted by a stranger or a casual friend with whom they are not intimate may be hit once or repeatedly but they do not have to be placed into a category before doctors, lawyers, family, counselors, etc. take their problem seriously. Again, it must be stated that establishing categories and terminology has been part of the effort to draw public attention to the seriousness of male violence against women in intimate relationships. Even though the use of convenient labels and categories has made it easier to identify problems of physical abuse, it does not mean the terminology should not be critiqued from a feminist perspective and changed if necessary.

Recently, I had an experience assisting a woman who had been brutally attacked by her husband (she never commented on whether this was the first incident or not), which caused me to reflect anew on the use of the term "battered woman." This young woman was not engaged in feminist thinking or aware that "battered woman" was a category. Her husband had tried to choke her to death. She managed to escape from him with only the clothes she was wearing. After she recovered from the trauma, she considered going back to this relationship. As a church-going woman, she believed that her marriage vows were sacred and that she should try to make the relationship work. In an effort to share my feeling that this could place her at great risk, I brought her Lenore Walker's *The Battered Woman* because it seemed to me that there was much that she was not revealing, that she felt alone, and that the experiences she would read about in the book would give her a sense that other women had experienced what she was going through. I hoped reading the book would give her the courage to confront the reality of her situation. Yet I found it difficult to share because I could see that her self-esteem had already been greatly attacked, that she had lost a sense of her worth and value, and that possibly this categorizing of her identity would add to the feeling that she should just forget, be silent (and certainly returning to a situation where one is likely to be abused is one way to mask the severity of the problem). Still I had to try. When I first gave her the book, it disappeared. An unidentified family member had thrown it away. They felt that she would be making a serious mistake if she began to see herself as an absolute victim which they felt the label "battered woman" implied. I stressed that she should ignore the labels and read the content. I believed the experience shared in this book helped give her the courage to be critical of her situation, to take constructive action.

Her response to the label "battered woman," as well as the responses of other women who have been victims of violence in intimate relationships, compelled me to critically explore further the use of this term. In conversation with many women, I found that it was seen as a stigmatizing label, one which victimized women seeking help felt themselves in no condition to critique. As in, "who cares what anybody is calling it—I just want to stop this pain." Within patriarchal society, women who are victimized by male violence have had to pay a price for breaking the silence and naming the problem. They have had to be seen as fallen women, who have failed in their "feminine" role to sensitize and civilize the beast in the man. A category like "battered woman" risks reinforcing this notion that the hurt woman, not only the rape victim, becomes a social pariah, set apart, marked forever by this experience.

A distinction must be made between having a terminology that enables women, and all victims of violent acts, to name the problem and categories of labeling that may inhibit that naming. When individuals are wounded, we are indeed often scarred, often damaged in ways that do set us apart from those who have not experienced a similar wounding, but an essential aspect of the recovery process is the healing of the wound, the removal of the scar. This is an empowering process that should not be diminished by labels that imply this wounding experience is the most significant aspect of identity.

As I have already stated, overemphasis on extreme cases of violent abuse may lead us to ignore the problem of occasional hitting, and it may make it difficult for women to talk about this problem. A critical issue that is not fully examined and written about in great detail by researchers who study and work with victims is the recovery process. There is a dearth of material discussing the recovery process of individuals who have been physically abused. In those cases where an individual is hit only once in an intimate relationship, however, violently, there may be no recognition at all of the negative impact of this experience. There may be no conscious attempt by the victimized person to work at restoring her or his well-being, even if the person seeks therapeutic help, because the one incident may not be seen as serious or damaging. Alone and in isolation, the person who has been hit must struggle to regain broken trust—to forge some strategy of recovery. Individuals are often able to process an experience of being hit mentally that may not be processed emotionally. Many women I talked with felt that even after the incident was long forgotten, their bodies remain troubled. Instinctively, the person who has been hit may respond fearfully to any body movement on the part of a loved one that is similar to the posture used when pain was inflicted.

Being hit once by a partner can forever diminish sexual relationships if there has been no recovery process. Again there is little written about ways folks recover physically in their sexualities as loved ones who continue to be sexual with those who have hurt them. In most cases, sexual relationships are dramatically altered when hitting has occurred. The sexual realm may be the one space where the person who has been hit experiences again the sense of vulnerability, which may also arouse fear. This can lead either to an attempt to avoid sex or to unacknowledged sexual withdrawal wherein the person participates but is passive. I talked with women who had been hit by lovers who described sex as an ordeal, the one space where they confront their inability to trust a partner who has broken trust. One woman emphasized that to her, being hit was a "violation of her body space" and that she felt from then on she had to protect that space. This response, though a survival strategy, does not lead to healthy recovery.

Often, women who are hit in intimate relationships with male or female lovers feel as though we have lost an innocence that cannot be regained. Yet this very notion of innocence is connected to passive acceptance of concepts of romantic love under patriarchy which have served to mask problematic realities in relationships. The process of recovery must include a critique of this notion of innocence which is often linked to an unrealistic and fantastic vision of love and romance. It is only in letting go of the perfect, no-work, happily-ever-after union idea, that we can rid our psyches of the sense that we have failed in some way by not having such relationships. Those of us who never focussed on the negative impact of being hit as children find it necessary to reexamine the past in a therapeutic manner as part of our recovery process. Strategies that helped us survive as children may be detrimental for us to use in adult relationships.

Talking about being hit by loved ones with other women, both as children and as adults, I found that many of us had never really thought very much about our own relationship to violence. Many for us took pride in never feeling violent, never hitting. We had not thought deeply about our relationships to inflicting physical pain. Some of us expressed terror and awe when confronted with physical strength on the part of others. For us, the healing process included the need to learn how to use physical force constructively, to remove the terror—the dread. Despite the research that suggests children who are hit may become adults who hit—women hitting children, men hitting women and children—most of the women I talked with not only did not hit but were compulsive about not using physical force.

Overall the process by which women recover from the experience of being hit by loved ones is a complicated and multi-faceted one, an area where there must be much more feminist study and research. To many of us, feminists calling attention to the reality of violence in intimate relationships has not in and of itself compelled most people to take the issue seriously, and such violence seems to be daily on the increase. In this essay, I have raised issues that are not commonly talked about, even among folks who are particularly concerned about violence against women. I hope it will serve as a catalyst for further thought, that it will strengthen our efforts as feminist activists to create a world where domination and coercive abuse are never aspects of intimate relationships.

Further Questions

1. Is it shocking to hear that (irrespective of sexual preference) most women have been hit at least once in a relationship? What does this say about present relationships?

2. Suppose a battered woman somehow escapes her battering situation. Will other people treat her as well as they would treat someone they believed had not been battered?

3. If a woman is being hit in a relationship, does she have reasons to remain in the relationship, for example, loyalty to her partner or to the relationship?

Battered Women of Color in Public Health Care Systems: Racism, Sexism, and Violence   IV.7

BETH E. RICHIE AND VALLI KANUHA

Beth E. Richie and Valli Kanuha describe the special situations of battered women of color. These women may try to conceal their injuries so as not to compromise the couple's standing in the community and the standing of the ethnic community itself. Men of color may arrive in court on allegations of domestic violence with bruises supposedly inflicted by police officers. Thus, issues of domestic violence on women of color often become subordinated to other concerns of the minority group. Women of color may have additional problems with the health care system, such as stereotyping, poor skills in English, or undocumented status in the country.

Reading Questions

1. Why is a battered woman of color sometimes torn between getting help for her problem and concealing it for the sake of her husband or boyfriend or for the ethnic community itself?

2. Do health care providers sometimes lose a valuable opportunity to help battered women of color by not acknowledging the battering? How would acknowledging the battering be helpful?

3. Should a pregnant woman be held liable for any damage inflicted on her fetus, even if her only fault is not leaving an abusive relationship?

INTRODUCTION

This chapter will address an important factor which is often ignored in our understanding and analysis of domestic violence. While our increasing knowledge of battered women is usually ap-plied in the context that "all women are vulnerable to male violence," the emphasis of this discussion will be on those differential social, economic, and cultural circumstances that render women of color, in particular, vulnerable to male violence at both individual and institutional

Abridgement of pp. 289–299 of Barbara Blair and Susan E. Caylett, eds., Wings of Gauze, *1996. Wayne State University Press. Reprinted by permission of the publisher.*

levels. In addition, this article will focus specifically on the experiences of battered women of color within the health care system, including hospitals, clinics, and public health agencies. As will be described in later sections, many women of color rely significantly on public health institutions not only for ongoing preventive health care and crisis intervention services but, more importantly, as a viable access point for other services and institutions, e.g., public welfare, housing assistance, legal advice, and so on. Thus the emphasis of this chapter is on the relationship between health care institutions and battered women of color, although similar critiques could be made about the inadequate response of other public institutions (such as religious organizations or the criminal justice system) to battered women of color. Finally, this essay will discuss some effective strategies and programs which address the unique and complex issues affecting women of color who are battered.

BALANCING OUR MULTIPLE LOYALTIES: SPECIAL CONSIDERATIONS FOR WOMEN OF COLOR AND VICTIMS OF DOMESTIC VIOLENCE

There are many stereotypes about women of color which affect not only our understanding of them as women, but particularly our analysis of and sensitivity to them with regard to domestic violence. For example, many portrayals of women of color espouse their inherent strengths as historical, matriarchal heads of households (Rudwick and Rudwick, 1971). While this stereotype of women of color as super homemakers, responsible family managers, and unselfish nurturers may be undisputed, such attributions do not mean that all (or most) women of color are therefore empowered and supported in their various family roles or have positions of leadership within their ethnic communities. Many women of color with whom we work state that

they face the burden either of having to be overly competent and successful or having to avoid the too-often painful reality of becoming "just another one of those horror stories or pitiful statistics on the front page of the newspaper." For women of color who are experiencing domestic violence, the implicit community and societal expectation to be strong and continue to care for themselves and their families results in their denying not only the actual existence of battering in their lives, but the extent and nature of that abuse (Richie, 1992). For example, one Korean woman who was repeatedly punched around her head and face by her husband reported that she used cosmetics extensively each day when she want to Mass with her husband, in order to assure protection of her own, as well as her husband's, dignity among their church and neighborhood friends. When she went to work as a typist in a white business, she was especially careful not to disclose evidence of her abuse, in order to protect both herself and her husband from her co-workers' judgments that "there was something wrong with Korean people."

While public policy makers are concerned about the rapidly escalating crime rate in this country, many leaders in cities predominated by communities of color are becoming increasingly concerned about the profile of those convicted for crimes, i.e., young boys and men of color. The predominance of men of color in correctional facilities (close to 90 percent of the penal population in some cities) has polarized everyone, from scholars to community leaders to policy makers. While most mainstream legislators and public health officials are reluctant to discuss it publicly, there is a rising belief that men of color are inherently problematic and socially deviant. More progressive analysts have ascribed criminal behavior among nonwhite males to historically racist social conditions that are reinforced by criminal, legal, and penal systems which disproportionately arrest and convict men of color at least in part because of their skin color (Kurtz, 1990).

There are no equally concerned dialogues about how women of color continue to be victims of crime more often than white women and about the disparate treatment they receive from not only racist, but sexist social systems. An African-American woman who works with battered women as a court advocate states unequivocally that battered women of color were usually treated less respectfully by prosecutors and judges than the white women with whom she works. In addition, when this same court advocate has raised this disparity with her African-American brothers and male friends in her community, she is often derided as being "one of those white women's libbers" who has betrayed "her own" by working on a problem like domestic violence, which will further stigmatize and destroy the men of color who are charged with battering. Unfortunately, this dialectic of the comparable oppression of women and men of color has resulted in a troubling silence about the needs of women of color and led to counterproductive discussions between women and men of color about the meaning and significance of domestic violence, specifically, and sexism in general.

For a battered woman of color who experiences violence at the hands of a man of color from her own ethnic group, a complex and troublesome dynamic is established that is both enhanced and compromised by the woman's relationship to her community. She is battered by another member of her ethnic community, whose culture is vulnerable to historical misunderstanding and extinction by society at large. For the battered woman, this means that she may be discriminated against in her attempt to secure services *while at the same time* feeling protective of her batterer, who might also be unjustly treated by such social institutions as the police and the judicial system. Most battered women of color are acutely aware of how the police routinely brutalize men of color, how hospitals and social services discriminate against men of color, and the ways men of color are

more readily labeled deviant than white men. In one Midwestern city, anecdotal reports from court and police monitors have shown that men of color awaiting arraignment for domestic violence charges frequently arrive in court with bruises supposedly inflicted by police officers. One Indian woman stated that when she saw her husband in court the morning after a battering incident, he looked just as bad as she did, with black eyes and bruises about his face. Feeling pity for him, she refused to testify, and upon release he told her of being beaten by police while being transported between the jail and the court house. Although the existence of police brutality is unfortunately not a new phenomenon, it is certainly compromised and complicated in the context of domestic violence, *especially* for men and women of color who are seeking help from this already devastating problem. For battered women of color, seeking help for the abuse they are experiencing always requires a tenuous balance between care for and loyalty to themselves, their batterers, and their communities.

The situation is further complicated by the fact that communities of color have needed to prioritize the pressing social, economic, and health problems which have historically plagued their people and neighborhoods. Because of sexism, the particular concerns of women typically do not emerge at the top of the list. The values of family stability, community self-determination, and protection of one's racial and ethnic culture are often seen as incompatible with addressing the needs of battered women within communities of color. Most of us who have worked in the domestic violence movement are well aware of the gross misconceptions that battering is just a woman's issue or that domestic violence in communities of color is not as serious as other problems. The most dangerous consequence, for battered women of color, however, is that they are often entrapped by these misconceptions and misguided loyalties and thus remain in the confines of violent and abusive households (Richie, 1985).

BATTERED WOMEN OF COLOR: HEALTH PROBLEMS AND HEALTH CARE

Women who are battered are often seriously hurt; their physical and psychological injuries are life-threatening and long-lasting. In one-third of all battering incidents, a weapon is used, and 40 percent result in the need for emergency medical attention (Stark et al., 1977). Research suggests that one-third of all adult female suicide attempts can be associated with battering, and 25 percent of all female homicide victims die at the hands of their husbands or boyfriends (Browne, 1987). More women are injured in their homes by their spouses or male partners each year than by accidents or illnesses (FBI, 1982).

It is not surprising, therefore, that most battered women report their first attempt to seek help is from a health care institution, even before contacting the police (Stark et al., 1977). This is especially true in communities of color, where police response is likely to be sporadic, at best (Davis, 1985). Yet research indicates that of those battered women using the emergency room for acute treatment of injuries related to an abusive incident, only one in ten was identified as battered (McLeer and Amwar, 1989). Similar findings have been cited for women using ambulatory care settings. A random sample of women seeking health maintenance visits at neighborhood health clinics revealed that 33 percent were battered women and less than 10 percent received safety information or counseling for domestic violence (Richie, 1985). The following story of Yolanda (a pseudonym) illustrates the role of health facilities in the lives of battered women.

> Yolanda is a forty-six-year old who receives primary health care from a neighborhood health clinic. She uses the services of the walk-in clinic two or more times each month, complaining of discomfort, sleeplessness, and fatigue. Yolanda never mentions that her boyfriend abuses her, but her clinic visits correspond directly

with the pattern of his alcohol binges. The staff of the clinic know about her boyfriend's mistreatment, because he sometimes comes to the clinic drunk and will threaten her if she does not leave with him.

For Yolanda, the clinic symbolizes a safe, public place of refuge. From her experience, she knows it is legitimate to seek assistance when one is sick, and she trusts health authorities to take care of her needs. Health providers lose an important opportunity for intervention when they do not offer assistance to Yolanda, especially since they have clear evidence that her boyfriend is violent toward her. She, in turn, feels that the violence must be hidden and that it is a source of shame, since her health care providers do not acknowledge it or offer to help.

For many battered women of color, the unresponsiveness of most health care institutions is symbolic of the overall reality of social disenfranchisement and deterioration in poor, non-white communities across the United States. While lack of quality, affordable housing is a major problem for many people of color, the majority of the homeless are women of color and their children (Perales and Young, 1988). The drug epidemic, particularly crack and heroin use, has had a significant impact on violence against women. There is growing anecdotal evidence to suggest that battered women are often forced to use drugs as part of the pattern of their abuse, yet there is a serious lack of treatment programs for women, particularly poor women with children (Chavkin, 1990). The spread of HIV and AIDS among many women of color has been compounded by the HIV infection rate among children of HIV-positive mothers. Many women with HIV report that negotiating for safer sex or clean needles is difficult when they are controlled by violent, coercive partners.

With regard to women and the social problems of drugs, homelessness, and AIDS, most public health officials have been quick to label women as the criminals, rather than the victims of a society that is disintegrating before our very eyes. When we add to the above the battering, rape, and psychological abuse of those same women who are homeless, drug addicted, and HIV-positive, it is clear that the health care system can be either a vehicle for assistance or a significant barrier for women who are seeking protection from a myriad of health and social problems.

The experience of Ana illustrates the interrelatedness that can occur between domestic violence, drug use, HIV infection, and the chronic and acute need for health care. Ana's husband was an injection drug user who had battered her severely throughout their ten-year marriage. He had been very ill for a period of months and had tested positive for HIV. Ana was already pregnant when her husband was tested, but he insisted that she carry through with the pregnancy. She was battered twice in the four months since she had gotten pregnant, and after one incident she was unable to get out of bed for two days. Her husband Daniel reportedly was concerned about the baby and took her to the emergency room of their local hospital. During the triage interview, the ER (Emergency Room) nurse noticed the tension between Ana and Daniel but was uncomfortable addressing it. The nurse later reported that she did not want to offend them by suggesting that they appeared to be having "marriage problems" because they were Hispanic, and she understood that Hispanics were embarrassed about discussing such matters with health professionals. After being admitted for observation, Ana began to complain of increased pains in her abdomen. After five days in the hospital, Ana hemorrhaged and lost her baby. At that time, she discovered that she had been tested for HIV and was seropositive. She returned home to a distraught and angry husband, who blamed the baby's death on her. She was beaten again and returned to the ER once more.

Ana's case illustrates one of the most troubling examples of the interface between health care and violence against women. With the long-standing lack of adequate and accessible prenatal care for poor women of color, pregnant women of color who are battered are especially vulnerable. Research indicates that 20 percent of all women who are battered experience the first incident during pregnancy (McFarland, 1989). The situation for pregnant battered women is further complicated by the troubling legal trend to hold women accountable for any damage inflicted upon a fetus in utero. If a pregnant women is battered and the fetus is harmed, she may be criminally liable for not leaving the abusive relationship. Not surprisingly, in most recent "fetal death" cases across the country, the women who are most severely punished are women of color (Pollitt, 1990).

As the health care system has labored under increased social and economical stress, specialized programs for women and for certain communities have also been curtailed. For battered women of color this trend has specific and dangerous affects. With a steady increase in immigrants from Central America, South America, and the Caribbean, battered women who do not have legal status in this country are destined to remain invisible and underserved. Because of their undocumented status and other significant barriers (such as language and cultural differences), many battered women of color are denied assistance by the same organizations established to protect them, e.g., public welfare, legal advocacy, and health clinics (Kanuha, 1987). One battered women's program specifically targeted to serve Caribbean women and their children reports that battered women who must use hospital services for their injuries often have to borrow Medicaid cards from other women in order to conceal their undocumented status. Staff from this same program describe the difficulty that one undocumented woman had even getting out of the house, much less to the hospital, as her batterer was rightfully suspicious that reports of his criminal behavior would also jeopardize *his* illegal status.

Most hospital-based crisis intervention programs do not have multi-lingual or multi-cultural staff who are trained in and sensitive to the special issues of women of color. For example, reliance on translators to communicate with non-English speaking women effectively compromises the confidentiality and protection of battered women who are immigrants, from small ethnic communities, or who must use their own family members as translators to describe painful and private incidents of violence in the home. There are numerous stories of women of color receiving insensitive treatment by health care staff who attribute domestic violence to stereotypes such as "I've heard you Latins have hot tempers" or "Asian women are so passive, it really explains why they get beaten by their husbands."

Finally, if a battered woman of color is also a lesbian, differently abled, or from any other group that is already stigmatized, her access to quality care from health providers may be further compromised. One battered lesbian who was an African American described a physician who was continually incredulous about her claims that a "pretty girl like her" would be beaten by her female lover. In fact, she stopped going to the hospital for emergency attention, even though she had no other health insurance, because she was angry at such homophobic treatment and therefore became increasingly reluctant to use the services of that hospital.

As long as health care institutions continue to be the primary, and usually first, access point for battered women of color, we must require them to institute ongoing training, education, and specialized programs, and to hire culturally knowledgeable staff to address the particular needs of this special group of women.

THE RESPONSE OF WOMEN OF COLOR

Despite the philosophical and political contradictions and the practical barriers described in the previous sections, women of color have actively and creatively challenged the discriminatory, institutional practices of health care and crisis intervention services. Against extremely difficult economic, cultural, and political odds, battered women of color and their advocates have initiated a broad-based response to violence against women in communities of color. Aspects of this response will be summarized in the remainder of the chapter.

One of the most significant developments in response to domestic violence in communities of color has been the creation of grassroots crisis intervention services by and for women of color. The majority of these programs have been organized autonomously from white women, privileging the analysis and experience of women of color by assuming the cultural, historical, and linguistic norms of Asian/Pacific Islander, Latin, African-American, Native-American, and other nonwhite cultures. Typically located in neighborhoods and communities of color, these programs have a strong emphasis on community organization and public education. While many of these programs struggle for financial support and recognition from mainstream public health agencies and feminist organizations, they endure in great part because they are grounded in a community-based approach to problem solving.

The Violence Intervention Program for Latina women and their children in the community of East Harlem and the Asian Women's Center in Chinatown are good examples of community-based programs in New York City. Refugee Women In Development (REFWID), in Washington, D.C., has a domestic violence component, as does Arco Iris, a retreat center for Native-American women and other women of color who have experienced violence in Arkansas. In Minnesota, women of color have created a statewide battered women's coalition called Black, Indian, Hispanic, and Asian Women In Action (BIHA). In California, California Women Of Color Against Domestic Violence organizes and publishes a newsletter, "Out Loud," and women of color from seven southern states have created The Southeast Women Of Color Task Force Against Domestic Violence. Nationally, the members of the Women Of Color Task Force of the National Coalition

Against Domestic Violence have provided national leadership training and technical assistance on the issues of battering and women of color, and their task force has served as a model for the development of programs for battered women of color across the country.

In addition to providing crisis intervention and emergency shelter services to battered women, these community based programs and statewide coalitions for women of color are involved in raising the issue of battering within other contexts of social justice efforts. Representatives of grassroots battered women's programs are often in leadership roles on such issues as reproductive freedom, immigration policy, lesbian rights, criminal justice reform, homelessness, AIDS policy, and other issues that affect women of color. The National Black Women's Health Project in Atlanta is a good example of this.

Finally, in the past several years there has been a proliferation of literature on violence against women by scholars and activists who are women of color. Seal Press's New Leaf Series published Evelyn C. White's *Chain, Chain Change: for Black Women Dealing with Physical and Emotional Abuse* and Myrna Zambrano's *Mejor Sola Que Mal Acompanada*. Another good example of analysis by and for battered women of color is a publication by the Center For Domestic And Sexual Violence in Seattle, *The Speaking Profits Us: Violence Against Women of Color,* a collection of papers edited by Mary Violet Burns. Kitchen Table, Women of Color Press in Albany, New York, has been a leader in publishing writing by women of color, addressing the issue of violence against women in the Freedom Organizing pamphlet series and in many other works (Smith, 1985).

By providing direct crisis intervention services, educating communities of color, advocating on broader feminist and social justice issues and publishing culturally relevant resources, Asian/Pacific Islanders, Latinas, Native-Americans, African Americans, Caribbeans, and other women of color have demonstrated a strong commitment to addressing violence against women. Our contri-

butions have significantly enhanced both the conventional research on battered women and the progressive work of the battered women's movement, challenging the accepted analysis that violence against women has equivalent effects on all women. We must continue to develop community-based programs that are culturally relevant and responsive to the complexity of experiences faced by women of color, including inadequate health care, unemployment, homelessness, a failing educational system, and violence. Equally important, we must continue to work within our own culture to challenge those traditions, assumptions, and values that reinforce male domination and ignore women's needs. In so doing, the struggle to end violence against women of color will include individual liberation as well as social reform. For us, the most compelling motivation for continuing this effort comes from the courage, commitment, and endurance that battered women of color have shown in their personal and collective struggles. On a daily basis they persist in defying the limits that violence, sexism, and racism impose on their lives. Our response must be to let their stories challenge and inspire us—women of color, battered women, white women, and men alike—to work actively to end individual and institutional violence against women.

NOTE

1. The women described in this essay are referred to anonymously or by pseudonyms to protect their safety and privacy. Their stories are both composites and individual accounts of women with whom the authors have worked.

REFERENCES

Browne, A. 1987. *When Battered Women Kill.* New York: Free Press.

Chavkin, W. 1990. "Drug Addiction and Pregnancy: Policy Crossroads." *American Journal of Public Health,* 80 (4):483–87.

Davis, A. 1985. *Violence against Women and the Ongoing Challenge to Racism.* Latham, N.Y.: Kitchen Table Press.

Federal Bureau of Investigation. 1982. *Uniform Crime Reports.* Washington, D.C.: Department of Justice.

Kanuha, V. 1987. "Sexual Assault in Southeast Asian Communities: Issues in Intervention." *Response,* 10:3–4.

Kurtz, H. 1990. "Jail City: Behind Bars with New York's 20,000 Inmates." *New York Magazine.* April 23, 1990.

McFarlane, J. 1989. "Battering During Pregnancy: Tip of an Iceberg Revealed." *Women and Health,* 15 (3):69–84.

McLeer, S., and R. Amwar. 1989. "A Study of Battered Women Presenting in an Emergency Department." *American Journal of Public Health,* 79 (1):65–66.

Perales, C., and L. Young, eds. 1988. *Too Little Too Late: Dealing with the Health Needs of Women in Poverty.* New York: Harrington Press.

Pollitt, K. 1990. "A New Assault on Feminism." *Nation,* 250:409–11.

Richie, B. 1985. "Battered Black Women: A Challenge of the Black Community." *Black Scholar,* 16:40–44.

Richie, B. 1992. "An Exploratory Study of the Link between Gender Identity Development, Violence Against Women, and Crime among African-American Battered Women." Ph.D. diss., The Graduate School and University Center, City University of New York.

Rudwick, B., A. Meier, and E. Rudwick, eds. 1971. *Black Matriarchy: Myth or Reality.* Belmont, Calif.: Wadsworth Publishing.

Smith, B., ed. 1985. *Home Girls: A Black Feminist Anthology.* Latham, N.Y.: Kitchen Table Press.

Stark, E., A. Flintcraft and W. Frazier. 1977. "Medicine and Patriarchal Violence: The Social Construction of a 'Private Event.'" *International Journal of Health Services.* 9 (3):461–94.

White, E. 1985. *Chain, Chain Change: For Black Women Dealing with Physical and Emotional Abuse.* Seattle: Seal Press.

Zambrano, M. 1985. *Mejor Sola Que Mal Acompanada: Para la Mujer Golpeada/For the Latina in an Abusive Relationship.* Seattle: Seal Press.

Further Questions

1. What kind of training should health care personnel be required to undergo to alert them to the special needs of battered women and to help them resolve their problems?

2. How can battered women of color be helped through grass-roots organizations in the community such as emergency shelters, crisis intervention, and counseling?

3. What would you like to see done in a community to help battered women? What kinds of special facilities would be helpful for battered women of color?

Further Readings for Part IV: Love and Relationships

Jessica Benjamin. *The Bonds of Love: Psychoanalysis, Feminism, and the Problem of Domination* (New York, NY: Pantheon, 1988). Freudian explanation of the appeal of domination and submission and the consequent difficulty men and women have treating each other as equals.

Martin S. Bergman. *The Anatomy of Loving: The Story of Man's Quest to Know What Love Is* (New York: NY: Columbia University Press, 1987). History of man's concept of love, ancient Egypt through the present.

Lawrence A. Blum. *Friendship, Altruism and Morality* (New York, NY: Routledge & Kegan Paul, 1980). Develops a morality built on concern for others, focusing on friendship.

Jeffrey Blustein. *Care and Commitment* (New York, NY: Oxford University Press, 1991). Scholarly discussion of issues in caring, integrity, and intimacy.

Robert Brown. *Analyzing Love* (New York, NY: Cambridge University Press, 1987). Interesting analyses of concepts of falling in love, being in love, the object of one's love, etc.

Francesca M. Cancian. *Love in America: Gender and Self-development* (New York, NY: Cambridge University Press, 1987). Examination of how many American couples combine self-development with commitment.

Jacqueline B. Carr. *Crisis in Intimacy: When Expectations Don't Meet Reality* (Pacific Grove, CA: Brooks/Cole, 1988). A self-help book, but one especially high in intellectual content.

Richard Christie and Florence L. Geis. *Studies in Machiavellianism* (New York, NY: Academic Press, 1970). The "mach" is the unit that measures how well manipulators fare in personal encounters. Well-written, scholarly, entertaining.

Rosalind Coward. *Female Desire* (London: Paladin, 1984). Follows de Beauvoir in arguing that female love is structured by the female gender role and oppressive for that reason.

Valerian J. Derlega and Alan L. Chaikin. *Sharing Intimacy: What We Reveal to Others and Why* (Englewood Cliffs, NJ: Prentice-Hall, 1975). A discussion of self-disclosure, its costs, and benefits.

Ilham Dilman. *Love and Human Separateness* (New York, NY: Basil Blackwell, 1987). Discussion of theories of love according to which love divides or unites human beings.

Kate Fillion. *Lip Service: The Truth About Women's Darker Side in Love, Sex and Friendship* (New York, NY: Harper Collins, 1996). Women who think they are better than men usually end up feeling worse about themselves.

Mark Fisher. *Personal Love* (London: Duckworth, 1990). Nice, basic level discussion of aspects of personal love.

Mark Fisher and George Stricker, eds. *Intimacy* (New York, NY: Plenum Press, 1982). Multifaceted approach to intimacy.

Marilyn Friedman. *What Are Friends For? Feminist Perspectives on Personal Relationships and Moral Theory* (Ithaca, NY: Cornell University Press, 1993). How friendship can contribute to our personal lives.

Marilyn Frye. *The Politics of Reality: Essays in Feminist Theory* (Trumansburg, NY: The Crossing Press, 1983). Many of these essays offer sound, well-developed insights into problems women have in their relationships with men.

Paul Gilbert. *Human Relationships* (Cambridge, MA: Basil Blackwell, 1991). Love, sex, loving friends, "close encounters," etc.

Carol Gilligan. *In a Different Voice* (Cambridge, MA: Harvard University Press, 1982). Controversial book claiming women's experience gives them a distinct basis for morality and personal relationships, which has been neglected by male-dominated psychology.

George Graham and Hugh LaFollette, eds. *Person to Person* (Philadelphia, PA: Temple University Press, 1989). Good, readable collection of essays on the nature of personal relationships and the features of good relationships.

Vernon W. Grant. *Falling in Love: The Psychology of the Romantic Emotion* (New York, NY: Springer Publishing Co., 1976). Psychological theory brought to bear on falling in love. Non-Freudian approach.

C. Hendrick and S. Hendrick. *Liking, Loving and Relating* (Belmont, CA: Wadsworth, 1982).

Sarah Lucia Hoagland. *Lesbian Ethics: Toward New Value* (Palo Alto, CA: Institute of Lesbian Studies, 1988).

bell hooks. *Ain't I a Woman? Black Women and Feminism* (Boston, MA: South End Press, 1984).

bell hooks. *From Margin to Center* (Boston, MA: South End Press, 1984). All of bell hooks' books contain excellent insights into sexism in personal relationships as well as good thinking on racism.

J. F. M. Hunter. *Thinking About Sex and Love* (Toronto: Macmillan Canada, 1980). Musings that sometimes stop short of making a solid point.

Søren Kierkegaard. *Either/Or: A Kierkegaard Anthology,* Robert Bretall, ed. (Princeton, NJ: Princeton University Press, 1946). Romance is immediate, founded on nothing, untested, and thus inferior to committed, conjugal love.

Bonnie Kreps. *Authentic Passion: Loving Without Losing Yourself* (Toronto: McLelland and Stewart, 1990). Men who write on love seem positive about it and fairly sure of what they are talking about. Women tend to write paperbacks, not explaining what love is but warning the (presumably female) reader of love's dangers ("losing yourself") and giving advice on how to avoid them. This effort is more intellectual, more creative, and more positive about love than most of the other paperback guides on love by women.

Joseph A. Kuypers. *Man's Will to Hurt: Investigating the Causes, Supports and Varieties of His Violence*. (Halifax, NS: Fernwood Publishing, 1992). Contends that male violence serves men's self-interest which makes it difficult for men to see problems with it.

Hugh La Follette. *Personal Relationships: Love, Identity, and Morality* (Cambridge, MA: Blackwell Publishers Inc., 1996). Careful and detailed analysis of aspects of personal relationships.

Harriet Goldhor Lerner. *The Dance of Intimacy: A Woman's Guide to Courageous Acts of Change in Key Relationships* (New York, NY: Harper & Row, 1989). Best-seller by the author of *The Dance of Anger*. A little on the practical, non-intellectual side.

Myriam Miedzian. *Boys Will Be Boys: Breaking the Link Between Masculinity and Violence* (New York, NY: Doubleday 1991).

Gilbert Meilander. *Friendship: A Study in Theological Ethics* (Notre Dame, IN: University of Notre Dame Press, 1981). A development of the virtues of friendship in the tradition of Aristotle and Aquinas.

Nel Noddings. *Caring: A Feminine Approach to Ethics and Moral Education* (Berkeley, CA: University of California Press, 1984). Controversial claim that women's moral awareness centers around caring.

David L. Norton and Mary F. Kille, eds. *Philosophies of Love* (Totowa, NJ: Rowman and Allanheld, 1971). Anthology of writings on romantic love, eros, agape, "Tristanism," friendship, fellow feeling, and other love topics.

Michael Paluk, ed. *Other Selves: Philosophers on Friendship* (Indianapolis, IN: Hackett, 1986). Historically oriented; Aristotle, Plato, Emerson, etc.

Janice Raymond. *A Passion for Friends* (Boston, MA: Beacon Press, 1986). Aristotelian friendship forms a model for relationships, especially lesbian relationships.

Adrienne Rich. *On Lies, Secrets and Silence: Selected Prose, 1966–1978* (New York, NY: W. W. Norton and Co., Virago Press, 1979). Features "Women and Honor: Some Notes on Lying," an argument that patriarchy forces women to take refuse in dishonorable behavior.

Lillian B. Rubin. *Intimate Strangers: Men and Women Together* (New York, NY: Harper & Row, 1983). Much-read book on difficulties with intimacy in heterosexual relationships.

Lillian B. Rubin. *Just Friends: The Role of Friendship in Our Lives* (New York, NY: Harper & Row, 1985). A sequel to *Intimate Strangers;* much of it again focused on heterosexual relationships.

Ronald Sharp, *Friendship and Literature* (Durham, NC: Duke University Press, 1989). Analysis of friendship as gift exchange. Argues that friendship creates roles enabling us to relate to one another.

Irving Singer, ed. *The Nature of Love* (Chicago, IL: University of Chicago Press, 1987). Three volume set of renditions of love by major figures, ending with some of Singer's own ideas.

Guy Siriello. *Love and Beauty* (Princeton, NJ: Princeton University Press, 1989). Loosely described experience of love and of the beloved, relating these to morality, reproduction, and the rest of the world.

Alan Soble, ed. *Eros, Agape and Philia: Readings in the Philosophy of Love* (New York, NY: Paragon House, 1989). Nice, well-balanced collection of writings.

Alan Soble. *The Structure of Love* (New Haven, CT: Yale University Press, 1990). Elaborate tour through various facets of love, leaving the reader somewhat out of breath.

Robert C. Solomon. *About Love: Reinventing Romance for Our Times* (Lanham, MD: Rowman and Littlefield, 1994). Explores many interesting questions about romantic love.

Richard Taylor. *Having Love Affairs* (Buffalo, NY: Prometheus Books, 1982). Defense of adultery and other forms of teacher-student liaisons.

Laurence Thomas. *Living Morally: A Psychology of Moral Character* (Philadelphia, PA: Temple University Press, 1989). Careful development of a morality based partially on altruism and friendship, with the claim that moral flourishing is essential to human flourishing.

Robert Trevas, Arthur Zucker and Donald Borchert, eds. *Philosophy of Sex and Love: A Reader* (Upper Saddle River, NJ: Prentice-Hall Inc., 1997). Thinkers address a wide variety of topics in the area.

Dwight Van de Vare, Jr. *Romantic Love: A Philosophical Inquiry* (University Park, PA: Pennsylvania State University Press, 1981). Love as a social institution; love as used by individuals, singly and collectively.

Paul J. Wadell. *Friendship and the Moral Life* (Notre Dame, IN: University of Notre Dame Press, 1989). Expansive view of friendship and morality to the point of the possibility of being friends with God.

R. Winch. *Mate Selection: A Study of Complementary Needs* (New York, NY: Harper & Row, 1958). Development of the old idea of genders as being different and complementary and thus male gender fitting neatly onto female to make a good relationship.

Julia T. Wood, ed. *Gendered Relationships* (Mountain View, CA: Mayfield Publishing Company, 1996). Good sections on gendered personal relationships and gendered romantic relationships.

VIOLENCE IN PERSONAL RELATIONSHIPS

Pauline B. Bart and Eileen Gail Moran, eds. *Violence Against Women: The Bloody Footprints* (Thousand Oaks, CA: Saye Publications, 1993). Violence against women, including wife-battering and sexual assault.

Douglas J. Besharov, ed. *Family Violence: Research and Public Policy Issues* (Washington, DC: The AEI Press, 1990).

David Finkelhor, Richard S. Gelles, Gerald T. Hotaling, and Murray A. Straus, eds. *The Dark Side of Families: Current Family Violence Research* (Beverly Hills, CA: Sage Publications, 1983).

Stanley G. French, ed. *Interpersonal Violence, Health and Gender Politics*, 3rd edition (Chicago and Boston: McGraw-Hill Ryerson Ltd, 1998). A variety of topics in the area explored from theoretical and personal viewpoints.

Stanley G. French, Wanda Teays and Laura M. Purdy, eds. *Violence Against Women: Philosophical Perspectives* (Ithaca, NY: Cornell University Press, 1998). Contributors consider rape, battering, sexual harassment, pornography, prostitution, and international policies on violence against women.

Robert L. Hampton, ed. *Black Family Violence: Current Research and Theory* (Lexington, MA: Lexington Books, 1991).

Gerald T. Hotaling, David Finkelhor, John R. Kirkpatrick, and Murray A. Straus, eds. *Coping with Family Violence: Research and Policy Perspectives* (Newbury Park, CA: Sage Publications, 1988).

Barry Levy, ed. *Dating Violence: Young Women in Danger* (Seattle, WA: The Seal Press, 1991).

Mary Lystad, ed. *Violence in the Home: Interdisciplinary Perspectives* (New York, NY: Brunner/Mazel Publishers, 1986).

Gordon W. Russell, ed. *Violence in Intimate Relationships* (New York: PMA Publishing Corporation, 1988).

Anson Shupe, William A. Stacey, and Lonnie R. Hazelwood. *Violent Men, Violent Couples: The Dynamics of Domestic Violence* (Lexington, MA: Lexington Books, 1987).

Daniel Jay Sonkin, Del Martin, and Lenore E. Auerbach, eds. *The Male Batterer: A Treatment Approach* (New York, NY: Springer Publishing Company, 1985).

William A. Stacey and Anson Shupe. *The Family Secret: Domestic Violence in America* (Boston, MA: Beacon Press, 1983).

Murray A. Straus, Richard Gelles, et al. *Physical Violence in American Families: Risk Factors and Adaptations to Violence in 8,145 Families* (New Brunswick, NJ: Transaction Publishers, 1990).

Ron Thorne-Finch. *Ending the Silence: The Origins and Treatment of Male Violence Against Women* (Toronto, ON: University of Toronto Press, 1992).

Gillian A. Walker. *Family Violence and the Women's Movement: The Conceptual Politics of Struggle* (Toronto, ON: University of Toronto Press, 1992).

Leonore E. Walker. *The Battered Woman* (New York, NY: Harper & Row, 1979).

Leonore E. Walker. *Terrifying Love: Why Battered Women Kill and How Society Responds* (New York, NY: Harper Collins, 1989).

Suggested Moral of Part IV

Romantic relationships can incorporate undesirable elements. Hidden mechanisms can trigger power and control by one of the participants. Also, violence can become a clear danger in these relationships. To live well, we need to be able to pursue relationships in which we can avoid these faults, which are costs presently sustained mainly by women.

Part V

Bonds

Introduction

A ROMANTIC RELATIONSHIP CAN RESULT IN A COMMITMENT. Our present paradigm for this bond is heterosexual marriage as it has evolved in the Judaeo-Christian religion and in law. The writers in this part analyze this bond and point the way for extending it to homosexual unions as well.

Graham explores some of the forms the marital bond can take; Mendus explains faithfulness in marriage; Staples discusses relationships of black men and black women, including that of marriage; Sullivan argues for the institution of gay marriage, and Weston for family bonds among gays and lesbians; de Beauvior finds serious flaws in the traditional marriage, especially in the position of the wife.

V.1   Commitment and the Value of Marriage

GORDON GRAHAM

Gordon Graham outlines two kinds of marriage that have developed within Christianity. One is based upon legitimate sex. The other is a spiritual union resulting from mutual commitment. He contrasts these ideas with the more modern view of personal marriage.

Reading Questions

1. Do you believe that sex is good only in marriage? Why or why not?
2. Do you think marriage, ideally, should be a union of two people, as distinguished from a relationship between two people?
3. Would you feel comfortable marrying someone you were not in love with?

. . . THE QUESTION "What is commitment to another person?" seems much too direct to be approachable. There is, however, a less direct approach whereby we inquire into commitment through what is perhaps its only unmistakable institutional form: marriage. Many aspects of this very ancient institution warrant attention in their own right, but examination of them, I believe, will also throw light on the modern notion of commitment.

MAKING RELATIONSHIPS WORK

I

We rarely stop to ask whether marriage is valuable and, if it is, what makes it so. Most of us just assume that it is and that some positive account of its value can be given. This assumption shows itself, very often, in our attitude to statistics relating to divorce, which are often presented in a manner suggesting that a rise in the divorce rate is a social problem. But it is a problem only if there is something lamentable about the collapse of a marriage. If there is not, an increasing number of divorces is no more a problem than an increasing number of tennis matches.

Of course when we speak of divorce as a problem we usually make at least one of two hidden assumptions. We assume that divorce brings with it unhappiness. If so, what worries us, strictly, is not increasing divorce but a rise in the amount of unhappiness. The end of a marriage, on this view is not lamentable *in itself*. Alternatively, we assume that lifelong marriage is some sort of ideal, so that the more divorces there are, the less this ideal is being realized. This is the more interesting assumption because it raises the question whether marriage *is* an ideal.

To answer it, we obviously need to say something about what marriage is, and here another interesting feature of modern thinking comes to the fore. As a human institution marriage has taken many different forms, and some of them

Abridged from "Commitment and the Value of Marriage" in Person to Person, *George Graham and Hugh LaFollette, eds. (Philadelphia: Temple University Press, 1989). pp. 199–212. Reprinted by permission of the publisher.*

are quite alien to our ways of thinking—marriage by arrangement and capture, marriages of the dead, marriages to inanimate objects, all of which are recorded in human history. These are not, however, the institutions modern Western supporters of marriage have in mind. What they mean to endorse is not marriage itself, but one form of it, roughly a relationship of sexual fidelity to one member of the opposite sex entered into voluntarily, unconditionally, and for good, regardless of how the future, including the future of the relationship, may go. It is the last part that is specially important because it is this that makes marriage a relationship entered into "for better, for worse, for richer, for poorer, in sickness and in health, till death do us part," and because it is here that we can see why some people have thought marriage to be a kind of institutionalized commitment between people. . . .

II

. . . Broadly, there are two common Christian understandings of marriage as revealed in the New Testament and in the liturgy of the church. The first is what we might call the low theology of marriage. According to this view all sexual activities and relations are prima facie evil. The reasons for this low view of sex have varied, but in general this view is connected with the belief that all fleshly desires have a tendency to pull the individual away from the true joys of heaven, and by thus coming between man and God they take on the distinguishing character of sin. But though sex does have this sinful aspect, it is as plain as anything can be that human beings need sex, both for the procreation of children and for the satisfaction of natural (God-given) desires. For this reason God has *ordained* a special relationship—matrimony—in the context of which sex becomes good, in fact *holy*, because it now stands apart from any other sexual activity. Matrimony, then, is a set of conditions ordained by God under which alone sexual activity ceases to be sinful, and one of these conditions is lifelong fidelity to one partner.

To ask why lifelong fidelity should be one of the conditions of matrimony is to question the ordination of God, and though Christian theology has generally held that lifelong marriage is *good* for human beings and that this is the reason for its ordination, the final answer, as far as human beings are concerned, must be that lifelong fidelity is simply *ordained*. Its ultimate value for us must lie not in the fact that it makes us happy, which, as we know, it may or may not do, but in the fact that it provides for the satisfaction of our natural desires in a way that rescues us from sin.

This low theology might appear to make the institution of marriage of purely instrumental value rather than intrinsic value, but this is not strictly so. It is not that sex is made good *by* marriage, but that only *in* marriage is sex good. Marriage, on this view, we might say, is a constituent of the good life, not a means to it.

It is fairly clear on this low view what adultery is and why it is a ground for divorce. If only sex with one other person on the part of both parties throughout life can be good, sex with someone else on the part of either puts an end to that possibility. What is not so clear is whether remarriage is permissible, but however this may be, we can see easily enough why lifelong marriage is an ideal. It is that relationship alone under which a certain sort of purity is possible. And the desirability of that purity arises from its place in the Christian scheme of salvation, according to which, this life must be used as a preparation for the beatific vision of God. Of course, for those who have no understanding of salvation, this explanation will hardly be satisfactory, and in a more straightforward sense it will generally fail with those who knowingly prefer pleasure not purity. But to acknowledge this limitation is only to acknowledge that *all* explanations must stop somewhere and will not persuade those who are unwilling or unable to stop at that point.

The second Christian understanding of marriage, one more in keeping with the somewhat fleeting references to this subject in the Gospels perhaps, we might call the high view, because it appears to focus on metaphysical rather than moral features of marriage. (I do not mean to suggest that the two views are incompatible in any way.) On this view marriage is a sacrament and the resulting relationship, consummated in sexual relations, a wholly new entity, which is to say that the two parties to a marriage, by vowing fidelity to each other in the sight of God, bring something into existence, namely a unity of two persons in one. This may sound odd, but it does reflect ways of speaking with which we are quite familiar, as for instance the expression "united in matrimony." If, as has traditionally been said, such a sacrament can be performed only once within the lifetimes of the partners, under normal circumstances, divorce and remarriage are impossible; just as the chemicals that go to make up a compound (in contrast to a mixture) cannot be separated again, so the persons who make up a marriage are thereafter in some way inseparable.

It is plain that even the strictest interpretation of this sacramental character of marriage does not exclude *annulment,* which is quite different from *divorce.* When a marriage is annulled it is declared never to have been. When a divorce is granted the marriage is declared to be at an end, and on the high Christian view this is in reality impossible. It is not so much that those who have availed themselves of God's power to make of themselves a holy unity *ought* not to part company, but that in some deep sense they *cannot.*

The point may best be illustrated by comparing marriage with other relationships. If I have a brother, though I can of course ignore my responsibilities to him, I nonetheless stand in a relationship to him which only death can put to an end. I cannot decide to be a brother no longer. The parallel itself, however, suggests an alternative interpretation of the high view. The only sense of brother in which I cannot cease to be a brother is a biological one, and though "brother" generally has moral overtones, these overtones cannot be attributed to the biology

alone. In the moral sense, therefore, it may in extreme circumstances be possible for me to cease to be a father, mother, son, brother, or any other family relationship, a possibility that the legal institution of adoption formalizes. The biological relation, on this view, is normally a sufficient condition of the moral one, but not always. Similarly, those who subscribe to the sacramental theory may in fact admit the permissibility of divorce, on the ground that certain activities—adultery and cruelty are the commonest causes—can rupture the relationship, a rupture that may properly be reflected in law.

But whatever its attitude on divorce, it is clear that the high view also has its account of the value of marriage, namely that through it individuals may participate in a sacramental union of two persons in one, which, like every other sacrament, makes marriage an outward sign of inner grace.

Both these understandings of marriage have attendant problems, not least of which is their employment of language that many people find hard to grasp or sympathize with. It is not my business here, however, to urge the merits of either understanding, but only to point out that both go some way toward explaining why, on the Christian view, marriage based upon self-conscious vows of lifelong sexual fidelity is to be thought of as an ideal, and why its collapse, even if in some cases it is to be regarded as the only sensible course, is still a cause for regret. On the first view, it makes possible a certain sort of purity, and with the demise of a marriage that purity is lost. On the second, it is a new creation that is lost, and even if we allow the permissibility of divorce and remarriage, this remains a loss, just as the death of one child cannot be compensated for by the birth of another, on any but the crudest of utilitarian views.

It might be thought that the Christian account of marriage as elaborated here does *not* explain its value, partly because the theology remains obscure and partly because it gives us no account of the place of love in the relationship. Such a criticism misses the essential claim that the theology *goes some way* toward providing an explanation. To the question "What is valuable about marriage?" the answer may be given that it supplies the individual with a uniquely personal relationship to one other person. As a step in a process of explanation this answer may be of some value. But if, in response to the further question "What is that relationship?" we are obliged, for want of anything better, to answer, "The relationship of being married to them," then quite clearly we have learned nothing. We need something more at this point. And this is what Christian theology gives us, for on the first view it says "The relation of lawful sex" and in the second "Spiritual union." No one could claim that either answer settles all further queries, only that each provides *some* answer and suggests a direction for further inquiry.

That this further inquiry does not push us in the direction of love is not necessarily a weakness, because it may be that what is distinctively valuable in the relation between man and wife is *not* usefully thought of as love. Of course, on the Christian view, man and wife should love each other, but not more so than they should their children and indeed their neighbors and enemies. This is, of course, love in the sense of agape rather than eros. Whether in marriage there is some special role for romantic love is a question to which I shall return. At this point, however, I think enough has been said to throw some light on the uncertainty that so often surrounds secular views of marriage. For while they inherit the belief that in every divorce there is *some* cause for lamentation, at the same time they lack the background that enables them to explain why this is so. And this, or so I argue, reflects a further deficiency: their inability to explain the peculiar value of marriage in the first place. . . .

III

. . . Our modern view of marriage has been heavily influenced by romanticism, the belief that *feelings* are what make for authenticity. Under the influence of romanticism we find it difficult, as most other cultures have not, to see any value

in arranged marriages of convenience, since true marriage, it is thought, must rest upon love. And the highest form of love is the undying love of a Romeo and a Juliet. Marriage is an ideal, therefore, precisely because it expresses in institutional form the value of such love.

There are many objectionable features to this sort of romanticism, not least its unreality for most ordinary human beings, and its relegating the idea of love to the realm of romantic feeling. . . . But to see its limitations in the present context no detailed exploration of romanticism as a whole is required. We need only agree that on this conception, either true marriage consists just in the right state of feeling, in which case *vows* are irrelevant, or the appropriate loving relationship must exist independently of the vows expressed in formal marriage. If the former, the romantic conception has no place at all for self-conscious marriage as we have been considering it; and if the latter, since the loving relationship that the marriage vows exist to express may cease almost as soon as the vows are made, there may quickly be nothing for the marriage to express and hence no reason to persist with it. On the other hand, such a relationship may well exist outside solemnized marriages.

In fact this possibility suggests, curiously enough, that the romantic conception is better suited to *common* marriage, an institution around which most of Europe's marriage laws have grown up. In a common-law marriage no vows are made: the relationship is not even begun with the intention of permanence. It is its continuation that eventually results in its being given a certain legal status; and this being so, it seems natural to say that common marriage expresses or recognizes a pre-existing relationship. But of course the relationship it expresses *lacks* just the feature that marriage proper is supposed to have: the vow to lifelong fidelity.

The romantic conception of love and marriage, then, seems unable to supply the sort of background that would explain the value of marriage proper. This in itself, of course, is not a reason to reject romanticism, as many romantics saw, for it may be that to the true romantic, marriage as we commonly understand it is *not* something to which we should aspire. This is not a conclusion which many are as yet willing to accept, and for this reason, perhaps, equally familiar is an alternative response to the demand, one which rejects the romantic idea of love independent of marriage and focuses instead upon the idea of commitment. True love, we are sometimes told, is not so much the state of feeling that precedes marriage as the relationship that is itself formed by the initiation and persistence of marriage. On this account marriage expresses commitment to another person. Before we can see the limitations of this response we must explore a little further the notion of commitment.

When we speak of commitment to other people, we often have in mind a relationship that is *essentially* personal. This is to say, to be committed to others is thought to go beyond being related to them under some general category—such as clients, patients, customers, penitents—and to constitute a relationship with them as the individuals they are, which is personal in a way that all others are impersonal and is special precisely because of its personal character. This is one way in which commitment might be thought a reasonable substitute for the theological conceptions we have left behind. On the low theology outlined earlier, to be committed to someone in marriage is to be related to that person such that good sex is possible with that one and with no other. On the high view it is to be joined in a mystic unity. Either way, there is some other person to whom an individual stands in a unique relation that is itself constitutive of a life supremely valuable of human beings. In place of such an understanding, it is commitment that is to be seen as providing this unique personal relation to one other.

There is need for some greater clarification here, but we can usefully proceed on the assumption that the idea of commitment to another person does indeed mark an aspiration to a relationship that could hold only with that one person. This way of talking can be misunderstood. No doubt all relationships can be brought under the head of *some* general category which will determine certain duties between the related parties. The talk of commitment, it seems to me, does not need to deny this. It claims only that if *all* relationships are understood *solely* in this way, then an important aspect of human relationships, and what is a matter of fact valued about them, is left out of the picture.

For example, we are related to our doctors in certain institutional ways according to which they owe certain duties to us and we to them. The exercise of these duties is generally valuable, such that were they to die or leave town, we should certainly miss them, regret being without a doctor, and take steps to find another. But it may also be the case that we miss our own particular doctor, and whereas, in a sense, *anyone* may replace this one as a doctor, *no one* can replace this one as the person in my life.

Such a personal element may suffuse almost any relationship. This is not to say, however, that all such relationships contain an element of commitment. Commitment implies an active resolution which, though not incompatible with the ties of mutual pleasure, affection, admiration, and the like—we generally love and like those we are committed to—is nonetheless to be contrasted with them. Though we may commit ourselves to others *because* we love or admire them, we cannot sensibly speak of a resolve to regard with affection. . . . People can resolve to take care of others in a context of intimacy; and this we may, if we wish, call a resolve to love. There is nothing in the English language that prevents it. But it remains true that there are always spontaneous elements in personal relationships that in part determine the value of the relationship—I cannot delight in your company unless I am sometimes amused by you, and I cannot *resolve* to be amused. And so it is with those relationships of which it is common to speak of commitment.

Now, the idea we are concerned with considers marriage a relationship in which this personal element takes the form of the highest possible degree of commitment, a commitment that is legally or socially formalized, without, however, losing anything of its intensely personal character.

But this suggests a problem. How can commitment in the form of a marriage vow, which is a sort of promising or resolving, contrive to secure a relationship distinctive of its highly personal, and hence in part spontaneous, nature? It seems, on the present analysis, that it cannot. The best that can be said is that this sort of resolution, together with the legal relationship and the social recognition that result, can provide the means whereby the personal may be made more likely to flourish. To put it another way, commitment, and hence marriage, is in some sense an *instrument* in the development of a personal relationship. Thus we are brought to the second of the two justifications outlined earlier, that it promotes something of value.

It is a common view that the value of marriage lies chiefly in its being a means of promoting the interests of the two parties, where "interests" is widely understood, and to think of it in this way is to regard it as a contract. . . . marriage, understood as an unconditional contract, is by its nature a relationship entered into regardless of the future benefits to either party or to both. This means that, at the point of marrying, though the expectation that neither party will benefit from the marriage would be a reason not to enter into it, the acknowledged *possibility* of shared disbenefit cannot be understood to supply a condition under which the marriage will be terminated. It is precisely all such possibilities that are excluded by the unconditional nature of the marriage vows. But further, there seems no reason to suppose that contracts cannot properly, and without remainder, be dissolved upon the simple agreement of both parties *on any grounds whatever,* and this in itself suggests that marriage is not to be understood simply as a contract between two people voluntarily entered into. For to conceive of it thus, we might say, is to make it *too* instrumental.

It is here that the idea of commitment may be expected to do its most useful work, because we may plausibly suppose that, though it is correct to locate marriage in the general area of promising and to emphasize its formal character, it cannot adequately be treated as a contract, with the instrumental and impersonal overtones that this idea brings. And this gives us reason to think of marriage as an act of commitment. The question then is whether commitment fares better than contract.

A commitment, it might be said, *has* to be more than a fair-weather agreement. Otherwise there is nothing in it that may be tested; there is, in fact, no real element of commitment. This does not mean, however, that all commitments are quite without conditions, and it may in principle be both possible and prudent to explore and to detail the terms of all our commitments, even those we have to our nearest and dearest. But it is not always wise to do so. For example, if asked for a meal at a restaurant by a comparative stranger, I have no very good reason to suppose that I will not be left to foot the bill. But if what I hope for is the development of a firm friendship, I would be wise not to ask for assurances before accepting the invitation. Similarly or so it may be said, what we want in marrying is a long-term relationship of trust and intimacy with one other person; and in most cases, to spell out the precise conditions under which each party would be entitled to abandon the commitment would be a sure way to jeopardize the possibility of such a relationship from the outset. In other words, trust can only grow from trust, commitment from commitment.

This resulting view of marriage has much to commend it. It relies on no strange metaphysics and seems well adapted to the facts of modern marriage. And I am inclined to say that, so far as it goes, this appeal to commitment provides us with an intelligible view of it. But it does not make an ideal of the institution we have inherited. It does not do so because the permanence and exclusivity of the commitment matter only because the alternatives are, as a rule, best not thought of. Should it be the case, in any particular instance, that they *can* be thought of without detriment to the personal character of the relationship, they have no place at all in the account.

This is a matter of some importance because we can easily imagine couples making the sort of commitment that marriage requires, but allowing each other a measure of sexual freedom.

And we can also imagine, more easily if anything, a commitment which, though it has no express time limit, is not generally expected to last past childrearing. In such circumstances, the idea of commitment would still have an important part to play in the explanation of these marriages and what was valuable about them, but it would secure nothing of the character of marriage as Christianity conceives it. . . .

Further Questions

1. Would a bad sexual experience have been any better if you had been married to the person with whom you had it? Would a good one have been improved?

2. Do you agree that it is all right to dissolve a (childless) marriage whenever both parties agree to the dissolution? Could such dissolution be on any grounds they chose?

3. Is it appropriate to dissolve a (childless) marriage when neither party is getting anything out of it at the personal level? Would this mean that there had been some defect in the original commitment?

V.2   Marital Faithfulness

SUSAN MENDUS

Susan Mendus tries to disentangle confusions about marriage vows. The central problem is that these vows seem to promise feelings in the distant future, over which the person has no effective control. How can you promise to love someone fifty years hence?

Mendus is Lecturer in Philosophy and Morrell Fellow in Toleration at the University of York.

Reading Questions

1. Do you think that your love for someone is conditional on him or her not changing in any drastic way?

2. People do change, sometimes in drastic ways. If your feelings toward a person change as a result, do you plead that that individual has become a different person, hence not the person who was the original object of your feelings?

3. When you make commitments to people, do you usually couple them with "escape clauses" ("unless . . .")?

Abridged from "Marital Faithfulness" by Susan Mendus in Philosophy *(59) 1984, pp. 243–252 (Cambridge University Press). Reprinted by permission of the publisher and author.*

And so the two swore that at every time of their lives, until death took them, they would assuredly believe, feel and desire exactly as they had believed, felt and desired during the preceding weeks. What was as remarkable as the undertaking itself was the fact that nobody seemed at all surprised at what they swore.[1]

CYNICISM ABOUT THE PROPRIETY of the marriage promise has been widespread amongst philosophers and laymen alike for many years. Traditionally, the ground for suspicion has been the belief that the marriage promise is a promise about feelings where these are not directly under the control of the will. . . .

[For example, Bertrand Russell] tells of how his love for his wife "evaporated" during the course of a bicycle ride. He simply "realized," he says, that he no longer loved her and was subsequently unable to show any affection for her.[2] This, anyway, is the most familiar objection to the marriage promise: that it is a promise about feelings, where these are not directly under the control of the will.

A second objection to the marriage promise is that it involves a commitment which extends over too long a period: promising to do something next Wednesday is one thing, promising to do something fifty years hence is quite another, and it is thought to be improper either to give or to extract promises extending over such a long period of time. . . .

Claiming that long-term promises do not carry any moral weight seems to be another way of claiming that unconditional promises do not carry any moral weight. Such an unconditional promise is the promise made in marriage, for when I promise to love and to honor I do not mutter under my breath, "So long as you never become a member of the Conservative Party," or "Only if your principles do not change radically." . . .

[In "Later Selves and Moral Principles," Derek Parfit[3] seems to suggest] that all promises (all promises which carry any moral weight, that is) are, and can be, made only on condition that there is no substantial change in the character either of promisor or promisee: if my husband's character changes radically, then I may think of the man before me not as my husband, but as some other person, some "later self." Similarly, it would seem that I cannot now promise to love another "till death us do part," since that would be like promising that another person will do something (in circumstances in which my character changes fundamentally over a period of time) and I cannot promise that another person will do something, but only that *I* will do something. Thus all promises must be conditional; all promises must be short-term. For what it is worth, I am not the least tempted to think that only short-term promises carry any moral weight and it is therefore a positive *disadvantage* for me that Parfit's theory has this consequence. But even if it were intuitively plausible that short-term promises alone carry moral weight, there are better arguments than intuitive ones, and I hope I can mention some here.

The force of Parfit's argument is brought out by his "Russian nobleman" example, described in "Later Selves and Moral Principles".

> Imagine a Russian nobleman who, in several years will inherit vast estates. Because he has socialist ideals, he intends now to give the land to the peasants, but he knows that in time his ideals may fade. To guard against this possibility he does two things. He first signs a legal document, which will automatically give away the land and which can only be revoked with his wife's consent. He then says to his wife "If I ever change my mind and ask you to revoke the document, promise me that you will not consent." He might add "I regard my ideals as essential to me. If I lose these ideals I want you to think that I cease to exist. I want you to think of your husband then, not as me, but only as his later self. Promise me that you would not do as he asks."[4]

Parfit now comments:

> This plea seems understandable and if his wife made this promise and he later asked her to revoke the document *she* might well regard herself as in no way released from her commitment. It might seem to her as if she had

obligations to two different people She might think that to do what her husband now asks would be to betray the young man whom she loved and married. And she might regard what her husband now says as unable to acquit her of disloyalty to this young man—to her husband's earlier self. [Suppose] the man's ideals fade and he asks his wife to revoke the document. Though she promised him to refuse, he now says that he releases her from this commitment . . . we can suppose she shares our view of commitment. If so, she will only believe that her husband is unable to release her from the commitment if she thinks that it is in some sense not *he* to whom she is committed . . . she may regard the young man's loss of ideals as involving replacement by a later self.[5]

Now, strictly speaking, and on Parfit's own account, the wife should not make such a promise: to do so would be like promising that another person will do something, since she has no guarantee that *she* will not change in character and ideals between now and the time of the inheritance. Further, there is a real question as to why anyone outside of a philosophical example should first draw up a document which can only be revoked with his wife's consent and then insist that his wife not consent whatever may happen. But we can let these points pass. What is important here, and what I wish to concentrate on, is the suggestion that my love for my husband is conditional upon his not changing in any substantial way: for this is what the example amounts to when stripped of its special story about later selves. (In his less extravagant moods Parfit himself allows that talk of later selves is, in any case, a mere "façon de parler."[6]

The claim then is that all promises must be conditional upon there being no change in the character of the promisee: that if my husband's character and ideals change, it is proper for me to look upon him as someone other than the person I loved and married. This view gains plausibility from reflection on the fact that people can, and often do, give up their commitments. There is, it will be said, such an institu-

tion as divorce, and people do sometimes avail themselves of it. But although I might give up my commitment to my husband, and give as my reason a change in his character and principle, this goes no way towards showing that only short-term promises carry any moral weight, for there is a vital distinction here: the distinction between, on the one hand, the person who promises to love and to honor but who finds that, after a time, she has lost her commitment (perhaps on account of change in her husband's character), and, on the other hand, the person who promises to love and to honor only on condition that there be no such change in character. The former person may properly be said, under certain circumstances, to have given up a commitment; the latter person was never committed in the appropriate way at all. The wife of the Russian nobleman, by allowing in advance that she will love her husband only so long as he doesn't change in any of the aforementioned ways, fails properly to commit herself to him: for now her attitude to him seems to be one of respect or admiration, not commitment at all. Now she *does* mutter under her breath "So long as you don't become a member of the Conservative Party." But the marriage promise contains no such "escape clause." When Mrs. Micawber staunchly declares that she will never desert Mr. Micawber, she means just that. There are no conditions, nor could there be any, for otherwise we would fail to distinguish between respect or admiration *for the principles* of another and the sort of unconditional commitment to *him* which the marriage vow involves. There are many people whose ideals and principles I respect, and that respect would disappear were the ideals and principles to disappear, but my commitment to my husband is distinct from mere respect or admiration in just this sense, that it is not conditional on there being no change in his ideals and principles. I am now prepared to admit that my respect for another person would disappear were he revealed to be a cheat and a liar. I am not now prepared to admit that my love for my husband, my commitment to him, would disappear were he revealed to be a cheat and a liar. . . . Such is the case with commitment of the sort involved in the marriage vow. I promise to love and to honor and in so doing I cannot now envisage anything happening such as would make me give up that commitment. But, it might be asked, how can I be clairvoyant? How can I recognize that there is such a thing as divorce and at the same time declare that nothing will result in my giving up my commitment? The explanation lies in the denial that my claim . . . has the status of a prediction. My commitment to another should not be construed as a prediction that I will never desert that other. . . . But if my statement is not a prediction, then what is it? It is perhaps more like a statement of intention, where my claims about a man's intentions do not relate to his future actions in as simple a way as do my predictions about his future actions.

If I predict that A will do x and A does not do x, then my prediction is simply false. If, on the other hand, I claim that A intends to do x and he does not, it is not necessarily the case that my statement was false: for he may have had that intention and later withdrawn it. Similarly with commitment: if I claim that A is unconditionally committed to B, that is not a prediction that A will never desert B; it is a claim that there is in A a present intention to do something permanently, where that is distinct from A's having a permanent intention. Thus Mrs. Micawber's claim that she will never desert Mr. Micawber, if construed as a commitment to him, is to that extent different from a prediction that she will never desert him, for her commitment need not be thought never to have existed if she does desert him. Thus an unconditional commitment to another person today, a denial today that anything could happen such as would result in desertion of Mr. Micawber, is not incompatible with that commitment being given up at a later date.

In brief, then, what is wrong in Parfit's example is that the wife *now* allows that her commitment will endure only so long as there is no substantial change in character. She should not behave thus, because her doing so indicates that she has only respect for her husband, or admiration for his principles, not a commitment to him: she need not behave thus, as there can be such a thing as unconditional commitment, analogous to intention and distinct from prediction in the way described.

All this points to the inherent oddity of the "trial marriage." It is bizarre to respond to "wilt thou love her, comfort her, honor her, and keep her?" with "Well, I'll try." Again, the response "I will" must be seen as the expression of an intention to do something permanently, not a prediction that the speaker will permanently have that intention.

A further problem with the Russian nobleman example and the claim that only short-term promises carry any moral weight is this: When the wife of the Russian nobleman allows in advance that her commitment to her husband will cease should his principles change in any substantial way, she implies that a list of his present principles and ideals will give an exhaustive explanation of her loving him. But this is not good enough. If I now claim to be committed to my husband I precisely cannot give an exhaustive account of the characteristics he possesses in virtue of which I have that commitment to him: if I could do so, there would be a real question as to why I am not prepared to show the same commitment to another person who shares those characteristics (his twin brother, for example). Does this then mean that nothing fully explains my love for another and that commitment of this sort is irrationally based? I think we need not go so far as to say that: certainly, when asked to justify or explain my love I may point to certain qualities which the other person has, or which I believe him to have, but in the first place such an enumeration of qualities will not provide a complete account of why I love him, rather it will serve to explain, as it were, his "lovableness." It will make more intelligible my loving him, but will not itself amount to a complete and exhaustive explanation of my loving him.

Further, it may well be that in giving my list of characteristics I cite some which the other person does not, in fact, have. If this is so, then the explanation may proceed in reverse order: The characteristics I cite will not explain or make intelligible my love, rather, my love will explain my ascribing these characteristics. A case in point here is Dorothea's love for Casaubon, which is irrationally based in that Casaubon does not have the characteristics and qualities which Dorothea thinks him to have. Similarly, in the case of infatuation the lover's error lies in wrongly evaluating the qualities of the beloved. In this way Titania "madly dotes" on the unfortunate Bottom who is trapped in an ass's head, and addresses him thus:

> Come sit thee down upon this flowery bed
> While I thy amiable cheeks do coy
> And stick musk roses in thy sleek, smooth head
> And kiss thy fair, large ears my gentle joy.

and again

> I pray thee, gentle mortal, sing again.
> Mine ear is much enamoured of thy note;
> So is mine eye enthralled to thy shape,
> And thy fair virtue's force perforce doth move me
> On the first view, to say, to swear, I love thee.[7]

Both cases involve some error on the part of the lover: in one case the error is false belief about the qualities the beloved possesses; in the other it is an error about the evaluation of the qualities the beloved possesses. These two combine to show that there can be such a thing as a "proper object" of love. This will be the case where there is neither false belief nor faulty evaluation. They do not, however, show that in ascribing qualities and characteristics to the beloved the lover exhaustively explains and accounts for his love. The distinction between "proper" love and irrationally based love, or between "proper" love and infatuation, is to be drawn in terms of the correctness of beliefs and belief-based evaluations. By contrast, the distinction between love and respect or admiration is to be drawn in terms of the explanatory power of the beliefs in-

volved. In the case of respect or admiration the explanatory power of belief will be much greater than it is in the case of love. For this reason my respect for John's command of modal logic will disappear, and I am now prepared to admit that it will disappear, should I discover that my belief that he has a command of modal logic is false. Whereas I am not now prepared to admit that my commitment to and love for my husband will disappear if I discover that my beliefs about his qualities and characteristics are, to some extent, false. . . .

I turn now to a somewhat bizarre element in Parfit's talk of ideals. Parfit portrays the Russian nobleman as one who "finds" that his ideals have faded, as one who "loses" his ideals when circumstances and fortune change. What is bizarre in this talk is emphasized by the following extract from Alison Lurie's novel *Love and Friendship*:

> "But, Will, promise me something."
> "Sure."
> "Promise me you'll never be unfaithful to me."
> Silence.
> Emily raised her head, "You won't promise?" she said incredulously.
> "I can't, Emily. How can I promise how I'll feel for the next ten years? You want me to lie to you? You could change. I could change. I could meet somebody."
> Emily pulled away. "Don't you have any principles?" she asked.[8]

The trouble with the inappropriately named Will and the Russian nobleman in Parfit's example is that it is doubtful whether either man has any genuine principles at all. Each is portrayed as almost infinitely malleable, as one whose principles will alter in accordance with changing circumstances. The point about a moral principle however is that it must serve in some sense to rule out certain options as options at all. In his article "Actions and Consequences," John Casey refers us to the example of Addison's Cato who, when offered life, liberty, and the friendship of Caesar if he will surrender, and is asked to name his terms, replies:

Bid him disband his legions,
Restore the Commonwealth to liberty,
Submit his actions to the public censure
And stand the judgement of a Roman Senate.
Bid him do this and Cato is his friend.[9]

The genuine principles which Cato has determine that certain options will not ultimately be options at all for him. To say this, of course, is not to deny that life and liberty are attractive and desirable to him. Obviously he is, in large part, admirable precisely because they are attractive to him and yet he manages to resist their allure. The point is rather that not *any* sort of life is desirable. The sort of life he would, of necessity, lead after surrender—a life without honor—is not ultimately attractive to him and that it is not attractive is something which springs from his having the principles he does have. What Cato values above all else is honor and his refusal to surrender to Caesar is a refusal to lead life without honor. By contrast, when the Russian nobleman draws up a legal document giving away his inheritance, we may suspect that he is concerned not with an honorable life or with a life which he now conceives of as honorable, but rather with his present principle. Where Cato values a certain sort of life, the Russian nobleman values a certain principle. It is this which is problematic and which generates, I believe, the bizarre talk of ideals fading. For Cato's adherence to his principles is strengthened, if not guaranteed, by the fact that he treats a certain sort of life as an end in itself and adopts the principle he does adopt because they lead to that end. The Russian nobleman, however, is portrayed more as a man who finds the principle important than as a man who finds the life to which the principle leads important. Obviously, in either case there may be temptation and inner struggle, but the temptation is less likely to be resisted by the Russian nobleman than by Cato, for the nobleman will find his principle undermined and threatened by the prospect of affluence, which is attractive to him. His ideals will fade. For Cato, on the other hand, things are not so simple. He is not faced by a choice between two things, each of which he finds attractive. The fact that he treats a life of honor as an end in itself precludes his finding life attractive under *any* circumstances. For him, life will ultimately be attractive and desirable only where it can be conducted honorably. Nevertheless, he finds life attractive and desirable, but this means only that if he surrenders he will have *sacrificed* his ideals, not that his ideals will have faded. Thus, the nobleman is a victim, waiting for and guarding against attack upon his principles; Cato is an agent who may sacrifice his principles after a struggle, but not one who would find that they had altered.

In conclusion, then, the claim that the marriage vow is either impossible or improper is false. It is possible to commit oneself unconditionally because commitment is analogous to a statement of intention, not to a prediction or a piece of clairvoyance. It is proper, since if we refuse to allow such unconditional commitment, we run the risk, of failing to distinguish between, on the one hand, sentimentality and commitment and, on the other hand, respect or admiration and commitment. Further, it is simply not true that I am helpless in circumstances in which I find my commitment wavering: this is because my principles will initially serve to modify my view of the opportunities which present themselves, so that I simply will not see certain things as constituting success because my principles are such as to exclude such things being constitutive of success. In this way, my principles determine what is to count as a benefit and what is to count as an opportunity. As Shakespeare has it:

Some glory in their birth, some in their skill,
Some in their wealth, some in their body's
    force,
Some in their garments though new fangled ill:
Some in their hawks and hounds, some in their
    horse.
And every humour has his adjunct pleasure,
Wherein it finds a joy above the rest,
But these particulars are not my measure.
All these I better in one general best.

Thy love is better than high birth to me.
Richer than wealth, prouder than garments cost,
Of more delight than hawks and horses be:
And having these of all men's pride I boast.
Wretched in this alone, that thou may'st take
All this way, and me most wretched make.[10,11]

NOTES

1. Thomas Hardy, *Jude the Obscure*.

2. Bertrand Russell, *Autobiography* (London: George Allen and Unwin, 1967–1969).

3. Derek Parfit, "Later Selves and Moral Principles" in *Philosophy and Personal Relations*, A. Monte-fiore (ed.) (London: Routledge and Kegan Paul, 1973), 144.

4. *Ibid.*, 145.

5. *Ibid.*, 145–146.

6. *Ibid.*, 14, 161–162.

7. W. Shakespeare, *A Midsummer Night's Dream*, Acts III and I.

8. Alison Lurie, *Love and Friendship* (Harmondsworth: Penguin, 1962), 329–330.

9. As quoted in J. Casey, "Actions and Consequences," from *Morality and Moral Reasoning*, J. Casey (ed.) (London: Methuen, 1971), 201.

10. W. Shakespeare, Sonnet 91.

11. I wish to thank my colleague, Dr. Roger Woolhouse, for many helpful discussions on the topic of this paper.

Further Questions

1. Do you think that there is such a thing as discovering that you no longer have a commitment to a person to whom you once made the commitment?

2. Is a trial marriage, in which you *try* to love, honor, and so on someone else, a bizarre idea?

3. Is a person who cannot promise to be faithful to another too malleable?

4. Do you think marriage vows statements of intention, rather than predictions, as Mendus suggests?

V.3   Black Men/Black Women: Changing Roles and Relationships

ROBERT STAPLES

Robert Staples mentions some economic and social forces that preclude marriage as an option between black men and black women. Sometimes black couples "date," but these same forces preclude even "dating" among many blacks. In addition, black men may misuse their power over black women in any coupling arrangement.

Staples is author of numerous books and articles focusing on black society and culture in the United States.

"*Black Men/Black Women: Changing Roles and Relationships From Black Masculinity.*" The Black Male's Role in American Society *(Oakland, CA: Black Scholar Press, 1982). Chapter 7. Reprinted by permission of the author and publisher.*

Reading Questions

1. Would you avoid a legal marriage with someone who had no skills, education, or steady income? Would you consider having some other sort of relationship with him or her instead?
2. According to your understanding of "dating," is this activity possible only if the two people on the "date" have a certain amount of money? Must the person with the money be the man?
3. To secure a "date," does someone need to spend a lot of money and time on clothes, cosmetics, hairstyling, and so on? Is this cost greater for one gender than it is for the other?

THE DECADE OF THE SEVENTIES was witness to a number of changes in marriage and the family. Considering the sanctity of the nuclear family as an American institution, the changes that transpired were only short of revolutionary. In 1979 almost half of the women in the 20 to 24 year-old age bracket were still single, compared with only 28 percent in 1960. Even in the later years, 25 to 29, 20 percent of them remained unmarried in 1979. During the period 1970 to 1979, the ratio of divorced persons per 1,000 husbands and wives in intact marriages increased by 96 percent from 47 per 1000 to 92 per 1,000.[1] As startling as these figures may be, they do not begin to mirror the changes in single and marital status and fertility behavior among the Afro-American population. The majority of Afro-Americans, over the age of 18, are no longer in intact marriages. About 47 percent of black men and 56 percent of black women are not married and living with a spouse. Almost half (48.7 percent) of all black families are headed by a single parent. The majority of black children are born out-of-wedlock and only a minority of black children live in a two-parent household.[2] Thus, at the end of the seventies, the black family had undergone a radical transformation. The nuclear family is no longer the assumed structure. This fact raises the question of why and how the transformation occurred.

It is clear that the white American family is changing in the same direction but the magnitude of these changes have been much greater for black Americans. Seemingly, blacks have come almost full circle to the period of slavery when marriage was denied them. However, after the demise of "the peculiar institution," they married in record numbers. By the beginning of the twentieth century, three out of four adult blacks were members of a nuclear family. About 90 percent of all black children were born in wedlock during that same period.[3] Even in the more recent era, black women over 65 years of age had a higher rate of marriage (96.5) than comparable white women (93.1).[4] Historically, a legal marriage was employed as a device by which status was determined. Blacks were considered respectable or non-respectable based on whether they were legally married or cohabitating. My guess is that the black American's desire to be in a nuclear family has not changed but the conditions which permit fulfillment of that desire have been altered significantly.

BLACK SINGLES

The increase in black singles is consistent with the constraints on the supply of eligible mates available for and interested in a monogamous marriage. Not only is there an excess of one million adult black women (over age 18) in the black population but the institutional decimation of black men leaves working-class black women with an extremely low supply of desirable men (i.e. employed and mentally stable) from which to choose. This is particularly true of men who reach the age of thirty and are single or divorced. Paradoxically, there is a larger number of never-married black men at lower-class levels than there are similar black women.[5]

In the lower classes, these men are without skills, education, and a steady income. Thus, it makes sense in terms of daily economic security for black women to avoid a legal marriage with such men. They may live with these men and have children by them; but, as one black woman asserted, "Without marriage I know I've got security. My welfare check keeps coming as long as I am not married. Otherwise I don't know if he's going to keep his job or if he's going to start "acting up" and staying out drinking and fooling around with other women. This way I might not have the respectability of marriage, but at least I know how much I got."

Many of the stable black marriages are among couples in the black working class. These are the blacks who finished high school but have less than four years of college. The men in this group tend to be dependent on the wife's income to maintain a decent standard of living. Because they avoid the harsh economic repression of black males in the underclass, it seems easier for them to maintain a stable marriage and average standard of living. Often, they are the "silent majority," the men who are unrepresented in the literature and general stereotypes about black males.

When we ascend the socioeconomic scale, the men between the ages 35 to 54 years[6] in the middle class are more likely to remain single than their female counterparts, at least those with five years of college or more. Many of those men are exclusive homosexuals, for whom a legal marriage is not possible.

Among the black middle class (i.e., 4 years of college or more), the shortage of black males is complicated by a number of factors. Assuming a woman wants to marry a male of comparable education, there were only 339,000 black male college graduates for 417,000 black female college graduates in 1977. Moreover, the eligible pool of college educated black men is further reduced by homosexuality, interracial marriages, and the fact that many of them marry women with less than a college education. As a result, among blacks (ages 35–54) with 5 years or more

of college, there are 52,000 eligible women for only 15,000 men. To illustrate the seriousness of the problem, the census bureau lists 15,000 divorced black women in that same category and *no* black males (actually less than 500).[7] Small wonder, then, that competition among black women is keen for that low supply of college-educated black males. And, it is the competition for those men that largely explains their high divorce rate. The marriages of these black males often are disrupted by "the other woman." We see it in the statistics which show that black women are more likely than white women to marry men who are four and more years their senior and who have been married before.[8]

THE COST OF BEING MALE AND SINGLE

It is commonplace to hear of families cutting back on expenses to cope with the increasing cost of goods and services. Reducing their expenditure is easily accomplished among married couples since they perceive themselves as an inseparable unit with the same goals. But, there is another group whose expenses continue to rise. This group consists of individuals whom we typically refer to as the swinging single men. Among blacks, they are more than a crowd—they are almost the majority of adult black men. As of 1979, almost half of the black men, ages 18 and above, had never been married, or are separated, divorced, or widowed. Approximately 47 percent of adult black men and 56 percent of comparable black women are eligible for the "take-out, make-out" game known as dating.[9] Yet due to age, poverty, children, or lack of opportunity, the majority of black singles do not go out on dates—at least not very often.

Dating, in fact is a relatively new concept to most blacks. Prior to the desegregation of public facilities, there were few places to go. Most blacks met in the church, school, or neighborhood, and spent leisurely evenings sitting on their front porches. Marriage followed soon afterwards. Presently, blacks are more likely to remain unmarried for a longer period of time, especially those who are considered middle class. Almost a third of the black women who go to college remain unmarried past the age of thirty. Men with the same educational background tend to marry at an earlier age but a high divorce rate throws many of them back into the singles world.[10] And, the purpose of dating has changed. No longer is it solely a form of courtship, especially for men, where each person's intent is to explore the potential for marriage or a stable relationship. Some still use it to serve that function. However, a large number of men and women view it as recreation, a free night's entertainment, a time for sexual seduction and status enhancement.

While the purpose of dating has changed considerably, the roles have not altered that much. Men are still expected to bear the costs of dating. Why this tradition continues to exist is somewhat of a mystery. Few college-educated black women live at home with their parents, bereft of any visible means of support, and in fact, college-educated black women earn 90 percent of the income of their male peers. One answer is that it is a self-serving interpretation of a custom designed for an earlier era and it is one that has been largely unaffected by the women's liberation movement. It is a sacrosanct tradition with a great deal of force behind it. Men who violate that tradition are labelled as cheap. The ability to escort a woman in style is often the measure of the man, especially in this inflationary period. Dr. Joyce Brothers once commented that when economic times are hard, women look for signs of a man's socioeconomic status. When we were in a period of economic prosperity, women were attracted to men with sex appeal as exhibited in snappy apparel such as tight-fitting pants and open chested shirts. Now, it is the three piece suit, signaling arrival, which turns women on.

For middle-class black men, appealing to women can be an expensive proposition. The higher status clothes and car can be very expen-

sive outlays. Most good quality suits cost at least $500. The "right" kind of car (e.g., Porsche, BMW, Mercedes) sells for twenty thousand dollars and above. Since the initial attraction of the sexes to each other is based on external, visible factors, those accoutrements are necessary. A man's possession of money is important but not as important as his willingness to spend it. One black woman, a 33-year-old college professor, once called a man she dated "cheap." When asked why, she cited the case of their initial meeting at a bar where she sat with three female companions. After ordering a drink and talking to them for a period of time, the bill for $34 arrived. To their surprise, he insisted on paying only for his own drink and not picking up the entire tab.

The more formal dating situations can be quite expensive. An investment counselor, Ray Devoe has constructed a "cost of loving index." Using 1954 as his base year, he calculated that the cost of dating has increased twice as much as the advance in the consumer price index—340 percent vs. 172 percent. And, the cost of an average date is now about $43.[11] Of course, it can be higher or lower, expending on the choice of activity and location. Since women may judge men on their willingness to spend, a "cheap date" may be costly. There is a cadre of women who do not know any cheap forms of entertainment and an equal number who do not appreciate them. As one woman, a 34-year-old nurse, told me: "the one time you don't worry about being on a diet is when a man is picking up the tab." And, how many men look first at the prices on a restaurant menu and multiply by two before they consider a choice of food? Going out to eat is often necessary since many younger black women (southern women being an exception) do not know how to cook. A man living in the expensive urban centers, such as New York, Boston, Washington, and San Francisco, and planning on going to the theatre, having dinner and drinks, must also figure on paying $100 for the night. As the investment counselor has noted, "the dating game doesn't come cheap.

And, carried to an excess, it can quickly bankrupt you."[12]

There are several anticipated consequences of the cost of dating. As many women reported to me, they do not get many invitations for dates. Some men go out with other men and split expenses down the middle. It is not uncommon to go to concerts, plays, restaurants and see men grouped with men, women with women, and some men alone. Another common complaint of the women was that men simply dropped by their homes and wanted to watch television, get high, or otherwise hang out. As one woman reported to me, "the only place men ever took me was from the living room into the bedroom."* And that is yet another consequence of the rising cost of dating. Men become sexually aggressive faster because they cannot afford to prolong dating for an extended period of time. One man, a 37-year-old lawyer, told me: "I can't see taking a woman out and spending $50 for the night's entertainment. There was this one women whose taste ran to French restaurants. Not only did she order the most expensive dish on the menu and a bottle of expensive wine but I even had to pay for the Perrier she ordered. After getting the bill of $89, I was determined to get some reward for my money." Such an attitude led one woman, a 32-year-old social worker, to ask the question: "Are women expected to screw for their supper? All a man gets for taking me out is the 'pleasure of my company.'"

Considering the cost of dating, only a certain category of men can and will engage in it for long periods of time. A noticeable trend is toward women in their twenties and thirties dating men in their late forties and early fifties. When I asked one woman, a 32-year-old specialist in multicultural education, why she dated so many men in their forties, she replied, "because you don't have to pick up the tab for your own dinner. They come from the old school

and know how to treat a woman. Besides, they know if they want to date a woman 15 years their junior, they have to spend money on her." These older men, of course, are often at the peak of their earning power, some are recently divorced and new to the dating game. Also, some men are in positions where they can write off the costs of dating on expense accounts or as tax deductions.

Women, however, are not spared the expense of dating or finding a man. Since a man's willingness to spend money on her is often based on how attractive she is, she must lay out fairly large sums of money for cosmetics, hairstyling, and fashionable clothes. Since fashions in clothes and hairstyles fluctuate almost yearly, they are a considerable expense for her.[13] Moreover, many women incur the costs of going to places in order to meet men. Even if a woman goes with a girlfriend to a bar or club, she generally pays her own way. Then, there is the conference circuit. Some women save their pennies all year in order to attend the annual meetings of the National Medical or Bar Association, and as a result, many predominantly black conferences have a disproportionate number of women in attendance, in relationship to their numbers in the profession. Most of the men, however, are married and, therefore, "single for the conference only."

Hence, dating is not just a case of men paying and women receiving. Furthermore, as men and women enter into stable relationships, they often stay home together or she invites him over to dinner. And, there are increasing instances of women sharing the cost of the evening's entertainment. Ann Arbor, Michigan, a college town, was the only city where this seemed to be the norm. After having coffee with a young woman there. I picked up the bill for $1.10 and she asked if I wanted her to pay for her cup of coffee. When I said no, she replied that you had to do that in Ann Arbor since the men were quick to pick out the cost of their meal and pay only that amount. Possibly Ann Arbor's practice may be the harbinger of the future. If not, the cost of dating in the future will have outpriced most black men. Based

*Unless otherwise identified or footnoted, quotes are taken from the black singles data. See Chapter Six [of *Black Masculinity*] for a description of the study.

on my own calculations, a man who remains single and "dates" steadily for twenty years can expect to spend almost $75,000 for dating alone.

There are a few other costs that blacks must pay for all the singles in their midst. In the past, many black families maintained a decent or middle class standard of living through the double wages of both husband and wife. Since there are no longer as many black husband/wife couples, the standard of living has decreased for blacks. According to the Bureau of the Census report, between 1976 and 1978, the proportion of black families with two or more earners declined from 48 to 46 percent. The proportion of white families with two or more earners remained at 55 percent. While that may be attributed to a decline in the employment status of black women, only 48 percent of the adult black women were reported as married and living with a spouse in 1976. That was a considerable decline from the 66 percent who were married, with spouse present, in 1950. The difference that marriage makes is illustrated in the figures that show black husband/wife families (husband under 35 years old), in the North and West, in which both spouses were earners and achieved incomes equal to those of their white peers in 1976. On the other hand, the median income of the black family (which includes singe parent households) declined from 60 percent of white family income in 1974 to 57 percent in 1977.[14]

Unmarried blacks who share the American dream of owning their own home may have to forget it. Presently, the average home seems to be available only to two wage families. According to recent surveys, over 54 percent of home buyers relied on two incomes to buy a house in 1979. And, among first time buyers, those families in which the wife was employed accounted for 64 percent of the total.[15] Few single blacks have the income required to meet the monthly mortgage payments for most new homes. Ironically, it is, in part, the dramatic increase in the number of singles that accounts for the rapid rise in housing prices.[16] In the last decade the number of households increased more than twice as fast as the number of people in them. In 1978, more than half of all households consisted of only one or two individuals. In other words, the housing that used to accommodate a husband/wife couple must now be doubled to house the unmarried individual.

Interestingly enough, it may also be economic factors that will stem the tide of increasing singleness. More and more blacks seem to be gravitating toward marriage this year. Certainly inflationary trends combined with an economic recession have forced many of them to seek the security of a stable relationship as opposed to a casual dating lifestyle. Women used to seek security in marriages, then began to seek it in jobs. As the job picture, especially for blacks, became more bleak *and* uncertain, they are again looking to marriage for security. Another factor is that the high cost of dating insures only the most attractive women (and sometimes not them) a steady pool of men willing to bear those expenses. Perforce, many black women are remaining at home alone or going out primarily with other women. Dating may be an idea whose time has come and gone.

Many blacks will continue to remain unmarried due to demographic factors. There remains in the black community an imbalance in the sex ratio, resulting from the institutional decimation of black men, who cannot get jobs and who wind up on drugs, in the military, or prison or dead at a young age. The black singles world is characterized by a large proportion of men who are uneducated, with low incomes, and an equally disproportionate number of women with college degree and high incomes. Until some of our values change, it is evident that few of the former will be dating the latter. As has often been the case, economics is a strong determinant of one's marital status.

UNFAITHFUL WOMEN AND JEALOUS MEN

After hunger and sex, sexual jealousy is one of the strongest passions experienced by homo sapiens. Jealousy does not exist in every culture and emerged in Western culture as a result of the development of private property.[17] Certainly it is a common emotion among Americans. Jealousy of one's mate is a major cause of marital disruption and interpersonal violence. It is such a destructive emotion that therapists generally attempt to label it as a pathological state of mind. Various theories attribute jealousy to low self-esteem, misanthropy, personal unhappiness, etc. While it seems obvious that much jealousy is irrational, we rarely hear about rational jealousy and the social forces that promote jealousy. If absolute fidelity is required from a mate, what are the chances that it will be given? In today's society, the chances are fairly low. This fact will give rise to jealous suspicions that are unfounded in particular but true in general. Hence, it is incumbent upon us to examine infidelity as well as sexual jealousy in order to understand their relationship to one another.

Although little has been written about it, sexual jealousy is not unknown in the black community. Indeed, one study found that 40 percent of blacks, whose marriages had terminated, gave as at least one of the reasons, often as the only reason, jealousy and infidelity.[18] One pronounced difference in black jealousy is that these suspicious attitudes are not that uncommon to men. In the same study previously cited, black men felt that a wife would search for sexual gratification elsewhere if relations did not go well.[19] And, that belief is confirmed in the findings of Bell that almost half of his black female subjects believed that a married woman would be justified in running around.[20] The Rainwater study found that 31 percent of the divorced women in the survey admitted to at least one extramarital affair.[21] In another study of college-educated black divorcees, 54 percent believed that their ex-husbands had engaged in extramarital sexual activity.[22]

It must be emphasized that infidelity per se is seldom the cause of divorce, especially when women terminate the marriage. Lower income women may divorce a man who is unfaithful *and* also fails to support his family. Both violations of societal norms may be too much for her to bear. Among middle-class blacks, male infidelity may be tolerated if he is taking care of home (i.e., sexual and financial needs are satisfied). Lower income black males may be more tolerant of extramarital sexual activity by their wives. Often, they are more dependent upon their wives for certain services and do not have the economic wherewithal to insure a wife's fidelity. On the other hand, college-educated black males are more likely to terminate a marriage if the wife is known to be unfaithful. The norms of his class require him to save face by the rejection of the wandering wife. A lesser-educated male may resort to physical abuse to bring the unfaithful wife in line.

However, it is often jealousy, not the act of infidelity, that is a disruptive force in male/female relationships. An act of infidelity is a *fait accompli* and known to both parties. Jealousy is the nagging suspicion that one's partner is unfaithful. It may be based on reality or be a reflection of other psychological forces. At best, it can be an emotionally draining experience for both partners. He may experience anxiety and anger over the feeling that she is consorting with other men. If his suspicions are untrue, she may be pained by his lack of trust in her, the constant accusations, and even constraints on her movements and emotions. There are numerous cases of women who eventually were unfaithful in retaliation for the male partner's unfounded suspicions about their fidelity.

While jealousy can be a destructive force in a relationship, there are social forces that have given rise to its increase among married *and* unmarried couples. One of them is the permanent availability of many individuals in American society.[23] Even marriage is no longer seen as a permanent alliance as people constantly exit from relationships in the search for somebody better, the perfect mate. It is common, for instance, for married men who get a divorce to remarry another woman within a year. Often, that woman was a sexual partner during the course of his marriage. While her presence may not have been the dominant factor in the marital disruption, her availability (and pressure) certainly contributed to his willingness to dissolve the marriage. Thus, jealousy that is rooted in the fear of losing one's partner is not totally unfounded.

Another social force impinging on attitudes of jealousy are the changes in the female role. Infidelity was once considered a male practice, with female infidelity subject to all the scorn a society could muster. Various studies indicate that 50–60 percent of wives will engage in extramarital sexual activity during the course of their marriages.[24] In general, women have not engaged in extramarital sex for the same reasons as men—sexual variety and recreation. Often, they were "forced" to do so because of the husband's neglect, sexual incompetency, or blatant infidelity. These remain the dominant reasons for infidelity but the sexual revolution and its concomitants have produced a new kind of woman.

We should be clear on what the sexual revolution was all about. It eroded the double sexual standard but did not eliminate all its aspects. Women had been totally denied the pleasures of sex except within the context of marriage. And even today, they still are subject to a different set of standards than men. Men do not expect women to have the same number of sexual partners or variety of sexual experiences as males. And, they are expected to be discrete in the sexual liaisons they do have. At the same time, the legacy of the double standard has provided women with more opportunities for sexual outlets than most men. It is still men who are the buyers and women who are the sellers in the sexual marketplace. For women whose values allow permissive sexual activity, there is no shortage of partners in a sellers' market. Male sexual jealousy may be shaped by this knowledge of a woman's greater chances for sexual adventures. She neither has to wine and dine in order to obtain a sexual consort nor do many men require a commitment from her before indulging in coitus. As one woman remarked, "it's easier to get a man in bed than a drink of water."

Many women have asserted their sexual rights and opportunities. According to one survey, (1) 54 percent of the married women had had extramarital affairs, (2) 55 percent had engaged in sex on their lunch hours, (3) 48 percent had made love with more than one man in the same day, (4) 82 percent had seduced a man at least once.[25] Again, we can see the visible evidence of sexual liberalization among women and the natural concomitant is increased male jealousy. For example, the increase of women in the labor force has brought men and women into contact with each other in heretofore unprecedented ways. A major problem of integrating police cars with male and female officers has been the jealousy of the spouse over such an arrangement. This is especially a problem among white-collar workers, where there is ample time for socializing on the job and discretionary time for having sexual affairs.

Another social arrangement that promotes sexual jealousy is the increase in opposite sex friendships. Many of these friendships are platonic and provide an enriching experience in heterosexual communication and interaction. Others are a mask for cheating on one's partner—married or otherwise. Women are more likely to have such friendships since men tend to keep their affairs underground. A woman's male friends are often former lovers who may turn out to be future lovers as well. Some are current lovers masquerading as platonic friends. When one relationship is ended, the woman's next mate is frequently a man who was formerly a "friend." A woman may use a man who is a platonic friend as a reserve lover for the future in case her present relationship does not work out. It is the contact with these men and former lovers that generates much male jealousy.

Women may define boundaries for their male friends that prohibit sexual contact but give the appearance of infidelity. One of the most common examples is permitting male guests to stay overnight in their homes, sometimes sharing the same bed with them. We encountered one woman who could not understand her boyfriend's jealousy. It seems that she told him of her relationship with several men over a period of time. While involved with one man, she allowed another man to pay her air fare to a conference in another city. The man, although married, was a former lover and they slept in the same hotel room without engaging in sex. While at that conference, she invited another man to visit her and stay at her house. By the time of his visit, she was involved with her present boyfriend who objected to the man's visit. The man came anyway and she did not have sexual relations with him. Yet, she had created a low level of trust in her current lover, and her continued contact with former lovers did nothing to ameliorate his sexual jealousy.

Coming into contact with former lovers can be a common problem in the black community. Middle-class blacks are fewer in numbers and the places they frequent are the same. Thus, there are numerous cases of black singles dating the friend of a friend. In any social gathering of middle-class blacks, an individual's past, present, and future lovers may be present. Because this social incest is so pervasive, it may be difficult to maintain a positive image when so much is known about one's sexual affairs. Perforce, indiscreet men may make known their previous sexual affairs with a particular woman, often "passing" her on to their male running partners. Lately, men with lusty sexual appetites have been discussed by their sexual partners and been labeled as "male whores." Women may eschew such a man because "he's been had by everybody." Sleeping around, then, becomes a problem for both sexes. And, it contributes to feelings of sexual jealousy, and social embarrassment, when a mate's previous sexual liaisons are well known.

Women have the greatest cause for sexual jealousy since studies have estimated that as many as 90 percent of American males have had extramarital affairs. While most have no intention of leaving their wives, the "other woman" can be the precipitant force in the termination of a deteriorating marriage.[26] Black women, in particular, face stiff competition for the few available and desirable men. Most of the desirable black males are already married, but some

single black women realize that nothing is forever. If unable to find an unattached man, they are not reluctant to seek one who belongs to another woman. As a result, many married black women resign themselves to accepting a man's infidelity, as long as he is not disrespectful. Others adopt the motto, "What's good for the goose is good for the gander." They, too, engage in extramarital affairs although they tend to be more discreet in their sexual liaisons.

The consequences of such a reaction and counter-reaction are predictable. Even in relationships where fidelity is the norm, sexual jealousy may occur. Jealousy may be more a cause of marital disruption than actual infidelity. There is ample evidence that it is a contributory cause to the 130 percent increase in divorces among blacks during the 1970s.[27] Moreover, it has created a low level of trust among blacks engaged in intimate relationships. Single black women are all too aware of the many married men who approach them for dates and sexual favors. Certainly, it is not surprising that many of them see all men as being incapable of having a monogamous marriage. More to the point, they will have a low level of trust in their future husbands, especially if they were married when they embarked on their intimate association.

Sexual jealousy may have always been a reality. But, the current prevalence of infidelity is largely a product of the sexual revolution and the changes in women's roles. In earlier periods, married men were more faithful because there were few women available to them. Women were monogamous because they were economically dependent on men, and society punished their sexual transgressions in the harshest manner. A return to the constraints on women is not being argued here. The sexual revolution liberated America from its puritanical and hypocritical moral order and freed the female libido for fuller expression. Still, sexual jealousy is not just a function of negative psychological forces residing in the individual. In many ways it is a realistic reflection of the options people have for sexual variety in their lives and the social arrangements that promote infidelity.

SUMMARY

The problems black men and women have in their relationships often are shaped by external forces. Many have been unable to form a monogamous family due to structural impediments. In a society where money is the measure of the man, many black males are excluded as potential mates because they lack the economic wherewithal to support a family in a reasonable manner. Given the traditional role definitions for women, definitions internalized by many black males, the highly educated black woman finds herself victimized by the fact that she has a higher educational and income level than most of the black men in her pool of eligibles. Both of those factors are products of institutional racism and black history in America. Hence, the conflict between men and women may be more apparent than real. The real problem may be largely a demographic one with strong class overtones. There simply are not enough black men to go around, and the ones available are not regarded as viable mates. As Patrice Rushen, the singer, has stated, "I think it is just a way to divert our attention from the fact that we have things that must be done together to make some headway. We're not dealing in times that afford us the luxury of being able to feel there's a problem with black men that automatically creates a problem for the black woman and vice-versa. We have to look for where these problems come from—and we might find it ain't us."[28]

Regardless of the source of the problem, the high number of unmarried and divorced blacks signals that all is not well between black men and women. The unbalanced ratio of men to women and the greater degree of "power" given to men is a combustible combination that creates a potential problem. In men this power is often manifested as arrogance and insensitivity to women's needs. For women, feelings of insult and injury can add up to outrage. White racism may have been the force which shaped black relationships, and its spectre may remain with us for the foreseeable future. However, the future of the black family may rest upon those blacks who resist the notion that racism will determine their personal relationships. Otherwise, it seems clear that racism may have decisively determined the nature of the most intimate association between men and women. Then, their capacity to resist racism itself may be brought into question. A house divided against itself cannot stand.

NOTES

1. U.S. Bureau of the Census, "Marital Status and Living Arrangements: March 1980," Washington, D.C.: U.S. Government Printing Office, 1981.
2. Suzanne Bianchi and Reynolds Farley, "Racial Differences in Family Living Arrangements and Economic Well Being: An Analysis of Recent Trends," *Journal of Marriage and the Family* 41 (August 1979): 537–552.
3. Herbert Gutman, *The Black Family in Slavery and Freedom 1750–1925* (New York: Pantheon, 1976).
4. U.S. Bureau of the Census, "Marital Status and Living Arrangements: March 1973," Washington, D.C., U.S. Government Printing Office, 1974.
5. Paul C. Glick and Karen Mills, *Black Families: Marriage Patterns and Living Arrangements* (Atlanta: Atlanta University, 1974), p. 9.
6. U.S. Bureau of the Census, "Current Population Reports, Series p. 20, no. 314. Washington, D.C., U.S. Government Printing Office, 1978, p. 31. Most of the men in that class, however, are married.
7. Ibid.
8. Graham Spanier and Paul Glick, "Mate Selection Differentials Between Whites and Blacks in the United States," *Social Forces* 58 (August 1980).
9. U.S. Bureau of the Census, "Marital Status and Living Arrangements: March 1980," op. cit.
10. Ibid.
11. Quoted in Dan Dorfman, "Tempest in the Take-Out Game," *San Francisco Examiner,* November 18, 1979, pp. 3–13.
12. Ibid. Some very exclusive restaurants hand the female member of the duo a menu without prices listed, a practice that has drawn the protests of some feminists.
13. C.f. Beth Trier, "Beauty—Is It Only Pocketbook Deep?" *San Francisco Chronicle,* June 12, 1980, p. 43.
14. Bianchi and Farley, op. cit.
15. "Home Buying Needs Working Wife," *San Francisco Sunday Examiner and Chronicle,* May 18, 1980, p. 34.

16. "S.F. Economist Traces Housing Crisis," *San Francisco Sunday Examiner and Chronicle*, April 20, 1980.

17. Frederick Engels, *The Origin of the Family, Private Property, and the State* (Chicago: Charles W. Kerr, 1920).

18. Lee Rainwater, *Behind Ghetto Walls* (Chicago: Aldine, 1970), p. 63.

19. Ibid.

20. Robert Bell, "Comparative Attitudes About Marital Sex Among Negro Women in the United States, Great Britain, and Trinidad," *Journal of Comparative Family Studies I.* (Autumn); 71–81.

21. Rainwater, *Behind Ghetto Walls* (Chicago: Aldine, 1970), p. 63.

22. William M. Chavis and Gladys J. Lyles, "Divorce Among Educated Black Women," *Journal of the National Medical Association* 67 (March 1975): 128–134.

23. Bernard Farber, *Kinship and Family Organization* (New York: John Wiley and Sons, 1966).

24. "Sex Lives of Cosmopolitan Readers," *San Francisco Chronicle*, August 4, 1980, p. 1.

25. Ibid.

26. Lewis Yablonsky, "How Infidelity Can Strengthen Ailing Marriages," *The Detroit Free Press*, February 15, 1979, p. 5-C.

27. Robert Staples, *The World of Black Singles: Changing Patterns of Male-Female Relations* (Westport, Connecticut: Greenwood Press, 1981).

28. Patrice Rushen quoted in *Jet Magazine*, April 10, 1980, p. 30.

Further Questions

1. Would you prefer to marry someone whose education is comparable to yours? If this is not possible, would you prefer to marry someone with more or less education?

2. Does a man's spending a lot of money on a woman justify his becoming sexually aggressive toward her at the end of the evening?

3. Is it rational to demand absolute fidelity from a mate? If so, is infidelity itself a sufficient reason for breaking off the marriage or relationship? Does the answer to this question depend on the gender of the person who has been unfaithful?

4. If persons of your gender who are more attractive than you are available, do you think of the possibility of losing your partner to one of them, either temporarily or permanently?

5. Would you consider becoming involved with someone who has had many sexual affairs? Would whether you expected to meet the previous partners make a difference? Would you give a different answer if you were of the other gender?

V.4   Is "Straight" to "Gay" as "Family" Is to "No Family"?

KATH WESTON

Kath Weston outlines a gay and lesbian understanding of "family." A nonprocreative sexual identity precludes a definition of "family" in terms of sexual intercourse and genealogy. Without implying that gay or lesbian identity is itself chosen, Weston calls the nonheterosexual analog to heterosexual marriage "families we choose."

Is "Straight" to "Gay" as "Family" Is to "No Family"? Abridged from "Exiles From Kinship." in Families We Choose: Lesbians, Gays, Kinship, *Second Edition by Kath Weston (New York: Columbia University Press, 1997), pp. 21–41. Reprinted by permission of the author.*

Weston teaches in the Department of Social and Behavioral Sciences at Arizona States University West. *Families We Choose: Lesbians, Gays, Kinship,* from which this selection was taken, is her first book.

Reading Questions

1. Does "family" just have one definition? If so, what is it? If not, what are they?
2. Must "family" (past, present, or future) have a biological component? If so, what is it?
3. What do you think of the idea held by the conservative element of society that lesbians and gays are a threat to "the family," and perhaps to "society" as well?

FOR YEARS, and in an amazing variety of contexts, claiming a lesbian or gay identity has been portrayed as a rejection of "the family" and a departure from kinship. In media portrayals of AIDS, Simon Watney (1987:103) observes that "we are invited to imagine some absolute divide between the two domains of 'gay life' and 'the family,' as if gay men grew up, were educated, worked and lived our lives in total isolation from the rest of society." Two presuppositions lend a dubious credence to such imagery: the belief that gay men and lesbians do not have children or establish lasting relationships, and the belief that they invariably alienate adoptive and blood kin once their sexual identities become known. By presenting "the family" as a unitary object, these depictions also imply that everyone participates in identical sorts of kinship relations and subscribes to one universally agreed-upon definition of family.

Representations that exclude lesbians and gay men from "the family" invoke what Blanche Wiesen Cook (1977:48) has called "the assumption that gay people do not love and do not work," the reduction of lesbians and gay men to sexual identity, and sexual identity to sex alone. In the United States, sex apart from heterosexual marriage tends to introduce a wild card into social relations, signifying unbridled lust and the limits of individualism. If heterosexual intercourse can bring people into enduring association via the creation of kinship ties, lesbian and gay sexuality in these depictions isolates individuals from one another rather than weaving them into a social fabric. To assert that straight people "naturally" have access to family, while gay people are destined to move toward a future of solitude and loneliness, is not only to tie kinship closely to procreation, but also to treat gay men and lesbians as members of a nonprocreative species set apart from the rest of humanity (cf. Foucault, 1978).

It is but a short step from positioning lesbians and gay men somewhere beyond "the family"—unencumbered by relations of kinship, responsibility, or affection—to portraying them as a menace to family and society. A person or group must first be outside and other in order to invade, endanger, and threaten. My own impression from fieldwork corroborates Frances FitzGerald's (1986) observation that many heterosexuals believe not only that gay people have gained considerable political power, but also that the absolute number of lesbians and gay men (rather than their visibility) has increased in recent years. Inflammatory rhetoric that plays on fears about the "spread" of gay identity and of AIDS finds a disturbing parallel in the imagery used by fascists to describe syphilis at mid-century, when "the healthy" confronted "the degenerate" while the fate of civilization hung in the balance (Hocquenghem 1978). . . .

At the height of gay liberation, activists had attempted to develop alternatives to "the family," whereas by the 1980s many lesbians and gay men were struggling to legitimate gay families as a form of kinship. When Armistead Maupin spoke at a gathering on Castro Street to welcome home two gay men who had been held hostage in the Middle East, partners who had stood with arms around one another upon their release, he congratulated them not only for their safe return, but also as representatives of a new kind of family. Gay or chosen families might incorporate friends, lovers, or children, in any combination. Organized through ideologies of love, choice, and creation, gay families have been defined through a contrast with what many gay men and lesbians in the Bay Area called "straight," "biological," or "blood" family. If families we choose were the families lesbians and gay men created for themselves, straight family represented the families in which most had grown to adulthood.

What does it mean to say that these two categories of family have been defined through contrast? One thing it emphatically does *not* mean is that heterosexuals share a single coherent form of family (although some of the lesbians and gay men doing the defining believed this to be the case). I am not arguing here for the existence of some central, unified kinship system vis-à-vis which gay people have distinguished their own practice and understanding of family. In the United States, race, class, gender, ethnicity, regional origin, and context all inform differences in household organization, as well as differences in notions of family and what it means to call someone kin.[1] . . .

KINSHIP AND PROCREATION

Since the time of Lewis Henry Morgan, most scholarly studies of familial relations have enthroned human procreation as kinship's ultimate referent. According to received anthropological wisdom, relations of blood (consanguinity) and marriage (affinity) could be plotted for any culture on a universal genealogical grid. Generations of field-workers set about the task of developing kinship charts for a multitude of "egos," connecting their subjects outward to a network of social others who represented the products (offspring) and agents (genitor/genetrix) of physical procre-

ation. In general, researchers occupied themselves with investigations of differences in the ways cultures arranged and divided up the grid, treating blood ties as a material base underlying an array of cross-cultural variations in kinship organization.

More recently, however, anthropologists have begun to reconsider the status of kinship as an analytic concept and a topic for inquiry. What would happen if observers ceased privileging genealogy as a sacrosanct or objective construct, approaching biogenetic ties instead as a characteristically Western way of ordering and granting significance to social relations? After a lengthy exercise in this kind of bracketing, David Schneider (1972, 1984) concluded that significant doubt exists as to whether non-Western cultures recognize kinship as a unified construct or domain. Too often unreflective recourse to the biogenetic symbolism used to prioritize relationships in Anglo-European societies subordinates an understanding of how particular cultures construct social ties to the project of crosscultural comparison. But suppose for a moment that blood is not intrinsically thicker than water. Denaturalizing the genealogical grid would require that procreation no longer be postulated as kinship's base, ground, or centerpiece.

Within Western societies, anthropologists are not the only ones who have implicitly or explicitly subjected the genealogical grid to new scrutiny. By reworking familiar symbolic materials in the context of nonprocreative relationships, lesbians and gay men in the United States have formulated a critique of kinship that contests assumptions about the bearing of biology, genetics, and heterosexual intercourse on the meaning of family in their own culture. Unlike Schneider, they have to set out to deconstruct kinship as a privileged domain, or taken issue with cultural representations that portray biology as a material "fact" exclusive of social significance. What gay kinship ideologies challenge is not the concept of procreation that informs kinship in the United States, but the belief that procreation *alone* constitutes kinship, and that "nonbiological" ties must be patterned after a biological model (like adoption) or forfeit any claim to kinship status.

In the United States the notion of biology as an indelible, precultural substratum is so ingrained that people often find it difficult to take an anthropological step backward in order to examine biology as symbol rather than substance. For many in this society, biology is a defining feature of kinship: they believe that blood ties make certain people kin, regardless of whether those individuals display the love and enduring solidarity expected to characterize familial relations. Physical procreation, in turn, produces biological links. Collectively, biogenetic attributes are supposed to demarcate kinship as a cultural domain, offering a yardstick for determining who counts as a "real" relative. Like their heterosexual counterparts, lesbians and gay men tended to naturalize biology in this manner. . . .

Not all cultures grant biology this significance for describing and evaluating relationships. To read biology as symbol is to approach it as a cultural construct and linguistic category, rather than a self-evident matter of "natural fact." At issue here is the cultural valuation given to ties traced through procreation, and the meaning that biological connection confers upon a relationship in a given cultural context. In this sense biology is no less a symbol than choice or creation. Neither is inherently more "real" or valid than the other, culturally speaking.

In the United States, Schneider (1968) argues, "sexual intercourse" is the symbol that brings together relations of marriage and blood, supplying the distinctive features in terms of which kinship relations are defined and differentiated. A relationship mediated by procreation binds a mother to a daughter, a brother to a sister, and so on, in the categories of genitor or genetrix, offspring, or members of a sibling set. Immediately apparent to a gay man or lesbian is that what passes here for sex per se is actually the *hetero*sexual union of two differently gendered persons. While all sexual activity among heterosexuals certainly does not lead to the

birth of children, the isolation of heterosexual intercourse as a core symbol orients kinship studies toward a dominantly procreative reading of sexualities. For a society like the United States, Sylvia Yanagisako's and Jane Collier's (1987) call to analyze gender and kinship as mutually implicated constructs must be extended to embrace sexual identity.

The very notion of gay families asserts that people who claim nonprocreative sexual identities and pursue nonprocreative relationships can lay claim to family ties of their own without necessary recourse to marriage, childbearing, or childrearing.[2] By defining these chosen families in opposition to the biological ties believed to constitute a straight family, lesbians and gay men began to renegotiate the meaning and practice of kinship from within the very societies that had nurtured the concept. Theirs has not been a proposal to number gay families among variations in "American kinship," but a more comprehensive attack on the privilege accorded to a biogenetically grounded mode of determining what relationships will *count* as kinship. . . .

FROM BIOLOGY TO CHOICE

Upon first learning the categories that framed gay kinship ideologies, heterosexuals sometimes mentioned adoption as a kind of limiting case that appeared to occupy that borderland between biology and choice. In the United States, adopted children are chosen, in a sense, although biological offspring can be planned or selected as well, given the widespread availability of birth control. Yet adoption in this society "is only understandable as a way of creating the social fiction that an actual link of kinship exists. Without biological kinship as a model, adoption would be meaningless" (Schneider 1984:55). Adoption does not render the attribution of biological descent culturally irrelevant (witness the many adopted children who, later in life, decide to search for their "real" parents). But adoptive relations—unlike gay families—pose no fundamental challenge to either procreative interpretations of kinship or the culturally standardized time of a family assembled around a core of parent(s) plus children.

Mapping biological family and families we choose onto contrasting sexual identities (straight and gay, respectively) places these two types of family in a relation of opposition, but *within* that relation, determinism and implicitly differentiates biology from choice and blood from creation. Informed by contrasting notions of free will and the fixedness often attributed to biology in this culture, the opposition between straight and gay families echoes old dichotomies such as nature versus nurture and real versus ideal. In families we choose, the agency conveyed by "we" emphasizes each person's part in constructing gay families, just as the absence of agency in the term "biological family" reinforces the sense of blood as an immutable fact over which individuals exert little control. Likewise, the collective subject of families we choose invokes a collective identity—who are "we" if not gay men and lesbians? In order to identify the "we" associated with the speaker's "I," a listener must first recognize the correspondence between the opposition of blood to choice and the relation of straight to gay.

Significantly, families we choose have not built directly upon beliefs that gay or lesbian identity can be chosen. Among lesbians and gay men themselves, opinions differ as to whether individuals select or inherit their sexual identities. In the aftermath of the gay movement, the trend has been to move away from the obsession of earlier decades with the etiological question of what "causes" homosexuality. After noting that no one subjects heterosexuality to similar scrutiny, many people dropped the question. Some lesbian-feminists presented lesbianism as a political choice that made a statement about sharing their best with other women and refusing to participate in patriarchal relations. In everyday conversations, however, the majority of both men and women portrayed their sexual identities as either inborn or a predisposition

developed very early in life. Whether or not to act on feelings already present then became the only matter left to individual discretion. "The choice for me wasn't being with men or being a lesbian," Richie Kaplan explained. "The choice was being asexual or being with women."

In contrast, parents who disapproved of homosexuality could convey a critical attitude by treating gay identity as something elective, especially since people in the United States customarily hold individuals responsible for any negative consequences attendant upon a "free choice." One man described with dismay his father's reaction upon learning of his sexual identity: "I said, 'I'm gay.' And he said, 'Oh. Well, I guess you made your choice.'" According to another, "My father kept saying, 'Well, you're gonna have to live by your choices that you make. It's your responsibility.' What's there to be responsible [about]? I was who I *am*." When Andy Wentworth disclosed his gay identity to his sister,

> She asked me, how could I *choose* to do this and to ignore the health risks . . . implying that this was a conscious, "Oh, I'd like to go to the movies today" type of choice. And I told her, I said, "Nobody in their right mind would go through this *hell* of being gay just to satisfy a whim." And I explained to her what it was like growing up. Knowing this other side of yourself that you can't tell anybody about, and if anybody in your family knows they will be upset and mortified.

Another man insisted he would never forget the period after coming out when he realized that he felt good about himself, and that he was not on his way to becoming "the kind of person that they're portraying gay people to be." What kind of person is that, I asked. "Well, you know, wicked, evil people who *decide* that they're going to be evil."

Rather than claiming an elective gay identity as its antecedent, the category "families we choose" incorporates the meaningful *difference* that is the product of choice and biology as two relationally defined terms. If many gay men and lesbians interpreted blood ties as a type of social connectedness organized through procreation, they tended to associate choice and creativity with a total absence of guidelines for ordering relationships within gay families. Although heterosexuals in the Bay Area also had the sense of creating something when they established families of their own, that creativity was often firmly linked to childbearing and childrearing, the "pro-" in procreation. In the absence of a procreative referent, individual discretion regulated who would be counted as kin. For those who had constructed them, gay families could evoke utopian visions of self-determination in the absence of social constraint. . . .

Gone are the days when embracing a lesbian or gay identity seemed to require a renunciation of kinship. The symbolic groundwork for gay families, laid during a period when coming out to relatives witnessed a kind of institutionalization, has made it possible to claim a sexual identity that is not linked to procreation, face the possibility of rejection by blood or adoptive relations; yet still conceive of establishing a family of one's own.

NOTES

1. On the distinction between family and household, see Rapp (1982) and Yanagisako (1979).

2. See Foucault (1978) on the practice of grouping homosexuality together with other nonprocreative sex acts, a historical shift that supplanted the earlier classification of homosexuality with adultery and offenses against marriage. According to Foucault, previous to the late eighteenth century acts "contrary to nature" tended to be understood as an extreme form of acts "against the law," rather than something different in kind. Only later was "the unnatural" set apart in the emerging domain of sexuality, becoming autonomous from adultery or rape. See also Freedman (1982:210): "Although the ideological support of the separation of [erotic] sexuality and reproduction did not appear until the twentieth century, the process itself began much earlier."

REFERENCES

Bourdieu, Pierre. 1977. *Outline of a Theory of Practice*. New York: Cambridge University Press.

Cook, Blanche Wiesen. 1977. "Female Support Networks and Political Activism: Lillian Wald, Crystal Eastman, Emma Goldman." *Chrysalis* 3:44–61.

FitzGerald, Frances. 1986. *Cities on a Hill: A Journey Through Contemporary American Cultures*. New York: Simon & Schuster.

Foucault, Michel. 1978. *The History of Sexuality*. Vol. 1. New York: Vintage.

Freedman, Estelle B. 1982. "Sexuality in Nineteenth-Century America: Behavior, Ideology, and Politics." *Reviews in American History* 10:196–215.

Hocquenghem, Guy. 1978. *Homosexual Desire*. London: Alison & Busby.

Rapp, Rayna. 1982. "Family and Class in Contemporary America: Notes Toward an Understanding of Ideology." In Barrie Thorne with Marilyn Yalom, eds., *Rethinking the Family*, pp. 168–187. New York: Longman.

Schneider, David M. 1968. *American Kinship: A Cultural Account*. Englewood Cliffs, N.J.: Prentice-Hall.

———. 1972. "What Is Kinship All About?" In Priscilla Reining, ed., *Kinship Studies in the Morgan Centennial Year*. Washington, D.C.: Anthropological Society of Washington.

———. 1984. *A Critique of the Study of Kinship*. Ann Arbor: University of Michigan Press.

Silverstein, Charles. 1977. *A Family Matter: A Parents' Guide to Homosexuality*. New York: McGraw-Hill.

Watney, Simon. 1987. *Policing Desire: Pornography, AIDS, and the Media*. Minneapolis: University of Minnesota Press.

Yanagisako, Sylvia Junko and Jane Fishburne Collier. 1987. "Toward a Unified Analysis of Gender and Kinship." In Jane Fishburne Collier and Sylvia Junko Yanagisako, eds., *Gender and Kinship: Essays Toward a Unified Analysis*, pp. 14–50. Stanford: Stanford University Press.

Further Questions

1. Homosexual unions are chosen. Does this mean that heterosexual ones are *not* chosen? Explain.

2. Are heterosexual unions established, at least in part, for the purpose of procreation? If so, does this mean childless heterosexual marriages and heterosexual unions lack something? Explain.

3. Should your sexual orientation make a difference in your place in the family into which you were born? Why or why not?

V.5   Virtually Normal

ANDREW SULLIVAN

Andrew Sullivan argues that marriage as a social and public recognition of a private commitment ought to be equally accessible to homosexuals. Homosexuals, as well as heterosexuals, need the anchor for emotional stability and economic security that marriage provides. Like heterosexuals, homosexuals need to feel that their emotional orientation is about the ability to love and be loved as complete, imperfect human beings.

Sullivan is a former editor of *The New Republic*.

Reading Questions

1. Why is domestic partnership an inadequate substitution for marriage, either gay or lesbian or straight?

2. Should procreation be a required part of marriage so that only fertile heterosexuals intending to have children can enter into marriage? Is there evidence that gays and lesbians make inferior parents to single parents or no effective parents?

3. Would heterosexuals be more sympathetic toward homosexual marriage if they would consider what it would be like to date without even the possibility of marriage and to believe that their love and attractions were all illicit?

THE CENTERPIECE of [the] new [homosexual] politics . . . is equal access to civil marriage. . . .

This is a question of formal public discrimination, since only the state can grant and recognize marriage. If the military ban deals with the heart of what it means to be a citizen, marriage does even more so, since, in peace and war, it affects everyone. Marriage is not simply a private contract; it is a social and public recognition of a private commitment. As such, it is the highest public recognition of personal integrity. Denying it to homosexuals is the most public affront possible to their public equality.

This point may be the hardest for many heterosexuals to accept. Even those tolerant of homosexuals may find this institution so wedded to the notion of heterosexual commitment that to extend it would be to undo its very essence. And there may be religious reasons for resisting this that, within certain traditions, are unanswerable. But I am not here discussing what churches do in their private affairs. I am discussing what the allegedly neutral liberal state should do in public matters. For liberals, the case for homosexual marriage is overwhelming. As a classic public institution, it should be available to any two citizens.

Some might argue that marriage is by definition between a man and a woman; and it is difficult to argue with a definition. But if marriage is articulated beyond this circular fiat, then the argument for its exclusivity to one man and one woman disappears. The center of the public contract is an emotional, financial, and psychological bond between two people; in this respect, heterosexuals and homosexuals are identical. The heterosexuality of marriage is intrinsic only if it is understood to be intrinsically procreative; but that definition has long been abandoned in Western society. No civil marriage license is granted on the condition that the couple bear children; and the marriage is no less legal and no less defensible if it remains childless. In the contemporary West, marriage has become a way in which the state recognizes an emotional commitment by two people to each other for life. And within that definition, there is no public way if one believes in equal rights under the law, in which it should legally be denied homosexuals.

Of course, no public sanctioning of a contract should be given to people who cannot actually fulfill it. The state rightly, for example, withholds marriage from minors, or from one adult and a minor, since at least one party is unable to understand or live up to the contract. And the state has also rightly barred close family relatives from marriage because familial emotional ties are too

strong and powerful to enable a marriage contract to be entered into freely by two autonomous, independent individuals, and because incest poses a uniquely dangerous threat to the trust and responsibility that the family needs to survive. But do homosexuals fall into a similar category? History and experience strongly suggest they don't. Of course, marriage is characterized by a kind of commitment that is rare—and perhaps declining—even among heterosexuals. But it isn't necessary to prove that homosexuals or lesbians are less—or more—able to form longterm relationships than straights for it to be clear that at least some are. Moreover, giving these people an equal right to affirm their commitment doesn't reduce the incentive for heterosexuals to do the same.

In some ways, the marriage issue is exactly parallel to the issue of the military. Few people deny that many homosexuals are capable of the sacrifice, the commitment, and the responsibilities of marriage. And indeed, for many homosexuals and lesbians, these responsibilities are already enjoined—as they have been enjoined for centuries. The issue is whether these identical relationships should be denied equal legal standing, not by virtue of anything to do with the relationships themselves but by virtue of the internal, involuntary nature of the homosexuals involved. Clearly, for liberals, the answer to this is clear. Such a denial is a classic case of unequal protection of the laws.

But perhaps surprisingly, . . . one of the strongest arguments for gay marriage is a conservative one. It's perhaps best illustrated by a comparison with the alternative often offered by liberals and liberationists to legal gay marriage, the concept of "domestic partnership." Several cities in the United States have domestic partnership laws, which allow relationships that do not fit into the category of heterosexual marriage to be registered with the city and qualify for benefits that had previously been reserved for heterosexual married couples. In these cities, a variety of interpersonal arrangements qualify for health insurance, bereavement leave, insurance, annuity and pension rights, housing rights (such as rent-control apartments), adoption and inheritance rights. Eventually, the aim is to include federal income tax and veterans' benefits as well. Homosexuals are not the only beneficiaries; heterosexual "live-togethers" also qualify.

The conservative's worries start with the ease of the relationship. To be sure, potential domestic partners have to prove financial interdependence, shared living arrangements, and a commitment to mutual caring. But they don't need to have a sexual relationship or even closely mirror old-style marriage. In principle, an elderly woman and her live-in nurse could qualify, or a pair of frat buddies. Left as it is, the concept of domestic partnership could open a Pandora's box of litigation and subjective judicial decision making about who qualifies. You either are or you're not married; it's not a complex question. Whether you are in a domestic partnership is not so clear.

More important for conservatives, the concept of domestic partnership chips away at the prestige of traditional relationships and undermines the priority we give them. Society, after all, has good reasons to extend legal advantages to heterosexuals who choose the formal sanction of marriage over simply living together. They make a deeper commitment to one another and to society; in exchange, society extends certain benefits to them. Marriage provides an anchor, if an arbitrary and often weak one, in the maelstrom of sex and relationships to which we are all prone. It provides a mechanism for emotional stability and economic security. We rig the law in its favor not because we disparage all forms of relationship other than the nuclear family, but because we recognize that not to promote marriage would be to ask too much of human virtue.

For conservatives, these are vital concerns. There are virtually no conservative arguments either for preferring no social incentives for gay relationships or for preferring a second-class relationship, such as domestic partnership, which really does provide an incentive for the decline of traditional marriage. Nor, if conservatives are concerned by the collapse of stable family life, should they be dismayed by the possibility of gay parents. There is no evidence that shows any deleterious impact on a child brought up by two homosexual parents, and considerable evidence that such a parental structure is clearly preferable to single parents (gay or straight) or no effective parents at all, which, alas, is the choice many children now face. Conservatives should not balk at the apparent radicalism of the change involved, either. The introduction of gay marriage would not be some sort of leap in the dark, a massive societal risk. Homosexual marriages have always existed, in a variety of forms; they have just been euphemized. Increasingly they exist in every sense but the legal one. As it has become more acceptable for homosexuals to acknowledge their loves and commitments publicly, more and more have committed themselves to one another for life in full view of their families and friends. A law insitutionalizing gay marriage would merely reinforce a healthy trend. Burkean conservatives should warm to the idea.

It would also be an unqualified social good for homosexuals. It provides role models for young gay people, who, after the exhilaration of coming out, can easily lapse into short-term relationships and insecurity with no tangible goal in sight. My own guess is that most homosexuals would embrace such a goal with as much (if not more) commitment as heterosexuals. Even in our society as it is, many lesbian and gay male relationships are virtual textbooks of monogamous commitment; and for many, "in sickness and in health" has become a vocation rather than a vow. Legal gay marriage could also help bridge the gulf often found between homosexuals and their parents. It could bring the essence of gay life—a gay couple—into the heart of the traditional family in a way the family can most understand and the gay offspring can most easily acknowledge. It could do more to heal the gay-straight rift than any amount of gay rights legislation.

More important, perhaps, as gay marriage sank into the subtle background consciousness of a culture, its influence would be felt quietly but deeply among gay children. For them, at last, there would be some kind of future; some older faces to apply to their unfolding lives, some language in which their identity could be properly discussed, some rubric by which it could be explained—not in terms of sex, or sexual practices, or bars, or subterranean activity, but in terms of their future life stories, their potential loves, their eventual chance at some kind of constructive happiness. They would be able to feel by the intimation of a myriad examples that in this respect their emotional orientation was not merely about pleasure, or sin, or shame, or otherness (although it might always be involved in many of those things), but about the ability to love and be loved as complete, imperfect human beings. Until gay marriage is legalized, this fundamental element of personal dignity will be denied a whole segment of humanity. No other change can achieve it.

Any heterosexual man who takes a few moments to consider what his life would be like if he were never allowed a formal institution to cement his relationships will see the truth of what I am saying. Imagine life without a recognized family; imagine dating without even the possibility of marriage. Any heterosexual woman who can imagine being told at a young age that her attraction to men was wrong, that her loves and crushes were illicit, that her destiny was singlehood and shame, will also appreciate the point. Gay marriage is not a radical step; it is a profoundly humanizing, traditionalizing step. It is the first step in any resolution of the homosexual question—more important than any other institution, since it is the most central institution to the nature of the problem, which is to say, the emotional and sexual bond between one human being and another. If nothing else were done at all, and gay marriage were legalized, 90 percent of the political work necessary to achieve gay and lesbian equality would have been achieved. It is ultimately the only reform that truly matters.

So long as conservatives recognize, as they do, that homosexuals exist and that they have equivalent emotional needs and temptations as heterosexuals, then there is no conservative reason to oppose homosexual marriage and many conservative reasons to support. So long as liberals recognize, as they do, that citizens deserve equal treatment under the law, then there is no liberal reason to oppose it and many liberal reasons to be in favor of it. So long as intelligent people understand that homosexuals are emotionally and sexually attracted to the same sex as heterosexuals are to the other sex, then there is no human reason on earth why it should be granted to one group and not the other. . . .

[L]ifting the marriage bar [is] simple, direct, and require[s] no change in heterosexual behavior and no sacrifice for heterosexuals. [It would] represent a politics that tackles the heart of prejudice against homosexuals while leaving bigots their freedom. This politics marries the clarity of liberalism with the intuition of conservatism. It allows homosexuals to define their own future and their own identity and does not place it in the hands of the other. It makes a clear, public statement of equality while leaving all the inequalities of emotion and passion to the private sphere, where they belong. It does not legislate private tolerance; it declares public equality. It banishes the paradigm of victimology and replaces it with one of integrity. . . .

It has become a truism that in the field of emotional development homosexuals have much to learn from the heterosexual culture. The values of commitment, of monogamy, of marriage, of stability are all posited as models for homosexual existence. And, indeed, of course, they are. Without an architectonic institution like that of marriage, it is difficult to create the conditions for nurturing such virtues, but that doesn't belie their importance.

It is also true, however, that homosexual relationships, even in their current, somewhat eclectic form, may contain features that could nourish the broader society as well. Precisely because there is no institutional model, gay relationships are often sustained more powerfully by genuine commitment. The mutual nurturing and sexual expressiveness of many lesbian relationships, the solidity and space of many adult gay male relationships, are qualities sometimes lacking in more rote, heterosexual couplings. Same-sex unions often incorporate the virtues of friendship more effectively than traditional marriages; and at times, among gay male relationships, the openness of the contract makes it more likely to survive than many heterosexual bonds. Some of this is unavailable to the male-female union: There is more likely to be greater understanding of the need for extramarital outlets between two men than between a man and a woman; and again, the lack of children gives gay couples greater freedom. Their failures entail fewer consequences for others. But something of the gay relationship's necessary honesty, its flexibility, and its equality could undoubtedly help strengthen and inform many heterosexual bonds.

In my own sometimes comic, sometimes passionate attempts to construct relationships, I learned something of the foibles of a simple heterosexual model. I saw how the network of gay friendship was often as good an emotional nourishment as a single relationship, that sexual candor was not always the same as sexual license, that the kind of supportive community that bolsters many gay relationships is something many isolated straight marriages could benefit from. I also learned how the subcultural fact of gay life rendered it remarkably democratic: In gay bars, there was far less socioeconomic stratification than in heterosexual bars. The shared experience of same-sex desire cut through class and race; it provided a humbling experience, which allowed many of us to risk our hearts and our friendships with people we otherwise might never have met. It loosened us up, and gave us a keener sense, perhaps, that people were often difficult to understand, let alone judge, from appearances. My heterosexual peers, through no fault of their own, were often denied these experiences. But they might gain from understanding them a little better, and not simply from a position of condescension.

As I've just argued, I believe strongly that marriage should be made available to everyone, in a politics of strict public neutrality. But within this model, there is plenty of scope for cultural difference. There is something baleful about the attempt of some gay conservatives to educate homosexuals and lesbians into an uncritical acceptance of a stifling model of heterosexual normality. The truth is, homosexuals are not entirely normal; and to flatten their varied and complicated lives into a single, moralistic model is to miss what is essential and exhilarating about their otherness.

This need not mean, as some have historically claimed, that homosexuals have no stake in the sustenance of a society, but rather that their role is somewhat different; they may be involved in procreation in a less literal sense: in a society's cultural regeneration, its entrepreneurial or intellectual rejuvenation, its religious ministry, or its professional education. Unencumbered by children, they may be able to press the limits of the culture or the business infrastructure, or the boundaries of intellectual life, in a way that heterosexuals, by dint of a different type of calling, cannot. Of course, many heterosexuals perform similar roles; and many homosexuals prefer domesticity to public performance; but the inevitable way of life of the homosexual provides an opportunity that many intuitively seem to grasp and understand.

Or perhaps their role is to have no role at all. Perhaps it is the experience of rebellion that prompts homosexual culture to be peculiarly resistant to attempts to guide it to be useful or instructive or productive. Go to any march for gay rights and you will see the impossibility of organizing it into a coherent lobby: Such attempts are always undermined by irony, or exhibitionism, or irresponsibility. It is as if homosexuals have learned something about life that makes them immune to the puritanical and flattering demands of modern politics. It is as if they have learned that life is fickle; that there are parts of it that cannot be understood, let alone solved; that some things lead nowhere and mean nothing; that the ultimate exercise of freedom is not a programmatic journey but a spontaneous one. Perhaps it requires seeing one's life as the end of a biological chain, or seeing one's deepest emotions as the object of detestation, that provides this insight. But the seeds of homosexual wisdom are the seeds of human wisdom. They contain the truth that order is in fact a euphemism for disorder; that problems are often more sanely enjoyed than solved; that there is reason in mystery; that there is beauty in the wild flowers that grow randomly among our wheat.

Further Questions

1. Have homosexuals something to learn from the heterosexual culture about marriage? Can heterosexuals gain an enriched sense of human relationships by learning about same-sex unions?
2. Would extending the institution of marriage to homosexuals mean that the roles in society of everyone, gay and straight, would be flattened to become all alike? Explain.
3. How would gay marriage influence the outlook on life of gay children? Could gay marriage help integrate the couple with their parents?

The Married Woman   V.6

SIMONE DE BEAUVOIR

Simone de Beauvoir attacks the gender role system in marriage. The system oppresses the woman and, through her, the man as well. She suggests that the remedy is to prohibit marriage as a "career" for women.

Other excerpts from Simone de Beauvoir's *The Second Sex* appear in Parts I, IV, and XII.

Reading Questions

1. In the social world, is the status of a married woman more legitimate than that of a single woman? Does the age of a single woman make any difference to whether she is socially legitimate?
2. Are housework, shopping, and cooking rewarding work, if these are all a person does? Does the amount of satisfaction a person gains from doing only this kind of work depend on the circumstances in which the work is done?
3. Do the parents of a woman (or man) have a right to put pressure upon her (or him) to marry?

MARRIAGE IS THE DESTINY traditionally offered to women by society. It is still true that most women are married, or have been, or plan to be, or suffer from not being. The celibate woman is to be explained and defined with reference to marriage, whether she is frustrated, rebellious, or even indifferent in regard to that institution. . . .

. . . [F]or both parties marriage is at the same time a burden and a benefit; but there is no symmetry in the situations of the two sexes; for girls marriage is the only means of integration in the community, and if they remain unwanted, they are, socially viewed, so much wastage. This is why mothers have always eagerly sought to arrange marriages for them. In the last century they were hardly consulted among middle-class people. They were offered to possible suitors by means of "interviews" arranged in advance. Zola describes this custom in *Pot-Bouille*.

> "A failure, it's a failure," said Mme Josserand, falling into her chair. M. Josserand simply said: "Ah!"
>
> "But," continued Mme Josserand in a shrill voice, "you don't seem to understand, I'm telling you that there's another marriage gone, and it's the seventh that has miscarried.
>
> "You hear," she went on, advancing on her daughter. "How did you spoil this marriage?"
>
> Bertha realized that it was her turn.
>
> "I don't know, Mamma," she murmured.
>
> "An assistant department head," her mother continued, "not yet thirty, and with a great future. A man to bring you his pay every month; substantial, that's all that counts. . . . You did something stupid, the same as with the others?"
>
> "No, Mamma, certainly not."
>
> "When you were dancing with him you disappeared into the small parlor."
>
> Bertha said in some confusion: "Yes, Mamma—and as soon as we were alone he wanted to act disgracefully, he hugged me and took hold of me like this. Then I got scared and pushed him against a piece of furniture."
>
> Her mother interrupted, furious again: "Pushed him against the furniture! You wretch, you pushed him!"
>
> "But, Mamma, he was holding on to me."

> "So? He was holding on to you, fancy that! And we send these simpletons to boarding school! What do they teach you, tell me! Ah, just for a kiss behind the door! Should you really tell us about such a thing, your parents? And you push people against furniture, and you spoil chances to marry!"
>
> She assumed a didactic air and continued:
>
> "That's the end, I give up, you are just stupid, my dear. Since you have no fortune, understand that you have to catch men some other way. The idea is to be agreeable, to gaze tenderly, to forest about your hand, to allow little intimacies without seeming to notice; in a word, you fish for a husband. . . . What bothers me is that she is not too bad, when she feels like it. Come, now, stop crying and look at me as if I were a gentleman courting you. See, you drop your fan so that when he picks it up he will touch your fingers. . . . And don't be stiff, let your waist bend. Men don't like boards. And above all don't be a ninny if they go too far. A man who goes too far is done for, my dear."
>
> Through the long evening of furious talk the girl was docile and resigned, but her heart was heavy, oppressed with fear and shame. . . .

In such circumstances the girl seems absolutely passive; she *is* married, *given* in marriage by her parents. Boys *get* married, they *take* a wife. They look in marriage for an enlargement, a confirmation of their existence, but not the mere right to exist; it is a charge they assume voluntarily. Thus they can inquire concerning its advantages and disadvantages, as did the Greek and medieval satirists; for them it is one mode of living, not a preordained lot. They have a perfect right to prefer celibate solitude; some marry late, or not at all.

In marrying, woman gets some share in the world as her own; legal guarantees protect her against capricious action by man but she becomes his vassal. He is the economic head of the joint enterprise, and hence he represents it in the view of society. She takes his name; she belongs to his religion, his class, his circle; she joins his family, she becomes his "half." She follows wherever his work calls him and determines their place of residence; she breaks more or less decisively with her past, becoming attached to her husband's universe; she gives him her person, virginity and a rigorous fidelity being required. She loses some of the rights legally belonging to the unmarred woman. Roman law placed the wife in the husband's hands *loco filiae*, in the position of a daughter; early in the nineteenth century the conservative writer Bonald pronounced the wife to be to her husband as the child is to its mother; before 1942 French law demanded the wife's obedience to her husband; law and custom still give him great authority, as implied in the conjugal situation itself.

Since the husband is the productive worker, he is the one who goes beyond family interest to that of society, opening up a future for himself through cooperation in the building of the collective future: he incarnates transcendence. Woman is doomed to the continuation of the species and the care of the home—that is to say, to immanence. The fact is that every human existence involves transcendence and immanence at the same time; to go forward, each existence must be maintained, for it to expand toward the future it must integrate the past, and while intercommunicating with others it should find self-confirmation. These two elements—maintenance and progression—are implied in any living activity, and for *man* marriage permits precisely a happy synthesis of the two. In his occupation and his political life he encounters change and progress, he senses his extension through time and the universe; and when he is tired of such roaming, he gets himself a home, a fixed location, and an anchorage in the world. At evening he restores his soul in the home, where his wife takes care of his furnishings and children and guards the things of the past that she keeps in store. But she has no other job than to maintain and provide for life in pure and unvarying generality; she perpetuates the species without change, she ensures the even rhythm of the days and the continuity of the home, seeing to it that the doors are locked. But she is allowed no direct influence upon the future nor

upon the world; she reaches out beyond herself toward the social group only through her husband as intermediary.

Marriage today still retains, for the most part, this traditional form. And, first of all, it is forced much more tyrannically upon the young girl than upon the young man. . . .

. . . A single woman in America, still more than in France, is a socially incomplete being even if she makes her own living; if she is to attain the whole dignity of a person and gain her full rights, she must wear a wedding ring. Maternity in particular is respectable only for a married woman; the unwed mother remains an offense to public opinion, and her child is a severe handicap for her in life.

For all these reasons a great many adolescent girls—in the New World as in the Old—when asked about their plans for the future, reply today as formerly: "I want to get married." But no young man considers marriage as his fundamental project. Economic success is what will bring him adult standing; such success may imply marriage—especially for the peasant—but it can also preclude it. The conditions of modern life—less stable, more uncertain than in the past—make the responsibilities of marriage especially heavy for the young man. Its benefits, on the other hand, have decreased, since it is easily possible for him to obtain board and room and since sexual satisfaction is generally available. No doubt marriage can afford certain material and sexual conveniences: it frees the individual from loneliness, it establishes him securely in space and time by giving him a home and children; it is a definitive fulfillment of his existence. But, for all that, the masculine demand is on the whole less than the feminine supply. A father can be said less to give his daughter than to get rid of her; the girl in search of a husband is not responding to a masculine demand, she is trying to create one. . . .

. . . The male is called upon for action, his vocation is to produce, fight, create, progress, to transcend himself toward the totality of the universe and the infinity of the future; but traditional marriage does not invite woman to transcend herself with him; it confines her in immanence, shuts her up within the circle of herself. She can thus propose to do nothing more than construct a life of stable equilibrium in which the present as a continuance of the past avoids the menaces of tomorrow—that is, construct precisely a life of happiness. In place of love, she will feel a tender and respectful sentiment known as conjugal love, wifely affection; within the walls of the home she is to manage, she will enclose her world; she will see to the continuation of the human species through time to come.

But no existent ever relinquishes his transcendence, even when he stubbornly forswears it. The old-time bourgeois thought that in preserving the established order, in showing its virtues through his own prosperity, he was serving God, his country, a regime, a civilization: to be happy was to fulfill his function as a man. Woman, too, must envisage purposes that transcend the peaceful life of the home; but it is man who will act as intermediary between his wife as an individuality and the universe, he will endue her inconsequential life of contingency with human worth. Obtaining in his association with his wife the strength to undertake things, to act, to struggle, he is her justification: She has only to put her existence in his hands and he will give it meaning. This presupposes a humble renunciation on her part; but she is compensated because, under the guidance and protection of masculine strength, she will escape the effects of the original renunciation; she will once more become essential. Queen in her hive, tranquilly at rest within her domain, but borne by man out into limitless space and time, wife, mother, mistress of the home, woman finds in marriage at once energy for living and meaning for her life. We must now see how this ideal works out in reality. . . .

The ideal of happiness has always taken material form in the house, whether cottage or castle; it stands for permanence and separation from the world. Within its walls the family is established as a discrete cell or a unit group and maintains its identity as generations come and go; the past preserved in the form of furnishings and ancestral portraits, gives promise of a secure future; in the garden the seasons register their reassuring cycle in the growth of edible vegetables; each year the same springtime with the same flowers foretells the return of immutable summer, of autumn with its fruits no different from the fruits of any other autumn: neither time nor space fly off at a tangent, they recur in their appointed cycles. In every civilization based on landed property an ample literature sings the poetry of hearth and home; in such a work as Henry Bordeaux's *La Maison* it sums up all the middle-class values: fidelity to the past, patience, economy, foresight, love of family and of the native soil, and so on. It often happens that the poets of the home are women, since it is woman's task to assure the happiness of the family group; her part, as in the time when the Roman *domina* sat in the atrium, is to be "lady of the house."

Today the house has lost its patriarchal splendor; for the majority of men it is only a place to live in, no longer freighted with the memory of dead generations, no longer encompassing the centuries to come. But still woman is all for giving her "interior" the meaning and value that the true house and home once had. In *Cannery Row* Steinbeck describes a vagrant woman who was determined to decorate with rugs and curtains the discarded engine boiler in which she lived with her husband; he objected in vain that the curtains were useless—"We got no windows." . . .

In domestic work, with or without the aid of servants, woman makes her home her own, finds social justification, and provides herself with an occupation, an activity, that deals usefully and satisfyingly with material objects—shining stoves, fresh, clean clothes, bright copper, polished furniture—but provides no escape from immanence and little affirmation of individuality. Such work has a negative basis: cleaning is getting rid of dirt, tidying up is eliminating disorder. And under impoverished conditions no satisfaction is possible; the hovel remains a hovel in spite of woman's sweat and tears: "nothing in the world can make it pretty." Legions of women have only this endless struggle without victory over the dirt. And for even the most privileged the victory is never final.

Few tasks are more like the torture of Sisyphus than housework, with its endless repetition: the clean becomes soiled, the soiled is made clean, over and over, day after day. The housewife wears herself out marking time: She makes nothing, simply perpetuates the present. She never senses conquest of a positive Good, but rather indefinite struggle against negative Evil. A young pupil writes in her essay: "I shall never have house-cleaning day"; she thinks of the future as constant progress toward some unknown summit; but one day, as her mother washes the dishes, it comes over her that both of them will be bound to such rites until death. Eating, sleeping, cleaning—the years no longer rise up toward heaven, they lie spread out ahead, gray and identical. The battle against dust and dirt is never won.

Washing, ironing, sweeping, ferreting out rolls of lint from under wardrobes—all this halting of decay is also the denial of life; for time simultaneously creates and destroys, and only its negative aspect concerns the housekeeper. Hers is the position of the Manichaeist, regarded philosophically. The essence of Manichaeism is not solely to recognize two principles, the one good, the other evil; it is also to hold that the good is attained through the abolition of evil and not by positive action. . . . [W]oman is not called upon to build a better world: her domain is fixed and she has only to keep up the never ending struggle against the evil principles that creep into it; in her war against dust, stains, mud, and dirt she is fighting sin, wrestling with Satan.

But it is a sad fate to be required without respite to repel an enemy instead of working toward positive ends, and very often the housekeeper submits to it in a kind of madness that may verge on perversion, a kind of sado-masochism. The maniac housekeeper wages her furious war against dirt, blaming life itself for the rubbish all living growth entails. When any living being enters her house, her eye gleams with a wicked light: "Wipe your feet, don't tear the place apart, leave that alone!" She wishes those of her household would hardly breathe; everything means more thankless work for her. Severe, preoccupied, always on the watch, she loses *joie de vivre*, she becomes overprudent and avaricious. She shuts out the sunlight, for along with that come insects, germs, and dust, and besides, the sun ruins silk hangings and fades upholstery; she scatters naphthalene, which scents the air. She becomes bitter and disagreeable and hostile to all that lives: the end is sometimes murder. . . .

The preparation of food, getting meals, is work more positive in nature and often more agreeable than cleaning. First of all it means marketing, often the bright spot of the day. And gossip on doorsteps, while peeling vegetables, is a gay relief for solitude; to go for water is a great adventure for half-cloistered Mohammedan women; women in markets and stores talk about domestic affairs, with a common interest, feeling themselves members of a group that—for an instant—is opposed to the group of men as the essential to the inessential. Buying is a profound pleasure, a discovery, almost an invention. As Gide says in his *Journal,* the Mohammedans, not knowing gambling, have in its place the discovery of hidden treasure; that is the poetry and the adventure of mercantile civilizations. The housewife knows little of winning in games, but a solid cabbage, a ripe Camembert, are treasures that must be cleverly won from the unwilling storekeeper; the game is to get the best for the least money; economy means not so much helping the budget as winning the game. She is pleased with her passing triumph as she contemplates her well-filled larder.

Gas and electricity have killed the magic of fire, but in the country many women still know the joy of kindling live flames from inert wood. With her fire going, woman becomes a sorceress; by a simple movement, as in beating eggs, or through the magic of fire, she effects the transmutation of substances: matter becomes food.

There is enchantment in these alchemies, there is poetry in making preserves; the housewife has caught duration in the snare of sugar, she has enclosed life in jars. Cooking is revelation and creation; and a woman can find special satisfaction in a successful cake or a flake pastry, for not everyone can do it: One must have the gift.

Here again the little girl is naturally fond of imitating her elders, making mud pies and the like, and helping roll real dough in the kitchen. But as with other housework, repetition soon spoils these pleasures. The magic of the oven can hardly appeal to Mexican Indian women who spend half their lives preparing tortillas, identical from day to day, from century to century. And it is impossible to go on day after day making a treasure hunt of the marketing or ecstatically viewing one's highly polished faucets. The male and female writers who lyrically exalt such triumphs are persons who are seldom or never engaged in actual housework. It is tiresome, empty, monotonous, as a career. If, however, the individual who does such work is also a producer, a creative worker, it is as naturally integrated in life as are the organic functions; for this reason housework done by men seems much less dismal; it represents for them merely a negative and inconsequential moment from which they quickly escape. What makes the lot of the wife-servant ungrateful is the division of labor which dooms her completely to the general and the inessential. Dwelling-place and food are useful for life but give it no significance: the immediate goals of the housekeeper are only means, not true ends. She endeavors, naturally, to give some individuality to her work and to make it seem essential. No one else, she thinks, could do her work as well; she has her rites, superstitions, and ways of doing things. But too often her "personal note" is but a vague and meaningless rearrangement of disorder.

Woman wastes a great deal of time and effort in such striving for originality and unique perfection; this gives her task its meticulous, disorganized, and endless character and makes it difficult to estimate the true load of domestic work. Recent studies show that for married women housework averages about thirty hours per week, or three fourths of a working week in employment. This is enormous if done in addition to a paid occupation, little if the woman has nothing else to do. The care of several children will naturally add a good deal to woman's work: A poor mother is often working all the time. Middle-class women who employ help, on the other hand, are almost idle; and they pay for their leisure with ennui. If they lack outside interests, they often multiply and complicate their domestic duties to excess, just to have something to do.

The worst of it all is that this labor does not even tend toward the creation of anything durable. Woman is tempted—and the more so the greater pains she takes—to regard her work as an end in itself. She sighs as she contemplates the perfect cake just out of the oven: "It's a shame to eat it!" It is really too bad to have husband and children tramping with their muddy feet all over her waxed hardwood floors! When things are used they are soiled or destroyed—we have seen how she is tempted to save them from being used; she keeps preserves until they get moldy; she locks up the parlor. But time passes inexorably; provisions attract rats; they become wormy; moths attack blankets and clothing. The world is not a dream carved in stone, it is made of dubious stuff subject to rot; edible material is as equivocal as Dali's fleshy watches: It seems inert, inorganic, but hidden larvae may have changed it into a cadaver. The housewife who loses herself in things becomes dependent, like the things, upon the whole world: Linen is scorched, the roast burns, chinaware gets broken; these are absolute disasters, for when things are destroyed, they are gone forever. Permanence and security cannot possibly be obtained through them. The pillage and bombs of war threaten one's wardrobes, one's house.

The products of domestic work, then, must necessarily be consumed; a continual renunciation is required of the woman whose operations are completed only in their destruction. For her to acquiesce without regret, these minor holocausts must at least be reflected in someone's joy or pleasure. But since the housekeeper's labor is expended to maintain the *status quo*, the husband, coming into the house, may notice disorder or negligence, but it seems to him that order and neatness come of their own accord. He has a more positive interest in a good meal. The cook's moment of triumph arrives when she puts a successful dish on the table: Husband and children receive it with warm approval, not only in words, but by consuming it gleefully. The culinary alchemy then pursues its course, food becomes chyle and blood.

Thus, to maintain living bodies is of more concrete, vital interest than to keep a fine floor in proper condition; the cook's effort is evidently transcended toward the future. If, however, it is better to share in another's free transcendence than to lose oneself in things, it is not less dangerous. The validity of the cook's work is to be found only in the mouths of those around her table; she needs their approbation, demands that they appreciate her dishes and call for second helpings; She is upset if they are not hungry, to the point that one wonders whether the fried potatoes are for her husband or her husband for the fried potatoes. This ambiguity is evident in the general attitude of the housekeeping wife: She takes care of the house of her husband, but she also wants him to spend all he earns for furnishings and an electric refrigerator. She desires to make him happy, but she approves of his activities only in so far as they fall within the frame of happiness she has set up. . . .

Marriage incites man to a capricious imperialism: the temptation to dominate is the most truly universal, the most irresistible one there is; to surrender the child to its mother, the wife to her husband, is to promote tyranny in the world. Very often it is not enough for the husband to be approved of and admired, for him to be counselor and guide; he issues commands, he plays the lord and master. All the resentments accumulated during his childhood and his later life, those accumulated daily among other men whose existence means that he is browbeaten and injured—all this is purged from him at home as he lets loose his authority upon his wife. He enacts violence, power, unyielding resolution; he issues commands in tones of severity; he shouts and pounds the table: This farce is a daily reality for his wife. He is so firm in his rights that the slightest sign of independence on her part seems to him a rebellion; he would fain stop her breathing without his permission. . . .

To "catch" a husband is an art; to "hold" him is a job—and one in which great competence is called for. A wise sister said to a peevish young wife: "Be careful, making scenes with Marcel is going to cost you your *job*." What is at stake is extremely serious: material and moral security, a home of one's own, the dignity of wifehood, a more or less satisfactory substitute for love and happiness. A wife soon learns that her erotic attractiveness is the weakest of her weapons; it disappears with familiarity; and, alas, there are other desirable women all about. . . .

A human relation has value only in so far as it is directly experienced; the relations of children to parents, for example, take on value only when they are consciously realized; it is not to be wondered at that conjugal relations tend to relapse from the condition of directly experienced emotion, and that the husband and wife lose their liberty of feeling in the process. This complex mixture of affection and resentment, hate, constraint, resignation, dullness, and hypocrisy called conjugal love is supposedly respected only by way of extenuation, whitewash. But the same is true of affection as of physical love: For it to be genuine, authentic, it must first of all be free.

Liberty, however, does not mean fickleness: A tender sentiment is an involvement of feeling which goes beyond the moment; but it is for the individual alone to determine whether his will in general and his behavior in detail are to be such as to maintain or, on the contrary, to break off the relation he has entered upon; sentiment is free when it depends upon no constraint from outside, when it is experienced in fearless sincerity. The constraint of "conjugal love" leads, on the other hand, to all kinds of repressions and lies. And first of all it prevents the couple from really knowing each other. Daily intimacy creates neither understanding nor sympathy. The husband respects his wife too much to take an interest in the phenomena of her psychic life that would be to recognize in her a secret autonomy that could prove disturbing, dangerous; . . . On the other hand, the wife does not know her husband; she thinks she perceives his true aspect because she sees him in his daily round of inessential circumstances; but man is first of all what he *does* in the world among other men. . . . As a woman has said: "One marries a poet, and when one is his wife the first thing to be noticed is that he forgets to pull the chain in the toilet." . . .

. . . The couple should not be regarded as a unit, a closed cell; rather each individual should be integrated as such in society at large, where each (whether male or female) could flourish without aid; then attachments could be formed in pure generosity with another individual equally adapted to the group, attachments that would be founded upon the acknowledgment that both are free.

This balanced couple is not a utopian fancy: such couples do exist, sometimes even within the frame of marriage, most often outside it. Some mates are united by a strong sexual love that leaves them free in their friendships and in their work; others are held together by a friendship that does not preclude sexual liberty; more rare are those who are at once lovers and friends but do not seek in each other their sole reasons for living. Many nuances are possible in the relations between a man and a woman: In comradeship, pleasure, trust, fondness, cooperation, love, they can be for each other the most abundant source of joy, richness, and power available to human beings. Individuals are not to be blamed for the failure of marriage: It is—counter to the claims of such advocates as Comte and Tolstoy—the institution itself, perverted as it has been from the start. To hold and proclaim that a man and a woman, who may not even have chosen each

other, *are in duty bound* to satisfy each other in every way throughout their lives is a monstrosity that necessarily gives rise to hypocrisy, lying, hostility, and unhappiness. . . .

Men are enchained by reason of their very sovereignty; it is because they alone earn money that their wives demand checks, it is because they alone engage in a business or profession that their wives require them to be successful, it is because they alone embody transcendence that their wives wish to rob them of it by taking charge of their projects and successes.

Inversely, the tyranny exercised by woman only goes to show her dependence: She knows that the success of the couple, its future, its happiness, its justification rest in the hands of the other; if she seeks desperately to bend him to her will, it is because she is alienated in him— that is, her interests as an individual lie in him. She makes a weapon of her weakness, but the fact remains that she is weak. Conjugal slavery is chiefly a matter of daily irritation for the husband; but it is something more deep-seated for the woman; a wife who keeps her husband at her side for hours because she is bored certainly bothers him and seems burdensome; but in the last analysis he can get along without her much more easily than she can without him; if he leaves her, she is the one whose life will be ruined. The great difference is that with woman dependency is interiorized: she *is* a slave even when she behaves with apparent freedom; while man is essentially independent and his bondage comes from without. If he seems to be the victim, it is because his burdens are most evident: Woman is supported by him like a parasite; but a parasite is not a conquering master. The truth is that just as—biologically—males and females are never victims of one another but both victims of the species, so man and wife together undergo the oppression of an institution they did not create. If it is asserted that *men* oppress *women*, the husband is indignant; he feels that *he* is the one who is oppressed—and he is; but the fact is that it is the masculine code, it is the society developed by the males and in their interest, that has established woman's situation in a form that is at present a source of torment for both sexes.

It is for their common welfare that the situation must be altered by prohibiting marriage as a "career" for woman. Men who declare themselves antifeminists, on the ground that "women are already bad enough as it is," are not too logical; it is precisely because marriage makes women into "praying mantises," "leeches," "poisonous" creatures, and so on, that it is necessary to transform marriage and, in consequence, the condition of women in general. Woman leans heavily upon man because she is not allowed to rely on herself; he will free himself in freeing her—that is to say, in giving her something to *do* in the world.

Further Questions

1. If a wife had sufficient income of her own and a place in the world that did not depend on her husband's position, would the problems de Beauvoir perceives in the traditional marriage be as likely to occur?

2. Can a woman make a weapon of her weakness? If so, how much is she to blame for doing so?

3. Is conjugal love difficult to maintain because spouses have constraints on them to remain in the marriage?

Further Readings for Part V: Bonds

Most libraries stock a large collection of books on marriage and the family because these institutions have been the subject of much study. The following is a small selection from the group, which the reader might find of special interest.

Ifi Amadiume. *Male Daughters, Female Husbands: Gender and Sex in an African Society* (Atlantic Highlands, NJ: Zed Books, 1987). Argument that family gender roles are flexible because they are reversed in a particular African society.

Robert M. Baird and Stuart E. Rosenbaum, eds. *Same Sex Marriage: The Moral and Legal Debate* (Amherst, NY: Prometheus Books, 1997). Lively attacks on and defenses of the idea of gay marriage.

Gloria Bird and Michael J. Sporakowski, eds. *Taking Sides: Clashing Views on Controversial Issues in Family and Personal Relationships* (Guilford, CT: The Dushkin Publishing Group, 1992). Short lively pieces on issues in marriage and parenthood.

Becky Butler. *Ceremonies of the Heart: Celebrating Lesbian Unions* (Seattle, WA: The Seal Press, 1990). Twenty-seven lesbian couples speak of affirming their commitment through wedding ceremonies.

Caroline Dryden. *Being Married, Doing Gender: A Critical Analysis of Gender Relationships in Marriage* (New York, NY: Routledge, 1999). An examination of equalities and inequalities in marriage.

Barbara Ehrenreich. *The Hearts of Men: American Dreams and the Flight from Commitment* (New York, NY: Anchor, Doubleday, 1983). Argues that the feminist movement was set in motion by men walking away from their roles as breadwinners and success machines. This action on men's part also caused the anti-feminist backlash.

Betty Friedan. *The Feminine Mystique* (New York, NY: Dell Publishing Co., 1963). "The problem that has no name" is the emptiness of the life of the suburban housewife.

Betty Friedan. *The Second State* (New York, NY: Summit Books, Simon and Schuster, 1986). Redesigning the family so as to better meet human needs.

Jean Schaar Gochros. *When Husbands Come Out of the Closet* (Binghamton, NY: The Haworth Press, 1989). How to cope with a gay husband, including strategies for handling the problem of AIDS.

Clyde Hendrick, ed. *Close Relationships: Development, Dynamics and Deterioration* (Newbury Park, CA: Sage Publications, 1989). What happens to relationships in the long run.

Søren Kierkegaard. "The Aesthetic Validity of Marriage" in *Either/Or,* Vol. 2, translated by Walter Lowrie (New York, NY: Anchor, Doubleday, 1959), pp. 3–157. The difference commitment makes in a relationship.

Mirra Komarovsky. *Blue-Collar Marriage* (New York, NY: Vintage Books, 1962). Classic analysis of working class families, including power configurations.

Susan Krieger. *The Mirror Dance: Identity in a Women's Community* (Philadelphia, PA: Temple University Press, 1983). Women's experiences in an all-woman community.

Demie Kutz. *For Richer, For Poorer: Mothers Confront Divorce* (New York, NY: Routledge, 1995). Rationalizes the choices of women to leave their marriages despite the resulting hardships.

Robert A. Lewis and Marvin B. Sussman, eds. *Men's Changing Roles in the Family* (New York, NY: The Haworth Press, 1986). Are times changing? This is an interesting study focusing on men's roles in the family.

Eleanor D. Macklin and Roger H. Rubin, eds. *Contemporary Families and Alternative Lifestyles: Handbook on Research and Theory* (Beverly Hills, CA: Sage Publications, 1983). Collection of interesting writings on non-traditional families.

David P. McWhirter and Andrew M. Mattison. *The Male Couple: How Relationships Develop* (Englewood Cliffs, NJ: Prentice-Hall, 1984). 156 gay couples are studied in 6 temporal stages of their relationships.

Robert C. L. Moffat, Joseph Grcic, and Michael D. Bayles, eds. *Perspectives on the Family* (Lewiston, NY: The Edwin Mellen Press, 1990). Philosophers and other thinkers look at family issues.

Hilde Lindemann Nelson, ed. *Feminism and Families* (New York, NY: Routledge, 1997). Viewpoints on families from feminist perspectives.

Ann Oakley. *The Sociology of Housework* (New York, NY: Pantheon Books, Random House, 1974). Analysis and (fairly negative) evaluation of housework.

Susan Moller Okin. *Justice, Gender and the Family* (New York, NY: Basic Books, 1989). How liberal theories of justice, Rawls' in particular, produce injustices for women in families.

Daniel Perlman and Steve Ducks, eds. *Intimate Relationships: Long Term Relationships* (Newbury Park, CA: Sage Publications, 1987).

Bertrand Russell. *Marriage and Morals* (London: George Allen and Unwin, 1929). A protest against tradition, considered shocking in its day.

John Scanzoni. *Shaping Tomorrow's Family: Theory and Policy for the 21st Century* (Newbury Park, CA: Sage Publications, 1983).

John Scanzoni, Karen Polenks, Jay Teachman, and Linda Thompson. *The Sexual Bond: Rethinking Families and Close Relationships* (Newbury Park, CA: Sage Publication, 1989).

Arlene Skolnick and Jerome H. Skolnick, ed. *Family in Transition* (Boston, MA: Little, Brown and Co., 3rd Edition, 1980).

Judith Stacey. *In the Name of the Family: Rethinking Family Values in the Postmodern Age* (Boston, MA: Beacon Press, 1996). Critique of family values as a support to the heterosexual, two-parent family.

Robert Staples, ed. *The Black Family: Essays and Studies,* 5th Edition (Belmont, CA: Wadsworth Inc., 1994). Writers address a wide variety of issues relating to the black family.

Mark Strasser. *Legally Wed: Same-Sex Marriage and the Constitution* (Ithaca, NY: Cornell University Press, 1997). Clear, well-written discussion of the legal issues concerning same-sex marriage.

Barrie Thorne with Marilyn Yalom, eds. *Rethinking the Family: Some Feminist Questions,* Revised edition (Boston, MA: Northeastern University Press, 1992). Varied strains of feminism speak to issues in contemporary families.

Kath Weston. *Families We Choose: Lesbians, Gays, Kinship,* 2nd Edition. (New York, NY: Columbia University Press, 1997). Nice analysis of San Francisco bay area notions of kinship for gays and lesbians. Should be encouragement to gays and lesbians everywhere.

Suggested Moral of Part V

Creating permanent bonds of commitment is important to many couples. Structures for doing so should not be limited to the traditional heterosexual marriage, with its specific gender roles. Many couples would benefit, personally and legally, from having options available that do not require specific gender roles and are not limited to heterosexual couples. Both members of a couple should think carefully about whether they want the traditional gender role structure, which can be oppressive to women.

Part VI

Sex and Sexuality

Introduction

RELATIONSHIPS ROOTED IN GENDER—romances and affairs, one-night stands, and marriages—clearly include sexual activity as an important component. Even when both members of a couple decide on total abstinence, they believe their decision has been made in an important area. The writers of the pieces in this section discuss sexual activity, its nature, and its very real problems.

Nozick gives an elaborate description of what he sees to be heterosexual sex; Rochlin and Baker show how our opinions about sex work their way into the language we use to talk about sex and sexuality. Steedman addresses the practice of male dominance in heterosexual sex; Mohr explains and defends the outing of gays. Frye describes her discussions with other lesbians about lesbian sex; Bassford and Bell address some of the issues raised by the presence of AIDS in society.

VI.1   Sexuality

ROBERT NOZICK

Robert Nozick has a well-developed view of sexual activity. Sexual activity with someone, he says, is the most intense way to relate to another person. Addressing himself to heterosexual sex, Nozick perceives distinct gender roles.

Another writing by Nozick from *The Examined Life* appears in Part IV.

Reading Questions

1. Would you liken the intensity of sexual activity to watching the end of a closely matched athletic contest or a suspense film, as Nozick does? Does this view suggest that an episode of sexual activity can include goals, and a possibility of "winners" and "losers"?
2. Nozick explains one traditional basic sexual script, roughly, penis, vagina, intercourse, orgasm. Is this script, in some way, central to sexual activity?
3. Is your orgasm the kind of event that can tell your partner how pleased you are with him or her, given that orgasms just happen (or, perhaps, just fail to happen)? If you don't have an orgasm, does this give your partner the message that you are *not* pleased with him or her?

THE MOST INTENSE WAY we relate to another person is sexually. Nothing so concentrates the mind, Dr. Johnson noted, as the prospect of being hanged. Nothing, that is, except sexual arousal and excitement: rising tension, uncertainty about what will happen next, occasional reliefs, sudden surprises, dangers and risks, all in a sequence of heightened attention and tension that reaches toward resolution. A similar pattern of excitement also occurs near the end of closely matched athletic contests and in suspense films. I do not say our excitement at these is at base covertly sexual. Yet the sexual is so preeminent an exemplar of the general pattern of excitement that these others also may hold sexual reverberations. However, only in sex is such intense excitement shared with the object and cause of it.

Sex is not simply a matter of frictional force. The excitement comes largely in how we interpret the situation and how we perceive the connection to the other. Even in masturbatory fantasy, people dwell upon their actions with others; they do not get excited by thinking of themselves or of themselves masturbating while thinking of themselves. What is exciting is interpersonal: how the other views you, what attitude the actions evidence. Some uncertainty about this makes it even more exciting. Just as it is difficult to tickle oneself, so too sex is better with an actual partner on the other end. (Is it the other person or the uncertainty that is crucial?)

Sex holds the attention. If any wanderings of the mind from the immediate sexual situation are permissible, it is only to other sexual fantasies. It bespeaks a certain lack of involvement to be ruminating then about one's next choice of automobile. In part, the focus of attention is on how you are touched and what you are feeling, in part on how you are touching the other person and what he or she is feeling.

At times we focus in sex upon the most minute motions, the most delicate brushing of a

---

Abridged from "Sexuality" in The Examined Life: Philosophical Meditations *(New York: Simon & Schuster). Copyright © 1989 by Robert Nozick. Reprinted by permission of Simon & Schuster.*

hair, the slow progress of the fingertips or nails or tongue across the skin, the slightest change or pause at a point. We linger in such moments and await what will come next. Our acuity is sharpest here; no change in pressure or motion or angle is too slight to notice. And it is exciting to know another is attuned to your sensations as keenly as you are. A partner's delicacy of motion and response can show knowledge of your pleasure and care about its details. To have your particular pleasures known and accepted, to linger in them for as long as you will without any rushing to another stage or another excitement, to receive another's permission and invitation to loll there and play together—*is* there such a thing as sex that is too slow?—to be told in this way that you are deserving of pleasure and worthy of it, can bring a profound sigh.

Not only are old pleasures sensitively and delicately awakened and explored, but one becomes willing to follow to somewhere new, in the hands and mouth and tongue and teeth of someone who has cared and caressed knowingly.

It is not surprising that profound emotions are awakened and expressed in sex. The trust involved in showing our own pleasures, the vulnerability in letting another give us these and guide them, including pleasures with infantile or oedipal reverberations, or anal ones, does not come lightly.

Sex is not all delicacy of knowledge and response to nuanced pleasure. The narrative that begins there, and occasionally returns, also moves along to stronger and less calibrated actions, not so much the taking of turns in attentiveness to each other's pleasures as the mutual growth of stronger and broader excitements—the move from the adult (or the infantile) to the animal. The passions and motions become fiercer and less controlled, sharper or more automatically rhythmic, the focus shifts from flesh to bones, sounds shift from moans and sighs to sharper cries, hisses, roars, mouths shift from tongue and lips to teeth and biting, themes of power, domination, and anger emerge to be healed in tenderness and to emerge yet again in ever stronger and more intense cycles.

In the arena of sex, our very strongest emotions are expressed. These emotions are not always tender and loving, though sometimes, perhaps often, they are. Such strong emotions bring equally strong ones, excited and exciting, in response. The partners see their strongest and most primitive emotions expressed and also contained safely. It is not only the other person who is known more deeply in sex. One knows one's own self better in experiencing what it is capable of: passion, love, aggression, vulnerability, domination, playfulness, infantile pleasure, joy. The depth of relaxing afterward is a measure of the fullness and profundity of the experience together, and a part of it.

The realm of sex is or can be inexhaustible. There is no limit to what can be learned and felt about each other in sex; the only limit is the sensitivity or responsiveness or creativity or daring of the partners. There always are new depths—and new surfaces—to be explored.

The one maxim is to experiment attentively: to notice what excites, to follow the other's pleasure where it is and goes, to lean into it, to play with variations around it, with stronger or more delicate pressures, in related places. Intelligence helps, too, in noticing whether what excites fits into a larger pattern or fantasy, in testing out that hypothesis and then, through congruent actions and words, sometimes ambiguous, in encouraging it. Through fresh experimentation one can bypass routinized or predictable pleasures. How nice that freedom, openness, creativity, daring, and intelligence—traits not always so amply rewarded in the larger world—bear such exceedingly sweet private fruits.

Sex also is a mode of communication, a way of saying or of showing something more tellingly than our words can say. Yet though sexual actions speak more pointedly than words, they also can be enhanced by words, words that name one's pleasure or lead ahead to greater intensity, words that narrate a fantasy or merely hint at exciting one that cannot comfortably be listened to.

Like musicians in jazz improvisation, sexual partners are engaged in a dialogue, partly scored, partly improvised, where each very attentively responds to the statements in the bodily motions of the other. These statements can be about one's own self and pleasures, or about one's partner's, or about the two of you together, or about what one would like the other to do. Whether or not they do so elsewhere in life, in sex people frequently and unconsciously do unto others as they would have others do unto them. By the placing or intensity or rate or direction of their pressures and motions they are constantly sending signals, often unawares, about what they want to receive. In manifold ways, also, some parts of the body can stand for or represent others, so that what happens, for example, at the mouth or ear (or palm or armpit or fingers or toes or bones) can intricately symbolize corresponding events elsewhere with coordinate excitement.

In verbal conversations, people speak in different voices, with different ideas, on different topics. In sexual conversation, too, everyone has a distinctive voice. And there is no shortage of new things two people can say, or older things that can be said newly or reminisced about. To speak of *conversations* here does not mean that the sole (nonreproductive) purpose of sex is communication. There is also excitement and bodily pleasure, desired for themselves. Yet these too are also important parts of the conversation, for it is through pleasurable excitement and the opening to it that other powerful emotions are brought into expression and play in the sexual arena.

In this arena, everything personal can be expressed, explored, symbolized, and intensified. In intimacy, we let another within the boundaries we normally maintain around ourselves, boundaries marked by clothing and by full self-control and monitoring. Through the layers of public defenses and faces, another is admitted to see a more vulnerable or a more impassioned you. Nothing is more intimate than showing another your physical pleasure, perhaps because we learned we had to hide it even (or especially) from our parents. Once inside the maintained boundaries, new intimacies are possible, such as

the special nature of the conversation new partners can have in bed after sex. (Might they engage in sex partly in order to have such unposed conversations?)

Is there a conflict between the desire for sexual excitement including orgasm and the deepest knowing of one's partner and oneself? A rush to immediately greater excitement, a focus upon everything else merely as a means to orgasm, would get in the way of deeply opening to another and knowing them. Everything in its proper time. The most intense excitement too can be a route to depth; people would not be so shaken by sex, so awed sometimes by what occurs, if their depths had stayed unplumbed.

Exciting for itself, orgasm also tells your partner how very pleased you are with him or her. When it takes a deeper form, when you allow yourself to become and appear totally without control, completely engulfed, you show the other, and show yourself too, the full extent of that other's power over you and of your comfort and trust in being helpless before him or her.

Pleasuring another feels best when it is an accomplishment, a surmountable challenge. Consequently, an orgasm is less satisfying to the giving partner when it comes too early or too late. Too early and it is no accomplishment, too late and only after very much effort, it states that the giving partner is not exciting and pleasing enough. The secret of success with orgasm, as with comedy, is timing.

Orgasm is not simply an exciting experience but a statement about the partner, about the connection to the partner; it announces that the partner satisfies you. No wonder partners care that it happen. Here, too, we can understand the punitive force of simultaneous orgasm, of feeling the most intense pleasure with and from the other person at the very moment that you are told and shown you intensely please him or her.

There are other statements, less about the whole person, more about parts. The penis can be made to feel a welcome entrant in the vagina; it can be kissed lovingly and unhurriedly; it can be made to feel nurturative; it can be delighted in and known for itself; in more exalted moments its fantasy is to be worshiped almost. Similarly, the sweetness and power of the vagina can be acknowledged in its own right, by tender kissing, long knowing, dwelling in the tiniest crevices and emitting those sounds this calls forth. Knowing a partner's body, meditating on the special energy of its parts without rushing anywhere else, also makes a statement the partner receives.

Unlike making love, which can be symmetrical, tender, and turn-taking all the way through, what we might (without any denigration) call "fucking" contains at least one stage where the male displays his power and force. This need not be aggressive, vicious, or dominating, although perhaps statistically it frequently slides into that. The male can simply be showing the female his power, strength, ferocity even, for her appreciation. Exhibiting his quality as a beast in the jungle, with a lion or tiger's fierceness, growling, roaring, biting, he shows (in a contained fashion) his protective strength. This display of force need not be asymmetrical, however. The female can answer (and initiate) with her own ferocity, snarls, hissing, scratching, growling, biting, and she shows too her capacity to contain and tame his ferocity. It is even more difficult to state in quite the right way matters of more delicate nuance, the special way a woman can at some point *give* herself to her partner.

In sexual intimacy, we admit the partner within our boundaries or make these more permeable, showing our own passions, capacities, fantasies, and excitements, and responding to the other's. We might diagram sexual intimacy as two circles overlapping with dotted lines. There *are* boundaries between the partners here, yet these boundaries are permeable, not solid. Hence, we can understand the oceanic feeling, the sense of merging, that sometimes occurs with intense sexual experience. This is not due merely to the excited feelings directed toward the other; it results from not devoting energy to maintaining the usual boundaries. (At climactic moments, are the boundaries dropped or are they made *selectively* permeable, lowered only for that particular person?)

Much that I have said thus far might apply to single sexual encounters, yet a sexual life has its special continuities over time. There is the extended being together over a full day or several, with repeated and varied intimacies and knowings, scarcely emerging or arising from the presence of the other with fuller knowledge and feelings fresh in memory as a springboard to new explorations. There are the repeated meetings of familiar partners who scarcely can contain their hunger for each other. There are the fuller enduring relationships of intimacy and love, enhancing the excitement, depth, and sweetness of sexual uniting and enhanced by it.

Not only can one explore in sex the full range of emotions, knowing one's partner and oneself deeply, not only can one come to know the two of you together in union, pursuing the urge to unite or merge with the other and finding the physical joy of transcending the self, not only is (heterosexual) sex capable of producing new life which brings further psychological significance to the act itself—perhaps especially saliently for women, who are able to become the carriers of life within them, with all its symbolic significance—but in sex one also can engage in metaphysical exploration, knowing the body and person of another as a map or microcosm of the very deepest reality, a clue to its nature and purpose.

Further Questions

1. If sex is communication, what exactly can be expressed through this form of activity?
2. If your mind wanders from the activity, is your side of it thereby impoverished? Explain.
3. Is it productive to think of heterosexual sex as having built-in gender roles? Is it sometimes a good idea to think of sex instead as an exchange, with no particular gender roles?

VI.2A   The Language of Sex: The Heterosexual Questionnaire

M. ROCHLIN

We can learn something about sexual activity and sexual orientation (homosexual and heterosexual) by looking into what we say about it. M. Rochlin applies the convention that we only question what we consider deviant to the issue of sexual orientation.

Reading Questions

1. Is homosexuality deviant, in need of explanation or questionable, in a way in which heterosexuality is not? Explain.
2. Answer some of the questions on the heterosexual questionnaire. (If you are not heterosexual, answer the questions on behalf of someone who is.)

1. What do you think caused your heterosexuality?

2. When and how did you decide you were a heterosexual?

3. Is it possible that your heterosexuality is just a phase you may grow out of?

4. Is it possible that your heterosexuality stems from a neurotic fear of others of the same sex?

5. If you have never slept with a person of the same sex, is it possible that all you need is a good Gay lover?

6. Do your parents know that you are straight? Do your friends and/or roommate(s) know? How did they react?

7. Why do you insist on flaunting your heterosexuality? Can't you just be who you are and keep it quiet?

8. Why do heterosexuals place so much emphasis on sex?

9. Why do heterosexuals feel compelled to seduce others into their lifestyle?

10. A disproportionate majority of child molesters are heterosexual. Do you consider it safe to expose children to heterosexual teachers?

11. Just what do men and women *do* in bed together? How can they truly know how to please each other, being so anatomically different?

12. With all the societal support marriage receives, the divorce rate is spiraling. Why are there so few stable relationships among heterosexuals?

13. Statistics show that lesbians have the lowest incidence of sexually transmitted diseases. Is it really safe for a woman to maintain a heterosexual lifestyle and run the risk of disease and pregnancy?

14. How can you become a whole person if you limit yourself to compulsive, exclusive heterosexuality?

15. Considering the menace of overpopulation, how could the human race survive if everyone were heterosexual?

16. Could you trust a heterosexual therapist to be objective? Don't you feel s/he might be inclined to influence you in the direction of her/his own leanings?

17. There seem to be very few happy heterosexuals. Techniques have been developed that might enable you to change if you really want to. Have you considered trying aversion therapy?

18. Would you want your child to be heterosexual, knowing the problems that s/he would face?

The Language of Sex: Our Conception of Sexual Intercourse   VI.2B

ROBERT BAKER

In this excerpt Robert Baker notes the asymmetry of terminology for heterosexual intercourse, reflecting active-passive gender roles. In addition, many terms for the female role in heterosexual intercourse also mean "harmed," suggesting that the man harms the woman in this type of activity.

Reading Questions

1. Why do you think so many terms for sexual intercourse can be used also to indicate harm?
2. In descriptions of sexual intercourse, the man is usually the grammatical subject and the woman is the grammatical object. Why do you think this is the case?

THERE ARE TWO PROFOUND INSIGHTS that underlie the slogan "men ought not conceive of women as sexual objects"; both have the generality of scope that justifies the universality with which the feminists apply the slogan; neither can be put as simply as the slogan. The first is that the conception of sexual intercourse that we have in this culture is antithetical to the conception of women as human beings—as persons rather than objects. (Recall that this is congruent with the fact we noted earlier that "man" can be substituted for "humanity," while "woman" cannot.)

Many feminists have attempted to argue just this point. Perhaps the most famous defender of this view is Kate Millett,[1] who unfortunately faces the problem of trying to make a point about our conceptual structure without having adequate tools for analyzing conceptual structures.

The question Millett was dealing with was conceptual—Millett, in effect, asking about the nature of our conception of sexual roles. She tried to answer this question by analyzing novels; I shall attempt to answer this question by analyzing the terms we use to identify coitus, or more technically, in terms that function synonymously

The Language of Sex: Our Conception of Sexual Intercourse. Abridged from "'Pricks and Chicks': A Plea for 'Persons'," in Philosophy and Sex, *Robert Baker and Frederick Elliston, eds. (Buffalo, NY: Prometheus Books, 1975), Reprinted by permission of the author and publisher.*

with "had sexual intercourse with" in a sentence of the form "A had sexual intercourse with B." The following is a list of some commonly used synonyms (numerous others that are not as widely used have been omitted, for example, "diddled," "laid pipe with"):

screwed
laid
fucked
had
did it with (to)
banged
balled
humped
slept with
made love to

Now, for a select group of these verbs, names for males are the subjects of sentences with active constructions (that is, where the subjects are said to be doing the activity); and names for females require passive constructions (that is, they are the recipients of the activity—whatever is done is done to them). Thus, we would not say "Jane did it to Dick," although we would say "Dick did it to Jane." Again, Dick bangs Jane, Jane does not bang Dick; Dick humps Jane, Jane does not hump Dick. In contrast, verbs like "did it with" do not require an active role for the male; thus, "Dick did it with Jane and Jane with Dick." Again, Jane may make love to Dick, just as Dick makes love to Jane; and Jane sleeps with Dick as easily as Dick sleeps with Jane. (My students were undecided about "laid." Most thought that it would be unusual indeed for Jane to lay Dick, unless she played the masculine role of seducer-aggressor.)

The sentences thus form the following pairs. (Those nonconjoined singular noun phrases where a female subject requires a passive construction are marked with a cross. An asterisk indicates that the sentence in question is not a sentence of English if it is taken as synonymous with the italicized sentence heading the column.[2]

Dick had sexual intercourse with Jane
Dick screwed Jane+

Dick laid Jane+
Dick fucked Jane+
Dick had Jane+
Dick did it to Jane+
Dick banged Jane+
Dick humped Jane+
Dick balled Jane(?)+
Dick did it with Jane
Dick slept with Jane
Dick made love to Jane

Jane had sexual intercourse with Dick
Jane was banged by Dick
Jane was humped by Dick
*Jane was done by Dick
Jane was screwed by Dick
Jane was laid by Dick
Jane was fucked by Dick
Jane was had by Dick
Jane balled Dick(?)
Jane did it with Dick
Jane slept with Dick
Jane made love to Dick
*Jane screwed Dick
*Jane laid Dick
*Jane fucked Dick
*Jane had Dick
*Jane did it to Dick
*Jane banged Dick
*Jane humped Dick

These lists make clear that within the standard view of sexual intercourse, males, or at least names for males, seem to play a different role than females, since male subjects play an active role in the language of screwing, fucking, having, doing it, and perhaps, laying, while female subjects play a passive role.

The asymmetrical nature of the relationship indicated by the sentences marked with a cross is confirmed by the fact that the form "__ed with each other" is acceptable for the sentences not marked with a cross, but not for those that require a male subject. Thus:

Dick and Jane had sexual intercourse with each other
Dick and Jane made love to each other
Dick and Jane slept with each other
Dick and Jane did it with each other

Dick and Jane balled with each other(*?)
*Dick and Jane banged with each other
*Dick and Jane did it to each other
*Dick and Jane had each other
*Dick and Jane fucked each other
*Dick and Jane humped each other
*(?)Dick and Jane laid each other
*Dick and Jane screwed each other

It should be clear, therefore, that our language reflects a difference between the male and female sexual roles, and hence that we conceive of the male and female roles in different ways. The question that now arises is, "What difference in our conception of the male and female sexual roles requires active constructions for males and passive for females?"

One explanation of the use of the active construction for males and the passive construction for females is that this grammatical asymmetry merely reflects the natural physiological asymmetry between men and women: the asymmetry of "to screw" and "to be screwed," "to insert into" and "to be inserted into." That is, it might be argued that the difference between masculine and feminine grammatical roles merely reflects a difference naturally required by the anatomy of males and females. This explanation is inadequate. Anatomical differences do not determine how we are to conceptualize the relation between penis and vagina during intercourse. Thus one can easily imagine a society in which the female normally played the active role during intercourse, where female subjects required active constructions with verbs indicating copulation, and where the standard metaphors were terms like "engulfing"—that is, instead of saying "he screwed her," one would say "she engulfed him." It follows that the use of passive constructions for female subjects of verbs indicating copulation does not reflect differences determined by human anatomy but rather reflects those generated by human customs.

What I am going to argue next is that the passive construction of verbs indicating coitus (that is, indicating the female position) can *also* be used to indicate that a person is being harmed. I am then going to argue that the metaphor involved would only make sense if we conceive of the female role in intercourse as that of a person being harmed (or being taken advantage of).

Passive constructions of "fucked," "screwed," and "had" indicate the female role. They also can be used to indicate being harmed. Thus, in all of the following sentences, Marion plays the female role: "Bobbie fucked Marion"; "Bobbie screwed Marion"; "Bobbie had Marion"; "Marion was fucked"; "Marion was screwed"; and "Marion was had." All of the statements are equivocal. They might literally mean that someone had sexual intercourse with Marion (who played the female role); or they might mean, metaphorically, that Marion was deceived, hurt, or taken advantage of. Thus, we say such things as "I've been screwed" ("fucked," "had," "taken," and so on) when we have been treated unfairly, been sold shoddy merchandise, or conned out of valuables. Throughout this essay I have been arguing that metaphors are applied to things only if what the term *actually* applies to shares one or more properties with what the term *metaphorically* applies to. Thus, the female sexual role must have something in common with being conned or being sold shoddy merchandise. The only common property is that of being harmed, deceived, or taken advantage of. *Hence we conceive of a person who plays the female sexual role as someone who is being harmed* (that is, "screwed," "fucked," and so on).

It might be objected that this is clearly wrong, since the unsigned terms do not indicate someone's being harmed, and hence we do not conceive of having intercourse as being harmed. The point about the unsigned terms, however, is that they can take both females and males as subjects (in active constructions) and thus *do not pick out the female role*. This demonstrates that we conceive of sexual roles in such a way that only females are thought to be taken advantage of in intercourse.

The best part of solving a puzzle is when all the pieces fall into place. If the subjects of the passive construction are being harmed, presumably the subjects of the active constructions are doing harm, and, indeed, we do conceive of these subjects in precisely this way. Suppose one is angry at someone and wishes to express malevolence as forcefully as possible without actually committing an act of physical violence. If one is inclined to be vulgar one can make the sign of the erect male cock by clenching one's fist while raising one's middle finger, or by clenching one's fist and raising one's arm and shouting such things as "screw you," "up yours," or "fuck you." In other words, one of the strongest possible ways of telling someone that you wish to harm him is to tell him to assume the female sexual role relative to you. Again, to say to someone "go fuck yourself" is to order him to harm himself, while to call someone a "mother fucker" is not so much a play on his Oedipal fears as to accuse him of being so low that he would inflict the greatest imaginable harm (fucking) upon that person who is most dear to him (his mother).

Clearly, we conceive of the male sexual role as that of hurting the person in the female role—but lest the reader have any doubts, let me provide two further bits of confirming evidence: one linguistic, one nonlinguistic. One of the English terms for a person who hurts (and takes advantage of) others is the term "prick." This metaphorical identification would not make sense unless the bastard in question (that is, the person outside the bonds of legitimacy) was thought to share some characteristics attributed to things that are literally pricks. As a verb, "prick" literally means "to hurt," as in "I pricked myself with a needle"; but the usage in question is as a noun. As a noun, "prick" is a colloquial term for "penis." Thus, the question before us is what characteristic is shared by a penis and a person who harms others (or, alternatively, by a penis and by being stuck by a needle). Clearly, no physical characteristic is relevant (physical characteristics might underlie the Yiddish metaphorical attribution "schmuck," but one would have to

analyze Yiddish usage to determine this); hence the shared characteristic is nonphysical; the only relevant shared nonphysical characteristic is that both a literal prick and a figurative prick are agents that harm people.

Now for the nonlinguistic evidence. Imagine two doors: in front of each door is a line of people; behind each door is a room; in each room is a bed; on each bed is a person. The line in front of one room consists of beautiful women, and on the bed in that room is a man having intercourse with each of these women in turn. One may think any number of things about this scene. One may say that the man is in heaven, or enjoying himself at a bordello; or perhaps one might only wonder at the oddness of it all. One does not think that the man is being hurt or violated or degraded—or at least the possibility does not immediately suggest itself, although one could conceive of situations where this was what was happening (especially, for example, if the man was important). Now, consider the other line. Imagine that the figure on the bed is a woman and that the line consists of handsome, smiling men. The woman is having intercourse with each of these men in turn. It immediately strikes one that the woman is being degraded, violated, and so forth—"that poor woman."

When one man fucks many women he is a playboy and gains status; when a woman is fucked by many men she degrades herself and loses stature.

Our conceptual inventory is now complete enough for us to turn to the task of analyzing the slogan that men ought not to think of women as sex objects.

I think that it is now plausible to argue that the appeal of the slogan "men ought not to think of women as sex objects," and the thrust of much of the literature produced by contemporary feminists, turns on something much deeper than a rejection of "scoring" (that is, the utilization of sexual "conquests" to gain esteem) and yet is a call neither for homosexuality or for puritanism.

The slogan is best understood as a call for a new conception of the male and female sexual roles. If the analysis developed above is correct, our present conception of sexuality is such that to be a man is to be a person capable of brutalizing women (witness the slogans "The Marines will make a man out of you!" and "The Army builds *men!*" which are widely accepted and which simply state that learning how to kill people will make a person more manly). Such a conception of manhood not only bodes ill for a society led by such men, but also is clearly inimical to the best interests of women. It is only natural for women to reject such a sexual role, and it would seem to be the duty of any moral person to support their efforts—to redefine our conceptions not only of fucking, but of the fucker (man) and the fucked (woman). . . .

NOTES

1. *Sexual Politics* (New York: Doubleday, 1971); but see also *Sisterhood Is Powerful*, ed. Robin Morgan (New York: Vintage Books, 1970).

2. For further analysis of verbs indicating copulation see "A Note on Conjoined Noun Phrases," *Journal of Philosophical Linguistics*, vol. 1, no. 2, Great Expectations, Evanston, Ill. Reprinted with "English Sentences Without Overt Grammatical Subject," in Zwicky, Salus, Binnick, and Vanek, eds., *Studies Out in Left Field: Defamatory Essays Presented to James D. McCawley* (Edmonton: Linguistic Research, Inc., 1971). The puritanism in our society is such that both of these articles are pseudoanonymously published under the name of Quang Phuc Dong; Mr. Dong, however, has a fondness for citing and criticizing the articles and theories of Professor James McCawley, Department of Linguistics, University of Chicago. Professor McCawley himself was kind enough to criticize an earlier draft of this essay. I should also like to thank G. E. M. Anscombe for some suggestions concerning this essay.

Further Questions

1. Answer some of the questions on the heterosexual questionnaire.

2. Is the "fact" that, grammatically, Dick can hump Jane but Jane cannot hump Dick due to gender roles in sex, or is this a mere grammatical matter of no importance?

3. "Prick" literally means "hurt." What does this indicate about male sexuality?

4. Did it ever occur to you that a sexual feeling, or response, might not be a positive occurrence in your life?

Who's on Top? Heterosexual Practices and Male Dominance During the Sex Act VI.3

MERCEDES STEEDMAN

Mercedes Steedman discusses "who's on top" in sexual activity in a patriarchal context. Men and women alike have ambiguous feelings about women taking sexual initiative or doing much of anything, sexually, outside the traditional sex act, intercourse.

Steedman teaches sociology at Laurentian University, Sudbury, Ontario.

Abridged from Buchbinder, Burstyn, Forbes, and Steedman: Who's on Top? The Politics of Heterosexuality, *Garamond Press, Toronto, 1987. Reprinted with the permission of Garamond Press and the author.*

Reading Questions

1. Is assertive sexual behavior in some way "unfeminine"?
2. Is it important that a man be more "knowledgeable" about sex than a woman is? If he is more "knowledgeable" about sex, what does he know that she doesn't know?
3. Is it important that women have orgasms? So important that it is sometimes a good idea for a woman to "fake" an orgasm?

. . . RECENT EVIDENCE from anatomical examination of male and female muscle construction in the genital area seems to indicate that the vasocongestion process (the engorgement of genital muscle tissue with blood) affects analogous muscles in the penile shaft and in the vaginal-labial system. The physiological processes of vasocongestion and myotonia (muscle spasm) are actually more similar for the two sexes than different.

Survey evidence has suggested that assertive sexual behaviour is still perceived as unfeminine by many women. As a result, women sacrifice sexual pleasure for fear of being perceived as "cheap." The good girl/bad girl dichotomy perpetuates the ideal of innocence as a component of femininity. Yet innocence and restraint are not effective behaviour if one is seeking to be orgasmic. Only 30 percent of Hite's sample reported orgasm through intercourse alone (Hite, 1976:229), and Seymour Fisher's study of 300 women (1972) reported a corresponding figure of only 20 percent. (Although other surveys show slightly higher figures for coital orgasm, it continues to be a minority response.) (See Fisher, 1973.)

SEXUAL POWER/SOCIAL POWER

Both men and women are asked to accept a code of social passivity for women during the act of coitus. Shere Hite comments on the contradictory message that men give here. "Although many men are very angry with women and suffer profound discomfort due to women's passivity regarding sex—possibly because of buried feelings of guilt and defensiveness, knowing that women are being exploited—most men do not overtly connect this with the need for improving women's status. Most men prefer to think that the problem is simply a lingering vestige of 'Victorian morality'—and prefer to believe that somehow women can be sexually 'free' even though they are not also economically and politically free" (Hite, 1981:736). As long as women remain economically dependent on men, it is risky for them to challenge or threaten men's masculinity in the bedroom. So there is collusion between men and women. Rubin encountered this attitude in her interviews with working-class wives: "One thing I know he likes is that he taught me mostly all I know about sex, so that makes him feel good." Rubin commented: "That seems a strange thing to say when you were married for some years before." The woman replied, "Yeah, I guess you'd think so. Well, you know, he likes to feel that way so why shouldn't he, and why shouldn't I let him?" (Rubin, 1976:142).

In addition, men and women alike continue to feel ambiguous about women's sexual aggression. Few studies have observed the man's reaction to a woman's assertiveness in the bedroom. Hunt's 1974 survey suggests that the norms for women's passivity are changing; he found that women did engage in a greater variety of sexual behaviour than they had some 20 years ago, but their comfort level in doing so seemed closely linked to their education, religiosity, urbanism, income, and age.[1] Allgeier and Fogel's 1978 study of coital positions and sex roles suggests that the changes observed by Hunt remain superficial. Their study of middle-class men and women found that "females rated the woman as dirtier, less respectable, less moral, less good, less desirable as a wife and less desirable as a mother when she was on top than when she was beneath the man during intercourse" (Allgeier and Fogel, 1978:589). Women (but not men) discriminated against the woman-on-top position, despite research evidence that suggests that women enjoy a higher orgasmic response rate when they are on top. A study of American university students conducted by Clinton Jessor (1978) found that women believed men would be "turned off" by women's sexual assertiveness, despite evidence that suggested the opposite to be true (Jessor, 1978:118–28). A woman's femininity is still partly perceived as residing in her receptivity, not in her control. Interestingly, this perception seems to influence women more than men. It would seem that the traditional dictates of appropriate, moral sex behaviour continue to outweigh reason and the dictates of "liberated" sexuality.

The thing is, there is more at stake here than a good orgasm. Men and women alike are caught up in the view that women must remain the standard-bearers for morally correct behaviour in our society, while pornography pushes the opposite view—that women are sexual aggressors and whores. Men and women alike live with these contradictory conceptions of women's sexuality, and the consequences are often confusing for both. One man said to Lillian Rubin: "It isn't that I mind her letting me know when she wants it, but she isn't very subtle about it. I mean, she could let me know in a nice, feminine way" (Rubin, 1976:143). Referring to oral sex, one respondent stated, "No, Alice isn't that kind of girl. Jesus, you shouldn't ask questions like that. She wasn't brought up to go for all that fancy stuff. ... There's plenty of women out there to do that kind of stuff with. You can meet them in any bar any time you want to. You don't have to marry those kind" (Rubin, 1976:141). The "liberated" sexuality of the eighties remains a cloak for traditional views of sexuality—and control of women. This control of women is maintained by the active suppression of their sexuality, by the ignoring of their sexuality, or by the rationalization of women's inability to reach orgasm

in the traditional sex act, and by a medicalized language that labels women's (and men's) behavior as "dysfunctional." "Sexual liberation" may have brought in some new rules, but the game remains the same.

Language further confuses the issue. The symbols and verbal clues we use ostensibly communicate real experience, yet they serve to maintain a certain image of sex. For example, the word "foreplay" suggests a prelude to a main event—penetration and orgasm. This language reinforces a conception of the sex act as sequential behaviour. A term such as "impotence" conveys a message about male sexual power (or the lack of it), and links men's power to their ability to maintain an erection. The public representation of the sensual intervenes in the intimate relations of the couple. Masculine dominance is reaffirmed in the erotic imagery of advertising and pornography. As the unreal becomes real, our perceptions of the sexes are distorted. The ad in *Penthouse* magazine for a life-size doll (called "Heaven") epitomizes this fantasy view of sexual experience: "Heaven has only one function in life, to please you, ... and her only passion is your endless pleasure, your total release!" The ad goes on to say, "In her sultry tones, she'll marvel at your body, plead for mercy when you hurt her, purr from the pleasure you give her and moan with ecstasy the instant she takes your manhood into her warm, willing mouth."[2] The image of feminine sexual submission portrayed here may seem extreme and distorted, but it does reinforce the point that male power is legitimized in popular sexual imagery, and that little room is accorded to female sexual expression.

The masculine dominance of sexual imagery continues to influence our conception of sexual arousal. Sexual images of women are usually constructed for and by the ignorant male observer, to serve as stimulants for solitary sex. As a result they portray women in passive and often vulnerable poses. They present an image of sexual arousal in women that is impossible to duplicate in the actual act of coitus. However, when women's sexual behaviour is perceived as assertive, as in the image of engulfment of the penis by the vagina, it is usually portrayed by pornographic imagery as threatening and castrating. The affirmation of female sexual power remains limited to images constructed by feminist cultural workers, and therefore outside the mainstream. The images that "teach" women what their sexual body language should be are the images of a masculine culture. Pornography, recently challenged by feminists, requires our serious examination for, as Roz Coward so succinctly puts it, "Pornography as a representation of the sexual sets up, reinforces, and sexualizes certain behaviors and certain images as erotic and sexual" (Coward, 1982:9–21).

Despite the expectation of intimacy during the sex act, the two sexes remain strangers. Many men remain uncertain of women's behaviour during the sex act; they often misinterpret the signals given by the woman. Hite reports men's accounts of how they know their partner has had an orgasm: "all the women I've ever known have uncontrollable erection of their nipples when they climax"; "she rapidly moves her hips, makes a sound deep in her throat, and smiles"; "she will become short-breathed and many times will dig her fingernails into my shoulders" (Hite, 1981:637–38). While these descriptions may accurately portray arousal states in women, they in no way represent orgasmic behaviour. . . .

The "discovery" of the female orgasmic potential has not served to free women from sexual repression, for this "discovery" has occurred within a climate of masculine dominance. What this has often meant, in effect, is that a woman's orgasm is used as an indicator of her partner's success as a lover. Given this, it is not surprising that 53 percent of Shere Hite's female informants reported "faking" orgasm at least some of the time (Hite, 1976:257). When a partner's manhood is at stake, a woman does not in fact have ownership of her orgasmic response (any

more than she has control over her economic life). Working-class women, more vulnerable to the dictates of men's egos, are quick to assess the significance of this. "I rarely have climaxes. But if it didn't bother my husband it wouldn't bother me. I keep trying to tell him that I know it is not his fault, that he's really a good lover. I keep telling him it's something the matter with me, not with him. But it scares me because he doesn't believe it, and I worry he might leave me for a woman who will have climaxes for him" (Rubin, 1976:152). . . .

NOTES

1. Hunt (1974:198); see also Petras (1978), for a review of these findings.

2. This ad often appears in *Penthouse*, under the title "Heaven Can't Wait."

BIBLIOGRAPHY

Allgeier, Elizabeth Rice, and Arthur F. Fogel. 1978. "Coital Positions and Sex Roles: Responses to Cross Sex Behavior in Bed." *Journal of Consulting and Clinical Psychology* 46 (no. 3):589.

Coward, R. 1982. "Sexual Violence and Sexuality." *Feminist Review* II (summer): 9–21.

Fisher, Seymour. 1973. *Understanding the Female Orgasm.* New York: Bantam.

Hite, Shere. 1976. *The Hite Report: A Nationwide Study on Female Sexuality.* New York: Macmillan.

Hite, Shere. 1981. *The Hite Report on Male Sexuality.* New York: Dell.

Hunt, Morton. 1974. *Sexual Behaviour in the 1970's.* Chicago: Playboy Press.

Jessor, Clinton J. 1978. "Male Responses to Direct Verbal Sexual Initiatives of Females." *Journal of Sex Research* 14 (no. 2):118–128.

Petras, J. 1978. *The Social Meaning of Human Sexuality.* Boston: Allyn & Bacon.

Rubin, Lillian Breslow. 1976. *Worlds of Pain.* New York: Basic Books.

Further Questions

1. Does male sexuality that is too much centered on penis performance run the risk of becoming too much oriented toward a goal and too isolated from other areas of human life?
2. Is the ideal human male always "ready" for sexual performance, whether or not he chooses to take the opportunity to perform?
3. Might sexuality be productively used in expressing attitudes and feelings other than male control or in playful or cooperative activity with one's partner?

The Outing Controversy: Privacy and Dignity in Gay Ethics   VI.4

RICHARD MOHR

Richard Mohr defends "outing" of gays and lesbians, making their sexual orientation publicly known: Outing is not a violation of a right to privacy because the secret of sexual orientation is not something covered by a right to privacy. In particular, a gay person who commits himself to keeping the secret of another gay person sacrifices the dignity of openness about gay existence which means being able to talk about what he believes is not vile and disgusting.

Mohr is Professor of Philosophy at the University of Illinois (Urbana) and, as an intellectual presence in North America, has been instrumental in bringing gay issues out of the closet.

Reading Questions

1. Does Mohr's distinction between sexual behavior, which is something an individual can claim as private, and sexual orientation, which is made known when an individual is "outed," sufficient for him to claim that no right to privacy need be violated when an individual is "outed"?
2. Is Mohr successful in showing that a gay who keeps his orientation a secret makes the secret dirty and devalues himself as a person?
3. Is Mohr correct in maintaining that a gay person who keeps the secret of another gay's orientation sacrifices his own dignity as a human being?

Mr. Naimy was helping pull the casket from the hearse, when his friend's father begged him to tell a relative that he had died of anything but AIDS. And please, emphasize that he was not gay.

"I told him I couldn't lie any more."[1]

Abridged from Chapter One of Gay Ideas *by Richard D. Mohr. Copyright © 1992 by Richard D. Mohr. Reprinted by permission of Beacon Press, Boston.*

I. DEFINITION AND THESES

"Outing" is making publicly acknowledged the sexual orientation of a homosexual without regard to whether the person is willing to have this information publicly acknowledged. It is making publicly acknowledged what most lesbians and gay men wish to be kept secret—their identity, what they are, possibly who they are. Usually outing will simply make a person's sexual orientation publicly known, but where a person's gayness is already publicly known but not publicly acknowledged—as in the case of the "open secret"—outing will disrupt the codes of silence that block public acknowledgment of gay lives.

With few exceptions, outing has been opposed in the gay press, and (to my knowledge) it has been universally opposed within the national gay litigative and political communities, including the National Gay and Lesbian Task Force. Others too have weighed in against outing: Fran Lebowitz, Mike Royko, Miss Manners, Randy Shilts, Barbara Bush, Eric Bentley, Joan Rivers, Jane Rule, Madonna, the National Organization of Women, and congressional anti-gay ringleader Representative William Dannemeyer.[2] And emotions run high. Fran Lebowitz, whose buddy Malcom Forbes was outed posthumously, calls outing "despicable" and "beneath contempt."[3]

II. PRIVACY VERSUS SECRECY

The most common argument deployed against outing is that outing violates the outed person's right to privacy. But, at heart, this argument, not much more than a slogan, confuses privacy and secrecy. Privacy, taken in a moral sense and put broadly, is control over the access that others have to one. Secrecy, broadly, is the intentional concealment of something, usually information. Control of access is the core of privacy; hiding is the core of secrecy.[4]

Further, when privacy is held to apply to something in a normative sense, the application in turn invokes certain norms. Indeed, any act, possession, or relation that is private *in a normative sense* invokes a right to it, a right barring unwanted access to it by others. Thus, not surprisingly, the term "privacy" occurs most frequently in the phrase "right to privacy." So when I say, for instance, that some occurrence of a sexual act is private (and mean thereby more than the simple description that it was performed out of sight), the act is covered by a right to privacy. No one, especially the state, can claim a right to spy on it or to prohibit its occurrence.[5]

III. GAY SECRECY AND GAY PRIVACY: THE CONTENT OF THE ALLEGED RIGHT AGAINST OUTING

Although normative privacy and secrecy overlap, there simply is no normative privacy, no content to the right to privacy, that covers the secret that is the closet. I will argue that no legitimate gay privacy interest is violated by making public the secret of someone's sexual orientation.

When I tell someone that someone else who does not want to be known as a homosexual is a homosexual, I convey a secret. That which is hidden is revealed. Metaphorically, I open the person's closet door to another, who sees the person inside as homosexual. It is the person's sexual orientation that I am revealing. I am saying that the person is someone whose erotic energies and sexual desires are directed toward members of the same biological sex as the person.

But the door that I open is not the door to the person's bedroom or to a cubicle at the baths. I am not revealing, making unhidden, the secrecy of the person's sexual *behavior*. I am not reporting, for instance, what could only have been gotten through spying, stealth, or coercion. I may simply have seen the person as a regular at a gay bar, or participating in a gay pageant or gay pride parade, or hanging out in gay areas of town, or working in a campaign for an openly gay candidate, or I may have read his name in gay newspapers. This catalog of "maybes" is not random. They are public events in which one Oliver Sipple participated prior to his thwarting a 1975 assassination attempt on President Gerald Ford. They are public events that a California appellate court cited as more than sufficient to dismiss summarily an invasion of privacy suit that Sipple lodged against the *San Francisco Chronicle,* whose columnist Herb Caen had undeniably implied that the ex-marine hero was gay.[8]

Vito Russo puts the distinction between sexual action and sexual identity nicely: "When I say my brother and his wife are heterosexual, that doesn't mean I'm talking about their sex lives. Likewise, when we say someone is gay, we're talking about *sexual orientation,* not their sexual activity. It's not our fault that every time someone says 'gay,' people think 'sex.' That's *their* twisted problem."[11] Moreover, when I say that Sally and Steve are married and that *those* are their children—claims that no one would think were invasions of privacy—I have actually conveyed more information and grounds for inferences about their actual sexual behavior than if I report that someone is gay. For the marriage commits the couple to having had intercourse, the consummation of marriage—that without which marriages are not marriages in Western civilization. And their children's existence presumptively implicates them as having left themselves open to HIV transmission in their sexual behavior. But the marriage and the children are completely compatible with Steve being entirely gay: his sex acts may have been possible only because he was fantasizing about having sex with a guy—although too, of course, he may never actually have done that.

It is sexual acts, and derivatively talk of them, not sexual orientations, that are protected by privacy. The reporting of sexual orientation does not violate any of the senses of privacy that are legitimately invoked in sexual matters. As we have seen, it does not violate privacy in its most central dimension as what is not to be spied on.[12] Nor obviously does it, like rape, violate rights to bodily integrity, which constitute another central part of our conception of normative privacy. Nor

does such reportage prevent one from fulfilling the crucial role that sexual behavior plays in central, personally affecting values: as the chief portal to ecstasy, as recurrent natural need, and as the near occasion of, undergirding for, and necessary prompt to marital love. Such central, personally affecting values are values that make up the private in the sense of the personal.[13] Nor does the reporting of sexual orientation violate privacy viewed as necessary sanctuary and repose in sexual behavior. Open gays have as much sanctuary and repose in their nonintruded on, nonreported on sex acts as closet cases do. All the senses of sexual privacy that are relevant to gays—the status of not being spied on, the integrity of the body, the importance of personally affecting values, and the need for sanctuary—all these were in fact violated by the Supreme Court's decision in *Bowers v. Hardwock,* which upheld against constitutional privacy challenge ten-year prison sentences for consensual "homosexual sodomy" performed in ones own bedroom.[14] But none of them is violated by outing.

IV. THE FORM OF THE ALLEGED RIGHT AGAINST OUTING

In addition to the failure of the alleged right against outing to be covered in its content by normative privacy, the right in question also has difficulties of form. Note that this putative right is not simply a garden-variety immunity right against others, that is, a right *not to be coerced by others* to do or not do something. In particular, the alleged right is not an unobjectionable immunity right against self-incrimination. For the outer is not forcing the outee to say anything about himself that he does not want to say. The outee is free to tell the truth, tell a lie, or remain silent. Indeed, all three options have been exercised by those outed. Rather, the alleged "no outing" right, unlike any common immunity right, is asserted as a positive demand-claim, that is, a right *to coerce others* to do or not do something. Specifically, the alleged right is a demand-claim that a specific person keep from repeating what he in fact knows about the closet case's identity—a right, that is, morally to place a gag order on someone. That the right asserted has both the general structure of a positive demand-claim and the specific form of a gag order should make it highly suspect.

A gag order squelches speech and so makes the purported right suspect as a direct violation of freedom of speech. There are, of course, culturally and constitutionally standard exceptions to rights of free speech: obscenity, slander (saying damaging falsehoods about a person), libel (printing damaging falsehoods about a person), and fighting words (those words that automatically, precognitively incite the hearer to strike out at the speaker present to hand). But none of these exceptions applies to outing.

. . . Third parties—parties with whom I have no contractual agreements—have no right to demand things of me. They cannot demand that I limit my independence—in the case of outing, my speaking and printing—for their sake even to the point of saving their lives. To claim that they can is to invert the totality of moral opinion of the West and to constitutionalize the Marxist view that my abilities exist simply as instruments to fulfill the needs of other people, whoever they may be.

The Secret's requirement that its keeper degrade himself means that, even if one could argue that the closet is a form of legitimate self-defense against unjust discrimination—could argue, that is, that there is no *duty* to come out, so that I cannot insist that you on your own come out—you still cannot insist that I keep your secret. For to require that keeping is to require that the out person do a double injustice to himself—to degrade himself and to force him to commit his life to the very values that keep him oppressed. The gay person who keeps another gay person's dirty little secret degrades himself, does an injustice to himself by going along with rather than resisting the values that oppress gays.

The web of omissions and commissions entailed in maintaining The Secret does not leave its keeper as an innocent bystander, who merely observes the immorality of others without participating in or enhancing it. The openly gay keeper of The Secret is morally *not* like those who working the fields, simply observed in the distance trains carrying Jews to the East; rather, the keeper is like those who, while not setting the trains in motion, nevertheless voluntarily serviced the trains on their way to the East.

IX. DIGNITY VERSUS HAPPINESS

An examination of the types of values variously lost and protected by the closet will show all the more clearly the moral permissibility of outing and the expectation that the gay person, living morally, will indeed out others. The closet case tries to assure his happiness by maintaining his closet. He collects nice antiques, buys nice clothes, drinks nice wines, and takes fun vacations that he might not be able to afford if he were openly gay. And he seeks out the regard of others. Regard feels nice. Love feels nice. But regard is not respect. One can have a warm regard for a painting. One can even love it. But one does not respect a painting. People have warm regard, even love, for their pets, but few people respect them. What the closet case does in maintaining his closet is to barter away his self-respect, his worthiness for respect, his dignity, for happiness, regard, and nonrespectful love.

To accept the closet is to have absorbed society's view of gays, to accept insult so that one avoids harm. Thereby one becomes a simulacrum—a deceptive substitute—of a person. One seems to be a moral agent with ends of one's own and an ability to revise them, but one really is simply a puppet to the values of society—the equivalent of the perpetually deferential "housewife" (of stereotype) who has no views but her husband's and who eventually loses even the ability to see things through any other eyes than his. To accept the closet is to be at best the "happy slave" (of stereotype) committed to the institution of slavery in the way a dog is committed to his food bowl.

Life in the closet is morally debased—and morally debasing. It frequently requires lying, but it always requires much more. Dan Bradley, president of the Legal Services Corporation under President Carter, elaborates:

> Always there was the coverup: Arranging for women with whom I was friendly and had shared my secret to brag about my virility to F.B.I. agents making a routine background check; keeping up a macho front with male colleagues; making sure I had a female escort for parties, and worrying about how to deal with homosexual issues in the legal services program. . . .
>
> The web of deceit I had so consciously and meticulously woven over the years made it possible for me to rationalize whatever I had to do to protect myself. You can rationalize the lies, the deceptions or whatever. There is no end of it.[37]

The life as lie chiefly entails a devolution of the person as person, as moral agent. The whiteness of the individual lies might be forgiven as self-defense, but the dirtiness of the secret that the lies maintain cannot be. The dirt is the loss of self, of personhood, the loss of that which makes human life peculiarly worth protecting to begin with.

The secret that the closet case wants to force on others is not a secret that is unique or peculiar to the individual (say, the secret that he really is the author whose nom de plume graces the dustjacket of many a mystery novel). Rather, the imposed secret is about his status, a status that he views as abject and that he shares with the others who are supposed to keep the secret for him. So, in abiding by the convention to keep the secret, the keeper commits to the view of gays that the convention presupposes: that gays are loathsome and disgusting, to be kept from sight, nauseating if touched or seen, filth always in need of being flushed away.

This abject condition is quite remote from valued privacy. The philosopher Ferdinand Schoeman has pointed out that violations of privacy are experienced similarly to violations of sacred objects and that the sharing of a privacy is like the revelation, in ritual, of a sacred objet. Outside

their religious context sacred objects may be quite humble, say, mere dollops of flour or a few bound twigs, the commercial value of which may be as little as nothing. Still, their violations are experienced as affronts, defilements, and pollutions.[38] But the closet case inverts this moral structure. The closet case and the society whose values he accepts do not view his violation as a defilement and pollution. Rather, he and society view his very existence—him—as an affront, as defilement and pollution. And his revelation of himself to his sacred band—his blood family—is not a wonderment but (he supposes) a horror.

The convention of The Secret would omit the openly gay person to a similar vision of gay people and so commit him to give up his own dignity for the happiness of the closeted gay person. To do that is the very inversion of moral life, in which nobility of character, as in the case, for example, of Freedom Riders, lies in sacrificing one's happiness so that dignity—one's own or others'—might be asserted. This is what civil disobedience does, yet the inverse does not hold. A person cannot be morally compelled to be debasedly servile, to sacrifice his dignity for the happiness of others. I cannot be morally compelled to eat dog shit even if to do so would comfort the lives of those who otherwise would commit suicide.

There are two exceptions to dignity-based outing. The first is if the outing violates some right of the outee. I cannot legitimately advance my dignity at the expense of other people's rights. But we have seen that there are no likely candidates for such rights that outing purportedly violates. And this is crucially important: Even if my actions in outing someone are a necessary condition for someone *else* violating the outee's rights—say, his right not to be harmed or his right not to be discriminated against—still, *my actions* are not violations of his rights any more so than are his great-great-grandfather's siring actions, which were also a necessary condition for the violations. Minus the siring or minus the outing, true, the violation would not have occurred, but the violator of the outee's rights is the bigoted employer, or whoever caused the violation, not those who merely provided some of the millions upon millions of necessary conditions for the violation.

The second circumstance that would make outing morally impermissible is if particular acts of outing objectively cause an overall loss of dignity—if, that is, dignity lost in others is greater than the dignity to be had both by the potential outer living morally and by the increase in overall gay dignity that attends outing's destruction of the code of silence that degrades all gays. This condition will rarely be met. Still, if it were the case (as it currently is not) that the government was shooting gays, I would morally be expected to suspend my dignity temporarily so that the current and prospective dignity of others is made possible.

Notice what will not count here against outing: any assertion of individual dignity that is dependant on upholding or giving effective voice to the prejudices of others or to other forces that degrade gays in general will not count toward an exception to outing. To lose a child in a custody case for prejudicial reasons is, to be sure, to suffer an indignity, but to insist on being closeted to protect one's parenting is simply to give effective voice to those social conditions that degrade gays in general. Or again, to remain a closeted member of a racial or ethnic minority community that despises gays is to avoid an indignity to be sure, but it also gives effective voice to prejudicial forces in the minority community that degrade all gays. A dignity may outweigh a dignity, as a pleasure or measure of happiness may not. But because the indignity bred and maintained by the convention of The Secret is so great and pervasive, it is unlikely that any individual indignity suffered will cancel the dignity gained in the convention's destruction through outing.

XII. OUTING AS "LIVING IN THE TRUTH"

In not leading a life of lies, in simply "living in the truth,"[44] one will make known the sexual orientation of others because one does not think, and rightly does not think, that there is anything wrong with being gay and because one will not play along with conventions that degrade gay existence, even if they are the conventions of gays themselves as a community of self-hating and self-oppressing persons. Self-hatred is the glue that holds together the convention of The Secret, which in turn generates the shame that underwriters self-hatred.

The core question in the outing debate is, "Whose values shall count?" Are the bigot's values to count—even or especially when bigots are the overwhelming majority? Or are the clues of pride and dignity as registered in the lives of openly gay people to count?

Vito Russo puts the core question thus: "What [outers are] saying is that if being gay is *not* disgusting, is *not* awful, then why can't we talk about it? After all, it's not an insult to call someone gay. Is it?"[45] Similarly: "The principle is really very simple. Either being gay is OK or it isn't. And allowing homosexuality to take its place as a normal part of the human sexual spectrum requires ceasing to treat it as a dirty little secret."[46]

Like civil disobedience, outing violates a community's conventions so that the community may come to live more morally. It violates a local or specific community-defining value in order that it may jog to foreground consciousness a community's higher or more overarching values, which it has failed to apply consistently. In this way, the culture's determinate but not fully realized general values are made concrete in the way people live. Outing violates a convention built on self-hatred as *the* lived experience among gays, the internalization of society's viewing of gays as scum. Outing appeals to and banks on a moral bet that, although many gays feel like they are shit and may even think they are shit, still they know they are not shit. Outing begins to show forth, in the proud gay person who refuses to participate in rituals of degradation, models of that knowledge in concrete lived form.

Those who have supported outing have usually done so on the utilitarian ground that those outed—statesmen, movie stars, and the like—will provide positive role models for gays, especially young gays. I suggest that these supporters of outing have picked the wrong models to prize. Outed people will frequently be spiritual basket cases in consequence of the effects of long years in the closet. Other people would not, or at least should not, want these people as models for their soul—however well known, bred, or heeled.[47]

Still, it will tend to be the case that famous people are outed simply because they are famous, not because they are especially worthy of punishment, owing, say, to their being hypocrites, oppressors of gays, whatever. The gayness of the famous is newsworthy. And gays need not feel embarrassed at contribution to the news. Indeed, the news has constitutional import. One of the tests for a group having enhanced rights under the equal protection clause is whether the group is subject to general incapacities that might legitimately be expected to warrant legal distinctions being drawn with respect to the group in general: "What differentiates sex from such nonsuspect statuses as intelligence or physical disability . . . is that the sex characteristic frequently bears no relation to ability to perform or contribute to society."[48] So if presidents, senators, CEOs, Nobel laureates, and such like are gay, that is important news whatever their political leanings, however dirty or clean their hands, and however mangled their self-perceptions.

But the gayness of average people is important news too. The California appellate court that heard Mr. Sipple's case pointed out several ways in which Mr. Sipple—just a typical, unassuming citizen—was newsworthy in his homosexuality. He was a gay ex-marine. That is relevant to military policy. It appeared that a thank-you note from President Ford to Sipple for saving the president's life was blocked or at least delayed because this man was gay. That is relevant to considerations of justice and decency. But further, Mr. Sipple, although just an average joe, had done lots of things to develop the gay community, through his work in Harvey Milk's campaigns, through his support work in the San Francisco drag ball scene, by participating in gay pride parades. And that is newsworthy too: Ordinary people can do extraordinary things. Indeed, Sipple's name had appeared several times in the gay press. Those opposed to outing can insulate such people as Sipple from outing only by condescendingly considering them "hapless nobodies."[49]

Further, when gays do bad things, especially to other gays, that unfortunately too is news and the evildoers are out-worthy for that reason—to clarify how the machinery of injustice operates—even if not for vindictive reasons. To take a personal example, a closeted colleague of mine voted against me on a fellowship matter in order to distance himself from me in the eyes of our department. Telling a verifiable story that this injustice had occurred would require making the person's sexual orientation known. Indeed, quite generally it is relevant to know that someone is leading a life as lie, is self-hating, is failing of his moral duties to himself. For such news ought to affect our understanding of the moral texture of the social universe, the dominant strata of which maintain their position in significant part by promoting self-hatred in minority groups while at the same time denying that self-hatred exists, so that, in turn, it will not count as evidence that oppression exists. My point then is that, even when vindictiveness and the urge to punish are firmly laid aside, it will still be the case that a person living in the truth will out nearly everyone he or she knows to be gay.

The comfort that the closet provides society stokes the convention of The Secret, by which in turn gays do most of the maintenance work in their own oppression. It is the shame-inducing Secret that is the chief dynamo of the closet's magnetic attraction. As long as The Secret is intact, the few people who are out are aberrant (even by gay standards) and are easily managed by society through the mechanisms of more and less subtle discriminations (a queer bashing here, a grant not given there, whatever does the trick). Being out, although necessary for gay progress, is nowhere near sufficient to achieve gay progress as long as the machinery by which gays are oppressed is left in place. Being out voluntarily is good. But no substantial gay progress will be made until the shame-enhancing Secret is abandoned. So gay progress requires both being publicly out and living in the truth, a necessary concomitant of which is that closet cases will be outed.

Some have thought that simply ending The Secret will itself usher in the gay millennium.[68] But it is not clear that ending The Secret alone will have the dramatic transformational effect that, say, the media's ending the secret about heterosexual liaisons seemed to have had on divorce and family law reform. For such reform, like currently secrecy-stalled euthanasia reform, provides options that the vast majority of people would probably want as permitted courses for themselves. It is far less clear that the vast majority of people want gay relations as a permitted option for themselves. More modestly, I think that, as a political strategy, outing is a way of getting gay people up to political speed, so that gays may play on an even field with other minorities and interest groups in the mechanisms of democracy. Ending the shame-drenched Secret would free the gay community from having to fight with one arm tied behind its back and much of its soul mired in self-hatred.

NOTES

1. *New York Times,* March 30, 1991, p. 8

2. *New York Times* March 27, 1990, p. A11; April 12, 1990, p. A11; *The Advocate,* #549, April 24, 1990, p. 37; #555, July 17, 1990, p. 9; #576, May 7, 1991, p. 50; Jane Rule, "Closet-Burning," from *Outlander* (Tallahassee, Fla.: Naiad, 1981), pp. 201–202.

3. *OutWeek* (New York), March 18, 1990, p. 4; *The Advocate,* #554, July 3, 1990, p. 63.

4. Here I am following Sissela Bok, *Secrets: On the Ethics of Concealment and Revelation* (New York: Pantheon, 1982), pp. 5–14.

5. For more detail, see Richard Mohr, *Gays/Justice—A Study of Ethics, Society, and Law* (New York: Columbia University Press, 1988), pp. 96–97.

8. *Oliver W. Sipple v. The Chronicle Publishing Co.,* 201 Cal. Rprt. 665

11. Vito Russo, letter, *Village Voice,* April 24, 1990, p. 4.

12. For elaborations and defenses of some of the claims about privacy in this paragraph, see Mohr, *Gays/Justice,* pp. 95–114.

13. It was this sense of privacy, e.g., that was held to protect abortion as a privacy right (*Roe v. Wade,* 410 U.S. 113, 152–53 [1973]).

37. *New York Times,* March 31, 1982, p. 24.

38. Ferdinand Schoeman, "Privacy and Intimate Information," in *Philosophical Dimensions of Privacy: An Anthology,* ed. Ferdinand Schoeman (Cambridge: Cambridge University Press, 1984), p. 406

44. In his unpublished 1991 paper "The Closet and the Ethics of Outing" (further information about this paper is available from Richard Mohr). Jerry McCarthy gives an extended account of the relevance to gay life of Vaclav Havel's vision of "living in the truth."

45. Russo, letter, p. 4.

46. Steve Berry, "Liz Smith Mon Amour," *OutWeek,* May 16, 1990, p. 44.

47. The editorial policy of *OutWeek* originally defended its outing of celebrities on the theory that such outing provided to gays, especially young ones, positive role models (*OutWeek,* #38, March 18, 1990, p. 4). Editor Michelangelo Signorile later gave a different, more interesting argument, one that moves in the spirit of John Stuart Mill's belief that the lives of alcoholics, drug addicts, and others who have made a botch of their lives, even in their botches, advance social utility—by showing others how *not* to live. In this new mode, Signorile asserts: "I agree that [those filled with shame and dragged out of the closet] are not going to be a good role model. But . . . they'll be a bad role model, which is very important too. The message will be 'Don't let this happen to you'" (*New York,* May 14, 1990, p. 94). If utilitarian arguments are called for, this is a pretty good one, although it should be remembered that increasing social utility is not enough to override right. So the argument will not succeed if there is a right to the closet.

48. *Frontiero v. Richarson,* 411 U.S. 677, 686 (1973).

49. "Many readers would quickly agree that snitching on other hapless nobodies is mean, pointless, and bad for the gay community in the long run" (Madsen, "Tattle," p. 42).

68. On secrets ended, see I Gabriel Rotello, "Tactical Considerations," *OutWeek,* May 16, 1990, p. 53.

Further Questions

1. Heterosexuals don't generally think of their sexual orientation as a private matter, something that others should respect as a secret. Is there a difference between heterosexuality and homosexuality that makes homosexuality a person's own private matter?

2. Sometimes someone can only keep his job (in teaching, say, or in the military) if it is not known that he is a homosexual. Do others have a right to make known his secret under these circumstances?

3. There are still negative feelings about homosexuality on the part of many people. Suppose you are gay. Do you have a good idea about how much of these negative feelings you would be willing to put up with in exchange for the dignity of being able to live openly as a homosexual?

Lesbian "Sex"   VI.5

MARILYN FRYE

Marilyn Frye gives a candid account of her understanding of lesbian "sex," much of which applies to women's sexuality more generally. Women's sexual experience has been relatively neglected, so they have no vocabulary in which to talk about, or think through, their sexual experiences.

Frye teaches philosophy and feminist theory at Michigan State University. Her writings are based directly on her life as a woman and lesbian. Other selections by Marilyn Frye appear in Parts I and IV.

Reading Questions

1. If you are a woman (and perhaps, a lesbian) how would you count the number of "times" you have had sex?
2. Is it discouraging to learn that each sexual experience of a long-term married heterosexual couple is, on average, about eight minutes long?
3. Would heterosexual women profit by doing what Frye suggests for lesbians: Discussing what we like in the area of sex in the context of a more general discussion of our favorite sorts of experience? Would men also learn something from this kind of discussion with each other?

THE REASONS THE WORD "SEX" is in quotation marks in my title are two: One is that the term "sex" is an inappropriate term for what lesbians do, and the other is that whatever it is that lesbians do that (for a lack of a better word) might be called "sex" we apparently do damned little of it. For a great many lesbians, the gap between the high hopes we had some time ago for lesbian

Reprinted from Lesbian Philosophies, *Jeffner Allen, Ed. (Albany: State University of New York Press, 1990). Reprinted by permission of the author.*

sex and the way things have worked out has turned the phrase "lesbian sex" into something of a bitter joke. I don't want to exaggerate this: Things aren't so bad for all lesbians, or all of the time. But in our communities* as a whole, there is much grumbling on the subject. It seems worthwhile to explore some of the meanings of the relative dearth of what (for lack of a better word) we call lesbian "sex."

Recent discussions of lesbian "sex" frequently cite the finding of a study on couples by Blumstein and Schwartz,[1] which is perceived by most of those who discuss it as having been done well, with a good sample of couples—lesbian, male homosexual, heterosexual non-married, and heterosexual married couples. These people apparently found that lesbian couples "have sex" far less frequently than any other type of couple, that lesbian couples are less "sexual" as couples and as individuals than anyone else. In their sample, only about one-third of lesbians in relationships of two years or longer "had sex" once a week or more; 47 percent of lesbians in long-term relationships "had sex" once a month or less, while among heterosexual married couples only 15 percent had sex once a month or less. And they report that lesbians seem to be more limited in the range of their "sexual" techniques than are other couples.

When this sort of information first came into my circle of lesbian friends, we tended to see it as conforming to what we know from our own experience. But on reflection, looking again at what has been going on with us in our long-term relationships, the nice fit between this report and our experience seemed not so perfect after all.

*When I speak of "we" and "our communities," I actually don't know exactly who that is. I know only that I and my lover are not the only ones whose concerns I address, and that similar issues are being discussed in friendship circles and communities other than ours (as witness, e.g., discussion in the pages of the *Lesbian Connection*). If what I say here resonates for you, so be it. If not, at least you can know it resonates for some range of lesbians and some of them probably are your friends or acquaintances.

It was brought to our attention during our ruminations on this that what 85 percent of long-term heterosexual married couples do more than once a month takes on the average 8 minutes to do.[2]

Although in my experience lesbians discuss their "sex" lives with each other relatively little (a point to which I will return), I know from my own experience and from the reports of a few other lesbians in long-term relationships, that what we do that, on average, we do considerably less frequently, takes, on average, considerably more than 8 minutes to do. It takes about 30 minutes, at the least. Sometimes maybe an hour. And it is not uncommon that among these relatively uncommon occurrences, an entire afternoon or evening is given over to activities organized around doing it. The suspicion arises that what 85 percent of heterosexual married couples are doing more than once a month and what 47 percent of lesbian couples are doing less than once a month is not the same thing.

I remember that one of my first delicious tastes of old gay lesbian culture occurred in a bar where I was getting acquainted with some new friends. One was talking about being busted out of the Marines for being gay. She had been put under suspicion somehow and was sent off to the base psychiatrist to be questioned, her perverted tendencies to be assessed. He wanted to convince her she had only been engaged in a little youthful experimentation and wasn't really gay. To this end, he questioned her about the extent of her experience. What he asked was, "How many times have you had sex with a woman?" At this, we all laughed and giggled: What an ignorant fool. What does he think he means, "times?" What will we count? What's to *count*?

Another of my friends, years later, discussing the same conundrum, said that she thought maybe every time you got up to go to the bathroom, that marked a "time." The joke about "how many times" is still good for a chuckle from time to time in my life with my lover. I have no memory of any such topic providing any such merriment in my years of sexual encounters and relationships with men. It would have been very rare indeed that we would not have known how to answer the question "How many times did you do it?"

If what heterosexual married couples do that the individuals report under the rubric "sex" or "have sex" or "have sexual relations" is something that in most instances can easily be individuated into countable instances, this is more evidence that it is not what long-term lesbian couples do . . . or, for that matter, what short-term lesbian couples do.

What violence did the lesbians do their experience by answering the same question the heterosexuals answered, as though it had the same meaning for them? How did the lesbians figure out how to answer the questions "How frequently?" or "How many times?" My guess is that different individuals figured it out differently. Some might have counted a two- or three-cycle evening as one "time" they "had sex"; some might have counted it as two or three "times." Some may have counted as "times" only the times both partners had orgasms; some may have counted as "times" occasions on which at least one had an orgasm; those who do not have orgasms or have them far more rarely than they "have sex" may not have figured orgasms into the calculations; perhaps some counted as a "time" every episode in which both touched the other's vulva more than fleetingly and not for something like a health examination. For some, to count every reciprocal touch of the vulva would have made them count as "having sex" more than most people with a job or a work would dream of having time for; how do we suppose those individuals counted "times?" Is there any good reason why they should *not* count all those as "times?" Does it depend on how fulfilling it was? Was anybody else counting by occasions of fulfillment?

We have no idea how the individual lesbians surveyed were counting their "sexual acts." But this also raises the questions of how heterosexuals counted *their* sexual acts. By orgasms? By *whose* orgasms? If the havings of sex by heterosexual married couples did take on the average 8 min-

utes, my guess is that in a very large number of those cases the women did not experience orgasms. My guess is that neither the women's pleasure nor the women's orgasms were pertinent in most of the individuals' counting and reporting the frequency with which they "had sex."

So, do lesbian couples really "have sex" any less frequently than heterosexual couples? I'd say that lesbian couples "have sex" a great deal less frequently than heterosexual couples: By the criteria that I'm betting most of the heterosexual people used to count "times," lesbians don't have sex at all. No male orgasms, no "times." (I'm willing to draw the conclusion that heterosexual women don't have sex either; that what they report is the frequency with which their partners had sex.)

It has been said before by feminists that the concept of "having sex" is a phallic concept; that it pertains to heterosexual intercourse, in fact, primarily to heterosex*ist* intercourse, that is, male-dominant-female-subordinate-copulation-whose-completion-and-purpose-is-the-male's-ejaculation. I have thought this was true since the first time the idea was put to me, some 12 years ago.[3] But I have been finding lately that I have to go back over some of the ground I covered a decade ago because some of what I knew then I knew too superficially. For some of us, myself included, the move from heterosexual relating to lesbian relating was occasioned or speeded up or brought to closure by our knowledge that what we had done under the heading "having sex" was indeed male-dominant-female-subordination-copulation-whose-completion . . . and so forth and it was not worthy of doing. Yet now, years later, we are willing to answer questionnaires that ask us how frequently we "have sex," and are dissatisfied with ourselves and with our relationships because we don't "have sex" enough. We are so dissatisfied that we keep a small army of therapists in business trying to help us "have sex" more.

We quit having sex years ago, and for excellent and compelling reasons. What exactly is our complaint now?

In all these years I've been doing and writing feminist theory I have not until very recently written, much less published, a word about sex. I did not write, though it was suggested to me that I do so, anything in the SM debates; I left entirely unanswered an invitation to be the keynote speaker at a feminist conference about women's sexuality (which by all reports turned out to be an excellent conference). I was quite unable to think of anything but vague truisms to say, and very few of those. Feminist theory is grounded in experience; I have always written feminist political and philosophical analysis from the bottom up, starting with my own encounters and adventures, frustrations, pain, anger, delight, etc. Sometimes this has no doubt made it a little provincial; but it has at least had the virtue of firm connection with *someone's* real, live experience (which is more than you can say for a lot of theory). When I put to myself the task of theorizing about sex and sexuality, it was as though I *had* no experience, as though there was no ground on which and from which to generate theory. But (if I understand the terminology rightly), I have in fact been what they call "sexually active" for close to a quarter of a century, about half my life, almost all of what they call one's "adult life," heterosexually, lesbianly, and autoerotically. Surely I have experience. But I seem not to have *experiential knowledge* of the sort I need.

Reflecting on all that history, I realize that in many of its passages this experience has been a muddle. Acting, being acted on, choosing, desiring, pleasure, and displeasure all akimbo: not coherently determining and connecting with each other. Even in its greatest intensity it has for the most part been somehow rather opaque to me, not fully in my grasp. My "experience" has in general the character more of a buzzing blooming confusion than of *experience*. And it has occurred in the midst of almost total silence on the part of others about their experience. The experience of others has for the most part also been opaque to me; they do not discuss or describe it *in detail* at all.

I recall an hours-long and heated argument among some eight or ten lesbians at a party a couple of years ago about SM, whether it is okay, or not. When Carolyn and I left, we realized that in the whole time not one woman had said one concrete, explicit, physiologically specific thing about what she actually *did*. The one arguing in favor of bondage: Did she have her hands tied gently with ribbons or scarves, or harshly with handcuffs or chains? What other parts of her body were or weren't restrained, and by what means? And what parts of her body were touched, and how, while she was bound? And what liberty did she still have to touch in return? And if she had no such liberty, was it part of her experience to want that liberty and tension or frustration, or was it her experience that she felt pleased or satisfied not to have that liberty . . . ? Who knows? She never said a single word at this level of specificity. Nor did anyone else, pro or con.

I once perused a large and extensively illustrated book on sexual activity by and for homosexual men. It was astounding to me for one thing in particular, namely, that its pages constituted a huge lexicon of *words;* words for acts and activities, their sub-acts, preludes and denouements, their stylistic variation, their sequences. Gay male sex, I realized then, is *articulate*. It is articulate to a degree that, in my world, lesbian "sex" does not remotely approach. Lesbian "sex" as I have known it, most of the time I have known it, is utterly *in*articulate. Most of my lifetime, most of my experience in the realms commonly designated as "sexual" has been prelinguistic, non-cognitive. I have, in effect, no linguistic community, no language, and therefore in one important sense, no knowledge.

In situations of male dominance, women are for the most part excluded from the formulation and validation of meaning and thereby denied the means to express themselves. Men's meanings, and no women's meanings, are encoded in what is presumed to be the whole population's language. (In many cases, both the men and women assume it is everyone's language.) The meanings one's life and experience might generate cannot come fully into operation if they are not woven into language: they are fleeting, or they hover, vague, not fully coalesced, nor connected, and hence not *useful* of explaining or grounding interpretations, desires, complaints, theories. In response to our understanding that there is something going on in patriarchy that it more or less well described by saying women's meanings are not encoded in the dominant languages and that this keeps our experience from being fully formed and articulate, we have undertaken quite deliberately to discover, complete, and encode our meanings. Such simple things as naming chivalrous gestures "insulting," naming Virginia Woolf a great writer, naming ourselves women instead of girls or ladies. Coining terms like "sexism," "sexual harassment," and "incestor." Mary Daly's new book is a whole project of "encoding" meanings, and we can all find examples of our own more local encodings.*

Meanings should arise from our bodily self-knowledge, bodily play, tactile communication, the ebb and flow of intense excitement, arousal, tension, release, comfort, discomfort, pain, and pleasure (and I make no distinctions here among bodily, emotional, intellectual, aesthetic). But such potential meanings are more amorphous, less coalesced into discrete elements of a coherent pattern of meanings, of an *experience,* than any other dimensions of our lives. In fact, there are for many of us *virtually no meanings* in this realm because nothing of it is crystallized in a linguistic matrix.†

What we have for generic words to cover this terrain are the words "sex," "sexual," and "sexuality." In our efforts to liberate ourselves from the stifling, women-hating, Victorian denial that women even *have* bodily awareness, arousal, excitement, orgasms and so on, many of us actively took these words for ourselves, and claimed that we *do* "do sex" and we *are* sexual and we *have* sexuality. This has been particularly important to lesbians because the very fact of "sex" being a phallocentric term has made it especially difficult to get across the idea that lesbians are not, for lack of a penis between us, making do with feeble and partial and pathetic half-satisfactions.‡ But it seems to me that the attempt to encode our lustiness and lustfulness, our passion and our vigorous carnality in the words "sex," "sexual," and "sexuality" has backfired. Instead of losing their phallocentricity, these words have imported the phallocentric meanings into and onto experience which is not in any way phallocentric. A web of meanings which pass emotional intensity, excitement, arousal, bodily play, orgasm, passion, and relational adventure back into a semantic center in male-dominant-female-subordinate-copulation-whose-completion-and-purpose-is-the-male's-ejaculation has been so utterly inadequate as to leave us speechless, meaningless, and ironically, according to the Blumstein and Schwartz report, "not as sexual" as couples or as individuals of any other group.

Our lives, the character of our embodiment, *cannot* be mapped back onto that semantic center. When we try to synthesize and articulate it by the rules of that mapping, we end up trying to mold our loving and our passionate carnal intercourse into explosive 8-minute events. That is not the timing and ontology of the lesbian body. When the only things that count as "doing it" are those passages of our interactions which most closely approximate a paradigm that arose from the meanings of the rising and

*I picked up the word "encoding" as it is used here from the novel *Native Tongue,* by Suzette Haden Elgin (New York: Daw Books, Inc., 1984). She envisages women identifying concepts, feelings, types of situations, etc., for which there are no words in English and giving them intuitively appropriate names in a women-made language called Laadan.

† Carolyn Shafer has theorized that one significant reason why lesbian SM occasioned so much excitement, both positive and negative, is that lesbians have been starved for language—for specific, detailed, literal, particular, bodily talk with clear non-metaphorical references to parts of our bodies and the ways they can be stimulated, to acts, postures, types of touch. Books like *Coming to Power* feed that need, and call forth more words in response.

‡ Asserting the robustness and unladylikeness of our passions and actions, some of us have called some of what we do "fucking."

falling penis, no wonder we discover ourselves to "do it" rather less often than do pairs with one or more penises present.

There are many cultural and social-psychological reasons why women (in white Euro-American groups, but also in many other configurations of patriarchy) would generally be somewhat less clear and less assertive about their desires and about getting their satisfactions than men would generally be. And when we pair up two women in a couple, it stands to reason that those reasons would double up and tend to make relationships in which there is a lowish frequency of clearly delineated desires and direct initiations of satisfactions. But for all the help it might be to lesbian bodies to work past the psychological and behavioral habits of femininity that inhibit our passions and pleasures, my suggestion is that what we have never taken seriously enough is the *language* which forecloses our meanings.

My positive recommendation is this: Instead of starting with a point (a point in the life of a body unlike our own) and trying to make meanings along vectors from that point, we would do better to start with a wide field of our passions and bodily pleasures and make meanings that weave a web across it. To begin creating a vocabulary that elaborates and expands our meanings, we should adopt a very wide and general concept of "doing it." Let it be an open, generous, commodious concept encompassing all the acts and activities by which we generate with each other pleasures and thrills, tenderness and ecstasy, passages of passionate carnality of whatever duration or profundity. Everything from vanilla to licorice, from puce to chartreuse, from velvet to ice, from cuddles to cunts, from chortles to tears. Starting from there, we can let our experiences generate a finer-tuned descriptive vocabulary that maps and expresses the differences and distinctions among the things we do, the kinds of pleasures we get, the stages and styles of our acts and activities, the parts of our bodies centrally engaged in the different kinds of "doing it," and

so on. I would not, at the outset, assume that all of "doing it" is good or wholesome, nor that everyone would like or even tolerate everything this concept includes; I would not assume that "doing it" either has or should have a particular connection with love, or that it hasn't or shouldn't have such a connection. As we explain and explore and define our pleasures and our preferences across this expansive and heterogeneous field, teaching each other what the possibilities are and how to navigate them, a vocabulary will arise among us and by our collective creativity.

The vocabulary will rise among us, of course, only if we talk with each other about what we're doing and why, and what it feels like. Language is social. So is "doing it."

I'm hoping it will be a lot easier to talk about what we do, and how and when and why, and in carnal sensual detail, once we've learned to laugh at foolish studies that show that lesbians don't have sex as often as, aren't as sexual as, and use fewer sexual techniques than other folks.

NOTES

This essay first appeared in *Sinister Wisdom*, vol. 35 (Summer/Fall 1988). In its first version this essay was written for the meeting of the Society for Women in Philosophy, Midwestern Division, November, 1987, at Bloomington, Indiana. It was occasioned by Claudia Card's paper, "Intimacy and Responsibility: What Lesbians Do," (published in the Institute for Legal Studies Working Papers, Series, 2, University of Wisconsin-Madison, Law School, Madison, WI 53706). Carolyn Shafer has contributed a lot to my thinking here, and I am indebted also to conversations with Sue Emmert and Terry Grant.

1. Philip Blumstein and Pepper Schwartz, *American Couples* (New York: William Morrow and Company, 1983).

2. Dotty Calabrese gave this information in her workshop on long-term lesbian relationships at the Michigan Womyn's Music Festival, 1987. (Thanks to Terry for this reference.)

3. By Carolyn Shafer. See pp. 156–157 of my book *The Politics of Reality* (The Crossing Press, 1983).

Further Questions

  1. When someone wonders what lesbians "do" in a sexual encounter, is he or she having problems thinking about a sexual situation that contains no penis?

  2. Discussions of "having sex" apparently caused a good deal of merriment in Frye's group of lesbians. If you cannot imagine this merriment in an all-male group, is this because men take themselves too seriously in the area of sex?

  3. Would men's thinking about sex benefit from hearing about the sexual experiences of women, couched in vocabulary developed by women? Explain.

Black Sexuality: The Taboo Subject   VI.6

CORNEL WEST

Cornell West describes the social mythology regarding black sexuality. Black men and women are depicted either as sexual threats who might overpower whites or as desexed subordinates. Black sexuality must cease to be a taboo subject in discussions of racial matters.

West is Professor of Religion and Director of Afro-American Studies at Princeton University.

Reading Questions

1. What do you say to someone who views black sexuality with disgust? Is it possible for black and white Americans to be on an equal basis, yet leave the mythologizing of black sexuality in place?

2. Many black Americans manifest self-contempt and self-hatred because they won't love their own bodies. How can this be viewed as a product of white supremacy?

3. Black institutions such as families, churches, and schools resisted white supremacy, but refused to deal with black sexuality. Why was this a "Faustian pact with white America"?

"Here," she said, "in this here place, we flesh; flesh that weeps, laughs; flesh that dances on bare feet in grass. Love it. Love it hard. Yonder they do not love your flesh. They despise it. They don't love your eyes; they'd just as soon pick em out. No more do they love the skin on your back. Yonder they flay it. And O my people they do not love your hands. Those they only use, tie, bind, chop off, and leave empty. Love your hands! Love them. Raise them up and kiss them. Touch others with them, pat them together, stroke them on your face 'cause they don't love that either. *You* got to love it, *You!* . . . This is flesh I'm talking about here. Flesh that needs to be loved."

Toni Morrison, *Beloved* (1987)

AMERICANS ARE OBSESSED WITH SEX and fearful of black sexuality. The obsession has to do with a search for stimulation and meaning in a fast-paced, market-driven culture; the fear is rooted in visceral feelings about black bodies fueled by sexual myths of black women and men. The dominant myths draw black women and men either as threatening creatures who have the potential for sexual power over whites, or as harmless, desexed underlings of a white culture. There is Jezebel (the seductive temptress), Sapphire (the evil, manipulative bitch) or Aunt Jemima (the sexless, long-suffering nurturer). There is Bigger Thomas (the mad and mean predatory craver of white women), Jack Johnson (the super performer—be it in athletics, entertainment, or sex—who excels others naturally and prefers women of a lighter hue), or Uncle Tom (the spineless, sexless—or is it impotent?—sidekick of whites). The myths offer distorted, dehumanized creatures whose bodies—color of skin, shape of nose and lips, type of hair, size of hips—are already distinguished from the white norm of beauty and whose feared sexual activities are deemed disgusting, dirty, or funky and considered less acceptable.

Yet the paradox of the sexual politics of race in America is that, behind closed doors, the dirty, disgusting, and funky sex associated with black people is often perceived to be more intriguing and interesting, while in public spaces talk about black sexuality is virtually taboo. Everyone knows it is virtually impossible to talk candidly about race without talking about sex. Yet most social scientists who examine race relations do so with little or no reference to how sexual perceptions influence racial matters. My thesis is that black sexuality is a taboo subject in white and black America and that a candid dialogue about black sexuality between and within these communities is requisite for healthy race relations in America.

The major cultural impact of the 1960s was not to demystify black sexuality but rather to make black bodies more accessible to white bodies *on an equal basis*. The history of such access up to that time was primarily one of brutal white rape and ugly white abuse. The Afro-Americanization of white youth—given the disproportionate black role in popular music and athletics—has put white kids in closer contact with their own bodies and facilitated more humane interaction with black people. Listening to Motown records in the sixties or dancing to hip hop music in the nineties may not lead one to question the sexual myths of black women and men, but when white and black kids buy the same billboard hits and laud the same athletic heroes the result is often a shared cultural space where some humane interaction takes place.

This subterranean cultural current of interracial interaction increased during the 1970s and 1980s even as racial polarization deepened on the political front. We miss much of what goes on in the complex development of race relations in America if we focus solely on the racial card played by the Republican Party and overlook the profound multicultural mix of popular culture that has occurred in the past two decades. In fact, one of the reasons Nixon, Reagan, and Bush had to play a racial card, that is, had to code their language about race, rather than simply call a spade a spade, is due to the changed *cultural* climate of race and sex in America. The classic scene of Senator Strom Thurmond—staunch segregationist and longtime opponent of interracial sex and marriage—strongly defending Judge Clarence Thomas—married to a white woman and an alleged avid consumer of white pornography—shows how this change in climate affects even reactionary politicians in America.

Needless to say, many white Americans still view black sexuality with disgust. And some continue to view their own sexuality with disgust. Victorian morality and racist perceptions die hard. But more and more white Americans are willing to interact sexually with black Americans *on an equal basis*—even if the myths still persist. I view this as neither cause for celebration nor reason for lament. Anytime two human beings find genuine pleasure, joy, and love, the stars smile and the universe is enriched. Yet as long as that pleasure, joy, and love is still predicted on myths of black sexuality, the more fundamental challenge of humane interaction remains unmet. Instead, what we have is white access to black bodies on an equal basis—but not yet the demythologizing of black sexuality.

This demythologizing of black sexuality is crucial for black America because much of black self-hatred and self-contempt has to do with the refusal of many black Americans to love their own black bodies—especially their black noses, hips, lips, and hair. Just as many white Americans view black sexuality with disgust, so do many black Americans—but for very different reasons and with very different results. White supremacist ideology is based first and foremost on the degradation of black bodies in order to control them. One of the best ways to instill fear in people is to terrorize them. Yet this fear is best sustained by convincing them that their bodies are ugly, their intellect is inherently underdeveloped, their culture is less civilized, and their future warrants less concern than that of other peoples. Two hundred and forty-four years of slavery and nearly a century of institutionalized terrorism in the form of segregation, lynchings, and second-class citizenship in America were aimed at precisely this devaluation of black people. This white supremacist venture was, in the end, a relative failure—thanks to the courage and creativity of millions of black people and hundreds of exceptional white folk like John Brown, Elijah Lovejoy, Myles Horton, Russell Banks, Anne Braden, and others. Yet this white dehumanizing endeavor has left its toll in the psychic scars and personal wounds now inscribed in the souls of black folk. These scars and wounds are clearly etched on the canvass of black sexuality.

How does one come to accept and affirm a body so despised by one's fellow citizens? What are the ways in which one can rejoice in the intimate moments of black sexuality in a culture that questions the aesthetic beauty of one's body? Can genuine human relationships flourish for black people in a society that assaults black intelligence, black moral character, and black possibility?

These crucial questions were addressed in those black social spaces that affirmed black humanity and warded off white contempt—especially in black families, churches, mosques, schools, fraternities, and sororities. These precious black institutions forged a mighty struggle against the white supremacist bombardment of black people. They empowered black children to learn against the odds and supported damaged black egos so they could keep fighting; they preserved black sanity in an absurd society in which racism ruled unabated; and they provided opportunities for black love to stay alive. But these grand yet flawed black institutions refused to engage one fundamental issue: *black sexuality*. Instead, they ran from it like the plague. And they obsessively condemned those places where black sexuality was flaunted: the streets, the clubs, and the dance-halls.

Why was this so? Primarily because these black institutions put a premium on black survival in America. And black survival required accommodation with and acceptance from white America. Accommodation avoids any sustained association with the subversive and transgressive—be it communism or miscegenation. Did not the courageous yet tragic lives of Paul Robeson and Jack Johnson bear witness to this truth? And acceptance meant that only "good" negroes would thrive—especially those who left black sexuality at the door when they "entered" and "arrived." In short, straggling black institutions made a Faustian pact with white America: Avoid any substantive engagement with black sexuality and your survival on the margins of American society is, at least, possible.

White fear of black sexuality is a basic ingredient of white racism. And for whites to admit this deep fear even as they try to instill and sustain fear in blacks is to acknowledge a weakness—a weakness that goes down to the bone. Social scientists have long acknowledged that interracial sex and marriage is the most *perceived* source of white fear of black people—just as the repeated castrations of lynched black men cries out for serious psychocultural explanation.

Black sexuality is a taboo subject in America principally because it is a form of black power over which whites have little control—yet its visible manifestations evoke the most visceral of white responses, be it one of seductive obsession or downright disgust. On the one hand, black sexuality among blacks simply does not include whites, nor does it make them a central point of reference. It proceeds as if whites do not exist, as if whites are invisible and simply don't matter. This form of black sexuality puts black agency center stage with no white presence at all. This can be uncomfortable for white people accustomed to being the custodians of power.

On the other hand, black sexuality between blacks and whites proceeds based on underground desires that Americans deny or ignore in public and over which laws have no effective control. In fact, the dominant sexual myths of black women and men portray whites as being "out of control"—seduced, tempted, overcome, overpowered by black bodies. This form of black sexuality makes white passivity the norm—hardly an acceptable self-image for a white-run society.

Of course, neither scenario fully accounts for the complex elements that determine how any particular relationship involving black sexuality *actually* takes place. Yet they do accent the crucial link between black sexuality and black power in America. In this way, to make black sexuality a taboo subject is to silence talk about a particular kind of power black people are perceived to have over whites. On the surface, this "golden" side is one in which black people simply have an upper hand sexually over whites given the dominant myths in our society.

Yet there is a "brazen" side—a side perceived long ago by black people. If black sexuality is a form of black power in which black agency and white passivity are interlinked, then are not black people simply acting out the very roles to which the racist myths of black sexuality confine them? For example, most black churches shunned the streets, clubs, and dance-halls in part because these black spaces seemed to confirm the very

racist myths of black sexuality to be rejected. Only by being "respectable" black folk, they reasoned, would white America see their good works and shed its racist skin. For many black church folk, black agency and white passivity in sexual affairs was neither desirable nor tolerable. It simply permitted black people to play the role of the exotic "other"—closer to nature (removed from intelligence and control) and more prone to be guided by base pleasures and biological impulses.

Is there a way out of this Catch-22 situation in which black sexuality either liberates black people from white control in order to imprison them in racist myths or confines blacks to white "respectability" while they make their own sexuality a taboo subject? There indeed are ways out, but there is no one way out for all black people. Or, to put it another way, the ways out for black men differ vastly from those for black women. Yet, neither black men nor black women can make it out unless both get out since the degradation of both are inseparable though not identical.

Black male sexuality differs from black female sexuality because black men have different self-images and strategies of acquiring power in the patriarchal structures of white America and black communities. Similarly, black male heterosexuality differs from black male homosexuality owing to the self-perceptions and means of gaining power in the homophobic institutions of white America and black communities. The dominant myth of black male sexual prowess makes black men desirable sexual partners in a culture obsessed with sex. In addition, the Afro-Americanization of white youth has been more a male than a female affair given the prominence of male athletes and the cultural weight of male pop artists. This process results in white youth—male and female—imitating and emulating black male styles of walking, talking, dressing, and gesticulating in relation to others. One irony of our present moment is that just as young black men are murdered, maimed, and imprisoned in record numbers, their styles have become disproportionately influential in shaping popular culture. For most young black men, power is acquired by stylizing their bodies over space and time in such a way that their bodies reflect their uniqueness and provoke fear in others. To be "bad" is good not simply because it subverts the language of the dominant white culture but also because it imposes a unique kind of order for young black men on their own distinctive chaos and solicits an attention that makes others pull back with some trepidation. This young black male style is a form of self-identification and resistance in a hostile culture; it also is an instance of machismo identity ready for violent encounters. Yet in a patriarchal society, machismo identity is expected and even exalted—as with Rambo and Reagan. Yet a black machismo style solicits primarily sexual encounters with women and violent encounters with other black men or aggressive police. In this way, the black male search for power often reinforces the myth of black male sexual prowess—a myth that tends to subordinate black and white women as objects of sexual pleasure. This search for power also usually results in a direct confrontation with the order-imposing authorities of the status quo, that is, the police or criminal justice system. The prevailing cultural crisis of many black men is the limited stylistic options of self-image and resistance in a culture obsessed with sex yet fearful of black sexuality.

This situation is even bleaker for most black gay men who reject the major stylistic option of black machismo identity, yet who are marginalized in white America and penalized in black America for doing so. In their efforts to be themselves they are told they are not really "black men," not machismo-identified. Black gay men are often the brunt of talented black comics like Arsenio Hall and Damon Wayans. Yet behind the laughs lurks a black tragedy of major proportions: the refusal of white and black America to entertain seriously new stylistic options for black men caught in the deadly endeavor of rejecting black machismo identities.

The case of black women is quite different, partly because the dynamics of white and black patriarchy affect them differently and partly because the degradation of black female heterosexuality in America makes black female lesbian sexuality a less frightful jump to make. This does not mean that black lesbians suffer less than black gays—in fact, they suffer more, principally owing to their lower economic status. But this does mean that the subculture of black lesbians is fluid and the boundaries are less policed precisely because black female sexuality in general is more devalued, hence more marginal in white and black America.

The dominant myth of black female sexual prowess constitutes black women as desirable sexual partners—yet the central role of the ideology of white female beauty attenuates the expected conclusion. Instead of black women being the most sought after "objects of sexual pleasure"—as in the case of black men—white women tend to occupy this "upgraded," that is, degraded, position primarily because white beauty plays a weightier role in sexual desirability for women in racist patriarchal America. The ideal of female beauty in this country puts a premium on lightness and softness mythically associated with white women and downplays the rich stylistic manners associated with black women. This operation is not simply more racist to black women than that at work in relation to black men; it also is more devaluing of women in general than that at work in relation to men in general. This means that black women are subject to more multilayered bombardments of racist assaults than black men in addition to the sexist assaults they receive from black men. Needless to say most black men—especially professional ones—simply recycle this vulgar operation along the axis of lighter hues that results in darker black women bearing more of the brunt than their already devalued lighter sisters. The psychic bouts with self-confidence, the existential agony over genuine desirability, and the social burden of bearing and usually nurturing black children under these circumstances breeds a spiritual strength of black women unbeknownst to most black men and nearly all other Americans.

As long as black sexuality remains a taboo subject, we cannot acknowledge, examine, or engage these tragic psychocultural facts of American life. Furthermore, our refusal to do so limits our ability to confront the overwhelming realities of the AIDS epidemic in America in general and in black America in particular. Although the dynamics of black male sexuality differ from those of black female sexuality, new stylistic options of self-image and resistance can be forged only when black women and men do so together. This is so not because all black people should be heterosexual or with black partners, but rather because all black people—including black children of so-called "mixed" couples—are affected deeply by the prevailing myths of black sexuality. These myths are part of a wider network of white supremacist lies whose authority and legitimacy must be undermined. In the long run, there is simply no way out for all of us other than living out the truths we proclaim about genuine humane interaction in our psychic and sexual lives. Only by living against the grain can we keep alive the possibility that the visceral feelings about black bodies fed by racist myths and promoted by market-driven quests for stimulation do not forever render us obsessed with sexuality and fearful of each other's humanity.

Further Questions

1. Why is black sexuality believed to be a form of black power over which whites have little control? Ought blacks to share this belief?

2. What are the advantages and disadvantages of the machismo identity assumed by many young black males?

3. How does the ideal of white female beauty cause a devaluing of black women?

VI.7   HIV Testing and Confidentiality

H. A. BASSFORD

H. A. Bassford addresses questions of testing for HIV infection as someone who has been so tested. Quarantine of HIV positive people is not justified, so there is little to warrant mandatory screening of whole populations. Instead, testing should be voluntary and confidential and should be combined with education about safe practices and voluntary contact tracing.

H. A. Bassford is University Professor of Philosophy and President of University College of the Fraser Valley, Abbotsford, BC.

Excerpted from Perspectives on AIDS: Ethical and Social Issues. *Christine Overall and William Zion, eds. (Don Mills, ON: Oxford University Press, 1991). P. 106–121. Reprinted by permission of the author.*

Reading Questions

1. What's to be said in favor of quarantine of the HIV positive, combined with mandatary testing? What is to be said against these two practices?
2. How easy will it be to educate people not to engage in behavior that is high risk for transmission of AIDS? What sorts of social programs should there be to implement such education?
3. Should voluntary testing for HIV be made available to anyone who wants it? How effective would attempts at contact tracing be? What safeguards for confidentiality should be set in place?

THE EXPERIENCE OF TESTING

UNLIKE MOST CANADIANS, I have been tested for HIV infection. At the end of a physical examination, I asked my family physician to authorize the test. He was somewhat taken aback, and explained to me that while there was much concern about AIDS, most members of the population had no good reason to be tested, since most people were not at risk. I told him I realized this, but still wished to be tested. This statement was not sufficient to persuade him. His sense of responsibility, both to his patients and to the public purse, would not allow him to order tests unless he believed there were medically acceptable reasons. With this, I explained my reasons, and he authorized the test.

I suspect that the reader is curious about why I needed to be tested. Normally, testing for disease is done in the presence of physical symptoms. The patient presents with an abnormality (e.g., lumps, shortness of breath, fever), and the physician tests for the presence of conditions that may cause these symptoms. But the curiosity in this case will not be about my physical symptoms. Rather it will be about my *social situation*. Am I gay, bisexual? Am I applying for a new job, for life insurance, to emigrate to another country? AIDS is a disease with very specific modes of transmission, most commonly involving sexual intercourse, so natural thought will be about my sexual orientation and habits. Thus the very mention of being tested for HIV infection will occasion speculation about intimate and private personal matters.

I work in a university, which is a more open and tolerant environment than most. But I dis-

covered that mentioning my having been tested carried social costs. At the minimum there were jokes about not coming near me. I encountered a wariness of expression, a stiffness of body when shaking hands or giving a hug, out-of-context speculations about other colleagues' sexual preferences, etc. These were mild reactions, but suggest the discomfort around AIDS, and the tendency to connect it with being gay, which carries with it the homophobic attitudes of our society. Rather than document these attitudes here, I shall take for granted the reader's awareness of them.[1] Everyone is aware of food preparers, flight attendants, or health-care workers (to mention three cases in the recent press) who have lost their jobs in Canada because of being HIV-positive. This has happened even given the epidemiological knowledge that the HIV virus is spread only by contact of the blood with infected semen or blood. To quote from the Surgeon General of the United States,[2]

> Everyday living does not present any risk of infection. You cannot get AIDS from casual social contact. . . . Casual social contact such as shaking hands, hugging, social kissing, crying, coughing or sneezing, will not transmit the AIDS virus. Nor has AIDS been contracted from swimming in pools or bathing in hot tubs or from eating in restaurants (even if a restaurant worker has AIDS or carries the AIDS virus). AIDS is not contacted from sharing bed linens, towels, cups, straws, dishes, or any other eating utensils. You cannot get AIDS from toilets, doorknobs, telephones, office machinery, or household furniture. You cannot get AIDS from body massages, masturbation, or any non-sexual contact.

Clearly, knowledge about the spread of AIDS has not made it possible for someone who is HIV-positive to live free from irrational social discrimination, should that knowledge become public. Accordingly, there are good reasons for not wishing to publicize one's seropositive status. And indeed, there are good reasons for not telling people even that one has been tested for the presence of HIV.

Sometimes, however, there are also good reasons for wanting to be tested. Although there is at present no cure for AIDS, there are increasing numbers of drugs and medical regimens (such as AZT) that can be effective in postponing the time between the onset of seropositivity and active AIDS. There are thus more and more reasons for medical management that make knowledge desirable. Furthermore, there is the general question of life planning. One of the characteristics of an autonomous, mature individual is the ability to make and live out a life plan. The presence of severe disease requires the rational person to restructure priorities and goals. This is clearly the case with HIV infection. Finally, there is the question of concern for others. A sexually active person may not want to put partners at risk, or may wish to be sure they are aware of the risk involved. Someone may be contemplating a monogamous relationship, and want to be sure it is safe to stop using the usual protective devices. A couple, or a woman, may want to make sure that there is no risk to a potential child. In all these cases, if there is a risk of infection, then there is reason to find out whether such infection is present. The question for the person who wishes a test is how to gain the knowledge without encountering the very real social problems I have delineated above.

PHYSICIAN CONFIDENTIALITY

. . . Principle six of the Canadian Medical Association Code of Ethics reads, "An ethical physician will keep in confidence information derived from his [sic] patient, or from a colleague, regarding a patient and divulge it only with the permission of the patient except when the law requires him to do so." In all ten provinces AIDS is a reportable disease, which means that the physician is legally required to report AIDS-related patient information, usually including the patient's identity, to the medical health officer. In six provinces HIV seropositivity is also reportable.[4] This means that the CMA partially exempts physicians from patient confidentiality in the case of AIDS and HIV seropositivity, extending the range of knowledge to another set of individuals.

This extension takes place because AIDS is a communicable disease, and as such is considered a danger to the public health; hence it falls within the purview of those whose job it is to protect the health of the public. In the case of communicable diseases, various means have traditionally been taken to effect public protection, including the collection of epidemiological data, education in prevention, voluntary or involuntary treatment or immunization, voluntary or involuntary screening, contact tracing, and quarantine of individuals or groups. Two problems accordingly arise for the person undergoing HIV testing. Will the public health system keep the desired confidences? Will that system itself subject patients to unwarranted coercion or invasions of privacy? I shall address these questions by first considering the moral propriety of the greatest interventions, involuntary mass-screening and quarantine, and then proceeding to examine the lesser interventions into patient privacy.

QUARANTINE

The most invasive response to AIDS has been that of Cuba, which has instituted the world's only nation-wide compulsory testing program. Those who test positive are subjected to lifetime quarantine in designated areas, where they are well-fed and well-housed, receive excellent medical care, and are allowed visits from family and friends. The quarantine is thus as humane as it is possible for any quarantine to be.[5] Nonetheless, the fact remains that those quarantined are being denied significant personal freedoms, based upon the need to protect the public from harm. Is this justified? I shall argue that it is not.

I propose two principles. The first I shall term the "foundational principle." The moral purpose of civil society is to allow people to live well: to have their physical necessities met, to develop their human potential, to share in the joys of community. Such a society works best when founded upon a principle of mutual trust and respect, with the rights to privacy, self-determination, and freedom being overridable only when other people's rights are deliberately or negligently infringed or when their safety is clearly threatened. Reflection will show that both criminal and tort law are based upon this principle. While the state can legitimately interfere with the behaviour of adults, it must shoulder the burden of proof by showing that one of the above conditions applies. In modern societies rights are adopted not out of a desire to let people selfishly pursue their own interests but rather out of a respect for people and a belief that they for the most part will handle their own affairs decently.

The second principle is as follows: when it is necessary to interfere with liberty, such interference should use the least restrictive alternative.[6] The point of this principle is straightforward. When there are two competing values, then even though one supersedes the other, there are cases wherein aspects of the other can be retained, and if possible they should be. To take an example from the current discussion, if public safety from a disease can be achieved by identifying and educating those spreading the disease rather than by identifying and quarantining them, then the proper path is to educate them.

With these principles in mind, let me now look at quarantine and universal mandatory testing. Is the public at risk of significant harm from those seropositive for HIV? It is clearly not at risk because of their mere physical presence in society. This could be the case with a virulent air-borne plague, with which people could become infected by merely being in the

same space as those already infected. This might have been the case for Mary Mallon (Typhoid Mary), who was quarantined in 1915 for the involuntary spread of typhoid fever. In such cases quarantine might be justified, even though those spreading the disease intend no harm whatsoever. However, the contagiousness of HIV is a very different matter. As my earlier reference to the Surgeon General of the United States has shown, AIDS is not spread by normal social contact. It is spread *only* through anal or vaginal sexual intercourse, or through the intermingling of blood through sharing intravenous needles, blood transfusions or major health-care accidents. People who have been found HIV-positive can produce infection, and thus cause harm, only by these means. Thus they can have their rights overridden only if they are engaging in these sorts of activities in ways which recklessly or purposely put others at risk.

But quarantine upon evidence of seropositivity presumes that all such individuals will in fact deliberately or negligently spread the disease. It presumes that everyone who is HIV-positive is of immoral and vicious character. Such a presumption is itself morally odious. It goes beyond even the prejudice that people with AIDS "deserve what they get" because they have engaged in "immoral" behaviour, and like this prejudice is reflective of the hysteria and homophobia that all too often have surfaced with respect to AIDS. It is also clearly factually false. Public health officers universally submit that the number of people with AIDS who want to spread the disease is extremely small.[7] Jeff Levi of the National Gay Task Force has put the reason clearly: "No one knows better than [those with AIDS] how terrible the disease is, and they wouldn't want to spread it."[8] To stigmatize people who are HIV-positive, and to quarantine them on unfounded presumptions of moral odiousness, flies in the face of the foundational principle of human society, and is accordingly not a morally acceptable practice.

This argument militates as well against preventive quarantine of any targeted high-risk group. Hemophiliacs, gays, or intravenous drug users (commonly mentioned as high-risk) are all groups made up of extremely varied individuals. Although some members of those groups may act viciously or recklessly, the great majority will not do so. Accordingly, even if such groups could be identified for mandatory testing (which would be very nearly impossible at best, and which would require massive state intervention into private behaviour), preventive quarantine of HIV-positive members of these groups would be morally wrong. Prediction of dangerousness has been found by the criminal justice system to be notoriously difficult, which is why preventive punishment has been rejected and only those found guilty of actually committing crimes have their liberty restricted. Such should be the case in the prevention of the spread of AIDS.

There are also empirical considerations concerning the testing procedures that militate against both universal testing and quarantine. The ELISA test, which is the most widely used, meets most epidemiological screening standards. However, for formal statistical reasons, its predictive value (the probability that a property is in fact present given a positive test result) decreases when the test is applied to the general population, in which the frequency of HIV infection is overall quite low.[9] In testing the general population of Canada, one-half to two-thirds of the positive results will be false positive. That is, more than one-half of the individuals who get a positive result will be virus-free. Retesting, or testing with one of the other available tests as well, will very significantly reduce the number of false positives, but the fact remains that the predictive value will never reach 100 percent. Reasonable numbers of false positives are acceptable in some cases. When the Red Cross screens all donated blood the presence of numbers of false positives means they will not use some blood that is safe to use. This loss is acceptable, given that sufficient blood is available and that they want to be very sure of screening out blood that is HIV-infected. However, if coercive measures are taken,

based upon test results, then significant numbers of people (especially when it is considered that entire populations are being tested) will be severely restricted, even though they cannot put anyone at risk. This result is not acceptable.

MANDATORY SCREENING

Moreover, given the moral non-viability of quarantine, there is little point to large-scale mandatory screening. What will it mean for the public health goal of halting the spread of the disease when people are identified as carrying AIDS antibodies? They can't be treated, for there is no treatment; they can't be quarantined or otherwise stigmatized, for this is immoral. What is left is the gathering of data for epidemiological study, contact tracing in order to warn others, and counselling those found to be seropositive so they will not spread the condition. I shall argue that the costs, both social and economic, are too high, given the possible results. Further, the same goals can be achieved just as well by less intrusive means, and so, by the principle of the least restrictive alternative, these are the means that should be used.

Let me look first at the costs. Testing the entire population would cost well over a hundred million dollars, purely in laboratory fees. It would require a massive increase in laboratory facilities, and a major bureaucracy and policing mechanism to see to it that the population complies with the testing requirement. This would not be cheap, either in dollars or in social costs. The entire population would go through the anxiety of waiting for results. Over half of those initially testing positive would be false positive; they and their relations would undergo immense stress while waiting retesting. Given that most people are not greatly at risk, and that risk can be very significantly reduced by voluntary changes in personal behaviour (safe sex, not sharing needles), one wonders if such stresses are justified.

The spectre of unnecessary suffering of the seropositive also arises once more. The largest seropositive group in Canada is composed of gay men, who as such have been historically subjected to much social and legal discrimination. They and others would legitimately fear that surveillance could easily turn to more restrictive actions. Additionally, it is hard to imagine that the public's already existing prejudice and fear would not increase if the government implemented a massive program based upon a perceived need to track down all possible sources of infection. Further, the mechanism required to complete the screening, given the numbers of people involved, and the size of the resulting government data bank, full of highly personal information, would make it extremely difficult, if not impossible, to maintain confidentiality. This would increase the already existing discriminatory practices with respect to employment, service delivery, housing, etc. Taken togther, these are very high moral costs.

But additionally there is the problem of whether the program could achieve its goals. People who fear or otherwise strongly oppose a program can hardly be expected to co-operate wholeheartedly with it. Some would try to evade the program completely; others would not volunteer information, or would deliberately misinform (e.g., officials will not know our sex partners unless we identify them); the co-operation necessary for successful counselling or education would not likely be forthcoming. Yet such cooperation is crucial if the program is to succeed. The point has been well put by David J. Mayo:[10]

> Since no vaccine or cure for AIDS is available, the most promising strategy available for cutting down on the transmission of AIDS now is the reduction of high-risk activities, and this can be achieved only through cooperation and education of high-risk groups about what activities are unsafe. This task is already well underway in the gay community in some cities, but is obviously frustrated by any antagonism between public officials and high-risk groups. Mutual trust is absolutely essential if individuals are to begin to listen to, believe, and finally

act on the advice of health professionals about what activities are unsafe. That is virtually impossible when those at risk are—or believe they are—stigmatized as "outsiders." That is the nearly unanimous belief of those who actually work in public health with victims of stigmatizing diseases, particularly diseases associated with stigmatized behaviour.

From all this it appears that the results of required screening contradict the goals of such screening. When the moral improprieties of mandatory testing are added, it becomes clear that alternative policies should be investigated.

EDUCATION AND SOCIAL SUPPORT

What is required is a policy that combines voluntary, truly confidential testing, comprehensive education and some supportive social programs. The primary goal, to reduce the spread of AIDS, can be accomplished if those who engage in potentially infective activities, whether HIV-positive or -negative, modify their behaviour patterns. There is clear evidence that carefully constructed educational programs can lead to safer sexual behaviour.[11] Especially effective are those programs conducted by, or in combination with, relevant community organizations. To quote from Ronald Bayer:

> it was stunning to find that in the face of the AIDS epidemic volunteer efforts undertaken by community organizations and funded in the most limited way by public agencies had apparently produced dramatic, even unprecedented changes in the sexual behaviour of gay men.[12]

Peer-group and other innovative educational techniques can help people to gain the knowledge and motivation to reassess the meaning of their behaviour, to act both in their own interest and out of concern of others. It must not be thought this is an easy process. Many men, surely including some readers of this paper, refuse to wear condoms. This is to refuse to accept responsibility for the results of their sexuality. Many women are socialized or coerced into compliance. Accordingly, successful educational programs to combat AIDS must do more than provide information; they must actively face deep-seated questions of gender and heterosexual sexual politics. Such programs may be expensive, although cheaper than quarantine and universal testing; but morally they are much preferable to the alternatives, not least because they address longstanding social injustices. When access to the physical means to change behaviour, such as needle-exchange programs and the placing of condom-vending machines in high-school washrooms, are combined with such educational programs, there can be significant progress towards slowing the spread of AIDS.

The notion of trust and co-operation should be emphasized here. The most successful programs are those wherein the government and the affected communities work together. In such cases those groups affected or most at risk can readily perceive that the authorities act out of concern for them, and do so in a context of respecting their personhood and sense of personal responsibility. This is also true with voluntary testing. The voluntary patient is more likely to work with the physician, and so to benefit from the physician's counselling or from the counseling arranged by the physician with relevant peer groups.

The opposite is the case with required testing. The coerced person will be seen as untrustworthy or unable to act autonomously. Being so seen does not tend to make one co-operative, nor does it engender the confidence and self-respect needed to cope with the situation. A voluntary testing program is consistent with the "foundation principle;" an involuntary one is not. Moreover, the results of voluntary testing, when combined with education, are at least as good. The conclusion is that voluntary testing with maintenance of primary physician confidentiality is the preferred social policy.

However, it might be argued that this conclusion is too strong. While the proposed program provides for better behaviour modification, it does not provide for proper collection of epidemiological data or for the contact tracing necessary to protect others. Because of this, some sort of mandatory testing, or at least required reporting to public health authorities of positive results, is necessary.

These considerations are not decisive. Epidemiological data are often essential to understanding and conquering a disease. It is important to know the ways in which the disease is spread and the ways in which individual instances of the disease develop. But the gathering of this information does not require officers of public health to know the identities of those whose cases provide data. The Centres for Disease Control in the United States, for example, have devised a reporting mechanism that allows reporting without the use of names or other personal identifiers, but that precludes duplicate reporting. Even though this method is more complex, it neither interferes with privacy nor produces non-compliance and false reporting, and so it is the morally proper choice.

This is also the case with contact tracing. The closest parallel is the use of contact tracing for venereal diseases, which has long been a standard practice. It has not, however, always been clearly successful, as Allan Brandt reports in his history of venereal disease in the United States:[13]

> The ultimate effect of case-finding remains difficult to evaluate. . . . Contact epidemiology clearly brought many unsuspecting individuals into treatment before they could spread their infections to others. But the knowledge that information regarding contacts would be sought by public health professionals also had the effect of encouraging some individuals to seek the aid of quacks or private practitioners who guaranteed absolute confidentiality. Indeed, most private physicians have resisted public health requirements that they report individuals suffering from venereal disease to public officials so that contacts can be approached.

While contact tracing did alert many, it drove others away from the health-care and education system. The Surgeon General of the United States believes that this can also happen with contact tracing for those who are HIV-positive, and for this reason opposes reporting to and training by public health departments.[14] It also can drive people away in another sense. Since affected communities are strongly opposed to this requirement, its imposition would not further the crucially needed community co-operation in education and counselling. As a social policy, public health contact tracing might well carry more cost than it produces benefits.

Moreover, a reasonable voluntary alternative exists. For the most part, officials will be able to find out who our sexual contacts are only if we tell them. Public health officers will be able to carry out their goal of contact tracing only if HIV-positive individuals volunteer the relevant information. In a coercive situation, fearing that friends and lovers will be "listed" or have their privacy dangerously invaded (think of a lover with a sensitive job), many will not volunteer accurate information. On the other hand, as I have emphasized often in this essay, most people do not want to cause harm to others. With appropriate counselling and support, it is reasonable to think that most will be willing to inform their sexual partners, even though this will sometimes be difficult for them. In some cases, people may find they need the help of their physician or a specially trained person in informing partners. This kind of help can be provided without keeping lists and with minimum loss of confidentiality.

While this voluntary method of contact tracing would not mean that all those at risk of infection would be informed, it should be as successful as the mandatary contact-tracing method. On the one hand, the mandatory method would inform, as the voluntary method would not, sexual partners of those who could not be persuaded to inform their partners themselves, but who could be coerced into giving their names. On the other hand, the mandatory method would not reach the sexual partners of those who would stay away from the system or would withhold information.

The mandatory method also alienates communities with whom co-operation is important. Given all this, and given that the voluntary system is far less invasive of privacy than the mandatory one, the principle of the least restrictive alternative prescribes opting for the voluntary system. With this result, the overall conclusion can now be stated. The best social policy for HIV-testing is one that makes testing voluntary, that maintains physician-patient confidentiality, and that does not involve mandatory reporting to or contact tracing by officers of public health.

I shall close with one general observation. The awful dilemmas just discussed, as well as many others around AIDS, often arise because of fears of having sexual practices and preferences revealed. Such fears are usually well founded, arising from the prejudices and intolerance of our society. AIDS is a terrible medical tragedy, but it focuses our attention upon a terrible social tragedy as well. So, while we can often sort out the morally least damaging path through the particular dilemmas of AIDS treatment, our goal should always be to change those social attitudes and conditions that cause them to arise.

NOTES

1. For an excellent study of AIDS and homophobia, see Denis Altman, *AIDS and the New Puritanism* (London: Pluto Press, 1986).

2. *Surgeon General's Report on Acquired Immune Deficiency Syndrome* (Washington, DC: United States Government), p. 21.

4. D. G. Casswell, "Disclosure by a Physician of AIDS-Related Patient Information: An Ethical and Legal Dilemma," *The Canadian Bar Review* 68, 2 (June 1989): 256–7.

5. Even though I shall be extremely critical of the quarantine program, it must be emphasized that this does not constitute an overall condemnation of Cuba's AIDS program. Cubans with AIDS all receive high-quality medical care, which cannot be said of any other Third World country. Indeed, the United States does not compare all that well in this particular. Given the

user-pay medical system, the fact that many people with AIDS live in big-city ghettos, and that many others exhaust their resources long before they no longer need medical care, many Americans with AIDS cannot be said to receive high-quality medical care.

6. This is a more general version of a principle proposed for public health restrictions in Lawrence O. Gostin, William J. Curran, and Mary E. Clark, "The Case Against Compulsory Casefinding in Controlling AIDS—Testing, Screening and Reporting," *American Journal of Law & Medicine* 12, 1: 24.

7. Ronald Bayer, *Private Acts, Social Consequences: AIDS and the Politics of Public Health* (New York: Free Press, 1989), pp. 146, 192, 198.

8. Ibid., p. 193.

9. The explanation of the relevant statistical concepts most accessible to the layperson can be found in

Kenneth R. Howe, "Why Mandatary Screening for AIDS is a Very Bad Idea," in Christine Pierce and Donald VanDeVeer, *AIDS: Ethics and Public Policy* (Belmont, CA: Wadsworth, 1988), pp. 140–149.

10. David J. Mayo, "AIDS, Quarantines, and Noncompliant Positives," in Pierce and VanDeVeer, pp. 117–118.

11. See, for example, Ronald O. Valdiserri, *et al.*, "AIDS Prevention in Homosexual and Bisexual Men: Results of Randomized Trial Evaluating Two Risk Reduction Interventions," *AIDS* 3, 1 (Jan. 1989): 21–26.

12. Bayer, p. 226. See also Altman, Ch. 5.

13. Allan M. Brandt, *No Magic Bullet: A Social History of Venereal Disease in the United States Since 1880* (New York: Oxford University Press, 1987), p.151.

14. *Surgeon General's Report*, p. 30.

Further Questions

1. What sorts of considerations would lead you to want to be tested for the AIDS virus? Whom would you want to know that you had been so tested and from whom would you want this information withheld? If you tested positive whom would you want to know this and whom would you not want to know?

2. What safeguards would you want to see in place before you identified your sexual contacts, in case you tested positive?

3. What systems would you like to see instituted that would offer treatment to the HIV infected, protect the non-infected, and do so with a maximum degree of confidentiality?

VI.8   Women and AIDS: Too Little, Too Late

NORA KIZER BELL

Nora Kizer Bell discusses the risk of women contracting AIDS through sexual contact. AIDS is, of course, the worst of the sexually transmitted diseases because it is a virus for which no cure is foreseeable. Of special interest in this writing is the discussion of the pregnant woman infected with AIDS.

Bell is Professor of Philosophy, The University of South Carolina (Columbia).

Abridged from "Women and AIDS: Too Little, Too Late," in Hypatia, *Volume 4, Number 3 (Fall 1989), pp. 3–22. Reprinted by permission of the author.*

Reading Questions

1. Does someone who has tested positive for HIV virus, or is otherwise in a high risk category (IV drug user, and so on), have an obligation to inform sexual partners about his or her status?
2. Under what circumstances, if any, is condom use not necessary or outweighed by the benefits of *not* using condoms?
3. If a pregnant woman discovers that she is HIV positive, should she have complete freedom of choice about whether to have an abortion?

. . . ALTHOUGH 90 PERCENT of reported AIDS cases continue to occur among homosexual men or intravenous drug users, a 1987 study notes a disproportional increase in cases of AIDS over the past three years among women who are heterosexual partners of bisexual men (16 percent) or of intravenous drug users (67 percent). From 1981 to 1986 reported cases of AIDS in women increased in parallel with cases in men, and although men with AIDS still clearly outnumber women with AIDS, there is one risk category in which women with AIDS outnumber men with AIDS by a significant margin: persons whose *only* risk factor is heterosexual contact with a person at risk (Guinan and Hardy, 1987).

The primary mode of transmission of HIV to women discerned by this study was intravenous drug use (52 percent). However, the second most common route of transmission to women (21 percent) was heterosexual contact with someone with AIDS. This compares to a mere 1 percent of nonhomosexual/bisexual men with AIDS who had this risk factor. Of a total of 456 adults with AIDS whose only risk factor was heterosexual contact with someone at risk, 84 percent were women. It is noteworthy that the proportion of women with AIDS in that risk category increased from 12 percent in 1982 to 26 percent in 1986 (Guinan and Hardy, 1987, 2040).

As Des Jarlais explains, since approximately 75 percent of IV drug users in the United States are males and since fully 95 percent of those males are predominantly heterosexual,

> there simply are not enough female IV drug users for the majority of the group to have their primary sexual relationships with other

IV drug users. The number of females who do not inject drugs themselves but are regular sexual partners of IV drug users has been estimated to be at least half as large as the number of IV drug users. These figures indicate that a large number of persons may become infected with the AIDS virus through the IV user without involvement with IV drugs themselves (1988, 3).

Acknowledging the decrease in HIV transmission among homosexual men, and in light of data such as the above, Guinan and Hardy argue that in the United States, at the present time, "a heterosexual woman is at greater risk for acquiring AIDS through sexual intercourse than is a heterosexual man" (1987, 2041). . . .

The increase in the numbers of heterosexually acquired cases of HIV among women is thought to be the result of two factors: (1) because there are more men than women who are infected, women are more likely than men to encounter an infected partner, and (2) it appears that the efficiency of transmission of the virus is greater from man to woman than from woman to man (Guinan and Hardy, 1987; Curran et al., 1988). . . .

In spite of the fact that cases of AIDS in women have been documented from the early stages of the epidemic in this country and elsewhere, their plight and their place in the epidemic received very little attention. Women weren't educated about their risk factors or about the possible risk to the developing fetus; they themselves wanted to avoid the stigma associated with having a "gay" disease (Ledger, 1987, 5). Women were, and still are, "omitted from AIDS brochures and media coverage, and eclipsed in medical research" (Murphy, 1988, 6). In campaigns promoting safe sex, men weren't reminded of their responsibilities to their *female* sex partners (Patton, 1988). Even today few persons are aware that AIDS is now the leading cause of death among women aged 25 to 29 in New York City (Bacon, 1987, 6).

Even though anti-gay sentiment generated a response to AIDS, that over-shadowed concerns affecting women, attempts to *combat* homophobia have also been disadvantageous to women.[1] Early in the epidemic, it became clear that disclosure of one's seropositivity had devastating psycho-social effects: job and housing discrimination, increased suicide rates, ostracism, termination of women's parental rights, refusal of health care workers to treat, and so on. For that reason, efforts were begun to develop policy that would be responsible to the privacy rights of persons with AIDS. As important as these efforts were, they had the effect of slowing pubic health efforts to institute partner notification and contact tracing (both public health strategies long acknowledged as effective in combating the spread of other sexually transmitted diseases).[2] A recognition of the psycho-social effects of a disclosure of one's seropositivity also led (rightfully) to a fear of any form of selective or mandatary testing, thus ruling out premarital or prenatal testing. In truth, it would have made more sense to expend resources on combating the underlying discrimination that made protections of confidentiality so important. However, even the time required to confront homophobia among policy makers and the public at large has led to an eclipse of the needs of women with AIDS.

Racism, unfortunately, is also implicated in the neglect of issues affecting women. A report from the CDC in October of 1988 indicated that 26 percent of AIDS cases were among blacks and another 15 percent among Hispanics (CDC, 1988). In addition, 53 percent of the women with AIDS are black, and approximately 51 percent of them are engaged either in intravenous drug use or prostitution (Murphy,

1988, 66; Curran and Jaffe et al., 1988, 611). Researchers report further that while 78 percent of the reported cases of AIDS in children younger than six years old are in children of color, children of color constitute only 21 percent of the nation's population in that age group (Osterholm and MacDonald, 1987).

The disparities in the risk for AIDS among blacks and Hispanics must be examined within the context of the social fabric in which AIDS infection occurs, and at the core of that fabric one finds the problems of poverty, drug abuse, teen pregnancy, lack of education, inadequate health care and social support services, prostitution, and child and spouse abuse. These social problems are not only deplorable, but as Osterholm and MacDonald point out, they are very complex. For example, while needle-sharing activities continue to be a problem among the urban poor, especially persons of color, the United States continues to lead the industrialized world in rates of teen pregnancy and birth rates. "In particular, the rate of black, never married women aged 15 through 19 years who are sexually active is almost 35 percent higher than that of white women" (Osterholm and MacDonald, 1987, 2737). Because the social and economic realities for women of childbearing age in the inner cities are not easily remedied, the great weight of female and pediatric AIDS will continue to fall on the communities of color, particularly in these urban settings.

The charges of racism and the complexity of class politics cannot be ignored in attempting to understand and combat the effect of AIDS on women, for women with AIDS represent the least advantaged groups in American society. Already disenfranchised, these women lack the means to command the public's attention to their lot. These women are *not* the idealized "victim" woman. They represent yet another segment of society that has traditionally been considered "disposable." As Murphy concludes, "[s]mall wonder, then, that their plight has received so little attention" (1988, 66).

There are, therefore, important ethical issues relating specifically to women with AIDS that remain to be addressed. In the concluding portion of this discussion I propose to enumerate and examine . . . issues related to recommending condom use . . . and issues surrounding birth control and reproduction.

CONDOM USE AND WOMEN

Michael Simpson in his work on feminist thanatology, has written of the "nearly universal and persistent relationship between women, sex, and danger" (1988, 202). Historically, women have been subject to dangerous sex; "the risks of pregnancy, childbirth, abortion, miscarriage, and the puerperium have limited woman's potential across the centuries" (Simpson, 1988, 20). Women have had to be the principal advocates for improved methods of contraception, for male contraception, for legalization of abortion, and so on.

Knowledge of women's social and moral history underlies the anger some women feel about the place given to their role in the AIDS epidemic. It is no wonder that Kaplan argues,

> if men and boys find out that women are united in feeling entitled to protection, that *all* women expect men to behave responsibly, and that we *all* insist on making sure that a man is not infected before we will sleep with him; if he knows that he is not going to get the kind of sex he wants unless he proves that he is not infected, then men's behavior will change. When the majority of women insist on safe sex or hold out on sex until they and their partners are ready to commit themselves to an exclusive relationship or marriage, when we stop buying the nonsense that asking him to wear a condom is healthy assertiveness, then men's behavior will change (Kaplan, 1988, 82).

Unfortunately, the concepts of "safe sex" and "just say no" (to sex and drugs) portend a blurring of the sex/death boundaries for women. Condom use is touted as a reasonable method for the prevention of HIV transmission during penetrative sex (Freidland and Klein, 1987,

1130), and promoting the use of condoms is said to be a "potentially useful" intervention for preventing HIV infection (Quinn, Glasser, et al., 1988, 202). A great deal of the education concerning condom use has been directed at women, and women have been advised to carry their own condoms. Some authors report that women now constitute 70 percent of the condom-buying market (Patton, 1988). Yet researchers discovered in one study that only 3 percent of men and 4 percent of women reported consistent use of condoms.

Unfortunately, many of the recommendations for AIDS education and condom use fail to take the experience of women into account. Male machismo is reported to lead some men to refuse condom use, preferring, in their words, "the greater thrill of unprotected sex" (Zucker, interview, 1988). While the lure and the excitement of the forbidden and the dangerous are familiar themes in literature and in philosophy, sexual intercourse during the AIDS epidemic can be seen to perpetuate the inequality of women's risk in heterosexual relationships.

In some cultural contexts, a woman's acquiescence to sex on demand is both expected and enforced. Hence, for many women, "just saying no" to sex (or to unprotected sex) has turned into a prescription for battering and other forms of abuse (Bacon, 1987, 6). Among the women who are most affected by AIDS, the fact that they are still in situations of unequal power has meant that they now face additional obstacles in ensuring their own bodily safety.

Long aware that condom use was *not* recognized as an effective means of birth control, women are *now* being told that condom use will effectively prevent AIDS transmission. Yet the rate of the condom's failure to protect against pregnancy was measured in a monthly cycle during which most women were fertile only a few days. Women are justifiably concerned that condoms are not a reasonable protection against a disease that can be transmitted every day of the month. Furthermore, many brochures on "safe sex" concentrate on describing ways to make the condom more palatable to the male sexual experience than they do either on ways to ensure the safety of the woman receptor or on sexual practices that are non-penetrative. The many public health messages recommending condom use have conveyed the impression that the male sexual experience is the primary focus. Lisa Bacon notes as well that reliable safe sex information for lesbians is neither widely distributed nor widely known to be available (1987, 6).

The noticeable absence of research efforts to develop better barriers to transmission for women and to publicize alternative methods of expressing one's sexuality is troubling and remains an important issue in the ethics of AIDS. . . .

While many in society express little compassion for the prostitute who acquires AIDS from her customer, few economic alternatives exist for women in prostitution, and even fewer exist for the drug addicted prostitute. A dehumanizing aspect of prostitution is that it is essentially an involuntary form of labor that grows out of the economically disadvantaged position in which women find themselves. Prostitution is a manifestation of a lack of respect for persons, primarily because those who must prostitute themselves have not been accorded the freedom of choice that accompanies being treated fully as a person.[3] In addition, because prostitutes are at the bottom of the heap in all these other ways, they are among those persons who are often least able to organize to protect themselves. It compounds the moral insult to allow women prostitutes to fall prey to HIV infected "johns" and to believe that that is their due. . . .

BIRTH CONTROL AND REPRODUCTION

Women with AIDS pose further complex ethical issues that involve examining both their reproductive options and their obligations in exercising those options. One such issue grows out of the fact that researchers have found that trends in women with AIDS are good predictors of trends in pediatric AIDS cases, especially among mothers in identifiable risk groups (Guinan and Hardy, 1987).

In approximately two-thirds (65 percent) of the pregnancies of women who are infected with the virus, infection is passed on to the infant, and close to 50 percent of those infants will have disease within two years. The outlook for these children is almost certain death (Koop, 1987, 4; Ledger, 1987, 5; Piot, Plummer, et al., 1988). Furthermore, about two-thirds of pediatric AIDS cases are the result of transmission from infected mother to child[4] (Koop, 1987, 4). More importantly, not only women with AIDS, but also women with ARC and women who are asymptomatic carriers of HIV infection have the potential to transmit the virus perinatally.

HIV infection can be passed from mother to infant in three ways; to the fetus *in utero* through fetal-maternal circulation, to the infant during labor and delivery, and to the infant through infected breast milk (Freidland and Klein, 1987, 1130; Curran, Jaffe, et al., 1988, 614; Piot, Plummer, et al., 1988, 575).

Further complicating this issue is the fact that AIDS not only diversely affects the child born to an infected mother, it also seems to accelerate the progression of disease in the pregnant woman herself (Murphy, 1988, 73). Sadly, for many women, especially those who are culturally and economically deprived, childbearing sometimes provides a sense of self-esteem and is sometimes culturally expected. Hence, many women who have borne an infected child continue to reproduce "despite intensive culturally specific counseling" (Wofsy, 1987, 33). A second pregnancy in an HIV infected mother, however, is even more likely to move her into full blown AIDS at the same time that it produces an infected infant (Murphy, 1988, 73). A tragic irony of these findings is that oral contraception is also a factor thought to increase a woman's susceptibility to sexually acquired HIV infection (Piot, Plummer, et al., 1988, 575).

In addition to the risk of infection by vaginal intercourse, women undergoing artificial insemination (AI) are in some danger of HIV infection. Although not a widely published fact, there are close to 10,000 AI births per year in the United States (Murphy, 1988, 73). This form of transmission is easily eliminable by instituting procedures for testing donor sperm; the ejaculate of first time donors can be frozen and the donor retested for antibody two to three months before the sperm is used (Ledger, 1987, 5). Such testing would continue to ensure that AI remains a legitimate reproductive option for women while protecting them and their unborn fetuses from HIV infection. . . .

One option, abortion, is itself a volatile issue that promises to "increase the difficulty of dealing with HIV infection in the population of pregnant women" (Osterholm and MacDonald, 1987, 2737). Contrary to what many right-to-life advocates might argue, there are quite compelling moral grounds for advocating that an infected women is justified in aborting a fetus she might be carrying: a prospective mother might be said to have an obligation to any potential child to spare it a certain and gruesome death, a prospective mother might be said to have an obligation to ensure and protect her own health for as long as she can (both for her own sake as well as for the sake of others, including the unborn fetus), and a prospective mother might be said to have an obligation to society not to bear children for whom society may have to provide.

The flip side of that argument, however, might suggest that, in the black context, for example, a prospective mother could be said to have a responsibility *to bear* her child, even with only a 35 percent survival possibility in order to maintain the integrity of the Black community.

However, while I acknowledge the necessity of understanding the political and cultural implications of testing and of counseling HIV infected women against reproducing, I believe it is equally important to the racial integrity of communities of color that transmission to their offspring be avoided where that is possible.

A real worry underlying both of these arguments is mandatory testing. For many women,

mandatory testing carries with it the specter of forced celibacy, prohibitions against procreation (accompanied by the potential of sanctions against violators), and even the threat of forced abortion.

Apart from evidence that suggests that mandatory testing would have the effect of driving underground those most in need of testing and counseling, it is unclear both what gains could be expected from forced testing in this context and whether such testing even has the potential of reaching those it purports to reach. Many of the women in populations identified as "at risk" either don't marry those who have fathered their offspring or can't afford prenatal care. There is the additional question of determining how such options might be enforced or punished. By imprisonment? By steep fines? By terminating parental rights? By the time an accurate diagnosis were made and the appropriate causal link established, those found to be violators (and victims) would likely be dead or dying. Further, given the current state of the art with respect to testing, the test results themselves may give women a false sense of security about their serological status. Under such circumstances, if testing were mandated, the end hoped for still might not be realized.

In short, that there are strong moral reasons for preventing further spread of AIDS to newborns and for preventing pregnancy in infected women does not imply that policy be *mandated* for accomplishing that end. Some authors even express concern over the domino effect such mandated policies would have on the logic for testing other groups (Patton, 1988).

There is yet another argument that needs to be examined, one that will be more familiar to those who have a long standing interest in issues affecting women: A woman must be allowed to weigh for herself the risks inherent in continuing a pregnancy if she is found to be seropositive—only she can evaluate the moral validity of her options.

Preserving women's rights to exercise reproductive choice is said to be important for the reason that the HIV status of the fetus of an infected mother, as well as of asymptomatic mothers who have infected partners, is still highly uncertain and often cannot be determined until some time after birth. Hence, this argument goes, while a woman might elect to terminate a pregnancy if she or her partner is discovered to be HIV infected, she might also justifiably choose to continue the pregnancy. If the prospective mother were carrying the child of a beloved and dying spouse, she might legitimately reason that the risk to the unborn is one that is justified in order to have a part of her spouse live on, or in order to give her own life more meaning, or for sociological and cultural reasons noted above (Murphy, 1988, 75).

While I do not believe that mandatory testing is either morally appropriate or enforceable, I do believe that it is morally irresponsible to argue in this case for preserving women's rights to exercise reproductive choice. It seems important to come down hard on someone who would choose a 65 percent risk of spreading AIDS.[5] Sentimentalism and sexism aside, it seems unconscionable for a person knowingly to risk transmitting a lethal disease to another. Imagine our anger if an HIV infected man or woman were to engage intentionally in unprotected sexual relations with an uninfected partner. It seems uncontroversial to claim that we would feel moral outrage at such an act. It seems equally uncontroversial to claim that we would find it morally objectionable for an infected person knowingly to donate blood. The risk of infecting others with a lethal disease is simply too great. It seems even more objectionable when one doesn't consent to exposing oneself to the risk. For that reason, in the case of a prospective mother who risks transmitting HIV to her fetus, electing to continue the pregnancy seems an even greater abuse of one's moral and sexual responsibility.

Some states have already acknowledged the moral force of claims such as the above by enacting legislation that would make it a criminal act for an individual to engage in intercourse with another without informing that partner of his/her seropositivity[6] (Dickens, 1988, 583).

Of course, apart from the fact that I'm unsure how to evaluate the enforceability of such laws, it is unrealistic to believe that their payoff will be found in dramatic behavior change. Given the social and cultural context in which most of these women find themselves, it is even less clear what would effect behavior change in seropositive women who continue to conceive. Even so, such laws represent important expressions of a public attitude that such behaviors are wrong and that personal accountability is part of an accepted public morality. Such laws will help shape the moral climate of AIDS.[7] . . .

NOTES

An earlier, much shorter statistical version of this paper will appear in *AIDS Education and Prevention*. In this paper I have chosen to address the more philosophical issues surrounding AIDS/HIV in women. I am extremely grateful to Laura Purdy, Becky Holmes, and the reviewers of this paper for their many helpful and provocative comments.

1. It is important to understand here that I do not lay the blame for this at the feet of the gay community. On the contrary, the gay community historically has been supportive of efforts to secure higher moral and political status for women.

2. I have argued elsewhere that AIDS does not fit the traditional communicable disease model. Hence, I am aware that partner notification and contact tracing have little in the way of treatment (and nothing in the way of a cure) to offer to those traced and notified. What contact tracing does offer is the information that one may have been exposed to the virus, and that, I would argue, is information essential for both men and women to have.

3. I am aware that there are number of feminist analyses of prostitution that discuss how racism keeps Black and Latino women on the streets and lets white women work less conspicuously indoors, and a number of discussions of prostitution as a legitimate form of employment. Although there are important similarities between antiprostitute sentiment and homophobic sentiment, I don't have the space in this paper, unfortunately, to do more than note that fact.

4. Other pediatric cases result from sexual abuse, drug abuse, adolescent intercourse, and hemophilia.

5. I am extremely grateful to my colleague Ferdy Schoeman for discussing the difficulties inherent in taking any position other than this. His suggestions throughout this section were most useful and illuminating.

6. Although Dickens notes that Florida and Idaho have introduced such legislation, I am personally aware that South Carolina has enacted such legislation. Dickens also notes that most jurisdictions have chosen to rely on existing criminal statutes to proscribe some behaviors of the HIV infected person.

7. There are seropositive people who knowingly have unprotected sex, however, just as there are cases of persons who know they have serious risk factors for HIV infection and who aren't seeking to learn their HIV status, yet continue to share sexual and drug using behaviors. I consider this to be morally irresponsible behavior.

REFERENCES

Bacon, Lisa. 1987. Lessons of AIDS: Racism, homophobia are the real epidemic. *Listen Real Loud.* 8(2): 5–6.

Curran, J., Jaffe, H., Hardy, A., Morgan, W., Selik, R., & Dondero, T. 1988. Epidemiology of HIV infection and AIDS in the United States. *Science* 239:610–616.

Des Jarlais, D. and Hunt, D. 1988. AIDS and IV drug use. *AIDS Bulletin* Feb. 1988: 3.

Dickens, B. M. 1988. Legal rights and duties in the AIDS epidemic. *Science* 239: 580–585.

Freidland, G. H. and Klein, R. S. 1987. Transmission of human immunodeficiency virus. *New England Journal of Medicine* 317(18): 1125–1135.

Guinan, M. E. and Hardy, A. 1987. Epidemiology of AIDS in women in the United States: 1981–1986. *JAMA* 257(15): 2039–2042.

Kaplan, H. S. 1988. No sex this year. *New Woman* January: 81–82.

Koop, C. E. 1987. *Report of the surgeon general's workshop on children with HIV infection and their families.* (Excerpts from keynote address.) Public Health Service; US Dept. of HHS. HRS-D-MC 87–1.

Ledger, W. A. 1987. AIDS and the obstetrician/gynecologist: commentary. *Information on AIDS for the Practicing Physician* 2: 5–6.

Murphy, J. S. 1988. Women with AIDS: Sexual ethics in an epidemic. In *AIDS: principles, practices, and politics.* I. Corless and M. Pitman-Lindemann, eds. Washington: Hemisphere.

Osterholm, M. and MacDonald, K. L. 1987. Facing the complex issues of pediatric AIDS: A public health perspective. *JAMA* 258(19): 2736–2737.

Patton, C. 1988. Resistance and the erotic: Reclaiming history, setting strategy as we face AIDS. *Radical Teacher* 68–78.

Piot, P., Plummer, F., Mhalu, F., Lamboray, J., Chin, J., & Mann, J. 1988. AIDS: An international perspective. *Science* 239: 573–579.

Quinn, T., Glasser, D., Canon, R., Matuszak, D., Dunning, R., Kline, R., Campbell, C., Israel, E., Fauci, A., & Hook, E. 1988. Human immunodeficiency virus infection among patients attending clinics for sexually transmitted diseases. *New England Journal of Medicine* 318(4): 197–203.

Simpson, M. 1988. The malignant metaphor: A political thanatology of AIDS. In *AIDS: principles, practices, and politics.* I. Corless and M. Pittman-Lindemann, eds. Washington: Hemisphere.

Wofsy, C. 1987. Intravenous drug abuse and women's medical issues. *Report of the surgeon general's workshop on children with HIV infection and their families.* Public Health Service: US Dept. of HHS. HRS-D-MC 87-1.

Zucker, L. 1988. Interview. USC. Columbia, SC.

Further Questions

1. Should IV drug users be counseled, given bleach to sterilize their needles, and so forth, in the interest of sexual partners to whom they might transmit the AIDS virus?

2. AIDS was first discovered in gays and is still known by some as "the gay plague." Does this way of thinking discourage us from noticing that other people are at risk?

3. Should sexually active people, for example, teenagers, be taught barrier methods of birth control, to slow down progression of the AIDS virus?

Further Readings for Part VI: Sex and Sexuality

Jeffner Allen, ed. *Lesbian Philosophies and Cultures* (Albany, NY: State University of New York Press, 1990). Lesbians write from a variety of perspectives.

Robert M. Baird and M. Katherine Baird, eds. *Homosexuality: Debating the Issues* (Amherst, NY: Prometheus Books, 1995).

Robert Baker and Frederick Elliston, eds. *Philosophy and Sex* (Buffalo, NY: Prometheus Books, New Revised Edition, 1984). Nice anthology covering many of the topics of *Gender Basics*.

Regina Barreca. *They Used to Call Me Snow White . . . But I Drifted: Women's Strategic Use of Humor* (New York, NY: Viking, Penguin, 1991). Chapter 6 is especially interesting in illustrating women's sexual preferences.

Judith Barrington, ed. *An Intimate Wilderness: Lesbian Writers on Sexuality* (Portland, OR: The Eighth Mountain Press, 1991). Erotic explorations by top lesbian writers.

Warren J. Blumenfeld, ed. *Homophobia: How We All Pay the Price* (Boston, MA: Beacon Press, 1992). How homophobia causes damage in all our lives.

Howard Buchbinder, Varda Burstyn, Dinah Forbes, and Mercedes Steedman. *Who's on Top? The Politics of Heterosexuality* (Toronto, ON: Garamond Press, 1987). Four excellent essays on contemporary heterosexual sex.

Bonnie Bullough, Vern L. Bullough and James Elias, eds. *Gender Blending* (Amherst, NY: Prometheus Books, 1997). Readable accounts of transgenderism, transexuality, and transvestitism.

Pat Califia. *Sex Changes: The Politics of Transgenderism* (San Francisco, CA: Cleis Press Inc., 1997). Contemporary history of transexuality.

Andrea Dworkin. *Intercourse* (New York, NY: Macmillan, The Free Press, 1987). How intercourse is a patriarchal institution that enslaves women.

Robert T. Francoeur, ed. *Taking Sides: Clashing Views on Controversial Issues in Human Sexuality* (Guilford, CT: The Dushkin Publishing Group, Inc., Third Edition, 1991). Interesting issues tackled in short writings.

Nancy Friday. *Women on Top: How Real Life Has Changed Women's Sexual Fantasies* (New York, NY: Simon and Schuster, 1991). Sexual fantasies of more than 150 women. Is this sample typical of all women?

Diana Fuss, ed. *Lesbian Theories, Gay Theories* (New York, NY: Routledge, 1991). Nice imaginative collection.

Stevi Jackson an Sue Scott, eds. *Feminism and Sexuality: A Reader* (New York, NY: Columbia University Press, 1996). Writers address key issues in the area of sexuality.

Morris B. Kaplan. *Sexual Justice: Democratic Citizenship and the Politics of Desire* (New York, NY: Routledge, 1997). Sustained argumentation supporting the claims of gays and lesbians to full citizenship.

Jonathan Ned Katz. *The Invention of Heterosexuality* (New York, NY: Penguin Books, 1996). Heterosexuality as a concept for dividing up and judging sexuality and people.

Celia Kitzinger. *The Social Construction of Lesbianism* (Newbury Park, CA: Sage Publications, Inc., [1987], 1989). Exploration of oppression of lesbians by traditional liberal thinking.

Christian McEwen and Sue O'Sullivan, eds. *Out the Other Side* (Freedom, CA: The Crossing Press, 1989). Coming directly to the point on a variety of lesbian issues.

Andy Metcalf and Martin Humphries, eds. *The Sexuality of Man* (Concord, MA: Pluto Press, 1985). Gay and straight men write on male desire, defenses against intimacy, and other topics.

Richard D. Mohr. *Gays/Justice: A Study of Ethics, Society and the Law* (New York, NY: Columbia University Press, 1988). Well-documented, encyclopedic account of social injustice to gays.

Richard D. Mohr. *Gay Ideas: Outings and Other Controversies* (Boston, MA: Beacon Press, 1992). Interesting issues involving gays.

Richard D. Mohr. *A More Perfect Union: Why Straight America Must Stand Up for Gay Rights* (Boston, MA: Beacon Press, 1994).

Timothy F. Murphy, ed. *Gay Ethics: Controversies in Outing, Civil Rights and Sexual Science* (Birmingham, NY: Haworth Press, Inc., 1994). Clear, careful analyses of a number of issues in gay ethics.

Adie Nelson and Barrie W. Robinson. *Gigolos and Madames Bountiful: Illusions of Gender, Power, and Intimacy* (Toronto, ON: University of Toronto Press, 1994).

Trudy Party and Sandee Potter, eds. *Women-Identified Women* (Palo Alto, CA: Mayfield Publishing Co., 1984). Lesbian issues; coming out, motherhood, the workplace, etc.

Julia Penelope. *Call me Lesbian: Lesbian Lives, Lesbian Theory* (Freedom, CA: The Crossing Press, 1992). Aspects of lesbian life, e.g., role playing, wimmin-only spaces, sado-masochism.

Suzanne Pharr. *Homophobia: A Weapon of Sexism* (Little Rock, AR: Chardon Press, The Women's Project, 1988). Discussion of effects of homophobia on lesbians, gay men, and heterosexual women.

Richard A. Posner. *Sex and Reason* (Cambridge, MA: Harvard University Press, 1992). Explanation of sexual practices according to concepts borrowed from economic theory. A form of sex is a rational response to a particular situation.

John Preston. *The Big Gay Book: A Man's Survival Guide for the 90's* (New York, NY: Penguin Books, 1991). 534 pages intended as a resource for gay men, e.g. how to join a gay band.

Michael Ruse. *Homosexuality: A Philosophical Inquiry* (Cambridge, MA: Basil Blackwell, 1990).

Roger Scruton. *Sexual Desire: A Moral Philosophy of the Erotic* (London: Free Press, 1986). Emotions are not founded on belief in the way in which attitudes are.

Lois Shawver. *And the Flag Was Still There: Straight People, Gay People and Sexuality in the U.S. Military* (Binghamton, NY: The Haworth Press, 1995).

Simon Shepherd and Nick Wallis, eds. *Coming on Strong: Gay Politics and Culture* (Boston, MA: Unwin and Human, 1989). Discussions of gay life.

Ann Snitow, Christine Stansell, and Sharon Thompson, eds. *Powers of Desire: The Politics of Sexuality* (New York, NY: Monthly Review Press, 1983). Issues in sexuality, including heterosexism and male domination.

Alan Soble, ed. *The Philosophy of Sex: Contemporary Readings* (Savage, MD: Rowman and Littlefield, 1991). Readings on sex and the issues sex raises.

Alan Soble. *Sexual Investigations* (New York, NY: New York University Press, 1996). Readable defense of a liberal theory of sexuality.

Catharine R. Stimpson and Ethel Spector Person. *Women, Sex and Sexuality* (Chicago, IL: University of Chicago Press, 1980). Notion of women as the "mirror image" of the man in sexuality problematized.

John Stoltenberg. *Refusing to Be a Man: Essays on Sex and Justice* (New York, NY: Penguin, 1990). Male sexuality and male mystique leads to rape, homophobia, and other social ills.

Sharon Dale Stone. *Lesbians in Canada* (Toronto, ON: Between the Lines, 1990). Problems and solutions in situations of lesbians.

C. A. Tripp. *The Homosexual Matrix* (New York, NY: McGraw Hill, Second Edition, 1987). Well-written and thoroughly researched by an associate of Dr. Alfred Kinsey.

Mariana Valverde. *Sex, Power, and Pleasure* (Toronto, ON: The Woman's Press, 1985). Heterosexuality, lesbianism, bisexuality, and the shaping of female desire.

Russell Vannoy. *Sex Without Love* (Buffalo, NY: Prometheus Books, 1980). An idea someone had to develop: sex is better without love.

Martin S. Weinberg, Colin J. Williams, and Douglas W. Prior. *Dual Attraction: Understanding Bisexuality* (New York, NY: Oxford University Press, 1995). Excellent thorough introduction to bisexuality.

Elizabeth Reba Weise, ed. *Closer to Home: Bisexuality and Feminism* (Seattle, WA: Seal Press, 1992). Bisexuals speak out.

Sue Wilkinson and Celia Kitzinger, eds. *Heterosexuality: A Feminism and Psychology Reader* (Newbury Park, CA: Sage Publications, 1993). The taken for granted sexual orientation receives scholarly exploration.

John Wilson. *Love, Sex and Feminism: A Philosophical Essay* (New York, NY: Praeger, 1980). Interesting topics like sexual insults.

READINGS ON AIDS

The ACT UP/New York Women and AIDS Book Group, eds. *Women, AIDS and Activism* (Toronto, ON: Between the Lines, 1990).

Charles Anderson and Patricia Wilkie, eds. *Reflective Helping in HIV and AIDS* (Bristol, PA: Open Court, 1992).

Marie Antoinette Brown and Gail M. Powell-Cope. *Caring for a Loved One with AIDS* (Seattle, WA: University of Washington, School of Nursing, Community Health, 1992).

Christine Overall and William P. Zion, eds. *Perspectives on AIDS: Ethical and Social Issues* (New York, NY: Oxford University Press, 1991). Thorough treatment of a wide variety of problems in the area of AIDS.

Christine Pierce and Donald Vandeveer, eds. *AIDS: Ethics and Public Policy* (Belmont, CA: Wadsworth Publishing Co., 1988). Readable writers tackle a number of interesting issues relating to the threat of AIDS.

Frederic G. Remer, ed. *AIDS and Ethics* (New York, NY: Columbia University Press, 1991).

Diane Richardson. *Women and AIDS* (New York, NY: Methuen, Inc., 1988).

Beth E. Schneider and Nancy E. Stoller, eds. *Women Resisting AIDS: Feminists Strategies of Empowerment* (Philadelphia, PA: Temple University Press, 1995). Women making a difference in AIDS prevention and care.

Robert Searles Walker. *AIDS Today, Tomorrow: An Introduction to the HIV Epidemic in America,* 2nd edition (Atlantic Highlands, NJ: Humanities Press International, Inc., 1994). Thoroughgoing warning about the present dangers of AIDS in America.

Suggested Moral of Part VI

Sex today is very much in the control of men and centers around male erection and orgasm. Women's sexual preferences have been ignored to the point that women have difficulties determining what they are or expressing them in language.

Thus a popular conception of heterosexual sex is something a man does to a woman for his pleasure alone. Lesbian sex then becomes an impossibility because no penis is present, and gay sex is unnatural because there are too many penises and no legitimate place to insert them. Men are pressured into equating their sexuality and masculinity with the activity of their penises.

This thinking sets the stage for situations where men control women through sexuality. Every legitimate episode of sex is pleasure for the man with no known pleasure for the woman, who functions only as a receptacle.

The female orgasm is not well understood by the lay practitioner of sex, man or woman. Even when it becomes a goal in a sexual episode, it is not thought of as being important to a woman's well being or gender identity as a man's orgasm is to a man. Women may thus be cast as "sex-objects" in heterosexual sex from the outset, as long as their role is understood as limited to their being bodies from which men receive sexual pleasure.

Part VII

Rape and Sexual Harassment

Introduction

RAPE AND SEXUAL HARASSMENT are, by definition, sexual actions that are perpetrated on a woman against her will. The writers in this part address themselves to why men do these things and why there is not more resistance (including public complaints) by women.

Beneke explains the mentality of men who rape; Warshaw examines date rape and acquaintance rape; Sanday describes a form of gang rape; an unknown author likens the treatment of a hypothetical theft victim to that of a rape victim; Dziech and Weiner discuss sexual harassment on the college campus; May describes the effects of sexual harassment upon both the harassers and their victims.

VII.1   Men on Rape

TIM BENEKE

Tim Beneke explains how the widespread threat of rape affects lives of women. He also mentions some ways in which men try to blame the women they raped for the rape.

Beneke, a writer living in the San Francisco Bay Area, is the author of *Men on Rape*, (New York: St. Martin's Press, 1982).

Reading Questions

1. How would your life be different if rape were suddenly to end? Would your answer be different if you were of the other gender?
2. Do you feel your clothes must be zipped, buttons done up, everything tucked in because of threat of rape? Is this a matter that would be different for the other gender?
3. Would you be friendlier to people, strangers in particular, if you were not afraid of being taken advantage of sexually? Once again, is this different for the other gender?
4. Is the heterosexual situation a power game won by a woman if she engages a man's interest but doesn't have sex with him, won by the man if sex does occur?

RAPE MAY BE America's fasted growing violent crime; no one can be certain because it is not clear whether more rapes are being committed or reported. It *is* clear that violence against women is widespread and fundamentally alters the meaning of life for women; that sexual violence is encouraged in a variety of ways in American culture and that women are often blamed for rape.

Consider some statistics:

- In a random sample of 930 women, sociologist Diana Russell found that 44 percent had survived either rape or attempted rape. Rape was defined as sexual intercourse physically forced upon the woman, or coerced by threat of bodily harm, or forced upon the woman when she was helpless (asleep, for example). The survey included rape and attempted rape in marriage in its calculations. (Personal communication)

- In a September 1980 survey conducted by *Cosmopolitan* magazine to which over 106,000 women anonymously responded, 24 percent had been raped at least once. Of these, 51 percent had been raped by friends, 37 percent by strangers, 18 percent by relatives, and 3 percent by husbands. Ten percent of the women in the survey had been victims of incest. Seventy-five percent of the women had been "bullied into making love." Writer Linda Wolfe, who reported on the survey, wrote in reference to such bullying: "Though such harassment stops short of rape, readers reported that it was nearly as distressing."

- An estimated 2–3 percent of all men who rape outside of marriage go to prison for their crimes.[1]

- The F.B.I. estimates that if current trends continue, one woman in four will be sexually assaulted in her lifetime.[2]

- An estimated 1.8 million women are battered by their spouses each year.[3] In extensive interviews with 430 battered women, clinical psychologist Lenore Walker, author of *The Battered Woman*, found that 59.9 percent had also been raped (defined as above) by their spouses. Given the difficulties many women had in admitting they had been raped, Walker estimates the figure may well be as high as 80 or 85 percent. (Personal communication.) If 59.9 percent of the 1.8 million women battered each year are also raped, then a million women may be raped in marriage each year. And a significant number are raped in marriage without being battered.

- Between one in two and one in ten of all rapes are reported to the police.[4]

- Between 300,000 and 500,000 women are raped each year outside of marriage.[5]

What is often missed when people contemplate statistics on rape is the effect of the *threat* of sexual violence on women. I have asked women repeatedly, "How would your life be different if rape were suddenly to end?" (Men may learn a lot by asking this question of women to whom they are close.) The threat of rape is an assault upon the meaning of the world; it alters the feel of the human condition. Surely any attempt to comprehend the lives of women that fails to take issues of violence against women into account is misguided.

Through talking to women, I learned: *The threat of rape alters the meaning and feel of the night*. Observe how your body feels, how the night feels, when you're in fear. The constriction in your chest, the vigilance in your eyes, the rubber in your legs. What do the stars look like?

How does the moon present itself? What is the difference between walking late at night in the dangerous part of a city and walking late at night in the country, or safe suburbs? When I try to imagine what the threat of rape must do to the night, I think of the stalked, adrenalated feeling I get walking late at night in parts of certain American cities. Only, I remind myself, it is a fear different from any I have known, a fear of being raped.

It is night half the time. If the threat of rape alters the meaning of the night, it must alter the meaning and pace of the day, one's relation to the passing and organization of time itself. For some women, the threat of rape at night turns their cars into armored tanks, their solitude into isolation. And what must the space inside a car or an apartment feel like if the space outside is menacing?

I was running late one night with a close woman friend through a path in the woods on the outskirts of a small university town. We had run several miles and were feeling a warm, energized serenity.

"How would you feel if you were alone?" I asked.

"Terrified!" she said instantly.

"Terrified that there might be a man out there?" I asked, pointing to the surrounding moonlit forest, which had suddenly been transformed into a source of terror.

"Yes."

Another woman said, "I know what I can't do and I've completely internalized what I can't do. I've built a viable life that basically involves never leaving my apartment at night unless I'm directly going some place to meet somebody. It's unconsciously built into what it occurs to women to do." When one is raised without freedom, one may not recognize its absence.

The threat of rape alters the meaning and feel of nature. Everyone has felt the psychic nurturance of nature. Many women are being deprived of that nurturance, especially in wooded areas near cities. They are deprived either because they cannot experience nature in solitude because of threat, or because, when they do choose solitude in nature, they must cope with a certain subtle but nettlesome fear.

Women need more money because of rape and the threat of rape makes it harder for women to earn money. It's simple: if you don't feel safe walking at night, or riding public transportation, you need a car. And it is less practicable to live in cheaper, less secure, and thus more dangerous neighborhoods if the ordinary threat of violence that men experience, being mugged, say, is compounded by the threat of rape. By limiting mobility at night, the threat of rape limits where and when one is able to work, thus making it more difficult to earn money. An obvious bind: Women need more money because of rape, and have fewer job opportunities because of it.

The threat of rape makes women more dependent on men (or other women). One woman said: "If there were no rape I wouldn't have to play games with men for their protection." The threat of rape falsifies, mystifies, and confuses relations between men and women. If there were no rape, women would simply not need men as much, wouldn't need them to go places with at night, to feel safe in their homes, for protection in nature.

The threat of rape makes solitude less possible for women. Solitude, drawing strength from being alone, is difficult if being alone means being afraid. To be afraid is to be in need, to experience a lack; the threat of rape creates a lack. Solitude requires relaxation; if you're afraid, you can't relax.

The threat of rape inhibits a woman's expressiveness. "If there were no rape," said one woman, "I could dress the way I wanted and walk the way I wanted and not feel self-conscious about the responses of men. I could be friendly to people. I wouldn't have to wish I was ugly. I wouldn't have to make myself small when I got on the bus. I wouldn't have to respond to verbal abuse from men by remaining silent. I could respond in kind."

If a woman's basic expressiveness is inhibited, her sexuality, creativity, and delight in life must surely be diminished.

The threat of rape inhibits the freedom of the eye. I know a married couple who live in Manhattan. They are both artists, both acutely sensitive and responsive to the visual world. When they walk separately in the city, he has more freedom to look than she does. She must control her eye movements lest they inadvertently meet the glare of some importunate man. What, who, and how she sees are restricted by the threat of rape.

The following exercise is recommended for men.

> Walk down a city street. Pay a lot of attention to your clothing; make sure your pants are zipped, shirt tucked in, buttons done. Look straight ahead. Every time a man walks past you, avert your eyes and make your face expressionless. Most women learn to go through this act each time we leave our houses. It's a way to avoid at least some of the encounters we've all had with strange men who decided we looked available.[6]

To relate aesthetically to the visual world involves a certain playfulness, spirit of spontaneous exploration. The tense vigilance that accompanies fear inhibits that spontaneity. The world is no longer yours to look at when you're afraid.

I am aware that all culture, is, in part, restriction, that there are places in America where hardly anyone is safe (though men are safer than women virtually everywhere), that there are many ways to enjoy life, that some women may not be so restricted, that there exist havens, whether psychic, geographical, economic, or class. but they are *havens,* and as such, defined by threat.

Above all, I trust my experience: No woman could have lived the life I've lived the last few years. If suddenly I were restricted by the threat of rape, I would feel a deep, inexorable depression. And it's not just rape; it's harassment, battery, Peeping Toms, anonymous phone calls, exhibitionism, intrusive stares, fondlings—all contributing to an atmosphere of intimidation in women's lives. And I have only scratched the surface; it would take many carefully crafted short stories to begin to express what I have only hinted at in the last few pages. I have not even touched upon what it might mean for a woman to be sexually assaulted. Only women can speak to that. Nor have I suggested how the threat of rape affects marriage.

Rape and the threat of rape pervades the lives of women, as reflected in some popular images of our culture.

"SHE ASKED FOR IT"— BLAMING THE VICTIM[7]

Many things may be happening when a man blames a woman for rape.

First, in all cases where a woman is said to have asked for it, her appearance and behavior are taken as a form of speech. "Actions speak louder than words" is a widely held belief; the woman's actions—her appearance may be taken as action—are given greater emphasis than her words; an interpretation alien to the woman's intentions is given to her actions. A logical extension of "she asked for it" is the idea that she wanted what happened to happen; if she wanted it to happen, she *deserved* for it to happen. Therefore, the man is not to be blamed. "She asked for it" can mean either that she was consenting to have sex and was not really raped, or that she was in fact raped but somehow she really deserved it. "If you ask for it, you deserve it," is a widely held notion. If I ask you to beat me up and you beat me up, I still don't deserve to be beaten up. So even if the notion that women asked to be raped had some basis in reality, which it doesn't, on its own terms it makes no sense.

Second, a mentality exists that says: A woman who assumes freedoms normally restricted to a man (like going out alone at night) and is raped is doing the same thing as a woman who goes out in the rain without an umbrella and catches a cold. Both are considered responsible for what happens to them. That men will rape is taken to be a legitimized given, part of nature, like rain or snow. The view reflects a massive abdication of responsibility for rape on the part of men. It is so much easier to think of rape as natural than to ac-

knowledge one's part in it. So long as rape is regarded as natural, women will be blamed for rape.

A third point. The view that it is natural for men to rape is closely connected to the view of women as commodities. If a woman's body is regarded as a valued commodity by men, then of course, if you leave a valued commodity where it can be taken, it's just human nature for men to take it. If you left your stereo out on the sidewalk, you'd be asking for it to get stolen. Someone will just take it. (And how often men speak of rape as "going out and *taking* it.") If a woman walks the streets at night, she's leaving a valued commodity, her body, where it can be taken. So long as women are regarded as commodities, they will be blamed for rape.

Which brings us to a fourth point. "She asked for it" is inseparable from a more general "psychology of the dupe." If I use bad judgment and fail to read the small print in a contract and later get taken advantage of, "screwed" (or "fucked over") then I deserve what I get; bad judgment makes me liable. Analogously, if a woman trusts a man and goes to his apartment, or accepts a ride hitchhiking, or goes out on a date and is raped, she's a dupe and deserves what she gets. "He didn't *really* rape her" goes the mentality— "he merely took advantage of her." And in America it's okay for people to take advantage of each other, even expected and praised. In fact, you're considered dumb and foolish if you don't take advantage of other people's bad judgment. And so, again, by treating them as dupes, rape will be blamed on women.

Fifth, if a woman who is raped is judged attractive by men, and particularly if she dresses to look attractive, then the mentality exists that she attacked him with her weapon so, of course, he counter-attacked with his. The preview to a popular movie states: "She was the victim of her own provocative beauty." Provocation: "There is a line which, if crossed, will *set me off* and I will lose control and no longer be responsible for my behavior. If you punch me in the nose then, of course, I will not be responsible for what happens: You will have provoked a fight. If you dress, talk, move, or act a certain way, you will have provoked me to rape. If your appearance *stuns* me, *strikes* me, *ravishes* me, *knocks me out,* etc., then I will not be held responsible for what happens; you will have asked for it." The notion that sexual feeling makes one helpless is part of a cultural abdication of responsibility for sexuality. So long as a woman's appearance is viewed as a weapon and sexual feeling is believed to make one helpless, women will be blamed for rape.

Sixth, I have suggested that men sometimes become obsessed with images of women, that images become a substitute for sexual feeling, that sexual feeling becomes externalized and out of control and is given an undifferentiated identity in the appearance of women's bodies. It is a process of projection in which one blurs one's own desire with her imagined, projected desire. If a woman's attractiveness is taken to signify one's own lust and a woman's lust, then when an "attractive" woman is raped, some men may think she wanted sex. Since they perceive their own lust in part projected onto the woman, they disbelieve women who've been raped. So long as men project their own sexual desires onto women, they will blame women for rape.

And seventh, what are we to make of the contention that women in dating situations say "no" initially to sexual overtures from men as a kind of pose, only to give in later, thus revealing their true intentions? And that men are thus confused and incredulous when women are raped because in their sexual experience women can't be believed? I doubt that this has much to do with men's perceptions of rape. I don't know to what extent women actually "say no and mean yes"; certainly it is a common theme in male folklore. I have spoken to a couple of women who went through periods when they wanted to be sexual but were afraid to be, and often rebuffed initial sexual advances only to give in later. One point is clear: The ambivalence women may feel about having sex is closely tied to the inability of men to fully accept them as sexual beings. Women have been traditionally punished for being

openly and freely sexual; men are praised for it. And if many men think of sex as achievement of possession of a valued commodity, or aggressive degradation, then women have every reason to feel and act ambivalent.

These themes are illustrated in an interview I conducted with a 23-year-old man who grew up in Pittsburgh and works as a file clerk in the financial district of San Francisco. Here's what he said:

"Where I work it's probably no different from any other major city in the U.S. The women dress up in high heels, and they wear a lot of makeup, and they just look really *hot* and really sexy, and how can somebody who has a healthy sex drive not feel lust for them when you see them? I feel lust for them, but I don't think I could find it in me to overpower someone and rape them. But I definitely get the feeling that I'd like to rape a girl. I don't know if the actual act of rape would be satisfying, but the *feeling* is satisfying.

"These women look so good, and they kiss ass of the men in the three-piece suits who are *big* in the corporation, and most of them relate to me like "Who are *you?* Who are *you* to even *look* at?" They're snobby and they condescend to me, and I resent it. It would take me a lot longer to get to first base than it would somebody with a three-piece suit who had money. And to me a lot of the men they go out with are superficial assholes who have no real feelings or substance, and are just trying to get ahead and make a lot of money. Another thing that makes me resent these women is thinking, "How could she want to hang out with somebody like that? What does that make her?"

"I'm a file clerk, which makes me feel like a nebbish, a nurd, like I'm not making it, I'm a failure. But I don't really believe I'm a failure because I know it's just a phase, and I'm just doing it for the money, just to make it through this phase. I catch myself feeling like a failure, but I realize that's ridiculous."

What exactly do you go through when you see these sexy, unavailable women?

"Let's say I see a woman and she looks really pretty and really clean and sexy, and she's giving off very feminine, sexy vibes. I think, 'Wow, I would love to make love to her,' but I know she's not really interested. It's a tease. A lot of times a woman knows that she's looking really good and she'll use that and flaunt it, and it makes me feel like she's laughing at me and I feel *degraded*.

"I also feel dehumanized, because when I'm being teased I just turn off, I cease to be human. Because if I go with my human emotions I'm going to want to put my arms around her and kiss her, and to do that would be unacceptable. I don't like the feeling that I'm supposed to stand there and take it, and to be able to hug her or kiss her; so I just turn off my emotions. It's a feeling of humiliation, because the woman has forced me to turn off my feelings and react in a way that I really don't want to.

"If I were actually desperate enough to rape somebody, it would be from wanting the person, but it would be a very spiteful thing, just being able to say, 'I have power over you and I can do anything I want with you,' because really I feel that *they* have power over *me* just by their presence. Just the fact that they can come up to me and just melt me and make me feel like a dummy makes me want revenge. They have power over me so I want power over them. .. ..

"Society says that you have to have a lot of sex with a lot of different women to be a real man. Well, what happens if you don't? Then what are you? Are you half a man? Are you still a boy? It's ridiculous. You see a whiskey ad with a guy and two women on his arm. The implication is that real men don't have any trouble getting women."

How does it make you feel toward women to see all these sexy women in media and advertising using their looks to try to get you to buy something?

"It makes me hate them. As a man you're taught that men are more powerful than women, and that men always have the upper hand, and that it's a man's society; but then you see all these women and it makes you think 'Jesus Christ, if we have all the power how come all the beautiful women are telling us what to buy?' And

to be honest, it just makes me hate beautiful women because they're using their power over me. I realize they're being used themselves, and they're doing it for money. In *Playboy* you see all these beautiful women who look so sexy and they'll be giving you all these looks like they want to have sex so bad; but then in reality you know that except for a few nymphomaniacs, they're doing it for the money; so I hate them for being used and using their bodies in that way.

"In this society, if you ever sit down and realize how manipulated you really are it makes you pissed off—it makes you want to take control. And you've been manipulated by women, and they're a very easy target because they're out walking along the streets, so you can just grab one and say, 'Listen, you're going to do what I want you to do,' and it's an act of revenge against the way you've been manipulated.

"I know a girl who was walking down the street by her house, when this guy jumped her and beat her up and raped her, and she was black and blue and had to go to the hospital. That's beyond me. I can't understand how somebody could do that. If I were going to rape a girl, I wouldn't hurt her. I might *restrain* her, but I wouldn't *hurt* her. . . .

"The whole dating game between men and women also makes me feel degraded. I hate being put in the position of having to initiate a relationship. I've been taught that if you've not been aggressive with a woman, then you've blown it. She's not going to jump on *you*, so *you've* got to jump on *her*. I've heard all kinds of stories where the woman says, 'No! No! No!' and they end up making great love. I get confused as hell if a woman pushes me away. Does it mean she's trying to be a nice girl and wants to put up a good appearance, or does it mean she doesn't want anything to do with you? You don't know. Probably a lot of men think that women don't feel like real women unless a man tries to force himself on her, unless she brings out the 'real man,' so to speak, and probably too much of it goes on. It goes on in my head that you're complimenting a woman by actually staring at her or by trying to get into her pants. Lately, I'm realizing that when I stare at women lustfully, they often feel more threatened than flattered."

NOTES

1. Such estimates recur in the rape literature. See *Sexual Assault* by Nancy Gager and Cathleen Schurr, Grosset & Dunlap, 1976, or *The Price of Coercive Sexuality* by Clark and Lewis, The Women's Press, 1977.

2. *Uniform Crime Reports,* 1980.

3. See *Behind Closed Doors* by Murray J. Strauss and Richard Gelles, Doubleday, 1979.

4. See Gager and Schurr (above) or virtually any book on the subject.

5. Again, see Gager and Schurr, or Carol V. Horos, *Rape,* Banbury Books, 1981.

6. From "Willamette Bridge" in *Body Politics* by Nancy Henley, Prentice-Hall, 1977, p. 144.

7. I would like to thank George Lakoff for this insight.

Further Questions

1. Do you still think actions speak louder than words, so that a woman can ask to be raped through the way she behaves, no matter what she says?

2. Is going out alone at night, for a woman, defying danger, as you would be going out into the rain without an umbrella?

3. Is walking on a sidewalk at night like leaving your stereo on the sidewalk, asking for it to be taken?

4. Does an overly trustful woman deserve what she gets, sexually?

5. Is a woman's dressing to look attractive a weapon she uses on the man's sexuality, so that he is blameless if he mounts a sexual counterattack?

6. If you, a woman, say "no" to sex, but later say "yes," does that prove that you meant "yes" all along?

VII.2   I Never Called It Rape

ROBIN WARSHAW

Robin Warshaw addresses date and acquaintance rape. The dating game often mandates that the man put pressure on the woman and the woman keep things in check, sexually. Men often fail to understand that a woman means "no" when she says it; alcohol and drugs do little to help the situation. Warshaw concludes with an account of how men are taught to rape.

Warshaw is a writer specializing in social issues; her work has appeared in *Ms.,* *Women's Day,* and other publications. This writing is from a longer work conducted under the auspices of *Ms.*

Reading Questions

1. Suppose dating involved a game, which the man wins if sexual activity occurs, the woman wins if it doesn't. Does this mean that a game has been set in place with the consent of both genders, or have men forced this game on women? Explain.
2. Is there such a thing as justifiable rape on a date, where the victim's behavior is responsible for triggering the man's action? If so, can a woman negate her rights to what happens to her body by behaving in a sexually provocative manner?
3. Is it surprising to hear that when men are raped, it is a frightening and painful experience for them as well?

WHY DATE RAPE AND ACQUAINTANCE RAPE ARE SO WIDESPREAD

RAPES BETWEEN MEN AND WOMEN who know each other are happening in big cities, small towns, and rural areas. They occur among all ethnic and religious groups, regardless of education or wealth. Many of these rapes are rooted in the social behavior men and women learn. . . .

Dating Rituals

This interaction comes into sharpest focus in traditional dating behavior where the male initiates the date by asking the woman out, with him paying all of the expenses or buying the liquor, food, or entertainment. When this happens, the man may expect sexual activity or intercourse, with or without a serious attachment between himself and the woman; she, on the other hand, may want intimacy only after a relationship has developed over a period of time. Even when the woman wants sex without a developed relationship, she may put up a protest because she has been trained that only "bad girls" have sex willingly. Her date, on the other hand, has learned from seeing such behavior (or from the advice of other men) that women often say no when they mean yes.

If the male is nonaggressive sexually, there's no problem. But if he is aggressive, the female enters into a contest with him—either because she really doesn't want to have sex with him or because she feels she must put up some resis-

tance to maintain a good reputation. Dating then becomes a game which each side tries to win. And date rape may be the result. . . .

And so the game is afoot from the outset of many traditional dates, with the man pressing his attempts at seduction and the woman keeping a check on how sexually involved the couple will become. This balance might be maintained for a long time in a way that is satisfactory to both people. But if the man moves from trying to cajole the woman into sexual activity to forcing her to comply by raping her, he may encounter what seems to him little resistance. That's because the woman's socialization has most likely taught her that she must not express her own wishes forcefully, that she should not hurt other people's feelings or reject them, that she should be quiet, polite, and never make a scene. And, as a girl, she has also learned not to be physical. . . .

Interpersonal Violence

All it takes to solidify the aggressor/victim relationship of the dating couple is the addition of a belief in using violence to deal with personal conflict. Studies show that may not be a great leap.

A Minnesota survey of 202 male and female college students revealed that, in dating relationships:

- nearly 13 percent had either slapped their date or been slapped
- 14 percent were pushed or did the pushing
- 4 percent were punched or did the punching

- 3.5 percent were struck with an object or did the striking
- 1.5 percent were choked or did the choking
- 1 percent were assaulted with a weapon or committed such an assault. . . .

Communication

Miscommunication contributes to the factual and perceptual fogs that cloud acquaintance-rape incidents. This miscommunication may occur because men and women often interpret behavior cues and even direct conversation differently. In general, men give a more sexual reading to behavior and conversation than women do. In a 1982 study conducted by Antonia Abbey of Northwestern University in Evanston, Illinois, male and female subjects watched a male and female actor talk to each other, and the males rated the female actor as being more seductive and promiscuous than did the women. Another study, this one with high school students in California, showed that males consistently rated various dating behaviors, types of dress, and dating activities as signals for sex more often than females did.

Male and female subjects in a 1983 research project read scenarios about college students who went on dates, then evaluated whether the date participants wanted sex from each other. Regardless of who had initiated the date, who had paid for it, or where the couple went, the male students were more likely than their female counterparts to think that the woman in the scenario wanted sex from the man she was with. "It seems likely that a man might misinterpret a woman's behavior and think that she is more interested in him than she really is," writes the study's author, Charlene L. Muehlenhard of Texas A&M University, College Station, Texas. Indeed, many men only ask a woman out after they've decided that they'd like to have sex with her, whereas many women view dates, especially the first few dates, as opportunities to socialize and learn more about the man.

Some people hope that improving the woman's ability to clearly communicate what she wants will naturally lead the man to understand how to proceed. Although the "deafness" of some males involved in acquaintance rapes may, in part, be due to not being told in a decisive way what the woman wants, many men simply discount what a woman is saying or reinterpret it to fit what they want to hear. They have been raised to believe that women will always resist sex to avoid the appearance of being promiscuous (and, indeed, some do), will always say "no" when they really mean "yes,"and always want men to dominate them and show that they are in control. Further, many men have been conditioned to simply ignore women—whether those women are responding positively to sexual interactions or pushing, fighting, kicking, crying, or otherwise resisting them.

When it comes to sexual relations, saying "no" is often meaningless when the words are spoken by a female.

Belief in the "Justifiable" Rape

The result of these conflicts in communication—the socialized "deafness" of men toward women and the likelihood that a man will interpret a situation to have stronger sexual overtones than a woman will—leads to the belief among many men (and some women) in "justifiable rape," somewhat along the lines of "justifiable homicide." In "justifiable rape," the victim's behavior is seen as being responsible for triggering the man's action. Although there is no legal concept as there is in "justifiable homicide," the idea of "justifiable rape" influences the opinions of everyone from the rape victim's own family to the jury who may sit in judgment of her attacker.

Recent studies show that men believe date rape is more justifiable if one of these circumstances occurs:

- the woman invites the man out on the date
- the man pays for the date
- she dresses "suggestively"
- they go to his place rather than to a movie
- she drinks alcohol or does drugs

Men with traditional attitudes toward women rate these situations as justifying rape significantly more often than do men who hold nontraditional attitudes.

The research also shows that many times men will feel "led on" while women will not have the slightest clue that their actions are being interpreted as sexual. In a 1967 study by Purdue's Eugene Kanin, sexually aggressive college men said they believed their aggression was justified if the woman was "a tease." A 1979 survey of California high school boys showed 54 percent thought rape was justifiable if the girl "leads a boy on."

In a study exploring correlations between people who rated rape as justifiable under certain circumstances and people who actually were involved in sexually aggressive incidents, Texas A&M's Muehlenhard found that men were much more likely than women to say that the woman had hinted beforehand that she wanted the man to ask her out. When she looked at just those subjects whose dates involved sexual aggression, Muehlenhard saw this difference in high relief: 60 percent of men reported that the woman had hinted she was interested in dating him; only 16 percent of the women said they had so hinted. Those men clearly felt "led on" by the women who refused them sex, a feeling which many of them may have regarded as justification for committing rape.

The Role of Alcohol and Drugs

It's impossible to consider why acquaintance rape is so widespread without mentioning the correlation between drug and alcohol use and sexual assault.

> *Ms.* **SURVEY STAT** About 75 percent of the men and at least 55 percent of the women involved in acquaintance rapes had been drinking or taking drugs just before the attack.

Although it is certainly possible to drink alcohol without becoming intoxicated, in many social settings—particularly those involving teenagers and young adults—getting drunk is the point of drinking. And because there is really no drug-taking corollary to drinking just one glass of beer, using drugs like marijuana, hashish, cocaine, crack, methamphetamines, LSD, angel dust, and heroin almost always means becoming intoxicated or "high," although the depth of that intoxication may vary from drug to drug.

As has been seen in federal highway safety tests, alcohol begins to affect people in negative ways long before they believe they are actually drunk. Alcohol and drugs distort reality, cloud judgment, and slow reactions, causing men and women to expose themselves to dangers or disregard social constraints that might otherwise influence them.

When intoxicated, a woman's perceptions about what is happening around her and to her become blurred. Her ability to resist an attack is lessened as her verbal and physical response mechanisms become sedated. She may rely on other people to take care of her, to see that she gets home safely, and to protect her from harm. Some men purposely "feed" a woman alcohol or drugs before forcing her to have sex to reduce her defenses. . . . Moreover, women who have become obviously drunk or high on their own often become targets for individual men or groups of men scouting for a victim. And the fact that a woman is drinking, even if she's not drunk, is often believed by men to be a justification for rape (since "good girls" aren't supposed to drink). It also makes police and prosecutors less inclined to press charges in acquaintance and date rapes.

An intoxicated man may become more sexually aggressive, more violent and less interested in what the woman wants than when he's sober. And many men who commit acquaintance rape excuse their acts because they were drunk or under the influence of drugs. . . .

MEN WHO RAPE WOMEN THEY KNOW

Rape is not natural to men. If it were, most men would be rapists and they are not. Nonetheless, the answers given by the male college students who participated in the *Ms.* study delineate a sobering incidence of sexual aggression and assault in a predominantly middle-class, educated population.

As was done for the women surveyed, the word "rape" was not used in questions asked of men about their sexual behavior; instead, descriptions of specific acts were given (for example, "Have you ever engaged in sexual intercourse with a woman when she didn't want to by threatening or using some degree of physical force?"). The final tally:

Ms. SURVEY STATS In the year prior to the survey, 2,971 college men reported that they had committed:

- 187 rapes;
- 157 attempted rapes;
- 327 episodes of sexual coercion;
- 854 incidents of unwanted sexual contact.

How Men Are Taught to Rape

"Rape is not some form of psychopathology that afflicts a very small number of men," says acquaintance-rape educator Py Bateman. "In fact, rape is not that different from what we see as socially acceptable or socially laudable male behavior."

What differentiates men who rape women they know from men who do not is, in part, how much they believe the dogma of what most boys learn it means to be male—"macho" in the worst sense of the word. Some researchers describe this variable as the "hypermasculinity" factor. Others have dubbed the men who embody this behavior "male zealots."

Nearly all men are exposed to this sexual indoctrination, but fortunately only some truly adhere to it. These beliefs are chiefly promulgated by other men: fathers, uncles, grandfathers, coaches, youth group leaders, friends, fraternity brothers, even pop stars. Boys are taught through verbal and nonverbal cues to be self-centered and single-minded about sex, to view women as objects from whom sex is taken, not as equal partners with wishes and desires of their own. Boys learn that they must initiate sexual activity, that they may meet with reluctance from girls, but if they just persist, cajole, and refuse to let up, that ultimately they will get what they want. They view their relationships with women as adversarial challenges and learn to use both their physical and social power to overcome these smaller, less important people. . . .

This is what most boys—not just future rapists—learn about being sexual. Little or no mention is made of sex as an interaction between two people who are mutually participating and enjoying it. And few boys have the benefit of learning what good sexual relations are by the example of the men around them. . . .

Language not only leads men to objectify women but to objectify—and so dissociate themselves from—their own sexual organs. The man's penis becomes his "tool" and often he might even give it a name. It thus becomes a creature of its own, with a mind of its own, so the man is absolved of responsibility for its actions. This concept meshes with the popular myth of the male sexual imperative: that is, that once he is sexually aroused, a man cannot stop himself from forcing sex on a woman. Such a belief provides a handy rationalization of a man to use to coerce a woman into having sex ("See what you've done to me? Now we've *gotta* do it."). Moreover, the dissociation of the man from his penis and the myth that he can't be held responsible once he has been turned on makes many date rapes the woman's fault, in the man's view, for arousing him and his "friend." (Belief in these myths isn't limited to men. Studies of male and female college students have shown that both groups believe that sex is a biological drive for men but not for women.)

Reinforcing the effect of language on promulgating hypermasculine sexual behavior are the messages transmitted through popular culture such as movies and television. These messages often mix aggression, force, and sex. In the film *Gone With the Wind* (based on a book written by a woman), Rhett Butler and Scarlett O'Hara are seen drinking and fighting, displaying much anger toward each other. Suddenly, he lifts her off her feet, carries her up that dramatic staircase, and (presumably) to bed. "What happens the next morning?" asks rape educator Bateman. "She's got a big smile on her face!" Proof positive that women really want it, especially if you knock them around a little bit and then physically overpower them.

Bateman also likes to cite a scene from the movie *Saturday Night Fever* as reinforcing the belief that women's wishes should be ignored. In that scene, star John Travolta has just offered to walk the woman of his dreams home (and, hopefully, into an intimate encounter), but she refuses. So he starts to walk away, in the direction of his house, as she turns to walk toward hers. She crosses the street, then turns back to him and calls out, "You shouldn't have asked. You should've just done it." The message to men Bateman says, is, "If you ask, you're gonna lose an opportunity."

Such scenarios are not dated relics. There are dozens and dozens of recent examples. In 1987, the television program *Moonlighting*, supposedly written for a bright and hip audience, focuses on the sexual tensions between its lead characters, Maddie Hayes and David Addison, played by the very appealing Cybill Shepherd and Bruce Willis. For two years, *Moonlighting* fans had watched as Maddie and David danced around the issue of getting together sexually, even though everyone knew they wanted to. Finally, the much-awaited night of consummation arrived; ABC even ballyhooed it in TV ads for days in advance. "What happened is they had a fight," Bateman says. "She calls him a bastard and slaps him across the face. He calls her a bitch. And then it's onto the floor, breaking furniture, sweeping vases of flowers off. It was scary. My heart was pounding. I was extremely depressed and distressed." The yuppie lovers battled angrily for several minutes before collapsing into sexual ecstasy. And out in TV viewerland, millions of boys and men saw that this is what women—even smart, independent women like Maddie—really want.

Every now and then there are glimmers of change. A 1988 *Cagney and Lacey* episode realistically dealt with date rape as a widespread phenomenon: The rapist was a successful businessman and the victim was a strong, independent, female cop. . . .

Male Victims

Perhaps the first question that pops up from the audience at workshops on date rape is, "Don't women rape men, too?" Behind that question is the natural defensiveness many men feel about the subject of rape, especially acquaintance rape. (Women often ask this question too, perhaps out of compassion for the discomfort the men in the workshop are feeling.)

The truth is, men *are* rape victims. Some experts estimate that 10 percent of the victims coming to rape-crisis centers are male even though men are far less likely to seek help after being raped than women. *But almost all male rape victims have been raped by other men.*

However, women do rape, as is known from child sexual-abuse cases. And a few women have raped men, as it is possible to stimulate even a terrified man into having an erection or rape him anally with an object. But the number of women who rape men is infinitesimally small.

The frequent asking of the question, though, demonstrates a certain need on the part of men to believe that women do commit rape and that it happens frequently. Indeed, during acquaintance-rape workshops, college men can often be heard chuckling about how much they wish it would happen to them. That's because they enjoy grade-B movie fantasies of what being assaulted would be like: Perhaps a squad of voluptuous cheerleaders might take them to be their sex prisoners.

Nothing could be further from reality. When men are raped, they are raped by other men, regardless of whether the victim or the assailant(s) are heterosexual or homosexual. It is a frightening, painful, emotionally scarring experience—in short, very like what happens to women who are raped. Men are often brutally beaten during the course of their attacks. They are raped by strangers who assault them on the street, break into their homes, or pick them up hitchhiking. Like women, they are also raped by acquaintances and, in the case of homosexual men, by dates. (Of course, also like women, men are raped as children by relatives, baby-sitters, and other adults.) . . .

Further Questions

1. Is miscommunication regarding whether the woman wants sex mainly the result of her not being able to communicate her intentions clearly or of her date's giving more of a sexual reading to the situation than she intends?

2. Is it true that "good girls" don't drink or take drugs, hence any woman who drinks or takes drugs on a date is inviting the man to rape her by ceasing to be a "good girl"?

3. Why do some people continue to suggest that, once aroused, a man finds it difficult or impossible to stop himself from forcing sex on a woman?

VII.3   Pulling Train

PEGGY R. SANDAY

Peggy R. Sanday describes the phenomenon of "pulling train" on college campuses. Men line up like train cars to take turns having sex with a single woman. The woman is an unwilling participant and so such an incident can be described as a "gang rape."

Reading Questions

1. If a woman is too weak to protest, too frightened of being harmed, too high on alcohol or drugs, or unconscious, can she willingly consent to sex with a series of men?

2. Can the victim of "pulling train" be fairly blamed for placing herself in a situation where it is accepted that male adolescent hormones are likely to get out of hand?

3. Can the sexuality of the men involved in "pulling train" be fairly labelled as "homo-eroticism"? If men are staging their sexual acts for each other to watch, why is the woman even necessary, especially if she is unconscious?

THIS ARTICLE DISCUSSES CERTAIN GROUP RITUALS of male bonding on a college campus, in particular, a phenomenon called "pulling train." According to a report issued by the Association of American Colleges in 1985, "pulling train," or "gang banging" as it is also called, refers to a group of men lining up like train cars to take turns having sex with the same woman (Ehrhart and Sandler, 1985, 2). This report labels "pulling train" as gang rape. Bernice Sandler, one of its au-

thors, recently reported that she had found more than seventy-five documented cases of gang rape on college campuses in recent years (*Atlanta Constitution,* 7 June 1988). Sandler labeled these incidents gang rape because of the coercive nature of the sexual behavior. The incidents she and Julie K. Ehrhart described in their 1985 report display a common pattern. A vulnerable young woman, one who is seeking acceptance or who is high on drugs or alcohol, is taken to a room. She

Abridged from "Pulling Train" in Fraternity and Gang Rape: Sex, Brotherhood and Privilege on Campus *by Peggy R. Sanday. New York University Press 1990. Reprinted by permission of the publisher.*

may or may not agree to have sex with one man. She then passes out, or is too weak or scared to protest, and a train of men have sex with her. Sometimes the young woman's drinks are spiked without her knowledge, and when she is approached by several men in a locked room, she reacts with confusion and panic. Whether too weak to protest, frightened, or unconscious, as has been the case in quite a number of instances, anywhere from two to eleven or more men have sex with her. In some party invitations the possibility of such an occurrence is mentioned with playful allusions to "gang bang" or "pulling train" (Ehrhart and Sandler, 1985, 1–2).

The reported incidents occurred at all kinds of institutions: "public, private, religiously affiliated, Ivy League, large and small" (ibid.). Most of the incidents occurred at fraternity parties, but some occurred in residence halls or in connection with college athletics. Incidents have also been reported in high schools. .. ..

Just a few examples taken from the Ehrhart and Sandler report (1985, 1–2) are sufficient to demonstrate the coercive nature of the sexual behavior.

> The 17-year old freshman woman went to the fraternity "little sister" rush party with two of her roommates. The roommates left early without her. She was trying to get a ride home when a fraternity brother told her he would take her home after the party ended. While she waited, two other fraternity members took her into a bedroom to "discuss little sister matters." The door was closed and one of the bothers stood blocking the exit. They told her that in order to become a little sister (honorary member) she would have to have sex with a fraternity member. She was frightened, fearing they would physically harm her if she refused. She could see no escape. Each of the brothers had sex with her, as did a third who had been hiding in the room. During the next two hours a succession of men went into the room. There were never less than three men with her, sometimes more. After they let her go, a fraternity brother drove her home. He told her not to feel bad about the incident because another

woman had also been "upstairs" earlier that night. (Large southern university)

> It was her first fraternity party. The beer flowed freely and she had much more to drink than she had planned. It was hot and crowded and the party spread out all over the house, so that when three men asked her to go upstairs, she went with them. They took her into a bedroom, locked the door and began to undress her. Groggy with alcohol, her feeble protests were ignored as the three men raped her. When they finished, they put her in the hallway, naked, locking her clothes in the bedroom. (Small eastern liberal arts college)

> A 19-year-old woman student was out on a date with her boyfriend and another couple. They were all drinking beer and after going back to the boyfriend's dorm room, they smoked two marijuana cigarettes. The other couple left and the woman and her boyfriend had sex. The woman fell asleep and the next thing she knew she awoke with a man she didn't know on top of her trying to force her into having sex. A witness said the man was in the hall with two other men when the woman's boyfriend came out of his room and invited them to have sex with his unconscious girlfriend. (Small midwestern college)

Although Ehrhart and Sandler boldly labeled the incidents they described as rape, few of the perpetrators were prosecuted. Generally speaking, the male participants are protected and the victim is blamed for having placed herself in a compromising social situation where male adolescent hormones are known, as the saying goes, "to get out of hand." For a number of reasons, people say, "She asked for it." As the above examples from the Ehrhart and Sandler report suggest, the victim may be a vulnerable young woman who is seeking acceptance or who is weakened by the ingestion of drugs or alcohol. She may or may not agree to having sex with one man. If she has agreed to some sexual activity, the men assume that she has agreed to all sexual activity regardless of whether she is conscious or not. In the minds of the boys involved the sexual behavior is not rape. On many campuses this opinion is shared by a significant portion of the campus community. .. . .

THE XYZ EXPRESS

I first learned about "pulling train" in 1983 from a student who was then enrolled in one of my classes. Laurel had been out of class for about two weeks. I noticed her absence and worried that she was getting behind on her work. When she came back to class she told me that she had been raped by five or six male students at a fraternity house after one of the fraternity's weekly Thursday night parties. Later, I learned from others that Laurel was drunk on beer and had taken four hits of LSD before going to the party. According to the story Laurel told to a campus administrator, after the party she fell asleep in a first-floor room and when she awoke was undressed. One of the brothers dressed her and carried her upstairs, where she was raped by "guys" she did not know but said she could identify if photographs were available. She asked a few times for the men to get off her, but to no avail. According to her account, she was barely conscious and lacked the strength to push them off her.

There is no dispute that Laurel had a serious drinking and drug problem at the time of the party. People at the party told me that during the course of the evening she acted like someone who was "high," and her behavior attracted quite a bit of attention. They described her as dancing provocatively to the beat of music only she could hear. She appeared disoriented and out of touch with what was happening. Various fraternity brothers occasionally danced with her, but she seemed oblivious to the person she was dancing with. Some of the brothers teased her by spinning her around in a room until she was so dizzy she couldn't find her way out. At one point during the evening she fell down a flight of stairs. Later she was pulled by the brothers out of a circle dance, a customary fraternity ritual in which only brothers usually took part.

After the other partyers had gone home, the accounts of what happened next vary according to who tells the story. The differences of opinion do not betray a Rashomon effect as much as they reflect different definitions of a common sexual event. No one disputes that Laurel had sex with at least five or six male students, maybe more. When Anna, a friend of the XYZ bothers, saw Laurel the next day and heard the story from the brothers, her immediate conclusion was that they had raped Laurel. Anna based her conclusion on seeing Laurel's behavior at the party and observing her the following day. It seemed to Anna that Laurel was incapable of consenting to sex, which is key for determining a charge of rape. Anna's opinion was later confirmed by the Assistant District Attorney for Sex Crimes, who investigated but did not prosecute the case.

The brothers claimed that Laurel had lured them into a "gang bang" or "train," which they preferred to call an "express." Their statements and actions during the days after the event seemed to indicate that they considered the event a routine part of their "little sister program," something to be proud of. Reporting the party activities on a sheet posed on their bulletin board in the spot where the house minutes are usually posted, Anna found the following statement, which she later showed me:

> Things are looking up for the [XYZ] sisters program. A prospective leader for the group spent some time interviewing several [brothers] this past Thursday and Friday. Possible names for the little sisters include [XYZ] "little wenches" and "The [XYZ] express."

. . . The ideology that promotes "pulling train" is seen in the discourse and practices associated with some parties on campus. Party invitations expressing this ideology depict a woman lying on a pool table, or in some other position suggestive of sexual submission. The hosts of the party promote behavior aimed at seduction. *Seduction* means plying women with alcohol or giving them drugs in order to "break down resistance." A drunken woman is not defined as being in need of protection and help, but as "asking for it." If the situation escalates into sexual activity, the brothers watch each other perform sexual acts and then brag about "getting laid." The event is referred to as "drunken stupidity, women chasing, and all around silliness." The drama enacted parodies the image of the gentleman. Its male participants brag about their masculinity and its female participants are degraded to the status of what the boys call "red meat" or "fish." The whole scenario joins men in a no-holds-barred orgy of togetherness. The woman whose body facilitates all of this is sloughed off at the end like a used condom. She may be called a "nympho" or the men may believe that they seduced her—a practice known as "working a yes out"—through promises of becoming a little sister, by getting her drunk, by promising her love, or by some other means. Those men who object to this kind of behavior run the risk of being labeled "wimps" or, even worse in their eyes, "gays" or "faggots."

The rationalization for this behavior illustrates a broader social ideology of male dominance. Both the brothers and many members of the broader community excuse the behavior by saying that "boys will be boys" and that if a woman gets into trouble it is because "she asked for it," "she wanted it," or "she deserved it." The ideology inscribed in this discourse represents male sexuality as more natural and more explosive than female sexuality. This active, "naturally" explosive nature of male sexuality is expected to find an outlet either in the company of male friends or in the arms of prostitutes. In these contexts men are supposed to use women to satisfy explosive urges. The women who satisfy these urges are included as passive actors in the enactment of a sexual discourse where the male, but not the female, sexual instinct is characterized as an insatiable biological instinct and psychological need.

Men entice one another into the act of "pulling train" by implying that those who do not participate are unmanly or homosexual. This behavior is full of contradictions because the ho-

moeroticism of "pulling train" seems obvious. A group of men watch each other having sex with a woman who may be unconscious. One might well ask why the woman is even necessary for the sexual acts the men stage for one another. As fraternity practices described in this book suggest, the answer seems to lie in homophobia. One can suggest that in the act of "pulling train" the polymorphous sexuality of homophobic men is given a strictly heterosexual form.

Polymorphous sexuality, a term used by Freud to refer to diffuse sexual interests with multiple objects, means that men will experience desire for one another. However, homophobia creates a tension between polymorphous sexual desire and compulsory heterosexuality. This tension is resolved by "pulling train": The brothers vent their interest in one another through the body of a woman. In the sociodrama that is enacted, the idea that heterosexual males are superior to women and to homosexuals is publicly expressed and probably subjectively absorbed. Thus, both homophobia and compulsory heterosexuality can be understood as strategies of knowledge and power centering on sex that support the social stratification of men according to sexual preference.

In group sex, homoerotic desire is simultaneously indulged, degraded, and extruded from the group. The fact that the woman involved is often unconscious highlights her status as a surrogate victim in a drama where the main agents are males interacting with one another. The victim embodies the sexual urges of the brothers; she is defined as "wanting it"—even though she may be unconscious during the event—so that the men can satisfy their urges for one another at her expense. By defining the victim as "wanting it," the men convince themselves of their heterosexual prowess and delude themselves as to the real object of their lust. If they were to admit to the real object, they would give up their position in the male status hierarchy as superior, heterosexual males. The expulsion and degradation of the victim both brings a momentary end to urges that would divide the men and presents a social statement of phallic heterosexual dominance.

By blaming the victim for provoking their own sexual aggression, men control and define acceptable and unacceptable female sexual behavior through the agency of fear. The fear is that a woman who does not guard her behavior runs the risk of becoming the target of uncontrollable male sexual aggression. Thus, although women are ostensibly the controlling agent, it is fear of the imagined explosive nature of male sexuality that ultimately reigns for both sexes. This fear instills in some men and women consciousness of their sexual and social identities.

In sum, the phenomenon of "pulling train" has many meanings. In addition to those meanings that have been mentioned, it is a bonding device that can permanently change a young man's understanding of masculinity. The bonding is accomplished by virtue of coparticipation in a "forbidden" act. As Ward Goodenough (1963) points out, sharing in the forbidden as part of initiation to a group is a powerful bonding device. For example, criminal gangs may require the initiate to perform a criminal act in order to be accepted as a member, an act that once performed is irrevocable. Participation in a "train" performs the same function of bonding the individual to the group and changing his subjectivity. Such bridge-burning acts of one kind or another are standard parts of ritualized identity-change procedures.

THE CONDITIONS PROMOTING "PULLING TRAIN"

We cannot assume that all entering college students have well-established sexual and social identities or ethical positions regarding sexual harassment and abuse. Recent research by psychologists on human subjectivity argues that subjectivity is dynamic and changes as individuals move through the life cycle. The evidence presented here suggests that the masculine subjectivity of insecure males may be shaped, or at least reinforced, by experiences associated with male bonding at college.

[One] example is fraternity initiation rituals in which young men who admit to feelings of low self-esteem upon entering the college setting are forced to cleanse and purify themselves of the despised and dirty feminine, "nerdy," "faggot" self bonded to their mothers. The ritual process in these cases humiliates the pledge in order to break social and psychological bonds to parental authority and to establish new bonds to the brotherhood. The traumatic means employed to achieve these goals induces a state of consciousness that makes abuse of women a means to renew fraternal bonds and assert power as a brotherhood. . . .

. . . Cross-cultural research demonstrates that whenever men build and give allegiance to a mystical, enduring, all-male social group, the disparagement of women is, invariably, an important ingredient of the mystical bond, and sexual aggression the means by which the bond is renewed (Sanday, 1981, 1986). As long as exclusive male clubs exist in a society that privileges men as a social category, we must recognize that collective sexual aggression provides a ready state on which some men represent their social privilege and introduce adolescent boys to their future place in the status hierarchy.

Why has the sexual abuse of women and the humiliation of generations of pledges been tolerated for so long? The answer lies in a historical tendency to privilege male college students by failing to hold them accountable. Administrators protect young men by dissociating asocial behavior from the perpetrator and attributing it to something else. For example, one hears adult officials complaining about violence committed by fraternity brothers at the same time they condone the violence by saying that "things got out of hand" because of alcohol, adolescence, or some other version of "boys will be boys." Refusing to take serious action against young offenders promotes the male privilege that led to the behavior in the first place. At some level, perhaps, administrators believe that by taking effective action to end all forms of abuse they deny young men a forum for training for masculinity. Where this is the case women students cannot possibly experience the same social opportunities or sense of belonging at college as their male peers, even though they spend the same amount of money for the privilege of attending. As colleges and universities face an increasing number of legal suits deriving from rape, murder, and the other forms of abuse reported in fraternities, athletic settings, and dorms, change is clearly imminent. . . .

REFERENCES

Ehrhart, Julie K., and Bernice R. Sandler. 1985. "Campus Gang Rape: Party Games?" Washington, D.C.: Project on the Status of Women, Association of American Colleges.

Goodenough, Ward Hunt. 1963. *Cooperation In Change*. New York: Russell Sage Foundation.

Sanday, Peggy Reeves. 1981. "The Socio-Cultural Context of Rape." *Journal of Social Issues* 37: 5–27.

———. 1986. "Rape and the Silencing of the Feminine." In *Rape: A Collection of Essays,* edited by Roy Porter and Sylvana Tomaselli. London: Basil Blackwell.

Further Questions

1. Is it the male bonding or the fact that this bonding privileges men as a group that requires the humiliation of women in "pulling train"?

2. Does a refusal to hold male students accountable in gang rape promote the male privilege that made the behavior possible in the first place?

3. Do women signal that they want to be gang raped by having too much to drink, taking drugs, or being too trustful of those who initiate the gang rape?

"The Rape" of Mr. Smith   VII.4

UNKNOWN

An unknown writer describes "the rape" of Mr. Smith in the form of a dialogue between Smith, a hold-up victim, and someone who is putting the type of questions to him that are usually asked a victim of a rape.

Reading Question

1. Draw some of the intended parallels between Smith and his interlocutor and a hypothetical rape victim and her interlocutor. Do these parallels show that rape victims can be questioned unreasonably when they attempt to report rapes? Give examples.

THE LAW DISCRIMINATES AGAINST RAPE VICTIMS in a manner which would not be tolerated by victims of any other crime. In the following example, a holdup victim is asked questions similar in form to those usually asked a victim of rape.

"Mr. Smith, you were held up at gunpoint on the corner of 16th & Locust?"

"Yes."

"Did you struggle with the robber?"

"No."

"Why not?"

"He was armed."

"Then you made a conscious decision to comply with his demands rather than to resist?"

"Yes."

"Did you scream? Cry out?"

"No. I was afraid."

"I see. Have you ever been held up before?"

"No."

"Have you ever given money away?"

"Yes, of course—"

"And did you do so willingly?"

"What are you getting at?"

"Well, let's put it like this, Mr. Smith. You've given away money in the past—in fact, you have quite a reputation for philanthropy. How can we be sure that you weren't *contriving* to have your money taken from you by force?"

"Listen, if I wanted—"

"Never mind. What time did this holdup take place, Mr. Smith?"

"About 11 P.M."

"You were out on the streets at 11 P.M.? Doing what?"

"Just walking."

"Just walking? You know that it's dangerous being out on the street that late at night. Weren't you aware that you could have been held up?"

"I hadn't thought about it."

"What were you wearing at the time, Mr. Smith?"

"Let's see. A suit. Yes, a suit."

"An *expensive* suit?"

"Well—yes."

"In other words, Mr. Smith, you were walking around the streets late at night in a suit that practically *advertised* the fact that you might be a good target for some easy money, isn't that so? I mean, if we didn't know better, Mr. Smith, we might even think you were *asking* for this to happen, mightn't we?"

"Look, can't we talk about the past history of the guy who *did* this to me?"

"I'm afraid not, Mr. Smith. I don't think you would want to violate his rights, now, would you?"

Naturally, the line of questioning, the innuendo, is ludicrous—as well as inadmissible as any sort of cross-examination—unless we are talking about parallel questions in a rape case. The time of night, the victim's previous history of "giving away" that which was taken by force, the clothing—all of these are held against the victim. Society's posture on rape, and the manifestation of that posture in the courts, help account for the fact that so few rapes are reported.

The Lecherous Professor: Sexual Harassment on Campus

VII.5

BILLIE WRIGHT DZIECH AND LINDA WEINER

Billie Wright Dziech and Linda Weiner address sexual harassment of students by faculty on campus. Women are especially vulnerable in campus situations and also are victims of considerable mythology. Faculty use harassment as a way of coping with their own problems. They can get away with it because of the mystique associated with the professoriate.

Reading Questions

1. What is it about student life and student-faculty relations that make students especially vulnerable to harassment by faculty?
2. Do you think that if you were a student being sexually harassed by a faculty member, you could make the proper authorities believe you? Why or why not?
3. Are women taken less seriously than men, hence a woman student's desire to be helped academically by a professor is more easily mistaken for sexual desire? Explain.

CONTEMPORARY COLLEGE WOMEN: MYTHS AND REALITIES

The Consenting Adult Myth

OCCASIONALLY THERE ARE WOMEN STUDENTS who are attracted to faculty. There are husbands and wives who were once teacher and student. These relatively few examples are cited again and again as proof that relationships between professors and students are private matters and that the concept of sexual harassment should give wide berth to such liaisons. The faculty role may be attractive to some, because it combines intellectual attainment and power, but being attracted to an individual's role and consenting to a relationship are vastly different.

If a professor becomes involved with a student, his standard defense is that she is a consenting adult. Few students are even in the strictest sense, consenting adults. A student can never be a genuine equal of a professor insofar as his professional position gives him power over her. Access to a student occurs not because she allows it but because the professor ignores professional ethics and chooses to extend the student-faculty relationship. Whether the student consents to the involvement or whether the professor ever intends to use his power against her is not the point. The issue is that the power and the role disparity always exist, making it virtually impossible for the student to act as freely as she would with a male peer.

In a normal romantic situation, both the man and woman make efforts to assess each other's reasons for pursuing the relationship, to understand their true feelings and desires, and to predict their own and the other's future behaviors and attitudes. In a faculty-student relationship,

---

344 PART SEVEN: RAPE AND SEXUAL HARASSMENT

the enormous role (and frequently age) disparity inhibits the woman so that she herself may have trouble understanding and predicting her feelings. . . . People who promote the consenting adult myth seldom mention that true consent demands full equality and full disclosure. Students lack not only power and equality; they are also frequent victims of professors' distortions of truth. A student may understand and agree to limits in her relationship with a professor, but faculty Casanovas usually forget to inform the woman that she is only one in a long procession of "consenters." . . .

Vulnerability

College women may suffer because of misconceptions about their behaviors and characters, but do they also somehow permit themselves to be sexually harassed? An important factor in understanding women's responses to harassment is the education and socialization of females. . . . The education system, from nursery school through college, reinforces women's dependency and reliance on authority. Women are taught submission, not aggression. They learn that being "good" implies not acting but reacting, not trusting oneself but entrusting oneself to the authorities—parents, clergy, teachers— that promise reward. Forced into a choice between a teacher's wishes and their own, some students do what they have learned to do best— defer, submit, agree. In their own peculiar ways, they once again act out the roles of "good little girls," doing what teacher says is best. . . .

In addition to the burdens imposed by sexual stereotyping, many women confront new and greater pressures upon entering college. College is not a particularly quiescent juncture in anyone's life. Alumni view the experience far differently from those who are living it. For most students, it is a time of uncertainty, pressure, and confusion, a time in which joy is counterbalanced by despair and achievement, by defeat. Students must decide successfully about academic programs, careers, and personal independence and relationships. College is a period of constant trial and judgment by oneself and others, in truth a far more harrowing experience than students care to admit. . . .

It should not surprise anyone that many women feel less self-confidence and control once they reach college. Most academic environments are patterned after male interests and male behavior. Since the turn of the century, cognitive rationality and the scientific mode of enquiry have dominated higher education. Women, socialized in humanistic and intuitive forms of knowledge, are at a psychological disadvantage in this kind of environment. The institution's emphasis on competition and intellectual aggressiveness runs counter to all that they have been taught.

There may be a link between women's vulnerability to sexual harassment and their diminished confidence and sense of control in academic settings. Because higher education is a male-dominated institution, college women are often treated less seriously. A man who hopes to become a physician is taken at his word. A woman elicits raised eyebrows and questions about her marriage and child-bearing plans. Her intentions meet with skepticism, so she is forced to prove herself and to endure more from faculty.

Nonassertive women are not the only likely victims for sexual harassers. The data is anecdotal, but there are overwhelming similarities in accounts of counselors, ombudsmen, and administrators who deal with the problem daily. Women who are experiencing serious stress are vulnerable, as are women uncertain about academic programs. Women who are loners, without visible friends, seem to be sought out by harassers. One ombudsman commented, "This will sound really crazy, but I think we tend to have more blondes coming to our office. They aren't beautiful or necessarily even pretty and I haven't kept a running count, but I'm almost sure that's the case." Others note that the nontraditional woman student, the individual attending college after some time has elapsed, also seems to be a target for the lecherous professor.

Harassers are influenced by multiple characteristics in women—physical characteristics, economic status, marital status. However, from analysis of stories of sexual harassment collected from college women, two particularly vulnerable groups arise: minority women and females enrolled in traditionally male fields. The reasons they attract harassers are easy to identify.

A racist stereotype of minority women is that they are "easier" and more responsive to sexual advances. For some males, the sexuality of women of a different race reportedly appears mysterious. Either of these conditions could account for what one counselor describes as some harassers "quick-target" attitude toward minority women. An even more insidious possibility is that the lecherous professor may sense the unease experienced by some minority women entering the academic environment. If the self-esteem of women students in general is on trial during college, then that of minority females is sorely threatened as they seek to establish credibility in institutions that are not only traditionally male but also white-dominated.

Women in nontraditional fields exhibit some of the uncertainty and vulnerability of minority women. Male-dominated disciplines are governed by a fraternity of men with strong credentials who until very recently were unaccustomed to the presence of women in their classrooms. Women entering these fields tend to be high achievers, often academically superior to their male counterparts. Disconcerted by this new situation, some male faculty are openly hostile to such women; others ignore them. At any rate, female students in engineering, architecture, accounting, medicine, law, and a variety of other historically male disciplines report discomfort in their environments.

The sense of being an intruder can have consequences beyond the classroom. Women who feel themselves "outsiders" are especially vulnerable to displays of interest or kindness from their instructors. Some faculty prey on the distress of such students for their own ends. One administrator observed, "These women feel like such pariahs that they'll hang onto any shred of human kindness and a lot of faculty are not beyond taking advantage of that fact."

A story told by a black woman professor of accounting reflects the environmental stress. She recalls her own freshman collegiate days when she was singled out by a faculty member who was very arrogant about his five degrees and his predominantly male profession. She was the only one in the class whom he did not address by first name; he preferred calling her, "Miss ____." At the end of the quarter he asked to speak with her after class. She was 17 at the time, and he was a middle-aged married man. She described her shock when he asked her to attend a dance with him: "I just looked him in the face and said, 'You're the wrong age, the wrong color; and if you want to take someone to a dance, it ought to be your wife.'"

Attempts at Coping

Whatever her age, appearance, race, or field of study, there is vulnerability in the student's status that makes sexual harassment by teachers a most intimate betrayal of trust. In case after case, students report their initial reactions as disbelief and doubt about the most blatant acts.

College is a time when students question their sexual identities and relationships and evaluate their values and self-images. Most see faculty on the other side of the threshold called maturity, part of the adult world, more parents than peers. Sexual harassment by faculty, even in its most impersonal, generalized forms injects a note of unexpected, incestuous sexuality that shocks the average woman student.

After shock comes the feeling of powerlessness. College professors are older, more adept verbally, more sophisticated socially, and certainly more knowledgeable about the workings of the college or university. A student at a Midwestern university asked, "Who was going to believe me? I was an undergraduate student and he was a famous professor. It was an unreal situation." A graduate student complained to her college counselor:

> What was it that I did that led him to believe I was interested in him in anything but a professional

sense? I am quite outgoing and talkative; could that be interpreted wrongly? I realized how utterly vulnerable I was in a situation like this . . . Everything that happened would be interpreted in his favor, if it ever became public. It would be said that I got my signals wrong, that he was just truly interested in helping me in my career.[1]

Closely related to women's feelings of powerlessness are those of guilt. Student victims report feeling responsible, feeling at fault somehow. Some have an almost childlike fear of having broken some rule they did not know. They wonder what they should have known or done to prevent the harassment. "I keep asking myself what I did to get him started. There were twenty-two other girls in the class. Why did he pick on me?" Michelle Y., a student at a southern university, asked.

Women recognize early that power and sexuality are equated by society. Some students are unsophisticated and fearful about the possibilities suggested by their sexuality; they may develop conflict about it and, correspondingly, guilt about their intentions and behaviors. They know that in cases of sexual harassment and rape someone always asks, "Did she encourage it?" and "Did she enjoy it?" The questions linger in the minds of even the most innocent and make them important to confront the harassment. Too many members of both sexes assume that women say "no" when they really mean "yes," that they secretly savor squeezing, patting, and pinching.

Men are not misunderstood or vulnerable to the same degree. An average woman of fifty would never be expected to whet the sexual appetite of a twenty-year-old male, and he would not be accused of seducing her. But people believe a twenty-year-old female can easily be transported to rapture by the attentions of a fifty-year-old male. After a while, the culturally induced confusion makes some women actually begin to doubt their own motivations. They then discover that their abusers prey on their uncertainties.

Paramount in the minds of many student victims is fear of what will happen if they resist or report the professor's behaviors. Victims often believe that the authority of the professor equals power over their futures—in a sense, their lives. Ambivalent about her academic capabilities, the typical student may be devastated when a professor, the symbol of intellect, treats her as if she has only a body and no mind. Even the best students worry about reprisals by the harasser and his associates. They fear that grades, jobs, careers, and sometimes even their physical safety will be threatened. Kelly H., a pre-med student, observed:

It's easy for someone else to say I should do something about Dr. ____, but how can I? He was the first person at ____ to take my work seriously. At least I think it's my work that made him notice me. He's the one who's pushing for me to get into med school. If I refuse him, then I ruin my whole life.

Another repeated reaction of women victims is their ambivalence about and sometimes sympathy for the harasser. Women students, especially if they are considering making a formal complaint, worry about the professor's career marriage, and future. Over and over, they comment, "I don't want anything bad to happen to him." A major source of this guilt is the harasser himself; when confronted by a student, harassers often distract them with discussions of personal and professional costs professor pay. Students may also feel guilty because they are flattered by the professor's interest in them. They may find him physically and socially unattractive, but being the object of attention from an older man can be a heady experience. A student may worry that she is stepping out of her proper place by affecting a faculty life, or she may have a certain amount of gratitude for the interest he has in her. This, as much as compassion, may lead to students' frequent pleas that deans or counselors "make sure he doesn't get in a lot of trouble." . . .

Often women who do acknowledge the seriousness of harassment try to cope through avoidance. They invent appointments, enlist the presence of friends, cut class, or even hide to prevent encounters. Another tactic is "dressing down," trying to appear asexual and unattractive to avoid notice. Each of these maneuvers is a passive-aggressive strategy; the student attempts to control external factors in the environment because she realizes she cannot control the professor.

Avoidance strategies indicate that students are sensitive to the power imbalance. They take friends to meetings with harassers because another person can provide reinforcement. They avoid meetings with harassers by claiming obligations equally important to those imposed by faculty. In both cases, students are trying to convince themselves and to communicate to their professors that powers can be offset.

Dressing down is a form of avoidance that demonstrates women's use of clothing to symbolize self-perceptions. A woman may make herself unattractive to escape the attention of an undesirable male, but dressing down may also be a way of declaring feelings of inferiority and victimization. It can express self-doubt as well as desire to deal with a threatening situation. Making oneself unattractive can be a way of declaring, "I don't feel good about myself. I feel inadequate and incompetent to cope with this problem." . . . "Staying away" is not as simple as it sounds. Staying away means that women are forced to drop courses, to alter schedules, sometimes to change majors or colleges because they feel they have no other recourse. Frequently they transfer to other institutions without admitting their reasons. Worst of all, there are students so unable to withstand harassment and so estranged from the institution that the only solution they discover is leaving school. There is no way to determine the number who eventually adopt this drastic measure. Few colleges have adequate exit interviews of graduates, dropouts, or transfers, so information about sexual harassment is not likely to be collected and assessed by proper authorities. Nevertheless, counselors in a variety of schools state emphatically that the number of women who leave college because of harassment is substantial. . . .

Much is heard from educators concerned about the reputations and livelihoods of those accused of harassment, but there is little discussion of the long-term effects it has on the women abused. Sexual harassment obviously has the power to damage careers; women leave colleges every day because they cannot deal with it. It alters their attitudes toward institutions and may have longlasting effects on their perceptions of men and sex. Perhaps most insidious are its influences upon the self-images of those forced to endure it. Higher education has been able to ignore consequences of sexual harassment because the victim's damage and pain are often felt years later, long after women have left the institutional environment and forfeited their claims to its protection.

THE LECHEROUS PROFESSOR: A PORTRAIT OF THE ARTIST

* * *

Although there is limited evidence of the number of harassers who may be "loose" on the nation's campuses, one point is clear. They are tolerated because society doubts that men are capable of sexual restraint. Sexual harassers are often defended with the shrugged observation, "After all, they're only human." A middle-aged professor, notorious for pursuing sexual relations with female students, offered a variation on this view: "If you put me at a table with food [with coeds], I eat."

The appeal to "human nature" is a reminder that even in an era of ostensible sexual liberalism and freedom, both men and women suffer and stereotypes die hard. Even in the 1980s, society has not freed itself of the Victorian notion that men are creatures barely capable of controlling their bestial appetites and aggressions. All the contemporary rhetoric about liberating the sexes from stereotypes has done little to change the popular view of the male as a kind of external tumescence, forever searching and forever unsatisfied.

Such an attitude demeans the notion of "human." To be human does not mean that a man is at the mercy of his genitalia. Whatever it is that constitutes "humanness" is located in the mind and heart, not the libido. "Human" implies reason, compassion, control—all the qualities that distinguish college professors from their cats and dogs. Without these, they are "only animal," a defense few find appealing. Sexual harassment unquestionably harms females, but men are equally debased when it is allowed to flourish. On the college campus, a very small number of men damage the reputations of colleagues who perform difficult tasks for relatively low wages without "succumbing" to the "irresistible" temptations of women students. . . .

Regardless of the role he assumes or the type of harassment in which he engages, the lecherous professor always controls the circumstances surrounding the student victim. Sexual harassment is a power issue, and the power of the professoriate is enormous. . . . Sexual harassers are people who misuse the power of their positions to abuse members of the opposite sex. Higher education tends to discuss their behavior in the abstract—as if it were unrelated to real-life human beings. But sexual harassment cannot be understood or curtailed until professors are subjected to the same scrutiny as students. What motivates a man with so much education and power over others to act abusively toward women? . . .

It is difficult to determine how the media developed the image of the sexy college professor with the corduroy jacket and the ever-present pipe. He may be alive and well on the silver screen and in the pages of best-sellers, but he is not in abundance at the faculty club or meetings of the American Association of University Professors. The typical professor does not resemble Fred MacMurray, Elliot Gould, Donald Sutherland, or any other of the Hollywood types who have portrayed him over the years. If there is a star who most resembles the typical accounting, art history, or seventeenth-century literature professor, it would have to be Woody Allen. . . .

. . . In popular myth and movies, college professors live in Victorian houses with wood-burning fireplaces, oak staircases, and paneled, book-lined studies. In reality, many drive secondhand cars, consider themselves fortunate to afford tract housing, and wonder how they will accumulate enough money to send their own children to college. A party of professors often means moving the department or college meeting to someone's basement family room to nibble cheddar cheese and drink wine from Styrofoam cups. This scenario is not all that bleak unless one considers the discrepancy between the ideal and actual worlds of academics. College professors are the people who teach others to appreciate expensive and sophisticated equipment, books, art, theater, and music—all that society recognizes as manifestations of "the good life"—and who cannot really afford them for themselves or their families.

In *The Male Mid-Life Crisis,* Nancy Mayer pointed out that "in America success has always meant making money and translating it into status or fame,"[2] and the relationship between financial success, power, and sexuality is a frequent topic of psychologists and organization specialists. In their article "The Executive Man and Women: The Issue of Sexuality," Bradford, Sargent, and Sprague observed:

> An important aspect of the sense of self-identity for both males and females is their masculinity and femininity . . . How do males assert their sexuality? Teenagers resort to fist-fighting . . . playing football, and competing against one another to see who can consume more beer or have more dates. While this may do for youth, an educated adult must find more discreet and indirect proofs . . . For many men, work serves as the major vehicle defining their identity, including sexual identity . . . Status and pay of the job also bear an element of sexuality . . . [Men] strive to advance, build up their programs, and compete in meetings partially to obtain status and financial records that connote masculine success, but also to affirm their masculinity more directly.[3]

A professor who sees himself in a static or unsuccessful professional and financial position may choose to exert his masculinity in negative ways. Feelings of frustration and defeat can be displaced onto the women students under his control. He can affirm his authority by being openly abusive to them, or he can turn to them for solace and ego-gratification. The dean of students at a very selective liberal arts college considered such displacement significant in some sexual harassment:

> I guess you might say that many men consider access to females one of the perks of the profession. If you don't make a lot of money, if you can't go to Europe without scrimping and sacrificing, if publication of your dream book seems less and less a reality and even promotion becomes a vain hope, life looks fairly dim. It's also not hard to see why some of these men turn to students for comfort or excitement or whatever it is their egos need. Sometimes they're abusive to students because that's a way to deal with their own anger and despair. It's not right, but it's one of the realities we have to live with.

Midlife Crisis

The frustration and confusion inherent in professional crisis are similar to and sometimes synonymous with those of midlife crisis. Not surprisingly, midlife crisis is the most frequently—if not the only—explanation offered for sexually harassing behavior. Peter A., professor at a large Massachusetts university, voiced this common defense:

> Another problem, and one not easily dismissed, is the fact that many of us are in our thirties and forties and are watching our youth slip away at the very time we're in extremely close contact with women who are just coming into bloom. Let me tell you, it's not easy to hit the beginning of a midlife crisis when you're surrounded by nubile twenty-year-olds.[4]

If a man is going to follow the traditional pattern for male midlife crisis, academe is the best of all possible worlds in which to be. Mayer described this period in the male's life:

> In response to wrenching change, a man at this stage of life is struggling to revise his own self-image and find dignity in the face of undeniable limitations. More than ever, he needs the

confirmation of being seen as a powerful and desirable man—a need that the nubile girl is uniquely suited to satisfy. Our culture's most obvious symbol of hot-blooded sexuality, she can meet the aging male's intensified need for reassurance both in public and in private . . .

> Seeking refuge from the harsh assaults of this midlife period and release from heightened anxieties that haunt and perplex them, [some men in middle age] confirm their manhood through the worshipful gaze of a nubile girl—who mirrors back an image of their most potent self. Contrary to popular wisdom, men in their middle years are generally drawn to younger women not because they want to recapture their youth, but because they need to reconfirm their maturity . . .

> This, then, is the single most seductive reason for the appeal of the nubile girl: A yielding innocent on whom a man can project whatever fantasy he craves, she makes him feel not merely potent, but also omnipotent. A soothing balm indeed. Where else, after all, can the aging male find a sexual partner who will offer applause and adulation without demanding reciprocal attentions? Who will satisfy his emotional need without requiring him to cater to hers? Only the young can afford to be so selfless.[5]

The enormous advantage that college professors have over men in similar situations is that for them, the stage is already set. Not only are there more than enough "nubile girls" from whom to choose, but they are women who have already been conditioned to regard the teacher as intellectually omnipotent. As individual desires and needs change over time, a wife who is a peer may become intellectually, professionally, or emotionally menacing; the attraction to a younger woman may be in her lack of competition or threat. A person with whom the professor has no shared history is cleaner, less complicated. If she is also a student, she exhibits all of the deference that comes with discrepancies in roles, experience, and sophistication. A male confused about responding to an older woman's demands may find those of female students more manageable and less intense.

The middle-aged professor suffering from sexual insecurity may find college women especially appealing sexually. Older women may pose not only intellectual and professional threats but also—and perhaps more important—very real sexual pressure. Their sexual demands are greater, and they increase the anxiety of the male in crisis. One man explained to Mayer:

> One thing that's true, though, I think you can get a younger woman to respond to you very strongly. She's going to be less appraising than an older woman. She's had less experience. There are fewer men in her life to which she can compare you. You can dominate her more, sort of impose your myth on her. And you can feel you're initiating her into all sorts of things and blowing her mind and enslaving her—or whatever the hell it is that you want to do with a woman.[6]

The professor whose sexual insecurity contributes to his harassment of students can easily delude himself. He has heard that women students today are freer and engage in intercourse earlier, so taboos about despoiling or deflowering the innocent can be rationalized. At the same time, women students are, by and large, young and lacking the sexual experience of older, more demanding women. Thus the student seems "safe," a novice flattered by the attentions of the professor who can introduce her to the mysterious pleasures of adult sexuality. And the harasser can delude himself into believing that he has done no harm and that the student is responding to his sexuality rather than his position.

Even when sexual activity with the student is the end of harassment, it is not the only motivation. Mayer noted that contemporary social scientists, ". . . in contrast to Freud, who said all human actions were shaped by sexual needs . . . now suggest the opposite: that sexual activity is often motivated by other needs. Non-sexual needs."[7] At any point in a man's life cycle, but especially during midlife, one such need may be competition with other males. The college professor at forty is in an unusual position: He is surrounded by physically desirable young women, as well as by young men in their physical prime. If he has been reared in traditional fashion, he knows that beyond all the myths about male friendships, the truth is that males are taught to relate to one another in one way—competition. Fasteau was clear on this point:

> Competition is the principal mode by which men relate to each other—at one level because they don't know how else to make contact, but more basically because it is the way to demonstrate, to themselves, and others, the key masculine qualities of unwavering toughness and the ability to dominate and control. The result is that they inject competition into situations which don't call for it.[8]

The classroom may be one such situation. Male students represent youth, virility, vigor, uncircumscribed futures—everything the man in midlife crisis may feel himself lacking. Added to this may be the professor's doubts about the masculinity of his profession. The males he teaches in the 1980s are interested in careers in high technology, business, engineering, law, and medicine. His own profession is not especially popular—not only because it does not pay well but also because many men do not view it as particularly masculine. A study by David F. Aberle and Kaspar Naegele found, for instance, that middle-class fathers rejected academic careers for their sons because they did "not consider the academic role to exemplify appropriate masculine behavior."[9] The exception was a father who replied that such a role would be appropriate for his son who was shy, bookish, and needed women to care for him. . . .

The harasser lives by an outlaw code. Relying upon colleagues' reluctance to intervene in student-faculty relationships and the romantic notion that eccentricity is tolerable in academe, he has failed to read the signs of change. Higher education may accept idiosyncratic dress, manners, speech, and interests, but sexual harassment is different from these—less superficial and more threatening to the profession. Once professors realize that their own reputations suffer with that of the harasser, male college professors are likely to find the "eccentricity" of the lecherous professor less tolerable and less deserving of defense.

NOTES

1. Eileen Shapiro, "Some Thoughts on Counseling Women Who Perceive Themselves to Be Victims of Non-Actionable Sex Discrimination: A Survival Guide," in "Sexual Harassment: A Hidden Issue," *On Campus with Women,* Project on the Status and Education of Women (Washington, D.C.: American Association of College, 1978), p. 3.

2. Nancy Mayer, *The Male Mid-Life Crisis* (New York: New American Library, 1978), p. 164.

3. David Bradford, Alice Sargent, and Melinda Sprague, "The Executive Man and Woman: The Issue of Sexuality," *Bringing Women Into Management,* eds.

Francine Gordon and Myra Strober (New York: McGraw-Hill, 1975), pp. 18–19.

4. Harry Zehner, "Love and Lust on Faculty Row," *Cosmopolitan,* April 1982, p. 273.

5. Mayer, pp. 107, 111–13.

6. Mayer, p. 108.

7. Mayer, p. 107.

8. Mark Feigen Fasteau, *The Male Machine* (New York: McGraw-Hill, 1974), p. 11.

9. David F. Aberle and Kaspar Naegele, "Middle-Class Fathers' Occupational Role and Attitudes Toward Children," *American Journal of Orthopsychiatry* 22 (1952): 366.

Further Questions

1. Do we have reason to feel sorry for faculty who harass? Sorry enough to overlook the harassment?

2. Middle-aged male professors sometimes think of themselves as sexually irresistible to young students, while this thought rarely occurs in the mind of a middle-aged female professor. Any explanations?

3. Could part of an older professor's interest in a younger student be that he is trying to prove himself as desirable as younger male students?

Sexual Harassment and Solidarity   VII.6

LARRY MAY

Larry May distinguishes two types of sexual harassment of women. One is where a man in a position of power threatens the woman's job security, work evaluation, or promotion if she refuses a sexual advance. The second is a man's creation of a hostile environment for a woman by sexualizing it through sexual suggestions, sexual innuendos, disparaging remarks about her gender, or other behavior that affects her relations with her supervisors or co-workers. Both types of sexual harassment constitute discrimination against women and are forms of male bonding effected at women's expense.

May is Professor of Philosophy at Washington University, St. Louis.

Reading Questions

1. Is there any type of situation in which a person is not coerced or harmed when her position in the workplace will be adversely affected if she refuses a sexual advance?
2. What type of force is applied to women on the job when they are exposed to sexual offers, sexual remarks, or unfavorable comments on their gender? How does this become a form of discrimination against women?
3. How does the exhibition of a *Playboy* centerfold in the workplace become a basis of male solidarity and a form of exclusion for women?

SEXUAL HARASSMENT, LIKE RAPE, seems obviously wrong. Yet, many men are not as willing to condemn it as they are willing to condemn rape. In part, this is no doubt due to the fact that it is less clear what are the boundaries of the concept of harassment, where some putative forms of harassment are not easily distinguished from "horse play" or pranksterism.[1] But it may also be due to the fact that men are reluctant to condemn practices which have for so long functioned to build solidarity among men.[2] The *Playboy* centerfold pinned to the bulletin board at a workplace has at least two functions. It is a constant source of erotic stimulation for the men who work there, and it is a constant source of embarrassment and annoyance for many of the women, a clear sign that this is not the kind of place for them, but that it is a place for men.

In this chapter I wish to examine sexual harassment in its various forms, seeking a basis for moral criticism of it. In addition to more standard criticisms, largely parallel to those developed in law, I offer a new critique that calls attention to the way that sexual harassment promotes male solidarity and also thereby often excludes women from full and equal participation in various practices and contexts. . . .

I SEXUAL INTIMIDATION

The case of *Alexander v. Yale University* was the first sexual harassment lawsuit to concern an educational rather than a workplace setting.[3] The case concerned a female student at Yale University who alleged that one of her male political science professors threatened to *lower* her grade on a term paper (from a B to a C) unless she slept with him. The student, who was hoping to go to law school, felt intimidated by the proposal but did not capitulate. After her initial accusation, other women came forward with similar stories about this particular political science professor. The professor denied these other charges but admitted discussing grades with the student who sued. He claimed that he had offered to *raise* the student's grade (from a C to a B) if she slept with him, but that she had simply declined his offer. Since, on his view, the grade had remained what the student had earned, no harm had been done to the student. No foul, no harm.

This case raised difficulties with the way that sexual harassment had been previously understood. Previously, sexual harassment was thought by the courts to involve five elements:

1. a sexual advance
2. by a person in a more powerful position
3. made to a person in a less powerful position
4. against the second person's will
5. which adversely affected
   a. retention of job
   b. evaluation
   c. promotion

At least according to the version of the story told by the political science professor, the student had not been adversely affected, and so the fifth element of sexual harassment was not present.

Sexual harassment was understood to be harmful in that it constituted an unjustified form of intimidation, much like blackmail. But the attorneys who defended the Yale student felt that a different model was needed given the group-oriented nature of the offense. So they seized on the idea that sexual harassment like that directed at the student was a form of sex discrimination and thus harmful as a form of degradation. But what if the facts were as alleged by the professor, was there any discrimination against or degradation of the student? This seemed not to be like blackmail, since there was no clear indication that she would be rendered worse off if she turned down the professor's proposal.

If the facts were as the student alleged, then this was an egregious case of sexual intimidation. No one who understands the purpose of educational institutions would countenance the idea of a male professor threatening to give a student less than she deserved unless the student did something so utterly outside the realm of academic achievement as providing sexual favors. Worse than this is the idea of a male professor abusing his power and authority over often naive students for his own personal gain. And worse yet is the idea that a man could extort sex from an otherwise unwilling female by threatening to do something undeserved to harm her career prospects. For all these reasons, sexual harassment of the sort alleged by the student is clearly morally wrong.

If we believe the male political science professor, something morally wrong has occurred as well, although somewhat less clearly so. On his version he offered to give the student a grade better than she deserves, and so he seemingly did not threaten to harm her undeservedly. But there was an indication that the female student may have been harmed which can be seen in that she would not have wanted to have such proposals made in the first place. The student was put in the position of having her sexuality count as a basis of academic achievement. This had a negative impact on the educational environment in which the student resided.[4] I have elsewhere argued that this was indeed a form of sex discrimination which effectively coerced the student,

even though there was no direct threat to her, at least if we believe the professor's story.[5]

The professor's "offer" changes the range of options that the student previously had in a way which makes her post-offer situation worse than it was in the pre-offer state. The student could no longer proceed as before, thinking of her options in a purely academic way. And in this sense she is disadvantaged, perhaps even coerced, in that she is made to accept a set of options that she would not otherwise choose. When such proposals get made, the well is poisoned, and it is no longer possible for the student to think of herself as merely a student and not also as a sex object.[6] In the case of sexual harassment, seen as either a direct threat or as a seemingly innocent sexual offer, harm has occurred.

Laurence Thomas has challenged my analysis of sexual harassment in offer situations. He contends that not all examples of sexual offers contain veiled threats or can be characterized as situations that the woman would prefer not to be in. He gives an example: "Deborah is Peter's secretary. Peter offers to pay Deborah so many dollars per week, in addition to her present salary, if she would be his exclusive sexual partner. The money would come out of his own pocket."[7] Thomas stipulates that there is no veiled threat here, and no one is under psychological duress. In the case in question, Thomas "is not inclined to think that there is a moral wrong here."[8] His rationale is expressed in this blunt statement: "It simply cannot be the case that we should not enter into any interaction if there is the possibility that it might become morally explosive."[9]

It seems to me, however, that Peter has done something morally suspect by introducing sex into the workplace. Even though Deborah can take the offer or leave it, she cannot, on her own, return to a situation where her relationship with Peter was strictly professional. By turning the offer down, she does not return to the previous state of affairs because of the way that Peter's offer has changed the relationship between them and set the stage for abuses of

Peter's authority.[10] This much Thomas admits; yet he claims that we cannot stop acting just because it might turn out that abuse could occur. But he has focused on only one aspect of the problem, the possibility that things might turn ugly. What he has missed is that the relationship has changed, nearly irrevocably, in a way that is out of Deborah's control.

In some cases of sexual offers, or sexual innuendos, nothing straightforward coercive occurs, but there may be reasons nonetheless to think that a moral wrong has occurred. The moral wrong concerns the way that a person's options are restricted against that person's will. It is morally wrong not only to make a person's options worse than they were before, but also to limit them undeservedly if this is against the person's will. In this latter case, it is not the worsening of the situation but rather the way that it is undeservedly taken out of the control of the woman which makes it morally suspect. To put the point starkly, sexual harassment normally involves a restriction of options which also restricts autonomy.[11] In the straightforwardly coercive cases of sexual harassment, autonomy is restricted because a woman is forced to accede to a man's wishes or risk harm to herself. In some subtler cases of sexual harassment, autonomy is restricted in that a change in relationship is effected against the wishes of the woman, possibly to her detriment. But even if it is not to her detriment, she has been undeservedly forced into a situation that she has not chosen. In the next sections I will explore in more detail the moral harms of some of the subtle cases of sexual harassment.

II HOSTILE ENVIRONMENTS

In 1993 the United States Supreme Court gave its clearest support to a relatively new basis for understanding the harm of sexual harassment which is closer to the basis I have just suggested than is the intimidation model, although with several important differences. The Court carefully enunciated a doctrine that held that sexual harassment can be harmful in that it produces a hostile or abusive work environment for a person because of her gender.[12] I want to explore various theoretical issues that are implicated in this new approach to sexual harassment, where the older mode of intimidation and blackmail is by and large abandoned. I am especially interested in how this new model affects our understanding of male behavior in educational and workplace settings.

Here are some of the relevant facts of the case of *Harris v. Forklift Systems, Inc.*

> Teresa Harris worked as a manager at Forklift Systems, Inc., an equipment rental company, from April 1985 until 1987. Charles Hardy was Forklift's president. The magistrate found that, throughout Harris's time at Forklift, Hardy often insulted her because of her gender and often made her the target of unwanted sexual innuendos. Hardy told Harris on several occasions, in the presence of other employees, "You're a woman, what do you know" and "We need a man as the rental manager"; at least once, he told her she was "a dumb ass woman." Again, in front of others, he suggested that the two of them "go to the Holiday Inn to negotiate [Harris's] raise." Hardy occasionally asked Harris and other female employees to get coins from his front pants pocket. He threw objects on the ground in front of Harris and other women, and asked them to pick them up. He made sexual innuendos about Harris's and other women's clothing.[13]

This pattern of harassment was not aimed at extracting a particular form of behavior, such as a sexual favor. It was not straightforwardly coercive, but nonetheless something seems morally wrong about Hardy's actions.

What Hardy did was to create an environment in which it was very difficult for his female employees to be taken seriously as equals to their male counterparts. Justice Sandra Day O'Connor, delivering the opinion of the court, considered this case an example of a "discriminatorily abusive work environment." This new standard "takes a middle path between making actionable any conduct that is merely offensive, and requiring the conduct to cause a tangible psychological injury." A hostile environment is, according to O'Connor, not something that can be defined with mathematical precision, but it can be determined by "looking at .... the frequency of the discriminatory conduct; its severity; whether it is physically threatening or humiliating, or a mere offensive utterance; and whether it unreasonably interferes with an employee's work performance."

The harm of a hostile work environment is relatively clear. Again, according to O'Connor, a "discriminatorily abusive work environment, even one that does not seriously affect employees' psychological well-being, can and often will detract from employees' job performance, discourage employees from remaining on the job, or keep them from advancing in their careers." Even without a showing of these specific harms, O'Connor rightly pointed to the denial of "workplace equality" which is broadly guaranteed by Title VII of the Civil Rights Act of 1964.[14] The key here is that this form of behavior treats men differently from women, subjecting only the women to these risks.

The chief harm of sexual harassment is indeed that it discriminates against women by subjecting women to "run a gauntlet of sexual abuse in return for the privilege of being allowed to work and make a living"[15] and thereby demeans them. Sexual harassment, even of the more subtle variety, normally changes the work environment against the wishes of the women. And this creates a difference between male and female employees. Women are forced to be seen as both workers and sexual objects, while men are free either to be seen as only workers or to be seen as workers and sexual objects. The environmental change effected by sexual harassment discriminates against women, generally to their detriment.

What if the changes in the work environment are welcome? What if a particular woman wishes to be able to advance by the use of sexual favors? To go back to Thomas's example, what if

Deborah wishes to be able to supplement her income by doing sexual favors, on the side, for her boss? Does it still make sense to say that the environment is discriminatory? I believe the answer to this question is yes. But I'm not so sure that the environment is always hostile or abusive. In order to see this one needs to think about the way that women in the workplace, or in an educational setting, will be affected as a group. The environment is discriminatory because of the way that only women have had their options restricted in respect to the kind of relationships they can have with their male bosses. Normally only women, not men, are the ones whose appearance and sexual characteristics matter and who will be judged according to non-work-related, sexual criteria.

In my view the court has done well to focus on the discriminatory environment, rather than intimidation, created by even subtle examples of sexual harassment. But it has potentially led us astray by calling that environment hostile or abusive. Surely in the most egregious cases, such as that of Charles Hardy and Teresa Harris at Forklift Systems, Inc., the discriminatory work environment does become abusive. But in the more subtle cases, this is not necessarily so, and yet the environment is still discriminatory, and morally suspect for that reason. When more subtle forms of sexual harassment occur, such as when a *Playboy* centerfold is displayed in a common room, women are treated in a way that men are not, and even if some women find this to be welcome it still puts them at a competitive disadvantage in terms of being taken as seriously as their male counterparts with regard to job performance. Their sexuality is considered, illegitimately, to be relevant to job performance, and other, legitimate, bases of job performance are put on the same level as this illegitimate basis, thereby tainting the legitimate bases. This situation has been forced upon them and is, generally speaking, contrary to the autonomy of the women in question.

Sex discrimination can be morally wrong on at least three counts: Women are degraded; they are treated unfairly; or they are denied a certain amount of autonomy over their lives. When women seem to welcome differential status in a given context, as in the case of Deborah welcoming the opportunity to make more money by sleeping with her boss, it can appear that women are gaining autonomy rather than losing it. But this is not the case. For what is being lost is the choice of whether to be treated only as a worker and not also as a sex object. In most contexts this loss of control brings more harm to the woman's autonomy than the possible gain from being given more attention or allowed to use one's sexuality to gain certain advantages. What counts as "job related" or "meritorious" has undergone a sometimes subtle shift, to the detriment of women workers.

III FEMALE EXCLUSION FROM FULL PARTICIPATION

One of the things often ignored in discussions of sexual harassment is how it promotes male solidarity, especially a solidarity that keeps women in an inferior position and excludes them from full and equal participation in a practice. Think of a very minor form of sexual harassment, at least as compared to that suffered in the *Harris* or *Alexander* cases, namely, a *Playboy* centerfold placed on a locker door in an employee work area. Such an act is not likely to cause serious psychological distress to female employees, and it is not some kind of quid pro quo attempt to extort sexual favors. Nevertheless it resembles these more egregious acts in excluding women from full and equal participation in a work environment with their male colleagues, as we will see.

How is it that even such seemingly innocuous acts as posting the *Playboy* centerfold in a common area can contribute to a form of male bonding and solidarity that is aimed at, or at least has the known effect of, making females feel unwelcome?[16] My analysis is explicitly group oriented. The various forms of sexual harassment share, it seems to me, the effect of creating an environ-

ment in which women feel excluded. In this respect sexual harassment is best understood as a harm perpetrated by men against women. To see why this is a group-based problem as well as an interpersonal problem, one needs to recognize that putting the poster on the wall is a signal to any woman who enters the room that women are to be viewed as comparable to the woman in the centerfold picture—to be gawked at, drooled over, and reduced to the measurements of their breasts and buttocks—not welcome here as equals to men.

Even in the most egregious cases, sexual harassment often appears to be merely an interpersonal problem. One party, typically a male, is proposing sex to another party, typically a female, and the female does not welcome such a proposal but again, one needs to realize that in many of these cases, including *Alexander v. Yale* and *Harris v. Forklift Systems, Inc.,* the woman who sues is normally not the only one being harassed. Other female students or employees often come forward to allege the same behavior toward them by the same male. The multiple victims of sexual harassers make it unlikely that theirs is only an interpersonal problem between an individual male and an individual female.

The type of behavior characteristic of sexual harassment rarely relates to the differences of individual women. The underling attitudes of the men in question are contempt or at least condescension toward all or most women, not merely toward the one who is currently being harassed. In the next section we will see in more detail how this works when we examine the case of a heterosexual male who harasses a homosexual male. The thing that links the two cases is that exclusion is occurring because a person fails to occupy a certain category, not because of one's unique characteristics. A group-based harm has occurred whenever there is harm directed at a person because of features that that person shares with other members of a group.[17]

Indeed it is common for sexual harassment to promote male solidarity in educational or employment contexts. Think again of the *Playboy* centerfold displayed in a prominent place in an auto mechanics's work area. If a woman should stray into the work area by mistake or in order to find the mechanic working on her car, she will be alerted right away that this is a male-only domain. Indeed, it may be the practice of the fellow mechanics to touch the breasts of the woman in the picture or to pat her buttocks as they enter or leave the work area, especially when women are present. Here is a good example of how pornographic images can be used to isolate women and separate them from men, but this image also solidifies bonds of men with men. Such a practice is obviously much less morally offensive than actually touching the breasts or patting the buttocks of real women in the workplace. But these practices serve as a reminder that the same thing could happen to women who stumble into the wrong place at the wrong time.

Here is another case.[18] A male graduate student displays a *Playboy* centerfold on a bulletin board in an office that houses half a dozen teaching assistants in philosophy, some of whom are women. The male students gather and comment on the physical dimensions of the centerfold woman's breasts and buttocks, laughing and joking and comparing the dimensions of the centerfold woman to those of their fellow female graduate students. The women find this behavior either annoying or humiliating or both. One woman finds it increasingly difficult to go into the office, knowing that her male colleagues may be discussing the dimensions of her breasts and buttocks. Another woman who complains finds herself the subject of ridicule for her lack of camaraderie.

In both of these cases male bonding and solidarity are furthered by excluding women from full and equal participation. Of course, it is not necessarily the intention of these men or of these practices to exclude women, although this is at least a reasonable thing to expect. The exclusion is by and large the unintended, but foreseen, consequence of the practices that build solidarity. But this is not a necessary result of building male solidarity. . . . Indeed, men often find themselves

today under siege because their practices of bonding have so publicly excluded women in ways that have deprived women of opportunities to advance, compete, and cooperate in the larger society. Men have been challenged in this domain, both in the courts and in various other public forums. It is not male solidarity that is the culprit, but the forms of harassment that have both supported the bonding between men, and also excluded women from full and equal participation with males.

One may wonder if it is always wrong for one group to adopt practices that have the effect of excluding another group. To answer this question one needs to think seriously about the moral principles that would be implicated in such exclusion. Exclusion is not always morally wrong or even suspect. But when exclusion affects a whole category of people and there is no reasonable basis for it, then it is morally suspect. The principle of moral equality is implicated whenever like cases are not treated alike. Excluding one group of people from a domain without good reason is a paradigmatic example of morally suspicious treatment. While it is obviously quite common for one group of people to exclude another group, moral criticism is appropriate when the exclusion is done for arbitrary reasons, especially if it perpetuates a pattern of exclusion in the larger society.

Is it necessary that there be a past pattern of exclusion for a current particular instance of sexual harassment to constitute group-based harm to women? This is a complex question that cannot be easily answered. Implicated here is the question whether harassment of a man by a female superior would constitute harm to men as a group. In part the answer could be obvious. If the man is sexually harassed merely for being a man, where other men have been similarly treated, then the man is clearly harmed in a discriminatory way and, in some sense, so are men as a group. But without the pattern of adverse treatment it is unclear that men as a group are *significantly* harmed by this seemingly isolated act by a woman. What makes sexual harassment a form of morally harmful sexual discrimination is that it contributes to a particular pattern of subordination.

If we are discussing these issues in a legal context, it is probably a mistake to say that a past pattern of exclusion is necessary for legally actionable harm because on this construal a judge who does not see the pattern of past behavior will be entitled to disregard any current harm. But in the moral context, where we are not relying on judges who must decide whether to allow a suit to go forward, it is more reasonable to think that patterns of past discrimination are relevant to the assessment of harmfulness of what one man does to a female subordinate. While sexual harassment is often a form of group-based harm it is not always so, and the harms involved in sexual harassment are not completely captured by focusing on the group. This point will become clearer, I hope, in light of some nonstandard examples of sexual harassment in the next section.

IV DISCRIMINATION AND HARASSMENT

I wish to investigate two cases of harassment that complicate the preceding analysis because of the sexual orientation of the people involved. I begin with a brief examination of a hypothetical case, then move on to a more developed treatment of an actual case and a variation on that case. The first case involves a bisexual man who harasses both men and women indifferently. The second case is that of a heterosexual man who harasses another man whom he believes to be a homosexual. A consideration of these cases will allow us to achieve a more adequate understanding of the moral harm involved in excluding someone on grounds of sexuality. A variation on the latter case, where the supervisee is actually a homosexual, is especially interesting for even though it does not involve harassment by a man of a woman, it nonetheless involved harassment of one person whose group, homo-

sexual males is subordinated on grounds of sexuality, by another person whose group, heterosexual males, is dominant. A consideration of this case also relates to the previous section's discussion of how sexual harassment contributes to male solidarity.

In the case of a bisexual man who sexually harasses both men and women indifferently, we can begin to see whether it matters morally that the harassment is based on men's historical dominance of women.[19] This harasser does not treat women differently from men, so there is no disparate treatment of women and therefore it appears that there is no sex discrimination occurring either. This case contrasts with the case of the male boss who simply harasses (in the sense of "gives a hard time to") every one of his employees equally; the harassment itself may be morally problematic, but not because of its connection with sexuality. The male bisexual harasser seemingly harasses men and women indiscriminately, but the harassment is on sexual grounds and takes a sexual form, either making sexual propositions or engaging in sexual jokes and ridicule that change the workplace environment.

It seems fair to say that the male bisexual harasser is engaging in sexual harassment since his behavior places both men and women in uncomfortable, and unwanted, positions, undeservedly restricting their autonomy. His propositions indicate that he views sexual favors as appropriate criteria in judging job performance. Insofar as the employees wish that this were not the case, the work environment has been rendered hostile. But the hostility is muted by the fact that this does not appear to be part of a larger pattern of hostile treatment by bisexuals in the larger society. What makes sexual harassment so problematic morally is that it contributes to a larger social problem, namely, the discriminatory treatment of women by men.

The male bisexual harasser does engage in sexual harassment, which creates a hostile work environment, but he does not engage in sex discrimination. Even though he sexually harasses women in the workplace, creating a hostile work environment for them, even sexually intimidating them in some cases, his behavior does not necessarily contribute to a society-wide pattern of sex discrimination. The main reason for this, of course, is that he does not treat the men in his employ any differently. This is not to deny that the women may respond quite differently from their male colleagues to his propositions, because of differential socialization. And this socialization may make things worse for the women, who find it harder to resist the propositions than the men. But the acts of the bisexual harasser are not themselves instances of sex discrimination and hence do not violate the moral principle of equal treatment and equal respect.[20]

Now consider a case of a heterosexual male who harasses a male supervisee. A recent case arose in Springfield, Illinois.

> The suit alleges that the supervisor, John Trees, created "a sexually offensive and hostile work environment" at a Transportation Department facility in Springfield, repeatedly making comments in front of other workers indicating he believed that [Jim] Shermer was a homosexual. . . . Shermer isn't gay, the suit says. He alleges he "suffered emotional distress to his reputation, embarrassment, humiliation and other personal injuries," as a result of Trees' behavior. . . . A federal judge in Springfield dismissed the suit in August [1996], in part because of the state's novel argument: As a man on an all-male work crew, it was intrinsically impossible for Shermer to prove he was the victim of sexual discrimination, a necessary component of sexual harassment.[21]

I am inclined to agree with the judge in this case. There is no sex discrimination here because not all, or any other, men are being treated similarly by the supervisor, and there is no indication that the supervisee is being harassed because he is male.

In a variation of the above case, where the heterosexual male supervisor was harassing a homosexual male, we can begin to see whether it matters morally that harassment is directed at women for it to be pernicious. Here the history of the discriminatory treatment of homosexual men by the larger society makes the act of sexual harassment of a homosexual man more like the standard cases of men harassing women than like the original case, one heterosexual male harassing another, or like the hypothetical case of the male bisexual harasser. But even in this case, sexual harassment is not a form of sex discrimination, because it is not directed at someone by virtue of being a member of a certain gender group. As long as heterosexual men are not subjected to the same mistreatment, then it is not clear that the mistreatment is based on belonging to a gender group. But it may be discriminatory nonetheless if it turns out that the harasser only mistreats homosexual men, and no others, and such mistreatment is arbitrary.

Illegal discrimination occurs whenever one group is arbitrarily and adversely treated differently from another. Harassment of homosexual men is a clear example of discrimination even though it is not a form of sex discrimination. Discrimination against homosexuals is still in the stage of being quite blatant in most of Western society. The acts of gay bashing and ridicule of gay lifestyles occur largely unabated and unchallenged. In this sense discrimination against homosexuals is in a different stage, and perhaps a worse stage, from that of discrimination against women. The main way to see that it is, is to think about discrimination as a form of exclusion from full and equal participation in social practices. Discrimination against homosexuals, especially men, is so virulent that it virtually excludes this group from mainstream society in ways that are not now true for the way discrimination against women works.

Discrimination against women and discrimination against homosexual men share this much: they are both instances of dominant males excluding from full and equal participation those who are different from them and thereby building solidarity within the dominant group. But such solidarity is morally problematic, especially when it is purchased by virulent antihomosexual behavior and attitudes. When solidarity is purchased by strong exclusion, two sorts of moral wrong occur. First, of course, there is harm to the excluded group, and its members. Second, the group that does the excluding is also morally harmed and, in this sense, harms itself by its irrational aggression and anger, emotional responses that make it much harder for its members to know and do what is right and hence to attain certain moral virtues.

Aggression and anger often block one's ability to perceive a moral situation correctly. Indeed, the kind of exclusion-oriented aggression and anger characteristic of discrimination against homosexual men have made it very difficult for heterosexual men to recognize their behavior as discriminatory and their attitudes as displaying a lack of respect for fellow humans. Exclusion of one group by another is not always, but quite often, associated with characterizing the excluded group as one which is deserving of its exclusion. In the case of discrimination against homosexual men in Western society, and also in many areas of the non-Western world, the exclusion has been joined by strong emotional reactions directed against the "pernicious" life-styles of gay men. These strong emotional reactions have created moral harms both for those harassed but also, interestingly, for those who do the harassing.

NOTES

1. I do not mean to dismiss the difficulty of distinguishing innocent pranks from those that constitute harassment. But I will sidestep this question and employ examples that seem clearly to be more than innocent pranks.

2. Throughout this chapter I use the term "solidarity" to refer to the phenomenon first discussed theoretically by Émile Durkheim as "cohesiveness within a group." See chap. 2, "Solidarity and Moral Support," in May, *The Socially Responsive Self*.

3. *Alexander v. Yale University*, 459 F.Supp. I (D. Conn. 1977), 631 F.2d 178 (2d Cir. 1980). The courts ruled the case moot since the student had al-

ready graduated and other students were not clearly adversely affected by the harassment of one of their friends.

4. I am assuming that female students generally do not want to have their sexuality become a basis for academic success. Cynics might dispute this assumption, but I have never met a female student who took such a cynical view.

5. John C. Hughes and Larry May, "Sexual Harassment," *Social Theory and Practice* 56 (Fall 1980).

6. See Larry May and John C. Hughes, "Is Sexual Harassment Coercive?" in *Moral Rights in the Workplace*, ed. Gertrude Ezorsky (Albany: State University of New York Press, 1987). One of the main problems is that the woman no longer has at least one choice she had before, namely, to be regarded just as a student. Even if she doesn't mind being seen as a sex object, there is a problem in that her position in an academic community is being defined in a way over which she has no control.

7. Laurence Thomas, "On Sexual Offers and Threats," in *Moral Rights in the Workplace*, ed. Ezorsky, p. 125.

8. Ibid., p. 126.

9. Ibid.

10. For instance, Peter may be motivated to look more or less favorably on Deborah's job performance based on how well they are getting along sexually. There is another way to view this whole business that I also find helpful. It might be that the mutually trusting relationship that Peter and Deborah had is now shattered because neither can now trust the other to be "objective" about work-related matters. I am grateful to Ed Soule for providing this complementary way of seeing the damage that is done merely by Peter making the offer.

11. See my discussion of the harm that occurs when options are restricted in section II: Conceptualizing Harm, in Chapter 4.

12. This doctrine was first embraced, by a unanimous Supreme Court, in *Meritor Savings Bank v. Vinson*, 477 U.S. 57, 106 S.Ct. 2399, 91 L.Ed.2d 49 (1986).

13. *Harris v. Forklift Systems, Inc.* 114 S.Ct. 367 (1993).

14. Ibid.

15. This is a quotation from the Eleventh Circuit Court of Appeals ruling in *Henson v. Dundee*, quoted by Chief Justice William Rehnquist in *Meritor Savings Bank v. Vinson*.

16. Esther Nevarez, who counsels employers for the New Jersey Division of Civil Rights, put the point quite well when she said that such behavior "affects the esprit de corps in an office because it eliminates certain groups of people from participating." She was quoted in Trip Gabriel, "New Issue at Work: On-Line Sex Sites," *New York Times,* June 27, 1996, B4.

17. See my discussion on this point in May, *The Morality of Groups.*

18. Both the case of the mechanic and that of the graduate student are based on examples of which I have had personal experience.

19. This hypothetical case is loosely based on several actual cases I have heard about in the last ten years.

20. This is not to say that nothing morally suspicious has occurred here. The case I have described clearly involved an abuse of power by the bisexual harasser.

21. Kevin McDermott, "Same-Sex Suit Pits Man vs. Male Boss," *St. Louis Post-Dispatch,* October 13, 1996, D1, 11.

Further Questions

1. Is a bisexual man who sexually harasses both men and women less culpable than a man who harasses women only? Explain.

2. Suppose a heterosexual man harasses a homosexual man. Is the type of harm done to the homosexual the same as that done to women by men harassers? Why or why not?

3. Sometimes men complain that they can't flirt in the workplace or ask their coworkers for dates because their behavior might be interpreted as sexual harassment. Is an interpretation of such behavior as sexual harassment justified in all such cases?

4. Sometimes we hear that human life is naturally sexual and so the workplace is sexual along with other settings. Women who don't like this should leave. What is your reaction?

Further Readings for Part VII Rape and Sexual Harassment

Constance Backhouse and Leah Cohen. *Sexual Harassment on the Job* (Englewood Cliffs, NJ: Prentice-Hall, 1981).

Helen Benedict. *Recovery: How to Survive Sexual Assault for Women, Men, Teenagers and Their Friends* (New York, NY: Doubleday, 1985).

Timothy Beneke. *Men on Rape* (New York, NY: St. Martin's Press, 1982). Interviews with men on sexual violence.

Susan Brownmiller. *Against Our Will: Men, Women, and Rape* (New York, NY: Simon and Schuster, 1975). Well-written classic: sustained argument that rape threatens all women and is a crime of violence and power.

Emilie Buchwald, Pamela Fletcher, Martha Roth, eds. *Transforming a Rape Culture* (Minneapolis, MN: Milkweed Editions, 1993). Analysis of cultural factors that promote rape and proposals for remedies.

Anja Angelica Chan. *Women and Sexual Harassment: A Practical Guide to the Legal Protections of Title VII and the Hostile Environment Claim* (Binghamton, NY: Harrington Park Press, 1994). Sexual harassment in the law.

Lorenne M. G. Clark and Debra J. Lewis. *Rape: The Price of Coercive Sexuality* (Toronto, ON: Women's Educational Press, 1977). Conflict between two social attitudes towards rape: moral outrage and "wink-wink."

Rohan Collier. *Combatting Sexual Harassment in the Workplace* (Bristol, PA: Open University Press, 1995). Reasons sexual harassment occurs and methods for combatting it.

Billie Wright Dziech and Linda Weiner. *The Lecherous Professor: Sexual Harassment on Campus.* 2nd Edition (Urbana, IL: University of Illinois Press, 1990). Still a classic in its field.

Lin Farley. *Sexual Shakedown: The Sexual Harassment of Women on the Job* (New York, NY: McGraw-Hill, 1978). Mechanisms of sexual harassment of white women, black women, older women, waitresses, etc.

Leslie Francis, ed. *Date Rape: Feminism, Philosophy and the Law* (University Park, PA: The Pennsylvania State University Press, 1996). "Communicative sex" becomes the model for condemning aggressive and coercive sex.

Nicholas Groth with Jean Birnbaum. *Men Who Rape: The Psychology of the Offender* (New York, NY: Plenum Press, 1979).

Rita Gunn and Candice Minch. *Sexual Assault: The Dilemma of Disclosure: The Question of Conviction* (Winnipeg, MB: University of Manitoba Press, 1988). Responses of significant others and the criminal justice system to reports of sexual assault.

Linda E. Ledray. *Recovery from Rape* (New York, NY: Henry Holt and Co., 1986). Handbook for rape survivors.

Silvia Levine and Joseph Koenig, ed. *Why Men Rape: Interviews with Convicted Rapists* (Toronto, ON: Macmillan Canada, 1980). Based on National Film Board of Canada's "Why Men Rape." Rather terrifying.

Catharine A. MacKinnon. *Sexual Harassment of Working Women: A Case of Sex Discrimination* (New Haven, CT: Yale University Press, 1979).

Gregory M. Matoesian. *Reproducing Rape: Domination through Talk in the Courtroom* (Chicago, IL: The University of Chicago Press, 1993). The patriarchal domination of women is perpetuated in the rape trial courtroom.

Diana E. H. Russell. *The Politics of Rape: The Victim's Perspective* (New York, NY: Stein and Day, 1975).

———. *Sexual Exploitations* (Beverly Hills: Sage Publications, 1984).

———. *Rape in Marriage* (Bloomington, IN: Indiana University Press, Expanded Edition, 1990). One out of 7 married women is raped by her husband. Why?

Peter Rutter. *Understanding and Preventing Sexual Harassment: The Complete Guide* (New York, NY: Bantam Books, 1996). Anecdotal and readable guide to sexual harassment.

Amber Coverdale Sumrall and Dena Taylor, eds. *Sexual Harassment: Women Speak Out* (Freedom, CA: The Crossing Press, 1992). Women's experiences in their own voices. Dedicated to Anita Hill.

Edmund Wall, ed. *Sexual Harassment: Confrontations and Decisions* (Buffalo, NY: Prometheus Books, 1992). Opposing viewpoints on issues in the area of sexual harassment.

Robin Warshaw. *I Never Called It Rape: The Ms. Report on Recognizing, Fighting and Surviving Date and Acquaintance Rape,* 2nd Edition (New York, NY: Harper and Row, 1994).

Suggested Moral of Part VII

If sex (at least as it is understood by men) is in the control of men, as the writings in part VI suggest, it is a small step to men's using such sex, or threats of same, as weapons against women to keep them in a position of subordination. Rape is an action motivated mainly by power, not sexuality. Sex can also be used as a way of harassing women, either explicitly by threats or less explicitly by suggestions and innuendos, on a sustained basis, of sexual activity.

Part VIII

Sex for Sale

Introduction

PART VII DISCUSSED MEN USING SEX, as they understand it, to subordinate and control women. One question of this present section is whether paying a woman for sex she otherwise would not want changes the coercive elements in the sexual situation. Prostitution and pornography are the two chief ways of exchanging sex for money.

d'Aaran, a former prostitute, describes prostitution from the inside; Ericsson defends prostitution and Pateman argues against his defense; MacKinnon claims that pornography eroticizes wrongful treatment of women, Cowan considers the questions of whether violent or degrading pornography harms women; Steinberg maintains that pornography functions to furnish material for male fantasies.

VIII.1   I'm a Hooker: Every Woman's Profession

TERI-LEE D'AARAN

Teri-Lee d'Aaran describes the twelve years she spent as a prostitute. She argues that being paid gives a woman some control in a sexual situation. She claims, however, that she will always be a hooker, because she is a woman living in a world controlled by men.

D'Aaran now lives in Waterloo, Ontario, speaking to groups about her life as a prostitute and working for feminist causes.

Reading Questions

1. Can receiving money for work enhance the value of the work? Can it enhance the value perceived in the work?
2. Can participating in bargaining over pay for work give a worker more control over her working conditions?
3. Is a client of a prostitute deceiving his wife? Would it be better if he told his wife he was having sex with a prostitute? Why or why not?

LIFE ON THE STREET is as hard as the concrete on which the prostitute walks. With every client, she has fears of being robbed, beaten, raped, or even murdered. With these elements of danger constantly surrounding her, why would a woman choose this way of life? Why was I a hooker for almost 12 years?

I

Receiving money for sex in which she has no other interest gives a prostitute an opportunity to take some control, not only of the act itself, but of her body and her life. Men have placed themselves in a situation of power in all aspects of human life, including sex. They see women as performers of services, e.g, housekeeper and caregivers of men and children. Prostitutes are bodies, available to perform sexual services on an occasional basis. The prostitute gains some control of the situation by only agreeing to have sex for a set price, paid in advance, in a place she knows to be safe for her. Receiving money also lessens her feeling of being "cheap" and "easy." If a client (or "date") has paid the correct price, he is not getting anything cheap, and since handing over money puts him to some trouble and expense, the hooker's services have not been easy to acquire. Special difficulties can arise for him when the price that will suit both of them must be arrived at through bargaining. The hooker is in a better position during such bargaining processes because she can walk away if things get too rough or too difficult. He, on the other hand, has some investment in seeing that a bargain is struck, because he has taken the initiative. His male pride is on the line, even when other options are available nearby. Some men like to brag to other men about having been with a hooker, which indicates that striking an agreement with a hooker raises a man's status with other men.

A hooker is, ordinarily, nothing more to her date than an outlet for his sexuality. He has no other feelings for her, nor does he care about her in particular. She just happens to be available, willing, and convenient. In most cases the two will never see each other again. His lack of feeling is no secret to the hooker, even though there is an unspoken understanding that this will not be mentioned. By turning the event into a commercial transaction, the prostitute shields herself from the impact of sex without caring.

The prostitute also has a moral advantage over her date. She can be completely honest about herself with him, as well as with most other people about her profession. Her date knows he is not the first and that there will be others after him, perhaps within half an hour, depending on circumstances. He, on the other hand, always seems to have something to hide, if not from her, from his wife and family. He can hardly go home and talk about his recent sexual activity with a prostitute.

Moreover, while a hooker has taken no vows of fidelity to anyone, the date must consider his marital vows to his wife. Did he not promise to "forsake all others"? He is not being completely honest, even with himself, in refusing to admit the full implications of the double standard he maintains. Should his wife have sex with someone else, this would make her a bitch, a slut, just plain trash. His infidelities, by contrast, are continuing proof of his manhood, his attractiveness to women, and his ability to have anyone he wants. Also, he is not admitting his lack of concern for his wife. If he really still cares about his wife, what is he doing with a prostitute while his wife waits for him at home? What about the money he has spent on the prostitute, which could have gone to his wife instead? (Some men, in fact, take a cut from their pay checks before they are sent to the bank to conceal such expenditures from their wives.) The man's only defense is that it is "his" money to spend any

way he wants. Often he claims he has done more than enough for his wife in keeping a roof over her head and paying the family bills. In his convoluted reasoning, he may even fly into a rage with his wife if she as much as asks him whether he's been with another woman.

Not all clients of prostitutes are formally married, but most are in relationships in which there is expectation of fidelity, caring, and exclusivity.

II

It is a mistake to think of a hooker as selling her body to a client. If she had done so, he would have bought her outright and would then have to take her home, sell her to someone else, or dispose of her in the nearest trash can. None of this was part of the bargain struck between hooker and client, and usually this is not something he wants, anyway. This leaves the prostitute with full ownership of her body before, during, and after the activity contracted for. At most, she rents out her body, in exchange for cash, prepaid, according to the terms of the agreement struck. However, since hookers have so little personal involvement in their work (although, as mentioned, they do not discuss this with clients), it might be better to think of them as performing sexual services in exchange for an agreed-upon fee.

Dates are usually physically stronger than hookers. And so, it often happens that they will take by force more than was agreed-upon and paid for. This is "rape," according to my understanding of the term. Rape is any form of sex forced on a woman against her will; the reasons why a woman is or is not willing are not relevant. If a prostitute is willing to do something in the area of sex in exchange for money, then she is not being raped. If, however, she is forced to do something that she is not willing to do, or is only willing to do if paid, and payment has not taken place, she has been raped. That sex is her profession makes no difference, since rape is not about sex anyway. It is, as we know, about male power and continued control of women. The only difference between rape and other uses of male power (beatings, threats, etc.) is that in rape male power is exercised by violating a woman's sexuality. I have never forced a man into sex against his will and cannot understand why it is so important to men that they do this, not only to me, but to many other women as well.

III

The constant presence of male power and control in the life of every woman is what leads me to say that all women are, like me, hookers. A woman in a bank or restaurant is working for an agreed-upon payment. However, the bank or restaurant is no different from the streets in male control of payment for work done. On the streets, pimps set the prices for all hookers of a particular service. Regardless of whether a hooker works for a pimp, she is in trouble if she overcharges or undercharges, relative to this fee schedule. Only men can be pimps. It is not possible for a woman to break through the "ceiling" that separates pimps from hookers. How is this situation different from that in a bank or restaurant?

I rented out my body for sexual services while other women rent out their talents of counting money or clearing tables. Or women may be wives at home or wives who go home after work to work again under male-controlled conditions. I did sex work, but then, so does a woman in an office who is required to be pleasing to men in appearance and who is subject to sexual harassment. And so, I maintain, all women are hookers.

A hooker can get off the streets, but it is a decision she must make by herself in the absence of any counseling. I was fortunate, in a way. A year after I left the streets, my best friend died. I was put into counseling because it was noticed that not only was I suffering from grief but also a lot of unresolved anger. I have stayed in counseling, gone back to school for retraining, have my own apartment, a part-time job with a moving company, and a family of three cats. I miss the excitement of the streets, but not enough to go back to the dangers and uncertainties I know I would find there. I hope other prostitutes who want to get out will meet with my luck. However, I still think of myself as a hooker, because I will always be a woman.

Further Questions

1. This writer argues that there is no difference between doing sex work under conditions controlled by men and any other sort of work under male control. Do you agree with her?

2. Is rape *any* form of sex without consent, and does it matter *why* the other person does not consent to sex?

3. Ought conditions be made better for prostitutes? For example, ought there to be established safe places where they can take their clients?

Charges Against Prostitution:
An Attempt at a Philosophical Assessment

VIII.2A

LARS O. ERICSSON

Lars O. Ericsson and Carol Pateman, the author of selection VIII.2B, have fundamental disagreements about what prostitution is and whether the prostitute is oppressed in her work. The debate centers on the nature of the transaction between
prostitute and client.

Ericsson teaches at the Filosofiska Institionen, Stockholms Universitet, Stockholm.

Reading Questions

The following questions apply to selections VIII.2A and VIII.2B.
1. What exactly does a prostitute sell in selling sexual services: her labor, her body, her submission, or something else?
2. Is sexual desire a basic need (like that of food and shelter) so that as long as this need
   is unfulfilled by consenting partners, it is necessary to have prostitution available as an
   alternative?
3. Is a prostitute oppressed mainly because of her oppressive working conditions or by her
   relations with her clients?

PERSONALLY, I MUST CONFESS that I, upon reflection, am no more able to see that coition for a fee
is intrinsically wrong than I am able to see that
drunkenness is. There is something fanatic about
both of these views which I find utterly repelling.
If two adults voluntarily consent to an economic
arrangement concerning sexual activity and this
activity takes place in private, it seems plainly absurd to maintain that there is something intrinsically wrong with it. In fact, I very much doubt
that it is wrong at all. To say that prostitution is
intrinsically immoral is in a way to refuse to give
any arguments. The moralist simply "senses" or
"sees" its immorality. And this terminates rational
discussion at the point where it should begin. . . .

[Also], the comparison between sexual love and
mercenary lovemaking is both pointless and naive.

That lovers have very little need for the services of
hustlers is at best a silly argument against prostitution. Most couples are not lovers. A great number
of persons do not even have a sexual partner. And
not so few individuals will, in any society, always
have great difficulties in finding one. What is the
point of comparing the ideal sex life of the sentimentalist with the sexual services of prostitutes in
the case of someone whose only alternative to the
latter is masturbation? Is there any reason to think
that mercenary sex must be impersonal, cold, and
impoverished compared with autosex?

By this I do not wish to contend that the typical customer is either unattractive, physically or
mentally handicapped, or extremely shy. There
is abundant empirical evidence showing that the
prostitute's customers represent all walks of life

Abridged from "Charges Against Prostitution: An Attempt at a Philosophical Assessment," in Ethics, Volume 90
(April 1980), pp. 335–366. Reprinted by permission of The University of Chicago Press and the author.

and many different types of personalities.[1] That the typical "John" is a male who for some reason cannot find a sexual partner other than a prostitute is just one of the many popular myths about harlotry which empirical studies seem unable to kill. Approximately 75 percent of the customers are married men,[2] most of whom are "respectable" taxpaying citizens.

This brings us to another aspect of the sentimentalist charge. It is not seldom a tacit and insidious presupposition of the sentimentalist's reasoning that good sex equals intramarital sex, and that bad sex equals extramarital—especially prostitutional—sex. This is just another stereotype, which deserves to be destroyed. Concerning this aspect, Benjamin and Masters make the following comment: "The experience with a prostitute is probably ethically, and may be esthetically, on a higher level than an affectionless intercourse between husband and wife, such as is all too common in our present society."[3] The demarcation line between marital and mercenary sex is not quality but the contrasting nature of the respective legal arrangements. Furthermore, we must not think that the quality—in terms of physical pleasure—of the sex services of prostitutes varies any less than the quality of "regular" sex. The best prostitutional sex available is probably much better from the customer's point of view than average marital sex.

[Finally,] I would like to counter the charge that the prostitute-customer relationship is bad on the ground that it involves the selling of something that is too basic and too elementary in human life to be sold. This is perhaps not a sentimentalist charge proper, but since it seems to be related to it I shall deal with it here.

Common parlance notwithstanding, what the hustler sells is of course not her body or vagina, but sexual *services*. If she actually did sell herself, she would no longer be a prostitute but a sexual slave. I wish to emphasize this simple fact, because the popular misnomer certainly contributes to and maintains our distorted views about prostitution.

But is it not bad enough to sell sexual services? To go to bed with someone just for the sake of money? To perform fellatio on a guy you neither love nor care for? In view of the fact that sex is a fundamental need, is it not wrong that anyone should have to pay to have it satisfied and that anyone should profit from its satisfaction? Is it not a deplorable fact that in the prostitute-customer relationship sexuality is completely alienated from the rest of the personality and reduced to a piece of merchandise?

In reply to these serious charges I would, first, like to confess that I have the greatest sympathy for the idea that the means necessary for the satisfaction of our most basic needs should be free, or at least not beyond the economic means of anyone. We all need food, so food should be available to us. We all need clothes and a roof over our heads, so these things should also be available to us. And since our sexual desires are just as basic, natural, and compelling as our appetite for food, this also holds for them. But I try not to forget that this is, and probably for a long time will remain, an *ideal* state of affairs.

Although we live in a society in which we have to pay (often dearly) for the satisfaction of our appetites, including the most basic and natural ones, I still do not regard food vendors and the like with contempt. They fulfill an important function in the imperfect world in which we are destined to live. That we have to pay for the satisfaction of our most basic appetites is no reason for socially stigmatizing those individuals whose profession it is to cater to those appetites. With this, I take it, at least the nonfanatical sentimentalist agrees. But if so, it seems to me inconsistent to hold that prostitution is undesirable on the ground that it involves the selling of something that, ideally, should not be sold but freely given away. Emotional prejudice aside, there is on *this* ground no more reason to despise the sex market and those engaged in it than there is to despise the food market and those engaged in it.

But still, is there not an abyss between selling meat and selling "flesh"? Is there not something private, personal, and intimate about sex that makes it unfit for commercial purposes? Of course, I do not wish to deny that there are great differences between what the butcher does and what the whore does, but at the same time it seems to me clear that the conventional labeling of the former as "respectable" and the latter as "indecent" is not so much the result of these differences as of the influence of cultural, especially religious and sexual, taboos. That the naked human body is "obscene," that genitalia are "offending," that menstrual blood is "unclean," etc., are expressions of taboos which strongly contribute to the often neurotic way in which sex is surrounded with mysteriousness and secrecy. Once we have been able to liberate ourselves from these taboos we will come to realize that we are no more justified in devaluating the prostitute, who, for example, masturbates her customers, than we are in devaluating the assistant nurse, whose job it is to take care of the intimate hygiene of disabled patients. Both help to satisfy important human needs, and both get paid for doing so. That the harlot, in distinction to the nurse, intentionally gives her client pleasure is of course nothing that should be held against her!

As for the charge that in the prostitute-customer relationship sexuality is completely alienated from the rest of the personality—this is no doubt largely true. I fail to see, however, that it constitutes a very serious charge. My reason for this is, once again, that the all-embracing sex act represents an ideal with which it is unfair to compare the prostitute-customer relationship, especially if, as is often the case, such an all-embracing sex act does not constitute a realizable alternative. Moreover, there is no empirical evidence showing that sex between two complete strangers must be of poor quality. . . .

. . . Is harlotry an unequal practice? And if so, in what precisely does its inequality consist? . . . [One] way of interpreting this allegation is to say that prostitution constitutes exploitation of the female sex, since harlots are being exploited by, inter alia, sex capitalists and customers, and a majority of harlots are women. This interpretation of the allegation merits careful study and I shall therefore in the first instance limit my discussion to the capitalist exploitation of prostitutes.

It is of course true that not all prostitutes can be described as workers in the sex industry.

Some are in point of fact more adequately described as small-scale private entrepreneurs. Others are being exploited without being exploited by sex capitalists. Those who can be regarded as workers in the sex industry—the growing number of girls working in sex clubs and similar establishments for instance—are, of course, according to Marxist theory, being exploited in the same sense as any wage worker is exploited. But exploitation in this Marxist sense, although perhaps effective as an argument against wage labor in general, is hardly effective as an argument against prostitution.

There is no doubt, however, that practically all harlots—irrespective of whether they are high-class call girls, cheap streetwalkers, or sex-club performers—are being exploited, economically, in a much more crude sense than that in which an automobile worker at General Motors is being exploited. I am thinking here of the fact that all of them—there are very few exceptions to this—have to pay usury rents in order to be able to operate. Many are literally being plundered by their landlords—sex capitalists who often specialize in letting out rooms, flats, or apartments to people in the racket. Not a few prostitutes also have to pay for "protection" to mafiosi with close connections to organized crime.

What makes all this possible? And what are the implications of the existence of conditions such as these for the question of the alleged undesirability of prostitution? With respect to the first of these questions the answer, it seems to me, is that the major culprit is society's hypocritical attitude toward harlotry and harlots. It is this hypocrisy which creates the prerequisites for the sex-capitalist exploitation of the prostitutes. Let me exemplify what I mean by society's hypocritical—and, I might add, totally inconsistent—attitude here. On the one hand, most societies, at least in the West (one deplorable exception is the United States), have followed the UN declaration which recommends that prostitution in itself should not be made illegal.[4] One would therefore expect that someone who pursues a legal activity would have the right to rent the necessary premises to advertise her services, and so on. But not so! The penal code persecutes those who rent out rooms, apartments, and other premises to prostitutes. And an editor of a Swedish newspaper was recently convicted for having accepted ads from "models" and "masseuses." In what other legal field or branch would contradictions such as these be considered tolerable? None, of course! One of the first to point out this double morality of society was Alexandra Kollontay, who as early as 1909 wrote; "But if the state tolerates the prostitutes and thereby supports their profession, then it must also accept housing for them and even—in the interest of social health and order—institute houses where they could pursue their occupation."[5] And the most incredible of all is that the official motivation for outlawing persons prepared to provide harlots with the premises necessary for their legal activity is a paternalistic one: so doing is in the best interest of the hustlers themselves, who would otherwise be at the mercy of unscrupulous landlords! In practice, the risk of being thrown in jail of course scares away all but the unscrupulous individuals, who can charge sky-high rents (after all they take a certain risk) and who often are associated with the criminal world. How can anyone, therefore, be surprised at the fact that not so few hustlers display "antisocial tendencies"?

The conclusion I draw from this is that the crude economic exploitation of the prostitutes is not an argument against prostitution. It rather constitutes an accusation against the laws, regulations, and attitudes which create the preconditions for that exploitation. Society cannot both allow harlotry and deprive harlots of reasonable working conditions (as a concession to "common decency") and still expect that all will be well.

[Another] way of interpreting the charge that prostitution is unequal in the sense that it places a burden on women that it does not place on men is to say that whores are being oppressed, reified, and reduced to a piece of merchandise by their male customers. To begin with the last version of this charge first, I have already pointed out the obvious, namely, that whores do not sell themselves. The individual hooker is not for sale, but her sexual services are. One could therefore, with equal lack of propriety, say of any person whose job it is to sell a certain service that he, as a result thereof, is reduced to a piece of merchandise. I cannot help suspecting that behind this talk of reduction to a piece of merchandise lies a good portion of contempt for prostitutes and the kind of services they offer for sale.

As for the version according to which the whore is reified—turned into an object, a thing—it can be understood as the view that the customer does not look upon the prostitute as a human being but as "a piece of ass." He is not interested in her as a person. He is exclusively interested in her sexual performance. . . . [However], since when does the fact that we, when visiting a professional, are not interested in him or her as a person, but only in his or her professional performance, constitute a ground for saying that the professional is dehumanized, turned into an object? . . .

Both men and women need to be liberated from the harness of their respective sex roles. But in order to be able to do this, we must liberate ourselves from those mental fossils which prevent us from looking upon sex and sexuality with the same naturalness as upon our cravings for food and drink. And, contrary to popular belief, we may have something to learn from prostitution in this respect, namely, that coition resembles nourishment in that if it can not be obtained in any other way it can always be bought. And bought meals are not always the worst. . . .

NOTES

1. See Harry Benjamin and R. E. L. Masters, *Prostitution and Morality* (New York: Julian Press, 1964), chap. 6.

2. Ibid.

3. Ibid., p. 208.

4. United Nations, *Study on Traffic in Persons and Prostitution* (New York, 1959).

5. A. Kollontai, *Brak i semeinaja problema* [Marriage and the family problem] (1909); author's translation, p. 46.

Defending Prostitution: Charges Against Ericsson   VIII.2B

CAROL PATEMAN

Pateman has written extensively on philosophy and feminism and teaches political science at the University of California, Los Angeles. Here she disagrees with what Ericsson says in selection VIII.2A.

. . . SERVICES AND LABOR POWER are inseparably connected to the body and the body is, in turn, inseparably connected to the sense of self. Ericsson[1] writes of the prostitute as a kind of social worker, but the services of the prostitute are related in a more intimate manner to her body than those of other professionals. Sexual services, that is to say, sex and sexuality, are constitutive of the body in a way in which the counseling skills of the social worker are not (a point illustrated in a backhanded way by the ubiquitous use by men of vulgar terms of female sexual organs to refer to women themselves). Sexuality and the body are, further, integrally connected to conceptions of femininity and masculinity, and all these are constitutive of our individuality, our sense of self-identity. When sex becomes a commodity in the capitalism market so, necessarily, do bodies and selves. The prostitute cannot sell sexual services alone; what she sells is her body. To supply services contracted for, professionals must act in certain ways, or use their bodies; to use the labor power he has bought the employer has command over the worker's capacities and body; to use the prostitute's "services" her purchaser must buy her body and use her body. In prostitution, because of the relation between the commodity being marketed and the body, it is the body that is up for sale. . . .

. . . Certainly, sexual impulses are part of our natural constitution as humans, but the sale of "sexual services" as a commodity in the capitalist market cannot be reduced to an expression of our natural biology and physiology. To compare the fulfillment of sexual urges through prostitution to other natural necessities of human survival, to argue from the fact that we need food, so it should be available, to the claim that "our sexual desires are just as basic, natural, and compelling as our appetite for food, [so] this also holds for them" . . . is, to say the least, disingenuous. What counts as "food" varies widely, of course in different cultures, but, at the most fundamental level of survival there is one obvious difference between sex and other human needs. Without a certain minimum of food, drink, and shelter, people die; but, to my knowledge, no one has yet died from want of sexual release. Moreover, sometimes food and drink are impossible to obtain no matter what people do, but every person has the means to find sexual release at hand.

To treat prostitution as a natural way of satisfying a basic human need, to state that "bought meals are not always the worst" . . . . neatly, if vulgarly, obscures the real, social character of contemporary sexual relations. Prostitution is not, as Ericsson claims, the same as "sex without love or mutual affection" . . . .

The latter is morally acceptable *if* it is the result of mutual physical attraction that is freely expressed by both individuals. The difference

Abridged from "Defending Prostitution: Charges Against Ericsson" in Ethics, *Volume 93 (April 1983), pp. 561–565. Reprinted by permission of The University of Chicago Press and the author.*

between sex without love and prostitution is not the difference between cooking at home and buying food in restaurants; the difference is that between the reciprocal expression of desire and unilateral subjection to sexual acts with the consolation of payment: it is the difference for women between freedom and subjection.

To understand why men (not women) demand prostitutes, and what is demanded, prostitution has to be rescued from Ericsson's abstract contractarianism and placed in the social context of the structure of sexual relations between women and men. Since the revival of the organized feminist movement, moral and political philosophers have begun to turn their attention to sexual life, but their discussions are usually divided into a set of discrete compartments which take for granted that a clear distinction can be drawn between consensual and coercive sexual relationships. However, as an examination of consent and rape makes graphically clear,[2] throughout the whole of sexual life domination, subjection, and enforced submission are confused with consent, free association, and the reciprocal fulfillment of mutual desire. The assertion that prostitution is no more than an example of a free contract between equal individuals in the market is another illustration of the presentation of submission as freedom. Feminists have often argued that what is fundamentally at issue in relations between women and men is not sex but power. But, in the present circumstances of our sexual lives, it is not possible to separate power from sex. The expression of sexuality and what it means to be feminine and a woman, or masculine and a man, is developed within, and intricately bound up with, relations of domination and subordination.

Ericsson remarks that "the best prostitutional sex available is probably much better from the customer's point of view than average marital sex." . . . It is far from obvious that it is either "quality" or the "need" for sex, in the commonsense view of "quality" and "sex," that explains why three-quarters of these customers are husbands. In the "permissive society" there are numerous ways in which men can find sex without payment, in addition to the access that husbands have to wives. But, except in the case of the most brutal husbands, most spouses work out a modus vivendi about all aspects of their lives, including the wife's bodily integrity. Not all husbands exercise to the full their socially and legally recognized right—which is the right of a master. There is, however, another institution which enables all men to affirm themselves as master. To be able to purchase a body in the market presupposes the existence of masters. Prostitution is the public recognition of men as sexual masters; it puts submission on sale as a commodity in the market. . . .

NOTES

1. L. O. Ericsson, "Charges against Prostitution: An Attempt at a Philosophical Assessment," *Ethics* 90, no. 3 (1980): 335–366.

2. C. Pateman, "Women and Consent," *Political Theory* 8 (1980): 149–168.

Further Questions

The following questions apply to selections VIII.2A and VIII.2B.

1. Prostitution exists and most prostitutes of heterosexual clients are women. What does this indicate about gender relations in the area of sex?

2. Are sex and sexual activity more closely connected with our ideas of our bodies than are the things we do with other parts of our bodies?

3. Do you agree with Ericsson that "bought meals [that is, bought sexual encounters] are not always the worst"?

Francis Biddle's Sister: Pornography, Civil Rights, and Speech

VIII.3

CATHARINE MACKINNON

Catharine MacKinnon maintains that pornography sexualizes and thereby promotes some of the worst elements of human life; rape, abuse, battery, etc. In other words, pornography eroticizes men's control of women.

MacKinnon is presently on the faculty of the University of Michigan Law School, and has published extensively on legal issues from a feminist perspective.

Reading Questions

1. Does pornography promote bad gender relations, and control of women by men in particular, by making these seem "sexy"?
2. Does pornography depict forms of sex, or particular sexual practices, that contain disturbing, demeaning, or harmful elements?
3. Does pornography set out a script for men to follow in sexual relations with women and, by implication, a message that a woman should comply with various male-initiated sexual practices, whether she wants to or not?

. . . PORNOGRAPHY SEXUALIZES RAPE, battery, sexual harassment, prostitution, and child sexual abuse; it thereby celebrates, promotes, authorizes, and legitimizes them. More generally, it eroticizes the dominance and submission that is the dynamic common to them all. It makes hierarchy sexy and calls that "the truth about sex"[1] or just a mirror of reality. Through this process pornography constructs what a woman is as what men want from sex. This is what the pornography means.

Pornography constructs what a woman is in terms of its view of what men want sexually, such that acts of rape, battery, sexual harassment, prostitution, and sexual abuse of children become acts of sexual equality. Pornography's world of equality is a harmonious and balanced place.[2] Men and women are perfectly complementary and perfectly bipolar. Women's desire to be fucked by men is equal to men's desire to fuck women. All the ways men love to take and violate women, women love to be taken and violated. The women who most love this are most men's equals, the most liberated; the most participatory child is the most grown-up, the most equal to an adult. Their consent merely expresses or ratifies these preexisting facts.

The content of pornography is one thing. There, women substantively desire dispossession and cruelty. We desperately want to be bound, battered, tortured, humiliated, and killed. Or, to be fair to the soft core, merely taken and used.

This is erotic to the male point of view. Subjection itself, with self-determination ecstatically relinquished, is the content of women's sexual desire and desirability. Women are there to be violated and possessed, men to violate and possess us, either on screen or by camera or pen on behalf of the consumer. On a simple descriptive level, the inequality of hierarchy, of which gender is the primary one, seems necessary for sexual arousal to work. Other added inequalities identify various pornographic genres or subthemes, although they are always added through gender: age, disability, homosexuality, animals, objects, race (including anti-Semitism), and so on. Gender is never irrelevant.

What pornography *does* goes beyond its content: It eroticizes hierarchy, it sexualizes inequality. It makes dominance and submission into sex. Inequality is its central dynamic; the illusion of freedom coming together with the reality of force is central to its working. Perhaps because this is a bourgeois culture, the victim must look free, appear to be freely acting. Choice is how she got there. Willing is what she is when she is being equal. It seems equally important that then and there she actually be forced and that forcing be communicated on some level, even if only through still photos of her in postures of receptivity and access, available for penetration. Pornography in this view is a form of forced sex, a practice of sexual politics, an institution of gender inequality.

From this perspective, pornography is neither harmless fantasy nor a corrupt and confused misrepresentation of an otherwise natural and healthy sexual situation. It institutionalizes the sexuality of male supremacy, fusing the erotization of dominance and submission with the social construction of male and female. To the extent that gender is sexual, pornography is part of constituting the meaning of that sexuality. Men treat women as who they see women as being. Pornography constructs who that is. Men's power over women means that the way men see women defines who women can be. Pornography is that way. Pornography is not

imagery in some relation to a reality elsewhere constructed. It is not a distortion, reflection, projection, expression, fantasy, representation, or symbol either. It is a sexual reality. . . .

In this approach, the experience of the (overwhelmingly) male audiences who consume pornography is therefore not fantasy or simulation or catharsis but sexual reality, the level of reality on which sex itself largely operates. Understanding this dimension of the problem does not require noticing that pornography models are real women to whom, in most cases, something real is being done; nor does it even require inquiring into the systematic infliction of pornography and its sexuality upon women, although it helps. What matters is the way in which the pornography itself provides what those who consume it want. Pornography *participates* in its audience's eroticism through creating an accessible sexual object, the possession and consumption of which *is* male sexuality, as socially constructed; to be consumed and possessed as which, *is* female sexuality, as socially constructed; pornography is a process that constructs it that way.

The object world is constructed according to how it looks with respect to its possible uses. Pornography defines women by how we look according to how we can be sexually used. Pornography codes how to look at women, so you know what you can do with one when you see one. Gender is an assignment made visually, both originally and in everyday life. A sex object is defined on the basis of its looks, in terms of its usability for sexual pleasure, such that both the looking—the quality of the gaze, including its point of view—and the definition according to use become eroticized as part of the sex itself. This is what the feminist concept "sex object" means in this sense, sex in life is no less mediated than it is in art. Men have sex with their image of a woman. It is not that life and art imitate each other; in this sexuality, they *are* each other.

To give a set of rough epistemological translations, to defend pornography as consistent with the equality of the sexes is to defend the subordination of women to men as sexual equality. What in the pornographic view is love and romance looks a great deal like hatred and torture to the feminist. Pleasure and eroticism become violation. Desire appears as lust for dominance and submission. The vulnerability of women's projected sexual availability, that acting we are allowed (that is, asking to be acted upon), is victimization. Play conforms to scripted roles. Fantasy expresses ideology, is not exempt from it. Admiration of natural physical beauty becomes objectification. Harmlessness becomes harm. Pornography is a harm of male supremacy made difficult to see because of its pervasiveness, potency, and principally, because of its success in making the world a pornographic place. Specifically, its harm cannot be discerned, and will not be addressed, if viewed and approached neutrally, because it *is* so much of "what is." In other words, to the extent pornography succeeds in constructing social reality it becomes invisible as harm. If we live in a world that pornography creates through the power of men in a male-dominated situation, the issue is not what the harm of pornography is, but how that harm is to become visible. . . .

We define pornography as the graphic sexually explicit subordination of women through pictures or words that also includes women dehumanized as sexual objects, things, or commodities; enjoying pain or humiliation or rape; being tied up, cut up, mutilated, bruised, or physically hurt; in postures of sexual submission or servility or display; reduced to body parts, penetrated by objects or animals, or presented in scenarios of degradation, injury, torture; shown as filthy or inferior; bleeding, bruised, or hurt in a context that makes these conditions sexual. Erotica, defined by distinction as not this, might be sexually explicit materials premised on equality.[3] We also provide that the use of men, children, or transsexuals in the place of women is pornography.[4] The definition is substantive in that it is sex-specific, but it covers everyone in a sex-specific way, so is gender neutral in overall design.

There is a buried issue within sex discrimination law about what sex, meaning gender, is. If sex is a *difference*, social or biological, one looks to see if a challenged practice occurs along the same lines; if it does, or if it is done to both sexes, the practice is not discrimination, not inequality. If, by contrast, sex has been a matter of *dominance*, the issue is not the gender difference but the difference gender makes. In this more substantive, less abstract approach, the concern with inequality is whether a practice *subordinates* on the basis of sex. The first approach implies that marginal correction is needed; the second requires social change. Equality, in the first view, centers on abstract symmetry between equivalent categories; the asymmetry that occurs when categories are not equivalent is not inequality, it is treating unlikes differently. In the second approach, inequality centers on the substantive, cumulative disadvantagement of social hierarchy. Equality for the first is nondifferentiation; for the second, nonsubordination.[5] Although it is consonant with both approaches, our antipornography statute emerges largely from an analysis of the problem under the second approach.

To define pornography as a practice of sex discrimination combines a mode of portrayal that has a legal history—the sexually explicit—with an active term that is central to the inequality of the senses—subordination. Among other things, subordination means to be in a position of inferiority or loss of power, or to be demeaned or denigrated.[6] To be someone's subordinate is the opposite of being their equal. The definition does not include all sexually explicit depictions *of* the subordination of women. That is not what it says. It says, this which *does* that: the sexually explicit that subordinates women. . . .

The harm of pornography, broadly speaking, is the harm of the civil inequality for the sexes made invisible as harm because it has become accepted as the sex difference. Consider this analogy with race: if you see Black people as different, there is no harm to segregation; it is merely a recognition of that difference. To neutral principles, separate but equal was equal. The injury of racial separation to blacks arises "solely because [they] choose to put that construction upon it."[7] Epistemologically translated: how you see it is not the way it is. Similarly, if you see women as just different, even or especially if you don't know that you do, subordination will not look like subordination at all, much less like harm. It will merely look like an appropriate recognition of the sex difference.

Pornography does treat the sexes differently, so the case for sex differentiation can be made here. But men as a group do not tend to be (although some individuals may be) treated the way women are treated in pornography. As a social group, men are not hurt by pornography the way women as a social group are. Their social status is not defined as *less* by it. So the major argument does not turn on mistaken differentiation, particularly since the treatment of women according to pornography's dictates makes it all too often accurate. The salient quality of a distinction between the top and the bottom in a hierarchy is not difference, although top is certainly different from bottom; it is power. So the major argument is: subordinate but equal is not equal. .. . .

The first victims of pornography are the ones in it. To date, it has only been with children, and male children that the Supreme Court has understood that before the pornography became the pornographer's speech it was somebody's life.[8] This is particularly true in visual media, where it takes a real person doing each act to make what you see. This is the double meaning in a statement one ex-prostitute made at our hearing: "[E]very single thing you see in pornography is happening to a real woman right now."[9] Linda Marchiano, in her book *Ordeal*,[10] recounts being coerced as "Linda Lovelace" into performing for *Deep Throat*, a fabulously profitable film,[11] by being abducted, systematically beaten, kept prisoner, watched every minute, threatened with her life and the lives of her family if she left, tortured, and kept under constant psychological intimidation and duress. . . .

What would justice look like for these women?[12] Linda Marchiano said, "Virtually every time someone watches that film, they are watching me being raped. . . ."[13]

NOTES

1. Michel Foucault, "The West and the Truth of Sex," 20 *Sub-Stance* 5 (1978).

2. This became a lot clearer to me after reading Margaret Baldwin, "The Sexuality of Inequality: The Minneapolis Pornography Ordinance," 2 *Law and Inequality: Journal of Theory and Practice* 629 (1984). This paragraph is directly indebted to her insight and language there.

3. *See, e.g.,* Gloria Steinem, "Erotica v. Pornography," in *Outrageous Acts and Everyday Rebellions* 219 (1983).

4. . . . No definition can convey the meaning of a word as well as its use in context can. However, what Andrea Dworkin and I mean by pornography is rather well captured in our legal definition: "Pornography is the graphic sexually explicit subordination of women, whether in pictures or in words, that also includes one or more of the following: (i) women are presented dehumanized as sexual objects, things, or commodities; or (ii) women are presented as sexual objects who enjoy pain or humiliation; or (iii) women are presented as sexual objects who experience sexual pleasure in being raped; or (iv) women are presented as sexual objects tied up or cut up or mutilated or bruised or physically hurt; or (v) women are presented in postures of sexual submission, servility, or display; or (vi) women's body parts including but not limited to vaginas, breasts, and buttocks—are exhibited, such that women are reduced to those parts; or (vii) women are presented as whores by nature; or (viii) women are presented being penetrated by objects or animals; or (ix) women are presented in scenarios of degradation, injury, torture, shown as filthy or inferior, bleeding, bruised, or hurt in a context that make these conditions sexual." Pornography also includes "the use of men, children, or transsexuals in the place of women." Pornography, thus defined, is discrimination on the basis of sex and, as such, a civil rights violation. This definition is a slightly modified version of the one passed by the Minneapolis City Council on December 30, 1983.

Minneapolis, Minn., Ordinance amending tit. 7, chs. 139 and 141, Minneapolis Code of Ordinances Relating to Civil Rights (Dec. 30, 1983). The ordinance was vetoed by the mayor, reintroduced, passed again, and vetoed again in 1984. . . . The Indianapolis City and County Council passed a version of it eliminating subsections (i), (v), (vi), and (vii), and substituting instead as (vi) "women are presented as sexual objects for domination, conquest, violation, exploitation, possession, or use, or through postures or positions of servility or submission or display." Indianapolis, Ind., City-County General Ordinance No. 35 (June 11, 1984) (adding inter alia, ch. 16, § 16-3(q)(6) to the Code of Indianapolis and Marion County) . . .

5. *See* Catharine A. MacKinnon, *Sexual Harassment of Working Women* 101–41 (1979).

6. For a lucid discussion of subordination, *see* Andrea Dworkin, "Against the Male Flood: Censorship, Pornography, and Equality," 8 *Harvard Women's Law Journal 1* (1985).

7. See *Plessy v. Ferguson,* 163 U.S. at 551; Herbert Wechsler, "Toward Neutral Principles of Constitutional Law," 73 *Harvard Law Review 1* (1959) at 33.

8. *Ferber,* 458 U.S. 747 (1982).

9. *Public Hearings on Ordinances to Add Pornography as Discrimination Against Women,* Committee on Government Operations, City Council, Minneapolis, Minn. (Dec. 12–13, 1983) [hereinafter cited as *Hearings*]. All those who testified in these hearings were fully identified to the City Council. II *Hearings* 75 (testimony of a named former prostitute).

10. Linda Lovelace and Michael McGrady, *Ordeal* (1980).

11. As of September, 1978, *Deep Throat* had grossed a known $50 million worldwide. . . . Many of its profits are untraceable. The film has also recently been made into a home video cassette.

12. This question . . . draw[s] directly on [a s]peech by Andrea Dworkin, in Toronto, Feb. 1984 (account told to Dworkin), reprinted in *Healthsharing,* Summer 1984, at 25.

13. I *Hearings* 56.

Further Questions

1. What does it mean to claim that women are portrayed as "sex objects" in certain forms of pornography?

2. Does pornography sexualize male supremacy? Discuss, with reference to some examples.

3. What does it mean to deny that pornography is mere fantasy and maintain that it portrays sexual reality?

Pornography: Conflict Among Feminists   VIII.4

GLORIA COWAN

Gloria Cowan addresses the questions of whether violent pornography harms women and of whether degrading pornography harms women. She cites studies showing that viewing violent pornography increases aggression toward women in a laboratory setting, desensitization toward presented rape victims, and belief in rape myths to the effect that woman incite rape and enjoy it when it happens. Exposure to degrading pornography leads to acceptance of sexual coercion and increases the tendency of men to say they would rape if they could get away with it.

Cowan is Professor of Psychology at California State University, San Bernardino.

Reading Questions

1. Is the evidence that violent pornography harms women sufficient for taking action against such pornography? What sort of action should be taken?
2. Is the evidence that degrading pornography harms women sufficient for taking action against such pornography? Action of what sort?
3. Are women faced with a dilemma of either doing nothing about pornography or joining the puritanical segment of society and demanding censorship?

FEMINISTS DISAGREE about pornography. One issue concerns whether it contributes to violence against women. Susan Brownmiller (1975) argues that it provides the propaganda machine that teaches men to hate women. Deriving from this is a debate over whether the harm caused by pornography warrants government control. . . .

DOES VIOLENT PORNOGRAPHY HARM WOMEN?

Social scientists do not agree about the effects of pornography on behavior or attitudes. Some researchers, such as Donnerstein, Linz, and Penrod (1987), believe that only violent pornography causes harm, while others (Zillmann, 1989) believe that nonviolent common pornography is harmful as well. Whether something is "harmful" depends, of course, on one's values. Harm may be physical—rape and other acts of sexual violence—or attitudinal, that which encourages rape-supportive beliefs, attitudes, and values in society at large. From a feminist framework, the primary issue is whether degrading and violent pornography *leads to* subordination of or violence toward women.

Different types of pornographic material have different effects. The evidence on violent pornography is less controversial than that on degrading/dehumanizing/common pornogra-

phy. Research has shown that the viewing of violent sexually explicit material affects aggressive behavior, attitudes regarding the legitimacy of violence against women, and emotions and judgments regarding victims of violence.

In several studies using primarily male college student volunteers, exposure to violent pornography increased aggression toward females in a laboratory setting (in Linz, Donnerstein, & Penrod, 1987). The aggression, it should be noted, is typical of the type of aggression studied in experiments by social psychologists—administering electric shock to a (female) confederate under the guise of providing feedback in a learning experiment. Thus, this laboratory research has demonstrated a link between violent pornography and laboratory aggression, not between violent pornography and rape.[3]

Another effect of exposure to violent pornography is desensitization, which is the blunting or lessening of emotional responses after repeated exposure to some stimulus or event. When male college students are exposed to violent pornography and then given a mock rape trial to view or read about, those exposed to violent pornography are more likely to see the victim as less injured than those exposed to other types of films or to control groups (Linz, Donnerstein, & Penrod, 1984). Desensitization may be among the most important effects of repeated exposure to sexually violent pornography because if members of a community have been desensitized to sexual violence by viewing it in media, they might tend to see a real victim of sexual violence, e.g., a rape victim, as not injured.

Exposure to violent pornography also affects beliefs in rape myths. The scenarios in pornography that suggest women enjoy being dominated and respond orgasmically to violence support the rape myths that women may incite rape in various ways and even want or enjoy rape. Portrayals that show women enjoying rape and other forms of sexual violence lead to increased acceptance of rape myths in both men and women (Malamuth & Check, 1985). Men who initially expressed some proclivity to rape (who report they would rape if they would not be caught and punished) were most likely to increase in their level of rape myth acceptance after exposure to violent pornography (Malamuth & Check, 1985). The effects on rape myth acceptance have been shown to occur several days after exposure to sexually violent films (Malamuth & Check, 1981). The link between violent pornography and sexual violence is indirect, based as it is on controlled research in a laboratory setting. Although we cannot say that pornography causes rape, we can say that pornography causes the types of attitudes rapists hold. Violent pornography increases beliefs in rape myths, and belief in rape myths is a predictor of self-reported sexual aggression (Malamuth, 1986).

Nonlaboratory evidence is also available, though limited and often controversial. This includes testimonials by rapists of adult women, child molesters, and prostitutes of the role of pornography in their lives. For example, Silbert and Pines (1984), in a study of street prostitutes, discovered a significant relationship between violent pornography and sexual abuse in the reports of these prostitutes. Although they were not asked directly about pornography, of 193 prostitutes who had been raped, 24 percent mentioned that the rapist had insisted that the prostitutes perform and enjoy extreme acts of violence that the rapist had seen or had read. Diane Russell (1982), in a telephone study of

rape incidence among a random sample of 930 women in the San Francisco area, found that 10 percent reported that they had been upset by being asked by their partner to imitate pornography seen or read. Twenty-four percent of the women who had been raped by their husbands or partners reported being asked to perform acts viewed or read in pornography.

Research on imprisoned sex offenders' use of pornography is inconclusive, although some suggest correlations between sex crimes and pornography consumption (Marshall, 1989). Sex offenders are exposed to explicit pornography at an earlier age (six to ten) than nonoffenders. Marshall (1988) found that over one-third of rapists and nonfamilial child molesters used pornography immediately prior to at least one of their offenses. Familial sex offenders (incest perpetrators) used pornography less than rapists and nonfamilial pedophiles. While a significant number of nonoffenders also use rape pornography and entertain thoughts of raping women, Marshall (1989) suggests that "pornography has a negative influence on these (rapists and child molesters) men" (p. 210).

A controversial area of research is on the relationship between availability of pornography and the incidence of sex crimes at the aggregate level. Court (1984) has shown a relationship between the availability of pornography and sex crimes, including rape, across selected societies. Kutchinsky (1991), however, found no relation between sexual violence and the availability of pornography in Denmark, Sweden, Germany, and the United States. Two U.S. studies found a strong relationship between rape rates and the per capita sales of men's magazines such as *Playboy* even when important demographic differences were taken into account (Baron & Straus, in Marshall, 1989; Scott & Schwalm, 1988).[4] Using 1980 data, sociologists Jaffee and Straus (1987) examined reported rape rates in forty-one states as related to the circulation rates of eight leading sexually explicit magazines. Sex magazine circulation was found to have a significant relationship with the rate of reported rape even when important factors such as marital status, urban-rural location, socio-economic status, and political liberalism were controlled.

The problem with studies of the relationship between sex crimes and the availability of, and likely exposure to, pornography is, of course, that we cannot draw the inference that the availability of pornography causes sex crimes because some third factor may cause both sex crimes and tolerance of pornography. The examination of the relationship between exposure to pornography and sex crimes is useful; however, much of this work has not yet precisely identified the category of pornography most related to sexual violence, nor has it examined the relationship between availability of pornography and desensitization and attitude effects.

DOES DEGRADING PORNOGRAPHY HARM WOMEN?

Various experimental studies have suggested that exposure to degrading/dehumanizing/common pornography has negative attitudinal and emotional effects, if not behavioral effects. Zillmann (1982, 1989) and Zillmann and Bryant (1984) have found that exposure to "common"[5] pornography for six sessions created a number of changes in both female and male viewers' attitudes and emotions. These effects include trivialization of rape and increased acceptance of sexual coercion, decreased support of the women's movement, promotion of sexual callousness toward women,[6] and changes in traditional values, such as promotion of pre- and extramarital sex, increased doubts about the value of marriage and of having female children, and the increased perception of popularity of less common sexual practices (sadomasochism and violent sex). Zillmann and Bryant (1988) also found that exposure to common pornography increased male and female viewers' dissatisfaction with their partner's sexual appearance, behavior, and affection.

Check and Guloien (1989) compared the effects of violent pornography, nonviolent but dehumanizing pornography,[7] and erotica on male college students and nonstudents in Toronto, Canada. They found that exposure to both sexually violent pornography and to dehumanizing pornography, but not erotica, increased the tendency of men to say they would rape if they could be assured that they would not be caught and punished compared to control participants who had not been exposed to pornography. These findings were strongest for men who scored high on a psychoticism scale[8] and men who habitually consumed pornography.

Recent unpublished work on the effects of degrading or dehumanizing pornography (Stock, 1993) shows negative emotional effects of this type of material. Wendy Stock (1993) found that for both male and female college students, the viewing of unequal sex, using the dominance, objectification, and penis worship materials from the Cowan and Dunn (1994) study cited previously, led to more negative mood states (depression, hostility, confusion) than exposure to either mere female availability without inequality (female hypersexuality, availability, and lack of discrimination), violent pornography, or sexually explicit erotica that depicts mutuality. Among the female students specifically, exposure to both nonviolent but degrading (unequal) pornography and violent pornography increased negative moods compared to erotica and availability. Negative ratings of unequal material were significantly higher than ratings of the violent material. Stock's research supports the conclusion that subordination, rather than sexual availability, degrades women. She found that women respond negatively to both violent and degrading material. Nonviolent material can have a stronger effect on moods and devaluation than violent material.

Wendy Stock (1993) has been exploring women's real world experiences with pornography. Among college women, 42.4 percent responded affirmatively to items related to partners either showing or describing pornography to them and either asking or forcing them to act out behaviors from pornography. Of 233 college women, 16.3 percent indicated they have been upset by someone trying to get them to do what they have seen in pornographic pictures, movies, or books. Many women reported experiencing negative feelings when exposed to pornography: uncomfortable 74.7 percent; embarrassed, 73.4 percent; disgusted, 51.5 percent; repulsed, 41.2 percent; degraded, 38.6 percent; objectified, 29.6 percent; upset, 29.6 percent; nauseated, 26.6 percent; unattractive, 26.2 percent; inadequate, 26.2 percent; and angry, 35.3 percent.

The evidence on the effects of both violent and nonviolent but degrading pornography is as controversial among researchers as the issue of pornography is among feminists. Although it has not been demonstrated that exposure to pornography directly causes rape, the evidence that violent pornography and degrading pornography contribute to attitudes condoning and trivializing sexual violence is well documented. The source of disagreement among researchers is on what, specifically, in pornography is harmful. Is it the sex, the violence, the inequality, or the fusion of sex and violence? Researchers also disagree on the generality of the findings and the implications of the findings.

WHAT IS TO BE DONE?

The questions of what to do about pornography has become a debate over censorship. This has deflected attention from the issues of how to reduce violence against women. Concerns about freedom of speech have been especially acute in the United States, where an impossible dilemma is created for many feminists. Marilyn French (1991) notes,

> Even as women are told that restraining the pervasive violence against women in films means censorship, American culture censors other depictions of violence and *licences* white male violence against all others; most particularly it licenses male violence against women. The subliminal message is clear; male violence

is legitimate; the mark of a man; women are prey. Women face a dilemma: we can be nice and say nothing or we can join Jesse Helms and his fellow unpalatable puritans in demanding censorship. This is a false couching of the problem. We need to address the real one. (p. 32)

Pornography can be regarded as "hate" speech; it expresses hatred of women. Where to draw the line on hate speech has become an important issue in connection with political correctness and freedom of expression. In an article on racist speech, Mari J. Matsuda (1989) argues against an absolutist First Amendment position due to the harm experienced by victims of hate speech individually and the harm of perpetuating racism in general. Pornography is both sexist and racist.

Censorship of pornography in the United States exists now only in the area of child pornography. Although obscenity and pornography share sexual explicitness in common, pornography is a broad term and, as noted, can be broken into different categories. Obscenity, a legal term, is narrowly defined and is based on moral offensiveness to community standards, not potential harm to women. States have the right to enforce obscenity law, and some are doing so. Enforcement of obscenity law is not censorship because censorship involves the concept of *prior restraint*. Prior restraint means that the government cannot impose restraints on the publication of speech that has not been first proven illegal (Kaminer, 1980). Thus, each piece of pornography has to be individually judged obscene. While a harm-to-women interpretation that includes degrading and dehumanizing pornography as exceeding community standards could be added to obscenity law, as it has been in Canada, the enforcement procedure would still be tedious.

For many feminists, censorship and obscenity laws as they are currently defined are not the answers, but surely silence is not the answer either. As MacKinnon (1991, p. 11) said: "We are not supposed to talk about the way pornography hurts women. Pornography's actions are protected as speech, but our speech against it is silenced as action."[11] Women cannot afford to be silent about pornography in fear of being labeled as sexual prudes. Pornography is more about dehumanization and violence than it is about sex. As we have learned from the study of rape, incest, battering, and harassment speaking out is the first step in resisting the victimization and devaluation of women.

Notes

3. In these studies, the aggressive behavior was measured almost immediately after subjects viewed the violent pornography (Donnerstein, Penrod, & Linz, 1987). Also, in the laboratory experimental studies of pornography effects, participants are randomly assigned to the film viewing conditions, sometimes a neutral nonsexual and nonviolent film, and, in other studies, a sexual but nonviolent film and a violent but nonsexual film, thus eliminating systematic differences between the different exposure groups. Outside the laboratory, people who choose to watch pornography are likely to be different in many respects than those who do not choose to watch pornography. In several studies (Malamuth, Check, & Briere, 1986; Demare, Briere, & Lips, 1988), the types of men most likely to be sexually aroused by depictions of sexual violence were more likely to say that they would rape and were more accepting of an ideology justifying male dominance over women and aggression against women.

4. Baron (1990) has reported that States having higher rates of pornography magazine circulation are also higher on indicators of gender equality. Baron suggests that both pornography and equality of women are more likely in states with greater political tolerance.

5. As noted previously, Zillmann (1989) attributes the effects in his studies to the portrayal of women as sexually insatiable and available.

6. Linz, Donnerstein, and Penrod (1988) report that they have been unable to replicate the Zillmann and Bryant findings regarding exposure to nonviolent pornography and sexual callousness toward women. Further, they found no effects of either the X-rated nonviolent or R-rated extremely violent films on such beliefs and attitudes about women.

7. Check and Guloien (1989) define dehumanizing pornography as that which portrays women as "hysterically responsive to male sexual demands, ver-

bally abused, dominated, and degraded, and treated as a plaything with no human qualities other than her physical attributes" (p. 163).

8. Psychoticism measures include items that indicate feelings of isolation, thought control by others, obsessive thoughts, and other extreme ideations.

11. The idea expressed by MacKinnon and her supporters is that pornography shows real violence happening to real people and is more than speech. This statement also implies that attempts to redress the harm done to women by pornography is taken more seriously than the harm of pornography itself.

References

Baron, Larry. 1990. Pornography and gender equality: An empirical analysis. *Journal of Sex Research* 27: 363–380.

Brownmiller, Susan. 1975. *Against our will: Men, women, and rape.* New York: Simon & Schuster.

Check, James V. P., and Ted. H. Guloien. 1989. Reported proclivity for coercive sex following repeated exposure to sexually violent pornography, nonviolent dehumanizing pornography, and erotica. In Dolf Zillmann & Jennings Bryant (Eds.), *Pornography: Research advances and policy considerations* (pp. 159–84). Hillsdale, NJ: Lawrence Erlbaum.

Court, John H. 1984. Sex and violence: a ripple effect. In Neil M. Malamuth & Edward Donnerstein (Eds.), *Pornography and sexual aggression* (pp. 143–72). New York: Academic Press.

Cowan, Gloria, & Kerri F. Dunn. 1994. What themes in pornography lead to perceptions of the degradation of women? *Journal of Sex Research, 31,* 11–21.

Donnerstein, Edward, Daniel Linz, & Steven Penrod. 1987. *The question of pornography: Research findings and policy implications.* New York: The Free Press.

French, Marilyn. 1991. A choice we never chose. *The Women's Review of Books* 8(10–11):31–32.

Jaffee, David, & Murray A. Straus. 1987. Sexual climate and reported rape: A state-level analysis. *Archives of Sexual Behavior* 16: 107–23.

Kaminer, Wendy. 1980. Pornography and the First Amendment: Prior restraints and private actions. In Laura Lederer (Ed.), *Take back the night* (pp. 241–47). New York: William Morrow.

Kutchinsky, Berl. 1991. Pornography and rape: Theory and practice? *International Journal of Law and Psychiatry* 14:47–64.

Linz, Daniel, Edward Donnerstein, & Steven Penrod. 1984. The effects of multiple exposures to filmed violence against women. *Journal of Communication* 34:130–147.

Linz, Daniel, Edward Donnerstein, & Steven Penrod. 1987. The findings and recommendations of the Attorney General's Commission on Pornography: Do the psychological "facts" fit the political fury? *American Psychologist* 42:946–953.

Linz, Daniel, Edward Donnerstein, & Steven Penrod. 1988. Effects of long-term exposure to violent and sexually degrading depictions of women. *Journal of Personality and Social Psychology* 55:758–768.

MacKinnon, Catherine A. Summer. 1991. To quash a lie. *Smith Alumnae Quarterly*, 11–14.

Malamuth, Neil. 1986. Predictors of naturalistic sexual aggression. *Journal of Personality and Social Psychology* 50:953–962.

Malamuth, Neil, & James V. P. Check. 1981. The effects of mass media exposure on acceptance of violence against women: A field experiment. *Journal of Research in Personality* 15:436–446.

Malamuth, Neil, & James V. P. Check. 1985. The effects of aggressive pornography on belief of rape myths: Individual differences. *Journal of Research in Personality* 19:299–320.

Malamuth, Neil M., James V. P. Check, & John Briere. 1986. Sexual arousal in response to aggression: Ideological, aggressive, and sexual correlates. *Journal of Personality and Social Psychology* 18:438–453.

Marshall, W. L. 1988. The use of sexually explicit stimuli by rapists, child molesters, and non-offenders. *Journal of Sex Research* 25:267–288.

Marshall, W. L. 1989. Pornography and sex offenders. In Dolf Zillmann & Jennings Bryant (Eds.), *Pornography: Research advances and policy considerations* (pp. 215–234). Hillsdale, NJ: Lawrence Erlbaum.

Matsuda, Mari J. 1989. Public response to racist speech: Considering the victim's story. *Michigan Law Review* 87:2320–2381.

Russell, Diana H. 1982. *Rape in marriage.* New York: Macmillan.

Scott, Joseph E.,& Loretta A. Schwalm. 1988. Rape rates and the circulation rates of adult magazines. *Journal of Sex Research 24:* 241–250.

Silbert, Mimi H., & Ayala M. Pines. 1984. Pornography and sexual abuse of women. *Sex Roles* 10:857–868.

Stock, Wendy. 1993. The effects of pornography on women. Paper presented at Speech, Equality, and Harm Conference, Chicago, March 1993, and annual meeting of the Society for the Scientific Study of Sex, Chicago, November 5, 1993.

Zillmann, Dolf. 1982. Pornography, sex callousness and the trivialization of rape. *Journal of Communication* 32:10–21.

Zillmann, Dolf. 1989. Effects of prolonged consumption of pornography. In Dolf Zillmann & Jennings Bryant (Eds.), *Pornography: Research advances and policy considerations* (pp. 127–57). Hillsdale, NJ: Lawrence Erlbaum.

Zillmann, Dolf, & Jennings Bryant. 1984. Effects of massive exposure to pornography. In Neil M. Malamuth & Edward Donnerstein (Eds.), *Pornography and sexual aggression* (pp. 115–138). New York: Academic Press.

Zillmann, Dolf, & Jennings Bryant. 1988. Pornography's impact on sexual satisfaction. *Journal of Applied Social Psychology* 18:438–453.

Further Questions

1. At least one study has found no relation between sexual violence and the availability of pornography in Denmark, Sweden, Germany, and the United States. Must violent pornography be proven to cause rape before any steps are taken to remove it from the market?

2. Women have been reported as having negative feelings when exposed to pornography. Also, some women complain about someone trying to get them to do what is portrayed in pieces of pornography. Should these feelings be taken into account when assessing the impact of pornography on a population?

3. Why has pornography been called "hate" speech, expressing hatred of women. What kinds of action are appropriate reactions to hate speech of this sort?

VIII.5   The Roots of Pornography

DAVID STEINBERG

David Steinberg notes that pornography is not about our real selves but about our fantasies and unfulfilled desires. Because of social conditioning, women's sexual desire is truncated. Pornography fulfills men's fantasy of women possessed with desire for sex with them.

Steinberg is author, editor, and publisher of sex-positive, erotic photography and writing. He has been active in the California and national feminist men's movements for the past twenty years.

Reading Questions

1. Is the expectation that men be sexual initiators burdensome for men? Who, exactly, expects this of men?
2. Does pornography, which portrays sex between people but very little else, alienate people from their sexual selves?
3. Does pornography, at the same time, validate sex and sexual feeling in a somewhat puritanical society?

IT IS STRIKING THAT in the midst of so much vehement debate on the subject of pornography, there is so little discussion of, or attempt to understand, the nature of the pornographic phenomenon itself. The *Hite Report on Male Sexuality* notes that eighty-nine percent of its respondents report some involvement with pornography. Something basic is going on here.

What is it that makes pornography so popular among American men and, increasingly, among American women? Why does it sell? What does pornography accomplish, or seem to accomplish, for the tens of millions of people who are its market?

For myself, and for virtually all the men I have talked to, pornography is essentially a tool for masturbation, a fantasy enhancer. This is important to remember. Pornography is not about partner sex, not about sexual reality, not about our real lovers and mates, not about our real selves. Though women I have talked to consistently fear that their male lovers expect them to look and act like *Playboy* models or porn stars, I believe that the vast majority of men who use pornography are clear about the difference between images and real people, between archetypes and human beings, between the jet-setters and the rest of us.

To be effective, then, pornography must be good masturbation material. It must address our longings, our unfulfilled desires, the sexual feelings that have power in fantasy precisely because they are unsatisfied in our real lives. So what are some of these unresolved sexual issues addressed by men through pornography?

From my point of view, the most important single issue that welds men so forcefully to pornography is that of sexual scarcity. Although attitudes are changing, most heterosexual men still experience sex from the perspective of scarcity. Men seem to want sex more than women. Men try to get women to have sex with them. Or, more subtly: Men seem to respect sexual desire more than women do. Men feel resistance to sexual desire from women, expressed as fear, reluctance, disinterest, even revulsion.

Women, sadly, have been handed (and have generally accepted) the cultural role of being the final defenders of puritan antisex. Sexual desire is evil, they are told, or at least low. Men desire. Women—higher, more spiritual beings than men—are to distrust and defend themselves against male desire and will be severely punished if they do not. Women are not to enjoy being the focus for male desire and certainly ought not desire sex for its own sake.

Women are taught to experience sexual desire only in the context of emotional commitment or expression of affection, not as simple bodily hunger. Lust is, by definition, unwomanly. To be a lustful woman—especially a lustful young woman—still carries slutty connotations that few women want to engage.

Let me be clear that I am in no way blaming women for this situation. Nor am I trying to invalidate the many reasons women are protective of themselves sexually—ranging from fear of pregnancy, to fear of rape, to fear of mother, to fear of losing the respect of other women or of men. I am simply noting that we live in a sex economy that produces an ongoing pool of surplus male desire, a culture that fears even the best of male desire, a world that gives men precious little opportunity to be desired, feel desirable, feel attractive and appreciated for our sexual natures.

A closely related issue, one that is perhaps even more significant emotionally, is that of rejection. Even in progressive, "liberated," "enlightened" circles, and certainly in the dominant culture, men still carry the burden of being the sexual initiators, the desirers, and thus, inevitably, the rejected ones. A difficult, dangerous, and painful job but, as they say, somebody has to do it.

I believe that we are only beginning to appreciate the significance of the emotional work men must do to be able to repeatedly express sexual interest and initiative to those who are being taught to reject us. Warren Farrell, author of *Why Men Are the Way They Are,* suggests that men's attempts to deal psychologically with rejection have a lot to do with our need to objectify women—that it is less painful to be rejected by an object than by a thinking, feeling human being. I think he's right.

In any case, fear of rejection, and the resulting negative feelings about ourselves as sexual beings and about our sexual desirability, are difficult aspects of sexual manhood all men grapple with, usually with only partial success. The residue is part of the emotional material we take to pornography.

I believe that these issues—sexual scarcity, desire for appreciation and reciprocation of desire, and fear of being sexually undesirable—are the central forces that draw men to pornography. While violent imagery, by various estimates, accounts for only three to eight percent of all pornography, images that address scarcity, female lust, and female expression of male desirability account for at least seventy-five percent of porn imagery.

Pornography is a vehicle men use to help us fantasize sexual situations that soothe these wounds. The central themes are available, lusty sex, focused on *our* desirability, involving archetypal images of the very women who must represent our felt undesirability in real life. When we buy pornographic magazines, take them to the safety and privacy of our bedrooms and masturbate to their images (or when we masturbate to the images of these same women on screen), we vent the frustrations born of scarcity, the sexual fears born of rejection, and the sexual insecurity born of being so seldom appreciated by women for our specifically sexual existence.

And which images most effectively accomplish this for us? Images of women who are openly desirous of sex, who look out at us from the page with all the yearning we know so well yet so rarely receive from our partners. Images of women hungry for sex *with us,* possessed by desire *for us.* Women hungry to get their hands on our bodies or get our hands on theirs. Receptive women who greet our sexual desire not with fear and loathing but with appreciation, even gratitude. And glamorous women whose mere bestowal of sexual attention mystically proves our sexual worth.

Is it any wonder that such a sexual world is attractive to so many men? The problem, however, is that although the pornographic fantasies may be soothing in the moment, they often contribute to bad feelings about ourselves over time. This depends on the specific images, what we do with them, and how we feel about ourselves to begin with. But in general, the more the imagery of pornography confirms who we are as sexual people, the better we will probably feel about our sexual energies afterward. Conversely, the more we are told that to be sexually desirable we need to be other than who we really are, the worse we will feel.

From this point of view, much of pornography is likely to affect us negatively (although, again, not all—and we do get to pick and chose among the offerings). Michael Castleman, in his book *Sexual Solutions,* notes how seldom pornography includes "any kissing, handholding, caressing, massages, reciprocal undressing, tenderness or discussion of lovemaking preferences." It is sad that pornography speaks so little about softness, vulnerability, uncertainty, intimacy—all of which we know to be important parts of our sexual reality.

But the likelihood that pornography may alienate us from our sexual selves, or the fact that it fails to offer more than temporary relief from our sexual wounds, should not blind us to the very real and valid feelings that attract us to the medium in the first place.

Besides, not all of our attraction to pornography is rooted in pain and fear, and not all of pornography's effects are negative. Pornography is still the medium that most vociferously advocates free and diverse sexual expressiveness, a radical stance in our culture, which is still essentially puritanical and sex-negative. Pornography still serves as an arena for adolescents to get validation and approval for their emerging sexual feelings, whose power far exceeds what society is unwilling to endorse as proper. Pornography is still an ally for those of us who choose to fight for the full recognition and admiration of our sexual natures in the face of the growing forces of sexual repression.

Pornography is the one arena that is not afraid of the penis, even when erect, that does not find sperm disgusting, that shows pictures of men ejaculating in slow motion, even as other films emphasize the beauty of birds flying or dolphins leaping. And it is in the world of pornography where much of traditional male hatred and fear of vaginas has been redirected toward vaginal appreciation, through what writer Michael Hill calls "graphic and realistic depictions of the cunt as beautiful, tasty, wonderful to smell and touch."

In addition, pornography, for all its *mis*information, is still an important source of real and useful sexual information as well. The "G" spot and the normalcy of female ejaculation have been introduced to mass culture not by sex therapists but by the porn network. Dozens of magazines, and now a feature-length film, have taught men these important aspects of *female* pleasure. Mass acceptance of oral and anal sex as normal sexual practices has been accelerated by the repeated, indeed casual, depiction of these acts in hundreds of porn films.

Porn films in general offer real learn-by-watching information (the information we should all receive as emerging adults, but don't) on all kinds of sexual practices—as long as we bring a critical eye to tell the fake from the real (there's plenty of both), and the friendly from the nasty (also both well-represented). And if we want to encourage our sexual imagination, going to see a variety of sex loops will give us plenty of food for thought, and plenty of support for what we may feel to be our unique infatuations.

Finally, I think it is important to acknowledge that pornography provides a victimless outlet for the basic sexual rage that seems to sit within so many men, whether we like it or not. This is the rage that sadly gets vented at specific women through rape and other forms of sexual assault. It will not go away from the social psyche, pornography or no pornography.

For all the terrible pain this rage has brought to women, we must understand that at the core of this feeling there is a righteous anger: the anger at having our naturally exuberant, lively, pleasurable sexual feelings twisted, stunted, denied, and used against us. This anger needs to be acknowledged, respected, and redirected away from women, toward its appropriate targets: antisexual religious teachings, sex-phobia in general, the complex of societal institutions intent on denying us all the natural exploration of one of life's greatest miracles.

Respecting the roots of male sexual anger may be as uncomfortable for us as respecting the roots of our attraction to pornography. But both are important to own and affirm. If we can respect the core of what attracts us to pornography, we can begin to find ways to have that core more effectively addressed by the sexual materials we use. On the other hand, if we think that every time we're drawn to pornography we only express the worst of ourselves as men, we will both hate ourselves and become trapped in repeating and self-defeating cycles of guilt and rebellion.

What is needed, in my opinion, is not an attempt to drive pornography underground, socially or psychically. If pornography becomes outlawed (again), it, like prostitution, will only come to represent the notion that sex is dirty, even more strongly than it does today. What is needed instead is the development of sexual materials that take the *best* of the pornographic tradition—sexual openness, exploration, and celebration—and add to these egalitarian values, imagination, artfulness, respect of ourselves, and respect for the power and beauty of sex itself.

We need sexual materials that more fully address our real sexual needs and feelings, materials that help us feel better about ourselves, materials that enable us to resist the antisexual insanity that assaults us every day. We need material with which we can identify without contradicting our best sexual intuitions—photographs and stories whose beauty affirms our own sexual power and worth.

Happily, we can now point to the beginning of such materials. In the past few years, a group of us have developed an erotic theater show, *Celebration of Eros,* a dramatic presentation of poetry and prose with four slide shows set to music, to celebrate the best of our erotic natures. I have also recently edited an extensive hardcover collection of high-quality erotic photography, writing, and drawing, *Erotic by Nature* (Shakti Press/Red Alder Books). Excellent collections of erotic writing by women have recently been edited by Susie Bright (*Herotica,* Down There Press), Laura Chester (*Deep Down,* Faber & Faber), and Lonnie Barbach (*Pleasures: Erotic Interludes,* Doubleday). *Yellow Silk,* a journal for erotic arts whose motto is "all persuasions, no brutality," is in its seventh year of publication. *On Our Backs,* a San Francisco magazine of "entertainment of the adventurous lesbian," is to my knowledge the first explicitly feminist sex magazine anywhere.

We need more. We need what Paula Webster calls "a truly radical feminist pornography-erotica." Recent thinking and writing among the sex radicals of the feminist movement are an encouraging start toward understanding what such a feminist pornography might look like. Hopefully, before too long, when we and our sons and daughters go out to buy some sexual stimulation, we'll all be able to feel good about what we bring home.

Further Questions

1. Is it natural, in some sense, to want a lot of sex, so that lack of sexual desire must be due to social inhibition?

2. In introducing novel forms of sex, does pornography teach people things they should become aware of as possibilities?

3. Would it make sense for a man who wanted to vent his rage on women by rape or other forms of sexual assault to use pornography as an outlet instead?

Further Readings for Part VIII: Sex for Sale

Robert M. Baird and Stuart E. Rosenbaum, eds. *Pornography: Private Right or Public Menace* (Buffalo, NY: Prometheus Books, 1991).

Laurie Bell, ed. *Good Girls, Bad Girls: Sex Trade Workers and Feminists Face to Face* (Toronto, ON: Women's Press, 1987). Feminists and prostitutes speak on sex work, together and separately.

Deborah R. Brock. *Making Work, Making Trouble: Prostitution as a Social Problem* (Toronto, ON: University of Toronto Press, 1988). Why is prostitution considered a problem and for whom?

Vern Bullough and Bonnie Bullough. *Women and Prostitution: A Social History* (Buffalo, NY: Prometheus Books, 1987).

Susan G. Cole. *Pornography and the Sex Crisis* (Toronto: Amanita Enterprises, 1989). Pornography is sexuality socially constructed to maintain male power.

David Copp and Susan Wendell, eds. *Pornography and Censorship* (Buffalo, NY: Prometheus Books, 1983). Spectrum of perspectives on pornography, leaning toward the conservative end.

Frederique Delacoste and Priscilla Alexander, eds. *Sex Work: Writings by Women in the Sex Industry* (Pittsburg, PA: Cleis Press, 1987). Women in sex work speak for themselves, their experiences, and their attitudes toward what they do.

Edward Donnerstein, Daniel Linz, and Steven Penrod, eds. *The Question of Pornography* (New York, NY: Macmillan, The Free Press , 1987). Studies of degradation and violence in pornography.

Andrea Dworkin. *Pornography: Men Possessing Women* (New York, NY : Penguin, 1979). An all-bad view of pornography.

Susan M. Easton. *The Problem of Pornography: Regulation and the Right to Free Speed* (New York, NY: Routledge, 1994). The freedom of the individual versus the legal regulation of materials constituting incitement to sexual hatred.

Barbara Meil Hobson. *Uneasy Virtue: The Politics of Prostitution and the American Reform Tradition* (New York, NY: Basic Books, 1987). Researched in cell blocks, dusty corners of courthouses, etc.

Valerie Jenness. *Making It Work: The Prostitutes' Rights Movement in Perspective* (Hawthorne, NY: Aldine de Gruyter, 1993).

Laura Lederer, ed. *Take Back the Night: Women on Pornography* (New York, NY: Bantam Books, 1980).

Linda Lovelace. *Ordeal* (Secaucus, NJ: Citadel Press, 1980). Linda Marchiano writes of her coercion into "Linda Lovelace," the porn star.

Catharine A. MacKinnon. *Feminism Unmodified: Discourses on Life and Law* (Cambridge, MA: Harvard University Press, 1987). Pornography, rape, sexual harassment, and other issues discussed with all the stops let out.

———. *Only Words* (Cambridge, MA: Harvard University Press, 1993). Indictment of free-speech doctrine in matters of pornography and other hate propaganda.

Catharine A. MacKinnon and Andrea Dworkin, eds. *In Harm's Way: The Pornography Civil Rights Hearings* (Cambridge, MA: Harvard University Press, 1997). Victims of pornography give oral testimony.

Wendy McElroy. *XXX: A Woman's Right to Pornography* (New York, NY: St. Martin's Press, 1995). Argument that pornography benefits women and the feminist movement.

Richard B. Milner and Christina Andrea Milner. *Black Players: The Secret World of Black Pimps* (Boston, MA: Little, Brown and Co., 1972).

Gail Pheterson, ed. *A Vindication of the Rights of Whores* (Seattle, WA: Seal Press, 1989). Voices of prostitutes from around the world.

Helen Reynolds. *The Economics of Prostitution* (Springfield, IL: Charles C. Thomas, Publisher, 1986). Good discussion of incentives for prostitution.

Diana E. H. Russell, ed. *Making Violence Sexy: Feminist Views on Pornography* (Buckingham, England: Open Court University Press, 1993).

Carolyn See. *Blue Money* (New York, NY: David MacKay Co, Inc., 1974). Notes on porn stars and others in the porn trade.

Lynne Segal and Mary McIntosh, eds. *Sex Exposed: Sexuality and the Pornography Debate* (New Brunswick, NJ: Rutgers University Press, 1993).

John Stoltenberg. *What Makes Pornography "Sexy"?* (Minneapolis, MN: Milkweed Editions, 1994). Men are selected to do the pose in a pornographic photograph then talk about how it feels to pose.

D. Kelly Weisberg. *Children of the Night: A Study of Adolescent Prostitution* (Lexington, MA: Lexington Books, 1985).

Linda Williams. *Hard Core: Power, Pleasure and the Frenzy of the Visible* (Berkeley, CA: University of California Press, 1989). Diverse perspectives. What porn does, including what it does to women. Argues against censorship.

Suggested Moral of Part VIII

Women exchange sex for money, either as prostitutes or as subjects depicted in pornography. Although there is some reason to believe that what is sold is sexuality, most of these writers agree that subordination, or at least the appearance of it, is what men are really after. A thriving market in female subordination, of course, does little to put an end to it. We do have the idea that if there is a high demand for something in the market, there must be something valuable about it.

Part IX

Fertility Control: Contraception and Abortion

Introduction

THE WRITINGS IN THIS PART discuss whether there is a right to fertility control: contraception or abortion. Abortion is clearly the more serious matter, because the issue then is whether to terminate a form of human life that is developing into an infant; and an infant is expected to have a definite place in the human community.

Aquinas argues that procreative sex is the only legitimate form of sex; Radcliffe-Richards maintains that free contraceptives should be made available to anyone who wants them; Marquis claims that abortion wrongs the fetus; Thomson and Sherwin defend abortion; Timmins wants abortion to be available to and to be taken seriously by anyone who is carrying a handicapped fetus.

IX.1   The Purpose of Sex

ST. THOMAS AQUINAS

St. Thomas Aquinas articulates a creed we have come to associate with Roman Catholicism. Contraception is wrong because it frustrates the natural end of sexuality which is continuation of the human species. Hence no one has a right to use contraceptives.

Aquinas (c. 1224–1274) has been given a special position of respect in Roman Catholic scholarship. He was heavily influenced by Aristotle in his child-oriented approach to marriage.

Reading Questions

1. Do you think of semen as having a purpose, so that it would be a bad thing if semen were emitted under conditions where this purpose could not be fulfilled?
2. Suppose there is a tendency for men to remain with women after the sexual act. Would the explanation be that a woman could not, by herself, care for any offspring generated?
3. Does it then follow that marriage is the only appropriate context for sexual activity, and that contraceptives have no rightful place in human life?

THE REASON WHY SIMPLE FORNICATION IS A SIN ACCORDING TO DIVINE LAW, AND THAT MATRIMONY IS NATURAL

1. WE CAN SEE the futility of the argument of certain people who say that simple fornication is not a sin. For they say: Suppose there is a woman who is not married, or under the control of any man, either her father or another man. Now, if a man performs the sexual act with her, and she is willing, he does not injure her, because she favors the action and she has control over her own body. Nor does he injure any other person, because she is understood to be under no other person's control. So, this does not seem to be a sin.

2. Now, to say that he injures God would not seem to be an adequate answer. For we do not offend God except by doing something contrary to our own good, as has been said. But this does not appear contrary to man's good. Hence, on this basis, no injury seems to be done to God.

3. Likewise, it also would seem an inadequate answer to say that some injury is done to one's neighbor by this action, inasmuch as he may be scandalized. Indeed, it is possible for him to be scandalized by something which is not in itself a sin. In this event, the act would be accidentally sinful. But our problem is not whether simple fornication is accidentally a sin, but whether it is so essentially.

4. Hence, we must look for a solution in our earlier considerations. We have said that God exercises care over every person on the basis of what is good for him. Now, it is good for each person to attain his end, whereas it is bad for

The Purpose of Sex. From Summa Contra Gentiles Book Three *by St. Thomas Aquinas, Translated by Vernon J. Bourke. Translations copyright © 1956 by Doubleday, a division of Bantam Doubleday Dell Publishing Group, Inc. Used by permission of Doubleday, a division of Random House, Inc.*

him to swerve away from his proper end. Now, this should be considered applicable to the parts, just as it is to the whole being; for instance, each and every part of man, and every one of his acts, should attain the proper end. Now, though the male semen is superfluous in regard to the preservation of the individual, it is nevertheless necessary in regard to the propagation of the species. Other superfluous things, such as excrement, urine, sweat, and such things, are not at all necessary; hence, their emission contributes to man's good. Now, this is not what is sought in the case of semen, but, rather, to emit it for the purpose of generation, to which purpose the sexual act is directed. But man's generative process would be frustrated unless it were followed by proper nutrition, because the offspring would not survive if proper nutrition were withheld. Therefore, the emission of semen ought to be so ordered that it will result in both the production of the proper offspring and in the upbringing of this offspring.

5. It is evident from this that every emission of semen, in such a way that generation cannot follow, is contrary to the good for man. And if this be done deliberately, it must be a sin. Now, I am speaking of a way from which, *in itself,* generation could not result: such would be any emission of semen apart from the natural union of male and female. For which reason, sins of this type are called *contrary to nature*. But, if by accident generation cannot result from the emission of semen, then this is not a reason for it being against nature, or a sin as for instance, if the woman happens to be sterile.

6. Likewise, it must also be contrary to the good for man if the semen be emitted under conditions such that generation could result but the proper upbringing would be prevented. We should take into consideration the fact that, among some animals where the female is able to take care of the upbringing of offspring, male and female do not remain together for any time after the act of generation. This is obviously the case with dogs. But in the case of animals of which the female is not able to provide for the upbringing of offspring, the male and female do stay together after the act of generation as long as is necessary for the upbringing and instruction of the offspring. Examples are found among certain species of birds whose young are not able to seek out food for themselves immediately after hatching. In fact, since a bird does not nourish its young with milk, made available by nature as it were, as occurs in the case of quadrupeds, but the bird must look elsewhere for food for its young, and since besides this it must protect them by sitting on them, the female is not able to do this by herself. So, as a result of divine providence, there is naturally implanted in the male of these animals a tendency to remain with the female in order to bring up the young. Now, it is abundantly evident that the female in the human species is not at all able to take care of the upbringing of offspring by herself, since the needs of human life demand many things which cannot be provided by one person alone. Therefore, it is appropriate to human nature that a man remain together with a woman after the generative act, and not leave her immediately to have such relations with another woman as is the practice with fornicators.

7. Nor, indeed, is the fact that a woman may be able by means of her own wealth to care for the child by herself an obstacle to this argument. For natural rectitude in human acts is not dependent on things accidentally possible in the case of one individual, but, rather, on those conditions which accompany the entire species.

8. Again, we must consider that in the human species offspring require not only nourishment for the body, as in the case of other animals, but also education for the soul. . . . children must be instructed by parents who are already experienced people. Nor are they able to receive such instruction as soon as they are born, but after a long time, and especially after they have reached the age of discretion. Moreover, a long time is needed for this instruction. Then, too, because of the impulsion of the passions, through which prudent judgment is vitiated, they require not merely instruction but

correction. Now, a woman alone is not adequate to this task; rather, this demands the work
of a husband, in whom reason is more developed for giving instruction and strength is more
available for giving punishment. Therefore, in
the human species, it is not enough, as in the
case of birds, to devote a small amount of time
to bringing up offspring, for a long period of
life is required. Hence, since among all animals
it is necessary for male and female to remain together as long as the work of the father is
needed by the offspring, it is natural to the
human being for the man to establish a lasting
association with a designated woman, over no
short period of time. Now, we call this society
matrimony. Therefore, matrimony is natural for
man, and promiscuous performance of the sexual act, outside matrimony is contrary to man's
good. For this reason, it must be a sin.

9. Nor, in fact should it be deemed a slight
sin for a man to arrange for the emission of
semen apart from the proper purpose of generating and bringing up children, on the argument that it is either a slight sin, or none at all,
for a person to use a part of the body for a different use than that to which it is directed by
nature (say, for instance, one chose to walk on
his hands, or to use his feet for something usually done with the hands) because man's good
is not much opposed by such inordinate use.
However, the inordinate emission of semen is
incompatible with the natural good; namely, the
preservation of the species. Hence, after the sin
of homicide whereby a human nature already in
existence is destroyed, this type of sin appears to
take next place, for by it the generation of
human nature is precluded.

10. Moreover, these views which have just
been given have a solid basis in divine authority.
That the emission of semen under conditions in
which offspring cannot follow is illicit is quite
clear. There is the text of Leviticus (18:22–23):
"thou shalt not lie with mankind as with wom-
ankind . . . and thou shalt not copulate with any
beast." And in I Corinthians (6:10): "Nor the
effeminate, nor liers with mankind . . . shall possess the kingdom of God."

11. Also, that fornication and every performance of the act of reproduction with a person
other than one's wife are illicit is evident. For it
is said: "There shall be no whore among the
daughters of Israel, nor whoremonger among
the sons of Israel" (Deut. 23:17); and in Tobias
(4:13): "Take heed to keep thyself from all fornication, and beside thy wife never endure to
know a crime"; and I Corinthians (6:18): "Fly
fornication."

12. By this conclusion we refute the error of
those who say that there is no more sin in the
emission of semen than in the emission of any
other superfluous matter, and also of those who
state that fornication is not a sin. . . .

Further Questions

1. Is continuation of the human race so important that anything that intervenes with
this is so bad that only homicide is worse?

2. In times of underpopulation, producing many offspring betters a species' chances of
survival. Is the same true in situations where the problem is overpopulation?

3. Aquinas thinks that, in the human species, a single parent cannot normally care adequately for her offspring. Are conditions that encourage or preclude success as a single parent
so complex and so variable that Aquinas should not speak of a single array of such conditions
as being "normal."

Society and the Fertile Woman: Contraception IX.2

JANET RADCLIFFE-RICHARDS

Janet Radcliffe-Richards supports the right of any woman who wishes to separate sex and pregnancy to use contraception. In a situation of overpopulation, moreover, the taxpayer's dollars could scarcely be put to better use than providing free contraceptives to those who would not otherwise use them.

Radcliffe-Richards teaches philosophy at the Open University and at Oxford University.

Reading Questions

1. A husband wants (more) children; his wife does not. What's the best solution to this problem?
2. A state wants to increase its population. Should it be entitled to restrict access to contraception on these grounds? Which group would fare the worst under such restriction, and is it fair for the states to impose this kind of hardship on them?
3. I am a taxpayer. I do not want to subsidize people who want sex without children, by providing them with free contraceptives. Am I being reasonable? Would it be more reasonable if I were asked instead to help support children whose parents could not provide for them?

THE FREEDOM TO USE CONTRACEPTION

THE PROPOSITION that there should be no law preventing free access to contraceptives is a relatively uncontroversial one in nearly all civilized countries these days. At least, the main opposition to it usually comes from religious groups, and there is no space to discuss their views in a book like this one, because a challenge to their tenets calls for an analysis of the foundations of the religion itself, which has nothing to do with feminism.[1] However, even though the controversy about contraception has now receded a good deal it is still worth discussing the issues, because they do appear from time to time and it is as well to have properly thought-out arguments in readiness for their revival.

Roughly speaking, apart from the objections of religious groups, there seem to be three possible reasons for forbidding or controlling access to contraceptives. One is the fear that readily available birth control will encourage unsanctioned sex; one is the wish of some men to prevent their wives from using contraceptives (there are some who actually succeed); and one is the wish of a state to increase its population. The first two of these do not seem to be worth much discussion, given even the most basic principles about the rights of women. If a woman wants sex that is her own concern, and if it is possible to separate sex and pregnancy she should be allowed to. (It is, incidentally, rather ironic to see some people now wanting to preserve the threat of unwanted pregnancy to make women afraid of indulging in sex, when presumably the original

Excerpt from "Society and the Fertile Woman" in The Sceptical Feminist *by Janet Radcliffe-Richards (New York: Penguin Books, 1980), pp. 252–289. Reprinted by permission of the author.*

reason for the sanctions on sex was the likelihood of its resulting in pregnancy.) The case of a husband who wants children can be equally briefly dismissed. Any man whose wife wants no more children (or none at all) is no doubt entitled to find another woman to bear his children if he can, but at no point is he entitled to regard his wife as his property, to do as he likes with. The only situation worth discussing in any detail, therefore, is the third: the case of a state which wants to increase its population.

The desire to increase population happens from time to time. Nationalism is a thing which has always encouraged a high birth rate, from Sparta to Nazi Germany and beyond. As Kate Millett said, "population growth [is closely linked] with the ambitions of a military state; more children must be born to die for the country."[2] Expanding and developing countries also often want to increase their populations, so that there is more labour at hand for mines, factories, and agriculture. Racial minority groups may want to increase their numbers, so that they are not swamped by the majority. And in some places now, a new phenomenon, people are becoming so worried about the future age structure of the population that governments are beginning to think that if they do not encourage the birth of more children there will be no one to look after the present generation when it is old. Countries with such attitudes might perhaps try to present contraception, as Nazi Germany did.[3]

We may well object to nationalism, and given the general rate of increase of the world's population we may well object to any encouragement to increase populations at all. However, those issues are not feminist ones. The feminist question is whether, *if* it were legitimate to want to increase a population, it would be acceptable to do so by means of forbidding or limiting contraception. It is not enough to answer, as though it were obvious, that every woman has the right to whatever number of children she wants: that is the question at issue, and if we want to maintain that it ought to be so, arguments must be found. . . .

However, this can be done without difficulty. If a state wants more children what I should do is put its resources into making sure that all the women who want children can have them, because in that way the state gets what it wants by means of making sure that individuals get more of what they want. What it should certainly not do is forbid access to contraception, because that way *the people who get children are not the ones who want them most, but the ones who can least do without sex.* This sort of method of population increase lowers the level of well-being in society, because it forces parenthood on unwilling people and gives children the severe handicap of being unwanted. It also means that people who are absolutely determined to do without children are therefore forced to do without sex, which does them a great deal of harm and benefits nobody. And furthermore, if state money is going into customs inspectors and police and law courts to control people who do try to get contraceptives, it means that less is available for fertility clinics, childminders and other things which could help women who did want children to bear as many as possible. They too are therefore deprived of possible happiness.

In other words, a state which wants to increase its population has two alternative ways of going about it: it can get what it wants by means of making individuals happier, or by means of making them unhappy. To forbid contraception is to take the second of these options, and is therefore quite unacceptable. It may also be added as a corollary that since freedom to control reproduction is to the benefit of all, no child should be able to reach puberty without knowing that contraception is available and how to get it.

FREE CONTRACEPTIVES

That argument establishes that a state ought to allow free access to contraceptives, but it by no means justifies the feminist demand that contraceptives ought to be state-supplied from easily accessible clinics, and above all that they should be free. Perhaps it seems superfluous to argue that case now that in Britain we actually have a free state-supplied contraceptive service, but there are still people who oppose it, just as there are people who still oppose full sex education in schools, so it is as well to complete the battery of arguments on the feminist side. It is not at all obvious that contraception ought always to be free, especially in any country which did want to increase its population. It is no good just stating that the ability to separate sex and pregnancy is a basic human right, and presuming it is obviously true. It is very easy for people to draw up lists of things they would like and call them rights, but if other people are to be asked to work to supply the money to pay for them, they have to be justified with care.

The fact is that the people who say that they object to paying for other people's pleasures, tiresome as they usually are, have at least a *prima facie* case. For most people, certainly, it is an extremely good thing to be able to separate sex and procreation, because sex is such a good thing and being burdened with unwanted children such a very bad one, but not everyone needs to do it. Some people are not interested in sex, or are homosexual, or are sterile, or want children. Some people want more sex than others. But the way a free service is provided is more or less to collect taxes from *everyone* to provide contraceptives for the benefit only of the people who want them. If we are concerned with freedom, would it not be fairer to leave the people who do not want contraceptives to spend their money on something they themselves would like, rather than make them subsidize the indulgers in non-procreative sex? Should we not reduce taxes, and let people buy their own contraceptives? That is what an argument about *freedom* would suggest. (It is, of course, true that all kinds of other things are already paid for by all for the benefit of some, but each case of this should be justified; no *general* argument from freedom can provide it.)

Nevertheless it is possible to justify free contraception, not on any general grounds of fun-

damental rights and freedom, but on specific grounds arising out of times and circumstances.

In the first place, nearly everybody now is worried by the fact that our population is at present too *large*, both in the world as a whole and in our own country. *Obviously* the first thing to do about that is to make sure that, as the slogans say, every child is a wanted child. It is, therefore, well worth our while to make it easy for people to avoid having children, and not to force them to choose between contraceptives and other things like cigarettes or clothes, or food for the other children there are already. When the population needs reducing nobody should have to trust to luck or the safe period and hope for the best. This is one case where we can very easily achieve what is good for everyone by giving individuals more of what they want.

In the second place, however unfashionable it is to say such things, it is a simple fact that there is a pretty high correlation between the groups of people who, for whatever reason, cannot be bothered with contraception, those most likely to produce children who are going to be very expensive to the state in one way and another. Whatever uncharitable and imperceptive remarks people may make about leaving feckless parents to the consequences of their folly, no one can reasonably blame the children, or think that we ought to allow them to suffer. There are thousands or millions of women who can hardly be persuaded to take care even now that the service is free and are only too delighted to find obstacles between themselves and the clinic (which is not surprising, given the usual nature of clinics, but that is another matter). If contraceptives had to be paid for there would be no chance of these women's going anywhere near one.

It is beyond question that at present free contraception is one of the best investments of taxpayers' money there is, and people who are obsessed with the idea that they are paying for other people's pleasures should spend more time considering the other things they would have to pay for if they stopped paying for the pleasures. Or rather, they should realize that since people will have their pleasures anyway, paid for or not, what they are really paying for is lessening the bad consequences of those pleasures for *everyone*.

In conclusion, then, feminists have the best possible case for their insistence that contraception should be free and on demand. Its general *availability* is defensible on general moral grounds, and there are overwhelming practical arguments, in the present state of things, for making it free as well.

NOTES

1. If, for instance, someone says abortion is out of the question because the Bible says so, the first question to be asked is why one should take any notice of the Bible. That is obviously not a question to be tackled in a book on feminism. Since I can see no good reason to accept any claims of people to have direct knowledge of the will of God, any such arguments must be left out of the discussion.

2. Millett, *Sexual Politics*, p. 224.

3. Ibid., pp. 226–227.

Further Questions

1. My religious convictions are that contraception is wrong and I never use birth control. Do I have a right to force my views on others by making contraceptives unavailable to them? If I do so force others, what reason can I give them?

2. Is it primarily the responsibility of the woman to ensure that a pregnancy does not result from heterosexual intercourse? If it is her responsibility, is this because she is responsible for the fact that sexual activity occurred? Is it because she is the one who needs to be protected from pregnancy?

3. Does anyone ever have the right to ask anyone else not to use contraceptives because contraceptives would "spoil the moment" of sexual activity? If so, explain the circumstances which would make "the moment" more important than contraceptive protection.

IX.3   Why Abortion Is Immoral

DON MARQUIS

Don Marquis argues that what makes abortion wrong is that it constitutes loss of the fetus' future, one expected to be very much like our own. This makes most cases of contemplated abortion morally wrong, for the same reason that most killings are wrong.

Marquis works in applied ethics and teaches philosophy at the University of Kansas.

Reading Questions

1. What makes killing a person wrong? Do the same considerations make destroying a fetus wrong as well?

Abridged from Don Marquis, "Why Abortion Is Immoral," in The Journal of Philosophy, *1989, pp. 183–201. Reprinted by permission of the author and publisher.*

2. Under what circumstances is dying a bad thing? Is an aborted fetus a death that takes place under the same circumstances that make death of an adult a bad thing?
3. If it could be shown that a fetus, in its early stages, could not feel or think, would that make abortion permissible when the fetus was in those early stages?

II.

... WHAT PRIMARILY MAKES KILLING WRONG is neither its effect on the murderer nor its effect on the victim's friends and relatives, but its effect on the victim. The loss of one's life is one of the greatest losses one can suffer. The loss of one's life deprives one of all the experiences, activities, projects, and enjoyments that would otherwise have constituted one's future. Therefore, killing someone is wrong, primarily because the killing inflicts (one of) the greatest possible losses on the victim. To describe this as the loss of life can be misleading, however. The change in my biological state does not by itself make killing me wrong. The effect of the loss of my biological life is the loss to me of all those activities, projects, experiences, and enjoyments which would otherwise have constituted my future personal life. These activities, projects, experiences, and enjoyments are either valuable for their own sakes or are means to something else that is valuable for its own sake. Some parts of my future are not valued by me now, but will come to be valued by me as I grow older and as my values and capacities change. When I am killed, I am deprived both of what I now value which would have been part of my future personal life, but also what I would come to value. Therefore, when I die, I am deprived of all of the value of my future. Inflicting this loss on me is ultimately what makes killing me wrong. This being the case, it would seem that what makes killing *any* adult human being prima facie seriously wrong is the loss of his or her future. .. ..[1]

The claim that what makes killing wrong is the loss of the victim's future is directly supported by two considerations. In the first place, this theory explains why we regard killing as one of the worst of crimes. Killing is especially wrong because it deprives the victim of more than perhaps any other crime. In the second place, people with AIDS or cancer who know they are dying believe, of course, that dying is a very bad thing for them. They believe that the loss of a future to them that they would otherwise have experienced is what makes their premature death a very bad thing for them. A better theory of the wrongness of killing would require a different natural property associated with killing which better fits with the attitudes of the dying. What could it be?

The view that what makes killing wrong is the loss to the victim of the value of the victim's future gains additional support when some of its implications are examined. In the first place, it is incompatible with the view that it is wrong to kill only beings who are biologically human. It is possible that there exists a different species from another planet whose members have a future like ours. Since having a future like that is what makes killing someone wrong, this theory entails that it would be wrong to kill members of such a species. Hence, this theory is opposed to the claim that only life that is biologically human has great moral worth, a claim which many antiabortionists have seemed to adopt. This opposition, which this theory has in common with personhood theories, seems to be a merit of the theory.

In the second place, the claim that the loss of one's future is the wrong-making feature of one's being killed entails the possibility that the futures of some actual nonhuman mammals on our own planet are sufficiently like ours that it is seriously wrong to kill them also. Whether some animals do have the same right to life as human beings depends on adding to the account of the wrongness of killing some additional account of just what it is about my future or the futures of other adult human beings which makes it wrong to kill us. No such additional account will be offered in this essay. Undoubtedly, the provision of such an account would be a very difficult mater. Undoubtedly, any such account would be quite controversial. Hence, it surely should not reflect badly on this sketch of an elementary theory of the wrongness of killing that it is indeterminate with respect to some very difficult issues regarding animal rights.

In the third place, the claim that the loss of one's future is the wrong-making feature of one's being killed does not entail, as sanctity of human life theories do, that active euthanasia is wrong. Persons who are severely and incurably ill, who face a future of pain and despair, and who wish to die will not have suffered a loss if they are killed. It is, strictly speaking, the value of a human's future which makes killing wrong in this theory. This being so, killing does not necessarily wrong some persons who are sick and dying. Of course, there may be other reasons for a prohibition of active euthanasia, but that is another matter. Sanctity-of-human-life theories seem to hold that active euthanasia is seriously wrong even in an individual case where there seems to be good reason for it independently of public policy considerations. This consequence is most implausible, and it is a plus for the claim that the loss of a future of value is what makes killing wrong that it does not share this consequence.

In the fourth place, the account of the wrongness of killing defended in this essay does straightforwardly entail that it is prima facie seriously wrong to kill children and infants, for we do presume that they have futures of value. Since we do believe that it is wrong to kill defenseless little babies, it is important that a theory of the wrongness of killing easily account for this. Personhood theories of the wrongness of killing, on the other hand, cannot straightforwardly account for the wrongness of killing infants and young children. Hence, such theories must add special ad hoc accounts of the wrongness of killing the young. The plausibility of such ad hoc theories seems to be a function of how desperately one wants such theories to work. The claim

that the primary wrong-making feature of a killing is the loss to the victim of the value of its future accounts for the wrongness of killing young children and infants directly; it makes the wrongness of such acts as obvious as we actually think it is. This is a further merit of this theory. Accordingly, it seems that this value of a future-like-ours theory of the wrongness of killing shares strengths of both sanctity-of-life and personhood accounts while avoiding weaknesses of both. In addition, it meshes with a central intuition concerning what makes killing wrong.

The claim that the primary wrong-making feature of a killing is the loss to the victim of the value of its future has obvious consequences for the ethics of abortion. The future of a standard fetus includes a set of experiences, projects, activities, and such which are identical with the futures of adult human beings and are identical with the futures of young children. Since the reason that is sufficient to explain why it is wrong to kill human beings after the time of birth is a reason that also applies to fetuses, it follows that abortion is prima facie seriously morally wrong. . . .

Of course, this value of a future-like-ours argument, if sound, shows only that abortion is prima facie wrong, not that it is wrong in any and all circumstances. Since the loss of the future to a standard fetus, if killed, is, however, at least as great a loss as the loss of the future to a standard adult human being who is killed, abortion, like ordinary killing, could be justified only by the most compelling reasons. The loss of one's life is almost the greatest misfortune that can happen to one. Presumably abortion could be justified in some circumstances, only if the loss consequent on failing to abort would be at least as great. Accordingly, morally permissible abortions will be rare indeed unless, perhaps, they occur so early in pregnancy that a fetus is not yet definitely an individual. Hence, this argument should be taken as showing that abortion is presumptively very seriously wrong, where the presumption is very strong—as strong as the presumption that killing another adult human being is wrong.

III

How complete an account of the wrongness of killing does the value of a future-like-ours account have to be in order that the wrongness of abortion is a consequence? This account does not have to be an account of the necessary conditions for the wrongness of killing. Some persons in nursing homes may lack valuable human futures, yet it may be wrong to kill them for other reasons. Furthermore, this account does not obviously have to be the sole reason killing is wrong where the victim did have a valuable future. This analysis claims only that, for any killing where the victim did have a valuable future like ours, having that future by itself is sufficient to create the strong presumption that the killing is seriously wrong. . . .

IV.

. . . Paul Bassen[2] has argued that, even though the prospects of an embryo might seem to be a basis for the wrongness of abortion, an embryo cannot be a victim and therefore cannot be wronged. An embryo cannot be a victim, he says, because it lacks sentience. His central argument for this seems to be that, even though plants and the permanently unconscious are alive, they clearly cannot be victims. What is the explanation of this? Bassen claims that the explanation is that their lives consist of mere metabolism and mere metabolism is not enough to ground victimizability. Mentation is required.

The problem with this attempt to establish the absence of victimizability is that both plants and the permanently unconscious clearly lack what Bassen calls "prospects" or what I have called "a future life like ours." Hence, it is surely open to one to argue that the real reasons we believe plants and the permanently unconscious cannot be victims is that killing them cannot deprive them of a future life like ours; the real reason is not their absence of present mentation. . . .

. . . Suppose a severe accident renders me totally unconscious for a month, after which I recover. Surely killing me while I am unconscious victimizes me, even though I am incapable of mentation during that time. It follows that Bassen's thesis fails. Apparently, attempts to restrict the value of a future-like-ours argument so that fetuses do not fall within its scope do not succeed. . . .

VI.

The purpose of this essay has been to set out an argument for the serious presumptive wrongness of abortion subject to the assumption that the moral permissibility of abortion stands or falls on the moral status of the fetus. Since a fetus possesses a property, the possession of which in adult human beings is sufficient to make killing an adult human being wrong, abortion is wrong. . . .

. . . [T]his analysis can be viewed as resolving a standard prolem—indeed, *the* standard problem—concerning the ethics of abortion. Clearly it is wrong to kill adult human beings. Clearly, it is not wrong to end the life of some arbitrarily chosen single human cell. Fetuses seem to be like arbitrarily chosen human cells in some respects and like adult humans in other respects. The problem of the ethics of abortion is the problem of determining the fetal property that settles this moral controversy. The thesis of this essay is that the problem of the ethics of abortion, so understood, is solvable.

NOTES

1. I have been most influenced on this matter by Jonathan Glover, *Causing Death and Saving Lives* (New York: Penguin, 1977), ch. 3; and Robert Young, "What Is So Wrong with Killing People?" *Philosophy* I.IV, 210 (1979): 515–528.

2. "Present Sakes and Future Prospects: The Status of Early Abortion," *Philosophy and Public Affairs*, XI, 4 (1982): 322–326.

Further Questions

1. Suppose a dog, or some extraterrestrial life form, turns out to have expectations of a future of the same quality as members of our own species. Would it then be wrong to kill it? What features must nonhuman life forms possess in order to make killing them wrong?

2. If a pregnant woman knows that bringing her fetus to term will seriously compromise her future, as well as the futures of her other children, should she take this into account in deciding whether to have an abortion, or does only the fetus's future matter?

3. If a victim's future is what matters, do those with greater life expectancy (e.g., fetuses) matter more that older people who can expect to live only a few more years? If quality of a person's future matters, how bad must this future be expected to be before it is permissible to kill that person, or let him or her die?

IX.4   A Defense of Abortion[1]

JUDITH JARVIS THOMSON

Judith Jarvis Thomson asks you, the reader, to grant that the fetus is a person, then to compare a pregnancy to a situation where you find an ailing, unconscious violinist plugged into your kidneys where he must remain for nine months if he is to survive. As for the supposed difference that a pregnant woman is responsible for the condition of pregnancy, Thomson asks the reader to imagine that people seeds might drift into a house and take root because one of the screens is defective. Finally, she distinguishes a moral requirement that someone be given a certain kind of treatment from like actions of the Good Samaritan or Minimally Decent Samaritan variety.

Thomas is Professor of Philosophy at M.I.T.

Reading Questions

1. Suppose you wake up in the situation Thomson describes with an unconscious violinist plugged into your kidneys. Are you obliged to stay in bed plugged in for nine months? Compare this situation with that of a pregnancy.

2. Suppose that people are propagated by seeds that drift in the air and take root in carpets and upholstery. Are you obliged to care for a person seedling that managed to get in and plant itself despite the fact that you bought the very best window screens? Again, compare with a pregnancy.

3. What is the difference between someone having a moral right to certain treatment by you and the situation where this would be an action of a Good Samaritan or a minimally decent Samaritan? Apply this difference to a situation of a pregnancy.

MOST OPPOSITION TO ABORTION relies on the premise that the fetus is a human being, a person, from the moment of conception. The premise is argued for, but, as I think, not well. Take, for example, the most common argument. We are asked to notice that the development of a human being from conception through birth into childhood is continuous; then it is said that to draw a line, to choose a point in this development and say "before this point the thing is not a person, after this point it is a person" is to make an arbitrary choice, a choice for which in the nature of things no good reason can be given. It is concluded that the fetus is, or anyway that we had better say it is, a person from the moment of conception. But this conclusion does not follow. Similar things might be said about the development of an acorn into an oak tree, and it does not follow that acorns are oak trees, or that we had better say they are. Arguments of this form are sometimes called "slippery slope arguments"—the phrase is perhaps self-explanatory—and it is dismaying that opponents of abortion rely on them so heavily and uncritically.

I am inclined to agree, however, that the prospects for "drawing a line" in the development of the fetus look dim. I am inclined to think also that we shall probably have to agree that the fetus has already become a human person well before birth. Indeed, it comes as a surprise when one first learns how early in its life it begins to acquire human characteristics. By the tenth week, for example, it already has a face, arms and legs, fingers and toes; it has internal organs, and brain activity is detectable.[2] On the other hand, I think that the premise is false, that the fetus is not a person from the moment of conception. A newly fertilized ovum, a newly implanted clump of cells, is no more a person than an acorn is an oak tree. But I shall not discuss any of this. For it seems to me to be of great interest to ask what happens if, for the sake of argument, we allow the premise. How, precisely, are we supposed to get from there to the conclusion that abortion is morally impermissible? Opponents of abortion commonly spend most of their time establishing that the fetus is a person, and hardly any time explaining the step from there to the impermissibility of abortion. Perhaps they think the step too simple and obvious to require much comment. Or perhaps instead they are simply being economical in argument. Many of those who defend abortion rely on the premise that the fetus is not a person, but only a bit of tissue that will become a person at birth; and why pay out more arguments than you have to? Whatever the explanation, I suggest that the step they take is neither easy nor obvious, that it calls for closer examination than it is commonly given, and that when we do give it this closer examination we shall feel inclined to reject it.

I propose, then, that we grant that the fetus is a person from the moment of conception. How does the argument go from here? Something like this, I take it. Every person has a right to life. So the fetus has a right to life. No doubt the mother has a right to decide what shall happen in and to her body; everyone would grant that. But surely a person's right to life is stronger and more stringent than the mother's right to decide what happens in and to her body, and so outweighs it. So the fetus may not be killed; an abortion may not be performed.

It sounds plausible. But now let me ask you to imagine this. You wake up in the morning and find yourself back to back in bed with an unconscious violinist. A famous unconscious violinist. He has been found to have a fatal kidney ailment, and the Society of Music Lovers has canvassed all the available medical records and found that you alone have the right blood type to help. They have therefore kidnapped you, and last night the violinist's circulatory system was plugged into yours, so that your kidneys can be used to extract poisons from his blood as well as your own. The director of the hospital now tells you, "Look, we're sorry the Society of Music Lovers did this to you—we would never have permitted it if we had known. But still, they did it and the violinist now is plugged into you. To unplug you would be to kill him. But never mind, it's only for nine months. By then he will have recovered from his ailment, and can safely be unplugged from you." Is it morally incumbent on you to accede to this situation? No doubt it would be very nice of you if you did, a great kindness. But do you *have* to accede to it? What if it were not nine moths, but nine years? Or longer still? What if the director of the hospital says, "Tough luck, I agree, but you've now got to stay in bed, with the violinist plugged into you, for the rest of your life. Because remember this. All persons have a right to live, and violinists are persons. Granted you have a right to decide what happens in and to your body, but a person's right to life outweighs your right to decide what happens in and to your body. So you cannot ever be unplugged from him." I imagine you would regard this as outrageous, which suggests that something really is wrong with that plausible-sounding argument I mentioned a moment ago.

In this case, of course, you were kidnapped; you didn't volunteer for the operation that plugged the violinist into your kidneys. Can those who oppose abortion on the ground I mentioned make an exception for a pregnancy due to rape? Certainly. They can say that persons have a right to life only if they didn't come into existence because of rape; or they can say that all persons have a right to life, but that some have less of a right to life than others, in particular, that those who came into existence because of rape have less. But these statements have a rather unpleasant sound. Surely the question of whether you have a right to life at all, or how much of it you have, shouldn't turn on the question of whether or not you are the product of a rape. And in fact the people who oppose abortion on the ground I mentioned do not make this distinction, and hence do not make an exception in case of rape.

For we should now . . . ask what it comes to, to have a right to life. In some views having a right to life includes having a right to be given at least the bare minimum one needs for continued life. But suppose that what in fact *is* the

bare minimum a man needs for continued life is something he has no right at all to be given? If I am sick unto death, and the only thing that will save my life is the touch of Henry Fonda's cool hand on my fevered brow, then all the same, I have no right to be given the touch of Henry Fonda's cool hand on my fevered brow. It would be frightfully nice of him to fly in from the West Coast to provide it. It would be less nice, though no doubt well meant, if my friends flew out to the West Coast and carried Henry Fonda back with them. But I have no right at all against anybody that he should do this for me. Or again, to return to the story I told earlier, the fact that for continued life that violinist needs the continued use of your kidneys does not establish that he has a right to be given the continued use of your kidneys. He certainly has no right against you that *you* should give him continued use of your kidneys. For nobody has any right to use your kidneys unless you give him such a right; and nobody has the right against you that you shall give him this right—if you do allow him to go on using your kidneys, this is a kindness on your part, and not something he can claim from you as his due. Nor has he any right against anybody else that *they* should give him continued use of your kidneys. Certainly he had no right against the Society of Music Lovers that they should plug him into you in the first place. And if you now start to unplug yourself, having learned that you will otherwise have to spend nine years in bed with him, there is nobody in the world who must try to prevent you, in order to see to it that he is given something he has a right to be given.

There is another way to bring out the difficulty. In the most ordinary sort of case, to deprive someone of what he has a right to is to treat him unjustly. Suppose a boy and his small brother are jointly given a box of chocolates for Christmas. If the older boy takes the box and refuses to give his brother any of the chocolates, he is unjust to him, for the brother has been given a right to half of them. But suppose that, having learned that otherwise it means nine years in bed with that violinist, you unplug your-self from him. You surely are not being unjust to him, for you gave him no right to use your kid-neys, and no one else can have given him any such right. But we have to notice that in unplug-ging yourself, you are killing him; and violinists, like everybody else, have a right to life, and thus in the view we were considering just now, the right not to be killed. So here you do what he supposedly has a right you shall not do but you do not act unjustly to him in doing it.

The emendation which may be made at this point is this: the right to life consists not in the right not be killed, but rather in the right not to be killed unjustly. This runs a risk of circularity, but never mind: it would enable us to square the fact that the violinist has a right to life with the fact that you do not act unjustly toward him in unplugging yourself, thereby killing him. For if you do not kill him unjustly, you do not vio-late his right to life, and so it is no wonder you do him no injustice.

But if this emendation is accepted, the gap in the argument against abortion stares us plainly in the face: it is by no means enough to show that the fetus is a person, and to remind us that all per-sons have a right to life—we need to be shown also that killing the fetus violates its right to life, i.e., that abortion is unjust killing. And is it?

I suppose we may take it as a datum that in a case of pregnancy due to rape the mother has not given the unborn person a right to the use of her body for food and shelter. Indeed, in what pregnancy could it be supposed that the mother has given the unborn person such a right? It is not as if there were unborn persons drifting about the world, to whom a woman who wants a child says "I invite you in."

But it might be argued that there are other ways one can have acquired a right to the use of another person's body than by having been in-vited to use it by that person. Suppose a woman voluntarily indulges in intercourse, knowing of the chance it will issue in pregnancy, and then she does become pregnant; is she not in part re-sponsible for the presence, in fact the very exis-tence, of the unborn person inside her? No doubt she did not invite it in. But doesn't her partial responsibility for its being there itself give it a right to the use of her body?[7] If so, then her aborting it would be more like the boy's taking away the chocolates, and less like your unplug-ging yourself from the violinist—doing so would be depriving it of what it does have a right to, and thus would be doing it an injustice.

And then, too, it might be asked whether or not she can kill it even to save her own life: If she voluntarily called it into existence, how can she now kill it, even in self-defense?

The first thing to be said about this is that it is something new. Opponents of abortion have been so concerned to make out the indepen-dence of the fetus, in order to establish that it has a right to life, just as its mother does, that they have tended to overlook the possible sup-port they might gain from making out that the fetus is *dependent* on the mother, in order to es-tablish that she has a special kind of responsibil-ity for it, a responsibility that gives it rights against her which are not possessed by any inde-pendent person—such as an ailing violinist who is a stranger to her.

On the other hand, this argument would give the unborn person a right to its mother's body only if her pregnancy resulted from a voluntary act, undertaken in full knowledge of the chance a pregnancy might result from it. It would leave out entirely the unborn person whose existence is due to rape. Pending the availability of some further argument, then we would be left with the conclusion that unborn persons whose exis-tence is due to rape have no right to the use of their mothers' bodies, and thus that aborting them is not depriving them of anything they have a right to and hence is not unjust killing.

And we should also notice that it is not at all plain that this argument really does go even as far as it purports to. For there are cases and cases, and the details make a difference. If the room is stuffy, and I therefore open a window to air it, and a burglar climbs in, it would be absurd to say, "Ah, now he can stay, she's given him a right to the use of her house—for she is partially responsible for his presence there, having voluntarily done what enabled him to get in, in full knowledge that there are such things as burglars, and that burglars burgle." It would be still more absurd to say this if I had had bars installed outside my windows, precisely to prevent burglars from getting in, and a burglar got in only because of a defect in the bars. It remains equally absurd if we imagine it is not a burglar who climbs in, but an innocent person who blunders or falls in. Again, suppose it were like this: people-seeds drift about in the air like pollen, and if you open your windows, one may drift in and take root in your carpets or upholstery. You don't want children, so you fix up your windows with fine mesh screens, the very best you can buy. As can happen, however, and on very, very rare occasions does happen, one of the screens is defective; and a seed drifts in and takes root. Does the person-plant who now develops have a right to the use of your house? Surely not—despite the fact that you voluntarily opened your windows, you knowingly kept carpets and upholstered furniture, and you knew that screens were sometimes defective. Someone may argue that you are responsible for its rooting, that it does have a right to your house, because after all you *could* have lived out your life with bare floors and furniture, or with sealed windows and doors. But this won't do—for by the same token anyone can avoid a pregnancy due to rape by having a hysterectomy, or anyway by never leaving home without a (reliable!) army.

It seems to me that the argument we are looking at can establish at most that there are *some* cases in which the unborn person has a right to the use of its mother's body, and therefore *some* cases in which abortion is unjust killing. There is room for much discussion and argument as to precisely which, if any. But I think we should sidestep this issue and leave it open, for at any rate the argument certainly does not establish that all abortion is unjust killing.

5. There is room for yet another argument here, however. We surely must all grant that there may be cases in which it would be morally indecent to detach a person from your body at the cost of his life. Suppose you learn that what the violinist needs is not nine years of your life, but only one hour: All you need do to save his life is to spend one hour in that bed with him. Suppose also that letting him use your kidneys for that one hour would not affect your health in the slightest. Admittedly you were kidnapped. Admittedly you did not give anyone permission to plug him into you. Nevertheless it seems to me plain you *ought* to allow him to use your kidneys for that hour—it would be indecent to refuse.

Again, suppose pregnancy lasted only an hour, and constituted no threat to life or health. And suppose that a woman becomes pregnant as a result of rape. Admittedly she did not voluntarily do anything to bring about the existence of a child. Admittedly she did nothing at all which would give the unborn person a right to the use of her body. All the same it might well be said, as in the newly emended violinist story, that she *ought* to allow it to remain for that hour—that it would be indecent of her to refuse.

Now some people are inclined to use the term "right" in such a way that it follows from the fact that you ought to allow a person to use your body for the hour he needs, that he has a right to use your body for the hour he needs, even though he has not been given that right by any person or act. They may say that it follows also that if you refuse, you act unjustly toward him. This use of the term is perhaps so common that it cannot be called wrong; nevertheless it seems to me to be an unfortunate loosening of what we would do better to keep a tight rein on. Suppose that box of chocolates I mentioned earlier has not been given to both boys jointly, but was given only to the older boy. There he sits, stolidly eating his way through the box, his small brother watching enviously. Here we are likely to say "you ought not to be so mean. You ought to give your brother some of those chocolates." My own view is that it just does not follow from the truth of this that the brother has any right to any of the chocolates. If the boy refuses to give his brother any, he is greedy, stingy, callous—but not unjust. I suppose that the people I have in mind will say it does follow that the brother has a right to some of the chocolates, and thus that the boy does act unjustly if he refuses to give his brother any. But the effect of saying this is to obscure what we should keep distinct, namely the difference between the boy's refusal in this case and the boy's refusal in the earlier case, in which the box was given to both boys jointly, and in which the small brother thus had what was from any point of view clear title to half.

So my own view is that even though you ought to let the violinist use your kidneys for the one hour he needs, we should not conclude that he has a right to do so—we should say that if you refuse, you are, like the boy who owns all the chocolates and will give none away, self-centered and callous, indecent in fact, but not unjust. And similarly, that even supposing a case in which a woman pregnant due to rape ought to allow the unborn person to use her body of the hour he needs, we should not conclude that he has a right to do so; we should conclude that she is self-centered, callous, indecent, but not unjust, if she refuses. The complaints are no less grave; they are just different. However, there is no need to insist on this point. If anyone does wish to deduce "he has a right" from "you ought," then all the same he must surely grant that there are cases in which it is not morally required of you that you allow that violinist to use your kidneys, and in which he does not have a right to use them, and in which you do not do him an injustice if you refuse. And so also for mother and unborn child. Except in such cases as the unborn person has a right to demand it—and we were leaving open the possibility that there may be such cases—nobody is morally *required* to make large sacrifices, of health, of all other interests and concerns, of all other duties and commitments, for nine years, or even for nine months, in order to keep another person alive.

6. We have in fact to distinguish between two kinds of Samaritan: the Good Samaritan, and what we might call the Minimally Decent Samaritan. The story of the Good Samaritan, you will remember, goes like this:

> A certain man went down from Jerusalem to Jericho, and fell among thieves, which stripped him of his raiment, and wounded him, and departed, leaving him half dead.
>
> And by chance there came down a certain priest that way, and when he saw him, he passed by on the other side.
>
> And likewise a Levite, when he was at the place, came and looked on him, and passed by on the other side.
>
> But a certain Samaritan, as he journeyed, came where he was; and when he saw him he had compassion on him.
>
> And went to him, and bound up his wounds, pouring in oil and wine, and set him on his own beast, and brought him to an inn, and took care of him.
>
> And on the morrow, when he departed, he took out two pence, and gave them to the host, and said unto him, "Take care of him; and whatsoever thou spendest more, when I come again, I will repay thee."
>
> (Luke 10.30–35)

The Good Samaritan went out of his way, at some cost to himself, to help one in need of it. We are not told what the options were, that is, whether or not the priest and the Levite could have helped by doing less than the Good Samaritan did, but assuming they could have, then the fact they did nothing at all shows they were not even Minimally Decent Samaritans, not because they were not Samaritans, but because they were not even minimally decent.

These things are a matter of degree, of course, but there is a difference, and it comes out perhaps most clearly in the story of Kitty Genovese, who, as you will remember, was murdered while thirty-eight people watched or listened and did nothing at all to help her. A Good Samaritan would have rushed out to give direct assistance against the murderer. Or perhaps we had better allow that it would have been a Splendid Samaritan who did this, on the ground that it would have involved a risk of death for

himself. But the thirty-eight not only did not do this, they did not even trouble to pick up a phone to call the police. Minimally Decent Samaritanism would call for doing at least that, and their not having done it was monstrous.

After telling the story of the Good Samaritan, Jesus said "Go, and do thou likewise." Perhaps he meant that we are morally required to act as the Good Samaritan did. Perhaps he was urging people to do more than is morally required of them. At all events it seems plain that it was not morally required of any of the thirty-eight that he rush out to give direct assistance at the risk of his own life, and that it is not morally required of anyone that he give long stretches of his life—nine years or nine months—to sustaining the life of a person who has no special right (we were leaving open the possibility of this) to demand it.

Indeed, with one rather striking class of exceptions, no one in any country in the world is *legally* required to do anywhere near as much as this for anyone else. The class of exceptions is obvious. My main concern here is not the state of the law in respect to abortion, but it is worth drawing attention to the fact that in no state in this country is any man compelled by law to be even a Minimally Decent Samaritan to any person; there is no law under which charges could be brought against the thirty-eight who stood by while Kitty Genovese died. By contrast, in most states in this country women are compelled by law to be not merely Minimally Decent Samaritans, but Good Samaritans to unborn persons inside them. This doesn't by itself settle anything one way or the other, because it may well be argued that there should be laws in this country—as there are in many European countries—compelling at least Minimally Decent Samaritanism.[8] But it does show that there is a gross injustice in the existing state of the law. And it shows also that the groups currently working against liberalization of abortion laws, in fact working toward having it declared unconstitutional for a state to permit abortion, had better start working for the adoption of

Good Samaritan laws generally, or earn the charge that they are acting in bad faith.

8. My argument will be found unsatisfactory on two counts by many of those who want to regard abortion as morally permissible. First, while I do argue that abortion is not impermissible, I do not argue that it is always permissible. There may well be cases in which carrying the child to term requires only Minimally Decent Samaritanism of the mother, and this is a standard we must not fall below. I am inclined to think it a merit of my account precisely that it does *not* give a general yes or a general no. It allows for and supports our sense that, for example, a sick and desperately frightened fourteen-year-old schoolgirl, pregnant due to rape, may *of course* choose abortion, and that any law which rules this out is an insane law. And it also allows for and supports our sense that in other cases resort to abortion is even positively indecent. It would be indecent in the woman to request an abortion and indecent in a doctor to perform it, if she is in her seventh month, and wants the abortion just to avoid the nuisance of postponing a trip abroad. The very fact that the arguments I have been drawing attention to treat all cases of abortion, or even all cases of abortion in which the mother's life is not at stake, as morally on a par ought to have made them suspect at the outset.

Secondly, while I am arguing for the permissibility of abortion in some cases, I am not arguing for the right to secure the death of the unborn child. It is easy to confuse these two things in that up to a certain point in the life of the fetus it is not able to survive outside the mother's body; hence removing it from her body guarantees its death. But they are importantly different. I have argued that you are not morally required to spend nine months in bed, sustaining the life of that violinist; but to say this is by no means to say that if, when you unplug yourself, there is a miracle and he survives, you then have a right to turn round and slit his throat. You may detach yourself even if this costs him his life; you have no right to be guaranteed his death, by some other means, if unplugging yourself does not kill him.

There are some people who will feel dissatisfied by this feature of my argument. A woman may be utterly devastated by the thought of a child, a bit of herself, put out for adoption and never seen or heard of again. She may therefore want not merely that the child be detached from her, but more, that it die. Some opponents of abortion are inclined to regard this as beneath contempt—thereby showing insensitivity to what is surely a powerful source of despair. All the same, I agree that the desire for the child's death is not one which anybody may gratify, should it turn out to be possible to detach the child alive.

At this place, however, it should be remembered that we have only been pretending throughout that the fetus is a human being from the moment of conception. A very early abortion is surely not the killing of a person, and so is not dealt with by anything I have said here.

NOTES

1. I am very much indebted to James Thomson for discussion, criticism, and many helpful suggestions.

2. Daniel Callahan, *Abortion: Law, Choice and Morality* (New York, 1970), p. 373. This book gives a fascinating survey of the available information on abortion. The Jewish tradition is surveyed in David M. Feldman, *Birth Control in Jewish Law* (New York, 1968), Part 5; the Catholic tradition in John T. Noonan, Jr., "An Almost Absolute Value in History," in *The Morality of Abortion* ed. John T. Noonan, Jr. (Cambridge, Mass., 1970).

7. The need for a discussion of this argument was brought home to me by members of the Society for Ethical and Legal Philosophy, to whom this paper was originally presented.

8. For a discussion of the difficulties involved, and a survey of the European experience with such laws, see *The Good Samaritan and the Law,* ed. James M. Ratcliffe (New York, 1966)

Further Questions

1. Suppose that what Thomson needs to save her life is Henry Fonda's cool hand on her fevered brow. Does she have a right that he fly in and do this for her? Compare the situation of her right to life here with that of the violinist who needs to use your kidneys to stay alive and with that of the fetus *in utero*.

2. Does a woman's partial responsibility for a fetus' being inside her give it the right to use her body? Does this mean that a fetus whose existence is due to rape has no right to use his mother's body?

3. Is it sometimes indecent for a woman to request an abortion? Should a mother's desire for a child's death be satisfied if it is possible to detach the child from the mother alive?

IX.5   Abortion

SUSAN SHERWIN

Susan Sherwin gives a feminist perspective on abortion that makes the pregnant woman the focus of attention. A patriarchal society makes it even more important that a woman have the final say over controlling her reproductive life through abortion if that becomes necessary. The fetus is not an independent person but a being whose value is ascribed to it by the pregnant woman.

Sherwin is Professor of Philosophy at Dalhousie University, Halifax, Nova Scotia.

Reading Questions

1. Should there be general rules for when abortion is allowable or should the pregnant woman be allowed to come to her own conclusions on the matter? How feminist is the right answer to this question?
2. How is a woman's freedom to choose abortion related to her ability to control her own sexuality? Why is it naive to suppose that a woman can prevent an unwanted pregnancy by avoiding sexual intercourse?
3. Is the fetus an independent being whose status can determine the wrongfulness of abortion?

WOMEN AND ABORTION

THE MOST OBVIOUS DIFFERENCE between feminist and nonfeminist approaches to abortion lies in the relative attention each gives in its analysis to the interests and experiences of women. Feminist analysis regards the effects of unwanted pregnancies on the lives of women individually and collectively as the central element in the moral examination of abortion; it is considered self-evident that the pregnant woman is the subject or principal concerning abortion decisions. In many nonfeminist accounts, however, not only is the pregnant woman not perceived as central, she is often rendered virtually invisible. Nonfeminist theorists, whether they support or oppose women's right to choose abortion, generally focus almost all their attention on the moral status of the fetus.[2]

In pursuing a distinctively feminist ethics, it is appropriate to begin with a look at the role of abortion in women's lives. The need for abortion can be very intense; no matter how appalling and dangerous the conditions, women from widely diverse cultures and historical periods have pursued abortions. No one denies that if abortion is not made legal, safe, and accessible in our society, women will seek out illegal and life-threatening abortions to terminate pregnancies they cannot accept. Antiabortion activists seem willing to accept this cost, although liberals definitely are not; feminists, who explicitly value women, judge the inevitable loss of women's lives that results from restrictive abortion policies to be a matter of fundamental concern.

Antiabortion campaigners imagine that women often make frivolous and irresponsible decisions about abortion, but feminists recognize that women have abortions for a wide variety of compelling reasons. Some women, for instance, find themselves seriously ill and incapacitated throughout pregnancy; they cannot continue in their jobs and may face insurmountable difficulties in fulfilling their responsibilities at home. Many employers and schools will not tolerate pregnancy in their employees or students, and not every woman is able to put her job, career, or studies on hold. Women of limited means may be unable to take adequate care of children they have already borne, and they may know that another mouth to feed will reduce their ability to provide for their existing children. Women who suffer from chronic disease, who believe themselves too young or too old to have children, or who are unable to maintain lasting relationships may recognize that they will not be able to care properly for a child when they face the decision. Some who are homeless, addicted to drugs, or diagnosed as carrying the AIDS virus may be unwilling to allow a child to enter the world with the handicaps that would result from the mother's condition. If the fetus is a result of rape or incest, then the psychological pain of carrying it may be unbearable, and the woman may recognize that her attitude to the child after birth will be tinged with bitterness. Some women learn that the fetuses that they carry have serious chromosomal anomalies and consider it best to prevent them from being born with a condition that is bound to cause them to suffer. Others, knowing the fathers to be brutal and violent, may be unwilling to subject a child to the beatings or incestuous attacks they anticipate; some may have no other realistic way to remove the child (or themselves) from the relationship.[3]

Finally, a woman may simply believe that bearing a child is incompatible with her life plans at the time. Continuing a pregnancy may have devastating repercussions throughout a woman's life. If the woman is young, then a pregnancy will likely reduce her chances of pursuing an education and hence limit her career and life opportunities: "The earlier a woman has a baby,

it seems, the more likely she is to drop out of school; the less education she gets, the more likely she is to remain poorly paid, peripheral to the labor market, or unemployed, and the more children she will have" (Petchesky 1985, 150). In many circumstances, having a child will exacerbate the social and economic forces already stacked against a woman by virtue of her sex (and her race, class, age, sexual orientation, disabilities, and so forth). Access to abortion is necessary for many women if they are to escape the oppressive conditions of poverty.[4]

Whatever the specific reasons are for abortion, most feminists believe that the women concerned are in the best position to judge whether abortion is the appropriate response to a pregnancy. Because usually only the woman choosing abortion is properly situated to weigh all the relevant factors, most feminists resist attempts to offer general, abstract rules for determining when abortion is morally justified.[5] Women's personal deliberations about abortion involve contextually defined considerations that reflect their commitments to the needs and interests of everyone concerned, including themselves, the fetuses they carry, other members of their household, and so forth. Because no single formula is available for balancing these complex factors through all possible cases, it is vital that feminists insist on protecting each woman's right to come to her own conclusions and resist the attempts of other philosophers and moralists to set the agenda of these considerations. Feminists stress that women must be acknowledged as full moral agents, responsible for making moral decisions about their own pregnancies. Women may sometimes make mistakes in their moral judgments, but no one else can be assumed to have the authority to evaluate and overrule their judgments.[6]

Even without patriarchy, bearing a child would be a very important event in a woman's life, because it involves significant physical, emotional, social, and (usually) economic changes for her. The ability to exert control over the incidence, timing, and frequency of childbearing is often tied to a woman's ability to control most other things she values. Because we live in a patriarchal society, it is especially important to ensure that women have the authority to control their own reproduction.[7] Despite the diversity of opinion found among feminists on most other matters, most feminists agree that women must gain full control over their own reproductive lives if they are to free themselves from male dominance.[8]

Moreover, women's freedom to choose abortion is linked to their ability to control their own sexuality. Women's subordinate status often prevents them from refusing men sexual access to their bodies. If women cannot end the unwanted pregnancies that result from male sexual dominance, then their sexual vulnerability to particular men may increase because caring for an(other) infant involves greater financial needs and reduces economic opportunities for women.[9] As a result, pregnancy often forces women to become dependent on particular men. Because a woman's dependence on a man is assumed to entail her continued sexual loyalty to him, restriction of abortion serves to commit women to remaining sexually accessible to particular men and thus helps to perpetuate the cycle of oppression.

In contrast to most nonfeminist accounts, feminist analyses of abortion direct attention to how women get pregnant. Those who reject abortion seem to believe that women can avoid unwanted pregnancies "simply" by avoiding sexual intercourse. These views show little appreciation for the power of sexual politics in a culture that oppresses women. Existing patterns of sexual dominance mean that women often have little control over their sexual lives. They may be subject to rape by their husbands, boyfriends, colleagues, employers, customers, fathers, brothers, uncles, and dates, as well as by strangers. Often the sexual coercion is not even recognized as such by the participants but is the price of continued "good will"—popularity, economic survival, peace, or simple acceptance. Many women have found themselves in circum-

stances where they do not feel free to refuse a man's demands for intercourse either because he is holding a gun to her head or because he threatens to be emotionally hurt if she refuses (or both). Women are socialized to be compliant and accommodating, sensitive to the feelings of others, and frightened of physical power; men are socialized to take advantage of every opportunity to engage in sexual intercourse and to use sex to express dominance and power. Under such circumstances, it is difficult to argue that women could simply "choose" to avoid heterosexual activity if they wish to avoid pregnancy. Catharine MacKinnon neatly sums it up: "The logic by which women are supposed to consent to sex [is]: preclude the alternatives, then call the remaining option 'her choice'" (MacKinnon, 1989, 192).

Furthermore, women cannot rely on birth control to avoid pregnancy. No form of contraception that is fully safe and reliable is available, other than sterilization; because women may wish only to avoid pregnancy temporarily, not permanently, sterilization is not always an acceptable choice. The pill and the IUD are the most effective contraceptive means offered, but both involve significant health hazards to women and are quite dangerous for some.[10] No woman should spend the thirty to forty years of her reproductive life on either form of birth control. Further, both have been associated with subsequent problems of involuntary infertility, so they are far from optimal for women who seek to control the timing of their pregnancies.

The safest form of birth control involves the use of barrier methods (condoms or diaphragms) in combination with spermicidal foams or jelly. But these methods also pose difficulties for women. They are sometimes socially awkward to use. Young women are discouraged from preparing for sexual activity that might never happen and are offered instead romantic models of spontaneous passion; few films or novels interrupt scenes of seduction for a partner to fetch contraceptives. Many women find their male partners unwilling to use barrier methods of contraception, and they often find themselves in no position to insist. Further, cost is a limiting factor for many women. Condoms and spermicides are expensive and not covered under most health care plans.[11] Only one contraceptive option offers women safe and fully effective birth control: barrier methods with the backup option of abortion.[12]

From a feminist perspective, the central moral feature of pregnancy is that it takes place in women's bodies and has profound effects on women's lives. Gender-neutral accounts of pregnancy are not available; pregnancy is explicitly a condition associated with the female body.[13] Because only women experience a need for abortion, policies about abortion affect women uniquely. Therefore, it is important to consider how proposed policies on abortion fit into general patterns of oppression for women. Unlike nonfeminist accounts, feminist ethics demands that the effects of abortion policies on the oppression of women be of principal consideration in our ethical evaluations.

THE FETUS

In contrast to feminist ethics, most nonfeminist analysts believe that the moral acceptability of abortion turns entirely on the question of the moral status of the fetus. Even those who support women's right to choose abortion tend to accept the premise of the antiabortion proponents that abortion can be tolerated only if we can first prove that the fetus lacks full personhood.[14] Opponents of abortion demand that we define the status of the fetus either as a being that is valued in the same way as other humans and hence is entitled not to be killed or as a being that lacks in all value. Rather than challenging the logic of this formulation, many defenders of abortion have concentrated on showing that the fetus is indeed without significant value (Tooley, 1972; Warren, 1973); others, such as L. W. Summer (1981), offer a more subtle account that reflects the gradual development of fetuses and

distinguishes between early fetal stages, where the relevant criterion for personhood is absent, and later stages, where it is present. Thus the debate often rages between abortion opponents, who describe the fetus as an "innocent," vulnerable, morally important, separate being whose life is threatened and who must be protected at all costs, and abortion supporters, who try to establish that fetuses are deficient in some critical respect and hence are outside the scope of the moral community. In both cases, however, the nature of the fetus as an independent being is said to determine the moral status of abortion.

The woman on whom the fetus depends for survival is considered as secondary (if she is considered at all) in these debates. The actual experiences and responsibilities of real women are not perceived as morally relevant to the debate, unless these women too, can be proved innocent by establishing that their pregnancies are a result of rape or incest.[15] In some contexts, women's role in gestation is literally reduced to that of "fetal containers"; the individual women disappear or are perceived simply as mechanical life-support systems.[16]

The current rhetoric against abortion stresses that the genetic makeup of the fetus is determined at conception and the genetic code is incontestably human. Lest there be any doubt about the humanity of the fetus, we are assailed with photographs of fetuses at various stages of development that demonstrate the early appearance of recognizably human characteristics, such as eyes, fingers, and toes. Modern ultrasound technology is used to obtain "baby's first picture" and stimulate bonding between pregnant women and their fetuses (Petchsky, 1987). That the fetus in its early stages is microscopic, virtually indistinguishable to the untrained eye from fetuses of other species, and lacking in the capacities that make human life meaningful and valuable is not deemed relevant by the self-appointed defenders of the fetus. The antiabortion campaign is directed at evoking sympathetic attitudes toward a tiny, helpless being whose life is threatened by its own mother; the fetus is characterized as a being entangled in an adversarial relationship with the (presumably irresponsible) woman who carries it (Overall, 1987). People are encouraged to identify with the "unborn child," not with the woman whose life is also at issue.

In the nonfeminist literature, both defenders and opponents of women's right to choose abortion agree that the difference between a late-term fetus and a newborn infant is "merely geographical" and cannot be considered morally significant. Daniel Callahan (1986), for instance, maintains a pro-choice stand but professes increasing uneasiness about this position in light of new medical and scientific developments that increase our knowledge of embryology and hasten the date of potential viability for fetuses; he insists that defenders of women's right to choose must come to terms with the question of the fetus and the effects of science on the fetus's prospects apart from the woman who carries it. Arguments that focus on the similarities between infants and fetuses, however, generally fail to acknowledge that a fetus inhabits a woman's body and is wholly dependent on her unique contribution to its maintenance, whereas a newborn is physically independent, although still in need of a lot of care.[17] One can only view the distinction between being in or out of a woman's womb as morally irrelevant if one discounts the perspective of the pregnant woman; feminists seem to be alone in recognizing the woman's perspective as morally important to the distinction.[18]

In antiabortion arguments, fetuses are identified as individuals; in our culture, which views the (abstract) individual as sacred, fetuses qua individuals are to be honored and preserved. Extraordinary claims are made to establish the individuality and moral agency of fetuses. At the same time, the women who carry these fetal individuals are viewed as passive hosts whose only significant role is to refrain from abortion or harming their fetuses. Because it is widely believed that a woman does not actually have to do anything to protect the life of her fetus, pregnancy is often considered (abstractly) to be a tolerable burden to protect the life of an individual so like us.[19]

Medicine has played its part in supporting these attitudes. Fetal medicine is a rapidly expanding specialty, and it is commonplace in professional medical journals to find references to pregnant women as "the maternal environment." Fetal surgeons now have at their disposal a repertoire of sophisticated technology that can save the lives of dangerously ill fetuses; in light of the excitement of such heroic successes, it is perhaps understandable that women have disappeared from their view. These specialists see the fetuses as their patients, not the women who nurture the fetuses. As the "active" agents in saving fetal lives (unlike the pregnant women, whose role is seen as purely passive), doctors perceive themselves as developing independent relationships with the fetuses they treat. Barbara Katz Rothman observes: "The medical model of pregnancy, as an essentially parasitic and vaguely pathological relationship, encourages the physician to view the fetus and mother as two separate patients, and to see pregnancy as inherently a conflict of interests between the two" (Rothman, 1986, 25).

Perhaps even more distressing than the tendency to ignore the woman's agency altogether and view her as a passive participant in the medically controlled events of pregnancy and childbirth is the growing practice of viewing women as genuine threats to the well-being of the fetus. Increasingly, women are described as irresponsible or hostile toward their fetuses, and the relationship between them is characterized as adversarial. Concern for the well-being of the fetus is taken as license for doctors to intervene to ensure that women comply with medical "advice." Courts are called upon to enforce the doctors' orders when moral pressure alone proves inadequate, and women are being coerced into undergoing unwanted cesarean deliveries and technologically monitored hospital births (Annas, 1982; Rodgers, 1989; Nelson and Milliken, 1990). Some states have begun to imprison women for endangering their fetuses through drug abuse and other socially unacceptable behaviors (Annas, 1986). Mary Anne Warren reports that a bill was recently introduced in an Australian state that makes women liable to criminal prosecution "if they are found to have smoked during pregnancy, eaten unhealthful foods, or taken any other action which can be shown to have adversely affected the development of the fetus" (Warren, 1989, 60).

In other words, some physicians have joined antiabortion campaigners in fostering a cultural acceptance of the view that fetuses are distinct individuals who are physically, ontologically, and socially separate from the women whose bodies they inhabit and that they have their own distinct interests. In this picture, pregnant women are either ignored altogether or are viewed as deficient in some crucial respect, and hence they can be subject to coercion for the sake of their fetuses. In the former case, the interests of the women concerned are assumed to be identical with those of the fetus; in the latter, the women's interests are irrelevant, because they are perceived as immoral, unimportant, or unnatural. Focus on the fetus as an independent entity has led to presumptions that deny pregnant women their roles as active independent, moral agents with a primary interest in what becomes of the fetuses they carry. The moral question of the fetus's status is quickly translated into a license to interfere with women's reproductive freedom.

A FEMINIST VIEW OF THE FETUS

Because the public debate has been set up as a competition between the rights of women and those of fetuses, feminists have often felt pushed to reject claims of fetal value, in order to protect women's needs. As Kathryn Addelson (1987) has argued, however, viewing abortion in this way "rips it out of the context of women's lives." Other accounts of fetal value are more plausible and less oppressive to women.

On a feminist account fetal development is examined in the context in which it occurs, within women's bodies, rather than in the isolation of imagined abstraction. Fetuses develop in specific pregnancies that occur in the lives of particular women. They are not individuals housed in generic female wombs or full persons at risk only because they are small and subject to the whims of women. Their very existence is relationally defined, reflecting their development within particular women's bodies; that relationship gives those women reason to be concerned about them. Many feminists argue against a perspective that regards the fetus as an independent being and suggest that a more accurate and valuable understanding of pregnancy would involve regarding the pregnant women "as a biological and social unit" (Rothman, 1986, 25).

On this view, fetuses are morally significant, but their status is relational rather than absolute. Unlike other human beings, fetuses do not have any independent existence; their existence is uniquely tied to the support of a specific other. Most nonfeminist accounts have ignored the relational dimension of fetal development and have presumed that the moral status of fetuses could be resolved solely in terms of abstract, metaphysical criteria of personhood as applied to the fetus alone (Tooley, 1972; Warren, 1973). Throughout much of the nonfeminist literature, commentators argue that some set of properties (such as genetic heritage, moral agency, self-consciousness, language use, or self-determination) will entitle all who possess it to be granted the moral status of persons. They seek some feature by which we can neatly divide the world into moral persons (who are to be valued and protected) and others (who are not entitled to the same group privileges).

This vision, however, misinterprets what is involved in personhood and what is especially valued about persons. Personhood is a social category, not an isolated state. Persons are members of a community, and they should be valued in their concrete, discrete, and different states as specific individuals, not merely as conceptually undifferentiated entities. To be a morally significant category, personhood must involve personality as well as biological integrity.[20] It is not sufficient to consider persons simply as Kantian atoms of rationality, because persons are embodied, conscious beings with particular social histories. Annette Baier has developed a concept of persons as "second persons," which helps explain the sort of social dimension that seems fundamental to any moral notion of personhood:

> A person, perhaps, is best seen as one who was long enough dependent upon other persons to acquire the essential arts of personhood. Persons essentially are *second* persons, who grow up with other persons. . . . The fact that a person has a life *history,* and that a people collectively have a history depends upon the humbler fact that the person has a childhood in which a cultural heritage is transmitted, ready for adolescent rejection and adult discriminating selection and contribution. Persons come after and before other persons (Baier, 1985, 84–5).

Persons, in other words, are members of a social community that shapes and values them, and personhood is a relational concept that must be defined in terms of interactions and relationships with others.[21]

Because humans are fundamentally relational beings, it is important to remember that fetuses are characteristically limited in the "relationships" in which they can "participate"; within those relationships, they can make only the most restricted "contributions."[22] After birth human beings are capable of a much wider range of roles in relationships with a broad variety of partners; that very diversity of possibility and experience leads us to focus on the abstraction of the individual as a constant through all these different relationships. Until birth, however, no such variety is possible, so the fetus must be understood as part of a complex entity that includes the woman who currently sustains the fetus and who will, most likely, be principally responsible for it for many years to come.

A fetus is a unique sort of human entity, then, for it cannot form relationships freely with others, and others cannot readily form relationships with it. A fetus has a primary and particularly intimate sort of "relationship" with the woman in whose womb it develops; connections with any other persons are necessarily indirect and must be mediated through the pregnant woman. The relationship that exists between a woman and her fetus is clearly asymmetrical, because she is the only party to it who is capable of even considering whether the interaction should continue further; the fetus is wholly dependent on the woman who sustains it, whereas she is quite capable of surviving without it.

Most feminist views of what is valuable about persons reflect the social nature of individual existence. No human, especially no fetus, can exist apart from relationships; efforts to speak of the fetus itself, as if it were not inseparable from the woman in whom it develops, are distorting and dishonest. Fetuses have a unique physical status—within and dependent on particular women. That gives them also a unique social status. However much some might prefer it to be otherwise, no one other than the pregnant woman in question can do anything to support or harm a fetus without doing something to the woman who nurtures it. Because of this inexorable biological reality, the responsibility and privilege of determining a fetus's specific social status and value must rest with the woman carrying it.

Many pregnancies occur to women who place a very high value on the lives of the particular fetuses they carry and choose to see their pregnancies through to term, despite the possible risks and costs involved; it would be wrong of anyone to force such a woman to terminate her pregnancy. Other women, or some of these same women at other times, value other things more highly (for example, their freedom, their health, or previous responsibilities that conflict with those generated by the pregnancies), and so they choose not to continue their pregnancies. The value that women ascribe to individual fetuses varies dramatically from case to case and may well change over the course of any particular pregnancy. The fact that fetal lives can neither be sustained nor destroyed without affecting the women who support them implies that whatever value others may attach to fetuses generally or to specific fetuses individually should not be allowed to outweigh the ranking that is assigned to them by the pregnant women themselves.

No absolute value attaches to fetuses apart from their relational status, which is determined in the context of their particular development. This is not the same, however, as saying that they have no value at all or that they have merely instrumental value, as some liberals suggest. The value that women place on their own fetuses is the sort of value that attaches to an emerging human relationship.

Nevertheless, fetuses are not persons because they have not developed sufficiently in their capacity for social relationships to be persons in any morally significant sense (that is, they are not yet second persons). In this way they differ from newborns, who immediately begin to develop into persons by virtue of their place as subjects in human relationships; newborns are capable of some forms of communication and response. The moral status of fetuses is determined by the nature of their primary relationship and the value that is created there. Therefore, feminist accounts of abortion emphasize the importance of protecting women's rights to continue or to terminate pregnancies as each sees fit.

NOTES

2. Technically, the term "fetus" does not cover the entire period of development. Medical practitioners prefer to distinguish between differing stages of development with such terms as "conceptus," "embryo" (and, recently, "pre-embryo"), and "fetus." Because these distinctions are not relevant to the discussion here, I follow the course common to discussions in bioethics and feminism and use the term "fetus" to cover the entire period of development from conception to the end of pregnancy through either birth or abortion.

3. Bearing a child can keep a woman within a man's sphere of influence against her will. The Canadian news media were dominated in the summer of 1989 by the story of Chantel Daigle, a Quebec woman who faced injunctions granted to her former boyfriend by two lower courts against her choice of abortion before she was finally given permission for abortion by the Supreme Court of Canada. Daigle's explanation to the media of her determination to abort stressed her recognition that if she was forced to bear this child, she would never be free from the violent father's involvement in her life.

4. Feminists believe that it is wrong of society to make childbearing a significant cause of poverty in women, but the reality of our social and economic structures in North America is that it does. In addition to their campaigns for greater reproductive freedom for women, feminists also struggle to ensure that women receive greater support in child-rearing; in efforts to provide financial stability and support services to those who provide care for children, feminists would welcome the support of those in the antiabortion movement who sincerely want to reduce the numbers of abortions.

5. Among the exceptions here, see Overall (1987), who seems willing to specify some conditions under which abortion is immoral (78–79).

6. Critics continue to base the debate on the possibility that women might make frivolous abortion decisions; hence they want feminists to agree to setting boundaries on acceptable grounds for choosing abortion. Feminists, however, should resist this injunction. There is no practical way of drawing a line fairly in the abstract; cases that may appear "frivolous" at a distance often turn out to be substantive when the details are revealed. There is no evidence to suggest that women actually make the sorts of choices worried critics hypothesize about: for example, the decision of a woman eight-months pregnant to abort because she wants to take a trip or gets in "a tiff" with her partner. These sorts of fantasies, on which demands to distinguish between legitimate and illegitimate personal reasons for choosing abortion rest, reflect an offensive conception of women as irresponsible. They ought not to be perpetuated. Women seeking moral guidance in their own deliberations about choosing abortion do not find such hypothetical discussions of much use.

7. In her monumental historical analysis of the early roots of Western patriarchy, Lerner (1986) determined that patriarchy began in the period from 3100 to 600 B.C., when men appropriated women's sexual and reproductive capacity; the earliest states entrenched patriarchy by institutionalizing the sexual and procreative subordination of women to men.

8. Some women claim to be feminist yet oppose abortion; some even claim to offer a feminist argument against abortion (see Callahan, 1987). For reasons that I develop in this chapter, I do not believe a thorough feminist analysis can sustain a restrictive abortion policy, although I do acknowledge that feminists need to be wary of some of the arguments proposed in support of liberal policies on abortion.

9. The state could do a lot to ameliorate this condition. If it provided women with adequate financial support, removed the inequities in the labor market, and provided affordable and reliable child care, pregnancy need not so often lead to a woman's dependence on a particular man. That it does not do so is evidence of the state's complicity in maintaining women's subordinate position with respect to men.

10. The IUD has proven so hazardous and prone to lawsuits, it has been largely removed from the market in the United States (Pappert, 1986). It is also disappearing from other Western countries but is still being purchased by population-control agencies for use in the developing world (LaCheen, 1986).

11. For a more detailed discussion of the limitations of current contraceptive options, see Colodny (1989); for the problems of cost, see esp. 34–35.

12. See Petchesky (1985), esp. chap. 5, where she documents the risks and discomforts associated with pill use and IUDs and the increasing rate at which women are choosing the option of diaphragm or condom, with the option of early, legal abortions as backup.

13. Eisenstein (1988) has developed an interesting account of sexual politics, which identifies the pregnant body as the central element in the cultural subordination of women. She argues that pregnancy (either actual or potential) is considered the defining characteristic of all women, and because it is not experienced by men, it is classified as deviance and considered grounds for different treatment.

14. Thomson (1971) is a notable exception to this trend.

15. Because she was obviously involved in sexual activity, it is often concluded that the noncoerced woman is not innocent but guilty. As such, she is judged far less worthy than the innocent being she carries within her. Some who oppose abortion believe that an unwanted pregnancy is a suitable punishment for "irresponsible" sex.

16. This seems reminiscent of Aristotle's view of women as flowerpots where men implant the seed with all the important genetic information and the movement necessary for development and the woman's job

is that of passive gestation, like the flowerpot. See Whitbeck (1973) and Lange (1983).

17. Some are so preoccupied with the problem of fetuses being "stuck" in women's bodies that they seek to avoid this geographical complication altogether, completely severing the ties between woman and fetus. For example, Bernard Nathanson, an antiabortion activist with the zeal of a new convert, eagerly anticipates the prospect of artificial wombs as alternative means for preserving the lives of fetuses and "dismisses the traditional reverence for birth as mere 'mythology' and the act of birth itself as an 'insignificant event'" (cited in McDonnell, 1984, 113).

18. Cf. Warren (1989) and Tooley (1972).

19. The definition of pregnancy as a purely passive activity reaches its ghoulish conclusion in the increasing acceptability of sustaining brain-dead women on life-support systems to continue their functions as incubators until the fetus can be safely delivered. For a discussion of this trend, see Murphy (1989).

20. This apt phrasing is taken from Petchesky (1985), 342.

21. E.g., Held (1987b) argues that personhood is a social status, created by the work of mothering persons.

22. Fetuses are almost wholly individuated by the women who bear them. The fetal "contributions" to the relationship are defined by the projections and interpretations of the pregnant woman in the latter stages of pregnancy, if she chooses to perceive fetal movements in purposeful ways (e.g., "it likes classical music, spicy food, exercise").

REFERENCES

Addelson, Kathryn Payne. 1987. "Moral Passages." In *Women and Moral Theory*, ed. Eva Feder Kittay and Diana T. Meyers. Totowa, N.J.: Rowman & Littlefield.

Annas, George J. 1982. "Forced Cesareans: The Unkindest Cut of All." *Hastings Center Report* 12(3): 16–17, 45.

————. 1986. "Pregnant Women as Fetal Containers." *Hastings Center Report* 16(6): 13–14.

Baier, Annette C. 1985. *Postures of the Mind: Essays on Mind and Morals*. Minneapolis: University of Minnesota Press.

Callahan, Daniel. 1986. "How Technology Is Reframing the Abortion Debate." *Hastings Center Report* 16(1): 33–42.

Callahan, Sidney. 1987. "A Pro-Life Feminist Makes Her Case." *Utne Reader,* March/April, 104–114.

Colodny, Nikki. 1989. "The Politics of Birth Control in a Reproductive Rights Context." In *The Future of Human Reproduction,* ed. Christine Overall. Toronto: Women's Press.

Eisenstein, Zillah R. 1988. *The Female Body and the Law.* Berkeley: University of California Press.

Held, Virginia. 1987b. "Feminism and Moral Theory." In *Women and Moral Theory. See* Addelson 1987.

LaCheen, Cary. 1986. "Pharmaceuticals and Family Planning: Women Are the Target." In *Adverse Effects.* See Balasubrahmanyan 1986.

Lange, Lynda. 1983. "Woman Is Not a Rational Animal: On Aristotle's Biology of Reproduction." In *Discovering Reality.* See Harding and Hintikka, 1983.

Lerner, Gerda. 1986. *The Creation of Patriarchy.* New York: Oxford.

McDonnell, Kathleen. 1984. *Not an Easy Choice: A Feminist Re-examines Abortion.* Toronto: Women's Press.

MacKinnon, Catharine. 1989. *Toward a Feminist Theory of the State.* Cambridge: Harvard University Press.

Murphy, Julien S. 1989. "Should Pregnancies Be Sustained in Brain-Dead Women? A Philosophical Discussion of Postmortem Pregnancy." In *Healing Technology.* See Beck-Gernsheim, 1989.

Nelson, Lawrence J., and Nancy Milliken. 1990. "Compelled Medical Treatment of Pregnant Women: Life, Liberty, and Law in Conflict." In *Ethical Issues in the New Reproductive Technologies,* ed. Richard T. Hull. Belmont, Calif.: Wadsworth.

Overall, Christine. 1987. *Ethics and Human Reproduction: A Feminist Analysis.* Boston: Allen & Unwin.

Pappert, Ann. 1986. "The Rise and Fall of the IUD." In *Adverse Effects. See* Balasubrahmanyan 1986.

Petchesky, Rosalind Pollak. 1985. *Abortion and Woman's Choice: The State, Sexuality, and Reproductive Freedom.* Boston: Northeastern University Press.

———. 1987. "Foetal Images: The Power of Visual Culture in the Politics of Reproduction." In *Reproductive Technologies.* See Doyal, 1987.

Rodgers, Sandra. 1989. "Pregnancy as Justification for Loss of Juridical Autonomy." In *Future of Human Reproduction.* See Colodny, 1989.

Rothman, Barbara Katz. 1986. "Commentary: When a Pregnant Woman Endangers Her Fetus." *Hastings Center Report* 16(1): 25.

Sumner, L. W. 1981. *Abortion and Moral Theory.* Princeton: Princeton University Press.

Thomson, Judith Jarvis. 1971. "A Defense of Abortion." *Philosophy and Public Affairs* 1(1): 47–66.

Tooley, Michael. 1972. "Abortion and Infanticide." *Philosophy and Public Affairs* 2(1): 37–65.

Warren, Mary Anne. 1973. "On the Moral and Legal Status of Abortion." *The Monist* 57: 43–61.

———. 1989. "The Moral Significance of Birth." *Hypatia* 4: 46–65.

Warren, Virginia L. 1989. "Feminist Directions in Medical Ethics." *Hypatia* 4(2): 73–87.

Whitbeck, Carolyn. 1973. "Theories of Sex Difference." *Philosophical Forum* 5(1, 2): 54–80.

Further Questions

1. Ought the pregnant woman be the sole focus of attention in reaching a decision on an abortion? Should the father have a say in whether an abortion is to take place? What sort of say?

2. Is finding a perfectly reliable method of birth control a realistic alternative to permitting abortions?

3. What are the differences between fetuses and newborns? Are they slight enough so that a woman should be forced to bring a pregnancy to completion?

IX.6   What about Us?

BRENDA TIMMINS

Brenda Timmins argues that women should have unrestricted access to abortion as well as to contraception because parents have serious problems accepting and caring for children with handicaps. She writes a compelling, first-hand description of what life is like for such children.

At the time of writing this selection Timmins was a student in the *Gender Issues* course at the University of Waterloo.

Reading Questions

1. If you thought you might be expecting a child with a fetal defect, would you try to get a prenatal diagnosis? What role would the results play in your decision about whether to have an abortion?
2. If a prenatal diagnosis revealed that the fetus was seriously handicapped, would you choose to have an abortion? How would you justify your decision to someone else?
3. What role should the other parent play in making decisions about prenatal testing or abortion? Which parent should have the final say in case the two cannot reach agreement?

AS LONG AS WOMEN do not have unrestricted access to contraception and abortion, they will not have the same freedoms as men in matters of sexuality. It is a basic injustice for one gender to have less freedom than the other in this area, especially in light of the possibility that sexual activity may result in a defective fetus.

In the National Film Board's "Prenatal Diagnosis: To Be or Not To Be,"[1] a film about prenatal testing for fetal defects and subsequent choice of abortion, only parents and doctors were interviewed. Most of these parents were happy to care for their children in spite of their children's handicaps and were able to express themselves in positive ways. This was also true in other documentary films on this subject I have seen in the past. However, films with this orientation give the impression that this is the whole story, furnishing material for comfortable journalism supported by the medical community.

I have considerable evidence that a group that should be included is left out of this process. I would like to see handicapped children who have reached adulthood interviewed on film about the effects their conditions had on their families. As a member of this group, I will present in writing my own experiences and what they meant to me.

I spent the year 1967 as a patient on the Serious Surgical Ward at the Hospital for Sick Children in Toronto. During that year I had the opportunity to speak at some length with other seriously handicapped children. These conversations developed spontaneously in response to surrounding events.

On my third day on the floor, one of the children died. The standard procedure on the floor required the children to stay wherever they were, with the door closed, until after the body was removed. I was startled to realize that children as

young as four were quite familiar with this procedure. This happened frequently. Naturally it left
the children in a somber mood. One eight-year-
old boy said quietly, "His family will be okay
now." Every single one of us knew the meaning
of this statement.

During that year, I saw that children very
quickly became accustomed to being institutionalized as long as the routines were reliable
and there were playmates, fun, and mischief.
On our ward there were no rules. I was familiar
with the numerous rules elsewhere in the hospital and soon realized that we had both more
staff and no rules for a reason. Sometimes at
night, the staff would move our strykers and
stretchers into the hallway, side by side, and the
patients would hold hands and try to sleep.
"Trying to save electricity," the staff told us.
"Trying to save lives," we thought. During my
stay, not one parent stayed through the night.

Most of the children on that ward were surprisingly happy. Aside from the pain of surgery
and treatments, there were few problems. The
entire environment was designed to fill the
needs of the handicapped children. There were
no bullies because bullies were removed by the
gigantic, authoritarian head nurse. There was
lots of food, TV, and books. Regular patterns
emerged that were beneficial to all. We became
family by necessity.

During that year, I witnessed enormous acts
of compassion among the children on this otherwise all-boys' ward. (I was the only girl.) I
have not seen such acts of compassion since.
Sunday School was a dry affair and, in order to
escape these weekly meetings, the children
would bring their pillows, braces, and IV stands
to my room and sit on the floor while I read to
them. At fifteen, I was the oldest patient on the
floor. As I read, they would turn the pages, and
we would talk.

Most of the boys were happier to be in hospital than at home. Sundays brought episodes of
unusual behaviour from almost everyone because that was visiting day for parents. My reading became crucial to the children's well-being

on Sundays. They would come to and go from
my room all during the day, beginning at 6:00
A.M., to report to the others on whether I was
well enough to read that particular Sunday. The
children's relationships with their parents were
not healthy. The amount of conflict in their
families was enormous, and the children were
quite aware of the fact that their inabilities and
deformities were at the core of the conflict.
Handicapped children are a terrible inconvenience to everyone concerned.

*"Fake a seizure. They'll put you in isolation.
Then your parents won't stay!"* advised one very
experienced nine-year-old to another. The boys'
visits with unhappy parents were stiff and formal
because communication was so difficult. Those
children whose parents did not visit were just as
anxious as those who had Sunday adrenal visits.
One ten-year-old girl from another ward was in
hospital for six months; in that time her parents
did not visit her once. Her parents lived only a
few kilometres away in Oakville. Some of the
children wandered off the floor on Sundays,
hoping to get lost elsewhere in the hospital to
avoid their parents. The children were protecting
themselves and each other as best they could.

My own parents would visit once a month and
would find the floor of my room covered with
horribly deformed children who would not leave
the room until I read their entire stack of books.
Along with most of the other fathers, my own father had difficulty relating to deformed children
(me included, of course) and would soon leave.
After my parents left, the smallest children would
start to giggle. My parents' departure was perceived as another success in our community!

One delightful ten-year-old was second-gen-
eration Italo-Canadian, who referred to his
family as "the mourners." The women in the
family would dress in black and come to the
hospital every day to cry over this first-born
son. (The men in the family did not come to the
hospital.) This boy was relegated to a wheelchair. Unfortunately, the visitors from his extended family could see only the wheelchair.
This exceptional boy was funny, musical, spoke

three languages, and possessed unusual peace-making skills, demonstrated by his mediating conflicts on the ward. He was painfully aware of the controversy his disability caused his family, and he was far happier in his institutional setting.

One boy, who had survived many operations to enable him to walk, refused to try to walk after a final successful operation. This refusal caused quite a stir in the ward. He would not take a step and said he preferred to remain in his chair. This controversy (survivor vs. medical staff) went on for weeks, until finally the boy would not speak to anyone about walking. The adults involved were puzzled by his silence. In particular, his parents were angry with him for his "attitude." The truth of the matter was that he did not want to go home. His parents were fighting all the time over what to do about him. Because of long periods of hospitalization, he didn't know his siblings very well and was happier where he was.

In this type of setting, nonfunctioning bodies quickly became a commonality. We were instant comrades. We helped each other, as best we could, to get through surgery, which was quite often worse than anyone on the outside would be able to imagine. There were many deaths, and everyone understood that we were only temporary companions.

Most of the children on this life-and-death ward were happy to be alive. However, they were all painfully aware of the struggles their families were going through concerning them. The problem affected not only anguished parents but also siblings, grandparents, aunts, and uncles. Deformities can cast a dark shadow on families and can seriously damage even the strongest of family bonds. Marriages broke down. There was widespread neglect and alcoholism as well as battering of the handicapped children themselves.

Handicapped children do cost money. At that time, average medical insurance covered 80 percent of hospital stays. In my own case, experimental surgery cost $100,000 (in 1967 dollars) for use of staff and the largest operating theatre.

In conjunction with operating room costs, there were the cost of drugs and a room at $500 a day. My parents refused to give their consent for my surgery because they did not want to pay the remaining 20 percent. Although they had real estate holdings that could have been liquidated, this was too high a cost for the surgery that would extend my life. Finally, the threat of court order and police arriving at the door made it possible for me to have reconstructive surgery. Mine was not the only family falling apart for financial reasons connected with the costs of rehabilitating a handicapped child.

Suppose now that, before I was born, prenatal tests like amniocentesis were available to assess problematic pregnancies. Suppose also that abortion was readily available as an option. Should such tests reveal a serious difficulty in the developing fetus, then the parents of children like me would have had some choice as to whether to let us make an unwelcome appearance in the family. My parents' lives would have been much happier had I emerged in another family. My sister and brother would not have had to live through years of unending violence, conflict, and emotional neglect while my parents waged an enormous battle against me and the medical authorities, only to lose this battle in the end.

Parents in families like mine don't want to talk about responsibilities like me. Their inability to cope and continuing intolerance are not key subjects for average parents like mine. As well, both the handicapped children and their siblings do not want to discuss these matters. The doctors do not want to talk to these parents any more than is absolutely necessary. This could be why there are no interviews on film recording this type of situation. So why should anyone be expected to see the importance of prenatal testing and making abortion available as an option? It would be advantageous for parents at risk of producing handicapped children to talk to the children's adult counterparts to help them with such difficult decisions. If parents made an informed decision to bring a deformed fetus to term, they would very likely have an easier time coping afterwards. There would also be an opportunity to prepare other members of the family for the postnatal situation.

Although parenthood is not an issue for me, if I were faced with the decision to abort a severely handicapped child, I would not hesitate to do so.

I would like to close with a positive anecdote. One quiet day in the ward, an eight-year-old boy and I were playing checkers. Now this was quite a feat because I was on a stryker frame and he was in a wheelchair. Another boy was making the moves for me because I couldn't reach the board. These games took hours and required enormous cooperation. The eight-year-old had never walked. After eighteen hip ball/socket operations, the doctors had finally found a material that his body did *not* reject. The boy had never really considered walking and thought the doctors were "pretty stupid"

not to get him straightened out in eighteen tries. Finally, the doctors got it right!

I was with this boy when he took his first steps, and watched his life suddenly turn around. We spent the afternoon talking about what this meant. He knew I had been mobile in the past, and he wanted to talk about running and what you were supposed to do with your arms when you ran. We talked about walking in mud, sand, and water. He wanted to know what to do if you "just fall over" sometimes. We covered running shoes, flip flop sandals, grass, sand castles, etc. Before leaving the hospital, he walked into my room to say goodbye and left surrounded by a loving, joyful family.

NOTE

1. "Prenatal Diagnosis: To Be or Not To Be" National Film Board, 1981, Canada.

Further Questions

1. Are we being unrealistic about the possibilities of fetal defects, believing that every child born will be a healthy child? If so, how should our lack of realism be corrected?

2. Are we realistic in our expectations regarding whether we are prepared to accept and care for a handicapped child? If we do decide to institutionalize a handicapped child after it is born, how would we justify such a decision?

3. What can be done for handicapped children, who are not accepted by their parents, other than keeping them in hospitals and other institutions on a long-term basis?

Further Readings for Part IX: Fertility Control: Contraception and Abortion

BOOKS

Lynn S. Baker, MD. *The Fertility Fallacy: Sexuality in the Post Pill Age* (New York, NY: Holt, Rinehart and Winston, 1981). The fallacy is believing that fertility can be controlled by social policy. With the advent of "the pill," biological fertility control is here to stay, the only question being how we will use it.

Daniel Callahan. *Abortion: Law, Choice and Morality* (New York, NY: The Macmillan Co., 1970). Callahan calls abortion a "nasty problem" and attacks it from a multitude of perspectives.

Anne Collins. *The Big Evasion: Abortion, The Issue That Won't Go Away* (Toronto: Lester and Orpen Dennys, 1985).

John Connery, S.J. *Abortion: The Development of the Roman Catholic Perspective* (Chicago, IL: Loyola University Press, 1970).

Gary Crum and Thelma McCormack. *Abortion: Pro-Choice or Pro-Life* (Washington, DC: The American University Press, 1970). Each author takes a side in heated debate.

David M. Feldman. *Birth Control in Jewish Law: Marital Relations, Contraception, and Abortion as Set Forth in the Classic Texts of Jewish Law* (New York University Press, 1968).

Jay L. Garfield and Patricia Hennessey, ed. *Abortion: Moral and Legal Perspectives* (Amherst, MA: University of Massachusetts Press, 1984).

Mark A. Graber, *Rethinking Abortion: Equal Choice, the Constitution, and Reproductive Politics* (Princeton, NJ: Princeton University Press, 1996). Argument for "equal choice" in matters of abortion set in detailed legal analysis of the present and recent past.

Beverly Wildung Harrison. *Our Right to Choose: Toward a New Ethic of Abortion* (Boston, MA: Beacon Press, 1983). Develops a new theology to mesh with the new ethic.

Thomas W. Hilger, Dennis J. Horan, and David Mall, eds. *New Perspectives on Abortion* (Frederick, MD: University Publications of America, Inc., 1981).

Jane E. Hodgson, ed. *Abortion and Sterilization: Medical and Social Aspects* (New York, NY: Academic Press , 1981).

Helen B. Holmes, Betty B. Hoskins, and Michael Gross, eds. *Birth Control and Controlling Birth: Women-Centered Perspectives* (Clifton, NJ: Humana Press, 1980).

Sumi Hoshiko, ed. *Our Choices: Women's Personal Decisions about Abortions* (Binghamton, NY: Harrington Park Press, 1993). Women in a wide variety of situations demonstrate the importance of abortion as an option.

Stanley Johnson. *Life Without Birth* (Boston, MA: Little, Brown and Co., 1970). Voluntary family planning as a solution to world population explosion.

Hans Lostra. *Abortion: The Catholic Debate in America* (New York, NY: Irving Publishers, 1985). Balanced, critical approach.

Kristin Luker. *Abortion and the Politics of Motherhood* (Berkeley, CA: University of California Press, 1984). Argument that moral positions on abortion are tied to other social values, particularly those of the individual and the family.

Henry Morgantaler, MD. *Abortion and Contraception* (Don Mills, ON: General Publishing Co., 1982). Canada's prime mover in establishing abortion clinics speaks to the medical and ethical issues.

Bernard N. Nathanson, MD with Richard Ostling. *Aborting America* (New York, NY: Doubleday Inc., 1979). Director of the largest abortion clinic in the world explains some years later to the public his experiences, his doubts, his final conclusions.

Rosaline Pollack Petchesky. *Abortion and Women's Choice: The State Sexuality and Reproductive Freedom* (New York, NY: Longman, 1984).

Margaret Sanger. *Motherhood in Bondage* (New York, NY: Brentano's Publishers, 1928). Early activist for contraception publishes some of her correspondence, e.g., "I was married when I was fifteen, have been married only four years, and have three children already. . . ."

———. *The New Motherhood* (London: Jonathan Cape, 1922).

———. *Women and the New Race* (New York, NY: Blue Ribbon Books, 1920).

Janet E. Smith. *Humanae Vita: A Generation Later* (Washington, DC: The Catholic University of America Press, 1991). Discussion and defense of Pope Paul VI's encyclical condemning contraception.

L. W. Sumner. *Abortion and Moral Theory* (Princeton, NJ: Princeton University Press, 1981). A philosopher tries to strike a moderate position.

Edward D. Tyler, ed. *Birth Control: A Continuing Controversy* (Springfield, IL: Charles C. Thomas, Publisher, 1967). Doctors and other professionals discuss issues.

Martha C. Ward. *Poor Women, Powerful Men: America's Great Experiment in Family Planning* (Boulder, CO: Westview Press, 1986). Is family planning the answer to such problems as poor women with dead babies?

Robert G. Weisbord. *Genocide: Birth Control and the Black American* (Westport, CT: Greenwood Press, 1975.

J. Philip Wogaman, ed. *The Population Crisis and Moral Responsibility* (Washington, DC: The Public Affairs Press, 1973). Issues addressed by ethicists, theologians, and population experts.

ARTICLES AND ANTHOLOGIES ON ABORTION BY PHILOSOPHERS

Marshall Cohen, et al, eds. *The Rights and Wrongs of Abortion* (Princeton: Princeton University Press, 1974). Reprints of articles from *Philosophy and Public Affairs* by John Finnis, Judith Jarvis Thompson, Michael Tooley, and Roger Wertheimer.

Susan Dwyer and Joel Feinberg, eds. *The Problem of Abortion,* Third Edition (Belmont, CA: Wadsworth Publishing Co., 1997). Collection of the classical writings on abortion, mostly by philosophers.

Joel Feinberg. "Abortion" in *Matters of Life and Death: New Introductory Essays in Moral Philosophy,* Tom Regan, ed. (New York, NY: Random House, 1981).

Steven Ross. "Abortion and the Death of the Fetus" in *Philosophy and Public Affairs* II (1982), pp. 232–245.

Mary Anne Warren. "On the Moral and Legal Status of Abortion" in *The Monist* 51 (January 1973), pp. 43–61.

Suggested Moral of Part IX

Even if contraception and abortion can be classified together as "fertility control," abortion is much more controversial, because it destroys a form of life that is developing into a human baby.

What is known now as the right-to-life, or pro-life, position holds that abortion is morally wrong for this reason. Pro-life advocates, in fact, hold that abortion is so seriously wrong that the state must protect the fetus from being destroyed by abortion for much the same reasons as it must protect the life of any innocent person who is incapable of protecting it himself.

The other position on abortion calls itself pro-choice because its central contention is that the pregnant woman herself, not the state, should have the final choice on whether she is allowed to have an abortion. Believers in pro-choice may or may not believe that abortion is morally wrong. (Usually they believe that earlier abortions are morally better than late abortions and that, under ideal circumstances, only those who wanted children would conceive them.) Their reason for being pro-choice is that, however wrong an abortion may be, it is morally worse to deprive a woman of the choice of having one. The basis of a woman's right to make the choice is, first, that the abortion or pregnancy is something that will happen in her body; and, second, that she has only two alternatives after the child is born: giving the child to some unknown person to raise, perhaps never seeing it again, or taking the main responsibility of raising it herself (since, as the writers of Part XI argue, raising a child is still very much a responsibility of the mother). It must also be added that state "protection" of the life of the fetus can often result in illegal abortion with death of the fetus and high likelihood of substantial damage to, or death of, the mother as well.

The main question regarding abortion, then, is whether the state can force a pregnant woman to become a mother, in the name of protecting the life of something that is not yet a baby, but will develop into one if an abortion does not take place. This is not an easy question to answer, as the writings in Part IX show.

Most feminists, however, place a higher value on the quality of life for the pregnant woman than on protection of the process of bringing a fetus to term as a baby. Only through assurance that women are not burdened with unwanted pregnancies and unwanted children to raise can women and men have equal access to what human life has to offer, including the option of heterosexual intercourse. The prochoice position then, must be the suggested moral of Part IX.

Part X

Reproduction: Hi Tech/Low Tech

Introduction

EVEN THOUGH THERE HAS BEEN SOME TALK of male gestation and laboratory gestation of human infants, pregnancy and delivery are still activities only of women. Writers in this section react in various ways to this situation.

Steinem suggests new attitudes toward menstruation in a hypothetical situation where men, not women, menstruated; Overall argues for a childbirth unencumbered by unnecessary technology and hospital procedures; Homstein considers artificial insemination by a donor as an option for lesbians and for women more generally; Glover, et al. discuss surrogate motherhood.

X.1   If Men Could Menstruate

GLORIA STEINEM

Gloria Steinem speaks to the possibility of men menstruating. She argues that this would put menstruation in an entirely different light from the somewhat shameful cast it has at present.

Steinem is a feminist activist who has written numerous books and articles in the area. Another selection by Steinem appears in Part XII.

Reading Questions

1. If menstruation, in the ordinary course of events, happens once a month to every woman of a particular age, and if other forms of bleeding do not call for concealment, why are efforts made to conceal menstrual blood from the public eye?
2. Should premenstrual syndrome be taken seriously enough so that any woman who suffers from it has access to medical relief, or even time off from work if she needs it? Is menstruation taken too seriously if women are automatically thought to be incapacitated while menstruating?
3. Menstruation has traditionally been taken to mark the onset and cessation of womanhood. Does it make much sense to treat only that part of a woman's life when she menstruates as her era of being a *real* woman? In what respects, if any, is a nonmenstruating woman lacking full properties of womanhood?

LIVING IN INDIA made me understand that a white minority of the world has spent centuries conning us into thinking a white skin makes people superior, even though the only thing it really does is make them more subject to ultraviolet rays and wrinkles.

Reading Freud made me just as skeptical about penis envy. The power of giving birth makes "womb envy" more logical, and an organ as external and unprotected as the penis makes men very vulnerable indeed.

But listening recently to a woman describe the unexpected arrival of her menstrual period (a red stain had spread on her dress as she argued heatedly on the public stage) still made me cringe with embarrassment. That is, until she explained that, when finally informed in whispers of the obvious event, she had said to the all-male audience, "and you should be *proud* to have a menstruating woman on your stage. It's probably the first real thing that's happened to this group in years!"

Laughter. Relief. She had turned a negative into a positive. Somehow her story merged with India and Freud to make me finally understand the power of positive thinking. Whatever a "superior" group has will be used to justify its superiority, and whatever an "inferior" group has will be used to justify its plight. Black men were given poorly paid jobs because they were said to be "stronger" than white men, while all women were relegated to poorly paid jobs because they were said to be "weaker." As the little boy said when asked if he wanted to be a lawyer like his mother, "Oh, no, that's women's work." Logic has nothing to do with oppression.

So what would happen if suddenly, magically, men could menstruate and women could not?

Clearly, menstruation would become an enviable, boastworthy, masculine event:

Men would brag about how long and how much.

Young boys would talk about it as the envied beginning of manhood. Gifts, religious ceremonies, family dinners, and stag parties would mark the day.

To prevent monthly work loss among the powerful, Congress would fund a National Institute of Dysmenorrhea. Doctors would research little about heart attacks, from which men were hormonally protected, but everything about cramps.

Sanitary supplies would be federally funded and free. Of course, some men would still pay for the prestige of such commercial brands as Paul Newman Tampons, Muhammad Ali's Rope-a-Dope Pads, John Wayne Maxi Pads, and Joe Namath Jock Shields—"For Those Light Bachelor Days."

Statistical surveys would show that men did better in sports and won more Olympic medals during their periods.

Generals, right-wing politicians, and religious fundamentalists would cite menstruation ("*men*struation") as proof that only men could serve God and country in combat ("You have to give blood to take blood"), occupy high political office ("Can women be properly fierce without a monthly cycle governed by the planet Mars?"), be priests, ministers, God Himself ("He gave this blood for our sins"), or rabbis ("Without a monthly purge of impurities, women are unclean").

Male liberals or radicals, however, would insist that women are equal, just different; and that any woman could join their ranks if only she were willing to recognize the primacy of menstrual rights ("Everything else is a single issue") or self-inflict a major wound every month ("You *must* give blood for the revolution").

Street guys would invent slang ("He's a three-pad man" and "give fives" on the corner with some exchange like, "Man, you lookin' *good!*"

"Yeah, man, I'm on the rag!"

TV shows would treat the subject openly. (*Happy Days:* Richie and Potsie try to convince Fonzie that he is still "The Fonz," though he has missed two periods in a row. *Hill Street Blues:* The whole precinct hits the same cycle.) So would newspapers. (SUMMER SHARK SCARE THREATENS MENSTRUATING MEN. JUDGE CITES MONTHLIES IN PARDONING RAPIST.) and so would movies. (Newman and Redford in *Blood Brothers!*)

Men would convince women that sex was *more* pleasurable at "that time of the month." Lesbians would be said to fear blood and therefore life itself, though all they needed was a good menstruating man.

Medical schools would limit women's entry ("they might faint at the sight of blood").

Of course, intellectuals would offer the most moral and logical arguments. Without that biological gift for measuring the cycles of the moon and planets, how could a woman master any discipline that demanded a sense of time, space, mathematics—or the ability to measure anything at all? In philosophy and religion, how could women compensate for being disconnected from the rhythm of the universe? Or for their lack of symbolic death and resurrection every month?

Menopause would be celebrated as a positive event, the symbol that men had accumulated enough years of cyclical wisdom to need no more.

Liberal males in every field would try to be kind. The fact that "these people" have no gift for measuring life, the liberals would explain, should be punishment enough.

And how would women be trained to react? One can imagine right-wing women agreeing to all these arguments with a staunch and smiling masochism. ("The ERA would force housewives to wound themselves every month": Phyllis Schafly. "Your husband's blood is as sacred as that of Jesus—and so sexy, too!": Marabel Morgan.) Reformer and Queen Bees would adjust their lives to the cycles of the men around them. Feminists would explain endlessly that men, too, needed to be liberated from the false idea of Martian aggressiveness, just as women needed to escape the bonds of "menses-envy." Radical feminists would add that the oppression of the nonmenstrual was the pattern for all other oppressions. ("Vampires were our first freedom fighters!") Cultural feminists would exalt a female bloodless imagery in art and literature. Socialist feminists would insist that, once capitalism and imperialism were overthrown, women would menstruate, too. ("If women aren't yet menstruating in Russia," they would explain, "it's only because true socialism can't exist within capitalist encirclement.")

In short, we would discover, as we should already guess, that logic is in the eye of the logician. (For instance, here's an idea for theorists and logicians: If women are supposed to be less rational and more emotional at the beginning of our menstrual cycle when the female hormone is at its lowest level, then why isn't it logical to say that, in those few days, women behave the most like the way men behave all month long? I leave further improvisations up to you.)[1]

The truth is that, if men could menstruate, the power justifications would go on and on.

If we let them.

NOTE

1. With thanks to Stan Pottinger for many of the improvisations already here.

Further Questions

1. If men were the only ones who menstruated, would they take it as a status symbol and brag about it, as Steinem suggests? (If so, think of some possible examples of this in addition to the ones given by Steinem.)

2. Menstrual blood is traditionally thought of as unclean. Do you think Steinem is correct in saying that if men menstruated, menstruation would be treated as a necessity to purge impurities? What do "unclean" and "impurities" mean in the preceding question?

3. Would hypothetical menstruating men look down on hypothetical nonmenstruating women because the latter are not synchronized with the universe and hence lacking in understanding of much of anything, as Steinem suggests? How might synchronization with the universe contribute to understanding it?

Childbirth

CHRISTINE OVERALL

Christine Overall believes that a pregnant woman should be the one who makes the final decisions about the birth of her baby. She claims that putting medical personnel in charge of decisions is of dubious benefit to the baby and can negate the value of the birthing experience as a meaningful, self-affirming event for the woman.

Overall teaches philosophy at Queen's University, Kingston, Ontario. *Ethics and Human Reproduction* was her first book, and she has written on a wide number of feminist issues.

Reading Questions

1. Do you see childbirth as a situation in which the baby's needs, as perceived by medical personnel, ought to take precedence over the pregnant woman's wishes? If some of the pregnant woman's wishes should take precedence, which wishes are they?
2. Quoting Bayles, Overall speaks of an "ethically ideal childbirth," as being a vaginal delivery with healthy mother and child. Does this mean that someone has done something wrong (and, if so, who?) if either the mother or child is damaged in delivery, or if the delivery is by caesarean section?
3. Do you think that childbirth can be one of the high points of a woman's life, especially if she gives birth with very little intervention on the part of medical personnel? If so, exactly what makes this a high point? Are women who don't give birth, or don't give birth in this way, missing something important in life?

CONFLICT BETWEEN PREGNANT WOMAN AND FETUS

. . . ACCORDING TO "the medical belief in an adversary relationship between the mother and the baby,"

> the baby must be stopped from ripping its mother apart, and the surgical scissors [performing an episiotomy, that is, a cut in the mother's perineum] are considered to be more gentle than the baby's head. At the same time, the mother must be stopped from crushing her baby, and the obstetrical forceps are seen as being more gentle than the mother's vagina.[1]

Thus in a 1984 discussion paper of the Ontario Medical Association (OMA) entitled "Issues Relating to Childbirth,"[2] the pregnant woman and her fetus (and, later, the baby) are seen as adversaries competing to get their needs filled. The pregnant woman is primarily a container or environment for the fetus; her interests are often different from—even in conflict with—those of her fetus. The paper states,

> We are . . . beginning to see claims for dual medical-legal rights and new responsibilities, one set for the mother and an increasingly well-defined set for the fetus. There is a growing need to discuss how we are going to resolve

Abridged from "Childbirth," in Ethics and Human Reproduction: A Feminist Analysis *(Winchester, MA: Allen and Unwin, Inc., 1987), pp. 88–110. Reprinted by permission of the author.*

social conflicts between the rights of the mother and the rights of the fetus and newborn. Quite separately, appropriate and useful medical care for the fetus will require the mother to assume some risks without any benefit to herself since for some procedures she is the only route to the fetus.[3]

There are a number of problems with this type of approach to the pregnant woman/fetus relationship. First, seeing the pregnant woman as the "route to the fetus" has the effect of literally depersonalizing her, reducing her to a mere environment in which the fetus grows. It obscures the fact that she is, or ought to be, an independent and autonomous adult, with full decison-making powers and legal rights to determine what occurs to and within her own body. The discussion paper's approach appears to demote the pregnant woman to a derivative ontological and moral status, making questions of her safety and well-being secondary to questions about the safety and well-being of the fetus. . . .

. . . [T]he antifeminist perspective on childbirth sees the alleged conflict between pregnant woman and fetus as an unequal struggle: The pregnant woman is the potential oppressor of her fetus. During birth she must therefore voluntarily abdicate her power over it, and if she will not, the resolution of this unequal conflict requires the oppression of the pregnant woman by medical and legal authorities.

What sorts of sacrifice are expected of pregnant women in the process of birth? First, parturient women are ordinarily expected to abandon any preference they may have for birthing at home. In most of the Western world, and particularly in North America, women are supposed to give birth in a hospital. Moreover, they are not permitted much choice in their attendants at birth; in particular, they are often prevented (and again, this is a special problem in North America) from having the services of midwives, and even close friends and relatives (other than her husband, if she has one) are not allowed to be present.

Giving birth in the hospital requires further sacrifices of the parturient women. She must often accept extensive technological intervention in her labor, sometimes at the expense of lack of personal attention from birth "attendants." For example, she may be left *unattended* except for the presence of a fetal heart monitor, which gives the misleading impression that she is being watched. External monitors require straps around the woman's abdomen and impose limitations on her movements during labor. Internal monitors require electrodes that are passed through the woman's vagina and are clipped or screwed into the fetus's scalp.[4]

Additional medical interventions in the course of a hospital birth include the following:[5]

- Shaving of the perineal area
- Enemas
- Intravenous feeding
- Artificial induction of labor, which may in some cases, be done for the sake of the physician's convenience[6]
- Withholding of food and liquids during labor
- Stimulation of labor by means of oxytocin
- Analgesia and anesthesia
- Artificial rupture of membranes (amniotomy)
- Use of the lithotomy (horizontal supine) position and stirrups for delivery
- Episiotomy, which does not seem to reduce the incidence of tears,[7] and may even be associated with a greater incidence of lacerations
- Use of forceps
- Cesareans
- Postnatal separation of mother and infant

For the laboring woman a hospital birth can be an extraordinarily alienating experience:

> Her clothes are sent away and she wears a standard gown. Her name is appended a hospital number. She is cleansed (shaved, washed, and given an enema). Communication with her family and friends is monitored by the staff and

severely curtailed. Instruments are attached to her to monitor the child's heart beat. Drugs are given to partially anesthetize her. She is physically inspected mainly in the area of her genitals. She is expected to remain lying down and, at inspections, near delivery and afterwards, her legs are in straps which retain them in a raised and apart position.[8]

Thus the sacrifices inherent in many hospital births also include such psychological costs as loss of autonomy and self-esteem.[9]

Although these sacrifices are presented as being mainly for the sake of the fetus's welfare, in fact it is not entirely clear that the infant always, or even usually, benefits from them. Fetal heart monitors, to take just one example are inaccurate; they can create the impression of fetal distress, resulting in unnecessary procedures such as cesarean sections. The necessary immobilization may be uncomfortable for the woman and even detrimental to her and the fetus.[10] In general, it seems likely that the twentieth-century drop in infant mortality rates owes little to the procedures of hospital births and much to improved maternal diet, clean water, and adequate sanitation, housing, and working conditions.[11] There is no evidence of a causal relationship (in addition to a mere correlation) between the gradual drop in neonatal mortality rates in the last century and the rise in rates of hospital births.

Hence there is nothing self-evident about the value orientation exemplified in standard hospital birth practices. If some physicians regard the pregnant woman as a "route to the fetus" who during childbirth must sacrifice her interests to those of the fetus, they ought to *defend* that approach and not merely assume that it is legitimate. And so even if it is assumed, for the sake of argument, that on some occasions and in some circumstances (though certainly not all) the pregnant woman's interests and those of her fetus are not compatible, then the predominant question must be: To what degree, if at all, should the pregnant woman sacrifice her interests or permit them to be sacrificed? It is certainly not obvious that decisions about care for

pregnant woman and fetus should necessarily subordinate the woman's freedom, interests, and well-being to those of her fetus. . . .

Beyond its unquestioning emphasis upon the priority of fetal rights, a further problem with the assumption that there is a conflict between maternal and fetal rights and needs is that it is not at all obvious that fetus and pregnant women *should* in fact always be viewed as adversaries, competing to get their needs filled. . . . [O]rdinarily during the course of pregnancy activities and resources—for example, mild exercise, nourishing food, and unpolluted air—that are beneficial for the mother are also beneficial for the fetus. Conversely, activities and environments—such as smoking, dangerous work environments, and exposure to disease—that are harmful for the fetus are also harmful for the pregnant woman. This relationship of shared benefit and vulnerability does not cease during the activity of childbirth.

Furthermore, it is unlikely that a pregnant woman sees herself as being in competition with her fetus; on the contrary, women ordinarily want the best for their future baby and are willing to go to considerable lengths to secure it.[12] Although it is undoubtedly true that some women may be unhappy during pregnancy, or may fear (perhaps with very good reason) the process of giving birth, those women who are involved in preparing and planning for the circumstances of their child's birth certainly perceive themselves as acting on behalf of, and in the best interests of, their fetus. . . .

However, insofar as there is ever a necessity to override the pregnant woman's decisions—whether because of her lack of knowledge or lack of competence—this necessity would have to be demonstrated, and not simply assumed to hold in all cases. Surely in no other human relationship does an unrelated person believe he has grounds unilaterally to appoint himself another's advocate without prior invitation. Certainly such a belief runs counter to the general practice in most other aspects of parent/child relationships

This general practice is ably described by Paul Thompson in a discussion of the "*prima facie* prerogative [of parents] to choose on behalf of their children."[13] Thompson points out that there is a great range of activities in which it is justifiably assumed that parents have a legitimate right to determine their children's participation.[14] There is no general reason to suppose that childbirth is different; there are no compelling grounds (such as the expectation of great harm) to justify overriding the parent's prerogative. Hence insofar as the fetus needs an advocate, there is no reason to regard the physician rather than the pregnant woman as the appropriate advocate.

CONFLICT BETWEEN SAFETY AND OTHER VALUES

In his discussion of childbirth, Michael Bayles also criticizes the belief that the physician should be the advocate of the fetus. He describes it as follows:

> Many physicians claim that they best represent the interests of the fetus. They do not deny that almost all women are interested in the well-being of their baby, but the woman's interests can conflict with those of the baby. For example, the woman's interests in the psychological and social aspects of birth are probably greater than those of the child, and women might sacrifice the physical safety of the fetus for their own psychological fulfillment. Even if maternal-infant bonding is beneficial for the baby, it is not as important as its physical well-being. Moreover, it is precisely in the area of physical safety that physicians have expertise. Consequently, it is claimed, they should make the decisions about childbirth.[15]

Interestingly, although Bayles rejects the notion that the physician is the appropriate advocate for the fetus, he nevertheless accepts, along with many antifeminist theorists, the assumption that there may be a conflict between the psychological needs of the pregnant woman and the requirements of safety for her and the fetus. ... .

VALUES AND GOALS IN CHILDBEARING

The emphasis by nonfeminist and antifeminist writers on an alleged conflict between safety and psychosocial needs appears to be connected with two other basic beliefs. The first concerns the nature of risk-taking in childbirth, and the second concerns the significance of childbearing. To examine both of these requires some thought about the values and goals of childbirth.

A recurrent ideal cited in nonfeminist and antifeminist literature on birth is the health of the baby and the mother. From this point of view, "a 'successful' pregnancy is one which results in a physically healthy baby and mother as assessed in the period immediately following birth."[16] Bayles, for example, describes "the ethically ideal childbirth" as involving "a vaginal delivery with a healthy mother and infant."[17] The OMA Discussion Paper says that in the traditional system of provision of reproductive care by physicians, the physician's goal was "to facilitate the birth of a healthy baby"; hospitals attempted to "ensure efficient functioning of the hospital and safety of patients."[18] (This in itself is an interesting priority of values!)

As Bayles himself readily acknowledges, this quest for a healthy baby and mother is translated, in practice, into an all-out attempt to "make the best of the worst possible outcome, no matter what the likelihood of its occurring."[19] For example, while claiming that "the chances for a successful labor and delivery are certainly 98 out of 100 or greater,"[20] one physician states that if one is "interested in taking that 2 percent chance [of an unsuccessful birth outcome], then fetal monitoring is unnecessary. [But] if one is interested in optimizing the chances for *every* fetus, fetal monitoring is *essential*."[21] The quest is most clearly exemplified in the medical establishment's insistence that home birth is dangerous and that all births should take place in a hospital. The Ontario Medical Association asserts categorically that "planned home births involve increased and avoidable risks to the health of the mother, foetus, and newborn infant"; it therefore opposes without reservation all planned home births.[22] The American College of Obstetricians and Gynecologists has a similar position.[23]

Planned home births, however, have an impressive safety record,[24] comparing very favorably with hospital births in terms of both mortality and morbidity rates. Hence the fact that there is a low rate of unforeseeable risk in any birth (for instance, as a result of cord prolapse or postpartum hemorrhage[25]) does not morally justify approaching all births as if they involved the highest degree of risk.

> Probably 20 percent of births are to mothers with no high-risk factor identifiable before delivery, yet about 10 percent of perinatal deaths are to such mothers. To ensure that these unpredictable dangerous births take place in consultant hospitals, obstetricians recommend that all births should take place there, for they claim that the chances of a successful outcome are then improved. However valid the claim may be in individual cases, the available statistical evidence does not support it in general. It does not show that an increased rate of hospitalization promotes the objective of reducing overall mortality.[26]

Similarly, the low rate of unforeseeable risk to pregnant women and their fetuses of riding in automobiles does not justify enforced banishment from cars![27] It is impossible to eliminate all risks completely from human activities; an attempt must be made to make a realistic assessment of and preparation for possible dangers and, where possible, to reduce or compensate for them.

The fact that there may be an unforeseen negative outcome of one particular woman's birth choice—for example, in favor of home birth—does not by itself demonstrate that *all* similar choices are therefore unjustified. More important still, the occurrence of an unforeseen negative outcome is not even sufficient to show that the specific choice itself was unjustified. To see this, imagine the following analogous case. An individual decides to take her family for a car ride. The weather is fine, road conditions are

good, the woman drives carefully and defensively. Nevertheless an accident occurs and an occupant of the car is injured. The fact that an injury occurred does not show that the decision to take the car ride in the first place was unjustified. Given all of the foreseeable information at the time, and given the appropriate precautions the driver took, the car ride was an entirely justified activity. Similarly, if a low-risk mother chooses home birth and takes all appropriate precautions for the circumstances of the birth, then the fact that an unforeseen injury occurs is not sufficient to show that her choice was unjustified.

No studies exist to support the justification of universal hospitalization, and existing studies of the safety of home versus hospital are often misused by the medical profession.[28] Furthermore, as Paul Thompson points out,

> hospital birth, while reducing a number of risks which are present in home birth, introduces new risks and increases remaining risks. And .... it is not immediately obvious that the negative outcomes of the new risks introduced by hospital birth are more desirable than those of the risks of home birth which have been eliminated or reduced.[29]

Assessments both of what constitutes a benefit and of what constitutes a benefit substantial enough to warrant taking a risk to achieve it are value judgments.[30] Moreover, there is good evidence to suggest that contemporary medical practice creates what is regarded as a risk by defining certain conditions—such as having had three previous births—as high risk.[31] Hence the error in positions such as that of the OMA is that they fail to recognize that the mere acknowledgment of the possible existence of a risk does not by itself entail a particular course of action; a further evaluation of the significance of the risk is necessary, and such an evaluation is a moral, not a medical, judgment. Moreover, in light of the implausibility of assuming that pregnant woman and fetus are in conflict, it is not even very obvious that risks and benefits can or should be assessed separately for each of them.[32] . . .

Who ought to make decisions about the evaluation of risk in childbirth, and how should those decisions be made? I suggest that they should be made by the pregnant woman herself, through a process that places the childbirth event within the more general context of her life. Childbearing is not something that merely happens to women, but is a process in which women are (or can be) actively engaged. "Birth cannot simply be a matter of techniques for getting a baby out of one's body,"[33] and childbirth is not just a type of production.[34] Although hospitals do not reward, encourage, or even recognize competence in giving birth,[35] there is a very important conceptual and experiential difference between giving birth and being delivered. "When the *mother* is seen as delivering, then the attendant is assisting—aiding, literally attending. But when the *doctor* is delivering the baby, the mother is in the passive position of *being delivered*."[36]

It therefore seems unduly pessimistic to claim, as does Bayles, that "there does not appear to be any way to justify one attitude toward risk rather than another."[37] Evaluation of possible risk in childbirth, and of the importance of achieving a healthy baby and mother, requires dictating the birth event within the wider circumstances of the mother's life. This is not to say that the familiar antifeminist belief in a conflict between safety and psychosocial needs must be reinstated. Instead it is necessary to reconstruct, from the point of view of the laboring woman, the very nature of what have been called "psycho-social needs" and "psycho-social interests."[38] Is it correct to say that the pregnant woman seeks to "personally grow and experience to the fullest a basic aspect of [her] femininity"? Or that "childbirth is an opportunity for personal development and growth"?[39] Or, as Bayles remarks, that "women generally want childbirth to be a rewarding personal experience"?[40] . . .

The suggestion that the childbearing experience is central to a woman's life[41] need not be at all incompatible with a feminist perspective on birth. It is of course necessary to avoid pre-scribing, as so many writers have in the past,[42] what childbirth *must* be like, or how it *must* be experienced,[43] and to avoid describing it romantically as a necessarily transcendent, quasi-mystical experience. The point being made is not that a woman is incomplete without experiencing birth, nor that childbearing is women's natural work, nor even that childbirth is always a happy event.

Instead what is being pointed to is the simple fact that childbirth is, or can be, if not skewed in its meaning by a medical reconstruction, a powerful, self-affirming, and memorable event whose meaning is not isolated but resonates throughout all of the woman's subsequent experiences as a woman and as a mother.[44] Since women now tend to have fewer children and have few, if any, opportunities to participate in other women's births, childbirth is for most of those who undertake it a journey into the unknown. Giving birth is a chance to come to know oneself and one's strengths, and to weave that knowledge into a more general understanding of the significance of one's life. Insofar as a "rewarding personal experience" (to use Bayles's phrase) is sought by pregnant women, that experience arises not just from the relatively brief events surrounding birth but from the mother-baby relationship and from the integration of motherhood into the woman's life pattern.[45]

Hence the conclusion must be that, in general, decisions about the birth of her baby belong primarily to the pregnant woman herself, for whom the process is not some isolated medical emergency but a vital part of the living of her life. And although it is impossible to specify uniformly what all births ought to be like, it can at least be said that they should not be founded upon the belief that the pregnant woman's interests conflict with those of her fetus, or that safety requirements must conflict with psychological needs. Ordinarily childbearing need not and should not require sacrifices of the pregnant woman.

NOTES

1. Barbara Katz Rothman, *Giving Birth: Alternatives in Childbirth* (Harmondsworth, England: Penguin Books, 1984), p. 277.

2. OMA Committee on Perinatal Care, "Ontario Medical Association Discussion Paper on Directions in Health Care Issues Relating to Childbirth" (Toronto, 1984). Although the paper is said not to represent present OMA policy (p. 1), it can be taken as representative of standard medical views on childbearing and on the relationship of the pregnant woman to her fetus.

3. *Ibid.,* p. 12.

4. Sheila Kitzinger, "The Social Context of Birth: Some Comparisons between Childbirth in Jamaica and Britain," in *Ethnography of Fertility and Birth,* ed. Carol P. MacCormack (London: Academic Press, 1982), p. 183.

5. For a complete discussion, see Yvonne Brackbill, June Rice, and Diony Young, *Birth Trap: The Legal Low-Down on High-Tech Obstetrics* (St. Louis: C. V. Mosby, 1984). p. 1–38 and Doris Haire, "The Cultural Warping of Childbirth" (Seattle, WA.: International Childbirth Education Association, 1972).

6. Ronald R. Rindfuss, Judith L. Ladinsky, Elizabeth Coppock, Victor W. Marshall, and A. S. Macpherson, "Convenience and the Occurrence of Births: Induction of Labor in the United States and Canada," in *Women and Health: The Politics of Sex in Medicine,* ed. Elizabeth Fee (Farmingdale, N.Y.: Baywood, 1982), pp. 37–58.

7. Janice Armstrong, "The Risks and Benefits of Home Birth" (unpublished paper, 1982), p. 10.

8. A. D. Jones and C. Dougherty, "Childbirth in a Scientific and Industrial Society," in MacCormack, *Ethnography of Fertility and Birth,* p. 280.

9. Brackbill et al., *Birth Trap,* pp. 3–4.

10. Armstrong, "Risks and Benefits of Home Birth," p. 2.

11. C. P. MacCormack, "Biological, Cultural and Social Adaptation in Human Fertility and Birth: A Synthesis," in *Ethnography of Fertility and Birth,* pp. 18–19.

12. David Stewart and Lewis E. Mehl, "A Rebuttal to Negative Home Birth Statistics Cited by ACOG," in *21st Century Obstetrics Now!* I, 2nd ed., ed. Lee Stewart and David Stewart (Chapel Hill, N.C.: NAPSAC, 1977), p. 29.

13. Paul Thompson, "Home Birth: Consumer Choice and Restrictions of Physician Autonomy," *Journal of Business Ethics* 6 (1987): 76.

14. But, as will be argued in chapter 8 [of *Ethics and Human Reproduction,* Christine Overall, Boston: Unwin Hyman, 1987] those rights are not unlimited.

15. Michael D. Bayles, *Reproductive Ethics* (Englewood Cliffs, N.J.: Prentice-Hall, 1984), p. 80.

16. Hilary Graham and Ann Oakley, "Competing Ideologies of Reproduction: Medical and Maternal Perspectives on Pregnancy," in *Women, Health and Reproduction,* ed. Helen Roberts (London: Routledge & Kegan Paul, 1981), p. 54.

17. Bayles, *Reproductive Ethics,* p. 83.

18. "OMA Discussion Paper," p. 9.

19. Bayles, *Reproductive Ethics,* p. 80.

20. Henry Klapholz, "The Electronic Fetal Monitor in Perinatology," in Holmes et al., *Birth Control and Controlling Birth,* p. 167.

21. *Ibid.,* p. 173, my emphasis.

22. "OMA Discussion Paper," p. 30.

23. Richard H. Aubry, "The American College of Obstetricians and Gynecologists: Standards for Safe Childbearing," in Stewart and Stewart, *21st Century Obstetrics Now!,* p. 20.

24. Brackbill et al., *Birth Trap,* pp. 59–61; Gerard Alan Hoff and Lawrence J. Schneiderman, "Having Babies at Home: Is It Safe? Is it Ethical?" *Hastings Center Report* 15 (December 1985): 21.

25. Armstrong, "Risks and Benefits of Home Births," p. 4.

26. Marjorie Tew, "The Case against Hospital Deliveries: The Statistical Evidence," in *The Place of Birth,* ed. Sheila Kitzinger and J. A. Davis (Oxford: Oxford University Press, 1978), p. 65.

27. Compare Thompson, "Home Birth: Consumer Choice," pp. 75–78.

28. Stewart, "The Case for Home Birth," pp. 221–223.

29. Paul Thompson, "Childbirth in North America: Parental Autonomy and the Welfare of the Fetus," unpublished paper, Toronto, Ontario (1984): 5.

30. *Ibid.,* p. 10.

21. Barbara Katz Rothman, "Awake and Aware, or False Consciousness," in Romalis, *Childbirth : Alternatives to Medical Control,* p. 177.

32. As some recommend: e.g., Hoff and Schneiderman, "Having Babies at Home," p. 24.

33. Sheila Kitzinger, *The Experience of Childbirth* 3rd ed., (Harmondsworth, England: Penguin Books, 1972), p. 21; compare Kitzinger, *Women as Mothers,* p. 24.

34. Adrienne Rich, "The Theft of Childbirth," in *Seizing Our Bodies: The Politics of Women's Health,* ed.

Claudia Dreifus (New York: Vintage Books, 1977), p. 162.

35. Germaine Greer, *Sex and Destiny: The Politics of Human Fertility* (London: Secker & Warburg, 1984), p.17.

36. Rothman, *Giving Birth*, p. 174, her emphasis.

37. Bayles, *Reproductive Ethics*, p. 81.

38. "OMA Discussion Paper," p. 33.

39. *Ibid.*, pp. 22, 24.

40. Bayles, *Reproductive Ethics*, p. 83.

41. As Adrienne Rich points out ("The Theft of Childbirth," p. 152), at times Kitzinger takes this claim too far—when, for example, she refers to births as "perhaps the most important moments of their [women's] lives" (Kitzinger, *The Experience of Childbirth*, p. 20).

42. Richard W. Wertz and Dorothy C. Wertz, *Lying-In: A History of Childbirth in America* (New York: Schocken Books, 1977), pp. 188–189.

43. Lester Dessez Hazell's moving "Truths about Birth" remind us that each birth is unique (Lester Dessez Hazell, "Spiritual and Ethical Aspects of Birth: Who Bears the Ultimate Responsibility?" in Stewart and Stewart *21st Century Obstetrics Now!*, p. 259).

44. Kitzinger, *Giving Birth*, p. 31; Graham and Oakley, "Competing Ideologies of Reproduction," p. 54.

45. Graham and Oakley, p. 54; Rich, "The Theft of Childbirth," pp. 161–162. If, for example, she returns to work after she has ostensibly recovered from the birth, "she is not the same worker who left to bear a child. Asking her to continue as if nothing had happened is absurd" (Greer, *Sex and Destiny*, p. 13).

Further Questions

1. Are hospital procedures in birthing (for example, as described by Overall) humiliating experiences? If so, which procedures, and why are they humiliating?

2. If your baby were delivered by caesarean section, or if forceps were used on your baby's head during delivery, would you feel that you had somehow failed as a woman? What exactly does being a success as a woman have to do with delivering a baby in a certain way?

3. Since it is impossible to eliminate risk from all human activity (for example, riding in automobiles), is it silly to try to maximize safety for the infant during delivery by "making the best of the worst possible outcome" (Bayles)? If this idea is silly, what is a better idea?

X.3 Children by Donor Insemination: A New Choice for Lesbians

FRANCIE HORNSTEIN

Francie Hornstein describes her conception of a child by donor insemination. This possibility gives lesbians and heterosexual women without partners a new option in reproductive choice. In addition, self-insemination clinics offer women more control over the process of reproduction.

Hornstein has worked for reproductive choices for women and for lowering infant death rates among poor and minority communities since the late 1960s.

Francie Hornstein, "Children by Donor Insemination: A New Choice for Lesbians" from Test Tube Women: What Future for Motherhood? *edited by Rita Arditti, Renate Duelli, and Shelley Minden, published by Pandora Press, London, 1984. Reprinted by permission of the publisher.*

Reading Questions

1. Does the element of control a woman has in self-insemination (in selecting the donor and doing the insemination herself) make this an attractive option for women? For example, if you are (or were) a woman, would this be attractive for you?
2. What would you tell a child who was so conceived?
3. If you were in a permanent partnership with someone who would not be your child's biological parent, would the birth of your child pose potential problems in your relationship? If so, what kinds of problems?

IN SPITE OF THE MANY DIFFICULTIES involved in making any kind of far-reaching change, donor insemination has been an enormously exciting step in breaking through the constraints placed on women by sexist prohibitions. It has opened the door for allowing women to arrange their lives in a way that best suits their needs. For lesbians and some heterosexual women, donor insemination represents a new reproductive choice—and one which can remain in our control.

My decision to conceive a child by donor insemination was a long time coming. It was nearly seven years between the time I first considered the possibility and when I began trying to get pregnant. The one recurring reservation in what had become a passionate desire to have children was my fear for how the children would cope with being from a different kind of family.

I knew I would be sorry if I never had children; sorry not only for giving up a part of life I really wanted, but for not making a decision that I believed was right. I felt I was as worthy of having children as any other person. To not have children simply because I was a lesbian would have been giving up on a goal that was very dear to me.

I had always wanted to have children. I can remember when I was very young, as far back as elementary school, being afraid that I would never have children because I didn't think I would ever get married. Of course when I was eight years old I didn't realize that I was lesbian—I just could never imagine myself married to a man. Marrying a woman might have been more appealing, but that option was never presented to me.

No one has yet written a chronicle of feminist-controlled donor insemination, though some of us are beginning to collect information. It seems that small groups of women in different parts of the country began discussing and actually doing donor insemination beginning in the middle to late 1970s. For the most part, we were unaware of one another's existence. It wasn't until after several of us had children and either heard about each other through the grapevine or met at conferences that we began comparing notes.

I first tried donor insemination in 1973 while I was working at the Feminist Women's Health Center in Los Angeles. I was unable to use the services of the sperm bank because they would only accept married women as candidates for insemination. It was difficult finding donors and I was absorbed in long hours of work in the women's health movement, so the work involved in my getting pregnant was shelved for a few years. With the help of my co-workers and the encouragement of my lover, I finally began trying to get pregnant in 1977.

I think it was significant that I was working at the Feminist Women's Health Center at the time I got pregnant. It seemed particularly fitting that the same women who developed the practice of menstrual extraction, a procedure which could be used for early abortion, also were among the pioneers in the practice of self-help donor insemination. We figured if we could safely help a woman end her pregnancy without the help of physicians and patriarchal laws, we could certainly help women get pregnant.

My co-workers at the FWHC and I learned how to do the insemination in the same self-help way we learned about other aspects of women's health. We read medical journals and textbook articles, talked with physicians who did the procedure and combined that information with plain, down-to-earth common sense.

Finding donors was the most difficult part of the whole process for me. At the time I got pregnant, there was only one sperm bank in the city. It was owned and operated by a physician who had a private infertility practice and who was very conservative in selecting his clientele. He declined to make his services available to women who were not married, not to mention lesbians.

The only option open to us at the time was to find donors through our friends. I wanted to be able to give the children the option of knowing their father, so we preferred a situation in which the donor was known either to us or to a friend. Eventually, we were able to find donors.

The insemination itself was simple. All we had to do was have the donor ejaculate into a clean container, draw up the semen into a clean syringe (with the needle removed) and inject it into the vagina. We already knew how to do vaginal self-examination with a speculum, so we were familiar with the anatomy of the cervix, the opening of the uterus where the sperm needs to be put. Other women we later spoke with who didn't have access to medical supplies, such as syringes, improvised with common household items. A turkey baster, now synonymous with self-help insemination, works just fine. One innovative woman had her donor ejaculate into a condom, then she simply turned the condom inside-out in her vagina. Some women either insert a diaphragm or cervical cap to hold the semen near the cervix or they lie down for a half-hour or so after inserting the semen.

After our son was born, in the fall of 1978, my lover and I were asked to talk about our experiences at a variety of feminist conferences and programs. It was then that we began meeting other women who either had children or wanted to have children by donor insemination. Since that time, we have personally met women from several states and Canada and have heard about women from England and throughout Europe who are also having children by donor insemina-

tion, without the assistance of physicians. We have met two women who had children before 1978, but are sure there must be others. We had also heard that women in England had been using donor insemination for a number of years before women in the United States. A friend visited a woman in England who has a 12-year-old son conceived by donor insemination.

The majority of women we have met who have had children by donor insemination are lesbians, though there is now a growing number of single, heterosexual women who are choosing donor insemination as a way of getting pregnant. Some of these women prefer being single, but want to have children; others haven't yet met men they want to live with or have children with, but because of their age or other reasons, don't want to wait for marriage before having children.

Several feminist health groups have begun making donor insemination available to women who ordinarily would not be able to use the services of sperm banks. In 1978, the Feminist Women's Health Center in Los Angeles began a donor insemination program. A commercial sperm bank had just opened up in the city and the only requirement for obtaining sperm from them was a physician's order. The FWHC used their staff physicians to order sperm for women requesting insemination. The Vermont Women's Health Center and the Chelsea Health Center in New York City also assisted women in getting pregnant by donor insemination. In 1982, the Oakland Feminist Women's Health Center began their own sperm bank, the Sperm Bank of Northern California, tailor-making the health services to conform to their own feminist values and expectations rather than the medical model of the traditional sperm banks.[1]

The Oakland FWHC program varies from other sperm banks in a number of important ways. The aspects that distinguish their services are their willingness to provide sperm to any woman, regardless of her marital status, sexual preference, or physical disability; their provision of extensive, but non-identifying social and health background information of donors; a policy which permits women to examine a catalogue of donor information and to select their own donor; and possibly most important, a donor "release-of-information contract" which donors have the option of signing which gives their consent to provide their name to any children conceived from their sperm, when the child reaches the age of majority.

One thing the feminist health services have in common with one another is their attempt to demedicalize the procedure of donor insemination. In most instances, physicians do not perform the insemination. Although the feminist health workers are willing to assist their clients who ask for their help, they prefer to provide the information so that women can do the insemination themselves, most often with the help of lovers or friends.

The intention on the part of feminist health services who provide donor insemination is less a desire to branch out into additional services but rather a strong political statement in support of a woman's right to make her own reproductive decisions. The feminist clinics find themselves in the unique position of having physicians on staff who have access to commercial sperm banks and want to make the resource available to the community. But they are adamant about their belief that physicians should not make decisions for women about whether or not they will have children. Because of the services provided by the Oakland Feminist Women's Health Center and the other clinics, and the work of women who have done self-help donor insemination and who are talking publicly about their experiences, a great many women, particularly lesbians, are now able to have children by donor insemination.

In discussing women's rights to make reproductive decisions, the positive impact of self-help donor insemination cannot be underestimated. But the practice does not exist in isolation and carries its fair share of potential problems and unanswered questions.

A woman deciding to have children on her own terms and without the inclusion of an on-site father is seen as attacking the traditional no-tion of a proper family. In spite of the fact that a large proportion of children end up living with their mothers only, it remains more threatening to patriarchy for a woman to *choose* to set up such an arrangement than to merely end up that way as a result of divorce, desertion, or death.

While feminists are trying to make room for a variety of acceptable models for families, a number of patriarchal institutions are objecting to donor insemination as a means for creating a different kind of social unit. One incident is particularly illustrative of the reaction of the medical establishment and the state and local government to a woman's choosing to become pregnant by donor insemination.

In 1981, a woman in Milwaukee, Wisconsin, was inseminated by a physician and became pregnant. The woman was single and employed in a part-time job which did not provide health insurance coverage. She subsequently applied for medical assistance from the country social service agency for help in paying her maternity care bills. She was told that she would also qualify for Aid to Families with Dependant Children (AFDC) after her baby was born. The incident began the first public skirmish in the country about the rights of a single woman to have children by donor insemination.

The medical community was divided on the issue, with a number of outspoken physicians calling for a ban on the insemination of single women who could not prove financial stability. Although the physician who inseminated the woman held firm to his belief that a woman has the right to decide to bear children, the situation incensed other physicians and politicians who thought a single woman, especially a low-income single woman, had no right to intentionally have children.

Conservative politicians in the city and state governments called for actions ranging from a resolution for the county to file a paternity suit against the woman's physician to an amendment to a bill introduced into the state legislature which would have considered it unprofessional conduct for a physician to inseminate a woman under similar circumstances. The bill was vetoed by the governor.[2]

For the most part, women who are having children by donor insemination are not in such a public spotlight. Yet there are still a number of difficult issues we must face—even under the best of circumstances. We must all decide what to tell our children about their fathers. Our families, who may not share our feminist perspectives yet whose attachments we don't want to lose, often find it difficult to accept our lesbian families and our decisions to have children. Our children may well want to have contact or relationships with their fathers (in the event that they are known and can be located). We need to establish and protect the rights of partners of lesbians who may not be biological parents of the child, but who may be parents in every other sense of the word. And what do we do when a known donor who, after the baby is born, has a change of heart and wants more of a relationship with the child than was his original intention? These are all real issues that have and will continue to come up.

In addition to creating a new option for lesbians and other women who find that donor insemination is, for them, the best way to have children, it has been reassuring and exciting that a variety of support systems have grown right along with the numbers of women who have children by this method. Several feminist attorneys around the country have acquired considerable information about legal implications of donor insemination and have provided invaluable assistance to those of us having children. In many cities, women who have children or want to have children by donor insemination have started information and support groups.

The groups provide as much benefit for the children as for the mothers. Even though the children are still fairly young, they are growing up knowing that there are other children whose families are like theirs.

I think it is unwise and dishonest to gloss over many of the complex issues involved in donor insemination. Serious consideration and care must be taken for our children as they grow. Our children are not subjects in a social experiment but human beings with feelings whom we deeply love. There needs to be continuous support for mothers and for the rights of non-biological mothers who are part of the children's lives. We need to recognize the interests of the donors. But in the midst of trying to carve out new ways of doing things in an ethical way, we should also take joy in the fact that we have broken new ground. We have created new and important life choices for many people. We have taken back a little more of what is rightly ours—the chance to make decisions about how we will live our lives.

NOTES

1. Information about the Sperm Bank of Northern California was obtained in a personal communication with Laura Brown, Director of the Oakland Feminist Women's Health Center. The services of the Sperm Bank can be made available to interested people living outside the Northern California area. For more information write: Sperm Bank of Northern California, 2930 McClure Street, Oakland, CA 94609.

2. Facts about the Milwaukee, Wisconsin, donor insemination case were provided in a personal communication with Dan Wikler, Program in Medical Ethics, Center for Health Sciences, University of Wisconsin.

Further Questions

1. Donor insemination produces a separation between sex and reproduction, because the former is not necessary for the latter. Do you think perceiving them as separate processes, each with its own worth, is a good idea? Does it impair anything in the idea of sex with the aim of procreation that is worth preserving?

2. Does donor insemination undermine the ideal of the traditional family where children are conceived in marriage through sexual intercourse? Would it cause problems not found in a traditional family structure? If so, what problems would it cause?

3. Should children conceived by donor insemination qualify, along with their mothers, for full public assistance benefits? As a taxpayer, would you mind supporting these children and mothers through public assistance?

The Ethics of Surrogacy   X.4A

JONATHAN GLOVER ET AL., THE GLOVER REPORT TO THE EUROPEAN COMMISSION

This chapter of the report discusses some moral questions that arise if any form of surrogate motherhood is permitted.

Reading Questions

1. Suppose you wanted a child but for some reason, could not gestate one biologically. Under what circumstances would you think it morally permissible to have a surrogate mother gestate one for you?
2. Do you think a child is wronged in any way if he is gestated by a surrogate mother? If he is harmed in some way, is he better or worse off than if he had been adopted in a traditional manner?
3. Should potential surrogate mothers be screened? Should potential adoptive couples be screened? If so, in whose interest should such screening take place?

THE TWO CENTRAL QUESTIONS are whether surrogate motherhood is morally acceptable and whether it should be legally permitted. These questions are not identical, but they are related.

If any policy short of a total ban is adopted, the main further questions are these:

Should there be surrogacy contracts? Should they be legally enforceable either when the surrogate breaks the restrictions imposed on her during pregnancy, or when she changes her mind about handing over the child?

Should the contents of contracts be regulated, either to protect the surrogate from exploitation, or to protect the interests of the child?

Should there be screening of surrogate mothers? Possible problem cases include heavy smokers and people with severe psychological problems. They also include the sister or other close relation of the potential parent, who may be particularly likely to volunteer, but whose role might create family problems later.

"The Ethics of Surrogacy." Jonathan Glover, et al., Ethics of New Reproductive Technologies: The Glover Report to the European Commission. *DeKalb: Northern Illinois University Press, 1989. Used with permission of the publisher.*

What is the role of intermediaries, such as doctors, clinics, and agencies? Should there be profit-making agencies?

1. THE CASE FOR SURROGACY

Part of the case is straightforward. Surrogacy relieves childlessness. For women who have had repeated miscarriages, or who suffer from conditions making pregnancy dangerous, surrogacy may be the only hope of having a child.

Another, more problematic, argument appeals to the interests of the child who would not have existed without surrogacy.

Another argument appeals to liberty. Some strong justification is needed for preventing people from bearing children to help their sisters or friends. And a similar strong justification is needed for preventing people freely contracting to do this for someone for money. This argument relates to the legality of surrogacy, but does nothing to show that surrogacy is a good thing in itself. The central case for that has to rest on relieving the burden of childlessness.

2. THE CASE AGAINST SURROGACY

(a) The children: One line of thought appeals to the rights of the child. It appears in the Catholic document issued by the Congregation for the Doctrine of the Faith, which says that surrogacy "offends the dignity and the right of the child to be conceived, carried in the womb, brought into the world, and brought up by his own parents."

This case seems to us not overwhelming. Even if the child has a strong interest in being created sexually, to call this a *right* is to claim that it trumps *any* interests of the childless couple. This requires that being the child of a surrogate is such an indignity that, by comparison, relieving *any* degree of the potential parents' misery is to count for nothing. We have not found the powerful supporting argument this would need.

The objection is made even weaker by a further problem. For the potential child, the alternative to surrogacy may be nonexistence. It seems unlikely that the child will see surrogacy as so bad as to wish he or she had not been born at all. The "right" looks like one the child will later be glad was not respected. It is hard to see the case for giving this supposed interest any weight at all, let alone for saying that it justifies leaving people unwillingly childless.

Another argument appeals to the psychological effects of surrogacy on the child. If the surrogacy is paid for there is a danger that the child will think he or she has been bought. Also, it is sometimes suggested that surrogacy breaks a bond formed by the time of birth. Dr. John Marks, the chairman of the British Medical Association, has said: "By the time a baby is born there is a bond between the mother and the child. With surrogacy you break that bond. You are depriving the child of one natural parent. We think that is wrong" (The *Guardian* May 8, 1987). It is reported that the General Medical Council may ban doctors from involvement in surrogacy. This step has already been taken in West Germany.

The surrogate mother may well feel a bond between herself and the child. But is there reason to believe in any bond in the other direction before birth? Or could this be an illusion created by projecting the mother's feelings on to the foetus? If the child's feelings are a reason against surrogacy, the baby has to have, by the time of birth, highly specific feelings towards the particular woman who bears him. The evidence for this can charitably be described as slight.

Suppose, for the sake of argument, that there is such a bond. It is then undesirable to break it. But, where it is broken, is the child so harmed that it would have been better if he or she had not been born? For this is what banning surrogacy on these grounds seems to imply. We do not have such drastic thoughts about people who are adopted. The British Medical Association's Board of Science is quoted as saying that while adoption may be "the next best thing" for a child facing an uncertain future, any arrangement where a surrogate mother hands over the child "dooms it to second best from the start" (*The Independent,* May 8, 1987). But is it obvious here that no life at all is preferable to "second best"?

(b) Conflicts: The conflicts sometimes arising between the potential parents and the surrogate mother may harm the child, and this is part of the case against surrogacy.

(c) Effects on the family: Perhaps introducing a third party so intimately into the process of having children may weaken the institution of the family. (In West Germany, the report of the Benda Commission considers a legal ban on surrogacy with the exception of surrogacy by relatives.)

(d) The surrogate mother: The position of the surrogate mother varies, according to whether she is bearing a child to help a sister or friend, or has made a commercial arrangement. There is the criticism that surrogacy is an invasion of her bodily integrity. This criticism may be weaker if she willingly agreed than if she was forced into it by money problems. Sometimes she may bitterly regret having agreed to give away the baby. . . . [T]here is [also] a danger of her being exploited. Financial pressures may put her in a weak position to resist contractual conditions which give little weight to her interests.

Another important motive for volunteering to act as a surrogate seems to be the desire for friendship with the parents-to-be. As this is usually exactly what the parents-to-be do *not* want, it is an illusory objective. She wants friendship: she is treated as a provider of a service, and afterwards dismissed.

3. POLICY

Is surrogacy something to encourage or not? The Warnock Committee said, "The question of surrogacy presented us with some of the most difficult problems we encountered." We found this too. The central issue is the conflict between the interests of the childless couple and those of the surrogate mother.

Some members of the committee are opposed to surrogacy in principle, because of what the practice does to the surrogate mother. The invasion of her bodily integrity, the disappointment of any hopes for friendship with the family who receive the child, the psychological trauma of giving up the baby, and the possibility of regrets for the rest of her life, add up to a very strong case against surrogacy. There is also the possibility of ill effects on the surrogate's own family, particularly on her own children.

Other members of the committee share these anxieties, but are sufficiently impressed by the needs of infertile couples to think that some cases of surrogacy are beneficial. Whichever view we take, we agree both that surrogacy should not be illegal, and also that, if it *does* take place, it should be subject to certain restrictions.

A general legal ban would be unenforceable. Moreover there is a powerful consideration which also influenced the Warnock Committee: the birth of a child should not have a taint of criminality. We recommend that surrogacy should not itself be illegal.

The surrogate mother is notably vulnerable, and any acceptable arrangements for surrogacy must give her a lot of protection. The child should be protected against prolonged battles between the surrogate and the potential parents. These two considerations support restrictions which may in practice greatly reduce the frequency of surrogacy. While this will leave some infertile couples childless, we think this is a lesser evil than the ones such restrictions would be designed to avert.

4. AGENCIES AND REGULATION

Sometimes surrogates will be relations or friends helping people they know well. But there is a case for the option of making arrangements through a clinic or other agency. They will have more experience of the problems than the couple or the surrogate mother. They will know what should go into a contract. And they will be able to carry out any necessary screening either of couples or of surrogate mothers.

Where these agencies are public, they should operate on guidelines open to public inspection. If there are private agencies, they should be publicly inspected and licensed.

5. MAKING CONTRACTS UNENFORCEABLE AGAINST THE SURROGATE MOTHER

We think that the surrogate mother should remain free to decide for herself whether or not to have an abortion. And we think she should not be forced to hand over the child against her will. In these respects at least, any contract should not be enforceable against her.

This is mainly to protect the surrogate mother. But there are other reasons. If the contract were enforceable, a pregnant surrogate who started to change her mind might become depressed. This could be bad for the child. If a contract were enforced against a reluctant surrogate the couple might feel guilty, which could interfere with their relationship with the child. If the child found out (as would be likely in a system not based on anonymity), the relationship might again be disturbed.

6. THE CLAIMS OF THE BIOLOGICAL FATHER

This policy of unenforceability supports the claims of the surrogate mother against those of the biological father. In cases of dispute over the baby, some think that the father's right to his child should not be overridden. There are two main arguments for this: he has a right arising out of a contract freely entered into by the surrogate, and he *is* the biological father.

(a) The contract: This is partly a claim abut a legal right. In many countries, such contracts

are unenforceable, and so this legal right does not exist. The issue is whether they *should* be enforceable, and this cannot be settled by citing what the law happens to be.

Most legal systems refuse to recognize some kinds of contract, such as those in which people sell themselves into slavery. This refusal is a restriction of liberty: It excludes people's freedom to bind themselves in certain ways. It is a protection against people doing themselves great harm or giving away vital liberties. It is a form of "paternalism": restricting people's freedom in their own interests.

Some are opposed to all paternalism. Too much paternalism can be a danger to liberty. But the case of contracting to become a slave illustrates the difficulty of excluding all paternalism. Stopping people making enforceable slavery contracts protects one of their vital interests. It also protects far more freedom than it takes away. We think that these reasons (as well as the other nonpaternalist ones) apply to making surrogacy contracts unenforceable.

(b) The biological link: The other basis for the father's claim to take the child from the reluctant surrogate mother is that he *is* the biological father. This case also seems to us not decisive. The father is genetically linked to the child. But so, in one form of surrogacy, is the surrogate mother. And even in the other form, "womb leasing," she has still carried and given birth to the child. This too is a biological link, and often creates, on her side at least, an emotional link as well.

The father's interests are not negligible here. Because of the genetic link, he is likely to care a lot about the child. And, if the surrogate changes her mind, he and his partner will have the anguish of childlessness compounded by disappointed expectations.

But it is not obvious that, of the biological bonds, the genetic one should trump the others to give the father a right to the child. And, severe as the couple's disappointment is, we do not think it justifies forcing a woman to endure the anguish of being made to give up the child she has given birth to.

The possibility of the surrogate mother changing her mind should be accepted by the couple as one of the risks of this way of trying to overcome childlessness when embarking on it.

7. PROTECTING THE CHILD

If there is to be surrogate motherhood, the child needs protection from emotional damage. In every way things should be as normal for the child as possible. This is one reason why surrogacy should not be illegal. It cannot be good for children to know that their social parents or surrogate mother committed a crime through having them.

It is also surely bad for children if there are long legal battles over them. And even if the battles lasted only for a few months, the insecurity in the (social or surrogate) mother looking after the child could interfere with bonding, as would any transfer which then took place. These are further reasons for making the contract unenforceable in this respect against the surrogate mother. Her decision to keep the baby should be final.

But they are equally reasons for making her decision *not* to keep the baby final. Once the baby has been voluntarily handed over to the social parents, further upheavals around the child should be avoided. The social parents should be recognized as the legal parents beyond further challenge, even if the surrogate later changes her mind.

The surrogate mother should normally be regarded as having no right to a further relationship with the child who has been handed over. Visits or other contact could undermine the child's security about who his or her parents are. There are special cases, as when a relation or close friend acts as a surrogate. But, in other cases, we think that the child's interests require severance of the relationship to be the norm. (Though there is a case for the child having the right to be told on reaching maturity the identity of the surrogate mother. The case is like that for nonanonymity of donors already discussed.)

8. SCREENING POTENTIAL SOCIAL PARENTS

No individual should be put in the position of breaking the law by becoming a surrogate or by contracting with one. But agencies could adopt a policy of screening potential surrogates or potential parents, and it would be possible for *them* to be legally required to do so.

We think there should be a background presumption that reproductive help should be available to those who request it, subject to competing claims for resources, and with certain exceptions where special reasons apply. But, because of the special problems of surrogacy, particularly for the surrogate mother, we think that agencies should only help those who cannot have children in other ways, or where serious medical risks are involved. The desire not to interrupt a career does not seem sufficient reason for imposing the risk and traumas of surrogacy on another woman, even if she is prepared to accept them.

9. SCREENING POTENTIAL SURROGATE MOTHERS

There is now little screening of surrogate mothers. They are not easily found, and screening may seem just a way of reducing their number still further. But some screening, or at least counseling, would be in the interest of everyone. It is possible, for instance, that women who have been very promiscuous, or who have had a long series of unstable relationships, or who have been abandoned in childhood, are more likely to resist giving up the baby, or else to suffer from extreme depression over it.

Some screening would be on behalf of the potential surrogate herself. Apart from the psychological aspects, she may want to know that pregnancy will not carry any special health risks for her. The screening period might give her time to think about her decision, and about its implications for herself and for her family. The agency should provide her with counseling help during this period.

Some screening should be on behalf of the child. Heavy smokers, alcoholics, and other addicts may harm the child and these conditions should be grounds for exclusion. (*Grounds* for exclusion: Where surrogates are very hard to obtain, these grounds may *perhaps* be overridden. From the later perspective of the child, it may be better to have run those risks, or even to have suffered some harm, than not to have been born at all.)

Some screening should be on behalf of the potential parents. The kind of history linked with the surrogate changing her mind about handing over the baby seems a reasonable ground for exclusion. There are other grounds. In one case, a surrogate repeatedly extracted more money from the potential parents, threatening to kill herself unless they paid (Noel Keane and Denis Breo: *The Surrogate Mother,* New York, 1981, quoted in Peter Singer and Deane Wells: *The Reproduction Revolution,* Oxford, 1984, pages 116–117). No doubt it is hard to pick up this sort of thing in advance. but, where there is reason to suspect it, the potential parents would have reason to complain if the agency accepted the woman as a surrogate.

There are obviously difficulties in predicting who will be a good surrogate mother. Those rejected by agencies would be free to be surrogates by private arrangement. These comments about screening are intended as general guidance. Good agencies will revise their criteria in the light of their experience, and in the light of evidence collected in studies of other cases.

Further Questions

1. Suppose there were a legal ban on surrogacy and suppose, realistically, that it was not completely enforceable. Would children then illegally born of surrogates bear too much taint of criminality?

2. Is there ever sufficient reason for a biological father's claim to a child to take precedence over that of the surrogate mother in case both want the child after it is born?

3. Should you resort to surrogacy only if there is no other way you can have a child? Should you be required to have a partner if you are going to raise a child gestated by someone else?

X.4B   Having Children and the Market Economy

JONATHAN GLOVER ET AL., THE GLOVER REPORT TO THE EUROPEAN COMMISSION

This seventh chapter of the report discusses payment of surrogate mothers and semen donors and also whether there should be commercial agencies ("third parties") for surrogacy.

"Having Children and the Market Economy." Jonathan Glover et al. Ethics of New Reproductive Technologies: The Glover Report to the European Commission. *DeKalb: Northern Illinois University Press, 1989. Used with permission of the publisher.*

Reading Questions

1. If you were (or are) a man, would you consider donating semen to a sperm bank? Would whether you were paid influence your decision? If you were (or are) a woman, are there circumstances under which you would become an egg donor?
2. Suppose surrogate mothers were paid at an hourly rate better than that of a secretary. Would such payment make surrogates more or less exploited than if they were unpaid?
3. Would you consider a ban on sperm donation or surrogate motherhood a restriction on someone's liberty of earning a living in the way he or she chooses? If so, do you think these practices should be banned anyway because they exploit those who choose to engage in them?

WITH BOTH SURROGATE MOTHERS and semen donors, the question of payment comes up. We discuss these issues briefly, and then turn to the more important issue of whether there should be commercial agencies for surrogacy.

These may be straightforward questions about efficiency, to be answered by seeing what works best. In part, they are questions of that sort. But, entangled with those pragmatic problems are some deeper issues about what sort of society we want.

1. SEMEN DONORS

... [S]ome hospitals and sperm banks pay semen donors, while egg donors are rarely paid. Is it better when semen donors are also unpaid?

The case for payment is mainly that it brings in more donors, as the Necker Hospital found when it stopped paying. Payment also gives some recognition to the donor. And it is a way of ending the donor's involvement.

On the other hand, as with blood donation, payment may lead unsuitable people to apply, lying about their medical history (perhaps one of AIDS) in order to be paid (Richard Titmuss: *The Gift Relationship, From Human Blood to Social Policy,* London, 1970, chapter eight). And, although Necker Hospital found that unpaid donors were fewer, they are more diverse in their socioeconomic background.

There are further arguments against payment. By giving donors a "reason" to account for their donation, it may incline them to think less about the implications of what they are doing. Is our aim to obtain the maximum number of donors, no matter how, or do we want men to think about what they are going to do before they do it? Semen donation may mean nothing to the traditional anonymous medical student, but he can be motivated by payment. On the other hand, a man who has himself either experienced difficulty in having children or who has had an infertile couple in his family or among his friends, may be someone to whom donation makes very good sense. He may find reasons for giving semen without having to be motivated by money.

Payment also deprives donors of the chance of doing something purely for others. Blood donors sometimes say that paying for blood would debase the value of the act and make it feel less worth doing. Payment and non-payment seem to lead to two different conceptions of donation.

Our inclinations are strongly towards a non-commercial ethos for donation, and we are impressed by the ethos of some of the systems developed in France. An economic case is always easy to understand, as is a case based on a quantifiable change, such as a larger or smaller number of donors. But policies adopted for such reasons can have more subtle side-effects, often of a kind not easily measurable. The issues we are concerned with are not only about easily measurable effects, such as how many infertile couples are enabled to have children. What matters most is how these techniques can be used to enrich people and their relationships, rather than diminish them. The *central* focus of this report is not technology but people. And so we think it right to stress the way payment affects the psychology of donation, turning what could be an enriching act of altruism into an act more like selling an old motorbike. Every time we institutionalize the commercial solution rather than the altruistic one, we take a small step further towards a society where more relationships are permeated by the motive of economic gain.

Our preference for a non-commercial ethos is strong, both for semen donation and for egg donation. But we do not think the case against commercialism is powerful enough to justify a legal ban, which would anyway probably be unenforceable. We would like to see strong public campaigns for altruistic donation, bringing the plight of the infertile to the front of public attention. Only after such a policy has been tried should the market be thought of as a last resort policy to fill any remaining gap.

2. SHOULD SURROGATE MOTHERS BE PAID?

Surrogate mothers do something really important for the potential parents. Unlike semen donation, surrogacy involves a lot of inconvenience and some risk. Apart from women helping sisters or friends, unpaid surrogates are hard to find.

If surrogacy is to be available to childless people without altruistic sisters, payment may be hard to escape. There is again the question of whether we want to encourage the spread of the market into this area. Payment brings the danger of poor women being exploited. They may be pressured into surrogacy by their need of money. One way of making it less exploitative (apart from making the contract unenforceable, and excluding people who have health risks) would be to make the payment substantial. But, on the other hand, high pay may make it even harder for a woman needing money to resist.

In one way, the higher the pay the less the exploitation. But commercialism, with this pressure on poor women to embark on surrogacy they may later regret, seems a greater evil. It is better for fees to surrogates to be nonexistent or kept to a minimum. This may reduce drastically the number of surrogate mothers. That seems to us more acceptable than the commercial alternative. The payment of surrogates should not be illegal, as such a law would be unenforceable, and because of the need to avoid a child's birth being tainted with criminality.

3. COMMERCIAL AGENCIES

The payment of sperm donors or of surrogate mothers at all lets market forces into childbearing. But it does so in a small way. Commercial agencies create much more of the ethos of the market.

Some of the arguments against market forces appeal to the public interest. For instance monetary incentives may encourage medically unsuitable people to sell blood or semen. And, in the present context, where would-be parents have paid a surrogacy agency, they may be more willing to engage in lengthy legal battles, even at considerable psychological cost to the child.

There is a case against banning commercial surrogacy agencies. A ban restricts people's freedom to earn their living in the way they choose. It also restricts the freedom of others by making surrogacy less available. If the agencies meet a demand, making them illegal will frustrate it. If there is no demand, making them illegal may be said to be unnecessary, on the grounds that they will go out of business anyway.

The suggestion that, if there is no demand for their services, the agencies will go out of business is naive. Commercial organizations can often create a demand for previously unwanted products. (An issue then arises as to whether such supplier-induced demands should be taken less seriously than others.) But the central argument is the appeal to liberty. It is true that banning commercial agencies is a restriction of liberty. But so is any law. And any law is either unnecessary or else stops some people doing what they want to do. There is a presumption against restricting liberty. Are there reasons powerful enough to justify doing so in this case?

A major argument for banning commercial agencies is to protect surrogate mothers from being exploited. But, desirable as this is, it might be done by regulating how agencies operate. Regulation is still an interference with the market, but one easy to justify on principles similar to those used to prevent companies from operating factories that are unhealthy or unsafe to work in.

Many who oppose the extension of the market into this area would not be satisfied with commercial agencies being subject to controls to prevent exploitation. The opposition is not based only on worries about exploitation, but also stems from the idea that childbearing is simply not something to which buying and selling are appropriate.

There are two main arguments for limiting the market. One is based on equal access to certain basic goods. The other is linked to a preference for a society not dominated by money values.

(a) Equal access to basic goods: It is widely accepted that the services of the police should not depend on the citizen's ability to pay. Some of the arguments for non-commercial health systems have the same basis. Basic medical care and protection against crime are held to be such fundamental interests that they should be equally available to rich and poor. One argument against commercializing the new reproductive techniques would place help necessary for having children in this category of fundamental interests.

(b) Limiting the dominance of money values: Money is only a means of exchange for goods and services. But the dominance of money transactions can affect the values of a society, by making people less inclined to unpaid acts of altruism. And a society can be dominated by money in a different way: Wealth or income can increasingly colour people's relationships.

4. THE EXCLUSION OF COMMERCIAL AGENCIES

The case for equal access to basic goods carries some weight against commercial surrogacy agencies. But it could be questioned whether this kind of help with having children qualifies as one of the basic goods where money should be irrelevant. It would be perfectly consistent to think that essential medical treatment should be available equally, but to deny that this held for surrogacy.

The stronger argument seems to be that based on resisting the encroachments of commerce on the intimate relationships of parenthood. Even here the case can be questioned. If commercial agencies are banned, surrogacy will often be arranged through a non-commercial agency. And the intimate relationships to be protected are between man and woman, parents and children, not those with the non-commercial agency. So why should a commercial agency make any difference?

The difference is a matter of the way commercialism changes the way we see the things that are bought and sold. Almost inevitably they come to be seen as commodities. And some aspects of life seem particularly inappropriate to the market. Having children may be seen in this way because it is such a central part of our lives, and because it is bound up with such deep and intimate experiences. Comparisons with prostitution are made when surrogacy is commercialized.

Intimate and commercial relationships do not fit together easily. In relationships between friends or lovers, or in families (at least as they should be), we confront each other without calculating commercial gain, and do not assess each other mainly in terms of wealth. In families and between friends, gifts are more common than sales. This antagonism between intimacy and commerce is part of the reason why prostitution does not seem the ideal model of sexual partnership, and why other forms of commercialization of sex are tolerated rather than admired.

No doubt it is impossible to prevent individuals paying others for sex; but, if a large company set up as an agency for prostitution this might seem an unacceptable further step towards turning sex into a commodity. In a similar way, commercial surrogacy agencies can be seen as contributing to a society in which parenthood is seen as another commodity. And, because relationships are partly constituted by how they are seen, this threatens an unwelcome change in the relationship itself.

Because the commercialization of intimate relationships seems something to resist, and because restricting the liberty of commercial organizations seems less intrusive than restricting the liberty of individuals, we do not favour permitting commercial agencies for surrogacy.

The question of commercial agencies may be one of the few we have considered where there is room for a distinctively Western European approach. In the United States, there is a strong presumption in favour of the free market, while the countries of Eastern Europe operate with a strong presumption against it. Generalizations about people living in large geographical regions are obviously suspect, but in Western Europe there does seem to be a strong current of opinion favouring a society between these extremes. We think that the policy of discouraging payment to surrogates without imposing a legal ban, and of banning commercial agencies, fits this approach.

Further Questions

1. Is producing a child a basic human necessity, like the need for basic health care and protection against crime, so that new forms of reproduction, such as surrogate motherhood, should be available to as many persons as possible?

2. If a large company set up an agency for prostitution, would this be a step toward turning sex into a commodity? Do the same considerations apply to setting up large surrogacy agencies; i.e., would they tend to turn reproduction into a commodity?

3. If commercial surrogacy (agencies and exchange of money) is prohibited, would unpaid, private surrogacy arrangements be morally permissible?

Further Readings for Part X: Reproduction: Hi Tech/Low Tech

James Aiman. *Infertility: Diagnosis and Management* (New York, NY: Springer Verlag, 1984).

Rita Arditti, Renate Duelli Klein and Shelley Minden, eds. *Test-Tube Women: What Future for Motherhood?* (Boston, MA: Pandora Press, Routledge & Kegan Paul, 1984).

Michael D. Bayles. *Reproductive Ethics* (Englewood Cliffs, NJ: Prentice-Hall, 1984).

David R. Bomham, Maureen E. Dalton, and Jennifer C. Jackson, eds. *Philosophical Ethics in Reproductive Medicine* (New York, NY: Manchester University Press, 1990).

Thomas Buckley and Alma Gottlieb, ed. *Blood Magic: The Anthropology of Menstruation* (Berkeley, CA: The University of California Press, 1988).

C. O. Carter, ed. *Developments in Human Reproduction and Their Eugenic Implications* (New York, NY: Academic Press, 1983).

Ruth Chadwick, ed. *Ethics, Reproduction and Genetic Control* (New York, NY: Routledge, 1987).

Gena Corea. *The Mother Machine: Reproductive Technologies from Artificial Insemination to Artificial Womb* (New York, NY: Harper & Row, 1985).

Claudia Dreifus, ed. *Seizing Our Bodies: The Politics of Women's Health* (New York, NY: Vintage, Random House, 1977).

Anthony Dyson and John Harris, eds. *Experiments on Embryos* (New York, NY: Routledge, 1990).

Barbara Ehrenreich and Deidre English. *For Her Own Good: 150 Years of the Experts' Advice to Women* (Garden City, NY: Anchor Books, 1978).

Ellen Frankfort. *Vaginal Politics* (New York, NY: Quadrangle Books, 1972). Who controls women's reproductive systems?

Jonathan Glover et al. *Ethics of New Reproductive Technologies: The Glover Report to the European Commission* (DeKalb, IL: Northern Illinois Press, 1989). Especially recommended for its multifaceted, lucid approach to these issues.

Germaine Geer. *Sex and Destiny: The Politics of Human Fertility* (London: Secker and Warburg, 1984).

Helen B. Holmes. *The Custom-Made Child? Women-Centered Perspectives* (Clifton, NJ: Humana Press, 1981).

Sheila Kitzinger. *The Experience of Childbirth* (Harmondsworth, England: Penguin, 1974).

———. *The Complete Book of Pregnancy and Childbirth* (New York, NY: Alfred A. Knopf, 1980).

Miriam D. Mazor and Harriet F. Simon, eds. *Infertility: Medical, Emotional and Social Considerations* (New York, NY: Human Sciences Press, 1984).

Mary O'Brien. *The Politics of Reproduction* (London: Routledge & Kegan Paul, 1981).

Oliver O'Donovan. *Begotten or Made?* (New York, NY: Oxford: The Clarendon Press, 1984). Includes discussion of transsexual surgery.

Christine Overall. *Ethics and Human Reproduction: A Feminist Analysis* (Boston, MA: Unwin Hyman, 1987).

———, ed. *The Future of Human Reproduction* (Toronto, ON: The Women's Press, 1989). Examination of issues relating to the development of the new reproductive technologies.

Laura M. Purdy. *Reproducing Persons: Issues in Feminist Bioethics* (Ithaca, NY: Cornell University Press, 1996). Feminist perspectives on pregnancy, abortion, and the new reproductive technologies.

Helen Roberts, ed. *Women, Health and Reproduction* (New York, NY: Routledge & Kegan Paul, 1981).

Shelly Romalis, ed. *Childbirth: Alternatives to Medical Control* (Austin, TX: University of Texas Press, 1981).

Barbara Katz Rothman. *Giving Birth: Alternatives in Childbirth* (Harmondsworth, England: Penguin, 1984).

Joan Rothschild, ed. *Machine Ex Dea: Feminist Perspectives on Technology* (New York, NY: Pergamon Press, 1983).

Jocelynne A. Scutt, ed. *The Baby Machine: Reproductive Technology and the Commercialization of Motherhood* (London: The Merlin Press, 1990). Are women better or worse off with new reproductive technology?

William Walters and Peter Singer, eds. *Test Tube Babies: A Guide to Moral Questions, Present Techniques and Future Possibilities* (New York, NY: Oxford University Press, 1982).

Mary Warnock. *Question of Life: The Warnock Report on Human Fertilization and Embryology* (New York, NY: Basil Blackwell, 1984).

Mary Anne Warren. *Gendercide: The Implications of Sex Selection* (Totawa, NJ: Rowman and Allenheld, 1985). Will female fetuses be selected out?

Don P. Wolf and Martin M. Quigley. *Human In Vitro Fertilization and Embryo Transfer* (New York, NY: Plenum Press, 1984).

Joan Offerman Zuckerberg, ed. *Gender in Transition: A New Frontier* (New York, NY: Plenum Medical Book Co., 1989). New reproductive technologies strike at the heart of gender.

Suggested Moral of Part X

There are several ways of thinking about a woman's biological function in reproduction. One is that gestation and delivery are a source of esteem and self-worth. Therefore a woman should retain control over these processes. Allowing others (men, lawyers, doctors, and so on) to make decisions instead can cause self-alienation. However, there are other persons to consider in such decisions besides the woman herself. An undamaged baby, even if elaborate technology is required, is essential to a successful delivery. Moreover, new techniques that make surrogacy possible, with or without commercialization, raise new questions about a woman's using her reproductive capacity in the service of others, infertile couples in particular. Is putting the welfare of others ahead of her own in the area of reproduction yet another way in which a woman can suffer from oppression? If women are viewed as so much reproductive plumbing, this perspective and its consequences would be a form of oppression. However, it is not clear that new reproductive technology, or consideration of persons other than the woman herself, oppresses women in all cases. No clear moral emerges from Part X. Perhaps in the area of reproduction, technology has progressed faster than has our thinking about its proper use.

Part XI

Raising Children: Mothers and Fathers

Introduction

BEARING CHILDREN (GESTATION AND DELIVERY) and raising them (accompanying them from the delivery room to adulthood) are two separate domains, as contracted motherhood (surrogate motherhood), discussed in Part X, illustrated. Part X discussed the circumstances under which women should bear children. The writers in this part focus on the raising of children and the division of labor between the mother and father.

Stevens discusses *Marianismo,* the culture of the mother, in Latin America; Hochschild describes the second shift of work that many employed women must put in at home; Coltrane finds three different family roles for Chicano men; Hays explains intensive mothering; Collins discusses some of the features of black motherhood; Jenson recounts her years as a welfare mother; Crean describes some of the pressures that men bring upon women in child custody disputes.

XI.1   *Marianismo:* The Other Face of *Machismo* in Latin America

EVELYN P. STEVENS

Evelyn P. Stevens reports on *marianismo,* the feminine counterpart of *machismo* in Hispanic cultures, especially in Latin America. This secular set of beliefs and practices portrays the ideal woman as a mother, morally superior, patient, and with an infinite capacity for humility and self-sacrifice. The ideal of *marianismo* fits nicely with the ideal of *machismo* (aggressiveness, intransigence, and arrogance) in men and gives women some practical advantages that many are loathe to give up.

Stevens lived much of her life in Latin America. Her 1965 article on "machismo" in the *Western Political Quarterly* was the first scholarly treatment of this subject in U.S. social science literature.

Reading Questions

1. Is there a prevailing belief (even outside of Hispanic cultures) that women are expected to be patient, humble, and self-sacrificing with men, much as a mother would be with little boys? Is this expectation advantageous or disadvantageous to particular women? Illustrate your answer with some examples.
2. Is *marianismo* a beneficial force in keeping women out of the work place in times of high unemployment, and in giving a woman who does enter the work place a chance to tend a sick child and an opportunity to get low-cost care from her extended family? Are there disadvantages for a woman in being perceived primarily as a mother?

. . . IN THE INTEREST OF CLARITY in the following discussion, the term *machismo* will be used to designate a way of orientation which can be most succinctly described as the cult of virility. The chief characteristics of this cult are exaggerated aggressiveness and intransigence in male-to-male interpersonal relationships and arrogance and sexual aggression in male-to-female relationships.[1]

It has only been in the quite recent past that any attention has been focused on the other face of the problem. Women generally have maintained a discreet reserve with respect to the subject of *marianismo,* possibly because a very large segment of that group fears that publicity would endanger their prerogatives. A short time ago, however, a handful of male writers began to focus on this heretofore neglected pattern of attitudes and behavior. In this way, the term *hembrismo* ("femaleism") has been introduced by one observer, while *feminismo* has been used by another.

Marianismo is just as prevalent as *machismo* but it is less understood by Latin Americans themselves and almost unknown to foreigners.

Abridged and reprinted from "Marianismo: The Other Face of Machismo in Latin America," by Evelyn P. Stevens in Female and Male in Latin America: Essays, Ann Pescatello, editor, by permission of the University of Pittsburgh Press. © 1973 by University of Pittsburgh Press.

It is the cult of feminine spiritual superiority, which teaches that women are semidivine, morally superior to and spiritually stronger than men. It is this pattern of attitudes and behavior that will be the principal focus of attention in the present paper, but it will often be necessary to refer to the dynamic interplay between the two phenomena.

Both *marianismo* and *machismo* are New World phenomena with ancient roots in Old World cultures. Many of the contributing elements can be found even today in Italy and Spain, but the fully developed syndrome occurs only in Latin America.[3] . . .

Although all mestizo social classes are permeated with *machismo* and *marianismo* characteristics, the same statement does not hold true with respect to other ethnic groupings. Indigenous communities, while patriarchal in structure and value orientations, do not seem to share the *machismo-marianismo* attitudes as long as they retain their cultural "purity."

Marianismo is not a religious practice, although the word *marianismo* is sometimes used to describe a movement within the Roman Catholic church which has as its object the special veneration of the figure of the Virgin Mary. That cult, as it is practiced throughout the world, is rooted in very ancient religious observances that have evolved within the church itself, at times with the enthusiastic endorsement of ecclesiastical authorities and at other times with at least the tolerance of those authorities.

Marianismo, or *Mariology,* as most theologians prefer to call the religious movement, has provided a central figure and a convenient set of assumptions around which the practitioners of *marianismo* have erected a secular edifice of beliefs and practices related to the position of women in society. It is that edifice, rather than the religious phenomenon, which is the object of this study.

The roots of *marianismo* are both deep and widespread, springing apparently from primitive awe at woman's ability to produce a live human creature from inside her own body. This is the aspect of femininity which attracted the attention of the early artists who fashioned the Gravettian "venuses" of the upper Paleolithic era. In those small crude sculptures, the figures have enormous breasts and protruding bellies, as though they were pregnant. To the early men and women who posed the ontological question in its simplest terms—"Where did I come from?"—the answer must also have seemed simple, and on the basis of circumstantial evidence, woman was celebrated as being the sole source of life.

Archaeological research points to southern Russia, to the region around the Caspian Sea, as the source of inspiration for the cult of the mother goddess as we know it in the Western world, but not long afterward traces began to appear in the Fertile Crescent and the Indus Valley, as well as in Crete and the area around the Aegean Sea. During these early stages the female figure appeared alone, unaccompanied by any male figure, and for this reason she is sometimes described as the "unmarried mother."[4] . . .

Just how the excessive veneration of women became a distinguishing feature of Latin American secular society is difficult to determine. Two points are clear, however: This veneration parallels that which is rendered to the religious figure of the Virgin Mary, and the secular aspect is different both qualitatively and quantitatively from the attitude toward women which prevails in those very European nations where the religious cult is most prevalent.

Latin American mestizo cultures—from the Rio Grande to the Tierra del Fuego—exhibit a well-defined pattern of beliefs and behavior centered on popular acceptance of a stereotype of the ideal woman. This stereotype, like its *macho* counterpart, is ubiquitous in every social class. There is near universal agreement on what a "real woman" is like and how she should act. Among the characteristics of this ideal are semidivinity, moral superiority, and spiritual strength. This spiritual strength engenders abnegation, that is, an infinite capacity for humility and sacrifice. No self-denial is too great for the Latin American woman, no limit can be divined to her vast store of patience with the men of her world.[5] Although she may be sharp with her daughters—and even cruel to her daughters-in-law—she is and must be complaisant toward her own mother and her mother-in-law for they, too, are reincarnations of the great mother. She is also submissive to the demands of the men: husbands, sons, fathers, brothers.[6]

Beneath the submissiveness, however, lies the strength of her conviction—shared by the entire society—that men must be humored, for after all, everyone knows that they are *como niños* (like little boys) whose intemperance, foolishness, and obstinacy must be forgiven because "they can't help the way they are." These attitudes are expressed with admirable clarity by the editor of a fashionable women's magazine in Chile. When asked, "Is there any Chilean woman whom you particularly admire?" she answered, "Sincerely, I would mention a humble woman from the slums who did our laundry. She had ten children, and her husband spent his time drunk and out of work. She took in washing and ironing, and gave her children a good start in life. She is the typical Chilean woman of a [certain] sector of our society. She struggles valiantly until the end."[7]

But to the unalterable imperfection of men is attributable another characteristic of Latin American women: their sadness. They know that male sinfulness dooms the entire sex to a prolonged stay in purgatory after death, and even the most diligent prayerfulness of loving female relatives can succeed in sparing them only a few millennia of torture.

The sadness is evidenced in another highly visible characteristic of women. Custom dictates that upon the death of a member of her family, a woman shall adopt a distinctive mourning habit. The periods of mourning and the types of habit are rigidly prescribed. The death of a parent or husband requires lifetime full mourning: inner and outer clothing of solid black, unrelieved by even a white handkerchief. Deaths of brothers, sisters, aunts, and uncles require full mourning for three years, and those of more distant relatives require periods varying from three months to a year. After each period of full mourning ensues a prescribed period of "half-mourning" during which the grieving woman may at first wear touches of white with her black clothes, graduating with the passage of time to gray and lavender dresses.

Mourning is not simply a matter of dress. The affected person must also "show respect" for the deceased by refraining from any outward manifestation of happiness or joviality and to deny herself the company of others who may legitimately indulge in levity. This means abstention from attending parties, going to the cinema, or even watching television. Purists insist that cultural events such as concerts and lectures also fall under the ban.

Of course, these rules are supposed also to apply to men, but as "everybody knows" that they do not possess the spiritual stamina to endure such rigors, they usually render only token compliance with custom, often reduced to the wearing of a black armband for a short period. Although during mourning periods their women-ruled households are gloomy places, their escape to more joyful surroundings is condoned and often encouraged. Mistresses and other female companions "by the left" are not required to mourn.[8]

By the age of thirty-five, there are few women who have escaped the experience of at least a short period of mourning and by forty-five a large majority of women are destined to wear black for the rest of their lives. It is thus in the woman of middle age that we finally see all of the characteristics of full-blown *marianismo* coming into majestic flower. The author is familiar with the rather extreme case of a reputedly saintly Puerto Rican woman who had been widowed in her early twenties and who boasted that she had not attended the cinema since then, had never seen a television program, and had refused to pass the house in which her husband had died. Such exemplary devotion made the woman an object of general admiration, an example held up to the younger generation of more frivolous females.

As a result of this usage, the image of the Latin American woman is almost indistinguishable from the classic religious figure of the *mater dolorosa,* the tear-drenched mother who mourns for her lost son. The precursor of that figure can be found in the myths of many pre-Christian Mediterranean cultures: the earth goddess who laments the seasonal disappearance of her son and who sorrowfully searches for him until the return of spring restores him to her.[9]

Does this mean that all Latin American women conform to the stereotype prescribed by *marianismo?* Obviously not; as in most human societies, individual behavior often deviates widely from the ideal. But the image of the black-clad mantilla-draped figure, kneeling before the altar, rosary in hand, praying for the souls of her sinful menfolk, dominates the television and cinema screens, the radio programs, and the popular literature, as well as the oral tradition of the whole culture area. This is Latin America's chief export product, according to one native wit.[10]

The same culture provides an alternate model in the image of the "bad woman" who flaunts custom and persists in enjoying herself. Interestingly enough, this kind of individual is thought not be a "real woman." By publicly deviating from the prescribed norm, she has divested herself of precisely those attributes considered most characteristically feminine and in the process has become somewhat masculine.

This brings us to the question of sexual behavior and here, too, as might be expected, practice frequently deviates from prescription. The ideal dictates not only premarital chastity for all women but postnuptial frigidity. "Good" women do not enjoy coitus: they endure it when the duties of matrimony require it. A rich lexicon of circumlocutions is available to "real" women who find it necessary to refer to sexual intercourse in speaking with their priest, their physician, or other trusted confidant. "*Le hice el servicio,*" they may say ("I did him [my husband] the service").[11]

The norm of premarital chastity is confined principally to the urban and provincial middle class, as consensual unions predominate among peasants and urban slum dwellers. Nubility and sexual activity are frequently almost simultaneous events, although the latter occasionally precedes the former.[12]

Even in the middle- and upper-class society, norms of sexual behavior are often disregarded in practice. Premarital chastity is still highly prized, and many Latin American men take an unconscionable interest in the integrity of their fiancées' hymens. But the popular refrain, *el que hizo la ley hizo la trampa,* is particularly applicable in this context. A Peruvian woman writes with convincing authority that a large number of socially prominent young women in that country engage in coitus and then have surgical repair of the hymen performed in private hospitals—a practice that goes back at least to fifteenth-century Spain, when the operation was performed by midwives who often acted in the dual capacity of procuresses and mistresses of houses of assignation (see for example the *Tragicomedia de Calixto y Melibea,* the literary classic known popularly as *La Celestina*).[13]

An undetermined number of upper-middle and upper-class young women practice other varieties of sexual activity, calculated to keep the hymen intact. But a girl will usually engage in these variations only with her fiancé, and then largely as a stratagem for maintaining his interest in her until they are married. As long as he feels reasonably certain that his fiancée has not previously engaged in this kind of behavior with another man, a Latin American male may encourage or even insist on her "obliging" him in this way. But he must reassure himself that she is not enjoying it. A Peruvian journalist reveals the male insistence on the fiction of the frigidity of "good" women in such reported remarks as: "So-and-so is a bad woman; once she even made love with her husband in the bathtub," and "American women [*gringas*] are all prostitutes; I know one who *even takes the initiative*" (italics in original).[14]

At first glance, it may seem that these norms are imposed on women by tyrannical men—"male chauvinists," as contemporary English-speaking feminists would call them. But this assumption requires careful scrutiny, especially when it is remembered that during the preschool years the socialization of boys takes place almost entirely through the medium of women: mother, sisters, widowed or spinster aunts who live under one roof as part of the extended family, and female servants. From the women in the family a boy absorbs the attitudinal norms appropriate for his social class and from the servants, when he reaches adolescence—or often even before—he picks up the principal store of behavioral expertise which will suffice him in adult life. It is common practice for a prudent middle-class mestizo mother of a pubescent boy to hire a young female servant for general housework "and other duties," the latter expression being a euphemism for initiating the boy into adult heterosexual experience. "On such creatures," comments the writer previously cited, "a man lavishes his store of honorable semen and his Christian contempt."[15]

At this juncture it may be useful to ask ourselves a question suggested by the apparent contradiction posed by the foregoing material. On the one hand, our Latin American informants paint us a picture of the ideal woman which would inspire pity in the most sanguine observer. Woman's lot seems to be compounded of sexual frustration, intellectual stagnation, and political futility in a "repressive and *machista* society."[16] On the other hand, it is quite apparent that many women contribute to the perpetuation of the myths which sustain the patterns described. Why would they work against their own interests—if, indeed, they do? Might it not be possible that while employing a distinctive repertory of attitudes, they are as "liberated" as most of them really wish to be?

ALTERNATIVE MODELS

If we picture the options available to women, we can see that they cover a wide range including the ideal prescribed by myth and religion as well as an earthy and hedonistic life-style, and even occasionally a third variant characterized by an achievement-oriented puritan ethic. Some women choose to pattern their behavior after the mythical and religious ideal symbolized by the figure of the Virgin Mary. Others deviate from this ideal to a greater or lesser degree in order to obtain the satisfaction of their individual desires or aspirations. The ideal itself is a security blanket which covers all women, giving them a strong sense of identity and historical continuity.

As culture-bound foreigners, we are not qualified to define the interests of Latin American women. We cannot decide what is good for them or prescribe how they might achieve that good. If we were to ask whether, on the whole, Latin American women are happier and better "adjusted" (adjusted to what?) than, say, North American women, we would be forced to admit that the measurable data on which to base an answer are not available and probably never will be. It would appear then that the only meaningful question is whether the restrictions on individual action are so ironclad as to preclude any possibility of free choice.

Undeniably, the pattern of attitudes and behavior which we have described puts a distinctive stamp on Latin American society; certainly there are enormous pressures on individual women to conform to the prescriptions. Sometimes the results are tragic, both for the individual and for the society which is deprived of the full benefit of the individual's potential contribution. A notable example of this kind of tragedy is provided by the life and death of Sor Juana Inés de la Cruz of Mexico whose genius was denied and finally crushed by her ecclesiastical superiors.

But what of Manuela, the mistress of Simón Bolívar? Sublimely unconcerned with the stereotype of saintliness, she made her own decisions. The collective judgment of Latin American society accords her a measure of esteem not often associated with women who conform to the *marianismo* ideal.

The question of personal identity is much less troublesome to Latin American women than to their North American sisters. The Latin American always knows who she is; even after marriage she retains her individuality and usually keeps her family name tacking on her husband's name and passing both names on to her children. The fiction of unassailable purity conferred by the myth on saint and sinner alike makes divorce on any grounds a rather unlikely possibility, which means that married women are not often faced with the necessity of "making a new life" for themselves during middle age. When her husband indulges in infidelity, as the *machismo* norm expects and requires him to do, the prejudice in favor of the wife's saintliness guarantees her the support of the community.

In developing societies plagued by massive unemployment and widespread underemployment, economists might question the value of throwing larger numbers of women into the already overcrowded labor market. It is hard to assess the extent to which *marianismo* contributes to the present low participation of women in economically productive endeavors.[17] To assume that all or nearly all women would work outside the home if they were given the opportunity to do so is an example of the kind of thinking that sometimes vitiates the conclusions of militant feminists. My inquiries among a very small sample of women from several Latin American countries indicate that when a woman acquires expertise of a kind that is socially useful, she is quite likely to find a remunerative post in conditions far more favorable than her counterpart in, say, the United States or Western Europe. Expertise in Latin America is at such a premium that she will find little competition for a suitable post.

A Latin American mother is seldom faced with the dilemma, so publicized in the United States, of having to choose between her children or her paid job. When women work outside of their home, *marianismo* makes it plain that no employer, whether he or she be a corporation president, a university dean, or a government official, has the right to ask a mother to neglect a sick child in order to keep a perfect attendance record at the office, classroom, or factory. The granting of sick leave to the mother of a sick child is not so much a matter of women's rights as a matter of the employer's duty to respect the sacredness of motherhood which the individual woman shares with the Virgin Mary and with the great mother goddesses of pre-Christian times.

Middle-class women who have marketable skills also have fewer role conflicts because other female members of the extended family, and an abundant supply of low-cost domestic servants, are available for day-to-day care of dependent children. Non-working, married, middle-class women are far more fortunate than their North American counterparts; the Latin American women are free to shop or visit with friends as often as they like, without worrying about their children. The point is that as we simply do not know why only a small proportion of women work outside of the home in Latin America, we must leave open the possibility that a considerable number may have freely chosen to have their *marianismo* cake and eat it too.

CONCLUSION

This excursion into the realm of Latin American culture has revealed a major variant on the universal theme of male-female relationships. We have traced the major characteristics of these relationships as they have developed over thousands of years and as they are observed today. Our historical perspective enables us to see that far from being an oppressive norm dictated by tyrannical males, *marianismo* has received considerable impetus from women themselves. This fact makes it possible to regard *marianismo* as part of a reciprocal arrangement, the other half of which is *machismo*.

The arrangement is not demonstrably more "unjust" than major variants on the same theme in other parts of the world. While some individuals of both sexes have been "victimized" by the strictures, it appears that many others have been able to shape their own life-styles and derive a measure of satisfaction, sometimes because of and sometimes in spite of the requirements of the system.

It seems unlikely that this pattern of male-female relationships can persist indefinitely without undergoing important modification. The mestizos—precisely that part of Latin American society which is characterized by *machismo-marianismo*—are not a traditional group in the sense of that word used by anthropologists. All observable facets of Latin American mestizo society are experiencing the effects of rapid and far-reaching changes, from which the phenomenon we have described could hardly be exempt. In fact, some signs are already apparent that the current generation of middle-class university students hold somewhat different values with regard to relationships between the sexes than those of their parents. This was particularly evident during the 1968 student strike in Mexico, with reference to male-female role perceptions.

In my opinion, however, *marianismo* is not for some time yet destined to disappear as a cultural pattern in Latin America. In general, women will not use their vote as a bloc to make divorce more accessible, to abolish sex discrimination (especially preferential treatment for women), or to impose upon themselves some of the onerous tasks traditionally reserved for men. They are not yet ready to relinquish their female chauvinism.

NOTES

1. For a discussion of this term and its social and political implications, see Evelyn P. Stevens, "Mexican Machismo: Politics and Value Orientations," *Western Political Quarterly*, 18, no. 4 (December 1965), pp. 848–857.

2. *Mundo Nuevo*, no. 46 (April 1970), pp. 14–50, devotes an entire section to the topic of "Machismo y feminismo," in which several authors use the term *hembrismo*. Neither *feminismo* nor *hembrismo* seem to me as satisfactory as my own term *marianismo*, for reasons made plain by the text.

3. See for example Julian Pitt-Rivers, ed., *Mediterranean Countrymen, Essays in the Social Anthropology of the Mediterranean* (Paris and La Haye: Mouton, 1963).

4. See Edwin Oliver James, *The Cult of the Mother Goddess* (London: Thames and Hudson, 1959), and Erich Neumann, *The Great Mother: An Analysis of the Archetype* (New York: Pantheon Books, 1955).

5. Carl E. Batt, "Mexican Character: An Adlerian Interpretation," *Journal of Individual Psychology*, 5, no. 2 (November 1969), pp. 183–201. This author refers to the "martyr complex."

6. See Rogelio Díaz-Guerrero, "Neurosis and the Mexican Family Structure," *American Journal of Psychiatry*, 112, no. 6 (December 1955), pp. 411–417, and by the same author, "Adolescence in Mexico: Some Cultural, Psychological, and Psychiatric Aspects," *International Mental Health Research Newsletter*, 12, no. 4 (Winter 1970), pp. 1, 10–13.

7. Rosa Cruchaga de Walker and Lillian Calm, "Quién es la mujer chilena?" *Mundo Nuevo*, no. 46 (April 1970), pp. 33–38. The woman quoted in the interview is the wife of an engineer and the mother of two children. Although she professes to admire the laundress, she obviously does not emulate her life-style.

8. *Por la izquierda:* illicit.

9. James, *Cult of the Mother Goddess,* pp. 49 ff.

10. Salvador Reyes Nevares, "El machismo en Mexico," *Mundo Nuevo,* no. 46 (April 1970), pp. 14–19.

11. J. Mayone Stycos, *Family and Fertility in Puerto Rico* (New York: Columbia University Press, 1955). See also Theodore B. Brameld, *The Remaking of a Culture* (New York: Harper and Brothers, 1959).

12. Lloyd H. Rogler and August B. Hollingshead, *Trapped* (New York: John Wiley and Sons, 1965), pp. 133–47. See also the publications of Oscar Lewis on Mexico and Puerto Rico.

13. Ana María Portugal, "La peruana ¿'Tapada' sin manto?"L *Mundo Nuevo,* no. 46 (April 1970), pp. 20–27.

14. José B. Adolph, "La Emancipación masculina en Lima," *Mundo Nuevo,* no. 46 (April 1970), pp. 39–41.

15. Ibid., p. 39.

16. Portugal, "La peruana ¿'Tapada' sin manto?" p. 22.

17. Some representative figures for Mexico and other Latin American countries are given in Ifigenia de Navarrete's *La mujer y los derechos sociales* (Mexico: Ediciones Oasis, 1969).

Further Questions

1. Is it paradoxical that Latin *marianismo* comes into full flower only in the middle-aged woman whose children have reached adulthood? In particular, would a mother be better typified by a younger woman, since her (presumably) younger children require more care and attention?

2. Is a woman (Latin American or not) who is frivolous or exuberant and gets a lot of enjoyment out of life somewhat suspect? For example, if a woman enjoys sex or a large wardrobe of clothing, should we think she has overstepped the bounds of propriety?

3. If a woman (Latin American or not) has not borne and raised children of her own, should we think of her as irresponsible and not due full respect as a woman?

The Second Shift   XI.2

ARLIE HOCHSCHILD WITH ANNE MACHUNG

Arlie Hochschild describes a typical married woman with children and a job in the workplace as working a "second shift" at home after she finishes her work outside the home. The problem is that neither the workplace nor the institution of marriage has changed adequately to comfortably accommodate the relatively new working wife and mother.

Hochschild is Professor of Sociology at the University of California at Berkeley.

Reading Questions

1. What are the problems women encounter with having to work a "second shift"? Do women always have enough time for this shift?
2. How does the marriage of today help generate problems in women's "second shift"?
3. What is a "gender ideology," according to Hochschild, and how does it determine the type of marriage a woman wants and her desired role in the workplace?

A SPEED-UP IN THE FAMILY

SHE IS NOT THE SAME WOMAN in each magazine advertisement, but she is the same idea. She has that working-mother look as she strides forward, briefcase in one hand, smiling child in the other. Literally and figuratively, she is moving ahead. Her hair, if long, tosses behind her; if it is short, it sweeps back at the sides, suggesting mobility and progress. There is nothing shy or passive about her. She is confident, active, "liberated." She wears a dark tailored suit, but with silk bow or colorful frill that says, "I'm really feminine underneath." She has made it in a man's world without sacrificing her femininity. And she has done this on her own. By some personal miracle, this image suggests, she has managed to combine what 150 years of industrialization have split wide apart—child and job, frill and suit, female culture and male.

When I showed a photograph of a supermom like this to the working mothers I talked to in the course of researching this book, many responded with an outright laugh. One daycare worker and mother of two, ages three and five, threw back her head: "Ha! They've got to be *kidding* about her. Look at me, hair a mess, nails jagged, twenty pounds overweight. Mornings, I'm getting my kids dressed, the dog fed, the lunches made, the shopping list done. That lady's got a maid." Even working mothers who did have maids couldn't imagine combining work and family in such a carefree way. "Do you know what a baby *does* to your life, the two o'clock feedings, the four o'clock feedings?" Another mother of two said: "They don't show it, but she's whistling"—she imitated a whistling woman, eyes to the sky—"so she can't hear the din." They envied the apparent ease of the woman with the flying hair, but she didn't remind them of anyone they knew.

The women I interviewed—lawyers, corporate executives, word processors, garment pattern cutters, daycare workers—and most of their husbands, too—felt differently about some issues: how right it is for a mother of young children to work a full-time job, or how much a husband should be responsible for the home. But they all agreed that it was hard to work two full-time jobs and raise young children.

How well do couples do it? The more women work outside the home, the more central this question. The number of women in paid work has risen steadily since before the turn of the century, but since 1950 the rise has been staggering. In 1950, 30 percent of American women were in the labor force; in 1986, it was 55 percent. In 1950, 28 percent of married women with children between six and seventeen worked outside the home; in 1986, it had

risen to 68 percent. In 1950, 23 percent of married women with children under six worked. By 1986, it had grown to 54 percent. We don't know how many women with children under the age of one worked outside the home in 1950; it was so rare that the Bureau of Labor kept no statistics on it. Today half of such women do. Two-thirds of all mothers are now in the labor force; in fact, more mothers have paid jobs (or are actively looking for one) than non-mothers. Because of this change in women, two-job families now make up 58 percent of all married couples with children.[1]

Since an increasing number of working women have small children, we might expect an increase in part-time work. But actually, 67 percent of the mothers who work have full-time jobs—that is, thirty-five hours or more weekly. That proportion is what it was in 1959.

If more mothers of young children are stepping into full-time jobs outside the home, and if most couples can't afford household help, how much more are fathers doing at home? As I began exploring this question I found many studies on the hours working men and women devote to housework and childcare. One national random sample of 1,243 working parents in forty-four American cities, conducted in 1965–66 by Alexander Szalai and his coworkers, for example, found that working women averaged three hours a day on housework while men averaged 17 minutes; women spent fifty minutes a day of time exclusively with their children; men spent twelve minutes. On the other side of the coin, working fathers watched television an hour longer than their working wives, and slept a half hour longer each night. A comparison of this American sample with eleven other industrial countries in Eastern and Western Europe revealed the same difference between working women and working men in those countries as well.[2] In a 1983 study of white middle-class families in greater Boston, Grace Baruch and R. C. Barnett found that working men married to working women spent only three-quarters of an hour longer each week with their kindergarten-aged children than did men married to housewives.[3]

Szalai's landmark study documented the now familiar but still alarming story of the working woman's "double day," but it left me wondering how men and women actually felt about all this. He and his coworkers studied how people used time, but not, say, how a father felt about his twelve minutes with his child, or how his wife felt about it. Szalai's study revealed the visible surface of what I discovered to be a set of deeply emotional issues: What should a man and woman contribute to the family? How appreciated does each feel? How does each respond to subtle changes in the balance of marital power? How does each develop an unconscious "gender strategy" for coping with the work at home, with marriage, and, indeed, with life itself? These were the underlying issues.

But I began with the measurable issue of time. Adding together the time it takes to do a paid job and to do housework and childcare, I averaged estimates from the major studies on time use done in the 1960s and 1970s, and discovered that women worked roughly fifteen hours longer each week than men. Over a year, they worked an *extra month of twenty-four-hour days a year.* Over a dozen years, it was an extra year of twenty-four-hour days. Most women without children spend much more time than men on housework; with children, they devote more time to both housework and childcare. Just as there is a wage gap between men and women in the workplace, there is a "leisure gap" between them at home. Most women work one shift at the office or factory and a "second shift" at home.

Studies show that working mothers have higher self-esteem and get less depressed than housewives, but compared to their husbands, they're more tired and get sick more often. In Peggy Thoit's 1985 analysis of two large-scale surveys each of about a thousand men and women, people were asked how often in the preceding week they'd experienced each of twenty-three symptoms of anxiety (such as dizziness or hallucinations). According to the researchers' criteria, working mothers were more likely than any other group to be "anxious."

In light of these studies, the image of the woman with the flying hair seems like an upbeat "cover" for a grim reality, like those pictures of Soviet tractor drivers smiling radiantly into the distance as they think about the ten-year plan. The Szalai study was conducted in 1965–66. I wanted to know whether the leisure gap he found in 1965 persists, or whether it had disappeared. Since most married couples work two jobs, since more will in the future, since most wives in these couples work the extra month a year, I wanted to understand what the wife's extra month a year meant for each person, and what it does for love and marriage in an age of high divorce.

Inside the Extra Month a Year

The women I interviewed seemed to be far more deeply torn between the demands of work and family than were their husbands. They talked with more animation and at greater length than their husbands about the abiding conflict between them. Busy as they were, women more often brightened at the idea of yet another interviewing session. They felt the second shift was *their* issue and most of their husbands agreed. When I telephoned one husband to arrange an interview with him, explaining that I wanted to ask him about how he managed work and family life, he replied genially, "Oh, this will *really* interest my *wife.*"

It was a woman who first proposed to me the metaphor, borrowed from industrial life, of the "second shift." She strongly resisted the *idea* that homemaking was a "shift." Her family was her life and she didn't want it reduced to a job. But as she put it, "You're on duty at work. You come home, and you're on duty. Then you go back to work and you're on duty." After eight hours of adjusting insurance claims, she came home to put on the rice for dinner, care for her children, and wash laundry. Despite herself her home life *felt* like a second shift. That was the real story and that was the real problem.

One reason women take a deeper interest than men in the problems of juggling work with family life is that even when husbands happily shared the hours of work, their wives felt more *responsible* for home and children. More women kept track of doctors' appointments and arranged for playmates to come over. More mothers than fathers worried about the tail on a child's Halloween costume or a birthday present for a school friend. They were more likely to think about their children while at work and to check in by phone with the baby-sitter.

Partly because of this, more women felt torn between one sense of urgency and another, between the need to soothe a child's fear of being left at daycare, and the need to show the boss she's "serious" at work. More women than men questioned how good they were as parents, or if they did not, they questioned why they weren't questioning it. More often than men, women alternated between living in their ambition and standing apart from it.

As masses of women have moved into the economy, families have been hit by a "speed-up" in work and family life. There is no more time in the day than there was when wives stayed home, but there is twice as much to get done. It is mainly women who absorb this "speed-up." Twenty percent of the men in my study shared housework equally. Seventy percent of men did a substantial amount (less than half but more than a third), and 10 percent did less than a third. Even when couples share more equitably in the work at home, women do two-thirds of the *daily* jobs at home, like cooking and cleaning up—jobs that fix them into a rigid routine. Most women cook dinner and most men change the oil in the family car. But, as one mother pointed out, dinner needs to be prepared every evening around six o'clock, whereas the car oil needs to be changed every six months, any day around that time, any time that day. Women do more childcare than men, and men repair more household appliances. A child needs to be tended daily while the repair of household appliances can often wait "until I have time." Men thus have

more control over *when* they make their contributions than women do. They may be very busy with family chores but, like the executive who tells his secretary to "hold my calls," the man has more control over his time. The job of the working mother, like that of the secretary, is usually to "take the calls."

Another reason women may feel more strained than men is that women more often do two things at once—for example, write checks and return phone calls, vacuum and keep an eye on a three-year-old, fold laundry and think out the shopping list. Men more often cook dinner *or* take a child to the park. Indeed, women more often juggle three spheres—job, children, and housework—while most men juggle two—job and children. For women, two activities compete with their time with children, not just one.

Beyond doing more at home, women also devote *proportionately more* of their time at home to housework and proportionately less of it to childcare. Of all the time men spend working at home, more of it goes to childcare. That is, working wives spend relatively more time "mothering the house"; husbands spend more time "mothering" the children. Since most parents prefer to tend to their children than clean house, men do more of what they'd rather do. More men than women take their children on "fun" outings to the park, the zoo, the movies. Women spend more time on maintenance, feeding and bathing children, enjoyable activities to be sure, but often less leisurely or "special" than going to the zoo. Men also do fewer of the "undesirable" household chores: fewer men than women wash toilets and scrub the bathroom.

As a result, women tend to talk more intently about being overtired, sick, and "emotionally drained." Many women I could not tear away from the topic of sleep. They talked about how much they could "get by on" . . . six and a half, seven, seven and a half, less, more. They talked about who they knew who needed more or less. Some apologized for how much sleep they needed—"I'm afraid I need eight hours of sleep"—as if eight was "too much." They talked about the effect of a change in baby-sitter, the birth of a second child, or a business trip on their child's pattern of sleep. They talked about how to avoid fully waking up when a child called them at night, and how to get back to sleep. These women talked about sleep the way a hungry person talks about food.

All in all, if in this period of American history, the two-job family is suffering from a speed up of work and family life, working mothers are its primary victims. It is ironic, then, that often it falls to women to be the "time and motion expert" of family life. Watching inside homes, I noticed it was often the mother who rushed children, saying, "Hurry up! It's time to go," "Finish your cereal now," "You can do that later," "Let's go!" When a bath is crammed into a slot between 7:45 and 8:00 it was often the mother who called out, "Let's see who can take their bath the quickest!" Often a younger child will rush out, scurrying to be first in bed, while the older and wiser one stalls, resistant, sometimes resentful: "Mother is always rushing us." Sadly enough, women are more often the lightning rods for family aggressions aroused by the speed-up of work and family life. They are the "villains" in a process of which they are also the primary victims. More than the longer hours, the sleeplessness, and feeling torn, this is the saddest cost to women of the extra month a year.

MARRIAGE IN THE STALLED REVOLUTION

Each marriage bears the footprints of economic and cultural trends which originate far outside marriage. A rise in inflation which erodes the earning power of the male wage, an expanding service sector which opens up jobs for women, new cultural images—like the woman with the flying hair—that make the working mother seem exciting, all these changes do not simply go on *around* marriage. They occur *within* marriage, and transform it. Problems between husbands and wives, problems which seem "individual" and "marital," are often individual experiences of powerful economic and cultural shock waves that are not caused by one person or two. Quarrels that erupt, as we'll see, between Nancy and Evan Holt, Jessica and Seth Stein, Anita and Ray Judson result mainly from a friction between faster-changing women and slower-changing men, rates of change which themselves result from the different rates at which the industrial economy has drawn men and women into itself.

There is a "his" and "hers" to the economic development of the United States. In the latter part of the nineteenth century, it was mainly men who were drawn off the farm into paid, industrial work and who changed their way of life and their identity. At that point in history, men became more different from their fathers than women became from their mothers. Today the economic arrow points at women; it is women who are being drawn into wage work, and women who are undergoing changes in their way of life and identity. Women are departing more from their mothers' and grandmothers' way of life, men are doing so less.*

Both the earlier entrance of men into the industrial economy and the later entrance of women have influenced the relations *between* men and women, especially their relations within marriage. The former increase in the number of men in industrial work tended to increase the power of men, and the present growth in the number of women in such work has somewhat increased the power of women. On the whole, the entrance of men into industrial work did not destabilize the family whereas *in the absence of other changes,* the rise in female employment has gone with the rise in divorce. I will have more to say about the "his" and "hers" of economic history in Chapter 16. Here I'll focus on the current economic story, that which

---

*This is more true of white and middle-class women than it is of black or poor women, whose mothers often worked outside the home. But the trend I am talking about—an increase from 20 percent of women in paid jobs in 1900 to 55 percent in 1985—has affected a large number of women.

hangs over the marriages I describe in this book. Beneath the image of the woman with the flying hair, there has been a real change in women without much change in anything else.

The exodus of women into the economy has not been accompanied by a cultural understanding of marriage and work that would make this transition smooth. The workforce has changed. Women have changed. But most workplaces have remained inflexible in the face of the family demands of their workers and at home, most men have yet to really adapt to the change in women. This strain between the change in women and the absence of change in much else leads me to speak of a "stalled revolution."

A society which did not suffer from this stall would be a society *humanely* adapted to the fact that most women work outside the home. The workplace would allow parents to work part time, to share jobs, to work flexible hours, to take parental leaves to give birth, tend a sick child, or care for a well one. As Delores Hayden has envisioned in *Redesigning the American Dream*, it would include affordable housing closer to places of work, and perhaps community-based meal and laundry services. It would include men whose notion of manhood encouraged them to be active parents and share at home. In contrast, a stalled revolution lacks social arrangements that ease life for working parents, and lacks men who share the second shift.

The Top and Bottom of Gender Ideology

A gender strategy is a plan of action through which a person tries to solve problems at hand, given the cultural notions of gender at play. To pursue a gender strategy, a man draws on beliefs about manhood and womanhood, beliefs that are forged in early childhood and thus anchored to deep emotions. He makes a connection between how he thinks about his manhood, what he feels about it, and what he does. It works in the same way for a woman.

A woman's gender ideology determines what sphere she *wants* to identify with (home or work) and how much power in the marriage she wants

to have (less, more, or the same amount). I found three types of ideology of marital roles:—traditional, transitional, and egalitarian. Even though she works, the "pure" traditional wants to identify with her activities at home (as a wife, a mother, a neighborhood mom), wants her husband to base his at work, and wants less power than he. The traditional man wants the same. The "pure" egalitarian, as the type emerges here, wants to identify with the same spheres her husband does, and to have an equal amount of power in the marriage. Some want the couple to be jointly oriented to the home, others to their careers, or both of them to jointly hold some balance between the two. Between the traditional and the egalitarian is the transitional, any one of a variety of types of blending of the two. But, in contrast to the traditional, a transitional woman wants to identify with her role at work as well as at home. Unlike the egalitarian, she believes her husband should base his identity more on work than she does. A typical transitional wants to identify *both* with the caring for the home, and with helping her husband earn money, but wants her husband to focus on earning a living. A typical transitional man is all for his wife working, but expects her to take the main responsibility at home too. Most men and women I talked with were "transitional." At least, transitional ideas came out when I asked people directly what they believed.

The men and women I am about to describe seem to have developed their gender ideology by unconsciously synthesizing certain cultural ideas with feelings about their past. But they also developed their ideology by taking opportunity into account. Sometime in adolescence they matched their personal assets against the opportunities available to men or women of their type; they saw which gender ideology best fit their circumstances, and—often regardless of their upbringing—they identified with a certain version of manhood or womanhood. It "made sense" to them. It felt like "who they were." For example, a woman sizes up her education, intelligence, age, charm, sexual attractiveness, her dependency needs, her aspirations, and she matches these against her perception of how women like her are doing in the job market and the "marriage market." What jobs could she get? What men? What are her chances for an equal marriage, a traditional marriage, a happy marriage, any marriage? Half-consciously, she assesses her chances—chances of an interesting, well-paid job are poor? Her courtship pool has very traditional men? She takes these into account. *Then* a certain gender ideology, let's say a traditional one, will "make sense" to her. She will embrace the ideology that suits her perception of her chances. She holds to a certain version of womanhood (the "wilting violet," say). She identifies with its customs (men opening doors), and symbols (lacy dress, long hair, soft handshakes, and lowered eyes). She tries to develop its "ideal personality" (deferential, dependent), not because this is what her parents taught her, not because this corresponds to how she naturally "is," but because these particular customs now *make sense* of her resources and of her overall situation in a stalled revolution. The same principle applies to men. However wholehearted or ambivalent, a person's gender ideology tends to fit their situation.

Gender Strategies

When a man tries to apply his gender ideology to the situations that face him in real life, unconsciously or not he pursues a gender strategy.[2] He outlines a course of action. He might become a "superdad"—working long hours and keeping his child up late at night to spend time with him or her. Or he might cut back his hours at work. Or he might scale back housework and spend less time with his children. Or he might actively try to share the second shift.

The term "strategy" refers both to his plan of action and to his emotional preparations for pursuing it. For example, he may require himself to suppress his career ambitions to devote himself more to his children, or suppress his responsiveness to his children's appeals in the course of steeling himself for the struggle at work. He might harden himself to his wife's appeals, or he might be the one in the family who "lets" himself see when a child is calling out for help.

In the families I am about to describe, then, I have tried to be sensitive to the fractures in gender ideology, the conflicts between what a person thinks he or she ought to feel and what he or she does feel, and to the emotional work it takes to fit a gender ideal when inner needs or outer conditions make it hard.

As this social revolution proceeds, the problems of the two-job family will not diminish. If anything, as more couples work two jobs the problems will increase. If we can't return to traditional marriage, and if we are not to despair of marriage altogether, it becomes vitally important to understand gender strategies as the basic dynamic of marriage.

NOTES

1. U.S. Bureau of Labor Statistics, *Employment and Earnings, Characteristics of Families: First Quarter* (Washington, D.C.: U.S. Department of Labor, 1988).

2. Alexander Szalai, ed., *The Use of Time: Daily Activities of Urban and Suburban Populations in Twelve Countries* (The Hague: Mouton, 1972), p.668, Table B. Another study found that men spent a longer time than women eating meals (Shelley Coverman, "Gender, Domestic Labor Time and Wage Inequality," *American Sociological Review* 48 [1983]: 626). With regard to sleep, the pattern differs for men and women. The higher the social class of a man, the more sleep he's likely to get. The higher the class of a woman, the less sleep she is likely to get. (Upper-white-collar men average 7.6 hours sleep a night. Lower-white-collar, skilled and unskilled men all averaged 7.3 hours. Upper-white-collar women average 7.1 hours of sleep; lower-white-collar workers average 7.4; skilled workers 7.0 and unskilled workers 8.1.) Working wives seem to meet the demands of high-pressure careers by reducing sleep, whereas working husbands don't. For more details on the hours working men and women devote to housework and childcare, see the Appendix of this book.

3. Grace K. Baruch and Rosalind Barnett, "Correlates of Father's Participation in Family Work: A Technical Report," Working Paper no. 106 (Wellesley, Mass.:

Wellesley College Center for Research on Women, 1983), pp. 80–81. also see Kathryn E. Walker and Margret E. Woods, *Time Use: A Measure of Household Production of Goods and Services* (Washington, D.C.: American Home Economics Association, 1976).

2. The concept of "gender strategy" is an adaptation of Ann Swidler's notion of "strategies of action." In "Culture in Action—Symbols and Strate-gies," *American Sociological Review* 51 (1986): 273–286, Swidler focuses on how the individual uses aspects of culture (symbols, rituals, stories) as "tools" for constructing a line of action. Here, I focus on aspects of culture that bear on our ideas of manhood and womanhood, and I focus on our emotional preparation for and the emotional consequences of our strategies.

Further Questions

1. If you want to work an outside job and also want a marriage with children how do you plan to manage the two projects? What role do you envisage your spouse taking in the home?

2. If you and your spouse spend an equal amount of time and energy on your regular jobs but one of you spends more time on the household and children, do you find that a fair situation? If not, what do you plan on doing about it?

3. Is the answer to problems of the "double shift" for women to work only one shift, being either stay-at-home wives and mothers or unmarried and childless full-time members of the workforce? How likely is it that women would be happy with such a solution?

XI.3   Stability and Change in Chicano Men's Family Lives

SCOTT COLTRANE

Scott Coltrane seeks to explode the myth that Chicano men are too "macho" to in-volve themselves in household tasks and child-care. His subjects divided themselves into three groups: main provider families where the husband's work was held to be more important and paid better than his wife's; ambivalent co-providers where wife and husband had earnings more nearly equal; and full co-providers with nearly equal

Abridged from "Stability and Change in Chicano Men's Family Lives" in Men's Lives, *Michael S. Kimmel and Michael A. Messner, eds, 4th Edition (Needham Heights, MA: Allyn and Bacon, 1998.) pp. 520–536, Reprinted by permission of the author.*

This article is based on a study of dual-earner Chicano Couples conducted in 1990–1992 by Scott Coltrane with research assistance from Elsa Valdez and Hilda Cortez. Partial funding was provided by the Academic Senate of the University of California, Riverside, and the UCR Minority Student Research Internship Pro-gram. Included herein are analyses of unpublished interview excerpts along with selected passages from three published sources: (1) Coltrane, Family Man: Fatherhood, Housework, and Gender Equity *(New York: Oxford University Press, 1994); (2) Coltrane and Valdez, "Reluctant Compliance: Work/Family Role Alloca-tion in Dual-Earner Chicano Families," in Jane C. Hood (ed.),* Men, Work, and Family *(Newbury Park, CA: Sage, 1994) and (3) Valdez and Coltrane, "Work, Family, and the Chicana: Power, Perception and Equity," in Judith Frankel (ed.),* Employed Mothers and the Family Context *(New York: Springer, 1993).*

income and nearly equal hours spent on the job. Main provider husbands spent the least amount of time on children and household tasks and full co-providers spent the most, with ambivalent co-providers falling in between.

Coltrane is Associate Professor of Sociology at the University of California at Riverside.

Reading Questions

1. If a man makes a lot more money than his wife, is he justified in allocating to her the main part of the domestic tasks? How about if he works full-time and she works part-time?
2. If a man is perceived to be a failure in terms of his career aspirations, does this justify his performing more of the household tasks than if he were succeeding in terms of his chosen profession?
3. If the jobs of a couple are equally important, demand the same commitment of hours, and pay about the same, should the couple share housework and child-care equally?

ONE OF THE MOST POPULAR pejorative American slang terms to emerge in the 1980s was "macho," used to describe men prone to combative posturing, relentless sexual conquest, and other compulsive displays of masculinity. Macho men continually guard against imputations of being soft or feminine and thus tend to avoid domestic tasks and family activities that are considered "women's work." Macho comes from the Spanish *machismo,* and although the behaviors associated with it are clearly not limited to one ethnic group, Latino men are often stereotyped as especially prone toward macho displays.[1] This chapter uses in-depth interviews with twenty Chicano couples to explore how paid work and family work are divided. As in other contemporary American households, divisions of labor in these Chicano families were far from balanced or egalitarian, and husbands tended to enjoy special privileges simply because they were men. Nevertheless, many couples were allocating household chores without reference to gender, and few of the Chicano men exhibited stereotypical macho behavior.

Chicanos, or Mexican-Americans, are often portrayed as living in poor farm-worker families composed of macho men, subservient women, and plentiful children. Yet these stereotypes have been changing, as diverse groups of people with Mexican and Latin-American heritage are responding to the same sorts of social and economic pressures faced by families of other ethnic backgrounds. For example, most Chicano families in the United States now live in urban centers or their suburbs rather than in traditional rural farming areas, and their patterns of marital interaction appear to be about as egalitarian as those of other American families. What's more, Chicanos will no longer be a numerical minority in the near future. Because of higher-than-average birth rates and continued in-migration, by the year 2015 Chicano children will outnumber Anglos in many southwest states, including California, Texas, Arizona, and New Mexico.[2]

When family researchers study white couples, they typically focus on middle-class suburban households, usually highlighting their strengths. Studies of ethnic minority families, in contrast, have tended to focus on the problems of poor or working-class households living in inner-city or rural settings. Because most research on Latino families in the United States has not controlled for social class, wife's employment status, or recency of immigration, a narrow and stereotyped view of these families as patriarchal and culturally backward has persisted. In addition, large-scale studies of "Hispanics" have failed to distinguish between divergent groups of people with Mexican, Central American, South American, Cuban,

Puerto Rican, Spanish, or Portuguese ancestry. In contrast, contemporary scholars are beginning to look at some of the positive aspects of minority families and to focus on the economic and institutional factors that influence men's lives within these families.[3]

In 1990 and 1991, Elsa Valdez and I interviewed a group of twenty middle-class Chicano couples with young children living in Southern California. We were primarily interested in finding out if they were facing the same sorts of pressures experienced by other families, so we selected only families in which both the husband and the wife were employed outside the home—the most typical pattern among young parents in the United States today. We wanted to see who did what in these families and find out how they talked about the personal and financial pushes and pulls associated with raising a family. We interviewed wives and husbands separately in their homes, asking them a variety of questions about housework, child care, and their jobs. Elsewhere, we describe details of their time use and task performance, but here I analyze the couples' talk about work, family, and gender, exploring how feelings of entitlement and obligation are shaped by patterns of paid and unpaid labor.[4]

When we asked husbands and wives to sort sixty-four common household tasks according to who most often performed them, we found that wives in most families were responsible for housecleaning, clothes care, meal preparation, and clean-up, whereas husbands were primarily responsible for home maintenance and repair. Most routine child care was also performed by wives, though most husbands reported that they made substantial contributions to parenting. Wives saw the mundane daily housework as an ever-present burden that they had to shoulder themselves or delegate to someone else. While many wives did not expect the current division of labor to change, they did acknowledge that it was unbalanced. The men, although acknowledging that things weren't exactly fair, tended to minimize the asymmetry by seeing many of the short repetitive tasks associated with housekeeping as shared activities. Although there was tremendous diversity among the couples we talked to, we observed a general pattern of disagreement over how much family work the other spouse performed.

The sociologist Jesse Bernard provides us with a useful way to understand why this might be. Bernard suggested that every marital union contains two marriages—"his" and "hers."[5] We discovered from our interviews and observations that most of the husbands and wives were, indeed, living in separate marriages or separate worlds. Her world centered around keeping track of the countless details of housework and child care even though she was employed. His world centered around his work and his leisure activities so that he avoided noticing or anticipating the details of running a home. Husbands "helped out" when wives gave them tasks to do, and because they almost always complied with requests for help, most tended to assume that they were sharing the household labor. Because much of the work the women did was unseen or taken for granted by the men, they tended to underestimate their wives' contributions and escaped the full range of tensions and strains associated with family work.

Because wives remained in control of setting schedules, generating lists for domestic chores, and worrying about the children, they perceived their husbands as contributing relatively little. A frequent comment from wives was that their husbands "just didn't see" the domestic details, and that the men would not often take responsibility for anticipating and planning for what needed to be done. Although many of the men we interviewed maintained their favored position within the family by "not seeing" various aspects of domestic life and leaving the details and planning to their wives, other couples were in the process of ongoing negotiations and, as described below, were successful at redefining some household chores as shared endeavors.

Concerning their paid work, the families we interviewed reported that both husbands and wives had jobs because of financial necessity. The men made comments like, "we were pretty much forced into it," or "we didn't really have any choice." Although most of the husbands and wives were employed full-time, only a few accepted the wife as an equal provider or true breadwinner. Using the type of job, employment schedule, and earnings of each spouse, along with their attitudes toward providing, I categorized the couples into main-provider families and co-provider families.[6] Main-provider couples considered the husbands' job to be primary and the wife's job to be secondary. Co-provider couples in contrast, tended to accept the wife's job as permanent, and some even treated the wife's job as equally important to her husband's. Accepting the wife as an equal provider, or considering the husband to have failed as a provider, significantly shaped the couples' divisions of household labor.

MAIN-PROVIDER FAMILIES

In just under half of the families we interviewed, the men earned substantially more money than their wives and were assumed to be "natural" breadwinners, whereas the women were assumed to be innately better equipped to deal with home and children. Wives in all of these main-provider families were employed, but the wife's job was often considered temporary, and her income was treated as "extra" money and earmarked for special purposes.[7] One main-provider husband said, "I would prefer that my wife did not have to work, and could stay at home with my daughter, but finances just don't permit that." Another commented that his wife made just about enough to cover the costs of child care, suggesting that the children were still her primary responsibility, and that any wages she earned should first be allocated to cover "her" tasks.

The main-provider couples included many wives who were employed part-time, and some who worked in lower-status full-time jobs with wages much lower than their husband's. These women took pride in their homemaker role and

readily accepted responsibility for managing the household, although they occasionally asked for help. One part-time bookkeeper married to a recent law-school graduate described their division of labor by saying, "It's a given that I take care of children and housework, but when I am real tired, he steps in willingly." Main-provider husbands typically remained in a helper role: In this case, the law clerk told his wife, "Just tell me what to do and I'll do it." He said that if he came home and she was gone, he might clean house, but that if she was home, he would "let her do it." This reflects a typical division of labor in which the wife acts as household manager and the husband occasionally serves as her helper.[8]

This lawyer-to-be talked about early negotiations between he [sic] and his wife that seemed to set the tone for current smoldering arguments about housework:

> When we were first married, I would do something and she wouldn't like the way that I did it. So I would say, "OK, then, you do it, and I won't do it again." That was like in our first few years of marriage when we were first getting used to each other, but now she doesn't discourage me so much. She knows that if she does, she's going to wind up doing it herself.

His resistance and her reluctance to press for change reflect an unbalanced economy of gratitude.[9] When he occasionally contributed to housework or child care, she was indebted to him. She complimented him for being willing to step in when she asked for help, but privately lamented the fact that she had to negotiate for each small contribution. Firmly entrenched in the main-provider role and somewhat oblivious to the daily rituals of housework and child care, he felt justified in needing prodding and encouragement. When she did ask him for help, she was careful to thank him for dressing the children or for giving her a ten-minute break from them. While these patterns of domestic labor and inequities in the exchange of gratitude were long-standing, tension lurked just below the surface for this couple. He commented, "My wife gets uptight with me for agreeing to help out my mom, when she feels she can't even ask me to go to the store for her."

THE PROVIDER ROLE AND FAILED ASPIRATIONS

Wives performed most of the household labor in main-provider couples, but if main-provider husbands had failed career aspirations, more domestic work was shared. What appeared to tip the economy of gratitude away from automatic male privilege was the wife's sense that the husband had not fulfilled his occupational potential. For example, one main-provider husband graduated from a four-year college and completed two years of post-graduate study without finishing his Master's Thesis. At the time of the interview, he was making about $30,000 a year as a self-employed house painter, and his wife was making less than half that amount as a full-time secretary. His comments show how her evaluation of his failed or postponed career aspirations led to more bargaining over his participation in routine housework:

> She reminds me that I'm not doing what we both think I should be doing, and sometimes that's a discouragement. I might have worked a lot of hours and I'll come home tired, for example, and she'll say, "You've gotta clean the house," and I'll say, "Damn I'm tired, I'd like to get a little rest in," but she says "you're only doing this because it's been your choice." She tends to not have sympathy for me in my work because it was more my choice than hers.

He acknowledged that he should be doing something more "worthwhile," and hoped that he would not be painting houses for more than another year. Still, as long as he stayed in his current job, considered beneath him by both of them, she would not allow him to use fatigue from employment as a way to get out of doing housework:

> I worked about 60 hours a week the last couple of weeks. I worked yesterday [Saturday], and today—if it had been my choice—I would have drank beer and watched TV. But since she had a baby shower to go to, I babysitted my nephews. And since we had you coming, she kind of laid out the program: "You've gotta clean the floors, and wash the dishes, and do the carpets. So get to it buddy!" [Laughs.]

This main-provider husband capitulated to his wife's demands, but she still had to set tasks for him and remind him to perform them. In responding to her "program," he used the strategy of claimed incompetence that other main-provider husbands also used. While he admitted that he was proficient at the "janitorial stuff," he was careful to point out that he was incapable of dusting or doing the laundry:

> It's amazing what you can do when you have little time and you just get in and do it. And I'm good at that. I'm good at the big cleaning, I'm good at the janitorial stuff. I can do the carpet, do the floors, do all that stuff. But I'm no good on the details. She wants all the details just right, so she handles dusting, the laundry, and stuff like that. . . .You know, like I would have everything come out one color.

By re-categorizing some of the housework as "big cleaning," this husband rendered it accountable as mens' work. He drew the line at laundry and dusting, but he had transformed some household tasks, like vacuuming and mopping, into work appropriate for men to do. He was complying, albeit reluctantly, to many of his wife's requests because they agreed that he had not fulfilled "his" job as sole provider. He still yearned to be the "real" breadwinner and shared his hope that getting a better paying job would mean that he could ignore the housework:

> Sharing the house stuff is usually just a necessity. If, as we would hope in the future, she didn't have to work outside the home, then I think I would be comfortable doing less of it. Then she would be the primary house-care person and I would be the primary financial-resource person. I think roles would change then, and I would be comfortable with her doing more of the dishes and more of the

cleaning, and I think she would too. In that sense, I think traditional relationships—if traditional means the guy working and the woman staying home—is a good thing. I wouldn't mind getting a taste of it myself!

AMBIVALENT CO-PROVIDERS

Over half of the couples we interviewed were classified as co-providers. The husbands and wives in these families had more equal earnings and placed a higher value the wife's employment than those in main-provider families, but there was considerable variation in terms of their willingness to accept the woman as a full and equal provider. Five of the twelve husbands in the co-provider group were ambivalent about sharing the provider role and were also reluctant to share most household tasks. Compared to their wives, ambivalent co-provider husbands usually held jobs that were roughly equivalent in terms of occupational prestige and worked about the same number of hours per week, but because of gender bias in the labor market, the men earned significantly more than their wives. Compared to main-provider husbands, they considered their wives' jobs to be relatively permanent and important, but they continued to use their own job commitments as justification for doing little at home. Ambivalent co-provider husbands' family obligations rarely intruded into their work lives, whereas their wives' family obligations frequently interfered with their paid work. Such asymmetrically permeable work/family boundaries are common in single-earner and main-provider families, but must be supported with subtle ideologies and elaborate justifications when husband and wives hold similar occupational positions.[10]

Ambivalent co-provider husbands remained in a helper role at home, perceiving their wives to be more involved parents and assuming that housework was also primarily their wives' responsibility. The men used their jobs to justify their absence from home, but most also lamented not being able to spend more time with their families. For instance, one husband who worked full time as a city planner was married to a woman who worked an equal number of hours as an office manger. In talking about the time he put in at his job, he commented, "I wish I had more time to spend with my children, and to spend with my wife too, of course, but it's a fact of life that I have to work." His wife, in contrast, indicated that her paid job, which she had held for fourteen years, did not prohibit her from adequately caring for her three children, or taking care of "her" household chores. Ambivalent co-provider husbands did not perform significantly more housework and child care than main-provider husbands, and generally did fewer household chores than main-provider husbands with failed career aspirations.

Not surprisingly, ambivalent co-provider husbands tended to be satisfied with their current divisions of labor, even though they usually admitted that things were "not quite fair." One junior-high-school teacher married to a bilingual-education program coordinator described his reactions to their division of family labor:

> To be honest, I'm totally satisfied. When I had a first-period conference, I was a little more flexible; I'd help her more with changing 'em, you know, getting them ready for school, since I didn't have to be at school right away. Then I had to switch because they had some situation out at fifth-period conference, so that now she does it a little bit more than I do, and I don't help out with the kids as much in the morning because I have to be there an hour earlier.

This ambivalent co-provider clearly saw himself as "helping" his wife with the children, yet made light of her contributions by saying she does "a little bit more than I do." He went on to reveal how his wife did not enjoy similar special privileges due to her employment, since she had to pick up the children from day care every day, as well as taking them to school in the mornings:

> She gets out a little later than I do, because she's an administrator but I have other things outside. I also work out, I run, and that sort of gives me a time away, to do that before they all come here. I have community meetings in the

evenings sometimes, too. So I mean, it might not be totally fair—maybe 60/40—but I'm thoroughly happy with the way things are.

While he was "thoroughly happy" with the current arrangements, she thought that it was decidedly unfair. She said, "I don't like the fact that it's taken for granted that I'm available. When he goes out he just assumes I'm available, but when I go out I have to consult with him to make sure he is available." For her, child care was a given; for him, it was optional. He commented, "If I don't have something else to do, then I'll take the kids."

CO-PROVIDERS

In contrast, about a third of the couples we interviewed fully accepted the wife's long-term employment, considered her career to be just as important as his, and were in various stages of redefining household labor as men's work. Like the ambivalent couples discussed above, full co-provider spouses worked about the same number of hours as each other, but on the whole, these couples worked more total hours than their more ambivalent counterparts, though their annual incomes were a bit lower. According to both husbands and wives, the sharing of housework and child care was substantially greater for full co-providers than for ambivalent co-providers, and also much more balanced than for main-providers.

Like ambivalent co-providers, husbands in full co-provider families discussed conflicts between work and family and sometimes alluded to the ways that their occupational advancement was limited by their commitments to their children. One husband and wife spent the same number of hours on the job, earned approximately the same amount of money, and were employed as engineering technicians for the same employer. When we asked him how his family involvement had affected his job performance, he responded by saying, "It should, OK, because I really need to spend a lot more time learning my work, and I haven't really put in the time I need to advance in the profession. I would like to spend, I mean I *would* spend, more time if I didn't have kids. I'd like to be able to play with the computer or read books more often." Although he talked about conflicts between job and family, he also emphasized that lost work time was not really a sacrifice because he valued time with his children so highly. He did not use his job as an excuse to get out of doing child care or housework, and he seemed to value his wife's career at least as much as his own:

> I think her job is probably more important than mine because she's been at that kind of work a lot longer than I have. And at the level she is—it's awkward the way it is, because I get paid just a little bit more than she does, I have a higher position. But she definitely knows the work a lot more, she's been doing the same type of work for about nine years already, and I've only been doing this type of engineering work for about two-and-a-half years, so she knows a lot more. We both have to work, that's for sure.

Recognition of their roughly equivalent professional status and the need for two equal providers affected this couple's division of parenting and housework. The husband indicated the he did more child care and housework than his wife, and she gave him much credit for his efforts, but in her interview, she indicated that he still did less than half. She described her husband's relationship with their seven-year-old son as "very caring," and noted that he assists the boy with homework more than she does. She also said that her husband did most of the heavy cleaning and scrubbing, but also commented that he doesn't clean toilets and doesn't always notice when things get dirty. The husband described their allocation of housework by saying, "Maybe she does less than I do, but some of the things she does, I just will not do. I will not dust all the little things in the house. That's one of my least favorite things, but I'm more likely to do the mopping and vacuuming." This husband's comments also revealed some ongoing tension about whose housework standards should be maintained. He said, "She has high standards for cleanliness that you would have to be home to maintain. Mine tend to acknowledge that you don't always get at this stuff because you have other things to do. I think I have a better acceptance that one priority hurts something else in the background."

While this couple generally agreed about how to raise their son, standards for child care were also subject to debate. He saw himself as doing more with his son than his wife, as reflected in comments such as "I tend to think of myself as the more involved parent, and I think other people have noticed that, too." While she had only positive things to say about his parenting, he offered both praise and criticism of her parenting:

> She can be very playful. She makes up fun games. She doesn't always put enough into the educational part of it, though, like exploring or reading. . . . She cherishes tune-up time [job-related study or preparation], and sometimes I feel she should be using that time to spend with him. Like at the beach, I'll play with him, but she'll be more likely to be under the umbrella reading.

Like many of the other husbands, he went on to say that he thought their division of labor was unfair. Unlike the others, however, he indicated that he thought their current arrangements favored *her* needs, not his:

> I think I do more housework. It's probably not fair, because I do more of the dirtier tasks. . . . Also, at this point, our solution tends to favor her free time more than my free time. I think that has more to do with our personal backgrounds. She has more personal friends to do things with, so she has more outside things to do whereas I say I'm not doing anything.

In this family, comparable occupational status and earnings, coupled with a relatively egalitarian ideology, led to substantial sharing of both child care and housework. While the husband tended to take more credit for his involvement than his wife gave him, we can see a difference between their talk and that of some of the families discussed above. Other husbands sometimes complained about their wife's high standards, but they also treated housework, and even parenting, as primarily *her* duty. They usually resented being nagged to do more around the house and failed to move out of a helper role. Rarely did such men consider it *their* duty to anticipate, schedule, and take care of family and household needs. In this co-provider household, in contrast, the gendered allocation of responsibility for child care and housework was not assumed. Because of this, negotiations over housework and parenting were more frequent than in the other families. Since they both held expectations that each would fulfill both provider and caretaker roles, resentments came from both spouses—not just from the wife.

Our interviews suggest that it might be easier for couples to share both provider and home-maker roles when, like the family above, the wife's earnings and occupational prestige equal or exceed those of her husband. For instance, in one of the couples reporting the most sharing of child care and housework, the wife earned $36,000 annually as the executive director of a non-profit community organization and a consultant, and her husband earned $30,000 as a self-employed general contractor. This couple started off their marriage with fairly conventional gender-role expectations and an unbalanced division of labor. While the husband's ideology had changed somewhat, he still talked like most of the main-provider husbands:

> As far as the household is concerned, I divide a house into two categories: one is the interior and the other is the exterior. For the interior, my wife pushes me to deal with that. The exterior, I'm left to it myself. So, what I'm basically saying is that generally speaking, a woman does not deal with the exterior. The woman's main concern is with the interior, although there is a lot of deviation.

In this family, an egalitarian belief system did not precede the sharing of household labor. The wife was still responsible for setting the "interior" household agenda and had to remind her husband to help with housework and child care. When asked whether he and his wife had arguments about housework, this husband laughed and said, "All the time, doesn't everybody?"

What differentiated this couple from most others, is that she made more money than he did and had no qualms about demanding help from him. While he had not yet accepted the idea that interior chores were equally his, he reluctantly performed them. She ranked his contributions to child care to be equal to hers, and rated his contributions to housework only slightly below her own. While not eagerly rushing to do the cooking, cleaning, or laundry, he complied with occasional reminders and according to his wife, was "a better cleaner" than she was.

His sharing stemmed, in part, from her higher earnings and their mutual willingness to reduce his "outside chores" by hiring outside help. Unlike the more ambivalent co-providers who hired housekeepers to do "her" chores, this couple hired a gardener to work on the yard so they could both spend more time focusing on the children and the house. Rather than complaining about their division of labor, he talked about how he has come to appreciate his situation:

> Ever since I've known my wife, she's made more money than I have. Initially—as a man— I resented it. I went through a lot of head trips about it. But as time developed, I appreciated it. Now I respect it. The way I figure it is, I'd rather have her sharing the money with me than sharing it with someone else. She has her full-time job and then she has her part-time job as a consultant. The gardener I'm paying $75 per week, and I'm paying someone else $25 per week to make my lunch, so I'm enjoying it! It's self-interest.

The power dynamic in this family, coupled with their willingness to pay for outside help to reduce his chores, and the flexibility of his self-employed work schedule, led to substantial sharing of cooking, cleaning, and child care. Because she was making more money and working more hours than he was, he could not emulate other husbands in claiming priority for his provider activities.

SUMMARY AND DISCUSSION

For these dual-earner Chicano couples, we found conventional masculine privilege as well a considerable sharing in several domains. First, as in previous studies of ethnic minority families, wives were employed a substantial number of hours and made significant contributions to the household income. Second, like some who have studied Chicano families, we found that couples described their decision-making to be relatively fair and equal.[12] Third, fathers in these families were more involved in child rearing than their own fathers had been, and many were rated as sharing a majority of child care tasks. Finally, while no husband performed fully half of the housework, a few made substantial contributions in this area as well.

One of the power dynamics that appeared to undergird the household division of labor in these families was the relative earning power of each spouse, though this was modified by factors such as occupational prestige, provider role status, and personal preference. In just under half of the families, the wife earned less than a third of the family income, and in all of these families the husband performed little of the routine housework or child care. In two families, wives earned more than their husbands, and these two households reported sharing more domestic labor than others. Among the other couples who shared housework and child care, there was a preponderance of relatively balanced incomes. In the two families with large financial contributions from wives, but little household help from husbands, couples hired housekeepers to reduce the wives' household workload.

While relative income appeared to make a significant difference in marital power, we observed no simple or straightforward exchange of market resources for domestic services. Other factors like failed career aspirations or occupational status influenced marital dynamics and helped explain why some wives were willing to push a little harder for change in the division of household labor. In almost every case, husbands reluctantly responded to requests for help from wives. Only when wives explicitly took the initiative to shift some of the housework burden to husbands did the men begin to assume significant responsibility for the day-to-day operation of the household. Even when they began to share the housework and child care, men tended to do some of the less onerous tasks like playing with the children or washing the dinner dishes. When we compared these men to their own fathers, or their wives' fathers, however, we could see that they were sharing more domestic chores than the generation that preceded them.

Acceptance of wives as co-providers and wives' delegation of a portion of the homemaker role to husbands were especially important to creating more equal divisions of household labor in these families. If wives made lists for their husbands or offered them frequent reminders, they were more successful than if they waited for husbands to take the initiative. Remaining responsible for managing the home and children was cause for resentment on the part of many wives, however. Sometimes wives were effective in getting husbands to perform certain chores, like ironing, by stopping doing it altogether. For other wives, sharing evolved more "naturally," as both spouses agreed to share tasks or performed the chores that they preferred.

Economies of gratitude continually shifted as the ideology, career attachments, and feelings of entitlement of each spouse changed over time. For some main-provider families, this meant that wives were grateful for husbands' "permission" to hold a job, or that wives worked harder at home because they felt guilty for making their husbands do any of the housework. Main-provider husbands usually let their job commitments limit their family work, whereas their wives took time off from work to care for a sick child or to attend a parent-teacher conference.

Even in families where co-provider wives had advanced degrees and earned high incomes, some wives' work/family boundaries were more permeable than their husbands', like the program director married to a teacher who was a "perpetual" graduate student and attended "endless" community meetings. While she was employed more hours than he, and made about the same amount of money, she had to "schedule him" to watch the children if she wanted to leave the house alone. His stature as a "community leader" provided him with subterranean leverage in the unspoken struggle over taking responsibility for the house and children. His "gender ideology," if measured with conventional survey questions, would undoubtedly have been characterized as "egalitarian," because he spoke in broad platitudes about women's equality and was washing the dishes when we arrived for the interviews. He insisted on finishing the dishes as he answered my questions, but in the other room, his wife confided to Elsa in incredulous tones, "He *never* does that!"

In other ambivalent co-provider families, husbands gained unspoken advantage because they had more prestigious jobs than their wives, and earned more money. While these highly educated attorneys and administrators talked about how they respected their wives' careers, and expressed interest in spending more time with their children, their actions showed that they did not fully assume responsibility for sharing the homemaker or parenting role. To solve the dilemma of too little time and too many chores, two of these families hired housekeepers. Wives were grateful for this strategy, though it did not alter inequities in the distribution of housework and child care, nor in the allocation of worry.

In other families, the economy of gratitude departed dramatically from conventional notions of husband as economic provider and wife as nurturing homemaker. When wives' earnings approached or exceeded their husbands', economies of gratitude shifted toward more equal expectations, with husbands beginning to assume that they must do more around the house. Even in these families, husbands rarely began doing more chores without prodding from wives, but they usually did them "without complaining." Similarly, when wives with economic leverage began expecting more from their husbands, they were usually successful in getting them to do more.

Another type of leverage that was important, even in main-provider households, was the existence of failed aspirations. If wives expected husbands to "make more" of themselves, pursue "more important" careers, or follow "dream" occupational goals, then wives were able to get husbands to do more around the house. This perception of failed aspirations, if held by both spouses, served as a reminder that husbands had no excuse for not helping out at home. In these families, wives were not at all reluctant to demand assistance with domestic chores, and husbands were rarely able to use their jobs as excuses for getting out of housework.

The economies of gratitude in these families were not equally balanced, but many exhibited divisions of household labor that contradicted cultural stereotypes of macho men and male-dominated families. Particularly salient in these families was the lack of fit between their own class position and that of their parents. Most of the parents were Mexican immigrants with little education and low occupational mobility. The couples we interviewed, in contrast, were well-educated and relatively secure in middle-class occupations. The couples could have compared themselves to their parents, evaluating themselves to be egalitarian and financially successful. While some did just that, most compared themselves to their Anglo and Chicano friends and coworkers, many of whom shared as much or more than they did. Implicitly comparing their earnings, occupational commitments, and perceived aptitudes, husbands and wives negotiated new patterns of work/family boundaries and developed novel justifications for their emerging arrangements. These were not created anew, but emerged out of the popular culture in which they found themselves. Judith Stacey labels such developments the making of

the "postmodern family," because they signal "the contested, ambivalent, and undecided character of contemporary gender and kinship arrangements."[13] Our findings confirm that families are an important site of new struggles over the meaning of gender and the rights and obligations of men and women in each other and over each other's labor.

One of the most provocative findings from our study has to do with the class position of Chicano husbands and wives who shared household labor: white-collar, working-class families shared more than upper-middle-class professionals. Contrary to findings from nationwide surveys predicting that higher levels of education for either husbands or wives will be associated with more sharing, the most highly educated of our well-educated sample of Chicano couples shared only moderate amounts of child care and little housework.[14] Contrary to other predictions, neither was it the working-class women in this study who achieved the most balanced divisions of labor.[15] It was the middle occupational group of women, the executive secretaries, clerks, technicians, teachers, and mid-level administrators who extracted the most help from husbands. The men in these families were similarly in the middle in terms of occupational status for this sample—administrative assistants, a builder, a mail carrier, a technician—and in the middle in terms of income. What this means is that the highest status wives—the program coordinators, nurses, social workers, and office managers—were not able to, or chose not to, transform their salaries or occupational status into more participation from husbands. This was probably because their husbands had even higher incomes and more prestigious occupations than they did. The lawyers, program directors, ranking bureaucrats, and "community leaders" parlayed their status into extra leisure at home, either by paying for housekeepers or ignoring the housework. Finally, Chicana wives at the lowest end of the occupational structure fared least well. The teacher's aides, entry-level secretaries, day-care providers, and part-time employees did the bulk of the work at home whether they were married to mechanics or lawyers. When wives made less than a third of what their husbands did, they were only able to get husbands to do a little more if the men were working at jobs considered "below" them—a telephone lineman, a painter, an elementary-school teacher.

Only Chicano couples were included in this study but results are similar to findings from previous interviews with Anglo couples.[16] My interpretation is that the major processes shaping divisions of labor in middle-class Chicano couples are approximately the same as those sharing divisions of labor in other middle-class couples. This is not to say that ethnicity did not make a difference to the Chicano couples we interviewed. They grew up in recently immigrating working-class families, watched their parents work long hours for minimal wages, and understood firsthand the toll that various forms of racial discrimination can take. Probably because of some of these experiences, and their own more recent ones, our informants looked at job security, fertility decisions, and the division of household labor somewhat differently than their Anglo counterparts. In some cases, this can give Chicano husbands in working-class or professional jobs license to ignore more of the housework, and might temper the anger of some working-class or professional Chicanas who are still called on to do most of the domestic chores. If these findings are generalizable, however, it is those in between the blue-collar working-class and the upper-middle-class professionals that might be more likely to share housework and childcare.

Assessing whether these findings apply to other dual-earner Chicano couples will require the use of larger, more representative samples. If the limited sharing observed here represents a trend—however slow or reluctant—it could have far-reaching consequences. More and more Chicana mothers are remaining full-time members of the paid labor force. With the "postindustrial" expansion of the service and information sectors of the economy, Chicanos

and Chicanas will be increasingly likely to enter white-collar middle-class occupations. As more Chicano families fit the occupational profile of those we studied, we may see more assumption of housework and child care by Chicano men. Regardless of the specific changes that the economy will undergo, we can expect Chicano men and women, like their Anglo counterparts, to continue to negotiate for change in their work and family roles.

NOTES

1. For a discussion of how the term machismo can also reflect positive attributes of respect, loyalty, responsibility, and generosity, see Alfredo Mirandé, "Chicano Fathers: Traditional Perceptions and Current Realities," pp. 93–106, in *Fatherhood Today*, P. Bronstein and C. Cowan, eds. (New York: Wiley, 1988).

2. For reviews of literature on Latin-American families and projections on their future proportionate representation in the population, see Randall Collins and Scott Coltrane, *Sociology of Marriage and the Family* (Chicago: Nelson Hall, 1994); William A. Vega, "Hispanic Families in the 1980s," *Journal of Marriage and the Family* 52(1990): 1015–1024; and Norma Williams, *The Mexican-American Family* (New York: General Hall, 1990).

3. Maxine Baca Zinn, "Family, Feminism, and Race in America," *Gender & Society* 4(1990): 68–82; Mirandé, "Chicano Fathers"; Vega, "Hispanic Families"; and Williams, *The Mexican-American Family*.

4. See Coltrane, *Family Man: Fatherhood, Housework, and Gender Equity* (New York: Oxford University Press, 1994); Coltrane and Valdez, "Reluctant Compliance: Work/Family Role Allocation in Dual-Earner Chicano Families," in *Men, Work, and Family.* Jane C. Hood, ed. (Newbury Park, CA: Sage, 1994) and Valdez and Coltrane, "Work, Family, and the Chicana: Power, Perception and Equity," in *Employed Mothers and the Family Context*, Judith Frankel, ed. (New York: Springer, 1993). I thank Hilda Cortez, a summer research intern at the University of California, for help in transcribing some of the interviews and for providing insight into some of the issues faced by these families.

5. Jessie Bernard, *The Future of Marriage* (New York: World, 1972).

6. See Jane Hood, 1986. "The Provider Role: Its Meaning and Measurement." *Journal of Marriage and the Family* 48: 349–359.

7. Hood, "The Provider Role."

8. See Coltrane, "Household Labor and the Routine Production of Gender." *Social Problems* 35: 473–490.

9. I am indebted to Arlie Hochschild, who first used this term in *The Second Shift* (New York: Viking, 1987). See also Karen Pyke and Scott Coltrane, "Entitlement, Obligation, and Gratitude in Remarriage: Toward a Gendered Understanding of Household Labor Allocation."

10. I am indebted to Joseph Pleck for his conceptualization of "asymmetrically permeable" work/family boundaries ("The Work-Family Role System." *Social Problems* 24: 417–427).

12. See, for example, V. Cromwell and R. Cromwell, 1978. "Perceived Dominance in Decision Making and Conflict Resolution among Anglo, Black, and Chicano

Couples." *Journal of Marriage and the Family* 40: 749–760; G. Hawkes and M. Taylor, 1975. "Power Structure in Mexican and Mexican-American Farm Labor Families." *Journal of Marriage and the Family* 37: 807–881; L. Ybarra, 1982. "When Wives Work: The Impact on the Chicano Family." *Journal of Marriage and the Family* 44: 169–178.

13. Judith Stacey, 1990. *Brave New Families.* New York: Basic Books, p. 17.

14. See, for instance, Donna H. Berardo, Constance Shehan, and Gerald R. Leslie, "A Residue of Tradition: Jobs, Careers, and Spouses' Time in Housework." *Journal of Marriage and the Family* 49(1987): 381–390; Catherine E. Ross, "The Division of Labor at Home." *Social Forces* 65(1987): 816–833.

15. Patricia Zavella. 1987. *Women's Work and Chicano Families.* Ithaca, NY: Cornell University Press; Stacey, *Brave New Families.*

16. See, for example, Hochschild, *Second Shift;* Hood, *Two-Job Family;* Coltrane, *Family Man.*

Further Questions

1. If your work is not perceived to be as successful or as important as that of your spouse, does this mean that you should shoulder more of the household burdens? What if you are being paid less simply because women command less pay than men?

2. Do men have rights to think of domestic chores as optional while these chores are required for their wives? Who performs the chores if one spouse has higher standards for these chores than the other?

3. How good is a situation where a wife has to continually ask her husband to do certain things with the children or around the house? Is what matters his performance or the amount of initiative he took in getting his performance started?

XI.4 ## Love, Self Interest, Power, and Opposition: Untangling the Roots of Intensive Mothering

SHARON HAYS

Sharon Hays examines the rationale behind what she calls "intensive mothering," particularly that of women who also participate in the external workplace with its competitions for status and financial rewards. In this selection she explores the view

Abridged from "Love, Self Interest, Power, and Opposition: Untangling the Roots of Intensive Mothering" in The Cultural Contradictions of Motherhood *by Sharon Hays. (New Haven, CT: Yale University Press.) Copyright © 1996 Yale University Press. Reprinted by permission of the publisher.*

that women's intensive mothering serves the interests of the most powerful, namely, whites, upper classes, capitalist owners, and state leaders.

Hays is Assistant Professor of Sociology and Women's Studies at the University of Virginia.

Reading Questions

1. How are capitalists well-served by women's commitment to child rearing, both in the type of individual this produces and in the status in the workplace it affords women? Are there other possible systems of child rearing that would benefit capitalism equally well?
2. How are men advantaged by women's undertaking to do the main part of child rearing and housework? For some men, is there a better way for them to profit from the services of women?
3. Is intensive mothering primarily a middle-class and upper-class phenomenon, serving the interests of these classes?

RACHEL, WHO LIVES IN BOTH the public and private spheres, exemplifies the depth of the cultural contradictions of contemporary motherhood. As a woman, she has been taught that her primary responsibility is to maintain the logic that dominates family and intimate life, a logic requiring a moral commitment to unremunerated relationships grounded in affection and mutual obligations. As a mother, she knows that this includes taking individual responsibility for the maintenance of intensive methods on behalf of her innocent and "priceless" child. But as a paid working woman, she regularly experiences the logic that dominates the world of formal economic and political life, a logic emphasizing the individualistic, calculating, competitive pursuit of personal gain. And as a career woman, she has made a commitment to long-term, uninterrupted participation in that world. Given this commitment, the demands of intensive mothering seem to do nothing but drain away her time, interfere with her pursuit of financial rewards, diminish her status, and leave her feeling exhausted and inadequate by the end of her daily double shift. Yet Rachel does not give up on one commitment for the other but steadfastly juggles both. And, as I have shown, Rachel is not unique.

The fact that Rachel maintains these two commitments is a measure of the persistent strength of both the ethos of a rationalized market society and the ideology of intensive mothering. But, as

I have argued, theoretically speaking there are a number of reasons to believe that the logic of the market should be wining out and the ideology of intensive mothering fading away. . . .

In a larger social context that not only devalues intensive mothering but actually serves to undermine it, why hasn't this ideology been reconstructed to one more in line with the logic of instrumental rationality, profit maximization, and the practical needs of paid working mothers? Current scholarship on women and the family, though complex and diverse, can be synthesized, classified, and interpreted to yield three possible answers.

1. For some, this is the question of a cynical, uncaring academic who fails to recognize that intensive child rearing is actually based in the reality of children's needs—the growing historical recognition of which is a measure of progress in knowledge following from ongoing, and natural, parental love.

2. For other scholars, this is the question of an overly sentimental and gullible woman who ignores the fact that the ideology of intensive child rearing is actually disappearing, particularly among well-compensated working women who are now busy maximizing their self-interested gain.

3. Alternately [sic], it has been argued that this question and the two answers provided

above miss the point completely. Intensive mothering is neither a choice made by women nor a symbol of love and progress in society; rather, it is an indication of the power of men, whites, the upper classes, capitalists, and state leaders to impose a particular form of family life on those less powerful than themselves.

THE DIFFERENTIAL INTERESTS AT STAKE

One person's self-interested gain might be another person's loss—it all depends on whose ox is being gored. To predict the likelihood of winning or losing in this battle of oxen, one needs to determine who has the strongest oxen in the first place. In other words, while all people may in fact be self-interested, some people are in a better position than others to ensure that their interests are met. From this point of view, it is a mistake to focus on the profit-maximizing efforts of mothers themselves, since they are, after all, a relatively powerless group. Those who really benefit from the ideology of intensive mothering, as many scholars imply, are those who wield the most power economically, culturally, and politically—namely, men, whites, the upper classes, capitalist owners, and state leaders.

First, an ideological emphasis on particular family forms and models of child rearing may be implicated in attempts to maintain political stability and state power (e.g., Donzelot, 1979; Gordon, 1988; Platt, 1977; Stone, 1977; Zaretsky, 1982). The state has long attempted to regulate family matters and, ever since the Progressive Era, has been key in legislating and enforcing certain family forms. Welfare policies, tax laws, compulsory schooling, juvenile courts, and child labor laws, for example, have all contributed to the establishment of a particular form of parenting. To the extent that government officials have an interest in controlling potentially volatile populations and in sparing the coffers from the potential of new and multiple public demands, the internal logic of intensive mothering may be quite useful. A mother's ongoing dedication to educating the young in particular social norms helps to ensure the creation of law-abiding, tax-paying citizens, and the particularly time-consuming process of training children in self-discipline and individual responsibility makes a significant contribution toward sparing the state from future pressures to widen its welfare roles or raise the minimum wage or subsidize housing, childcare, or medical expenses. As Donzelot (1979) argues, social workers, public schools, the courts, and law-enforcement officers all contribute to training mothers and children at the same time that they serve government interests in "policing the family."[11] To the extent that this process runs smoothly, mothers will consider it their duty to send the kids to school, keep them off the streets, teach them obedience, and ensure that they grow up to be individuals who are, simultaneously, compliant in the face of authority and independent, individuals who consider themselves solely responsible for their own welfare.

Many scholars have also argued that capitalists are well served by women's commitment to child rearing (e.g., Acker, 1988; Bentson, 1984; Ehrenreich, 1989; Ehrenreich and English, 1978; Hartmann, 1981a; Kessler-Harris, 1982; Matthaei, 1982; Slater, 1976; Weiner, 1985; Zaretsky, 1976; Zuckerman, 1975). First, claiming that women's primary responsibility is to keep the home and raise the children helps convince women that they can be paid lower wages, since their earnings are only secondary to those of their husbands. Further, treating women as responsible for childcare means that the job of grooming young workers for the future is accomplished at a minimal cost to those who will employ them. The prolonged protection of childhood innocence that it contained in the logic of intensive mothering is useful to employers, since it includes the possibility of extensive schooling and thereby helps to create a flexible and well-trained labor force at a relatively low cost. The logic of meeting all the child's needs and desires means that mothers are encouraged to buy all those baby accessories, fancy toys, and children's designer fashions and, again, child-rearing techniques meant to instill self-discipline and a sense of personal responsibility are especially important in that they not only help in the development of self-motivated managers but also help create workers who will blame only themselves when they lose their jobs or find their wages inadequate. In addition, the permissive, child-centered nature of intensive mothering helps to create little consumers. Trained in having all their desires met, these children grow up hungry to buy every new commodity that capitalism produces.

Further, a major line of analysis implies that the ideology of intensive mothering serves men (e.g., Delphy, 1984; Hartmann, 1981a, 1981b; Kessler-Harris, 1982; Mainardi, 1970; Margolis, 1984; Matthaei, 1982; Polatnick, 1983; Ulrich, 1982; Weiner, 1985). As has been true since the days of the Puritans, the present-day model of appropriate child rearing frees men from having to do the grunt work of looking after the dirty, demanding, dependent beings that are their progeny. And the fact that women's responsibility for child rearing is part of a larger system that makes women responsible for all household chores means that men are often supplied with personal maids, chefs, and laundresses. More important perhaps, this system helps to ensure that men are spared from women's competition in the labor market. Those women who stay at home to care for children leave many openings for men, and even when women do work for pay, their identification with domesticity means that they tend to be segregated in those poorly paid occupations dubbed "women's work." Furthermore, the newer, more intensive version of mothering means that employed women work so hard at home and feel so responsible for the kids and so guilty about the hours they spend away that they do not have the time or the energy to compete with men for the more lucrative positions in the higher rungs of the career ladder. Finally, the ideology of intensive mothering

serves men in that women's commitment to this socially devalued task helps to maintain their subordinate position in society as a whole.

Child-rearing ideologies have also helped to maintain the privileged position of those who are native-born, those who are white, and those who are members of the middle and upper classes. Historically, ideas of appropriate child rearing were an integral part of the middle-class claim to superiority over the languishing, frivolous rich and the gaudy, untutored poor. Native-born whites of the dominant classes today have surely benefitted from the fact that they are the ones most likely to have the cultural and economic resources as well as the time to define and engage in the form of mothering that is considered proper. Recent immigrants and members of lower-income and nonwhite communities in the United States, on the other hand, are consistently placed at a practical, economic, and status disadvantage in these terms. Members of such groups may also thereby lower their children's chances for economic gain, since their child-rearing methods are, for instance, less likely to be valued and rewarded by the school system and less likely to provide the cultural capital necessary for a well-paying job. For much the same reasons, middle- and upper-class whites are not only liable to maintain the economic benefits connected to their class and race but also are likely to gain the advantage of a certain social legitimacy for their economically and culturally privileged position.[12]

The words of mothers offer little explicit help in confirming or denying this line of thought. In my small sample, Latinas and African-American women clearly recognize racial oppression, but these are the only groups that seem to argue that the injustice and oppression in their lives are systematic and straightforward. Although many working-class and poor women recognize inequality in the class system and a few rail against the very rich, most seem to accept the system as a relatively fair one in which nearly everyone has an equal opportunity to get ahead. Poor mothers are often dissatisfied with government bureaucracy, given that they suffer the weight of the welfare system, yet they also seem to be resigned that this is the price they must pay in order to receive assistance—after all, they imply, as individuals who control their own lives, they are ultimately responsible for their fate. Some paid working mothers are dissatisfied with the way their bosses treat them, with their inflexible schedules, with the size of their paychecks, or with the high cost of the children's toys and shoes, but none seem to feel that their child-rearing practices are controlled by the state and capitalism. On the other hand, since almost half of these women define themselves as feminists and nearly all express some resentment of men's incompetence or men's unwillingness to help domestically, one would suspect that they understand men as oppressors of a sort. But this attitude is actually a bit more complicated. When I asked these mothers, "Who do you think has it better, men or women?" many argue that a life of nurturing and child rearing is far preferable to a life of fighting wars and being primarily responsible for the financial support of the family.[13] Even male domination, in this sense, is not necessarily experienced as obvious or unambiguous. Above all, not one of the mothers I talked to understood her child-rearing efforts as an unjust burden or as a task imposed on her by others more powerful than herself.

These facts, however, do little to dent this argument. The power and the privileging of men, whites, the upper classes, the market, and the centralized state operate as interconnected system whose logics are necessarily hidden—since people might (and sometimes do) revolt if they recognize these systems as unjust. Ideological coercion, in this sense, is much more efficient and effective than physical coercion. These forms of ideological coercion are not so much the result of a self-conscious conspiracy but, rather, are developed over time through a process of trial and error. Arguments about "equal opportunity" and "individual responsibility" for one's social position, in these terms, are simply ideological mechanisms meant to disguise systematic injustice. So too is the ideology

of intensive mothering. It operates to convince women that they want (or at least should want) to commit themselves to a task that, in fact, ultimately serves those with the power to manipulate and control ideas.[14] The ideology of intensive child rearing, then, is both the result of and a form of *disguising* domination.

With this in mind, there are many indications that mothers are serving the interests of the powerful. The child-rearing techniques of lower-class, non-white, and immigrant women are treated as inferior, and, partly because of this, their children are less likely to get ahead (e.g., Bourdieu, 1977, 1984; Collins, 1971b; Lareau, 1987). Women in general do far more than their fair share of child rearing and housework, and there is much evidence that they spare men from heavier competition in the labor force. Mothers do attempt to raise their children as obedient citizens who will neither revolt against nor become dependent upon the state. And they are certainly producing workers for the future at a relatively low cost at the same time that they seem to be (perhaps unwittingly) training their kids to be heavy consumers of commercial goods.

This is, without a doubt, the most powerful argument for explaining why it is women rather than men who are held primarily responsible for child rearing.[15] It also provides a broader social context for understanding arguments about the love or self-interest of mothers. The explicit emphasis on nurturant and intensive maternal love is interpreted in relation to the social circumstances in which it arose and developed and is understood as part of an ideology initiated, elaborated, and maintained by the most powerful groups in society. By emphasizing the social reality of unequal gender relations, this analysis also allows one to recognize that women's "self-interested" attempts to gain status have long focused on ideologies valorizing motherhood precisely because this has been one of the few avenues for achieving status left open to women. In the same terms, the extent to which white, middle-class women have been successful in making their notions of appropriate child rearing salient has had much to do with their relative privilege. And, if one is trying to make sense of why paid work, efficiency, and the competition for monetary success are the primary goals that self-interested people would seek to maximize, then a recognition that a rationalized market society is the context in which they operate offers a good deal of clarification.

There are, however, problems and ambiguities in this explanation as well. The interests of men, capitalists, the state, the upper classes, and native-born whites, it could be argued, do not *necessarily* lead them to press for intensive child rearing. Arguably, the form of ideological coercion that would make the most sense is one that convinced women to dedicate themselves to efficiency above all—both in the maintenance of the household and in the pursuit of the best-paid work available to them. Children would then be sent elsewhere to be raised by others. Some men, after all, might want sexy wives cooking hearty meals instead of ones busy with diapers and covered with infant spittle—and at times they have been known to make this clear (e.g., Rubin, 1983). Women could also serve men quite well if they spent more of their time bringing home a larger portion of the family income. Capitalism could thus obtain full access to the energies of women in their prime productive years. It could also gain more customers by expanding the service industry in commercialized child care and boarding schools. And, theoretically at least, the child-care centers and boarding schools thus created could do a much more cost-effective job of preparing children for life in the market system—training them for future geographic mobility, helping them to develop the proper perspective on efficiency and the pursuit of profit, and preparing them more effectively for their respective futures as workers or managers by ranking and sorting them early on in accordance with their capabilities.[16] These "schools" for children could also serve the state well, allowing it to widen its net of regulation and control. White, middle-class women could then name themselves as the most efficient su-

perwomen of all, and their privileged economic position would serve as the glue to make that label stick.

In other words, the ideology of intensive motherhood is clearly not the only way for the powerful to ensure that their interests are met. And beyond this, one still needs to ask, if power actually does allow people to create and manipulate ideologies at will, why would those whose privilege relies on a society dominated by the logic of profit-oriented, competitive, and individualistic relations develop an ideology whose overall logic runs in contradiction to that system? This remains something of a mystery.

CULTURAL AMBIVALENCE

My argument about mothers' opposition to a traditionalized market society does not supersede or nullify arguments about unequal power relations or self-interested calculations of profit. Mothers are, in part, rational bookkeepers endeavoring to maximize their social assets and to organize their lives in efficient ways. Mothers are also social subordinates whose mothering, in part, serves the interests of those more powerful than themselves. But it would require a long theoretical stretch to simply explain away the ideology of intensive mothering as merely a cunning ploy devised to cover up the advantages that mothers seek or as solely a manipulative strategy meant to serve the powerful. Mothers operate in part according to a logic opposing that of self-interested gain—not because this is a necessity, not because they are irrational or selfless, and not because they are forced to, but because they are actively participating in a rejection of that logic. If women were simply calculating "rational actors" operating according to the logic that dominates in the marketplace, they could easily dispense with the ideology of intensive motherhood. And if they did so, there would be no cultural contradictions and motherhood would not hold the symbolic power that it does in our culture.

This way of opposing the logic of rationalized market societies is not necessarily a self-conscious opposition, it is not the opposition of isolated individuals, and, as I have noted, it is surely not the only form of such opposition. As Polanyi (1944) points out, if the self-regulating market alone determined the fate of the earth and its inhabitants, the earth would be polluted beyond recognition and the broken bodies of laborers would be strewn like garbage across the land. To stem this tide, Polanyi argues, people have engaged in a countermovement, a form of opposition to market logic that includes, for instance, the establishment of labor unions, worker-safety provisions, social security programs, welfare systems, environmental protection agencies, and national parks. People have not necessarily seen their work in establishing such programs and provisions as opposition to market logic, and their efforts are certainly not the work of isolated individuals. On a different level, the same is true of the form of opposition implicit in the ideology of intensive mothering. When women engage in this opposition, they generally do not make a self-conscious decision to oppose the system that values competitive individualism and material advantage. And although they do not engage in collective action per se, they are also not acting as isolated individuals. They act as members of a culture that maintains two contradictory ideologies, and their actions take place in the context of a social hierarchy that gives women primary responsibility for creating and maintaining nurturing ties.

The mothering relationship is not the only human relationship that holds symbolic power as a form of opposition. The ideologies of socially appropriate romantic love, friendship, and family ties, in particular, all treat considerations of financial profit, status seeking, and efficiency as taboo.[18] Of course, the same tensions that exist in the mothering relationship are present in love, friendship, and family relations. We know, for instance, that many people fall in love and establish friendships out of convenience, in attempts to heighten their own status of material gains, and as a way to exercise forms of power. And we know that people's level of commitment to family members is sometimes grounded in these same concerns. Although such practices point to significant realities, the cultural ideals that guide these relationships remain equally significant. The ideology guiding the relationship between mothers and children is, I would argue, particularly powerful in this regard, precisely because it is understood as more distant and more protected from market relationships than any other.

If mothering is one of the central practices meant to provide a crucial counterpoint to the corruption, impersonality, and individualistic competition of the larger society, the place that ordinary people in their everyday lives find hope for this sort of counterpoint has increasingly narrowed. Early in the history of this nation, citizens were understood as struggling to achieve some form of the common good, and mothers saw their role as instilling the values of virtuous citizenship in their children. Home, women, and mothers were imagined as a source of purity and goodness: home was sweet, women were pious, passionless, and pure, and mothers were unselfish, nurturing, and moral. But over time the image of a morally pure home was increasingly scarred as households were invaded by the logic of technical efficiency, juvenile courts and social workers, public schools, TV dinners and manufactured clothing, and visions of a competition for resources among family members. Claims to the virtue and moral righteousness of women were further tainted by a hesitancy to claim any single definition of morality as an absolute or shared one. More and more, at least some women seemed far from pious, passionless, and pure. In the present era the virtue of citizens has become a distant echo, as evidenced in widespread disenchantment with a political process perceived as competitive and corrupt. One of the few sources left for making the world a better place seems to be grounded in the ethic of maternal love and unselfishness and in children's apparent innocence, purity, and goodness.

Adding to this trend is the fact that as the implosion of self-interest and competition proceeds, ties of friendship, love, and family have come to seem increasingly tenuous. The more one begins to wonder if friends might be moving on to a better job or simply using those around them for their own gain, then the more one might expect the concern to establish lasting ties of mutual obligation and commitment to be centered on the family. The more divorce becomes the norm, the more unreliable and unstable relationships with adult family members seem, and the more that popular psychology advises people to pick and choose which adult family members they will remain close to, then the more one would expect people to seek out other friendships. But the more unreliable both friendships and adult family relationships become, the more one's attention comes to be focused on relations between mother and child. One mother implied this in her response to the question "How do you think you'd feel if you never had children?":

> I'd be really lonely. Because a husband, well, you can have two, three, four husbands, you know. Big deal. But your children are something that's a part of you. It's not the same with them. Because your husband will get up and leave one day and you can get another one. That's why.

And that's why, at least in part, the more the larger world becomes impersonal, competitive, and individualistic and the more the logic of that world invades the world of intimate relationships, the more intensive child rearing becomes.

To transform child rearing into shared work among social equals would require a revolution quite different from its predecessor [the Industrial Revolution]. But to the extent that we value at least portions of the ideology of intensive mothering, such a revolution is surely in order. Under current circumstances, our best hope for easing women's burden remains increased public power for women, higher public status for those involved in caregiving, and greater paternal participation in child rearing. All of these solutions are interrelated. The more public power women gain, the more they can demand that men take greater responsibility of child rearing and the more child rearing (and all it symbolizes) will likely come to be publicly valued. Given the greater share of public power among men currently, the more fathers participate in raising children, the more they will demand that child rearing be publicly valued. And as child rearing increases in public status, the more likely it is that men will participate in it. Finally, the more that men participate in child rearing and the more it is socially valued, the more likely it becomes that attempts to convince business leaders and legislators to provide subsidized child care, job sharing, flex time, and parental leave will meet with success.

The struggle, tensions, and contradictions will probably persist for some time to come, however. After all, even if we achieve these ends, the tensions between the values of parenthood and the values of the marketplace will not disappear. Such social revisions will simply mean that *both* men and women will experience in their daily lives the contradictions in modern society that now plague women primarily; both men and women will have to juggle the two commitments, and both will have to switch gears every day when they come home from their paying jobs. With this newfound sharing of responsibility, however, the cultural contradictions of parenthood will perhaps become more open to public view and be confronted more equally, by all.[19]

Notes

11. As Donzelot puts it, "Parents no longer have the right, as they had in the Dark Ages, to turn their children into failures" (1979: 225). Donzelot also points out that middle-class women have been particularly useful to the state, not only in their work of internally monitoring their own families but also in that they have regularly been enlisted in attempts to establish agencies meant to monitor the behavior of poor and working-class families.

12. In historical terms, this argument is implied by McGlone (1971), Ryan (1985), and Stansell (1987), among others. With reference to today's mothering, this argument is implied by many, including Anzaldua (1987); Bourdieu (1977); Bourdieu and Passeron (1977); Bowles and Gintis (1973, 1976); Chow (1989); Cliff (1983); Collins (1991); Glenn, Chang, and Forcey (1994); Joseph (1981); Lareau (1987); MacLeod (1987); Matute-Bianchi (1986); and Wilcox (1982). One could also add to this analysis the forms of power that undergird the systematic privileging of those with the "right" sexual orientation (e.g., Rich, 1983; Rubin, 1984).

13. More precisely, half state that women have it better, about one-third that men have it better, and the rest argue that neither men nor women have it better. Although I expected that they would respond to this question in terms of men's greater access to wealth and power, they instead answered in terms of whose life-style they would choose. It is also interesting to note that working-class and poor women were far more likely than middle-class women to say that men have it better, at the same time that middle-class mothers were far more likely to identify themselves as "feminists." These apparent contradictions clearly deserve further exploration.

14. See Chafetz (1990) and Jackman (1994) for versions of this argument.

15. This argument can also explain how forms of gender socialization and psychological processes that serve to reproduce certain types of mothering were first set in motion: both follow from male domination and the separation of spheres that attended the development of capitalism and the centralized states. Chodorow's (1974, 1978) and Benjamin's (1988) arguments about the reproduction of mothering fit into this framework and are also connected to arguments focusing on love. That is, both would argue that maternal love is very deep and emotionally powerful at the same time that they argue that the reason this love is maternal rather than parental is to be found in historically specific systems of domination. Rothman's (1989) view of mothering also fits with analyses of both love and unequal power. Unfortunately, I cannot do justice to the complexity and sophistication of their arguments here.

Since readers familiar with Chodorow's argument in particular will recognize the extent to which it could be used to explain intensive mothering, a further point of clarification may be in order. Her analysis of the complex psychoanalytic processes involved in parent-child relations and childhood-identity formation is the most powerful argument available for making sense of the way that the gendered nature of parenting is reproduced over generations and the fact that mothering seems such a deep and integral part of women's identities. This argument, however, cannot fully explain the development and persistence of intensive mothering. First, the ideology of intensive mothering is a far more elaborate set of beliefs than the emotional attachment that Chodorow describes. Second, the logic of Chodorow's argument would lead us to believe that the more women shared parenting with others (e.g., day care) and the more women had a chance to gain power and status in the world outside the home (e.g., paid work), the less attached to mothering they would become. As I have shown, this does not seem to hold true.

16. For a further analysis of why such practices would make perfect sense in modern market societies, see Bowles and Gintis (1976); Moore (1958); and Sennett (1970). Many Marxist feminists and socialist feminists have also implied that child rearing might be most equitably and effectively accomplished in a rationalized, institutional setting under the control of the state (e.g., Bentson, 1984; Firestone, 1984; Hartmann, 1981a; Kollantai, 1980). All these arguments challenge the widely accepted belief that children are best prepared for life in this society by currently prescribed child-rearing methods. Although the alternatives they propose may seem unacceptable, they do demonstrate that the value of today's child-rearing methods is not self-evident.

18. See Silver (1996) for a particularly nice rendition of friendship in these terms. Friendships are valued, he argues, precisely to the extent that they *invert* the norms of the larger society.

19. The question of making child rearing a public issue is a highly complex one, littered with land mines. To maintain child rearing as a private enterprise conducted by men and women in the (hypothetically) secluded haven of the home continues to absolve the public sphere from the values implied in the ideology of intensive mothering. On the other hand, many are appropriately concerned that the state and the marketplace, as they are presently constituted, would not provide appropriate leadership in a reconfiguration of family life. Attempts to find a compromise between these two extremes have not yet met with great success. Today, for instance, we find politicians simultaneously calling for a return to "family values" and for the substitution of welfare with "workfare." The tensions are apparent.

BIBLIOGRAPHY

Acker, Joan. 1988. "Class, Gender, and the Relations of Distribution." *Signs* 1 (3):473–497.

Anzaldua, Gloria. 1987. *Borderlands/La Frontera: The New Mestiza*. San Francisco: Spinsters/Aunt Lute.

Benjamin, Jessica. 1988. *The Bonds of Love: Psychoanalysis, Feminism, and the Problem of Domination*. New York: Pantheon Books.

Bentson, Margaret. 1984. "The Political Economy of Women's Liberation." Pp. 239–247 in *Feminist Frameworks: Alternative Theoretical Accounts of the Relations between Women and Men*, edited by Alison M. Jaggar and Paula S. Rothenberg. New York: McGraw-Hill.

Bourdieu, Pierre, 1977. "Cultural Reproduction and Social Reproduction." Pp. 487–511 in *Power and Ideology in Education*, edited by Jerome Karabel and A. H. Halsey. Oxford: Oxford University Press.

———. 1984. *Distinction: A Social Critique of the Judgment of Taste*. Translated by Richard Nice. Cambridge: Harvard University Press.

Bourdieu, Pierre, and Jean-Claude Passeron. 1977. *Reproduction in Education, Society and Culture*. London: Sage.

Bowles, Samuel, and Herbert Gintis. 1973. "IQ in the U.S. Class Structure." *Social Policy* 3:65–96.

Chafetz, Janet Saltzman. 1990. *Gender Equity: An Integrated Theory of Stability and Change*. Newbury Park: Sage.

Chodorow, Nancy. 1974. "Family Structure and Feminine Personality." Pp. 43–66 in *Woman, Culture, and Society,* edited by Michelle Z. Rosaldo and Louise Lamphere. Stanford: Stanford University Press.

———. 1978. *The Reproduction of Mothering*. Berkeley: University of California Press.

Chow, Esther Ngan-Ling. 1989. "The Feminist Movement: Where Are All the Asian American Women?" Pp. 362–377 in *Making Waves,* edited by Asian Women United of California. Boston: Beacon.

Cliff, Michelle. 1983. "If I Could Write This in Fire I Would Write This in Fire." Pp. 16–30 in *Home Girls: A Black Feminist Anthology,* edited by Barbara Smith. New York: Kitchen Table: Women of Color Press.

Collins, Patricia Hill. 1991. *Black Feminist Thought*. New York: Routledge.

Collins, Randall. 1971b. "Functional and Conflict Theories of Educational Stratification." *American Sociological Review* 36:1002–1019.

Delphy, Christine. 1984. *Close to Home: A Materialist Analysis of Women's Oppression*. Translated and edited by Diana Leonard. Amherst: University of Massachusetts Press.

Donzelot, Jacques. 1979. *The Policing of Families*. New York: Pantheon.

Ehrenreich, Barbara. 1989. *Fear of Falling: The Inner Life of the Middle-Class*. New York: HarperCollins.

Ehrenreich, Barbara, and Deirdre English. 1978. *For Her Own Good: Fifty Years of Experts' Advice to Women* New York: Doubleday.

Firestone, Shulamith. 1984. "The Dialectic of Sex." Pp. 136–143 in *Feminist Frameworks: Alternative Theoretical Accounts of the Relations between Women and Men,* edited by Alison M. Jaggar and Paula S. Rothenberg. New York: McGraw-Hill.

Glenn, Evelyn Nakano, Grace Chang, and Linda Rennie Forcey. 1994. *Mothering: Ideology, Experience, and Agency*. New York: Routledge.

Gordon, Linda. 1988. *Heroes of Their Own Lives: The Politics and History of Family Violence*. New York: Penguin.

Hartmann, Heidi. 1981a. "The Unhappy Marriage of Marxism and Feminism: Towards a More Progressive Union." Pp. 1–41 in *Women and Revolution: A Discussion of the Unhappy Marriage of Marxism and Feminism*, edited by Lydia Sargent. Boston: South End Press.

———. 1981b. "The Family as the Locus of Gender, Class, and Political Struggle: The Example of Housework." *Signs* 6 (3):366–394.

Jackman, Mary. 1994. *The Velvet Glove: Paternalism and Conflict in Gender, Class, and Race Relations*. Berkeley: University of California Press.

Joseph, Gloria. 1981. "The Incompatible Menage à Trois: Marxism, Feminism, and Racism." Pp. 91–107 in *Women and Revolution: A Discussion of the Unhappy Marriage of Marxism and Feminism,* edited by Lydia Sargent. Boston: South End Press.

Kessler-Harris, Alice. 1982. *Out to Work: A History of Wage-Earning Women in the United States*. Oxford: Oxford University Press.

Kollantai, Alexandra. 1980. "The Social Basis of the Woman Question." Pp. 58–73 in *Selected Writings of Alexandra Kollantai*, edited by A. Holt. New York: Norton.

Lareau, Annette. 1987. "Social Class Differences in Family-School Relationships." *Sociology of Education* 60:73–85.

MacCleod, Jay. 1987. *Ain't No Makin' It*. Boulder: Westview.

McGlone, Robert Elno. 1971. "Suffer the Children: The Emergence of Modern Middle-Class Family Life in America, 1820–1870." Ph.D. diss., University of California, Los Angeles.

Mainardi, Pat. 1970. "The Politics of Housework." Pp. 447–454 in *Sisterhood Is Powerful*, edited by Robert Morgan. New York: Vintage.

Margolis, Maxine. 1984. *Mothers and Such: Views of American Women and Why They Changed*. Berkeley: University of California Press.

Matthaei, Julie A. 1982. *An Economic History of Women in America*. New York: Schocken.

Matute-Bianchi, Maria Eugenia. 1986. "Ethnic Identities and Patterns of School Success and Failure among Mexican-Descent and Japanese American Students in a California High School: An Ethnographic Analysis." *American Journal of Education* 95:233–255.

Moore, Barrington, Jr. 1958. *Political Power and Social Theory: Six Studies*. Cambridge: Harvard University Press.

Platt, Anthony M. 1977. *The Child Savers: The Invention of Delinquency*. 2d ed. Chicago: University of Chicago Press.

Polanyi, Karl. 1944. *The Great Transformation*. Boston: Beacon.

Polatnick, M. 1983. "Why Men Don't Rear Children: A Power Analysis." Pp. 21–40 in *Mothering: Essays in Feminist Theory*, edited by Joyce Trebilcot. Savage, MD: Rowman and Littlefield.

Rich, Adrienne. 1983. "Compulsory Heterosexuality and Lesbian Existence." Pp. 177–205 in *Powers of Desire: The Politics of Sexuality*, edited by Ann Snitow, Christine Stansell, and Sharon Thompson. New York: Monthly Review Press.

Rothman, Barbara Katz. 1989. *Recreating Motherhood: Ideology and Technology in a Patriarchal Society*. New York: Norton.

Rubin, Gayle. 1984. "Thinking Sex: Notes for a Radical Theory of the Politics of Sexuality." Pp. 267–317 in *Pleasure and Danger*, edited by Carole S. Vance. New York: Routledge, Chapman, and Hall.

Rubin, Lillian B. 1983. *Intimate Strangers: Men and Women Together*. New York: Harper and Row.

Ryan, Mary P. 1985. *The Empire of the Mother: American Writing about Domesticity, 1830–1860*. New York: Harrington Park.

Sennett, Richard. 1970. *Families against the City: Middle Class Homes of Industrial Chicago, 1872–1890*. Cambridge: Harvard University Press.

Silver, Allan. 1996. "'Two Different Sorts of Commerce'—Friendship and Strangership in Civil Society." In *Public and Private in Thought and Practice: Perspectives on a Grand Dichotomy*, edited by Jeff Weintraub and Krishan Kumar. Chicago: University of Chicago Press.

Slater, Philip. 1976. *The Pursuit of Loneliness: American Culture at the Breaking Point*. Boston: Beacon.

Stansell, Christine. 1987. *City of Women: Sex and Class in New York, 1789–1860*. Chicago: University of Illinois Press.

Stone, Lawrence. 1977. *The Family, Sex and Marriage in England, 1500–1800*. New York: Harper and Row.

Ulrich, Laurel Thatcher. 1982. *Good Wives: Image and Reality in the Lives of Women in Northern New England, 1650–1750*. New York: Oxford University Press.

Weiner, Lynn Y. 1985. *From Working Girl to Working Mother: The Female Labor Force in the United States, 1820–1980*. Chapel Hill: University of North Carolina Press.

Wilcox, Kathleen. 1982. "Differential Socialization in the Classroom: Implications for Equal Opportunity." Pp. 270–309 in *Doing the Ethnography of Schooling*, edited by G. D. Spindler. New York: Holt, Rinehart, and Winston.

Zaretsky, Eli, 1976. *Capitalism, the Family, and Personal Life*. New York: Harper and Row.

———. 1982. "The Place of the Family in the Origins of the Welfare State." Pp. 188–224 in *Rethinking the Family: Some Feminist Questions*, edited by Barrie Thorne. New York: Longman.

Zuckerman, Michael. 1975. "Dr. Spock: The Confidence Man." Pp. 179–207 in *The Family in History*, edited by Charles E. Rosenberg. Philadelphia: University of Philadelphia Press.

Further Questions

1. Have you planned to raise your children according to the institution of intensive mothering? Have you felt a contradiction between this institution and the principles that structure the work place? How have you planned, or do you plan, to resolve this contradiction?

2. Is the mother-child tie special and more reliable than spousal or other family relationships and friendships? If so, does this give a woman a reason to make child rearing intensive?

3. What will it take for men to make the same investment in child rearing as women do presently? Will men's participation lead child-care to be more publicly valued and resolve some of the contradictions women presently encounter?

Black Women and Motherhood   XI.5

PATRICIA HILL COLLINS

Patricia Hill Collins discusses several important features of black motherhood. Because it might not be a good idea, or even possible, for the biological mother to assume sole care of a child, "other mothers" can share these responsibilities, often informally adopting the child. Black mothers pay special attention to their daughters, teaching them skills for surviving harsh circumstances and for transcending these circumstances if at all possible. Other mothers, in looking after the needs of all children in their care, can often find opportunities to become politically active on behalf of their communities.

Collins is Charles Phelps Taft Professor of Sociology in the Department of African-American Studies at the University of Cincinnati.

Reading Questions

1. Is it a good idea to have extended family and neighbors ready to share the responsibilities of child care when circumstances call for it? What would be some of these circumstances?
2. Should girls be brought up to expect that they will work when adults? Should they develop an affinity for education as a means of advancement in the world? Are such expectations more appropriate for some races and classes than others?
3. Would a concern for the children of a community be a good place to begin efforts of community service?

EXPLORING A BLACK WOMEN'S STANDPOINT ON MOTHERING

THE INSTITUTION OF BLACK MOTHERHOOD consists of a series of constantly renegotiated relationships that African-American women experience with one another, with Black children, with the larger African-American community, and with self. These relationships occur in specific locations such as the individual households that make up African-American extended family networks, as well as in Black community institutions (Martin and Martin, 1978; Sudarkasa, 1981b). Moreover, just as Black women's work and family experiences varied during the transition from slavery to the post-World War II political economy, how Black women define, value, and shape Black motherhood as an institution shows comparable diversity.

Black motherhood as an institution is both dynamic and dialectical. An ongoing tension exists between efforts to mold the institution of Black motherhood to benefit systems of race, gender, and class oppression and efforts by African-American women to define and value our own experiences with motherhood. The controlling images of the mammy, the matriarch, and the welfare mother and the practices they justify are designed to oppress. In contrast, motherhood can serve as a site where Black women express and learn the power of self-definition, the importance of valuing and respecting ourselves, the necessity of self-reliance and independence and a belief in Black women's empowerment. This tension leads to a continuum of responses. Some women view motherhood as a truly burdensome condition that stifles their creativity, exploits their labor, and makes them partners in their own oppression. Others see motherhood as providing a base for self-actualization, status in the Black community, and a catalyst for social activism. These alleged contradictions can exist side by side in African-American communities and families and even within individual women.

Embedded in these changing relationships are five enduring themes that characterize a Black women's standpoint on Black motherhood. For any given historical moment, the particular form that Black women's relationships with one another, children, community, and self actually take depends on how this dialectical relationship between the severity of oppression facing African-American women and our actions in resisting that oppression is expressed.

BLOODMOTHERS, OTHERMOTHERS, AND WOMEN-CENTERED NETWORKS

In African-American communities, fluid and changing boundaries often distinguish biological mothers from other women who care for children. Biological mothers, or Bloodmothers, are expected to care for their children. But African and African-American communities have also recognized that vesting one person with full responsibility for mothering a child may not be wise or possible. As a result, othermothers—women who assist bloodmothers by sharing mothering responsibilities—traditionally have been central to the institution of Black motherhood (Troester, 1984).

The centrality of women in African-American extended families reflects both a continuation of West African cultural values and functional adaptations to race and gender oppression (Tanner, 1974; Stack, 1974; Aschenbrenner, 1975; Martin and Martin, 1978; Sudarkasa, 1981b; Reagon, 1987). This centrality is not characterized by the absence of husbands and fathers. Men may be physically present and/or have well-defined and culturally significant roles in the extended family and the kin unit may be woman-centered. Bebe Moore Campbell's (1989) parents separated when she was small. Even though she spent the school year in the North Philadelphia household maintained by her grandmother and mother, Campbell's father assumed an important role in her life. "My father took care of me," Campbell remembers. "Our separation didn't stunt me or condemn me to a lesser humanity. His absence never made me a fatherless child. I'm not fatherless now" (p. 271). In woman-centered kin units such as Campbell's—whether a mother-child household unit, a married couple household, or a larger unit extending over several households—the centrality of mothers is not predicated on male powerlessness (Tanner, 1974, 133).

Organized, resilient, women-centered networks of bloodmothers and othermothers are key in understanding this centrality. Grandmothers, sisters, aunts, or cousins act as othermothers by taking on child-care responsibilities for one another's children. When needed, temporary child-care arrangements can turn into long-term care or informal adoption (Stack, 1974; Gutman, 1976). Despite strong cultural norms encouraging women to become biological mothers, women who choose not to do so often receive recognition and status from othermother relationships that they establish with Black children.

In African-American communities these women-centered networks of community-based child care often extend beyond the boundaries of biologically related individuals and include "fictive kin" (Stack, 1974). Civil rights activist Ella Baker describes how informal adoption by othermothers functioned in the rural southern community of her childhood:

> My aunt who had thirteen children of her own raised three more. She had become a midwife, and a child was born who was covered with sores. Nobody was particularly wanting the child, so she took the child and raised him . . . and another mother decided she didn't want to be bothered with two children. So my aunt took one and raised him . . . . they were part of the family. (Cantarow, 1980, 59).

Even when relationships are not between kin or fictive kin, African-American community norms traditionally were such that neighbors cared for one another's children. Sara Brooks, a southern domestic worker, describes the importance that the community-based child care a neighbor offered her daughter had for her: "She kept Vivian and she didn't charge me nothin either. You see, people used to look after each other, but now its not that way. I reckon

its because we all was poor, and I guess they put theirself in the place of the person that they was helpin" (Simonsen, 1986, 181). Brooks's experiences demonstrate how the African-American cultural value placed on cooperative child care traditionally found institutional support in the adverse conditions under which so many Black women mothered.

Othermothers are key not only in supporting children but also in helping bloodmothers who, for whatever reason, lack the preparation or desire for motherhood. In confronting racial oppression, maintaining community-based child care and respecting othermothers who assume child-care responsibilities serve a critical function in African-American communities. Children orphaned by sale or death of their parents under slavery, children conceived through rape, children of young mothers, children born into extreme poverty or to alcoholic or drug-addicted mothers, or children who for other reasons cannot remain with their bloodmothers have all been supported by othermothers, who, like Ella Baker's aunt, take in additional children even when they have enough of their own.

Young women are often carefully groomed at an early age to become othermothers. As a ten-year-old, civil rights activist Ella Baker learned to be an othermother by caring for the children of a widowed neighbor: "Mama would say, 'You must take the clothes to Mr. Powell's house, and give so-and-so a bath.' The children were running wild. . . . The kids . . . would take off across the field. We'd chase them down, and bring them back, and put 'em in the tub, and wash 'em off, and change clothes, and carry the dirty ones home, and wash them. Those kind of things were routine" (Cantarow, 1980, 59).

Many Black men also value community-based child care but exercise these values to a lesser extent. Young Black men are taught how to care for children (Young, 1970; Lewis, 1975). During slavery, for example, Black children under age ten experienced little division of labor. They were dressed alike and performed similar tasks. If the activities of work and play are any indication of the degree of gender role differentiation that existed among slave children, "the young girls probably grew up minimizing the difference between the sexes while learning far more about the differences between the races" (D. White, 1985, 94). Differences among Black men and women in attitudes toward children may have more to do with male labor force patterns. As Ella Baker observes, "my father took care of people too, but .... my father had to work" (Cantarow, 1980, 60).

Historically, community-based child care and the relationships among bloodmothers and othermothers in women-centered networks have taken diverse institutional forms. In some polygynous West African societies, the children of the same father but different mothers referred to one another as brothers and sisters. While a strong bond existed between the biological mother and her child—one so strong that, among the Ashanti for example, "to show disrespect towards one's mother is tantamount to sacrilege" (Fortes, 1950, 263)—children could be disciplined by any of their other "mothers." Cross-culturally, the high status given to othermothers and the cooperative nature of child-care arrangements among bloodmothers and othermothers in Caribbean and other Black societies gives credence to the importance that people of African descent place on mothering (Clarke, 1966; Shimkin et al., 1978; Sudarkasa, 1981a, 1981b).

Although the political economy of slavery brought profound changes to enslaved Africans, cultural values concerning the importance of motherhood and the value of cooperative approaches to child care continued. While older women served as nurses and midwives, their most common occupation was caring for the children of parents who worked (D. White, 1985). Informal adoption of orphaned children reinforced the importance of social motherhood in African-American communities (Gutman, 1976).

The relationship between bloodmothers and othermothers survived the transition from a slave economy to postemancipation southern rural agriculture. Children in southern rural communities were not solely the responsibility of their biological mothers. Aunts, grandmothers, and others who had time to supervise children served as othermothers (Young, 1970; Dougherty, 1978). The significant status women enjoyed in family networks and in African-American communities continued to be linked to their bloodmother and othermother activities.

The entire community structure of bloodmothers and othermothers is under assault in many inner-city neighborhoods, where the very fabric of African-American community life is being eroded by illegal drugs. But even in the most troubled communities, remnants of the othermother tradition endure. Bebe Moore Campbell's 1950s North Philadelphia neighborhood underwent some startling changes when crack cocaine flooded the streets in the 1980s. Increases in birth defects, child abuse, and parental neglect left many children without care. But some residents, such as Miss Nee, continue the othermother tradition. After raising her younger brothers and sisters and five children of her own, Miss Nee cares for three additional children whose families fell apart. Moreover, on any given night Miss Nee's house may be filled by up to a dozen children because she has a reputation for never turning away a needy child ("Children of the Underclass," 1989).

Traditionally, community-based child care certainly has been functional for African-American communities and for Black women. Black feminist theorist bell hooks suggests that the relationships among bloodmothers and othermothers may have greater theoretical importance than currently recognized:

> This form of parenting is revolutionary in this society because it takes place in opposition to the ideas that parents, especially mothers, should be the only childrearers. . . . This kind of shared responsibility for child care can happen in small community settings where people know and trust one another. It cannot happen in those settings if parents regard children as their "property," their possession. (1984, 144)

The resiliency of women-centered family networks illustrates how traditional cultural values—namely, the African origins of community-based child care—can help people cope with and resist oppression. By continuing community-based child care, African-American women challenge one fundamental assumption underlying the capitalist system itself: that children are "private property" and can be disposed of as such. Notions of property, child care, and gender differences in parenting styles are embedded in the institutional arrangements of any given political economy. Under the property model stemming from capitalist patriarchal families, parents may not literally assert that their children are pieces of property, but their parenting may reflect assumptions analogous to those they make in connection with property (J. Smith, 1983). For example, the exclusive parental "right" to discipline children as parents see fit, even if discipline borders on abuse, parallels the widespread assumption that property owners may dispose of their property without consulting members of the larger community. By seeing the larger community as responsible for children and by giving othermothers and other nonparents "rights" in child rearing, African-Americans challenge prevailing property relations. It is in this sense that traditional bloodmother/othermother relationships in women-centered networks are "revolutionary."

MOTHERS, DAUGHTERS, AND SOCIALIZATION FOR SURVIVAL

Black mothers of daughters face a troubling dilemma. On one hand, to ensure their daughters' physical survival, mothers must teach them to fit into systems of oppression. For example, as a young girl Black activist Ann Moody questioned why she was paid so little for the domestic work she began at age nine, why Black women domestics were sexually harassed by their white male employers, why no one would explain the activities of the National Association for the Advancement of Colored People to her, and why whites had so much more than Blacks. But her mother refused to answer her questions and actually chastised her for questioning the system and stepping out of her "place" (Moody, 1968). Like Ann Moody, Black daughters learn to ex-

pect to work, to strive for an education so they can support themselves, and to anticipate carrying heavy responsibilities in their families and communities because these skills are essential to their own survival and those for whom they will eventually be responsible (Ladner, 1972; Joseph, 1981). New Yorker Michele Wallace recounts: "I can't remember when I first learned that my family expected me to work, to be able to take care of myself when I grew up. . . . It had been drilled into me that the best and only sure support was self-support" (1978, 89–90). Mothers also know that if their daughters uncritically accept the limited opportunities offered Black women, they become willing participants in their own subordination. Mothers may have ensured their daughters' physical survival, but at the high cost of their emotional destruction.

On the other hand, Black daughters with strong self-definitions and self-valuations who offer serious challenges to oppressive situations may not physically survive. When Ann Moody became active in the early 1960s in sit-ins and voter registration activities, her mother first begged her not to participate and then told her not to come home because she feared the whites in Moody's hometown would kill her. Despite the dangers, mothers routinely encourage Black daughters to develop skills to confront oppressive conditions. Learning that they will work and that education is a vehicle for advancement can also be seen as ways of enhancing positive self-definitions and self-valuations in Black girls. Emotional strength is essential, but not at the cost of physical survival.

Historian Elsa Barkley Brown captures this delicate balance Black mothers negotiate by pointing out that the mothers' behavior demonstrated the "need to teach me to live my life one way and, at the same time, to provide all the tools I would need to live it quite differently" (1989, 929). Black daughters must learn how to survive in interlocking structures of race, class, and gender oppression while rejecting and transcending those same structures. In order to develop these skills in their daughters, mothers demonstrate varying combinations of behaviors devoted to ensuring their daughters' survival—such as providing them with basic necessities and protecting them in dangerous environments—to helping their daughters go further than mothers themselves were allowed to go.

This special vision of Black mothers may grow from the nature of work women have done to ensure Black children's survival. These work experiences have provided Black women with a unique angle of vision, a particular perspective on the world to be passed on to Black daughters. African and African-America women have long integrated economic self-reliance with mothering. In contrast to the cult of true womanhood, in which work is defined as being in opposition to and incompatible with motherhood, work for Black women has been an important and valued dimension of Afrocentric definitions of Black motherhood. Sara Brooks describes the powerful connections that economic self-reliance and mothering had in her childhood: "When I was about nine I was nursing my sister Sally—I'm about seven or eight years older than Sally. And when I would put her to sleep, instead of me going somewhere and sit down and play, I'd get my little old hoe and get out there and work right in the field around the house" (in Simonsen, 1986, 86)

Mothers who are domestic workers or who work in proximity to whites may experience a unique relationship with the dominant group. For example, African-American women domestics are exposed to all the intimated details of the lives of their white employers. Working for whites offers domestic workers a view from the inside and exposes them to ideas and resources that might aid in their children's upward mobility. In some cases domestic workers form close, long-lasting relationships with their employers. But domestic workers also encounter some of the harshest exploitation confronting women of color. The work is low paid, has few benefits, and exposes women to the threat and reality of sexual harassment. Black domestics could see the dangers awaiting their daughters.

Willi Coleman's mother used a Saturday-night hair-combing ritual to impart a Black women's standpoint on domestic work to her daughters:

> Except for special occasions mama came home from work early on Saturdays. She spent six days a week mopping, waxing and dusting other women's houses and keeping out of reach of other women's husbands. Saturday nights were reserved for "taking care of them girls" hair and the telling of stories. Some of which included a recitation of what she had endured and how she had triumphed over "folks that were lower than dirt" and "no-good snakes in the grass." She combed, patted, twisted and talked, saying things which would have embarrassed or shamed her at other times. (Coleman, 1987, 34)

Bonnie Thornton Dill's (1980) study of the child-rearing goals of domestic workers illustrates how African-American women see their work as both contributing to their children's survival and instilling values that will encourage their children to reject their proscribed "place" as Blacks and strive for more. Providing a better chance for their children was a dominant theme among Black women. Domestic workers described themselves as "struggling to give their children the skills and training they did not have; and as praying that opportunities which had not been open to them would be open to their children" (p. 110). But the women also realized that while they wanted to communicate the value of their work as part of the ethics of caring and personal accountability, the work itself was undesirable. Bebe Moore Campbell's (1989) grandmother and college-educated mother stressed the importance of education. Campbell remembers, "[they] wanted me to Be Somebody, to be the second generation to live out my life as far away from a mop and scrub brush and Miss Ann's floors as possible" (p. 83).

Understanding this goal of balancing the need for the physical survival of their daughters with the vision of encouraging them to transcend the boundaries confronting them explains many apparent contradictions in Black mother-daughter relationships. Black mothers are often described as strong disciplinarians and overly protective; yet these same women manage to raise daughters who are self-reliant and assertive. To explain this apparent contradiction, Gloria Wade-Gayles suggests that Black mothers

> do not socialize their daughters to be "passive" or "irrational." Quite the contrary, they socialize their daughters to be independent, strong and self-confident. Black mothers are suffocatingly protective and domineering precisely because they are determined to mold their daughters into whole and self-actualizing persons in a society that devalues Black women. (1984, 12)

African-American mothers place a strong emphasis on protection, either by trying to shield their daughters as long as possible from the penalties attached to their race, class, and gender status or by teaching them skills of independence and self-reliance so that they will be able to protect themselves. Consider the following verse from a traditional blues song:

> I ain't good lookin' and ain't got waist-long hair
>
> I say I ain't good lookin' and I ain't got waist-long hair
>
> But my mamma gave me something that'll take me anywhere.
>
> (Washington, 1984, 144)

Unlike white women, symbolized by "good looks" and "waist-long hair," Black women have been denied male protection. Under such conditions it becomes essential that Black mothers teach their daughters skills that will "take them anywhere."

Black women's autobiographies and fiction can be read as texts revealing the multiple ways that African-American mothers aim to shield their daughters from the demands of being Black women in oppressive conditions. Michele Wallace describes her growing understanding of how her mother viewed raising Black daughters in Harlem: "My mother has since explained to me that since it was obvious her attempt to protect me was going to prove a failure, she was determined to make me realize that as a black girl

in white America I was going to find it an uphill climb to keep myself together" (1978, 98). In discussing the mother-daughter relationship in Paule Marshall's *Brown Girl, Brownstones,* Rosalie Troester catalogues the ways mothers have aimed to protect their daughters and the impact this may have on relationships themselves:

> Black mothers, particularly those with strong ties to their community, sometimes build high banks around their young daughters, isolating them from the dangers of the larger world until they are old and strong enough to function as autonomous women. Often these dikes are religious, but sometimes they are built with education, family, or the restrictions of a close-knit and homogeneous community. . . . This isolation causes the currents between Black mothers and daughters to run deep and the relationship to be fraught with an emotional intensity often missing from the lives of women with more freedom. (1984, 13)

Michele Wallace's mother built banks around her headstrong adolescent daughter by institutionalizing her in a Catholic home for troubled girls. Wallace went willingly, believing "I thought at the time that I would rather live in hell than be with my mother" (1978, 98). But years later Wallace's evaluation of her mother's decision changed: "Now that I know my mother better, I know that her sense of powerlessness made it all the more essential to her that she take radical action" (p. 98).

African-American mothers try to protect their daughters from the dangers that lie ahead by offering them a sense of their own unique self-worth. Many contemporary Black women writers report the experience of being singled out, of being given a sense of specialness at an early age which encouraged them to develop their talents. My own mother marched me to the public library at age five, helped me get my first library card, and told me that I could do anything if I learned how to read. In discussing the works of Paule Marshall, Dorothy West, and Alice Walker, Mary Helen Washington observes that all three writers make special claims about the roles their mothers played in the development of their creativity:

"The bond with their mothers is such a fundamental and powerful source that the term 'mothering the mind' might have been coined specifically to define their experiences as writers" (1984, 144).

Black women's efforts to provide a physical and psychic base for their children can affect mothering styles and the emotional intensity of Black mother-daughter relationships. As Gloria Wade-Gayles points out, "mothers in Black women's fiction are strong and devoted . . . they are rarely affectionate" (1984, 10). For example, in Toni Morrison's *Sula* (1974), Eva Peace's husband ran off, leaving her with three small children and no money. Despite her feelings, "the demands of feeding her three children were so acute she had to postpone her anger for two years until she had both the time and energy for it" (p. 32). Later in the novel Eva's daughter Hannah asks, "Mamma, did you ever love us?" (p. 67). Eva angrily replies, "What you talkin' bout did I love you girl I stayed alive for you" (p. 69). For far too many Black mothers, the demands of providing for children in interlocking systems of oppression are sometimes so demanding that they have neither the time nor the patience for affection. And yet most Black daughters love and admire their mothers and are convinced that their mothers truly love them (Joseph, 1981).

Black daughters raised by mothers grappling with hostile environments have to come to terms with their feelings about the difference between the idealized versions of maternal love extant in popular culture and the strict and often troubled mothers in their lives. For a daughter, growing up means developing a better understanding that even though she may desire more affection and greater freedom, her mother's physical care and protection are acts of maternal love. Ann Moody describes her growing awareness of the cost her mother paid as a domestic worker who was a single mother of three. Watching her mother sleep after the birth of another child, Moody remembers:

> For a long time I stood there looking at her. I didn't want to wake her up. I wanted to enjoy and preserve that calm, peaceful look on her face, I wanted to think she would always be that happy. . . . Adline and Junior were too young to feel the things I felt and know the things I knew about Mama. They couldn't remember when she and Daddy separated. They had never heard her cry at night as I had or worked and helped as I had done when we were starving. (1968, 57)

Moody initially sees her mother as a strict disciplinarian, a woman who tries to protect her daughter by withholding information. But as Moody matures and better understands the oppression in her community, her ideas change. On one occasion Moody left school early the day after a Black family had been brutally murdered by local whites. Moody's description of her mother's reaction reflects her deepening understanding: "When I walked in the house Mama didn't even ask me why I came home. She just looked at me. And for the first time I realized she understood what was going on within me or was trying to anyway" (1968, 136).

Another example of a daughter's efforts to understand her mother is offered in Renita Weems's account of coming to grips with maternal desertion. In the following passage Weems struggles with the difference between the stereotypical image of the superstrong Black mother and her own alcoholic mother's decision to leave her children: "My mother loved us. I must believe that. She worked all day in a department store bakery to buy shoes and school tablets, came home to curse out neighbors who wrongly accused her children of any impropriety (which in an apartment complex usually meant stealing), and kept her house cleaner than most sober women" (1984, 256). Weems concludes that her mother loved her because she provided for her to the best of her ability.

Othermothers often help to defuse the emotional intensity of relationships between bloodmothers and their daughters. In recounting how she dealt with the intensity of her relationship with her mother, Weems describes the women teachers, neighbors, friends, and othermothers she turned to—women who, she observed, "did not have the onus of providing for me, and so had the luxury of talking to me" (1984, 27). Cheryl West's household included her brother, her lesbian mother, and Jan, her mother's lover. Jan became an othermother to West: "Yellow-colored, rotund, and short in stature, Jan was like a second mother. . . . Jan braided my hair in the morning, mother worked two jobs and tucked me in at night. Loving, gentle, and fastidious in the domestic arena, Jan could be a rigid disciplinarian. . . . To the outside world . . . she was my 'aunt' who happened to live with us. But she was much more involved and nurturing than any of my 'real' aunts" (1987, 43).

June Jordan offers an eloquent analysis of one daughter's realization of the high personal cost African-American women can pay in providing an economic and emotional foundation for their children. In the following passage Jordan offers a powerful testament of how she came to see that her mother's work was an act of love:

> As a child I noticed the sadness of my mother as she sat alone in the kitchen at night. . . . Her woman's work never won permanent victories of any kind. It never enlarged the universe of her imagination or her power to influence what happened beyond the front door of our house. Her woman's work never tickled her to laugh or shout or dance. But she did raise me to repeat her way of offering love and to believe that hard work is often the irreducible factor for survival, not something to avoid. Her woman's work produced a reliable home base where I could pursue the privileges of books and music. Her woman's work invented the potential of a completely different kind of work for us, the next generation of Black women: huge, rewarding hard work demanded by the huge, new ambitions that her perfect confidence in us engendered. (1985, 105)

COMMUNITY OTHERMOTHERS AND POLITICAL ACTIVISM

Black women's experiences as othermothers provide a foundation for Black women's political activism. Nurturing children in Black extended family networks stimulates a more generalized ethic of caring and personal accountability among African-American women who often feel accountable to all the Black community's children.

This notion of Black women as community othermothers of all Black children traditionally allowed African-American women to treat biologically unrelated children as if they were members of their own families. For example, sociologist Karen Fields describes how her grandmother, Mamie Garvin Fields, draws on her power as a community othermother when dealing with unfamiliar children: "She will say to a child on the street who looks up to no good, picking out a name at random, 'Aren't you Miz Pinckney's boy?' in that same reproving tone. If the reply is, 'No, *ma'am,* my mother is Miz Gadsen,' whatever threat there was dissipates" (Fields and Fields, 1983, xvii).

The use of family language in referring to members of the African-American community also illustrates this dimension of Black motherhood. In the following passage, Mamie Garvin Fields describes how she became active in surveying substandard housing conditions among African-Americans in Charleston. Note her explanation of why she uses family language:

> I was one of the volunteers they got to make a survey of the places where we were paying extortious rents for indescribable property. I said "we," although it wasn't Bob and me. We had our own home, and so did many of the Federated Women. Yet we still felt like it really was "we" living in those terrible places, and it was up to us to do something about them. (Fields and Fields, 1983, 195)

Black women frequently describe Black children using family language. In recounting her increasingly successful efforts to teach a boy who had given other teachers problems, my daughter's kindergarten teacher states, "You know how it can be—the majority of children in the learning disabled classes are *our children.* I know he didn't belong there, so I volunteered to take him." In their statements both women use family language to describe the ties that bind them as Black women to their responsibilities as members of an African-American community/family.

In explaining why the South Carolina Federation of Colored Women's Clubs founded a home of girls, Mrs. Fields observes, "We all could see that we had a responsibility for those girls: they were the daughters of our community coming up" (Fields and Fields, 1983, 197). Ms. Fields's activities as a community othermother on behalf of the "daughters" of her community represent an established tradition among educated Black women. Serving as othermothers to women in the Black community has a long history. A study of 108 of the first generation of Black club women found that three-quarters were married, three-quarters worked outside the home, but only one-fourth had children (Giddings, 1984). These women emphasized self-support for Black women, whether married or not, and realized that self-sufficient community othermothers were important. "Not all women are intended for mothers," declares an 1894 edition of the *Woman's Era*. "Some of us have not the temperament for family life. .... Clubs will make women think seriously of their future lives, and not make girls think their only alternative is to marry" (Giddings, 1984, 108).

Black women writers also explore this theme of the African-American community othermother who nurtures the Black community. One of the earliest examples is found in Frances Ellen Watkins Harper's 1892 novel *Iola Leroy*. By rejecting an opportunity to marry a prestigious physician and dissociate herself from the Black community, nearly white Iola, the main character, chooses instead to serve the African-American community. Similarly in Alice Walker's *Meridian* (1976) the main character rejects the controlling image of the "happy slave," the self-sacrificing Black mother, and chooses to become a community othermother. Giving up her biological child to the care of an othermother, Meridian gets an education, works in the civil rights movement, and eventu-

ally takes on responsibility for the children of a small southern town. She engages in a "quest that will take her beyond the society's narrow meaning of the word *mother* as a physical state and expand its meaning to those who create, nurture, and save life in social and psychological as well as physical terms" (Christian, 1985, 242).

Sociologist Cheryl Gilkes (1980, 1982, 1983b) suggests that community othermother relationships can be key in stimulating Black women's decisions to become community activists. Gilkes asserts that many of the Black women community activists in her study became involved in community organizing in response to the needs of their own children and of those in their communities. The following comment is typical of how many of the Black women in Gilkes's study relate to Black children: "There were a lot of summer programs springing up for kids, but they were exclusive ... and I found that most of *our kids* were excluded" (1980, 219). For many women what began as the daily expression of their obligations as community othermothers, as was the case for the kindergarten teacher, developed into full-fledged actions as community leaders.

This community othermother tradition also explains the "mothering the mind" relationships that can develop between Black women teachers and their Black women students. Unlike the traditional mentoring so widely reported in educational literature, this relationship goes far beyond that of providing students with either technical skills or a network of academic and professional contacts. bell hooks shares the special vision that teachers who see our work in community othermother terms can pass on to our students: "I understood from the teachers in those segregated schools that the work of any teacher committed to the full self-realization of students was necessarily and fundamentally radical, that ideas were not neutral, that to teach in a way that liberates, that expands consciousness, that awakens, is to challenge domination at its very core" (1989, 50). Like the mother-daughter relationship, this "mothering the mind" among Black women seeks to move toward the mutuality of a shared sisterhood that binds African-American women as community othermothers.

Community othermothers have made important contributions in building a different type of community in often hostile political and economic surroundings (Reagon, 1987). Community othermothers' actions demonstrate a clear rejection of separateness and individual interest as the basis of either community organization or individual self-actualization. Instead, the connectedness with others and common interest expressed by community othermothers models a very different value system, one whereby Afrocentric feminist ethics of caring and personal accountability move communities forward.

REFERENCES

Aschenbrenner, Joyce. 1975. *Lifelines, Black Families in Chicago.* Prospect Heights, IL: Waveland Press.

Brown, Elsa Barkley. 1989. "African-American Women's Quilting: A Framework for Conceptualizing and Teaching African-American Women's History." *Signs* 14(4): 921–29.

Campbell, Bebe Moore, 1989. *Sweet Summer: Growing Up with and without My Dad.* New York: Putnam.

Cantarow, Ellen. 1980. *Moving the Mountain: Women Working for Social Change.* Old Westbury, NY: Feminist Press.

"Children of the Underclass." 1989. *Newsweek* September 11, 16–27.

Christian, Barbara. 1985. *Black Feminist Criticism, Perspectives on Black Women Writers.* New York: Pergamon.

Clarke, Edith. 1966. *My Mother Who Fathered Me.* 2d ed. London: Allen and Unwin.

Coleman, Willi. 1987. "Closets and Keepsakes." *Sage: A Scholarly Journal on Black Women* 4(2): 34–35.

Dill, Bonnie Thornton. 1980. "'The Means to Put My Children Through': Child-Rearing Goals and Strategies among Black Female Domestic Servants." In *The Black Woman,* edited by La Frances Rodgers-Rose, 107–123. Beverly Hills, CA: Sage.

Dougherty, Molly C. 1978. *Becoming a Woman in Rural Black Culture.* New York: Holt, Rinehart and Winston.

Fields, Mamie Garvin, and Karen Fields. 1983. *Lemon Swamp and Other Places: A Carolina Memoir.* New York: Free Press.

Fortes, Meyer. 1950. "Kinship and Marriage among the Ashanti." in *African Systems of Kinship and Marriage,* edited by A. R. Radcliffe-Brown and Daryll Forde, 252–284. New York: Oxford University Press.

Giddings, Paula. 1984. *When and Where I Enter . . . The Impact of Black Women on Race and Sex in America.* New York: William Morrow.

Gilkes, Cheryl Townsend. 1980. "'Holding Back the Ocean with a Broom': Black Women and Community Work." In *The Black Woman,* edited by La Frances Rodgers-Rose, 217–232. Beverly Hills, CA: Sage.

———. 1982. "Successful Rebellious Professionals: The Black Woman's Professional Identity and Community Commitment." *Psychology of Women Quarterly* 6(3): 289–311.

———. 1983b. "Going Up for the Oppressed: The Career Mobility of Black Women Community Workers." *Journal of Social Issues* 39(3): 115–139.

Golden, Marita. 1983. *Migrations of the Heart.* New York: Ballantine.

Gutman, Herbert. 1976. *The Black Family in Slavery and Freedom, 1750–1925.* New York: Random House.

hooks, bell. 1984. *From Margin to Center.* Boston: South End Press.

———. 1989. *Talking Back: Thinking Feminist, Thinking Black.* Boston: South End Press.

Jordan, June. 1985. *On Call.* Boston: South End Press.

Joseph, Gloria. 1981. "Black Mothers and Daughters: Their Roles and Functions in American Society." In *Common Differences,* edited by Gloria Joseph and Jill Lewis, 75–126. Garden City, NY: Anchor.

Ladner, Joyce. 1972. *Tomorrow's Tomorrow.* Garden City, NY: Doubleday.

Lewis, Diane K. 1975. "The Black Family: Socialization and Sex Roles." *Phylon* 36(3): 221–37.

Martin, Elmer, and Joanne Mitchell Martin. 1978. *The Black Extended Family.* Chicago: University of Chicago Press.

Moody, Ann. 1968. *Coming of Age in Mississippi.* New York: Dell.

Morrison, Toni. 1974. *Sula.* New York: Random House.

Parker, Bettye J. 1979. "Mississippi Mothers: Roots." In *Sturdy Black Bridges,* edited by Rosann Bell, Bettye Parker, and Beverly Guy-Sheftall, 263–281. Garden City, NY: Anchor.

Reagon, Bernice Johnson. 1983. "Coalition Politics: Turning the Century." In *Home Girls—A Black Feminist Anthology,* edited by Barbara Smith, 356–368. New York: Kitchen Table Press.

———. 1978. "African Diaspora Women: The Making of Cultural Workers." In *Women in Africa and the African Diaspora,* edited by Rosalyn Terborg-Penn, Sharon Harley, and Andrea Benton Rushing, 167–180. Washington, DC: Howard University Press.

Shimkin, Demitri B., Edith M. Shimkin, and Dennis A. Frate, eds. 1978. *The Extended Family in Black Societies.* Chicago: Aldine.

Simms, Margaret C. 1988. *The Choices that Young Black Women Make: Education, Employment, and Family Formation.* Working Paper No. 190, Wellesley, MA: Center for Research on Women, Wellesley College.

Simonsen, Thordis, ed. 1986. *You May Plow Here: The Narrative of Sara Brooks."* New York: Touchstone.

Smith, Janet Farrell. 1983. "Parenting as Property." In *Mothering: Essays in Feminist Theory,* edited by Joyce Trebilcot, 199–212. Totawa, NJ: Rowman & Allanheld.

Stack, Carol D. 1974. *All Our Kin: Strategies for Survival in a Black Community.* New York: Harper & Row.

Sudarkasa, Niara. 1981a. "Female Employment and Family Organization in West Africa." In *The Black Woman Cross-Culturally,* edited by Filomina Chioma Steady, 49–64. Cambridge, MA: Schenkman.

———. 1981b. "Interpreting the African Heritage in Afro-American Family Organization." In *Black Families,* edited by Harriette Pipes McAdoo, 37–53. Beverly Hills, CA: Sage.

Tanner, Nancy. 1974. "Matrifocality in Indonesia and Africa and among Black Americans." In *Woman, Culture, and Society,* edited by Michelle Z. Rosaldo and Louise Lamphere, 129–156. Stanford: Stanford University Press.

Troester, Rosalie Riegle. 1984. "Turbulence and Tenderness: Mothers, Daughters, and 'Othermothers' in Paule Marshall's *Brown Girl, Brownstones.*" *Sage: A Scholarly Journal on Black Women* 1(2): 13–16.

Wade-Gayles, Gloria. 1984. "The Truths of Our Mothers' Lives: Mother-Daughter Relationships in Black Women's Fiction." *Sage: A Scholarly Journal on Black Women* 1(2): 8–12.

Wahlman, Maude Southwell, and John Scully. 1983. "Aesthetic Principles of Afro-American Quilts." In *Afro-American Folk Arts and Crafts,* edited by William Ferris, 79–97. Boston: G. K. Hall.

Walker, Alice. 1976. *Meridian.* New York: Pocket Books.

Wallace, Michele. 1978. *Black Macho and the Myth of the Superwoman.* New York: Dial Press.

Washington, Mary Hellen. 1984. "I Sign My Mother's Name: Alice Walker, Dorothy West and Paule Marshall." In *Mothering the Mind: Twelve Studies of Writers and Their Silent Partners,* edited by Ruth Perry and Martine Watson Broronley, 143–163. New York: Holmes & Meier.

———, ed. 1987. *Invented Lives: Narratives of Black Women 1860–1960.* Garden City, NY: Anchor.

Weems, Renita. 1984. "'Hush, Mama's Gotta Go Bye Bye': A Personal Narrative." *Sage: A Scholarly Journal on Black Women* 1(2): 25–28.

West, Cheryl. 1987. "Lesbian Daughter." *Sage: A Scholarly Journal on Black Women* 4(2): 42–44.

White, Deborah Gray. 1985. *Ar'n't I a Woman? Female Slaves in the Plantation South.* New York: W. W. Norton.

Young, Virginia Heyer. 1970. "Family and Childhood in a Southern Negro Community." *American Anthropologist* 72(32): 269–288.

Further Questions

   1. A network of othermothers puts women in central positions with regard to responsibility for children. Does this in any way diminish the role that fathers, or other male adults, can play in a child's life?

   2. If parents regard children as their property, to do with as the parents please, will it be difficult to initiate a system where responsibility for children is shared? If the two attitudes are not compatible, which is the better attitude?

   3. Do some of the things your mother did for you or for other children seem now to be rooted in love and concern, whereas they didn't seem so at the time?

Welfare: Exploding the Stereotypes   XI.6

RITA HENLEY JENSEN

Rita Henley Jensen discusses some of her experiences as a welfare mother. She also mentions some people with negative or unhelpful attitudes toward mothers on welfare.

Reading Questions

1. In what ways is it harmful for people to think of the typical welfare mother as being black? Does Jensen have a good strategy for combatting such beliefs?
2. Should welfare payments be in line with government estimates of the cost of living? Are mothers spending too much time on welfare so that they are an unnecessary cost to the government? How much time is too much?
3. How old must children on welfare be before their mother is required to sign up for job training? Should welfare mothers be permitted to delay training for a particular job to get a college education?

I AM A WOMAN. A white woman, once poor but no longer. I am not lazy, never was. I am a middle-aged woman, with two grown daughters. I was a welfare mother, one of those women society considers less than nothing.

I should have applied for Aid to Families with Dependent Children when I was 18 years old, pregnant with my first child, and living with a boyfriend who slapped me around. But I didn't.

I remember talking it over at the time with a friend. I lived in the neighborhood that surrounds the vast Columbus campus of Ohio State University. Students, faculty, hangers-on, hippies, runaways, and recent émigrés from Kentucky lived side by side in the area's relatively inexpensive housing. I was a runaway.

On a particularly warm midsummer's day, I stood on High Street, directly across from the campus' main entrance, with an older, more

Rita Henley Jensen "Welfare: Exploding the Stereotypes. In Ms. *magazine July/August 1995, Reprinted by permission of Ms. Magazine © 1995.*

sophisticated friend, wondering what to do with my life. With my swollen belly, all hope of my being able to cross the street and enroll in the university had evaporated. Now, I was seeking advice about how merely to survive, to escape the assaults and still be able to care for my child.

My friend knew of no place I could go, nowhere I could turn, no one else I could ask. I remember saying in a tone of resignation, "I can't apply for welfare." Instead of disagreeing with me, she nodded, acknowledging our mutual belief that taking beatings was better than taking handouts. Being "on the dole" meant you deserved only contempt.

In August 1965, I married my attacker.

Six years later, I left him and applied for assistance. My children were 18 months and five and half years old. I had waited much too long. Within a year, I crossed High Street to go to Ohio State. I graduated in four years and moved to New York City to attend Columbia University's Graduate School of Journalism. I have worked as a journalist for 18 years now. My life on welfare was very hard—there were times when I didn't have enough food for the three of us. But I was able to get an education while on welfare. It is hardly likely that a woman on AFDC today would be allowed to do what I did, to go to school and develop the kind of skills that enabled me to make a better life for myself and my children.

This past summer, I attended a conference in Chicago on feminist legal theory. During the presentation of a paper related to gender and property rights, the speaker mentioned as an aside that when one says "welfare mother" the listener hears "black welfare mother." A discussion ensued about the underling racism until someone declared that the solution was easy: all that had to be done was have the women in the room bring to the attention of the media the fact that white women make up the largest percentage of welfare recipients. At this point, I stood, took a deep breath, stepped out of my professional guise, and informed the crowd that I was a former welfare mother. Looking at my

white hair, blue eyes, and freckled Irish skin, some laughed; others gasped—despite having just acknowledged that someone like me was, in fact, a "typical" welfare mother.

Occasionally I do this. Speak up. Identify myself as one of "them." I do so reluctantly because welfare mothers are a lightning rod for race hatred, class prejudice, and misogyny. Yet I am aware that as long as welfare is viewed as an *African American* woman's issue, instead of a *woman's* issue—whether that woman be white, African American, Asian, Latina, or Native American—those in power can continue to exploit our country's racism to weaken and even eliminate public support for the programs that help low-income mothers and their children.

I didn't have the guts to stand up during a 1974 reception for Ohio state legislators. The party's hostess was a leader of the Columbus chapter of the National Organization for Women and she had opened up her suburban home so that representatives of many of the state's progressive organizations could lobby in an informal setting for an increase in the state's welfare allotment for families. I was invited as a representative of the campus area's single mothers' support group. In the living room, I came across a state senator in a just-slightly-too-warm-and-friendly state induced by the potent combination of free booze and a crowd of women. He quickly decided I looked like a good person to amuse with one of his favorite jokes. "You want to know how a welfare mother can prevent getting pregnant?" he asked, giggling. "She can just take two aspirin and put them between her knees," he roared, as he bent down to place his Scotch glass between his own, by way of demonstration. I drifted away.

I finally did get up my courage to speak out. It was in a classroom during my junior year. I was enrolled in a course on the economics of public policy because I wanted to understand why the state of Ohio thought it desirable to provide me and my two kids with only $204 per month—59 percent of what even the state itself said a family of three needed to live.

For my required oral presentation, I chose "Aid to Families with Dependent Children." I cited the fact that approximately two thirds of all the poor families in the country were white; I noted that most welfare families consisted of one parent and two children. As an audiovisual aid, I brought my own two kids along. My voice quavered a bit as I delivered my intro: I stood with my arms around my children and said, "We are a typical AFDC Family."

My classmates had not one question when I finished. I don't believe anyone even bothered to ask the kids' names or ages.

If I were giving this talk today, I would hold up a picture of us back then and say we still represent typical welfare recipients. The statistics I would cite to back up that statement have been refined since the 1970s and now include "hispanic" as a category. In 1992, 38.9 percent of all welfare mothers were white, 37.2 percent were black, 17.8 percent were "Hispanic," 2.8 percent were Asian, and 1.4 percent were Native American.

My report, however, would focus on the dramatic and unrelenting reduction in resources available to low-income mothers in the last two decades.

Fact: In 1970, the average monthly benefit for a family of three was $178. Not much, but consider that as a result of inflation, that $178 would be approximately $680 today. And then consider that the average monthly payment today is only about $414. That's the way it's been for more than two decades: the cost of living goes up (by the states' own accounting, the cost of rent, food, and utilities for a family of three has doubled), but the real value of welfare payments keeps going down.

Fact: The 1968 Work Incentive Program (the government called it WIN; we called it WIP) required that all unemployed adult recipients sign up for job training or employment once their children turned six. The age has now been lowered to three, and states may go as low as age one. What that means is you won't be able to attend and finish college while on welfare. (In most states a college education isn't considered job training, even though experts claim most of us will need college degrees to compete in the workplace of the twenty-first century.)

Fact: Forty-two percent of welfare recipients will be on welfare less than two years during their entire lifetime, and an additional 33 percent will spend between two and eight years on welfare. The statistics haven't changed much over the years: women still use welfare to support their families when their children are small.

When *U.S. News & World Report* did a major story on welfare reform this year, it featured large photographs of eight welfare recipients, seven of whom were women of color: six African Americans and one Latina or Native American (the text does not state her ethnicity). Describing the inability of welfare mothers to hold jobs (they are "hobbled not only by their lack of experience but also by their casual attitudes toward punctuality, dress, and coworkers"), the article offers the "excuse" given by one mother for not taking a 3 P.M. to 11 P.M. shift: "'I wouldn't get to see my kids,'" she told the reporter. You can't win for losing—should she take that 3-to-11 job and her unsupervised kids get in trouble, you can be sure some conservative would happily leap on her as an example of one of those poor women who are bad mothers and whose kids should be in orphanages.

Why don't the media ever find a white woman from Ohio or Iowa or Wisconsin, a victim of domestic violence, leaving the father of her two children to make a new start? Or a Latina mother like the one living in my current neighborhood, who has one child and does not make enough as a home health care attendant to pay for her family's health insurance? Or a Native American woman living on a reservation, creating crafts for pennies that will be sold by others for dollars?

Besides reinforcing stereotypes about the personal failings of welfare recipients, when my colleagues write in-depth pieces about life on welfare they invariably concentrate on describing welfare mothers' difficulties with the world at large: addictions, lack of transportation, dangerous neighbors, and, most recently, shiftless boyfriends who begin beating them when they do get jobs—as if this phenomenon were limited to relationships between couples with low incomes.

I wonder why no journalist I have stumbled across, no matter how well meaning, has communicated what I believe is the central reality of most women's lives on welfare: They believe all the stereotypes too and they are ashamed of being on welfare. They eat, breathe, sleep, and clothe themselves with shame.

Most reporting on welfare never penetrates the surface, and the nature of the relationship between the welfare system and the woman receiving help is never explored. Like me, many women fleeing physical abuse must make the welfare department their first stop after seeking an order of protection. Studies are scarce, but some recent ones of women in welfare-to-work programs across the U.S. estimate that anywhere from half to three fourths of participants are, or have been, in abusive relationships. And surveys of some homeless shelters indicate that half of the women living in them are on the run from a violent mate.

But if welfare is the means of escape, it is also the institutionalization of the dynamic of battering. My husband was the source of my and my children's daily bread and of daily physical and psychological attacks. On welfare, I was free of the beatings, but the assaults on my self-esteem were still frequent and powerful, mimicking the behavior of a typical batterer.

As he pounds away, threatening to kill the woman and children he claims to love, the abuser often accuses his victims of lying, laziness, and infidelity. Many times, he threatens to snatch the children away from their mother in order to protect them from her supposed incompetence, her laziness, dishonesty, and sexual escapades.

On welfare, just as with my husband, I had to prove every statement was not a lie. Everything had to be documented: how many children I had, how much I paid for rent, fuel, transportation,

electricity, child care, and so forth. It went so far as to require that at every "redetermination of need" interview (every six months), I had to produce the originals of my children's birth certificates, which were duly photocopied over and over again. Since birth certificates do not change, the procedure was a subtle and constant reminder that nothing I said was accepted as truth. Ever.

But this is a petty example. The more significant one was the suspicion that my attendance at Ohio State University was probably a crime. Throughout my college years, I regularly reported that I was attending OSU. Since the WIN limit at that time was age six and my youngest daughter was two when I started, I was allowed to finish my undergraduate years without having to report to some job-training program that would have prepared me for a minimum-wage job. However, my case-worker and I shared an intuitive belief that something just had to be wrong about this. How could I be living on welfare and going to college? Outrageous! Each day I awoke feeling as if I were in a race, that I had to complete my degree before I was charged with a felony.

As a matter of fact, I remember hearing, a short time after I graduated, that a group of welfare mothers attending college in Ohio were charged with food stamp fraud, apparently for not reporting their scholarships as additional income.

Batterers frequently lie to their victims—it's a power thing. Caseworkers do too. For example, when I moved to New York to attend graduate school and applied for assistance, I asked my intake worker whether I could apply for emergency food stamps. She told me there was no emergency food program. The kids and I scraped by, but that statement was false. I was unaware of it until welfare rights advocates successfully sued the agency for denying applicants emergency food assistance. In another case, when someone gave me a ten-year-old Opel so I could keep my first (very low paying) reporting job, my case-worker informed me in writing that mere possession of a car made me ineligible for welfare. (I appealed and won. The caseworker was apparently confused by the fact that although I was not allowed to have any assets, I did need the car to get to work. She also assumed a used car had to have some value. Not this one.)

Then there's the issue of sexual possessiveness: States rarely grant assistance to families with fathers still in the home. And as for feeling threatened about losing custody, throughout the time I was on welfare, I knew that if I stumbled at all, my children could be taken away from me. It is widely understood that any neighbor can call the authorities about a welfare mother, making a charge of neglect, and that mother, since she is less than nothing, might not be able to prove her competency. I had a close call once. I had been hospitalized for ten days and a friend took care of my children. After my return home, however, I was still weak. I would doze off on the sofa while the kids were awake—one time it happened when they were outside playing on the sidewalk. A neighbor, seeing them there unattended, immediately called the child welfare agency, which sent someone out to question me and to look inside my refrigerator to see if I had any food. Luckily, that day I did.

Ultimately, leaving an abusive relationship and applying for welfare is a little like leaving solitary confinement to become part of a prison's general population. It's better, but you are still incarcerated.

None of this is ever discussed in the context of welfare reform. The idiot state legislator, the prosecutor in Ohio who brought the charges against welfare mothers years ago, Bill Clinton, and Newt Gingrich all continue to play the race and sex card by hollering for welfare reform. They continue to exploit and feed the public's ignorance about and antipathy toward welfare mothers to propel their own careers. Sadly, journalists permit them to do so, perhaps for the same reason.

Lost in all this are the lives of thousands of women impoverished by virtue of their willingness to assume the responsibility of raising their children. An ex-boyfriend used to say that observing my struggle was a little like watching someone standing in a room, with arms upraised to prevent the ceiling from pressing in on her. He wondered just how long I could prevent the collapse.

Today, welfare mothers have even less opportunity than I did. Their talent, brains, luck, and resourcefulness are ignored. Each new rule, regulation, and reform makes it even more unlikely that they can use the time they are on welfare to do as I did: cross the High Streets in their cities and towns, and realize their ambitions. Each new rule makes it more likely that they will only be able to train for a minimum-wage job that will never allow them to support their families.

So no, I don't think all we have to do is get the facts to the media. I think we have to raise hell any way we can.

Our goal is simple: never again should there be a young woman, standing in front of the gates that lead to a better future, afraid to enter because she believes she must instead choose poverty and battery.

Further Questions

1. Should a mother be able to rely on welfare to get a fresh start in life after leaving an abusive husband or boyfriend?

2. Does the welfare system shame mothers too much by asking them periodically to document all their expenses? Should welfare mothers be threatened with loss of custody of their children if they are charged with child neglect?

3. Should possession of a car make a mother ineligible for welfare? Should welfare be denied if the father is still in the home?

XI.7A

Anna Karenina, Scarlett O'Hara, and Gail Bezaire: Child Custody and Family Law Reform

SUSAN CREAN

Susan Crean reveals some hypocrisy behind the claim that mothers are "natural childraisers." Should the parents separate, the father will often attempt to take custody of the child. This is exactly what happened to Anna Karenina, Scarlett O'Hara, and Gail Bezaire. (Gail Bezaire lost custody of her children because she was a lesbian, and after she abducted them from their father, who was abusing them, she was tried and sentenced for the abduction.)

Crean lives in Vancouver and travels widely. *In the Name of the Fathers* is her fourth book.

Reading Questions

1. In a custody dispute, the parent with more money often has more influence over the outcome. Is this fair? If not, what would be a fair way of settling a custody dispute?
2. If the child's best interests should be considered in a custody dispute, by what standards should these "best interests" be judged?
3. Should a parent's sexual conduct affect whether the parent wins custody of the child? Should it affect whether she or he has access to the child? Explain your answer.

* * *

UNLIKE MOTHERHOOD, custody is not a natural phenomenon. That is, it is a human invention—which is to say a patriarchal invention that apparently must have followed upon the discovery of biological paternity. As I imagine the evolution, it was marked by transition from an ideology of belonging—to clan, tribe, or family—which is essentially an expression of collective identity, to an ideology of ownership or the expression of possession by individuals. In other words, it developed out of the notion of practical responsibility (for that which one carries and cares for) into the power to control and to dispose of the lives of others. In that sense, custody is definitely related to the practice of slavery. To those people who

did not invent the idea but were forced to submit to it, child custody must at first have seemed as absurd as the idea of owning the land. . . .

. . . Motherhood may have been the most hallowed of female occupations, ordained by God and all his earthly bishops, but until the nineteenth century women had no legal rights whatsoever to their offspring. They lived with them and cared for them at the pleasure of their husbands, who could, and occasionally did, disown their wives, divorce them, or have them committed to institutions to separate them from their children permanently and against their will. In the rare instances where marriage breakdown led to divorce, every woman faced the real possibility of losing her children forever.

Abridged from "Anna Karenina, Scarlett O'Hara, and Gail Bezaire: Child Custody and Family Law Reform," pp. 12–53 in In the Name of the Fathers *by Susan Crean (Toronto, Ontario: Amanita Enterprises, 1988). Reprinted by permission of the publisher and author.*

If she "deserted" the matrimonial home she instantly became legally childless and property-less. Similarly, if she committed adultery she lost her dower rights and might well never see her children again. If she did, it was only because of her husband's generosity. . . .

From the 19th century we have the unforgettable story of Anna Karenina. In Tolstoy's novel the child loss at least is not hidden, even though it is subordinated to the larger theme of Anna's annihilation by the exploding forces of passion and social opprobrium. Anna commits the unpardonable sin of adultery. Her husband refuses to permit a divorce, so she cannot marry her lover Vronsky and is thereby sentenced to live in social limbo, a sentence which carries no parole and over which she has absolutely no control. The love-child she has with Vronsky is Karenina's according to law, and Vronsky himself has no paternal rights to his daughter or to any children he might have with Anna, an injustice he angrily laments. "Think of the bitterness and horror of such a position. Conceive the feelings of a man who knows that his children, the children of the woman he loves, will not be his, but will belong to someone who hates them, and will have nothing to do with them!"

Meanwhile Karenin forbids any contact between Anna and her son, Seriozha, and the boy is cruelly informed that his mother is dead. As well she might be described—for society refused to acknowledge the existence of women who strayed beyond the protection of husband; they were disqualified, defrocked, as wives and mothers. What else was there for Anna to be? Vronsky could go on being Vronsky, but Anna was branded a Scarlet Woman; she was conspicuous, tainted, and therefore ostracized. Like Niobe she tempted the fates by committing an act of love, in her case the unsanctioned love of another man. In nineteenth-century Russia she might as well have died. In the end, of course, she does die—by her own hand. Like Niobe she is turned to stone.

In another immensely popular epic about love and loss (and a child caught in between),

the plot includes a parental kidnapping which is so downplayed both in the novel and in its Hollywood rendition that few people even remember it. Margaret Mitchell's *Gone with the Wind* is a Harlequinesque romance about the stormy love affair between Scarlett O'Hara, stubborn southern belle, and Rhett Butler, professional rake and racketeer. However, it could just as accurately be described as the chronicle of a marriage coming apart at the seams—having never been made really, except in bed. Although the marital discord is in the league of *Who's Afraid of Virginia Woolf,* it is cushioned by genteel nostalgia and the magnificence of the antebellum American South. The relationship between Rhett and Scarlett is abusive, even violent, nonetheless. There is a scene of marital rape, lots of miscommunication and bridled anger and eventually Rhett takes off for England with their young daughter, Bonnie Blue, who had been living with Scarlett since her parents separated. In London, the child is inconsolable; she screams for her mother in her sleep, and Rhett is finally forced to take her home, whereupon she has an accident on her pony and is killed.

The earlier scenes of big, burly Rhett playing sensitive, loving father are now supplanted by the picture of a broken, despairing man, pushed to the edge of sanity by grief. Scarlett, however, gets next to no attention as the mother of the little girl, and even less sympathy. Throughout the film and the book, she is depicted as selfish and silly, albeit Irish and determined. A childish woman, she seems incapable of unconditionally loving anything but herself (and possibly the family estate, Tara). It is Rhett who gets the kudos for mothering, not Scarlett. Rhett is, naturally, the proverbial diamond in the rough, a thoroughly macho man who nevertheless displays uncommon tolerance and great forbearance. In a 180 degree reversal of stereotypes he ultimately commands sympathy as the aggrieved husband, and it is Scarlett who gets blamed for being flighty, insincere, and exhausting everyone's patience. And for failing to live up to the minimum standards of wife- and motherhood.

Whatever disasters befall her—her daughter's death, Rhett's desertion—are, it is broadly hinted, thoroughly deserved. So when Rhett gets around to uttering those frameable words, "Frankly, my dear, I don't give a damn," Scarlett is left to weep alone.

* * *

Ostensibly focusing on the needs of the children, custody disputes today typically focus on parents trying to "prove" each other unfit or incompetent. Such disputes provoke mudslinging matches in court and, as many family law lawyers will admit, the contest is far from fair or objective. Jeffrey Wilson, a Toronto lawyer who had championed the cause of children's rights for years, comments with chagrin: "This is a huge grey area—the child's best interests. For a long time it was thought to be custody by the father, then it was the mother, and today it is whoever bonds. Bonding is the in-thing with psychiatrists now and as sure as I am sitting here, it will be something else in ten years. I can still remember a case in the U.S. in the sixties in which a judge declared that 'mulatto kids' should go with their black parent rather than their white. The interpretations can be that ridiculous because 'best interests' can mean whatever you want it to mean. Like beauty, it is in the eye of the beholder." Wilson is not the only lawyer who frankly agrees that winning a custody suit has become a matter of money. Money won't guarantee a successful outcome, but lack of it has certainly lost many a case. "Basically," he says, "you can win a custody suit if you have enough money. And in my experience men enjoy doing battle in court more than women do and are better equipped to hire lawyers and to talk lawyers' language."

* * *

There are ways money talks in custody court. Judges routinely consider such things as a spouse's employment prospects, current income, and capital assets, which obviously relate to economics. Questions about who can provide the more stable home and who is the more stable parent can involve money as well. What

happens when disaster strikes or adversity befalls? As one judge said in a 1980 decision, "financially the father's proposal offers greater security, and although such financial security could, should the mother have custody, be compensated for by an award of maintenance, in any unexpected adversity the wife's proposal would lack this depth of security." In this case the child was awarded to the father. Similarly, a situation where the mother in fulfilling a traditional homemaker's role has not worked outside the home or has done part-time work, and where she now has to "retrain" and move into the work force full-time, can be a major upheaval in the domestic routine and could no doubt be interpreted as a destabilizing event. Some judges have seen it that way, awarding custody of children to a father because he has a second wife who can stay at home with the children, something their mothers can no longer afford to do.

* * *

Even though there was a time when marriage was supposed to be indissoluble and forever (as well as made in heaven), adultery by men was not in itself considered to be an attack or a betrayal. It was thought to be normal (though not necessarily nice) behaviour, thoroughly acceptable and forgivable. The law simply enshrined what men have been telling women for centuries: "But it didn't mean anything; it was like shaking hands." For long decades women were thus required by law to be more faithful and more forgiving than men, to believe in and dedicate their lives to the very idea of marriage. Even when her husband was long gone, the infamous "dum casta" clauses stipulated that her marital rights, such as they were, only obtained so long as she remained chaste. It sounds positively medieval to us now, but there are still vestiges of these "while chaste" provisions in many laws and although they are no longer directed to a particular gender they still do relate rights to a person's conduct. (Ontario's family law, for example, empowers the court to take the conduct of a spouse into account when deciding on the amount of maintenance to be ordered, if such conduct is deemed to have been "so unconscionable as to constitute a gross repudiation of the relationship." The Divorce Act also states that a person's past conduct shall not be a consideration for a court deciding custody "unless the conduct is relevant to the ability of that person to act as a parent of the child.")

To this day, people assume when a couple separates that the event puts the woman in such a precarious and vulnerable social position that she must watch herself and carefully guard her reputation. Free advice pours in unsolicited, with reminders about not allowing "other" men to visit overnight and not being seen with too many different male friends. Antique ideas and double standards hang about the culture like dustballs long after they have been cleared off the law books, which exasperates family law experts like Malcolm Kronby. In his handbook, *Canadian Family Law*,* Kronby writes: "I'd like to have a nickel for every woman who has been terrified by a threat from her husband that he'll take the children away, and she'll never see them again because she has been unfaithful. Even where the husband and wife have been separated for years, the threat still arises." It does happen, however, that women lose custody of their children because of circumstances which have little to do with their talents as parents or their track record as mothers. Conduct, as it is interpreted in Canadian courts, is very often a matter of appearances and sexual stereotypes. What is considered relevant behaviour in one parent may not be in the other. The law may have eliminated gender bias in its letter, but it cannot eliminate it in judges; and some rights are to this day dependent on a person's conduct.

* * *

The major change in the last decade has been the emergence of joint custody, a concept virtually unheard of before 1975 and a category which the Central Divorce Registry did not even include on its statistics-gathering forms until recently. Although it looks straightforward, the term joint custody can be misleading, for it refers only to legal guardianship, the right to make decisions about a child's upbringing, education, religion, language, and so forth. It does not require or necessarily entail shared physical custody or imply any regular involvement with the child by both parents. It should not therefore be mistaken for a co-parenting arrangement, although it can and sometimes does involve that. Joint custody can exist with one parent having no physical contact with the children or it can involve a man and woman co-operating in a fully-fledged shared parenting program where both individuals are equally involved and develop a new way of being parents together. Such an arrangement, however, does not actually need legal joint custody order to exist. A father does not have to have legal rights to his child to share in parenting. It does seem, though, that many men feel alienated by the label "non-custodial parent" and want a titular connection to their children, and the authority that goes with it, free and clear of their ex-wives' control. . . .

In the circumstances, it seems strange that fathers' rights groups are springing up just now, in the late eighties, claiming that the courts are biased in favour of mothers and against them as custodians. Mothers once more are obviously losing favour, and rather rapidly at that. Whatever "favour" they have had, in any case, came very late in history and has always been limited and provisional. Even during the recent heyday of the maternal presumption, there were legal principles at work in the justice system which favoured fathers—less well known perhaps, but there all the same—paternal presumption for older children and sons, for instance. A so-called bias against fathers could just as easily be interpreted as a fair reflection of the reality that women generally do have a more substantial and ongoing experience tending children than their husbands do and are, on the whole, more keenly interested in child-rearing. The fathers'

*Kronby, Malcolm C. *Canadian Family Law*. Toronto: Stoddart, 1986.

rights phenomenon begs for some answers and some questions: why is joint custody being championed? Is their cause or their claim about children?

* * *

The outcome of divorce can be crushing for many women, especially for those coming out of a long marriage or those who consciously chose to be full-time mothers and now find that their jobs have been eliminated without appeal, and that they must find work outside the home, delegate mothering to someone else and see the children in the spaces between work and housework. If, in the middle of the emotional turmoil surrounding separation and the complex reorganization of family and financial life, a woman is faced with the possibility of her husband suing for custody, it is easy to understand how she might give ground financially in order to stave off that threat of losing her children—to the point of accepting an unjust property settlement and or maintenance levels that are plainly inadequate. Indeed, family law practitioners report that custody is being dragged into financial negotiations more frequently, often enough that lawyers can no longer counsel their female clients that custody of their children is assured. It no longer is; and it never was absolutely guaranteed. With increasing regularity women go into the separation process telling their lawyers that "no, he'll never fight me for the children; he has no interest in custody," only to eat their words bitterly when he does precisely that a few months later. When things get sticky in settlement negotiations, given the poker-game mentality of these proceedings, custody is too valuable a chip to be kept out of play. The threat of a custody challenge is becoming a routine tactic, as in: "If that's the kind of money you expect, I can do it cheaper. I'll take the children," or "If you are going to demand this large a settlement, I'll sue you for custody."

I am not saying that all men who express interest in retaining custody are disingenuous or out for revenge. The tremendous change in family life over the past two decades in the wake of the sexual and feminist revolutions has affected men as well as women and children. As women questioned traditional marriage and motherhood, notions of fatherhood began to change too. As some men began to participate in the births of their children (their presence in hospital delivery rooms at one time being strictly prohibited, the very idea considered peculiar) and became more actively involved with childcare, naturally they would want to continue their close relationships with their children after separation. Indeed, hundreds, maybe thousands, of couples have organized such an arrangement for themselves privately and have simply worked out their own way of sharing the parenting by mutual agreement and co-operation. With or without help from lawyers, therapists, and friends, they have found ways to parent together while living apart, and formed a new type of relationship as parents. But then, these are not the people who are counted in custody statistics, and no one really knows how they have settled their affairs.

Further Questions

1. A father leaves all child care responsibilities to the mother until they separate, and then he insists that she cannot simultaneously earn a living and take care of the children. Why does he think he is able to?

2. What does "joint custody" of children mean if the divorcing couple are getting along so badly that they cannot make any joint decisions regarding the children's future?

The Anti-Feminist Backlash:
Or Why Custody Is a Fatherhood Issue   XI.7B

SUSAN CREAN

Susan Crean claims that "fathers' rights" advocates are not trying for nonsexist set-
tlements of custody, visiting rights, and support payments. Instead, they are trying to
make a case against mothers, claiming that it is women—not sexism in the family,
work force, and judicial system—who are the cause of family problems, both before
and after divorce.

Reading Questions

1. Is the role of supermom (wife, mother, and work-force participant) so demanding that a
   woman can be relieved to shed the first component of the role, that of being a wife? What
   do you think should be done about the predicament (overwork) of supermoms?
2. In a custody dispute, should the heterosexual nuclear family be perceived as the ideal
   situation in which to place a child? Which parent would most likely be awarded custody if
   this were the basis of the decision?

ADVOCATES FOR MEN'S RIGHTS have always been
with us in one guise or another, and "fathers'
rights" advocates have been on the scene for the
better part of a decade. Recently they have been
attracting mainstream attention, gathering
strength and visibility by taking on a broader
(and softer) political agenda. Since Manitoba
started the trend in provincial support payment
enforcement schemes, their lobbying efforts
have intensified and they have been successfully
getting stories into the papers which paint a picture of men as hard done by, misunderstood,
patient fathers-in-exile. Increasingly we are
hearing about men who are the innocent victims of malicious women and young girls who
make false accusations of sexual abuse against
them. By pressing for perfectly reasonable
things like paid paternity leave and tax deductions for unmarried fathers who do not live with
their children and contribute to their upkeep
without court orders, moreover, they are able
to curry the favour of public opinion and right-
thinking liberals who haven't yet glimpsed their
real agenda.

* * *

Despite the established facts that men are the
main perpetrators of violence and sexual abuse
in families and rarely participate in housework
or childcare, men's rights advocates would have
us believe that the only thing preventing them
from turning into kind and skilled parents after
they leave the marriage is their ex-wives. And it
is only the vindictiveness of their ex-wives that is
responsible for their children's problems after
separation. Tellingly, the target of men's rights
advocates' ire is not the male superstructure and
the discriminatory judicial system, but women.

* * *

Abridged from "The Anti-Feminist Backlash: Or Why Custody Is a Fatherhood Issue," p. 99–140 in In the
Name of the Fathers *by Susan Crean (Toronto, Ontario: Amanita Enterprises, 1988). Reprinted by permission of the publisher.*

516 PART ELEVEN: RAISING CHILDREN: MOTHERS AND FATHERS

The case for fathers' rights is a case against mothers; it is not a positive one attempting to deal with sexism from a male perspective; it denies that sexism even exists and blames the gross excesses of male behaviour (rape, abuse, and violence) on women. Instead of admitting the systemic discrimination which debilitates their ex-wives and families after divorce, they claim that the reverse is true, that women are the privileged ones in divorce. And always, whenever the men's rights movement speaks, there comes the sound of whining voices, accusations, and stories with villains and victims, no compassion or regret—only the hard, grim face of denial.

* * *

As many writers have reported, the division of labour in the home and the organization of the work force create a disincentive for men and career women to engage in child-rearing. As more women have entered the work force the social expectations for motherhood have simply expanded to include that work, effectively landing modern women with two full-time jobs without the support services obviously required. It means struggling to be Supermom, and it is no wonder that some women find it a relief to shed the third role (that of wife), if only because of the time and energy it requires. But in court, women who stray so much as a jot or a tittle from the straight and narrow ideal of motherhood are likely to find themselves in trouble.

* * *

If she is working-class and poor, a mother's chances of getting good legal advice are as slim as her chances of getting adequately paying work. If she lives in a rural community her isolation and distance from support services work against her. If she is lesbian, although Canadian courts are not supposed to deny custody on the grounds of sexual orientation, chances are her life will be scrutinized and a judge will declare her way of life prejudicial to her children.

Because custody decisionmakers have a picture of the ideal family (which is to say the heterosexual nuclear family) in the back of their minds, it is not surprising that many custody de-

cisions give the children to the parent who can offer the family set-up which most closely resembles it. Boyd* cites several cases where mothers who had to leave the home to work lost out to fathers who were also working full-time, but who could offer substitute female childcare. In one case the father was awarded custody on condition that his mother care for the child, which prompted Boyd's wry comment: "One wonders whether the grandmother herself should not have been competing with the mother for custody of the child." And she further notes, "Paternal grandparents are exhorted to assist fathers in parenting much more frequently than are maternal grandmothers, hinting that the courts view fathers as needing more help in performing childcare than do mothers." In another case, a young doctor who proposed to hire a housekeeper to care for his daughter was given custody, the rationale being that the mother would have to make a similar arrangement because she too was working, despite the fact that the child had been living with the mother for two years, and custody was only claimed by the father when she made a request for increased child support.

Boyd also found a marked tendency for the courts to overplay the contribution of fathers to childcare, often taking the least demonstration of interest as grounds for declaring him an excellent parent. Just as often, his actual contribution to childcare is never even investigated. While mothers are assumed to have difficulty in combining work and mothering, judges "fall over backwards so as not to give the impression they think employed fathers neglected their parenting." In one case Boyd cites, a father was given sole custody of his two young children although their mother was described as warm and demonstrative and he as highly controlled, disciplined, intellectual, and a solitary person. The judge noted, furthermore, that: "It is true that before the separation he did not devote as much time and attention to the children as [his wife] would have liked and that

*Boyd, Susan B. "Child Custody, Ideology and Female Employment," Unpublished paper, 1986.

he was preoccupied with his work and with achieving success. It is equally true, however, that he made a significant contribution to the care of the children and to the household even though with respect to the children, his undemonstrative nature may have made it appear that he was not as loving as he might have been." Asks Boyd: "Would a mother have been rewarded for similarly prioritizing her work over the needs of the children?" What about the children? Were they happy to be placed in the custody of their father? Have they found solace and security in the judge's assurance that he is really a much more loving man than he appears to them to be?

* * *

Of course, what this shows is that courts and their various professional attendants are very far removed from the everyday experience of most women and oblivious to the changes taking place in the practice and even the conceptualization of mothering by women. For instance, the idea of lesbian co-parenting is no longer an idea; it exists and by its existence reinvents the very idea of the family. The lesbian family is still based on a two-parent model, two adults connected by an emotional and sexual bond, although the child is the biological offspring of only one. It defies both the language and the conventions of heterosexual family life, and challenges the very definition of "mother." What does the word *mother* mean in such a context, (or, for that matter, the term *father* in a male homosexual family)?

For one thing, the lesbian family demonstrates how terribly narrow the term *mother* is; lesbian couples complain that when the impending birth is announced, people invariable ask who "the mother" is, meaning the biological mother. And what does it do for the verb "to mother"? Of course, fathering has also been undergoing change, attracting the attention of mental health professionals, researchers, and policymakers. As a social phenomenon it has acquired a certain cachet among some men who, for instance, no longer think it sissy work to change the kid's diaper or take her to daycare. Writer and broadcaster David Suzuki reports that one of the biggest responses he has ever had from the public was to a magazine piece he wrote about his experience taking primary care of his two small daughters. In many ways, fatherhood is an idea whose time has come, even though the public fascination with it is superficial—as superficial as is the statistical commitment of men to childcare and housework. It is, just the same, something the women's movement has always seen as valuable and necessary; but it arrived just as the divorce rate was exploding and as fathers were leaving their families in unprecedented numbers.

There is nothing to indicate that men as a group are more interested in, or capable of delivering, sound twenty-four-hour parenting than they ever were. The joys of fatherhood and the number of men engaging in it are being grossly exaggerated; and, while we all pay lip-service to the idea, we may be missing the point, which is that fatherhood is in crisis. The only people speaking up for it at the moment are fatherhood's greatest enemies: the men's rights activists who are only interested in post-marriage fatherhood as it reflects their personal power. Yet the men's rights phenomenon is having an insidious influence on the ideology and actions of the mainstream of which few people, including progressive men, are aware—an influence which threatens to make fatherhood just another word for patriarchy.

Further Questions

1. Suppose a child has been in the care of one parent for the duration of the child's life. Should custody of the child be transferred to the other parent because this other parent is now in a position to offer the child a better family set-up? If so, what features of the set-up would be relevant to transferring custody?

2. Should the sexual orientation of a parent make any difference to whether he or she becomes the custodial parent? Explain how, if at all, parental sexual orientation makes a difference in matters of custody.

3. If you are a man, do you plan to become actively engaged in care of your children (provided that you have children)? If so, what sorts of things do you plan to do in this area? Would your contributions to childcare be a sufficient basis for your claiming custody of the children if you and your wife should separate?

Further Readings for Part XI: Raising Children: Mothers and Fathers

Katherine Arnup, ed. *Lesbian Parenting: Living With Pride and Prejudice* (Charlottetown, P.E.I. Canada: Gynenergy books, 1995).

William R. Beer. *Househusbands: Men and Housework in American Families* (South Hadley, MA: J. F. Bergin Publishers, 1983). Housework: why men do it, how they like it, and why more men do not do it.

Jessie Bernard. *The Future of Motherhood* (New York, NY: Th Dial Press, 1974). Thorough critique of traditional attitudes toward maternity and a hopeful look toward its future.

Mary Frances Berry. *The Politics of Parenthood: Child Care, Women's Rights and the Myth of the Good Mother* (New York, NY: Penguin Books, 1999). 20th century history of parenthood in the U.S.

Bruno Bettelheim. *The Children of the Dream* (New York, NY: Avon Books , 1969). Somewhat idealized description of communal childrearing on an Israeli kibbutz.

Graham B. Blaine, Jr. *Are Parents Bad for Children?* (New York, NY: Coward, McCann and Goeghegan, 1973).

Jeffrey Blustein. *Parents and Children* (New York, NY: Oxford University Press, 182). Duties, responsibilities, and problems between parents and children.

John Bowlby. *Child Care and the Growth of Love* (Baltimore, MD: Penguin Books, 1973).

Paula J. Caplan. *Don't Blame Mother: Mending the Mother-Daughter Relationship* (New York, NY: Harper & Row, 1989). A psychologist takes a hard broom to Freudian cobwebs.

Nancy Chodorow. *The Reproduction of Mothering* (Berkeley, CA: University of California Press, 1978). Influential book arguing that mothering is doomed to repeat itself in daughters.

Brenda O. Daly and Maureen T. Reddy, eds. *Narrating Mothers: Theorizing Maternal Subjectivities* (Knoxville, TN: The University of Tennessee Press, 1991). What the experience of mothering is like under varying conditions.

Frederick Engels. *The Origin of the Family, Private Property and the State* (New York , NY: International, 1975). The patriarchal family is founded on private property. Women can be freed only through socialism.

Marilyn Fabe and Norman Wikler. *Up Against the Clock: Career Women Speak on the Choice to Have Children* (New York, NY: Random House, 1979).

Janet Finch. *Married to the Job: Wives' Incorporation in Men's Work* (Boston, MA: George Allen and Unwin, 1983). Taking on your husband's job and its impact on your life.

Martha Albertson Fineman. *The Neutered Mother, the Sexual Family and Other Twentieth Century Tragedies* (New York, NY: Routledge, 1995). Argument that nurturing tie between mother and child should be the focus of society's concern for "the family."

Martha Albertson Fineman and Isabel Karpin, eds. *Mothers in Law: Feminist Theory and the Legal Regulation of Motherhood* (New York, NY: Columbia University Press, 1995).

Sigmund Freud. "Femininity" (1933) in Jean Strouse, ed. *Women and Analysis* (New York, NY: Grossman, 1974). Girls' childhoods are so bad that their only hope of normality lies in becoming mothers.

Nancy Friday. *My Mother/My Self* (New York, NY: Delacorte, 1977). Popular book, so it must have struck a responsive chord in many women.

Barbara Furneaux. *Special Parents* (Children with Special Needs Series) (Philadelphia, PA: Open University Press, 1988). The impact of handicapped children on their parents.

Evelyn Nakano Glenn, Grace Chang, and Linda Rennie Forcey, eds. *Mothering: Ideology, Experience, and Agency* (New York, NY: Routledge, 1994). Social forces such as race and class have their impact upon the practice of mothering.

Tuula Gordon. *Feminist Mothers* (New York, NY: New York University Press, 1990). Patriarchal construction of motherhood can be combatted by an alternative ideology, feminism.

Geoffrey L. Greif. *Single Fathers* (Lexington, MA: Lexington Books, 1985). What happens when fathers have custody of their children.

Michael Hardy and Graham Crow, eds. *Lone Parenthood* (New York, NY: Harvestor Wheatsheaf, 1991). Coping with the constraints of single parenthood and creating opportunities within it.

Hilary Homans. *The Sexual Politics of Reproduction* (Brookfield, VT: Gower Publishing Co., 1985). Reproduction in a social context of male control.

Dwight J. Ingle. *Who Should Have Children?* (New York, NY: Bobbs-Merrill, 1973). Justification of selective population control.

Miriam M. Johnson. *Strong Mothers, Weak Wives: The Search for Gender Equality* (Berkeley, CA: University of California Press, 1988). Critique of popular ideas on motherhood.

Sheila B. Kamerman and Alfred J. Kahn. *Mothers Alone: Strategies for a Time of Change* (Dover, MA: Auburn House Publishing Co., 1988). Questions of going back to work, public support, personal life, etc.

Jane Price Knowles and Ellen Cole, eds. *Woman-Destined Motherhood* (Binghamton, NY: Harrington Park Press, 1990). Feminist perspective on the various thoughts and experiences of motherhood.

Edward Kruk. *Divorce and Disengagement: Patterns of Fatherhood Within and Beyond Marriage* (Halifax, Nova Scotia: Fernwood Publishing, 1993). Portrayal of the impact of divorce on non-custodial fathers.

Molly Ladd-Taylor and Laurie Umansky, eds. *"Bad" Mothers: The Politics of Blame in Twentieth-Century America* (New York, NY: New York University Press, 1998).

Jane Lazarre. *Beyond the Whiteness of Whiteness: Memoir of a White Mother of Black Sons* (Durham, NC: Duke University Press, 1996). A confrontation of white/racism through a white mother's love of her black sons.

Charlie Lewis and Margaret O'Brien, eds. *Reassessing Fatherhood: New Observations on Fathers and the Modern Family* (Newbury, CA: Sage Publications, 1987). How changes in the fatherhood role affect fathers' experiences.

Robert A. Lewis and Robert E. Salt, eds. *Men in Families* (Newbury Park, CA: Sage Publications, 1986). Response to Barbara Ehrenreich's *The Hearts of Men* (see Further Readings for Part V), attempting to explain why men want to be involved in marriage and parenthood.

Elaine Tyler May. *Barren in the Promised Land: Childless Americans and the Pursuit of Happiness* (New York, NY: Basic Books, Harper Collins, 1995). Aspects of childlessness in a nation obsessed with reproduction.

Martha McMahon. *Engendering Motherhood: Identity and Self-transformation in Women's Lives* (New York, NY: The Guilford Press, 1995). The effects of motherhood upon the way women undergo gendered experiences, and engendered identity.

Elizabeth A. Mulroy, ed. *Women as Single Parents: Confronting Institutional Barriers in the Courts, the Workplace and the Housing Market* (Dover, MA: Auburn House Publishing Co., 1988).

Uma Narayan and Julia T. Bartkowiak, eds. *Having and Raising Children: Unconventional Families, Hard Choices and the Social Good* (University Park, PA: The Pennsylvania State University Press, 1999).

Onora O'Neill and William Ruddick, eds. *Having Children: Philosophical and Legal Reflections on Parenthood* (New York, NY: Oxford University Press, 1979).

Adrienne Rich. *Of Women Born: Motherhood as Experience and Institution* (New York, NY: W. W. Norton, 1976). Discussion of motherhood in patriarchy, beginning with personal experience.

Bryan E. Robinson and Robert L. Barret. *The Developing Father: Emerging Roles in Contemporary Society* (New York, NY: The Guilford Press, 1986). Includes single fathers, stepfathers, gay fathers, and teenage fathers.

Barbara Katz Rothman. *Recreating Motherhood: Ideology and Technology in a Patriarchal Society* (New York, NY: W. W. Norton and Co., 1989). Woman-centered vision of reshaping technology to serve our purposes; includes more "fathering" on the part of men.

Sara Ruddick. *Maternal Thinking* (Boston, MA: Beacon Press, 1989). Maternal thinking can be done by women or men and can be directed at more situations than child raising.

Anna and Arnold Silverman. *The Case Against Having Children* (New York, NY: David MacKay Co., 1971). Don't have children for the wrong reasons. There are alternatives.

Joyce Trebilcot, ed. *Mothering: Essays in Feminist Theory* (Totowa, NJ: Rowman and Allenheld, 1984). Excellent collection of feminist writings on mothering.

Estela V. Welldon. *Mother, Madonna and Whore* (London: Free Association Books, 1988). Motherhood is sometimes chosen for unconscious, perverse reasons.

Suggested Moral of Part XI

One strand of tradition links womanhood strongly with motherhood. Through becoming mothers, bearing and raising children, some women gain a place in the world as well as esteem and respect from others. There are, however, disadvantages to child raising responsibilities, especially when a woman also wants a career in the workplace. One solution, which is meeting with resistance, especially from men, is for the mother and father to share these responsibilities. A common view is that children are better off when raised by their mother; however, this idea explodes in the legal system when the couple separates and the father attempts to take custody of the children, claiming that he would be a better parent. Should a woman become a mother with all these potential hazards in the path of motherhood?

Many women, quite understandably, have difficulties making decisions about whether to have children. But suppose the patriarchal elements infusing parenthood (discussed by the authors in this section) were eliminated and parents could make arrangements for the care of their children in the absence of such influences. Then a woman could choose to be a parent with the same freedom as a man. Under these circumstances, childcare might be more welcome by those choosing to undertake it and not perceived by the individual responsible for it as an unwanted interference with whatever else she wanted to do with her life.

Part XII

Youngsters and Oldsters

Introduction

AGEISM, OPPRESSION OF OLDER PEOPLE, has only recently come to public attention, even within feminism and movements of other oppressed groups. Relatively little has been written on this subject, despite the fact that aging affects everyone. The writings in this section address some of the problems of aging.

Steinem explains why young women are more conservative than older women; Lorde compares ageism to racism, classism, and sexism all of which are beliefs in the inherent superiority of one group to others. Moss complains of the social assignment of the aging woman to obsolescence; de Beauvoir describes the emptiness of the life of the older woman; MacDonald finds fault with the younger woman who cannot look her in the eye; Gerike discusses the social consequences of gray hair; Reeves describes possible strains on the dual career couple as they near retirement.

XII.1   Why Young Women Are More Conservative

GLORIA STEINEM

Gloria Steinem describes the typical mentality of younger women, the women on a college or university campus in particular. Their optimistic perspective, due partly to the value placed on them by patriarchal society, tends to make them lean toward conservatism. Many of them can be expected to develop a more realistic outlook on women's situations as they grow older.

Another selection by Steinem appears in Part X.

Reading Questions

1. As a young woman on a campus, do you feel that you are in a position of a consumer of services, paid for by you, your family, the government, or your institution's endowment? If so, do you think you have certain privileges as a consumer, relative to those who provide these services?
2. Is it true that male-dominated cultures place the most value on younger women because they have full potential for work, sex, and childbearing? If male dominance is not the source of value in younger women, what is? Or is youth not particularly valuable in a woman?
3. Do campus women sometimes participate in a female guilt trip in which they feel that if they are not studying hard and having a wonderful personal life at the same time, it is primarily their own fault? Give some examples of such guilt trips. Do men participate in these to the same extent as do women?

IF YOU HAD ASKED ME a decade or more ago, I certainly would have said the campus was the first place to look for the feminist or any other revolution. I also would have assumed that student-age women, like student-age men, were much more likely to be activist and open to change than their parents. After all, campus revolts have a long and well-publicized tradition, from the students of medieval France, whose "heresy" was suggesting that the university be separate from the church, through the anticolonial student riots of British India; from students who led the cultural revolution of the People's Republic of China, to campus demonstrations against the Shah of Iran. Even in this country, with far less tradition of student activism, the populist movement to end the war in Vietnam was symbolized by campus protests and mistrust of anyone over thirty.

It has taken me many years of traveling as a feminist speaker and organizer to understand that I was wrong about women; at least, about women acting on their own behalf. In activism, as in so many other things, I had been educated to assume that men's cultural pattern was the natural or the only one. If student years were the peak time of rebellion and openness to change for men, then the same must be true for women.

Why Young Women Are More Conservative. From Outrageous Acts and Everyday Rebellions *by Gloria Steinem. Copyright © 1983 by Gloria Steinem. © 1984 by East Toledo Productions, Inc. Reprinted by permission of Henry Holt and Company, Inc.*

In fact, a decade of listening to every kind of women's group—from brown-bag lunchtime lectures organized by office workers to all-night rap sessions at campus women's centers; from housewives' self-help groups to campus rallies—has convinced me that the reverse is more often true. Women may be the one group that grows more radical with age. Though some students are big exceptions to this rule, women in general don't begin to challenge the politics of our own lives until later.

Looking back, I realize that this pattern has been true for my life, too. My college years were full of uncertainties and the personal conservatism that comes from trying to win approval and fit into the proper grown-up and womanly role, whether that means finding a well-to-do man to be supported by or a male radical to support. Nonetheless, I went right on assuming that brave exploring youth and cowardly conservative old age were the norms for everybody, and that I must be just an isolated and guilty accident. Though every generalization based on female culture has many exceptions, and should never be used as a crutch or excuse, I think we might be less hard on ourselves and each other as students, feel better about our potential for change as we grow older—and educate reporters who announce feminism's demise because its red-hot center is not on campus—if we figured out that for most of us as women, the traditional college period is an unrealistic and cautious time. Consider a few of the reasons.

As students, women are probably treated with more equality than we ever will be again. For one thing, we're consumers. The school is only too glad to get the tuitions we pay, or that our families or government grants pay on our behalf. With population rates declining because of women's increased power over childbearing, that money is even more vital to a school's existence. Yet more than most consumers, we're too transient to have much power as a group. If our families are paying our tuition, we may have even less power.

As young women, whether students or not, we're still in the stage most valued by male-dominant cultures: We have our full potential as workers, wives, sex partners, and childbearers.

That means we haven't yet experienced the life events that are most radicalizing for women: entering the paid-labor force and discovering how women are treated there; marrying and finding out that it is not yet an equal partnership; having children and discovering who is responsible for them and who is not; and aging, still a greater penalty for women than for men.

Furthermore, new ambitions nourished by the rebirth of feminism may make young women feel and behave a little like a classical immigrant group. We are determined to prove ourselves, to achieve academic excellence, and to prepare for interesting and successful careers. More noses are kept to more grindstones in an effort to demonstrate newfound abilities, and perhaps to allay suspicions that women still have to have more and better credentials than men. This doesn't leave much time for activism. Indeed, we may not yet know that it is necessary.

In addition, the very progress into previously all-male careers that may be revolutionary for women is seen as conservative and conformist by outside critics. Assuming male radicalism to be the measure of change, they interpret any concern with careers as evidence of "campus conservatism." In fact, "dropping out" maybe a departure for men, but "dropping in" is a new thing for women. Progress lies in the direction we have not been.

Like most groups of the newly arrived or awakened, our faith in education and paper degrees also has yet to be shaken. For instance, the percentage of women enrolled in college and universities has been increasing at the same time that the percentage of men has been decreasing. Among students entering college in 1978, women *outnumbered* men for the first time. This hope of excelling at the existing game is probably reinforced by the greater cultural pressure on females to be "good girls" and observe somebody else's rules.

Though we may know intellectually that we need to have new games with new rules, we probably haven't quite absorbed such facts as the high unemployment rate among female Ph.D.s; the lower average salary among women college graduates of all races than among counterpart males who graduated from high school or less; the middle-management ceiling against which even those eagerly hired new business-school graduates seem to bump their heads after five or ten years; and the barrier-breaking women in nontraditional fields who become the first fired when recession hits. Sadly enough, we may have to personally experience some of these reality checks before we accept the idea that lawsuits, activism, and group pressure will have to accompany our individual excellence and crisp new degrees.

Then there is the female guilt trip, student edition. If we're not sailing along as planned, it must be *our* fault. If our mothers didn't "do anything" with their educations, it must have been *their* fault. If we can't study as hard as we think we must (because women still have to be better prepared than men), and have a substantial personal and sexual life at the same time (because women are supposed to care more about relationships than men do), then we feel inadequate, as if each of us were individually at fault for a problem that is actually culture-wide.

I've yet to be on a campus where most women weren't worrying about some aspect of combining marriage, children, and a career. I've yet to find one where many men were worrying about the same thing. Yet women will go right on suffering from the double role problem and terminal guilt until men are encouraged, pressured, or otherwise forced, individually and collectively, to integrate themselves into the "women's work" of raising children and homemaking. Until then, and until there are changed job patterns to allow equal parenthood, children will go right on growing up with the belief that only women can be loving and nurturing, and only men can be intellectual or active outside the home. Each half of the world will go on limiting the full range of its human talent.

Finally, there is the intimate political training that hits women in the teens and early twenties: the countless ways we are still brainwashed into assuming that women are dependent on men for our basic identities, both in our work and our personal lives, much more than vice versa. After all, if we're going to enter a marriage system that's still legally designed for a person and a half, submit to an economy in which women still average about fifty-nine cents on the dollar earned by men, and work mainly as support staff and assistants, or *co*-directors and *vice*-presidents at best, then we have to be convinced that we are not whole people on our own.

In order to make sure that we will see ourselves as half-people, and thus be addicted to getting our identity from serving others, society tries hard to convert us as young women into "man-junkies"; that is, into people who are addicted to regular shots of male-approval and presence, both professionally and personally. We need a man standing next to us, actually and figuratively, whether it's at work, on Saturday night, or throughout life. (If only men realized how little it matters *which* man is standing there, they would understand that this addiction depersonalizes them, too.) Given the danger to a male-dominant system if young women stop internalizing this political message of derived identity it's no wonder that those who try to kick the addiction—and, worse yet, to help other women do the same—are likely to be regarded as odd or dangerous by everyone from parents to peers.

With all that pressure combined with little experience, it's no wonder that younger women are often less able to support each other. Even young women who espouse feminist goals as individuals may refrain from identifying themselves as "feminist": it's okay to want equal pay for yourself (just one small reform) but it's not okay to want equal pay for women as a group (an economic revolution). Some retreat into individualized career obsessions as a way of avoiding this dangerous discovery of shared experience with women as a group. Others retreat into the safe middle ground of "I'm not a feminist but. . . ." Still others become politically active, but only on issues that are taken seriously by their male counterparts. . . .

This cultural pattern of youthful conservatism makes the growing number of older women going back to school very important. They are life examples and pragmatic activists who radicalize women young enough to be their daughters. Now that the median female undergraduate age in this country is twenty-seven because so many older women have returned, the campus is becoming a major place for cross-generational connections.

None of this should denigrate the courageous efforts of young women, especially women on campus, and the many changes they've pioneered. On the contrary, they should be seen as even more remarkable for surviving the conservative pressures, recognizing societal problems they haven't yet fully experienced, and organizing successfully in the midst of a transient student population. Every women's history course, rape hot line, or campus newspaper that is finally covering *all* the news; every feminist professor whose job has been created or tenure saved by student pressure, or male administrator whose consciousness has been permanently changed; every counselor who's stopped guiding women one way and men another; every lawsuit that's been fueled by student energies against unequal athletic funds or graduate school requirements: All those accomplishments are even more impressive when seen against the backdrop of the female pattern of activism. . . .

. . .[T]he definition of "political," on campus as elsewhere, tends to be limited to who's running for president, who's demonstrating against corporate investments in South Africa, or which is the "moral" side of some conventional revolution, preferably one that is thousands of miles away.

As important as such activities are, they are also the most comfortable ones when we're young. They provide a sense of virtue without much disruption in the power structure of our daily lives. Even when the most consistent energies on campus are actually concentrated around feminist issues, they may be treated as apolitical and invisible. Asked "What's happening on campus?" a student may reply, "The anti-nuke movement," even though that resulted in one demonstration of two hours, while student antirape squads have been patrolling the campus every night for two years and women's students have begun to transform the very textbooks we read.

No wonder reporters and sociologists looking for revolution on campus often miss the depth of feminist change and activity that is really there. Women students themselves may dismiss it as not political and not serious. Certainly, it rarely comes in the masculine sixties style of bombing buildings or burning draft cards. In fact, it goes much deeper than protesting a temporary symptom—say, the draft—and challenges the right of one group to dominate another, which is the disease itself.

Young women have a big task of resisting pressures and challenging definitions. Their increasing success is a miracle of foresight and courage that should make us all proud. But they should know that they, too, may grow more radical with age.

One day, an army of gray-haired women may quietly take over the earth.

Further Questions

1. As a young woman student, do you feel your main focus should be on proving yourself and preparing for an interesting successful career, especially if the presence of women is relatively new in your field? Are young men experiencing the same types of difficulty and, if so, to a greater or lesser extent than young women?

2. What, if anything, can be done for women who are "man-junkies," addicted to regular shots of male approval and presence to get on well in life? Are there men who are "woman-junkies" and, if so, what can be done to help them?

3. Do you find it difficult to call yourself "feminist" even though you share many goals with feminism? Is it more or less difficult to do this if you are a man?

XII.2   Age, Race, Class, and Sex: Women Redefining Difference

AUDRE LORDE

Audre Lorde believes that it too often happens that differences among people cause fear, loathing, rejection, and oppression. Ageism is a belief in the inherent superiority of one group of people over another, conjoined with a belief in the right to dominate the group thought inferior.

Another selection by Lorde appears in Part I.

Reading Questions

1. Do you think that ideas of young people are more suited to today's world than those of older people? Are young people more aware of social realities because they bring fresh ideas to what they find, or are older people better at assessing social realities because they have had more experience?

2. Suppose an older person sometimes despairs at young people's making the same mistakes her generation did, not having learned anything from past mistakes. Is she justified in doing so? Should young people pay more attention to what older people say, or are they better off making their own mistakes and learning from them?

3. If one group of people is oppressing another, is it the responsibility of the oppressed to speak up and make their voices heard by the oppressors? Does the oppressor group have any responsibilities to the oppressed to learn of their situation, such as asking the oppressed to speak and listening to them when they do?

MUCH OF WESTERN EUROPEAN HISTORY conditions us to see human differences in simplistic opposition to each other: dominant/subordinate, good/bad, up/down, superior/inferior. In a society where the good is defined in terms of profit rather than in terms of human need, there must always be some group of people who, through systematized oppression, can be made to feel surplus, to occupy the place of the dehumanized inferior. Within this society, that group is made up of Black and Third World people, working-class people, older people, and women.

As a forty-nine-year-old Black lesbian feminist socialist mother of two, including one boy,

Abridged from "Age, Race, Class, and Sex," in Sister Outsider by Audre Lorde (Freedom, CA: The Crossing Press, 1984). Reprinted by permission of the publisher.

and a member of an inter-racial couple, I usually find myself a part of some group defined as other, deviant, inferior, or just plain wrong. Traditionally, in american society, it is the members of oppressed, objectified groups who are expected to stretch out and bridge the gap between the actualities of our lives and the consciousness of our oppressor. For in order to survive, those of us for whom oppression is as american as apple pie have always had to be watchers, to become familiar with the language and manners of the oppressor, even sometimes adopting them for some illusion of protection. Whenever the need for some pretense of communication arises, those who profit from our oppression call upon us to share our knowledge with them. In other words, it is the responsibility of the oppressed to teach the oppressors their mistakes. I am responsible for educating teachers who dismiss my children's culture in school. Black and Third World people are expected to educate white people as to our humanity. Women are expected to educate men. Lesbians and gay men are expected to educate the heterosexual world. The oppressors maintain their position and evade responsibility for their own actions. There is a constant drain of energy which might be better used in redefining ourselves and devising realistic scenarios for altering the present and constructing the future.

Institutionalized rejection of difference is an absolute necessity in a profit economy which needs outsiders as surplus people. As members of such an economy, we have all been programmed to respond to the human differences between us with fear and loathing and to handle that difference in one of three ways: ignore it, and if that is not possible, copy it if we think it is dominant, or destroy it if we think it is subordinate. But we have no patterns for relating across our human differences as equals. As a result, those differences have been misnamed and misused in the service of separation and confusion.

Certainly there are very real differences between us of race, age, and sex. But it is not those differences between us that are separating us. It is rather our refusal to recognize those differences, and to examine the distortions which result from our misnaming them and their effects upon human behavior and expectation.

Racism, the belief in the inherent superiority of one race over all others and thereby the right to dominance. Sexism, the belief in the inherent superiority of one sex over the other and thereby the right to dominance. Ageism. Heterosexism. Elitism. Classism.

It is a lifetime pursuit for each one of us to extract these distortions from our living at the same time as we recognize, reclaim, and define those differences upon which they are imposed. For we have all been raised in a society where those distortions were endemic within our living. Too often, we pour the energy needed for recognizing and exploring difference into pretending those differences are insurmountable barriers, or that they do not exist at all. This results in a voluntary isolation, or false and treacherous connections. Either way, we do not develop tools for using human difference as a springboard for creative change within our lives. We speak not of human difference, but of human deviance.

Somewhere, on the edge of consciousness, there is what I call a *mythical norm*, which each one of us within our hearts knows "that it is not me." In america, this norm is usually defined as white, thin, male, young, heterosexual, christian, and financially secure. It is within this mythical norm that the trappings of power reside within this society. Those of us who stand outside that power often identify one way in which we are different, and we assume that to be the primary cause of all oppression, forgetting other distortions around difference, some of which we ourselves may be practising. By and large within the women's movement today, white women focus upon their oppression as women and ignore differences of race, sexual preference, class, and age. There is a pretense to a homogeneity of experience covered by the word *sisterhood* that does not in fact exist.

Unacknowledged class differences rob women of each other's energy and creative insight.

Recently a women's magazine collective made the decision for one issue to print only prose, saying poetry was a less "rigorous" or "serious" art form. Yet even the form our creativity takes is often a class issue. Of all the art forms, poetry is the most economical. It is the one which is the most secret, which requires the least physical labor, the least material, and the one which can be done between shifts, in the hospital pantry, on the subway, and on scraps of surplus paper. Over the last few years, writing a novel on tight finances, I came to appreciate the enormous differences in the material demands between poetry and prose. As we reclaim our literature, poetry has been the major voice of poor, working class, and Colored women. A room of one's own may be a necessity for writing prose, but so are reams of paper, a typewriter and plenty of time. The actual requirements to produce the visual arts also help determine, along class lines, whose art is whose. In this day of inflated prices for material, who are our sculptors, our painters, our photographers? When we speak of a broadly based women's culture, we need to be aware of the effect of class and economic differences on the supplies available for producing art.

As we move toward creating a society within which we can each flourish, ageism is another distortion of relationship which interferes with our vision. By ignoring the past, we are encouraged to repeat its mistakes. The "generation gap" is an important social tool for any repressive society. If the younger members of a community view the older members as contemptible or suspect or excess, they will never be able to join hands and examine the living memories of the community, nor ask the all important question, 'Why?' This gives rise to a historical amnesia that keeps us working to invent the wheel every time we have to go to the store for bread.

We find ourselves having to repeat and relearn the same old lessons over and over that our mothers did because we do not pass on what we have learned, or because we are unable to listen. For instance, how many times has this all been said before? For another, who would have believed that once again our daughters are allowing their bodies to be hampered and purgatoried by girdles and high heels and hobble skirts? .. . .

Further Questions

1. Is a normal person (a paradigm by which others are judged) white, thin, male, young, heterosexual, and financially secure? Is it disturbing when we don't meet one or more of these criteria? What is it that makes these criteria so important?

2. Within an oppressed group, how good are we at recognizing yet further forms of oppression that happen to those in the group other than ourselves? How can we increase our awareness of others' problems?

3. If we do not listen to older people and take them seriously, will we miss out on the "living memories" of our community? Are these "living memories" important for us to know about? Discuss, in connection with some examples.

It Hurts to Be Alive and Obsolete   **XII.3**

ZOE MOSS

Zoe Moss (a pseudonym she used for fear of losing her job for publishing this writing) speaks of the aging (43-year-old) woman, alive and obsolete. The world, she says, has no further use for her at that age.

Reading Questions

1. According to the media, is growing old one of the worst things that can happen to a woman? Give some examples. Does the media send the same message—or a different one—to men regarding aging?
2. Would a woman look out of place if she attended an important event wearing clothes that were five or six years out of date? Can a young woman defy fashion more easily than an older woman? Is it easier for men to keep wearing out-dated clothes than it is for women?
3. Is it more difficult for a woman to find companionship of any sort when she is over forty? If so, is this because she rejects other people or because they reject her? Would finding companionship be easier if she were a man?

WHAT, FAT, FORTY-THREE, and I dare to think I'm still a person? No, I am an invisible lump. I belong in a category labelled *a priori* without interest to anyone. I am not even expected to interest myself; A middle-aged woman is comic by definition.

In this commodity culture, we are urged and covered into defining ourselves by buying objects that demonstrate that we are, or which tell us that they will make us feel, young, affluent, fashionable. Imagine a coffee table with the best-sellers of five years ago carefully displayed. You giggle. A magazine that is old enough—say, a *New Yorker* from 1944 with the models looking healthy and almost buxom in their padded jackets—or a dress that is far enough gone not to give the impression that perhaps you had not noticed fashions had changed, can become campy and delightful. But an out-of-date woman is only embarrassing.

The mass media tell us all day and all evening long that we are inadequate, mindless, ugly, disgusting in ourselves. We must try to resemble perfect plastic objects, so that no one will notice what we really are. In ourselves we smell bad, shed dandruff, our breath has an odor, our hair stands up or falls out, we sag or stick out where we shouldn't. We can only fool people into liking us by using magic products that make us products, too.

Women, especially, are commodities. There is always a perfect plastic woman. Girls are always curling their hair or ironing it, binding their breasts or padding them. Think of the girls with straight hips and long legs skulking through the 1890s with its women defined as having breasts the size of pillows and hips like divans. Think of the Rubens woman today forever starving and dieting and crawling into rubber compression chambers that mark her flesh with livid lines and squeeze her organs into knots.

If a girl were to walk into a party in the clothes of just five or six years past, in the make-up and hairstyle of just that slight gap of time, no one would want to talk to her, no man would want to dance with her. Yet what has all that to do with even a man and a woman in bed? This is not only the middle class I am talking about. I have seen hippies react the same way to somebody wearing old straight clothes.

It is a joke, but a morbid one. My daughter has a girlfriend who always laughs with her hand up to her mouth because she is persuaded her teeth are yellow, and that yellow teeth are hideous. She seems somber and never will she enjoy a natural belly laugh. Most young girls walk around with the conviction that some small part of their anatomy (nose, breasts, knees, chin) is so large or so small or so misshapen that their whole body appears to be built around that part, and all of their activities must camouflage it.

My daughter is a senior in college. She already talks about her "youth" with a sad nostalgia. She is worried because she is not married. That she has not met anyone that she wants to live that close to, does not seem to figure in her anxiety. Everything confirms in her a sense of time passing, that she will be left behind, unsold on the shelf. She already peers into the mirror for wrinkles and buys creams and jellies to rub into her skin. Her fear angers me but leaves me helpless. She is alienated from her body because her breasts are big and do not stand out like the breasts of store mannequins. She looks twenty-one. I look forty-three.

I want to beg her not to begin worrying, not to let in the dreadful daily gnawing already. Everyone born grows up, grows older and ages every day until he dies. But every day in seventy thousand ways this society tells a woman that it is her sin and her guilt that she has a real living body. How can a woman respect herself when every day she stands before her mirror and accuses her face of betraying her, because every day she is, indeed, a day older.

Everything she reads, every comic strip, every song, every cartoon, every advertisement, every book and movie tells her that a woman over thirty is ugly and disgusting. She is a bag. She is to be escaped from. She is no longer an object of prestige consumption. For her to have real living sexual desires is obscene. Her touch is thought to contaminate. No man "seduces" a woman older than him: there is no conquest. It is understood she would be "glad for a touch of it." Since she would be glad, there can be no pleasure in the act. Either this society is mad or I am mad. It is considered incredible that a woman might have had experiences that are valuable or interesting and that have enriched her as a person. No, men may mature, but women just obsolesce.

All right, says the woman, don't punish me! I won't do wrong! I won't get older! Now, if a woman has at least an upper-middle-class income, no strong commitments such as a real career or a real interest in religion or art or politics; if she has a small family and hired help; if she has certain minimal genetic luck; if she has the ability to be infinitely fascinated by her own features and body, she may continue to present a youthful image. She can prolong her career as sexual object, lying about her age, rewriting her past to keep the chronology update, and devoting herself to the cultivation of her image. Society will reward her greatly. Women in the entertainment industry are allowed to remain sexual objects (objects that are prestigeful to use or own—like Cadillacs) for much of their lives.

To be told when you have half your years still to wade through and when you don't feel inside much different than you did at twenty (you are still you!—you know that!), to be told then that you are cut off from expressing yourself sexually and often even in friendship, drives many women crazy—even literally so.

Don't tell me that it is human nature for women to cease to be attractive early. In primitive society a woman who is still useful—in that by all means far more humane definition than ours—will find a mate, whom she may share as she shares the work with his other wives. Black women are more oppressed on the job and in almost every other way in this society than white women, but at least in the ghetto men go on assuming a woman is sexual as long as she thinks so too.

Earlier, mythology in which "the widow" is a big sex figure, French novels in which the first mistress is always an older woman, the Wife of Bath, all reinforce my sense that there is nothing natural about women's obsolescence.

I was divorced five years ago. Don't tell me I should have "held on to my husband." We let go with great relief. Recently he has married a woman in her late twenties. It is not surprising he should marry someone younger: most people in this society are younger than my ex-husband. In my job, most of the people I meet are younger than I am, and the same is true of people who share my interests, from skiing to resistance to the war against Vietnam.

When my daughter was little I stayed home, but luckily for me I returned to work when she entered school. I say luckily, because while I believe my ex-husband has an obligation to help our daughter, I would never accept alimony. I can get quite cold and frightened imagining what would have happened if I had stayed home until my divorce, and then, at thirty-eight, tried to find work. I used to eat sometimes at a lunchroom where the rushed and overworked waitress was in her late forties. She had to cover the whole room, and I used to leave her larger tips than I would give someone else because to watch her made me conscious of women's economic vulnerability. She was gone one day and I asked the manager at the cash register about her. "Oh, the customers didn't like her. Men come in here, they want to see a pretty face."

I have insisted on using a pseudonym in writing this article, because the cost of insisting I am not a cipher would be fatal. If I lost my job, I would have an incredible time finding another. I know I will never "get ahead." Women don't

move up through the shelves of a business automatically or by keeping their mouths shut. I could be mocked into an agony of shame for writing this—but beyond that, I could so easily be let go.

I am gregarious, interested in others, and I think, intelligent. All I ask is to get to know people and to have them interested in knowing me. I doubt whether I would marry again and live that close to another individual. But I remain invisible. I think stripped down I look more attractive on some abstract scale (a bisexual Martian judging) than my ex-husband, but I am sexually and socially obsolete, and he is not. Like most healthy women my face has aged more rapidly than my body, and I look better with my clothes off. When I was young, my anxiety about myself and what was to become of me colored all my relationships with men, and I was about as sensual as a clotheshanger. I have a capacity now for taking people as they are, which I lacked at twenty; I reach orgasm in half the time and I know how to please. Yet I do not even dare show a man that I find him attractive. If I do so, he may react as if I had insulted him: with shock, with disgust. I am not even allowed to be affectionate. I am supposed to fulfill my small functions and vanish.

Often when men are attracted to me, they feel ashamed and conceal it. They act as if it were ridiculous. If they do become involved, they are still ashamed and may refuse to appear publicly with me. Their fear of mockery is enormous. There is no prestige attached to having sex with me.

Since we are all far more various sexually than we are supposed to be, often, in fact, younger men become aware of me sexually. Their response is similar to what it is when they find themselves feeling attracted to a homosexual: they turn those feelings into hostility and put me down.

Listen to me! Think what it is like to have most of your life ahead and be told you are obsolete! Think what it is like to feel attraction, desire, affection toward others, to want to tell them about yourself, to feel that assumption on which self-respect is based, that you are worth something, and that if you like someone, surely he will be pleased to know that. To be, in other words, still a living woman, and to be told every day that you are not a woman but a tired object that should disappear. That you are not a person but a joke. Well, I am a bitter joke. I am bitter and frustrated and wasted, but don't you pretend for a minute as you look at me, forty-three, fat, and looking exactly my age, that I am not as alive as you are and that I do not suffer from the category into which you are forcing me.

Further Questions

1. Is growing older something that someone should be ashamed of, so that the symptoms should be hidden as much as possible? If there is shame about aging, what is its source? What, if anything, can be done about it?

2. Does society punish people, and women in particular, for getting older? If so, what forms does such punishment take? Is there anything we can do about it?

3. Is it worthwhile hanging onto a marriage that has become empty of content in order not to be alone in one's old age? If your answer depends on the circumstances, specify the circumstances under which it is or is not worthwhile. Is the answer the same for both genders?

XII.4   From Maturity to Old Age

SIMONE DE BEAUVOIR

Simone de Beauvoir describes the plight of the aging woman who has completed what tradition has expected of her. She married and raised children who are now able to do without her. Now, it seems, with half of her adult life before her, she has nothing left to do.

Other selections from de Beauvoir's *The Second Sex* appear in parts I, IV, and V.

Reading Questions

1. To what extent is a woman's social value dependent on her fertility and the erotic attractiveness only the relatively young possess? To what extent is this true of men as well?

2. Is growing old a horrible and depressing idea for most people? If so, why? Is there anything about growing old that we can look forward to?

3. As a woman, if you anticipate that you will have to spend part of the end of your life without a man, do you wonder what will become of you? Would you be less worried about being alone if you were a man? Do you think you will be able to look to other women for companionship?

THE INDIVIDUAL LIFE HISTORY of woman—because she is still bound up in her female functions—depends in much greater degree than that of man upon her physiological destiny; and the curve of this destiny is much more uneven, more discontinuous, than the masculine curve. Each period in the life of woman is uniform and monotonous; but the transitions from one stage to another are dangerously abrupt; they are manifested in crises—puberty, sexual initiation, the menopause—which are much more decisive than in the male. Whereas man grows old gradually, woman is suddenly deprived of her femininity; she is still relatively young when she loses the erotic attractiveness and the fertility which, in the view of society and in her own, provide the justification of her existence and her opportunity for happiness. With no future, she still has about one half of her adult life to live.

"The dangerous age" is marked by certain organic disturbances, but what lends them importance is their symbolic significance. The crisis of the "change of life" is felt much less keenly by women who have not staked everything on their femininity; those who engage in heavy work—in the household or outside—greet the disappearance of the monthly burden with relief; the peasant woman, the workman's wife, constantly under the threat of new pregnancies, are happy when, at long last, they no longer run this risk. At this juncture, as at many others, woman's discomforts come less from her body than from the anxious concerns she feels regarding it. The moral drama commonly begins before the physiological phenomena have appeared, and it comes to an end only after they have long since been done away with.

Long before the eventual mutilation, woman is haunted by the horror of growing old. The mature man is involved in enterprises more important than those of love; his erotic ardor is less keen than in the days of his youth; and since in him the passive qualities of an object are not called for, the changes in his face and body do not destroy his attractiveness. In woman, on the contrary, it is usually toward thirty-five, when all

inhibitions have been finally overcome, that full erotic development is attained. Then it is that her sexual desires are strongest and she most keenly wishes to have them satisfied; she has gambled much more heavily than man on the sexual values she possesses; to hold her husband and to assure herself of his protection, and to keep most of her jobs, it is necessary for her to be attractive, to please; she is allowed no hold on the world save through the mediation of some man. What is to become of her when she no longer has any hold on him? This is what she anxiously asks herself while she helplessly looks on at the degeneration of this fleshly object which she identifies with herself. She puts up a battle. But hair-dye, skin treatments, plastic surgery, will never do more than prolong her dying youth. Perhaps she can at least deceive her mirror. But when the first hints come of that fated and irreversible process which is to destroy the whole edifice built up during puberty, she feels the fatal touch of death itself.

One might think that the woman most ardently enraptured with her youth and beauty would be the one to be most disturbed; but not at all: the narcissist is too concerned with her person not to have foreseen its inevitable decline and made her preparations for retreat. She will suffer, to be sure, from her mutilation, but at least she will not be taken by surprise, and she will become adapted soon enough. The woman who has been forgetful of self, devoted, self-sacrificing, will be much more upset by the sudden revelation: "I had only one life to live; think what my lot has been, and look at me now!" To the astonishment of everyone, a radical change occurs in her: What has happened is that, dislodged from her sheltering occupations, her plans disrupted, she finds herself suddenly, without recourse, put face-to-face with herself. Beyond that milestone against which she has unexpectedly stumbled, it seems to her that there will be nothing more for her to do than merely survive her better days; her body will promise nothing; the dreams, the longings she has not made good, will remain forever unfulfilled. In this perspective she reviews the past; the moment has come to draw a line across the page, to make up her accounts; she balances her books. And she is appalled at the narrow limitations life has imposed upon her. . . .

. . .Sometimes she gives herself up to a dreamy and passive gloominess. But more often she suddenly undertakes to save her lost existence. She makes a show of this personality which she has just discovered in contrasting it with the meanness of her fate; she proclaims its merits, she imperiously demands that justice be done it. Matured by experience, she feels that at last she is capable of making her mark; she would like to get into action again. And first of all, she tries with pathetic urgency to turn back the flight of time. A woman of maternal type will assert that she can still have a child: she tries passionately to create life once again. A sensual woman will endeavor to ensnare one more lover. The coquette is more than ever anxious to please. One and all, they declare that they never felt so young. They want to persuade others that the passage of time has never really touched them; they begin to "dress young," they assume childish airs. The aging woman well knows that if she ceases to be an erotic object, it is not only because her flesh no longer has fresh bounties for men; it is also because her past, her experience, make her, willy-nilly, a person; she has struggled, loved, willed, suffered, enjoyed, on her own account. This independence is intimidating; she tries to disown it; she exaggerates her femininity, she adorns herself, she uses perfume, she makes herself all charm, all grace, pure immanence. She babbles to men in a childish voice and with naïve glances of admiration, and she chatters on about when she was a little girl; she chirps instead of talking, she claps her hands, she bursts out laughing. And she enacts this comedy with a certain sincerity. For her new interests, her desire to get out of the old routine and begin anew, make her feel that she is starting life again.

But in fact there is no question of a real start; she sees in the world no objectives toward which she might reach out in a free and effective manner. Her activity takes an eccentric, incoherent,

and fruitless form, because she can compensate only in a symbolic way for the mistakes and failures of the past. For one thing, the woman of the age we are considering will try to realize all her wishes of childhood and adolescence before it is too late: she may go back to her piano, take up sculpture, writing, travel, she may learn skiing or study foreign languages. She now welcomes with open arms—still before it is too late—everything she has previously denied herself. . . .

But the world has not been changed; the peaks remain inaccessible; the messages received—however brilliantly manifest—are hard to decipher; the inner illuminations fade; before the glass stands a woman who in spite of everything has grown one day older since yesterday. The moments of exaltation are succeeded by sad hours of depression. The organism manifests this rhythm because the decline of the female sex hormones is compensated for by an overactivity of the pituitary gland; but above all it is the psychological state that governs this alternation of mood. For the woman's restlessness, her illusions, her fervor, are only a defense reaction against the overruling fatality of what has been. Once more anguish is at the throat of the woman whose life is already done before death has taken her. . . .

It is in the autumn and winter of life that woman is freed from her chains; she takes advantage of her age to escape the burdens that weigh on her; she knows her husband too well to let him intimidate her any longer, she eludes his embraces, at his side she organizes a life of her own—in friendship, indifference, or hostility. If his decline is faster than hers, she assumes control of the couple's affairs. She can also permit herself defiance of fashion and of "what people will say"; she is freed from social obligations, dieting, and the care of her beauty. As for her children, they are old enough to get along without her, they are getting married, they are leaving home. Rid of her duties, she finds freedom at last. Unfortunately, in every woman's story recurs the fact we have verified throughout the history of woman: she finds this freedom at the very time when she can make no use of it. This recurrence is in no wise due to chance: Patriarchal society gave all the feminine functions the aspect of a service, and woman escapes slavery only at times when she loses all effectiveness. Toward fifty she is in full possession of her powers; she feels she is rich in experience; that is the age at which men attain the highest positions, the most important posts; as for her, she is put into retirement. She has been taught only to devote herself to someone, and nobody wants her devotion any more. Useless, unjustified, she looks forward to the long, unpromising years she has yet to live, and she mutters: "No one needs me!" .. . .

The actress, the dancer, the singer become teachers: they mold pupils; the intellectual—like Mme de Charrière in her Colombier retreat—indoctrinates disciples; the devotee gathers spiritual daughters about her; the woman of gallantry becomes a madam. If they bring an ardent zeal to their proselyting, it is never through pure interest in the field of effort; what they are passionately seeking is reincarnation in their protégées. Their tyrannical generosity gives rise to almost the same conflicts as those between mother and daughters united by ties of blood. It is also possible to adopt grandchildren; and grandaunts and godmothers readily play a role like that of the grandmother. But in any case it is very rare for a woman to find in her posterity—natural or adopted—a justification for her declining years: she fails to make the career of a single one of these young existences truly hers. Either she persists in the effort to take it over and is consumed in struggles and scenes that leave her disappointed and exhausted; or she resigns herself to no more than a modest participation, as usually happens. The older mother and the grandmother repress their ideas of domination, they conceal their resentments; they content themselves with whatever their children finally give them. But in that case they get little help from them. They are left to face the desert of the future without occupation, a prey to loneliness, regret, and boredom.

Here we come upon the sorry tragedy of the aged woman: She realizes she is useless; all her life long the middle-class woman has often had to solve the ridiculous problem of how to kill time. But when the children are grown, the husband a made man or at least settled down, the time must still be killed somehow. Fancywork was invented to mask their horrible idleness; hands embroider, they knit, they are in motion. This is no real work, for the object produced is not the end in view; its importance is trifling, and to know what to do with it is often a problem— one can get rid of it, perhaps, by giving it to a friend or to a charitable organization, or by cluttering the mantelpiece or center table. This is no longer a game that in its uselessness expresses the pure joy of living; and it is hardly an escape, since the mind remains vacant. It is the "absurd amusement" described by Pascal; with the needle or the crochet-hook, woman sadly weaves the very nothingness of her days. Water-colors, music, reading serve in much the same way; the unoccupied woman, in applying herself to such matters, is not trying to extend her grasp on the world, but only to relieve her boredom. An activity that does not open the future falls back into vain immanence; the idle woman opens a book and throws it aside, opens the piano only to close it, resumes her embroidering, yawns, and finally takes up the telephone. . . .

But it does happen that, in spite of everything, certain of the women we are considering are entirely committed to some enterprise and become truly effective; these women are no longer seeking merely to occupy their time, they have goals in view; producers in their own right, they are outside the parasitic category we are considering here. But this about-face is rare. The majority of these women, in their private or public activities, do not have in mind a result to be achieved, but merely some way of occupying themselves—and no occupant is worth while when it is only a means of killing time. Many of them are adversely affected by this; having behind them a life already finished, they are confused in much the same way as adolescents before whom life is not yet open; they feel no pull, around them in both cases is the wasteland; contemplating any action, they mutter: "What's the use?" But the adolescent male is drawn willy-nilly into a masculine way of life that discloses responsibilities, aims, values; he is thrown out into the world, he makes decisions, he commits himself to some enterprise. If it is suggested to the older woman that she should start out toward a new future, she will sadly reply that it is too late. Not that henceforth her time is limited, for a woman goes into retirement very early; but she lacks the spirit, the confidence, the hope, the anger, that would enable her to look round and find new goals.[1] She takes refuge in the routine that has always been her lot; repetition becomes her pattern. . . .

Old women take pride in their independence; they begin at last to view the world through their own eyes; they note that they have been duped and deceived all their lives; sane and mistrustful, they often develop a pungent cynicism. In particular, the woman who "has lived" knows men as no man does, for she has seen in man to the image on public view but the contingent individual, the creature of circumstance, that each man in the absence of her peers shows himself to be. She knows women also, for they show themselves without reserve only to other women: She has been behind the scenes. But if her experience enables her to unmask deceits and lies, it is not sufficient to show her the truth. Amused or bitter, the wisdom of the old woman still remains wholly negative: it is in the nature of opposition, indictment, denial; it is sterile. In her thinking as in her acts, the highest form of liberty available to the woman parasite is stoical defiance or skeptical irony. At no time of life does she succeed in being at once effective and independent.

NOTE

1. Few indeed are those, like Grandma Moses, the celebrated American painter, who take to new and fruitful work in their old age.—TR.

Further Questions

1. Do you look forward to an age when you will be retired from your tasks in life (children, job, and so forth)? At the same time do you fear that there will be nothing much to do (within your means) after all this is over? Does your answer to this question depend on your gender?

2. Will it be good or bad for you to reach a time in life when you can say "No one needs me!"? Would it be better or worse if you were of the other gender?

3. Do you believe that, at the end of life, the truth will be revealed, or that you will have learned falsehoods? Exactly what truth are you expecting to be revealed? What kinds of falsehoods do you expect to have learned?

Look Me in the Eye   XII.5

BARBARA MACDONALD

Barbara Macdonald and her partner, Cynthia Rich, went to a march to Take Back the Night. The monitor, a younger woman, took Barbara aside to ask her if she could keep up, but she could not look Barbara in the eye. After examining her own shame and anger, Barbara reflects on the history that led to this encounter.

Macdonald (b. 1913) is a lesbian feminist activist, writer, and lecturer who now lives in San Diego, CA. *Look Me in the Eye* has been widely influential in feminist theory on aging.

Reading Questions

1. Does the role of the mother in today's society in any way influence the way younger people view older women? Explain your answer with some examples.
2. Do some people find it difficult to look certain sorts of people in the eye (for example, old people, battered women, disabled people)? If so, what do you think the source of the difficulty is, and what do you propose as a solution?
3. Give some examples in which people, as individuals, personally neglect an older person. What do you think are the reasons for this type of attitude?

. . . WHERE ARE THE Susan B. Anthonys, the Carrie Nations, the Pankhursts today? These postmenopausal women were marching all over the place a hundred years ago, and no one was asking them if they could keep up. It was then I realized that this is probably the first time in history that the mass of rebelling angry women are so young. In the first wave in this country and in England, angry women in mid-life and older were marching and visible. In the photographs in Emmeline Pankhurst's *My Own Story,* I see older women marching with young women, and older women were smashing windows and setting fires all over London, and women in mid-life and older were going to prison and going on hunger strikes and being force fed. . . .

It is probably evidence of our growth and increasing strength that for the first time younger women make up the mass of the second wave. Made possible for the first time because young women are more knowledgeable than they were a hundred years ago, better read, and with more literature to read than ever before. And freer, because the younger woman of today is not caught in enforced heterosexual coupling until much later in her life and may, in fact, not choose heterosexuality. A hundred years ago, much of the radical feminist political action was probably not visible to most young women, who were in domestic servitude or were already burdened with unwanted pregnancies and small children, unable to read and with no way out. This increased visibility of young women is certainly due, in part, to the efforts of the older women of the first wave.

But the primary reason that the second wave is made up of young women is that the second wave rose out of a different time in patriarchal history—it rose out of a time of a patriarchally supported white middle class youth culture. This important difference in the two waves is not one that I can dismiss lightly with the popular observation that emphasis on youth neglects an older population. That is to trivialize what has been taking place since the first wave and the development of the youth culture. It does not make clear to me what happened to me in the Boston march. It does not explain to me why I do not have eye to eye contact with younger women as I enter my mid sixties, and it does not explain to me what happened to the older feminist activists who were such an important part of our earlier history.

In the first wave, when the angry older women were marching, most women were slaves to their husbands; as were his children whom he could put to work in factories, mines, or into domestic servitude as soon as they were strong enough. The mother had no real power over her life and no real power over the lives of her children. But it was profitable for the father to give the mother seeming authority over the children. In his absence, she represented his authority and kept the children in subjection. Frequently she was beaten by her husband for her children's insubordination, and she in turn beat the children to keep them in line.

But with the advent of child labor laws and children's rights, the father lost power over his children. Out from under the father's tyranny, the children were a burden and an expense instead of a source of income, and they became solely the woman's problem. The mother still had the care of the children, but now she had to try to control them without the father's power. Once the father had said to the mother, "I want them fed; feed them. I want them clothed for the workplace; clothe them. I want them God-fearing and industrious; teach them. I want them obedient; beat them." But now it was not in the father's interest to control the children, and he did not transfer his power to the mother. Instead, she was left powerless to protect herself from their battering demands. The children, out from under the tyranny of the father's rule, were free in their own way to tyrannize the powerless mother. Now it was the children who borrowed power from the father, who were saying to her, "Feed me, clothe me. Buy me everything. The fathers say you must." And indeed the fathers are saying clearly, "The children must have everything. If you are a good mother, your children's laundry will be Downy soft and perfumed. You will tempt your children's appetites and feel pride to hear them demand, 'More sausages, Mom.' You will send them out in white clothes to play in the mud to prove that you know how to wash their clothes cleaner than the woman next door. You will make sure the environment your children live in is scrubbed, polished, sanitized, and odorless. You will wipe their noses and bottoms with the softest tissue in the world, all the time rubbing your hands in lotion so your callouses and red cracks won't feel rough on your children's soft skin."

It seems to me that never in such a few years has the patriarchy been able to develop a new elite leisure class of consumers and a slave class to serve them—an elite class that stays out of the job market and does not threaten the father's job, but consumes endlessly to ensure his job.

A hundred years ago, the mother's value to the Fathers was that she raised God-fearing industrious children who could bring income into the family until they left home. Now the mother's value to the Fathers is that she raises children to expect the best, to be good consumers, to remain as children as long as possible and out of the job market and she hopes that society will value her for how well she serves them. The elitism of the children is still exploitation of the children. Now, instead of the exploitation by the single father, it is the exploitation by the collective Fathers. But the woman is still slave, and now she has two masters to serve.

Today, the evidence is all around us that youth is bonded with the patriarchy in the enslavement of the older woman. There would, in fact, be no youth culture without the powerless older woman. There can be no leisure elite consuming class unless it is off the back of someone. The older woman is who the younger women are better than—who they are more powerful than and who is compelled to serve them. This is not true of men; older men still have power, power to be president, power to be Walter Cronkhite, and power to marry younger women. Men are not the servants of youth; older women are.

The lines between the powerful and the powerless have always had to be very clearly drawn, and nowhere is this more evident than in the clothes of men, the young, and women. The clothes of the young woman are designed to, at least, give the illusion of power and freedom, and the clothes of the older woman are designed to make her look sexless, dowdy, and separated from the rest of society. Little boys and young men of high occasions dress fashionably like older men, in suit and vest, but no young woman dresses fashionably by imitating the dress of older women.

It becomes more clear that the present attitude of women in their twenties and thirties has been shaped since childhood by patriarchy to view the older woman as powerless, less important than the fathers and the children, and there to serve them both; and like all who serve, the older woman soon becomes invisible. . . .

I watched the 80 "Women to Watch in the '80s" go by in *Ms.* magazine last month, and I learned that there are only six women in their fifties worth watching and only one woman in her sixties worth watching. That's invisibility.

I find the whole line-up of women to watch in the 1980s very patriarchal and I would prefer not to see it at all. But worse, *Ms.* magazine asked older women to make the selection, a selection that excluded them. That's one way to get permission to oppress—ask the older woman, not to be co-equal, but to step aside for the younger woman. Sheila Tobias stepped aside by saying, "established women have the responsibility to boost others. One reason the first wave of feminism died out is that it failed to create new leaders."

To me something in her statement smacks of maternal self-sacrifice and invisibility: The young women asked Tobias to make herself invisible and she made herself invisible. Nor do I think that the first wave of feminism died because the women failed to create new leadership. I think it died because the women decided to put their own needs aside to help the good old boys win a war; and when they got ready to take up the struggle again, they discovered they were slave to two masters.

Given the nature of the question put to Tobias, it is not surprising that she responded in patriarchal language: the word *boost* suggests help on "the way up," someone on the bottom boosting another to a higher level. Such an image conjures up the possibility that the one being boosted may well have her foot on the booster. Such a word seems a long way from the beginnings of this second wave that consciously avoided hierarchical structure.

I hurt that the committee who selected the eighty women to watch tells me that I am invisible, that no sixty-five-year-old woman is still in process and worth watching; but they give no better message to the women who are pictured there in their forties, as it must be plain to them that they will be invisible in ten years, in their fifties and sixties.

Several months have gone by since Cynthia and I went to the Boston march, and I only begin to see how I came to be there at sixty-five in this particular time in our history and how the monitor came to be there. I only begin to see who we both are and how men are still defining our feelings about ourselves and each other.

—1979

Further Questions

1. Macdonald claims "youth is bonded with patriarchy in the enslavement of the older woman." What does this mean? If it is true, what are some examples of it in television ads, wording in media reports, and words and actions in daily life?

2. Is there an attitude that an older woman must serve others, or step aside for them, that is founded in expectations of this sort of deference from mothers? If so, is it paradoxical that a woman's status is lessened when she is perceived as a mother?

3. Are older persons avoided because aging is thought to be contagious? If so, is the avoidance of older women explained by the fact that their aging is perceived as more contagious than men's aging?

XII.6   On Gray Hair and Oppressed Brains

ANN E. GERIKE

Ann E. Gerike notes that coloring gray hair constitutes an attempt of an aging person to "pass" as a younger person with greater power, privilege, and prestige. Women must contend with the fact that aging is more negative for them than for men, and that gray hair is a significant feature in an aging appearance.

Gerike is a licensed consulting Psychologist in the state of Minnesota.

Reading Questions

1. Is a woman past menopause considered useless and asexual because she cannot bear children? Do older women become more assertive in a way that men perceive to be dangerous?

2. Do women try to look young to protect a husband or lover from the emotional reality of his own aging?

3. Can visibly gray hair endanger a woman's job or make it difficult for her to obtain a job? Are old women ignored or assumed to be unintelligent, uneducated, and incompetent?

GRAY HAIR IS UNIVERSALLY VIEWED as an indication of advancing age, though the age at which hair begins to gray varies widely among individuals. Changes in hair color begin sooner than most people realize. A study of Australian blood donors in 1965, for example, revealed that, by the time they were twenty-five, 22 to 29 percent of the men in the group and 23 to 35 percent of the women had some obvious graying (Parachini, 1987). The age at which people begin to gray seems to be genetically determined, as are the graying patterns.

Much of the gray effect is produced by the mixture of light and dark hairs, though as dark hair loses its color it is genuinely gray for a time. Blond hair, of course, "grays" much less

From Woman, Aging, and Ageism, Evelyn R. Rosenthal, ed. Copyright © 1990, The Haworth Press, Binghamton, NY, pp. 35–46. Reprinted by permission of the publisher.

noticeably than darker hair. The proportion of white to dark hairs has to be well over 50 percent before it begins to show decisively.

Little research has been done on the graying of hair, so most of what is known about it is assumption and guesswork. But the basic process appears to be the following:

> Each of the 100,000 hairs on the head is controlled by a hair bulb below the follicle at the deepest part of the root system. It is through the hair bulb that a variety of complex substances are channeled, creating each hair, mainly composed of a biochemical substance called keratin.
>
> In the hair roots and in the epidermis, millions of protein-producing pigment cells, called melanocytes, produce chemicals that determine the coloring of hair and skin. . . . The melanocytes, in turn, are responsible for chemistry that colors the hair that takes shape in the follicle and grows long enough, eventually, to be seen. . . .
>
> Melanin, the pigmentation chemical, has two components. The two basic colors predispose a hair to be dark or light or a shade between, depending on the proportion of each pigment that is genetically introduced into the hair-making process. Coloration is influenced by racial and ethnic factors, but virtually no research has been done on the existence of such influences in graying, . . .
>
> The color chemistry changes with age so that even a person who has no gray may find his or her natural hair coloring changing with advancing age. Many people experience a darkening in their coloring—directly attributable to the maturing function of the melanocytes and the varying production of melanin.
>
> With time . . . the melanocytes weaken and their pigment-producing chemistry begins to shut down. It is a gradual process and, for the period that the melanocyte is still functioning at reduced capacity, the bulb may produce a hair that is gray, or incompletely colored. In time, though, the melanocyte stops working and the hair bulb produces white hair. The process can also be influenced by a variety of diseases that prematurely—and sometimes reversibly—reduce enzyme chemistry and interfere with

pigment cells. In the vast majority of cases, age and the natural evolution melanocytes—culminating in their cessation of function—cause graying. (Parachini, 1987, p. 2C)

However interesting that explanation may be as a description of biological process, the graying of hair is interesting primarily for sociological, not biological reasons. For, of course, millions of women, and increasing numbers of men, color their hair because of the negative myths and stereotypes about aging which form the basis of ageism in our society. These negative attitudes are implicit in our language: "old" is assumed to connote incompetence, misery, lethargy, unattractiveness, asexuality, and poor health, while "young" is used to imply competence, happiness, vitality, attractiveness, sexuality, and good health. People are told they're "as young" (or "only as old") as they feel, and they are admonished to "keep themselves young." When they are ill, they are said to have aged; when they recover, they're told they look younger.

The coloring of gray hair disguises the physical feature associated with aging that is most obvious and most easily changed. Such hair dyeing, in our youth-oriented culture, represents the attempt of aging people to "pass" as members of a group with greater power, privilege, and prestige than the group to which they in truth belong. In that, it is similar to the widespread use of skin lighteners by many blacks in the time preceding the Civil Rights movement.

In a patriarchal society, the power and privilege of women reside in their utility to men. They must be able and willing to bear children, and be willing to remain in a subservient position. In such a society, women beyond the menopause are useless; they obviously cannot bear children. They may also be dangerous: with the growing assertiveness that often comes to women as they age, many are unwilling to remain subservient (Guttman, 1980; Melamed, 1983; Rubin, 1981). If a woman's choices are to be either useless or dangerous as she ages, it is perhaps no wonder many women prefer to use hair color as a means of concealing—or at least underplaying—their age.

Since traditional male socialization does not encourage men to acknowledge their "weaker" feelings, women have often taken on the role of caring for men's emotional as well as their physical needs. A 54-year-old man interviewed by Barbara Gordon for her book *Jennifer Fever* says: "Men are emotionally underdeveloped, and they want women to handle the emotional side of life for them" (Gordon, 1988, p. 100). In discussing feelings of vulnerability, Jean Baker Miller argues that "women provide all sorts of personal and social supports to help keep men going and to keep them and the total society from admitting that better arrangements are needed" (Miller, 1976, p. 32).

The fact that women expend far more time, money, and effort in attempts to retain a youthful appearance than do men may well represent an aspect of such emotional caretaking. By providing men their own age (usually their husbands, but sometimes their lovers) with a false-faced mirror of youth, they may be attempting to protect such men from the emotional reality of aging and eventual death. In the film *Moonstruck,* a white-haired Olympia Dukakis asks, "Why do men chase women?" and answers herself: "Because they fear death." I once heard a man say to his gray-haired wife, without rancor: "I only feel old when I look at you."

At the same time, of course, the woman may be protecting herself, or at least attempting to do so. A gray-haired or white-haired woman is often seen as motherly, and sexual attraction to the mother is taboo. In *About Men,* Phyllis Chesler writes:

> When a wife grows "old"—*as old as his mother once was*—a man must renounce his interest in Her once again. Only the blood of strange women, the blood of ever-younger women, can be pursued without incestuous guilt. (Chesler, 1978, p. 80)

If a woman believes that maintaining a youthful appearance in itself will enable her to attract or "keep" a man, however, she may well be disappointed. In Gordon's reports on a series of interviews with older men who are in relationships with younger women, she extracts their reasons for preferring such women: adoration, which they are unlikely to receive from an age peer; "liberation backlash"; the "scarring factor" of unhappy long-term marriages to women their own age; and "innocence." A 60-year-old lawyer says:

> I want someone young to love me. I want someone young and fresh and new to be attracted to me. I don't want a forty-five-year-old woman who looks great for her age, young for her age. No matter how great she looks, she's still forty-five. (Gordon, 1988, p. 100)

Fortunately, not all older men are so emotionally retarded. It will be interesting to see what kinds of attitudes today's young men, having grown up in a world where gender arrangements are changing, will have toward older women when they themselves grow old.

The assumption that women are no longer sexual beings when they have passed their childbearing years is clearly an aspect of patriarchy. The desexualizing effect of gray hair is well illustrated by the experience of a friend of mine who had grayed in her late teens and had never colored her hair. When she was in her late thirties she dyed her hair black, on a dare. The next day, when she went to the gym she had been attending for some time, she suddenly materialized for men who had not previously noticed her.

Such magical invisibility is not only sexual; it is pervasive, similar to that noted long ago for blacks by Ralph Ellison in *Invisible Man* (1952) and James Baldwin in *Nobody Knows My Name* (1961). The title of Barbara Macdonald's powerful treatise on ageism, *Look Me in the Eye* (1983), addresses the fact that, in most social circumstances, women as well as men seldom make eye contact with the old, whom they simply do not see. If old women are not ignored, they are often subjected to a condescending head-patting kindliness which suggests that its recipient is unintelligent, uneducated, and incompetent. That women should want to avoid such treatment as far as possible is understandable, and they may be able to avoid it for a time by coloring their gray hair.

Sexism in combination with ageism also causes women problems in the job market as they age. Many women dye their hair because they fear, perhaps with good reason, that they might lose their jobs, or find it difficult to obtain jobs, if their gray hair were visible. In many professional circles, gray hair on women is considered unprofessional. Office workers in particular are often chosen for youthful physical appearance. A story frequently heard from highly competent female clerical workers in their forties and fifties is of waiting for a job interview in competition with young inexperienced women, and seeing one of those women selected for the job (Leonard, 1982).

Interestingly, however, gray hair can be an advantage for a woman who is already in a position of authority. For example, a friend of mine who was a medical resident found her students much easier to manage when she let her naturally gray hair appear. I myself suspect that my almost-white hair gives me "clout," even though I entered my profession, clinical psychology, late in life. (One might assume that having gray or white hair would be an advantage for those working with an older population, as I do; but the majority of older women I know who work with the elderly dye their hair—perhaps out of fear of being identified with their clients?)

In the personal sphere, if not in that of employment, lesbians would seem to have less incentive than their straight sisters to dye their gray hair; lesbian women are less likely to be obsessed with youth and appearance than are heterosexual women (Doress & Siegal, 1987). But prejudices against *old* women are intact among most lesbians, as indicated in Macdonald's *Look Me in the Eye* (1983) and Baba Copper's *Over the Hill: Reflections on Ageism Between Women* (1988). Copper writes:

Lesbian youth worship differs little from heterosexual youth worship. The deprivation of sexual recognition between women which takes place after middle age (or the point when a woman no longer passes for young) includes withdrawal of the emotional work which women do to keep the flow of social interactions going: compliments, questions, teasing, touching, bantering, remembering details, checking back, supporting. (Copper, 1988, pp. 29–30).

Considering the combination of ageism with sexism, it is not surprising that far more women than men color their gray hair—45 percent of women in their forties and fifties (Doress & Siegal, 1987) and 8 percent of men (La Ferla, 1988). In a description of male and female ideals in advertising, the ideal woman's hair is "not gray," while that of the ideal man is "any color, even gray" (Melamed, 1983, p. 121). Hollywood "stars" over the age of fifty are living testimony to the sexist aspect of ageism: almost all of the men that age are gray or white-haired (and/or balding), while almost all of the women are blondes, brunettes, or redheads. Since women begin to gray sooner than men, that is obviously not a natural gender difference. Barbara Stanwyck, now gloriously white-haired, is one of the few film actresses who has never attempted to hide her age, by either word or deed.

Most of the older female actors on television dye their hair, including the woman most often cited as a role model for older women, 63-year-old Angela Lansbury, the star of "Murder She Wrote." Of the four older women on "Golden Girls," the two characters who do not color their hair are Sophia, a rude and inconsiderate woman in her eighties (whose rudeness is presumably funny because she is old), and her daughter Dorothy (Bea Arthur) who is very tall, deep-voiced, and powerful—clearly not the essence of traditional femininity.

The belief that aging is more negative for women than for men has a long history. Lois Banner, in *American Beauty,* her study of attitudes toward American women's physical appearance, quotes a *Harper's Bazaar* article from

1892 which noted that men did not have to look young to be appreciated; they could be considered attractive at any age. For women, "on some level their physical appearance would be judged and their approximation to a youthful standard measured" (Banner, 1983, p. 225).

Despite the advances of feminism, the ageist standards of appearance were seldom challenged before the last few years—probably because the majority of women in the latest wave of the movement could, until relatively recently, have considered themselves young. Now that the Baby Boom generation is entering middle age, however, that situation is beginning to change; the Boston Women's Health Collective, for example, with the publication of the excellent guide, *Ourselves, Growing Older,* has now acknowledged that women beyond menopause have both bodies and selves (Doress & Siegal, 1987).

In general, increasing attention is being paid to the "older [i.e., middle-aged] woman," with innumerable magazine stories and newspaper articles about well-known women (such as Diahann Carroll, Joan Collins, Jane Fonda, Ali McGraw) turning forty or even fifty, proclaiming that they have no problems with growing older. The message they give about age, however, is a mixed one: "It's all right to get older as long as you look as young as possible." (Can one imagine a Civil Rights movement with the slogan "Black is beautiful as long as you look as white as possible"?) That the normal physical signs of age, particularly wrinkles and gray hair, are unattractive is usually assumed without question. The assumption that women "lose their looks" as they age is implicit in the frequent description of a woman as "good-looking for a woman her age."

The film *Moonstruck* also contains a somewhat mixed message about gray hair. When Cher, as a supposedly dowdy woman, goes to her hairdresser to become transformed, the entire salon breathes a sign of relief that they can finally get rid of her "awful gray hair." But the Nicolas Cage character fell in love with her when her hair was still gray.

Another example of this ambivalence about age is the new magazine "for the woman who wasn't born yesterday," *Lear's.* Founded by Frances Lear, the ex-wife of the television producer Norman Lear, and launched in early 1988, it is a glossy magazine for "women over 40"—wealthy women. (As such, of course, it ignores the reality that the weighted mean of pooled median incomes for women age 45 and over is $7,550—Wang, 1988.) Though it does regularly include women's ages, and does indeed show faces with some visible wrinkles, gray hair is not in particular abundance. Frances Lear herself, as photographs indicate, is flamboyantly white-haired. But an examination of the first five issues reveals only one "cover woman" who may possibly have a few gray hairs; four have dark brown hair, and one light brown. Among the hundreds of women in the stories and advertisements, there are photographs of only thirty obviously gray-haired or white-haired women. (This total counts as one a photographic essay of a gray-haired yoga teacher—with a slim, taut, flexible body—in the second issue.) The possibility of progress is suggested by the sixth issue (January/February 1989), which includes four full-page close-up photographs of gray- and white-haired women in their sixties and seventies, with pores, wrinkles, and age lines attractively visible. (Interestingly, the second issue also contains an article about a totally dark-haired 70-year-old Mike Wallace. And three of the issues contain photo essays with full-page photographs of "good men," where wrinkles, gray and white hair, and baldness abound.)

One cannot, of course, blame editorial policy alone for the absence of women's gray hair in *Lear's;* many of the stories are about women who almost certainly color their hair. In that sense the magazine is simply reflecting a reality. Magazine articles which state that "Madison Avenue has given its OK for hair, at least, to look its age" (Salholz, 1985), and newspaper stories with titles such as "Gray definitely OK, more women believe" (Beck, 1988), appear occasionally, but the women who are cited in them as models of acceptable gray hair are most often relatively young women—the 34-year-old televison news reporter Kathleen Sullivan, and the 27-year-old model Marie Seznec, for example. The oldest gray-haired woman mentioned in any of them is 45-year-old Tish Hooker, who models for Germaine Monteil.

But there is no doubt that mainline fashion magazines no longer consign gray hair to total oblivion. As long ago as 1984, in a *Harper's Bazaar* issue headlined "Forty and Fabulous: How to Look Younger Every Day," two expert hair colorists recommended "making the gray work for the woman rather than fighting it." One of them suggested coloring the rest of the hair in imaginative ways and letting "one or two gray hairs show" ("Sensational Hair," 1984, pp. 238–239). They even included, at the suggestion of the magazine, advice for the occasional woman who might not want to cover her gray hair.

Older gray-haired models are not readily accepted for everyday fashion assignments. Kaylan Pickford, the top "mature" model in the country, says there is not enough work of her to earn a living. Despite her slim figure, she says she is most in demand for ads about laxatives, aspirin, denture cream, and arthritis or osteoporosis medications (Lindeman, 1988).

Ultimately, the coloring of gray hair by women is an endorsement of both ageism and sexism. It also serves to perpetuate both those forms of discrimination. The world is full of gray- and white-haired women who are living testimony to the advantages of age for women, but the power of their testimony is greatly muted by their dyed hair. Older women entering the job market would probably find it much easier to be hired if the older women in the work force were more visible.

I am not aware of any overt attempts by feminists to raise consciousness specifically on the issue of gray hair, and I am aware of no published feminist research on the subject. Elissa Melamed, in her book on ageism and its effects, *Mirror, Mirror: The Terror of Not Being Young* (1983), talks at length about cosmetic surgery and skin treatment and their ageist implications but dismisses hair dyeing with one sentence: "Covering gray is so simple and commonplace that there is no longer much emotional charge about it" (p. 134). (It is interesting, however, that in her fantasy about a pilot for a televison series, the 50-year-old heroine's hair is gray.)

Internalized ageism, an acceptance of the status quo, is no doubt one reason little has been written about gray hair; at earlier points in time, a male-dominated world was also considered "simple and commonplace." Another reason may be a reluctance to "blame the victim." Women clearly are the victims of ageism, and older women may be struggling to do their best in a world where they are disproportionately the victims of poverty. While it might theoretically be better for them to challenge ageism, they may be fighting other battles which consume most of their energy.

When most women reach their sixties and seventies (like the women in the sixth *Lear's* issue noted above), they are likely to give up on pretense and become more willing to look like their gray-haired and white-haired selves. (The fact that suicide rates for white women peak between the ages of 45 and 54—Melamed, 1983—and drop steadily thereafter is perhaps significant here.) Several shampoos are marketed especially to enhance gray and white hair. The advent in the White House of a defiantly white-haired First Lady may well increase the social acceptability of "old" hair.

One might postulate that feminist women, being more aware of sexism and the patriarchy, would be less likely than nonfeminist women to color their gray hair. Again, I know of no research on the subject. It does seem to me that I see many more gray-haired women in Minneapolis and St. Paul, a Mecca for feminists, than I did in Houston, where I lived previously. As women increasingly accept the reality that they have value in themselves, beyond their youth and their serviceability to men, they will naturally be less likely to attempt to hide the normal effects of their age. Just as women have produced a less sexist world, so they can challenge ageism to produce a world in which women do not feel compelled to hide their age with hair dyes, face lifts, and other expensive stratagems.

The advantages of leaving gray hair untouched are many. It saves a considerable amount of both time and money. The natural affinity of hair and skin color is preserved. Skin tone also naturally changes with age, and women who color their hair usually have to expend considerable time and effort to make their faces match their hair. Unfortunately, the combination of old face and young hair is often discordant.

Hair may gray in interesting patterns, which are lost when the gray hair is colored. Women who allow their hair its natural changes also often find themselves able to wear colors that did not suit them in their younger-haired days. And they can preserve both their hair and their health: the use of hair dyes can contribute to hair loss, especially when combined with other harsh hair treatments (Winning the Battle, 1984), and petroleum-based dyes, usually in dark shades, cause cancer in laboratory animals and may pose a danger to users (Doress & Siegal, 1987).

The greatest advantage, however, is that a woman who allows her hair to gray naturally is accepting herself for who she is. She is also, in effect, challenging the ageism of a society that tells her she should be ashamed of her age and should make every effort to disguise it. Just as blacks took a physical feature associated with their blackness—naturally kinky hair—and flaunted it in the Afro, challenging the limited white standards of physical attractiveness, so again women can flaunt their graying and white hair, challenging the blinkered standards of an ageist society.

In her fortieth year, talking about her hair (not about its grayness but its Blackness), Alice Walker wrote:

> Eventually, I knew precisely what hair wanted: it wanted to grow, to be itself, to attract lint, if that was its destiny, but to be left alone by anyone, including me, who did not love it as it was. . . . The ceiling at the top of my brain lifted; once again my mind (and spirit) could get outside myself. (Walker, 1988, p. 53)

She calls her essay "Oppressed Hair Puts a Ceiling on the Brain."

REFERENCES

Baldwin, J. (1961). *Nobody knows my name: More notes on a native son.* New York: Dial Press.

Banner, L. (1983). *American beauty.* New York: Knopf.

Beck, B. (1988, February 3). Gray definitely OK, more women believe. Houston (Texas) *Chronicle.*

Chesler, P. (1978). *About men.* New York: Simon & Schuster.

Copper, B. (1988). *Over the hill: Reflections on ageism between women.* Freedom, CA: Crossing Press.

Doress, P. B., & Siegal, D. L. (1987). *Ourselves, growing older: Women aging with knowledge and power.* New York: Simon & Schuster.

Ellison, R. (1952). *Invisible man.* New York: Random House.

Gordon, B. (1988, September). Why older men chase younger women. *New woman.* From *Jennifer Fever: Older men, younger women.* New York: Harper & Row.

La Ferla, R. (1988, January 17). Under cover: Going gray is going out. *New York Times Magazine.*

Leonard, F. (1982), with T. Sommers and V. Dean. *Not even for dogcatcher: Employment discrimination and older women.* Gray Paper No. 8. Washington, D.C.: Older Women's League.

Lindeman, B. (1988, February). Midlife beauty: The road to success for older models is a rough one. *Active Senior Lifestyles.* Kaylan Pickford has an autobiography, *Always a woman* (New York: Bantam), 1982.

Macdonald, B. (1983), with C. Rich. *Look me in the eye: Old women, aging and ageism.* San Francisco: Spinster's Ink.

Melamed, E. (1983). *Mirror, mirror: The terror of not being young.* New York: Simon & Schuster.

Miller, J. B. (1976). *Toward a new psychology of women.* Boston: Beacon Press.

Parachini, A. (1987, October 14). Scientists still haven't got to roots of gray hair. Minneapolis *Star-Tribune,* reprinted from the Los Angeles

Times. All factual information about hair presented here is from this article.

Rubin, L. B. (1981). *Women of a certain age: the midlife search for self.* New York: Harper & Row.

Salholz, E. (1985, January 28). The look of a "certain age." *Newsweek.*

Sensational Hair (1984, August). *Harper's Bazaar.*

Walker, A. (1988, June). Oppressed hair puts a ceiling on the brain. *Ms.*

Wang, C. (1988). *Lear's* magazine, "For the woman who wasn't born yesterday: A critical review." *The Gerontologist, 28,* 600–601.

Winning the battle against hair loss (1984, August). *Harper's Bazaar.*

Further Questions

1. Is it significant that almost all the women stars over fifty have colored hair while almost all the men that age are gray or white-haired?

2. The magazine *Lear's* is for "women over 40." Is it significant that there are few gray-haired or white-haired women in the stories and advertisements? How about the fact that older gray-haired women are not readily accepted anywhere for fashion advertisements?

3. Will aging women be less likely to try to hide their age with dye and face-lifts once they realize that they have value beyond their serviceability to men? Will a woman who allows her hair to gray naturally be accepting herself for who she is, age and all?

Women in Dual-Career Families and the Challenge of Retirement

XII.7

JOY B. REEVES

Joy B. Reeves surveys some of the issues that confront dual-career couples as they approach retirement. Among these issues are the management of household chores, use of leisure time, choice of friends, access to other family members such as grandchildren, loss of identity when work is given up, simultaneous versus sequential retirement, and the restructuring of personal responsibilities.

Reeves is Professor of Sociology and Chair of the Department of Sociology at Stephen F. Austin State University, Nacogdochas, Texas.

Reading Questions

1. How should household chores be allocated when a couple is nearing retirement? Should this allocation change when one person retires? Should it change when both people retire?
2. Suppose that the husband has retired and wants to use his leisure time to travel. His wife, however, wants to continue to work. How should the couple solve this dilemma?
3. What pressures on a dual-career couple might lessen after their retirement?

From Woman, Aging, and Ageism, *Evelyn R. Rosenthal, ed. Copyright © 1990, The Haworth Press, Binghamton, NY, pp. 119–132. Reprinted by permission of the publisher.*

ONE OF THE MOST SIGNIFICANT social movements of recent times is the movement of women into the work force. More women work outside of the home than ever before, and a large proportion (66 percent between the ages 18 and 44 years) are mothers (U.S. Department of Labor, 1985). As a result of occupational demand, the women's movement, and a more favorable ideological climate for women working outside of the home, women in the professions now outnumber men in the professions as defined by the U.S. Census Bureau (Andersen, 1988; p. 117). Since professional women tend to marry men in high-prestige occupations, the number of dual-career families is expected to increase (Pepitone-Rockwell, 1980). In this essay, dual-career family is defined as a type of family form in which married heterosexual couples with or without children pursue active family lives and full-time work careers rather than jobs. (A job is a typically salaried position with limited future mobility; a career usually requires more education and consists of steps leading to advancement within that career.) Researchers expect an upsurge in the growth of dual-career families approaching retirement age near the end of this century (Davidson, 1982).

Even though dual-career families are expected to increase in the future, very few researchers have studied mature dual-career families, the exceptions being Wartenberg and Ulbrich (1986), Anderson et al., (1980) and Jewson (1982). Here, I review the structural sources of strain younger dual-career families are likely to experience and then extend the analysis to older families whose members are about to retire or are retired. I hope to lay the groundwork for a theoretically informed empirical study of mature dual-career families, and identify needed areas of research on such families, with particular emphasis on older women.

REVIEW OF LITERATURE

I reviewed the literature on dual-career families and mature married professional women about to retire or who have already retired who may or may or may not be in dual-career families. All researchers agree that dual-career families are stress-producing, but there is no clear cut agreement by researchers on whether joining two careers in one family leads to a substantial change in family form or gender roles as a result of stress. The Rapoports (1971) claim the structure of dual-career families has the potential for producing greater gender equality. This position is espoused by Dizard (1968), Garland (1972), Miller (1972), Bailyn (1970), and Hertz (1986). Others say that dual career family structure does not necessarily change to one that is more egalitarian (Weingarten, 1978; Bird, 1979; Holmstrom, 1973; Keating & Cole, 1980; Kerchoff, 1966; Szinovacz, 1982). Knowledge about the extent of family structure and gender role change may be important in predicting successful adjustment to retirement by spouses, especially women, in dual-career families.

In an exploratory study of retired dual-career spouses, Wartenberg and Ulbrich (1981) found life satisfaction, as well as power and decision-making, are related to couple relationships prior to the husband's retirement. Wife's life satisfaction was also related to length of husband's retirement, perception of husband's attitudes toward her employment, and recent thoughts of divorce. While retired husbands tend to help more with household tasks, the wife continues to bear the responsibility for them, which conforms to the findings of younger spouses in dual-career families (Jewson, 1982). In a study that controlled for type of family, women in mature dual-career families were more likely than women in traditional families to have earned a private pension benefit and have social security benefits that exceeded the benefits to spouse of workers (Anderson et al., 1980). Retirement may be a welcome, satisfying change for women in dual-career families because they experience decreasing mobility at work as they age (Roberts, 1984), achieve less than their spouses professionally (Bryson & Bryson, 1980; Yogev, 1981), and experience sex discrimination at work (Benokratis & Feagin, 1986).

Not much exists in the literature on the subject of retired married professional women. Szinovacz (1982) produced the best compilation of the literature on this subject. In general, research shows work is meaningful to professional women (Atchley, 1976; Jacobson, 1974), retirement often does create a dilemma for women (Jewson, 1982; Foner & Schwab, 1981), and women are not often well rehearsed for retirement (Bock, 1984; Davidson, 1982; Behling et al., 1983). Retirement constitutes a crisis for many women in low-paying occupations who are single, divorced, widowed, or have husbands who did not adequately prepare for retirement in a financial sense. Only 67 percent of women aged 55 to 64 are married; the percentage drops to 47 percent between the ages of 65 and 74 years. Approximately 82 percent of men aged 55 to 74 years are married (Bock, 1984). Price-Bonham and Johnson (1982) reported that only 29 percent of married professional women in their sample had paid into any retirement fund of their own and that 40 percent of them opted not to participate in a retirement program. In general, professional women compared to men are less prepared for retirement (Behling et al., 1983).

The research is mixed as to whether or not professional women, compared to various populations such as men or non-professional women, look forward to retirement and make a positive adjustment. Some do (Cavaghan, 1981; Holahan, 1981; Foner & Schwab, 1981; Rosen & Palmer, 1981; Atchley, 1976; Campbell, 1979), and some do not (Price-Bonham & Johnson, 1982; Simpson et al., 1966). Positive retirement adjustment is significantly related to positive pre-retirement attitudes, a positive self-concept (Rosen & Palmer, 1982), and the orderliness or continuity of one's career (Simpson et al., 1966). When these factors are absent, retirement may not be a satisfying experience.

The lack of consistency in pre-retirement attitude and retirement satisfaction research calls for resolution. Few of the studies controlled for type of family form (dual-career vs. traditional.; egalitarian vs. traditional), gender identity of both spouse, and whether or not the spouses were in a female or male-dominated profession/occupation. These variables and how they interact with each other need to be considered in future retirement studies. More than likely some of the research inconsistencies arise from using nonrepresentative, specialized samples (nuns; academics; self-employed; social workers; education specialists), noncomparable units of analysis, and different data collection methods.

THEORETICAL FRAMEWORK AND ANALYSIS

From a family system perspective (Riley, 1983; Nye, 1976), the family is a system of interdependent roles. The social relationships among family members are never fixed, but change as the family members grow older, and as society, itself, changes. Family and work systems are interrelated; for most of us, renegotiation of work/family balance continues throughout work life. Renegotiation is intensified at times of transition, such as when a baby is born, the children leave home, or a spouse retires. Important role changes influence the family decison-making process, and the choices made at these points of transition will determine a new phase in the dual-career family, and with it a new pattern of stress (Bebbington, 1973).

A complex interrelationship exists among ideology, social structure, and behavior. When ideology, social structure and behavior are inconsistent, structural stress is produced and strain is experienced by individuals. Sometimes the strain is so great that social changes occur. A dual-career family is a relatively new type of family form whose members are subject to various strains because cultural patterns that permit adaptation at various stages of dual-career family life have not yet crystallized (Hunt & Hunt, 1982). Few middle-age spouses in dual-career families know what to expect in retirement because few older spouses have had experience with this type of family form. The Rapoports (1971), who expanded on the works of Goode (1960) and Wilensky (1962), identified five sources of structural stress in dual-career families: role overload, social network dilemmas, normative dilemmas, maintenance of personal identity, and role-cycling. I will review the Rapoports' analysis and extend it to mature dual-career spouses about to retire or already retired.

ROLE OVERLOAD AND SOCIAL NETWORK DILEMMAS

In dual-career families both spouses belong to a number of groups and therefore perform multiple roles. The necessity of the husband and wife to perform adequately all of the tasks in the domestic environment as well as their employment careers often results in role overload and social network dilemmas. Costs and strains are largely borne by women in dual-career families; where husbands are not supportive, the whole arrangement is exceedingly fragile (Johnson & Johnson, 1980). Perhaps this is why there is a higher divorce rate for dual-career spouses than for traditional spouses (Nadelson &Nadelson, 1980) or why in the recent past successful career women tended to be childless, divorced, or single (Astin, 1969; Hunt & Hunt, 1982).

According to the Rapoports (1971), dual-career families cope with this stress by curtailing nonessential social activities and leisure, especially on the part of the wife. When spouses limit social activities this tends to weaken their social networks and leaves the spouses more vulnerable in times of crisis. If these spouses, especially wives, restrict the size of their social circle and curtail their leisure in their younger married years, what kind of adjustment can we expect from these spouses in their retirement years when social networks and leisure are supposed to assume greater importance? Do spouses committed to a work ethic for twenty years just pick up a leisure lifestyle when they have had little or no experience with leisure?

People have to learn to value leisure just as they have to learn to value work; however, our culture, with its work ethic legacy, makes it especially difficult for professionals to appreciate leisure. In general, the research indicates people continue their life-style from pre-retirement to the retirement period; the aging process does not normally bring about a fundamental change in the type or quality of leisure behavior (Parker, 1983, p. 69). Lack of appreciation for an experience with leisure in pre-retirement years may constitute an especially potent source of stress in retirement for professional spouses in dual-career families.

How easy would it be for dual-career spouses to expand their social circle when for years they consciously held it to a minimum? A wide variety of friends can help individuals develop themselves as persons and can keep a marriage potentially interesting if new ideas and experiences derived from friends are shared with the spouse. Would dependence on a small circle of friends for social stimulation over an extended period of time tend to restrict personality expansion, inhibit a person from interacting in new social situations, and make for a less interesting marriage? Since role flexibility is greater in dual-career families than in traditional families, aging dual-career spouses may very well adapt more readily than traditional spouses to changes in their life-cycles and expand their social circles. Continuity and discontinuity in social patterns for couples in various types of family forms over time would seem to be a fruitful area of research.

NORMATIVE DILEMMAS

Normative dilemmas arise through discrepancies in the way people believe they ought to live and the way people actually live, producing stress for dual-career families. Spouses in dual-career families ideally support egalitarian relationships between spouses, but the society offers little support for such a relationship. This is why women, by and large, continue to follow their traditional priorities of fitting their employment schedules to their family responsibilities, rather than the reverse, as men do (Degler, 1980, p. 436). Hertz (1986), who studied only affluent dual-career spouses in corporate work settings, said high incomes were necessary for dual-career marriages to work, since services and goods must be purchased to make possible a more egalitarian lifestyle. The Rapoports (1971), who studied both affluent and nonaffluent dual-career spouses, concluded affluence is not a necessary condition for a workable dual-career family. Longitudinal studies that control for social class are needed to test this thesis more adequately.

Discrepancies between personal beliefs and social norms may be a particular source of stress to the professional wife in a dual-career family because society emphasizes wives' maternal and homemaking role. A husband who takes on domestic roles commits a less intense norm violation than a wife who delegates a large part of the child-rearing role to someone else (Rapoports, 1971). The Rapoports (1971) found spouses in dual-career families cope with this dilemma by selecting other couples who are most like themselves to be their friends. Dual-career spouses also tend to compartmentalize or segment their various roles to reduce the strain they experience in their lives. For example, women attempt to leave their family problems at home while they are at work and attempt to leave their work problems at the office when they are home.

Some norm dilemmas would seem to lessen considerably for retired dual-career spouses. For example, it would be unnecessary for retired spouses to insulate themselves from social criticism ("How can you be a good mother and also have a career?") by selecting other dual-career spouses as friends. Mature dual-career spouses can blend in easily with others who did not have a family lifestyle similar to theirs in earlier years. Work may no longer be a basis of identity for either retired spouse and consequently not serve as a criterion for selecting friends. Provided the

retired spouses can reactivate rusty interpersonal skills, and more discretionary time is available to them, retirement can be an opportunity for dual-career spouses to expand their social circle.

Other norm dilemmas may continue into retirement. Consider the continuity of women's care-taking/nurturant role. Dual-career women may choose to retire earlier than they had planned because they are expected to care for an elderly parent or other relatives. Hasty retirement may lack planning, and lack of pre-retirement planning negatively affects adjustment in retirement (Bock, 1984).

If dual-career spouses do not retire at the same time, dilemmas become evident in conflicts over household duties. Dual-career spouses must renegotiate their relationship when one spouse retires and repeat the process when the other retires. A spouse used to sharing household duties when he/she worked full-time may very well dislike assuming the full burden of household chores in retirement, yet the spouse who is still working may feel he/she should not have to do any household chores. Jewson's study (1982) of retired spouses in dual-career families indicates retired husbands tend to help more with household tasks, but the wife continues to bear the responsibility for them.

The Rapoports (1971) found parents in dual-career families were concerned with their children; they were not self-centered and anti-children, a sentiment often expressed by parents in traditional families about dual-career parents. Given this concern with children, and the fact that one of the perceived costs to women in this type of family structure is less involvement with children than desired, it is conceivable that as these women enter retirement years their children and grandchildren may become very important in deciding where to locate. If one or both spouses want to continue his/her professional life after retirement, such as write articles for publication or conduct workshops, how important would easy access to work facilities and grandchildren be to one or both members who have officially retired? The potential for conflict between work/family roles would continue to exist for the retired spouses, but its intensity is probably less severe than when they and their children were younger (Witt & Goodale, 1981).

MAINTENANCE OF PERSONAL IDENTITY

The Rapoports (1971) found spouses in dual-career families had problems with identity. Such problems stem from the socio-cultural definition of work as inherently "masculine" while homemaking and family rearing is "feminine." Implied is the idea that cultural confusion of gender roles results in psychological or even physical confusion, as reflected in impotence or frigidity (Bebbington, 1973).

Retirement can produce an identity crisis for a married professional woman because she has deliberately chosen to reject the position of full time housewife. Her return to an earlier rejected status may result in considerable strain for both her and her husband. As with professional men, her personal identity may in large part come from work. If both spouses retire concurrently, and both identify with their work, then retirement is likely to produce difficulty for the couple because both would be struggling simultaneously with identity problems. A wife in pain could hardly ease her husband's pain during their mutual transition to retirement or vice-versa. A profitable area of research would be to study personal identities of both spouses in dual-career families and how these may or may not change with various role transitions in the life-cycle.

ROLE-CYCLING DILEMMAS

Spouses in dual-career families experience problems relative to the timing of the demands associated with work and family roles. For example, when children are very young, the demands of the mother role may take priority over the demands of the work role. Spouses must decide

the best time periods for one or both partners to assume greater work responsibilities. Role-cycling dilemmas derive from organizational problems at critical stages in the life-cycle as when the dual-career couple decides to start a family or one of the partners decides to accept a more demanding career position. Since careers do not peak for women at the same time they do for men due to discrimination, late entry, delayed parenthood, and adjustment of career needs to family needs, there is a lack of integration of the three social systems (work system of wife; work system of husband; family system). It is this lack of integration that produces the role-cycling dilemmas for dual-career families. To what extent are these dilemmas increased or decreased as spouses in such families age?

As dual-career spouses enter retirement age, role-cycling dilemmas may become ever more problematic than when the spouses were younger. For example, the spouses may experience retirement at different times. Almost one-third of the wives whose husbands retired between the ages of 65 and 69 years had not yet retired (Fox, 1979). This situation increases the role complexity of the spouses. Due to a shorter pre-retirement employment history, married professional women may not be ready to retire when spouses wish to retire. One spouse may retire fully whereas the other may not retire at all or only partially.

Rather than just three social systems to consider in the cycling process, additional ones are added as the spouses age, such as the leisure systems of both husband and wife. Each spouse could have a separate leisure system, and both could share one. The spouse who works part-time or full time may not be available to share some of the leisure pursuits desired by the retired partner, such as frequent travel. Does the retired spouse take trips alone if the other spouse is unable to participate because of work commitments? Out of loneliness, the retired partner may pressure the working spouse to retire. Should a wife who delayed entry into the work world to please her husband also retire early so she can be a better companion to him? What happens to friendship circles of dual-career spouses when one spouse retires early? If dual-career spouses select other dual-career spouses for friends and the status of one partner changes, do the once compatible friends dissolve their friendship?

When spouses do not retire concurrently decisions about where to retire must be postponed. In addition, questions about who adjusts to whose time schedule are likely to occur. Does the retired spouse adjust to the spouse who is working? Even though most women in dual-career families adjust their schedules to fit their husband's schedule (Holmstrom, 1973; Bird, 1979; Weingarten, 1978; Lips, 1988), this may not be the case among mature women in this type of family. In the interest of equity these women may very well expect a shift on the part of their husbands (Bailyn, 1970).

Mature spouses in dual-career families may redefine their roles and possibly reexamine what retirement should be. Is retirement a time to be together with the spouse, a time to be less responsible to others, or a time to be more responsible to others? To what extent aging dual-career spouses hold compatible views on retirement should be researched.

Concurrent retirement of spouses in dual-career families may be less problematic than sequential retirement. And, because of this, it may be more common. A wife's attachment to the work force significantly raises the probability of her husband deferring retirement (Davidson, 1982; Anderson et al., 1980), and this may also increase the probability of concurrent retirement. Other factors that increase the probability of concurrent retirement are age of spouse, high economic status and amount of pension coverage (Henretta & O'Rand, 1983). Research indicates that dual-career spouses retire later than those who are not (Anderson et al., 1980), but we do not know why this is the case. An interesting area to explore would be the consequences of career couples following different retirement patterns.

CONCLUSION

The dual-career family form is stress-producing, but the nature and extent of stress may vary depending on the life-cycle of the partners involved. If our society becomes less stratified by sex, it will be easier to make a dual-career family work and this will encourage couples who "want to have it all" to consider adopting this type of family form. Whether or not this type of family form works well in the late years of life is largely unknown because too few spouses in dual-career families have reached this stage and of those who have, we know little about them. We need to pursue the neglected study of aging spouses in dual-career families to answer the many questions discussed here. In so doing we will contribute to the development of leisure, retirement, gender role, family, and gerontology theory, as well as facilitate the work of practitioners who develop programs for the aged, who are disproportionately women, and therapists, who counsel married couples contemplating marriage or divorce.

NOTES

Andersen, M. (1988). *Thinking about women.* New York: Macmillan.

Anderson, K., Clark R., and Johnson, T. (1989). "Retirement in dual-career families." In R. Clark (Ed.), *Retirement policy in an aging society* (pp. 109–127) Durham, NC: Duke University Press.

Astin, H. (1969). *The woman doctorate in America.* New York: Russell Sage.

Atchley, R. (1976). Adjustment to loss of job at retirement. *International Journal of Aging and Human Development 31*:204–211.

Bailyn, L. (1970). Career and family orientation of husband and wives in relation to mental happiness. *Human Relations 22*:97–113.

Bebbington, A.C. (1973). The function of stress in the establishment of the dual-career family. *Journal of Marriage and the Family 35*:530–537.

Behling, J., Kilty, K., and Foster, S. (1983). Scarce resources for retirement planning: A dilemma for professional women. *Journal of Gerontological Social Work* 5:49–60.

Benokratis, N., and Feagin, J. (1986). *Modern sexism*. New York: Prentice-Hall.

Bird, C. (1979). *The two-paycheck marriage*. New York: Pocket Books.

Bock, M. (1984). Retirement preparation needs of women. In H. Dennis (Ed.), *Retirement preparation* (pp. 129–140). Lexington, KY: Lexington Books.

Bryson, R., and Bryson, J. (1980). Salary and job performance difference in dual-career couples. In F. Pepitone-Rockwell (Ed.) *Dual-career couples* (pp. 241–259). London: Sage.

Campbell, S. (1979). Delayed mandatory retirement and the working women. *The Gerontologist* 19:257–263.

Cavaghan, P. (1981). *Social adjustment of women to retirement*. Unpublished doctoral dissertation, University of California, Davis.

Davidson, J. (1982). Issues of employment and retirement in the lives of women over age 40. In N. Osgood (Ed.), *Life after work* (pp. 95–114). New York: Praeger.

Degler, C. (1980). *At odds: Women and the family in America from the revolution to the present*. New York: Oxford University Press.

Dizard, J. (1968). *Social change in the family*. Chicago: University of Chicago Press.

Foner, A., and Schwab, K. (1981). *Aging and retirement*. Monterey, CA: Brooks/Cole.

Fox, J. (1979). Earnings replacement notes of retired couples: Findings from the retirement history study. *Social Security Bulletin* 42:17–39.

Garland, T. (1972). The better half: The male in the dual-career professional family. In C. Safilios-Rothschild (Ed.), *Toward a sociology of women* (pp. 199–216). Lexington, MA: Xerox College Publishing.

Goode, W. (1960). A theory of role strain. *American Sociological Review* 25:483–496.

Henretta, John C., and O'Rand, A. (1983). Joint retirement in the dual worker family. *Social Forces* 62: 504–520.

Hertz, R. (1986). *More equal than others: Women and men in dual-career marriages*. Berkeley: University of California Press.

Holmstrom, L. (1973). *The two-career family*. Cambridge, MA: Schenkman.

Holohan, C. (1981). Lifetime achievement patterns, retirement and life satisfaction of gifted aged women. *Journal of Gerontology* 36:741–749.

Hunt, J., and Hunt, L. (1982). The dualities of careers and families: New integration or new polarizations? *Social Problems* 29:499–510.

Jacobson, C. (1974). Rejection of the retiree role: A study of female industrial workers in their 50's. *Human Relations* 27:477–492.

Jewson, R. (1982). After retirement: An exploratory study of the professional woman. In M. Szinovacz (Ed.), *Women's retirement* (pp. 169–194). Beverly Hills: Sage.

Johnson, C., and Johnson, F. (1980). Parenthood, marriage and careers: Situational constraints and role strain. In F. Pepitone-Rockwell (Ed.), *Dual-career couples* (pp. 143–161). London: Sage.

Keating N., and Cole, P. (1980). What do I do with him 24 hours a day? Change in the housewife role after retirement. *The Gerontologist* 20:84–89.

Kerchoff, D. (1966). Family pattern and morale in retirement. In I. Simpson and J. McKinney (Ed.), *Social aspects of aging* (pp. 172–194). Durham, NC: Duke University Press.

Lips, H. (1988). *Sex and gender*. Mountain View, CA: Mayfield.

Miller, S. (1972). The making of a confused middle-aged husband. In C. Safilios-Rothschild (Ed.), *Toward sociology of women* (pp. 245–254). Lexington, MA: Xerox College Publishing.

Nadelson, C., and Nadelson, T. (1980). Dual-career marriages: benefits and costs. In F. Pepitone-Rockwell (Ed.), *Dual-career couples* (pp. 91–109). London: Sage.

Nye, F.I. (1976). *Rrole structure: An analysis of the family*. Beverly Hills: Sage.

Parker, S. (1983). *Leisure and work*. London: Allen and Unwin.

Pepitone-Rockwell, F. (Ed.) (1980). *Dual-career couples*. London: Sage.

Price-Bonham S., and Johnson, C. (1982). Attitudes toward retirement: A comparison of professional and nonprofessional married women. In M. Szinovacz (Ed.), *Women's retirement* (pp. 123–138). Beverly Hills: Sage.

Rapoport, R., and Rapoport, R.(1971). *Dual-career families*. Harmondsworth, England: Penguin Books.

Riley, M. (1983). The family in an aging society: A matrix of latent relationships. *Journal of Family Issues* 4:439–454.

Roberts, C. (1984). The role of employment in women's lives: Some findings from a British survey of women and employment. *Sociologie du Travail* 26:317–325.

Rosen, J., and Palmer, M. (1982). Retirement adaptations and self-concepts in professional women. Paper presented at the annual convention of the American Psychological Assoc., Washington, DC (Aug 23–27).

Simpson, I., Back, K., and McKinney, J. (1966). Orientation toward work and retirement. In I. Simpson and J. McKinney (Eds.), *Social aspects of aging* (pp. 45–54). Durham, NC: Duke University Press.

Szinovacz, M.(Ed.) (1982). *Women's retirement.* Beverly Hills: Sage.

U.S. Department of Labor (1985). *Employment and earnings* (Vol. 34). Washington DC: U.S. Government Printing Office.

Wartenberg, H., and Ulbrich, P. (1986). Women's timing of retirement and life satisfaction in dual-career families. Paper presented to International Sociological Association. U. of Miami. Coral Gables, Fl.

Weingarten, K. (1978). The employment pattern of professional couples and their distribution of involvement in the family. *Psychology of Women Quarterly* 3:43–53.

Wilkinsky, H. (1962). Life cycle, mark situations and social participation. In C. Tibbets and W. Donahue (Eds.), *Social aspects of aging* (pp. 40–56). New York: Columbia University Press.

Witt, P.,and Goodale, T. (1981). The relationship between farmers to leisure enjoyment and family stages. *Leisure Sciences* 4:29–49.

Yogev, S. (1981). Do professional women have egalitarian marital relationships? *Journal of Marriage and the Family* 43:865–871.

Further Questions

1. Could a wife have an identity crisis similar to that of her husband upon retirement if her identity came principally from her profession? What are possible ways of alleviating such identity crises?

2. Could the friendships of a couple undergo changes when one or both of them retires?

3. What issues concerning retirement should a prudent dual-career couple try to resolve before these issues come to a head and acquire the potential of disrupting their relationship?

Further Readings For Part XII: Youngsters and Oldsters

With people living longer, gerontology is expanding both in practice and as an area of study. There are, however, disappointingly few works that take the perspective of the aged person as a starting point. There are even fewer which take gender into account in aging, or which could be appropriately tagged as feminist in approach. The following selections are some works that attempt to orient themselves in these directions.

Sara Arber and Jay Ginn. "Gender and Later Life: A Sociological Analysis of Resources and Constraints" (Newbury Park, CA: Sage Publications, 1991). These authors claim that feminist sociologists neglect the elderly because they cannot relate them to their own experiences.

Lea Cohen. *Small Expectations: Society's Betrayal of Older Women* (Toronto: McClelland and Stewart, Ltd., 1984). Society rejects the old and is particularly disdainful of older women.

Baba Copper. *Over the Hill: Reflections on Ageism Between Women* (Freedom, CA: The Crossing Press, 1988). Should be required reading for all feminists.

Simone de Beauvoir. *The Coming of Age,* Patrick O'Brian, tr. (New York, NY: C. P. Putnam's Sons, 1972). Old age, both as experienced and as a social phenomenon.

Nancy D. Davis, Ellen Cole and Esther D. Rothblum, eds. *Faces of Women and Aging* (Binghamton, NY: Harrington Park Press, 1993). The challenges of late years of life and how women meet them.

Joseph L. Esposito. *The Obsolete Self: Philosophical Dimensions of Aging* (Berkeley, CA: The University of California Press, 1987). Experiences of aging and an explanation of how social forces shape perceptions of aging.

Ursual A. Falk. *On Our Own: Independent Living For Older Persons* (Buffalo, NY: Prometheus Books, 1989). Information, help, and vignettes on the challenges facing an older person living solo.

Janet Ford and Ruth Sinclair. *Sixty Years On: Women Talk About Old Age* (London: The Women's Press, Ltd., 1987). Old women in Britain speak of their experiences.

Betty Friedan. *The Fountain of Age* (New York, NY: Simon and Schuster, 1993). Friedan and others dispute the view that aging diminishes life.

J. Diane Garner and Susan O. Mercer, eds. *Women as They Age: Challenge, Opportunity and Triumph* (Binghamton, NY: The Haworth Press, Inc., 1989). Optimistic writers address issues in the area of women and aging.

J. Dianne Garner and Alice A. Young, eds. *Women and Healthy Aging: Living Productively in Spite of It All* (Binghamton, NY: The Haworth Press, 1993). Making the best of a life that includes aging and, possibly, disease.

Jewelle Taylor Gibbs. *Young, Black, and Male in America: An Endangered Species* (Westport, CT: Auburn House Publishing Company, 1988). Why young black males are "a population 'at risk' for an escalating cycle of deviance, dysfunction, and despair."

Jaber F. Gubrium, ed. *Time, Roles and Self in Old Age* (New York, NY: Human Sciences Press, 1976). Disengagement and retirement of older persons and the "generation gap" with younger persons.

John Hendricks and C. Davis Hendricks, eds. *Dimensions of Aging: Readings* (Cambridge, MA: Winthrop Publishers, 1979). Interdisciplinary problems approach to aging.

Margot Jeffreys, ed. *Growing Old in the Twentieth Century* (New York, NY: Routledge, 1989). Discusses issues like income, retirement, support networks, and racism.

Gerald A. Larue. *Geroethics: A New Vision of Growing Old in America* (Buffalo, NY: Prometheus Books, 1992). Ethical issues and suggested solutions for older people.

Gari Lesnoff-Caravaglia, ed. *Aging and the Human Condition* (New York, NY: Human Sciences Press, 1982). Interesting aspects of experiences of the elderly, e.g., time is perceived as a continuous present.

Barbara Macdonald with Cynthia Rich. *Look Me in the Eye: Old Women, Aging, and Ageism* (San Francisco, CA: Spinsters Book Co., expanded edition, 1991). Both writers combine ground-breaking feminist theory on ageism with direct personal experience.

Doris Marshall. *Silver Threads: Critical Reflections on Growing Old* (Toronto, ON: Between the Lines, 1987). Search for a new positive definition of growing old.

Mary Pipher. *Reviving Ophelia: Saving the Selves of Adolescent Girls* (New York, NY: Ballantine Books, 1994). Voices of girls and their parents speak to the loss of self in adolescence.

B. F. Skinner and M. F. Vaughan. *Enjoy Old Age: A Program of Self-Management* (New York, NY: W. W. Norton and Co., 1983). Fairly cheerless advice, much of which is denial of age, e.g., "Old people are boring when they talk about their illnesses."

Susan Sontag. . . . "The Double Standard of Aging" in *Saturday Review of the Society,* September 1977. Baba Copper calls this a "deeply ageist and heterosexist article."

Ruth Raymond Thorne. *Women and Aging: Celebrating Ourselves* (Binghamton, NY: Haworth Press, 1992). Better advice than Skinner/Vaughan on taking charge of your aging.

James E. Thornton and Earl R. Winkler, eds. *Ethics and Aging: The Right to Live, The Right to Die* (Vancouver: The University of British Columbia Press, 1988). Coming to terms with some problems of aging.

Margaret Urban Walker, ed. *Mother Time: Women, Aging and Ethics* (Lanham, MD: Rowman and Littlefield Publishers, Inc., 1999). Exploration into what is still a fairly novel territory.

Suggested Moral of Part XII

Aging is feared, not only because of possible physical debilitation, but also because an older person, especially if she is a woman, is often socially oppressed. Patriarchy causes both men and younger women to be oppressors of older women. Such oppression takes the form of excluding older women from an important part in family life, the workplace, and the community. An older woman is either invisible, a thing of the past, or a mother, rather than an integral part of the community. The role of "mother" seems particularly bad to younger women because these younger women often (correctly) believe that their own mothers betrayed them by preparing them to be used by men. Patriarchy is the root cause of silencing older women and excluding them from positions of power.

TO THE OWNER OF THIS BOOK:

I hope that you have found *Gender Basics: Feminist Perspectives on Women and Men*, Second Edition, useful. So that this book can be improved in a future edition, would you take the time to complete this sheet and return it? Thank you.

School and address: _____

_____

Department: _____

Instructor's name: _____

1. What I like most about this book is:_____

_____

_____

2. What I like least about this book is: _____

_____

_____

3. My general reaction to this book is: _____

_____

_____

4. The name of the course in which I used this book is: _____

_____

5. Were all of the chapters of the book assigned for you to read? _____

   If not, which ones weren't? _____

6. In the space below, or on a separate sheet of paper, please write specific suggestions for improving this book and anything else you'd care to share about your experience in using this book.

_____

_____

_____

OPTIONAL:

Your name: _____ Date: _____

May we quote you, either in promotion for [insert *Book title*, Edition here], or in future publishing ventures?

    Yes: _____ No: _____

    Sincerely yours,

    [insert *Author name(s)* here]